# High Frequency Trading and Limit Order Book Dynamics

This book brings together the latest research in the areas of market microstructure and high-frequency finance, along with new econometric methods to address critical practical issues in these areas of research. Thirteen chapters, each of which makes a valuable and significant contribution to the existing literature, have been brought together, spanning a wide range of topics including information asymmetry and the information content in limit order books, high-frequency return distribution models, multivariate volatility forecasting, analysis of individual trading behaviour, the analysis of liquidity, price discovery across markets, market microstructure models and the information content of order flow. These issues are central both to the rapidly expanding practice of high frequency trading in financial markets and to the further development of the academic literature in this area. The volume will therefore be of immediate interest to practitioners and academics.

This book was originally published as a special issue of *European Journal of Finance*.

**Ingmar Nolte** is a Reader in Finance at Lancaster University, UK. He held positions before at the University of Warwick, UK, and the University of Konstanz, Germany. His core research area is Financial Econometrics; he has published articles in the leading journals including the *Journal of Business & Economics Statistics*, *Journal of Financial Econometrics* and the *Journal of Applied Econometrics*.

**Mark Salmon** is Senior Scientist at BHDG Systematic Trading and has been a Visiting Professor at Cambridge University, UK, for the last three years Prior to joining BHDG he was Professor of Finance at Warwick Business School, UK, and prior to that a Professor at Cass Business School, UK, and the European University Institute, Italy. He has published widely in Finance, Economics, Econometrics and Statistics with papers in *Econometrica*, *The Annals of Statistics*, *The Journal of Econometrics*, *The Economic Journal*, *The Journal of Financial Markets*, *The Journal of Empirical Finance* amongst other places. He has also consulted with a number of financial institutions for many years, and was an advisor at the Bank of England for six years.

**Chris Adcock** is Professor of Financial Econometrics at the University of Sheffield, UK, and visiting Professor of Quantitative Finance at the University of Southampton, UK. His research interests are in portfolio selection, asset pricing theory and the development of quantitative techniques for portfolio management. He has acted as advisor to several international investment managers. He is founding editor of *The European Journal of Finance* and has been associate editor of several finance journals, and Series C and D of the Journal of the Royal Statistical Society. Current research projects are in downside risk, portfolio selection, skewness and option returns, with collaborations with universities in the UK, the European Union and China.

# High Frequency Trading and Limit Order Book Dynamics

*Edited by*
**Ingmar Nolte, Mark Salmon and Chris Adcock**

LONDON AND NEW YORK

First published 2015 by Routledge

2 Park Square, Milton Park, Abingdon, Oxon, OX14 4RN
605 Third Avenue, New York, NY 10017

*Routledge is an imprint of the Taylor & Francis Group, an informa business*

First issued in paperback 2020

*British Library Cataloguing in Publication Data*
A catalogue record for this book is available from the British Library

ISBN 13: 978-1-138-82938-1 (hbk)
ISBN 13: 978-0-367-73899-0 (pbk)

Typeset in Times New Roman
by RefineCatch Limited, Bungay, Suffolk

**Publisher's Note**
The publisher accepts responsibility for any inconsistencies that may have
arisen during the conversion of this book from journal articles to book chapters,
namely the possible inclusion of journal terminology.

**Disclaimer**
Every effort has been made to contact copyright holders for their permission to
reprint material in this book. The publishers would be grateful to hear from any
copyright holder who is not here acknowledged and will undertake to rectify
any errors or omissions in future editions of this book.

# Contents

CONTENTS

# Citation Information

The chapters in this book were originally published in *The European Journal of Finance*, volume 18, issues 9–10 (October-November 2012). When citing this material, please use the original page numbering for each article, as follows:

**Chapter 1**
*Introduction*
Ingmar Nolte and Mark Salmon
*The European Journal of Finance*, volume 18, issue 9 (October 2012) pp. i-iv

**Chapter 2**
*Limit order books and trade informativeness*
Hélena Beltran-Lopez, Joachim Grammig and Albert J. Menkveld
*The European Journal of Finance*, volume 18, issues 9–10 (October-November 2012) pp. 737–760

**Chapter 3**
*A forecast-based comparison of restricted Wishart autoregressive models for realized covariance matrices*
M. Bonato, M. Caporin and A. Ranaldo
*The European Journal of Finance*, volume 18, issues 9–10 (October-November 2012) pp. 761–774

**Chapter 4**
*A simple two-component model for the distribution of intraday returns*
Laura Coroneo and David Veredas
*The European Journal of Finance*, volume 18, issues 9–10 (October-November 2012) pp. 775–798

**Chapter 5**
*Liquidity determination in an order-driven market*
Jón Daníelsson and Richard Payne
*The European Journal of Finance*, volume 18, issues 9–10 (October-November 2012) pp. 799–822

**Chapter 14**

*The impact of aggressive orders in an order-driven market: a simulation approach*
Gunther Wuyts
*The European Journal of Finance*, volume 18, issues 9–10 (October-November 2012) pp. 1015–1038

Please direct any queries you may have about the citations to
clsuk.permissions@cengage.com

# Notes on Contributors

**Hélena Beltran-Lopez**, PNC Financial Services, Cleveland, USA

**Matteo Bonato**, UBS, Zurich, Switzerland

**Massimiliano Caporin**, Department of Economics, University of Padova, Italy

**Laura Coroneo**, Department of Economics and Related Studies, University of York, UK

**Jón Daníelsson**, Department of Finance and Financial Markets Group, London School of Economics, UK

**Alfonso Dufour**, ICMA Centre, Henley Business School, University of Reading, UK

**Joachim Grammig**, Department of Economics, Eberhard-Karls-University Tübingen, Germany

**Jinhui Luo**, ICBC, China

**Ian W. Marsh**, Cass Business School, City University, London, UK

**Albert J. Menkveld**, Department of Finance and Financial Sector Management, VU University Amsterdam, The Netherlands

**Teng Miao**, Casteel Capital, London, UK

**Minh Nguyen**, Sheffield University Management School, UK

**Sandra Nolte**, Lancaster University Management School, Lancaster University, UK

**Angel Pardo**, Department of Financial Economics, Universidad de Valencia, Spain

**Roberto Pascual**, Department of Business Economics, Universidad de las Islas Baleares, Palma, Spain

**Richard Payne**, Cass Business School, City University, UK

**A. Ranaldo**, Swiss Institute of Banking and Finance, University of St. Gallen, Zurich, Switzerland

**Erik Theissen**, Department of Business Administration, University of Mannheim, Germany

**David Veredas**, ECARES, Solvay Brussels School of Economics and Management, Université libre de Bruxelles, Brussels, Belgium

**Paolo Vitale**, Faculty of Economics, Università d'Annunzio, Italy

**Gunther Wuyts**, Faculty of Business and Economics, Department of Accountancy, Finance and Insurance, Katholieke Universiteit Leuven, Belgium

# Introduction

This book reflects the conference, 'Individual Decision Making, High Frequency Econometrics and Limit Order Book Dynamics', that took place at Warwick Business School in September 2009. The conference was organised by Roman Kozhan, Ingmar Nolte, Richard Payne and Mark Salmon with the aim of bringing together leading experts, academics, PhD students and members of the finance industry working in the areas of market microstructure, high-frequency finance and behavioural finance to discuss the latest research in these fields. Thirteen selected articles covering the state-of-the-art research in these areas have been brought together here after a rigorous refereeing process. Each paper makes a valuable and significant contribution to the existing literature and we hope that you will enjoy reading them.

*Beltran-Lopez, Grammig and Menkveld* analyse the link between information asymmetry and market liquidity. They study the importance of information asymmetry in limit order books based on a recent sample of 30 German DAX stocks and find that Hasbrouck's measure of trade informativeness Granger causes book liquidity, in particular that required to fill large market orders. They find that picking-off risk due to public news-induced volatility is more important for top-of-the book liquidity supply. In their multivariate analysis they control for volatility, trading volume, trading intensity and order imbalance to isolate the effect of trade informativeness on book liquidity.

*Bonato, Caporin and Ranaldo* focus within the class of realized covariance models on Wishart specifications and analyse the forecasting performance of parametric restrictions motivated by asset features such as their economic sector, book-to-market or price-earnings ratios. They consider a range of model comparison approaches that represent the most recent and up-to-date methods proposed in the literature. Their tests provide some evidence on the possible preference of restricted specifications over fully parameterized models.

*Coroneo and Veredas* model the conditional distribution of high-frequency financial returns by means of a two-component quantile regression model. Using three years of 30-minute returns, they show that the conditional distribution depends on past returns and on the time of the day. Two practical applications illustrate the usefulness of the model. First, they provide quantile-based measures of conditional volatility, asymmetry and kurtosis that do not depend on the existence of moments. They find seasonal patterns and time dependencies beyond volatility. Second, they estimate and forecast intraday Value at Risk and show that their two-component model is able to provide good risk assessments and to outperform GARCH-based Value at Risk methods.

*Daníelsson and Payne* exploit full-order level information from an electronic foreign exchange (FX) broking system to provide a comprehensive account of the determination of its liquidity. They not only look at bid–ask spreads and trading volumes, but also study the determination of order entry rates and depth measures derived from the entire limit order book. They find strong predictability in the arrival of liquidity supply/demand events. Further, in times of low (high) liquidity, liquidity supply (demand) events are more common. In times of high trading activity and volatility, the ratio of limit to market order arrivals is high but order book spreads and depth deteriorate. Their results are consistent with market order traders having better information than limit order traders.

*Daníelsson, Luo and Payne* investigate the dependence of FX rates on order flow for four major exchange rate pairs, EUR/USD, EUR/GBP, GBP/USD and USD/JPY, across sampling frequencies ranging from 5 minutes to 1 week. They discover strong explanatory power for all sampling frequencies and also uncover cross-market order flow effects, e.g. GBP exchange rates are very strongly influenced by EUR/USD order flow. They use the Meese and Rogoff framework to investigate the predictive power of order flow for exchange rate changes and show that the order flow specifications reduce RMSEs relative to a random walk for all exchange rates at high frequencies and for EUR/USD and USD/JPY at lower sampling frequencies.

*Dufour and Nguyen* analyse transaction data for euro-area sovereign bonds traded on the MTS electronic platforms. They measure the informational content of trading activity by estimating the permanent price response to trades. They find not only strong evidence of information asymmetry in sovereign bond markets, but also show the relevance of information asymmetry in explaining the cross-sectional variations of bond yields across a wide range of bond maturities and countries. Their results confirm that trades of more recently issued bonds and longer maturity bonds have a greater permanent effect on prices. They study the cross-section of bond yields and find that, after controlling for conventional factors, investors demand higher yields for bonds with a larger permanent trading impact. Interestingly, when investors face increased market uncertainty they require even higher compensation for information asymmetry.

*Marsh and Miao* consider the impact of FX order flows on contemporaneous and future stock market returns using a new database of customer order flows in the €-$ exchange rate market as seen by a leading European bank. They do not find clear contemporaneous relationships between FX order flows and stock market changes at high frequencies, but FX flows do appear to have significant power to forecast stock index returns over 1-minute to 30-minute horizons, after controlling for lagged exchange rate and stock market returns. The effects of order flows from financial customers on future stock market changes are negative, while the effects of corporate orders are positive. Their latter results are consistent with the premise that corporate order flows contain dispersed, passively acquired information about fundamentals. Thus, purchases of the dollar by corporate customers represent good news about the state of the US economy. Importantly, though, there also appears to be extra information in corporate flows which is directly relevant to equity prices over and above the impact derived from stock prices reacting to (predicted) exchange rate changes. Their findings suggest that financial customer flows only affect stock prices through their impact on the value of the dollar.

*Nolte* uses a panel survival approach to analyse the trading behaviour of FX traders. He focuses on a detailed characterisation of the shape of the disposition effect over the entire profit and loss region. Thereby he investigates the influence of trading characteristics such as special limit order strategies, trading success, size and investors' experience on the disposition effect. His main findings are that (i) the disposition effect has a non-linear shape. For small profits and losses, there is an inverted disposition effect, while for larger ones the usual positive disposition effect emerges. (ii) The inverted disposition effect is driven to a great extent by patient and cautious investors closing their positions with special limit orders (take-profit and stop-loss). The normal positive disposition effect is found to be intensified for impatient investors closing their positions actively with market orders. (iii) He shows that unsuccessful investors reveal a stronger inverse disposition effect and provides evidence that bigger investors are less prone to the disposition effect than smaller investors.

*Nolte and Nolte* examine how high-frequency trading decisions of individual investors are influenced by past price changes. Specifically, they address the question as to whether decisions to open or close a position are different when investors already hold a position compared to when they do not. Based on a unique dataset from an electronic FX trading platform, OANDA FXTrade, they find that investors' future order flow is (significantly) driven by past price movements and that these predictive patterns last up to several hours. This observation clearly shows that for high-frequency trading, investors rely on previous price movements in making future investment decisions. They provide clear evidence that market and limit orders' flows are much more predictable if those orders are submitted to close an existing position than if they are used to open one. This finding provides evidence for the existence of a monitoring effect, which has implications for theoretical market microstructure models and behavioural finance phenomena, such as the endowment effect.

*Pardo and Pascual* investigate the informativeness of iceberg orders, also known as hidden limit orders (HLOs). They analyse how the market reacts when the presence of hidden volume in the limit order book is revealed by the trading process. They use high-frequency book and transaction data from the Spanish Stock Exchange, including a large sample of executed HLOs. They show that just when hidden volume is detected, traders on the opposite side of the market become more aggressive, exploiting the opportunity to consume more than expected at the best quotes. However, neither illiquidity nor volatility increases in the short-term. They also find that the detection of hidden volume has no relevant price impact. Overall, their results suggest that market participants do not attribute any relevant informational content to the hidden side of liquidity.

*Theissen* reconsiders the issue of price discovery in spot and futures markets. He uses a threshold error correction model to allow for arbitrage opportunities to have an impact on the return dynamics. He estimates the model using quote midpoints and modifies the model to account for time-varying transaction costs. He finds that (a) the futures market leads in the process of price discovery and that (b) the presence of arbitrage opportunities has a strong impact on the dynamics of the price discovery process.

*Vitale* formulates a market microstructure model of exchange determination, which he employs to investigate the impact of informed trading on exchange rates and conditions in the FX market. With his formulation he shows how strategic informed agents influence exchange rates via both the portfolio-balance and information effects. He outlines the connection which exists between the private value of information, market efficiency, liquidity and exchange rate volatility. His model is also consistent with recent empirical research on the microstructure of FX markets.

*Wuyts* investigates resiliency in an order-driven market. On basis of a VAR model capturing various dimensions of liquidity and their interactions, he simulates the effect of a large liquidity shock, measured by a very aggressive market order. He shows that, despite the absence of market makers, the market is resilient. All dimensions of liquidity (spread, depth at the best prices and order book imbalances) revert to their steady-state values within 15 orders after the shock. For prices, a long-run effect is found. Furthermore, he finds that different dimensions of liquidity interact. Immediately after a liquidity shock, the spread becomes wider than in the steady state, implying that one dimension of liquidity deteriorates, while at the same time depth at the best prices increases, implying an improvement of another liquidity dimension. In subsequent periods, the spread reverts not only to the steady-state level but also the depth decreases. He also finds evidence for asymmetries in the impact of shocks on the ask and bid side. Shocks on the ask side have a stronger impact than shocks on the bid side. His final result is that resiliency is higher for less frequently traded stocks and stocks with a larger relative tick size.

Ingmar Nolte
*Lancaster University Management School, Lancaster University,*
*Bailrigg, Lancaster, LA1 4YX, UK*
Mark Salmon
*Faculty of Economics, University of Cambridge, Cambridge, CB3 9DD, UK*

# Limit order books and trade informativeness

Hélena Beltran-Lopez[a], Joachim Grammig[b] and Albert J. Menkveld[c]

*[a]Fifth Third Asset Management, Cleveland, USA; [b]Department of Economics, Eberhard-Karls-University Tübingen, Tübingen, Germany; [c]Department of Finance and Financial Sector Management, VU University Amsterdam, Amsterdam, The Netherlands*

In the microstructure literature, information asymmetry is an important determinant of market liquidity. The classic setting is that uninformed dedicated liquidity suppliers charge price concessions when incoming market orders are likely to be informationally motivated. In limit order book (LOB) markets, however, this relationship is less clear, as market participants can switch roles, and freely choose to immediately demand or patiently supply liquidity by submitting either market or limit orders. We study the importance of information asymmetry in LOBs based on a recent sample of 30 German Deutscher Aktienindex (DAX) stocks. We find that Hasbrouck's (1991) measure of trade informativeness Granger causes book liquidity, in particular that required to fill large market orders. Picking-off risk due to public news-induced volatility is more important for top-of-the book liquidity supply. In our multivariate analysis, we control for volatility, trading volume, trading intensity and order imbalance to isolate the effect of trade informativeness on book liquidity.

## 1. Introduction

The classic microstructure literature distinguishes liquidity suppliers and liquidity demanders, which naturally introduces information asymmetry. That is, liquidity suppliers trade against potentially privately informed liquidity demanders and charge them an increased price concession to protect themselves.[1] This deters uninformed, hedging-motivated liquidity demand and, in the extreme, might cause the market to break down. Information asymmetry thus reduces welfare (cf. Biais, Hillion and Spatt 2005, pp. 223–227). Easley, Hvidkjaer and O'Hara (2002) provide evidence that asymmetric information risk is priced, as stocks for which they estimate a high probability of informed trading have to offer higher expected returns.

With the advent of electronic limit order book (LOB) markets, however, the distinction between uninformed liquidity suppliers and potentially informed liquidity demanders became blurred. Investors arriving at the market can choose to demand liquidity through a market order, but they can also enter their trading interest in the book via a limit order. In the latter case they effectively supply liquidity. It is therefore unclear as to what extent the increased price concession due to information asymmetry, one of the cornerstones of classic microstructure, still matters for liquidity supply in electronic LOB markets.

We exploit a comprehensive sample of 30 index stocks traded in the LOB of the German Stock Exchange to empirically assess the effect of information asymmetry on the supply of liquidity. The main advantage is that the data come from a pure LOB market which, for these stocks, captures over 95% of the non-over the counter (OTC) order flow.

In a time-series approach, we relate Hasbrouck's (1991) informativeness measure to LOB liquidity. We find that trade informativeness Granger-causes price concessions for large market orders, but has little impact for average-size market orders. For top-of-the book liquidity supply, picking-off risk due to public news-induced volatility is more important. In a multivariate analysis of the impact of trade informativeness on book liquidity we allow for control variables such as realised volatility, trading intensity and trade size.

The main motivation for our study is to provide empirical evidence to feed the rapidly expanding theoretical literature on limit order markets. Recent LOB theory can be broadly classified into static and dynamic models. Static models strictly distinguish between liquidity suppliers and liquidity demanders. Only the latter have access to private information about the fundamental asset price. The LOB is the optimal market structure in this framework, as it fosters competition among suppliers of liquidity. In particular, Glosten (1994) shows that risk-neutral limit order submitters compete for supply so that, in equilibrium, the marginal order breaks even in terms of expected profit. Limit order traders incur adverse-selection costs as they trade against a (potentially) informed market order. Biais, Martimort and Rochet (2000) consider an extension with a limited number of strategic suppliers. They show that the Glosten result is obtained when their number goes to infinity. Seppi (1997) and Parlour and Seppi (2003) compare the LOB market with a hybrid market, where the LOB competes with a strategic specialist who has the privilege of *ex post* price improvement. Biais, Foucault and Salanié (1998) show how the LOB market is more likely to implement the competitive equilibrium of strategic suppliers when compared to a dealer or a floor market.

The class of dynamic LOB models does not distinguish *ex ante* between liquidity suppliers and demanders, but lets agents arrive randomly in the market to decide whether to submit a limit order (act as a liquidity supplier) or to submit a market order (act as a liquidity demander), or do nothing. These agents trade-off the cost of immediacy (to pay the spread) associated with a market order against the costs of a limit order submission, i.e. possibly infinitely delayed execution and picking-off risk. Picking-off risk occurs when limit orders are not monitored continuously, so that public information arrivals mechanically make limit buys execute more often when the value drops and make limit sells execute more often when the value rises. The agents in these dynamic models trade to lock in some private value orthogonal to common value innovations. Information is symmetric and there is no adverse-selection risk (cf. Parlour 1998; Foucault 1999; Hollifield, Miller and Sandås 2004, 2006; Goettler, Parlour and Rajan 2005; Foucault, Kadan and Kandel 2005; Rosu 2009). To the best of our knowledge, Goettler, Parlour and Rajan (2009) is the single exception as they propose a dynamic LOB model with adverse-selection risk.

One reason why dynamic LOB models abstract from adverse-selection risk is mathematical tractability, but Foucault, Kadan and Kandel (2005) and Rosu (2009) also justify the assumption with Huang and Stoll's (1997) finding that the majority of the bid-ask spread (88.8%) is due to non-informational frictions. We note that while dynamic LOB models do consider picking-off risk, this risk is fundamentally different from adverse-selection risk, as the latter involves a (potential) transfer of surplus from uninformed to informed traders and, therefore, potentially impedes trade. We henceforth interpret picking-off risk in the narrow sense of 'adverse' execution due to public information, consistent with dynamic LOB models. In real-world markets, such adverse execution might also be due to private information in the order flow. In our multivariate analysis, both aspects of adverse execution are accounted for by including a proxy for public news induced volatility (realised volatility) as a control variable along with Hasbrouck's (1991) measure of trade informativeness.

In addition to the time-series analysis of trade informativeness and liquidity supply, we also pursue a structural approach in order to test the Glosten (1994) model. For this test, we have a LOB in mind that quickly replenishes to equilibrium after each market order. We follow Sandås (2001) who tests the Glosten model using three months of data (starting Dec 1991) for 10 stocks traded on the Stockholm Stock Exchange (SSE). Formal tests performed by Sandås (2001) reject the model, but one could argue that the SSE market design is too different from the theoretical setting of the Glosten model in the first place. We believe our data are more appropriate because of three main reasons. First, the German electronic market covers over 95% of non-OTC trades, whereas the Swedish sample missed 'a significant fraction of the turnover' due to transactions on London's Stock Exchange Automated Quotation System (SEAQ) and National Association of Securities Dealers Automated Quotations (NASDAQ) (see Sandås 2001, p. 708). Second, entry as an implicit market maker through limit order activity is more attractive. The reason is that the German exchange, as opposed to the 1991 Stockholm exchange, does not charge for limit order submission or cancellation. Third, our more recent sample benefits from technological development since 1991. Early evidence of a quickly replenishing book is the high limit order activity that we measure in our data. We find that the ratio of limit to market orders is 6.1, which compares to a 1.7 ratio for Sandås' SSE sample.

Empirical evidence consistent with a replenishing 'Glosten'-book is that on poor book liquidity limit orders are more likely than market orders (cf. Biais, Hillion and Spatt 1995, Griffiths et al. 2000, Ahn, Bae and Chan 2001, Ranaldo 2004). This evidence, however, is also consistent with dynamic LOB models. There is, however, also some evidence in favour of a replenishing Glosten-book after *privately informed* market orders, which is harder to reconcile with current dynamic models that assume symmetric information. As for private information in market orders, Biais, Hillion and Spatt (1995) study the Paris LOB market and find that, along with the ask, the bid changes after a market buy, which indicates that market orders are informative. Bloomfield, O'Hara and Saar (2009) conduct an LOB market experiment and one of their findings is that informed traders use market orders relatively more often than noise traders or liquidity traders. As for a quickly replenishing book, Biais, Hillion and Spatt (1995, p. 1693) document that durations are 30% shorter after a large market order and interpret this finding as 'traders quickly place orders within the best quotes to supply liquidity at relatively advantageous prices and to obtain time priority' (p. 1683). Ranaldo (2004) reports a similar finding for the Swiss Stock Exchange. Finally, LOB markets are easily accessible, transparent electronic markets, and any profit opportunities in the book should therefore be quickly filled by outside liquidity providers.

There is also evidence against a quickly replenishing Glosten-LOB. For the hybrid NYSE market, Harrish and Hasbrouck (1996, p. 230) find that 'expected profits accruing to an off-the-floor trader who attempts to behave as a dealer are generally negative...'. In hybrid markets, though, limit orders are at a disadvantage relative to the specialist who can cream-skim arriving market orders, as she can decide *ex post* (i.e. after arrival) whether or not to supply liquidity (cf. Seppi 1997; Parlour and Seppi 2003).

Our main results can be summarised as follows. Consistent with Sandås's (2001) results, our formal tests also reject the structural model. The informativeness parameter, Glosten's $\alpha$, turns insignificant when based on the updating conditions for an equilibrium LOB. One interpretation is that book replenishment from transaction to transaction is noisy and potentially incomplete. This motivates our alternative approach that does not rely on a parametrised model, and uses the long-term price impact of trades to measure their informativeness. This approach finds empirical support for the main prediction of static LOB models that informativeness matters for book liquidity, which we measure through price concessions of market orders of different sizes. We find that large order price concessions are most sensitive to trade informativeness, as opposed to any of the control variables employed in the multivariate analysis, e.g. realised volatility. However, we also find that the bid-ask spread and the average-size order price concessions respond stronger to our proxy of market volatility, i.e. picking-off risk that is unrelated to private information.

These findings relate to two recent papers on the Island electronic crossing network, which has the additional feature of competition for order flow with other non-OTC venues, most notably the NASDAQ. Consistent with our findings, Hasbrouck and Saar (2007) document for a cross-section of securities that volatility is associated with lower depth in the book. We contribute by emphasising trade informativeness, where we control for volatility. And, Hasbrouck and Saar (2009) find that limit orders should not be viewed solely as 'patient' liquidity supply, as some 'fleeting' limit orders appear to hunt for hidden depth.

The remainder of the paper is organised as follows. Section 2 discusses the institutional background, the available data, and presents summary statistics. Section 3 reviews the Glosten (1994) model and estimates the structural parameters by generalized method of moments (GMM) following Sandås (2001). Section 4 studies time-varying trade informativeness using the Hasbrouck (1991) measure and conducts Granger causality tests to study whether high informativeness causes poor book liquidity or vice versa. In a multivariate analysis, we add control variables such as volatility, trade size, and duration to isolate the trade informativeness effect. Section 5 discusses the results and Section 6 concludes.

## 2.  Institutional background and data sample

### 2.1  *The XETRA LOB*

The German Stock Exchange (GSE) operates the electronic LOB XETRA according to trading rules that are similar to previously studied limit order markets, e.g. Euronext, the Hong Kong Stock Exchange and the Swedish Stock Exchange. We refer to Biais, Hillion, Spatt (1995) for a detailed description of these rules. Trading starts at 9 a.m. (Central European Time CET) with an opening auction and closes at 5.30 p.m. with a closing auction. Around noon, trading is interrupted for the 'mid-day' auction. For the Deutscher Aktienindex (DAX) 30 constituent stocks studied in this paper there are no designated market makers. Market orders larger than the depth available at the best quote automatically 'walk up the book'.

XETRA is quite close to the stylised setting analysed in Glosten's (1994) LOB model, but deviates in two ways. First, it allows for the so-called iceberg orders, which are similar to standard limit orders with the exception that part of the limit order volume is not displayed in the book. This hidden volume enjoys price priority over other limit orders, but not time priority. In the remainder of the paper, we focus on the results based on the visible book. For the sake of a robustness check, we also perform the analysis on the total book and find that the results are not affected. The second main difference to the Glosten framework is that the XETRA LOB faces some local, regional, and international competition for order flow. Parallel to the XETRA system, the German Stock Exchange maintains a trading floor which, by all means, functions as an upstairs market. Regional competition comes from smaller German exchanges. Finally, 11 of the 30 DAX stocks are cross-listed as American Depository Receipt (ADR) at the New York Stock Exchange (NYSE). However, we can safely ignore these alternative trading venues in the analysis as the

XETRA system has a market share of at least 95%. Our stocks also trade in an OTC market, but it is hard to measure the size of this market as trades do not need to be reported.

## 2.2 *Data and summary statistics*

From the GSE, we have received data on all XETRA order book events – entries, cancellations, revisions, expirations, partial-fills and full-fills of market, limit, and iceberg orders – for a three-month period, 2 January–31 March 2004. In this study, we focus on the 30 blue chip stocks in the German DAX index. We use the data to perform a real-time reconstruction of the order book sequences. For that purpose, we start with an initial state of the book each day and use all order events to re-build the book sequences for the remainder of the day, accounting for every event that changes the order book. Our reconstruction procedure permits distinguishing the visible and the hidden part of the order book.

Summary statistics in Table 1 show that XETRA trading is very active, in particular in terms of limit order submissions. For the average stock in the sample, the average daily number of limit orders submitted to the system is 12,785, i.e. 25 limit orders per minute. Of these submissions, 10,887 are cancelled prior to execution on the same day. The average number of trades per day is 2099, i.e. four trades per minute. These numbers suggest that limit order traders actively follow the market and submit orders to benefit from profit opportunities in the spirit of the Glosten-model. It is interesting to note that relatively many orders arrive as limit orders (as opposed to market orders or marketable limit orders) in comparison to what we know from previous studies. For the XETRA data, the limit to market order ratio is 6.1, whereas this ratio is, for example, 1.1 for the Paris Bourse in November 1991 and 1.7 for the Stockholm Stock Exchange (SSE) from December 1991 to February 1992 (cf. Biais, Hillion and Spatt 1995; Sandås 2001).

The descriptive statistics reveal three more interesting stylised facts of the data. First, we present the frequency of market orders that execute not only at the best quote, but also at prices strictly inside the book. We find that 15.2% of all market orders 'walk up the book', which demonstrates the relevancy of liquidity supply beyond the best quotes. Second, we find that bid-ask spreads are small, nine basis points on average, which is consistent with a very active and liquid market. Third, we find considerable cross-sectional variation and thus decide to sort the sample stocks into quartiles based on trade activity. Earlier work shows that informed trading is more important for small, less active stocks (cf. Easley et al. 1996).

## 3. Structural econometrics: the Glosten model

To study the importance of informativeness for book liquidity we first follow Sandås (2001) and estimate the structural parameters of the Glosten (1994) model. We briefly review the model and the implied moment conditions used for GMM estimation, and then present our estimates.

## 3.1 *General features of the model*

There are two types of agents in the market: liquidity suppliers and liquidity demanders. Liquidity suppliers are patient uninformed risk-neutral agents who submit limit orders to the book to maximise expected profit. Liquidity demanders submit market orders and may have private information about the value of the security. Liquidity demanders arrive randomly at the market and we organise our time line accordingly. The sequencing of events is such that between the arrival of market orders, the book is quickly updated by liquidity suppliers, as illustrated in the

Table 1. Characteristics of the stocks in the sample (DAX30 stocks).

| Ticker | Company name | Market cap. (Mill. €) | % Agg. trades | Daily nb. trades | Daily nb. subm. | Daily nb. cancel. | Price (€) | Spread (€) | Spread (%) | Activity quartile |
|---|---|---|---|---|---|---|---|---|---|---|
| ALV | Allianz | 33,805 | 21.4 | 4523 | 29,791 | 25,882 | 100.1 | 0.05 | 0.05 | Q1 |
| DTE | Deutsche Telekom | 34,858 | 5.0 | 4445 | 14,498 | 11,009 | 15.7 | 0.01 | 0.07 | |
| SIE | Siemens | 52,893 | 16.7 | 4418 | 23,659 | 19,920 | 64.0 | 0.03 | 0.05 | |
| DBK | Deutsche Bank | 38,228 | 19.3 | 3961 | 23,169 | 19,772 | 67.2 | 0.03 | 0.05 | |
| MUV2 | Muenchener Rueck | 16,396 | 20.7 | 3425 | 20,154 | 16,894 | 93.9 | 0.06 | 0.06 | |
| DCX | Daimlerchrysler | 30,316 | 14.5 | 3309 | 18,722 | 15,919 | 36.4 | 0.02 | 0.06 | |
| EOA | E.On | 33,753 | 13.6 | 2871 | 18,899 | 16,468 | 52.5 | 0.03 | 0.06 | |
| SAP | SAP | 27,412 | 21.9 | 2806 | 19,733 | 17,095 | 131.5 | 0.08 | 0.06 | Q2 |
| IFX | Infineon | 4790 | 8.6 | 2799 | 10,320 | 7744 | 11.6 | 0.01 | 0.10 | |
| BAS | Basf | 25,425 | 13.8 | 2580 | 18,211 | 15,898 | 43.3 | 0.03 | 0.06 | |
| VOW | Volkswagen | 9688 | 16.0 | 2545 | 13,474 | 11,273 | 39.2 | 0.03 | 0.07 | |
| BAY | Bayer | 15,911 | 12.4 | 2400 | 15,258 | 12,988 | 23.1 | 0.02 | 0.08 | |
| RWE | RWE | 12,653 | 13.0 | 2314 | 14,438 | 12,355 | 33.8 | 0.03 | 0.08 | |
| BMW | BMW | 12,211 | 14.4 | 2110 | 14,736 | 12,764 | 34.7 | 0.02 | 0.07 | |
| HVM | Bay.Hyp.Vereinsbank | 6629 | 15.0 | 1937 | 10,204 | 8293 | 18.7 | 0.02 | 0.11 | |
| SCH | Schering | 7055 | 16.2 | 1523 | 9,111 | 7669 | 40.8 | 0.04 | 0.09 | Q3 |
| CBK | Commerzbank | 7569 | 12.6 | 1450 | 11,922 | 10,476 | 15.4 | 0.02 | 0.11 | |
| LHA | Lufthansa | 4548 | 11.9 | 1352 | 8079 | 6780 | 14.2 | 0.02 | 0.12 | |
| DPW | Deutsche post | 6306 | 11.0 | 1315 | 6861 | 5666 | 18.2 | 0.02 | 0.11 | |
| TKA | Thyssen-Krupp | 6450 | 11.3 | 1262 | 7864 | 6672 | 15.9 | 0.02 | 0.13 | |
| MEO | Metro | 5018 | 15.7 | 1235 | 7975 | 6702 | 35.0 | 0.04 | 0.12 | |
| ALT | Altana | 3338 | 18.9 | 1095 | 7718 | 6609 | 48.6 | 0.05 | 0.10 | |
| TUI | TUI | 2025 | 17.6 | 1063 | 6767 | 5714 | 18.7 | 0.03 | 0.14 | |
| MAN | MAN | 2434 | 13.0 | 1057 | 7214 | 6235 | 27.7 | 0.03 | 0.12 | Q4 |
| CONT | Continental | 4060 | 13.5 | 1002 | 8036 | 7052 | 31.6 | 0.04 | 0.11 | |
| DB1 | Deutsche Boerse | 4847 | 18.4 | 982 | 6598 | 5698 | 46.9 | 0.04 | 0.10 | |
| ADS | Adidas-Salomon | 4104 | 20.1 | 980 | 8057 | 7105 | 92.6 | 0.08 | 0.09 | |
| LIN | Linde | 3448 | 15.8 | 896 | 8342 | 7454 | 43.6 | 0.05 | 0.11 | |
| HEN3 | Henkel | 3682 | 16.6 | 702 | 7989 | 7306 | 65.9 | 0.07 | 0.10 | |
| FME | Fresenius | 1944 | 16.7 | 621 | 5764 | 5195 | 54.0 | 0.07 | 0.13 | |
| | Average | 14,076 | 15.2 | 2099 | 12,785 | 10,887 | 44.5 | 0.04 | 0.09 | |

Notes: The statistics are computed based on market event data covering the sample period 2 January 2004–31 March 2004. Column market cap. gives the market capitalisation of the respective stock in million euros at the end of December 2003. % agg. trades is the percentage of total trading volume executed beyond the best quotes (aggressive trades). daily nb. trades denotes the average daily number of trades. Column daily nb. subm. reports the average number of order submissions per day, market orders excluded and daily nb. cancel. the average number of order cancellations per day. price (€), spread (€) and spread (%) are average midquote, spread and relative spread over the 3-month sample period. The stocks are sorted into four groups (activity quartiles, Q1–Q4) according to their trading frequency, i.e. by the column daily nb. trades. Horizontal lines separate the four groups.

following graph:

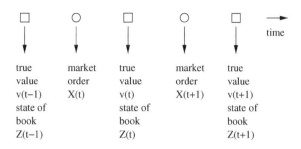

where $X_t$ is the signed market order size (number of shares), $v_t$ is the true value of the security after arrival of market order $X_t$, and $Z_t$ captures the state of the order book (e.g. bid–ask spread, depth at the best quote).

### 3.1.1 Liquidity demanders
The liquidity demander who arrives at time $t$ submits a market order of size $X_t$, a number that is positive for buys and negative for sells. We assume that buys and sells are equally likely and $X_t$ is independent from $X_s$ for $s \neq t$. For order size, we assume a symmetric, two-sided exponential distribution:

$$f(|X_t|) = \frac{1}{2\lambda}e^{|X_t|/\lambda}, \tag{1}$$

where $\lambda > 0$ is the average order size in absolute terms. To capture trade informativeness, we assume the following process for the true value of the security $v_t$ right after the arrival of the market order at event time $t$:

$$v_t = E[v_t|v_{t-1}, X_t] + \eta_t = c + v_{t-1} + \alpha X_t + \eta_t, \tag{2}$$

where $\eta_t$ accounts for the arrival of public information between the trades at event time $t$ and at $t - 1$. The key parameter in the model is $\alpha$, which captures the informativeness (with respect to the asset value) of the arriving market order. We refer to the parameter as Glosten's alpha.

### 3.1.2 Liquidity suppliers
We assume that liquidity suppliers incur fixed order-processing cost $\gamma$ when transacting with incoming market orders. They submit limit orders right after the arrival of market order $X_t$ at various prices until the marginal order at each of these prices breaks even. For example, suppose that price level $p_{1,t}$ is the lowest price above $v_t$ at which it is profitable to supply a limit sell of strictly positive quantity. Limit orders will fill the book at this price and the expected profit on the $q_{1,t}$th share at price level $p_{1,t}$, is determined by:

$$E[(p_{1,t} - E[v_{t+1}|X_{t+1}] - \gamma)I_{[X_{t+1}>q_{1,t}]}], \tag{3}$$

where $(p_{1,t} - E[v_{t+1}|X_{t+1}])$ is the difference between the price the limit order trades at and the expected fundamental value conditional on the next market order $X_{t+1}$. $I_{[X_{t+1}>q_{1,t}]}$ is an indicator function that is one if $X_{t+1}$ is larger than $q_{1,t}$ – in which case the limit order executes – and zero otherwise. A zero expected profit condition on the last unit (as the queue clears according to first-come-first-served time priority) determines the equilibrium depth $q_{1,t}$ at the best ask price $p_{1,t}$. Once the equilibrium depth is reached, limit order traders will consider submitting a unit at the next price on the grid, one tick above $p_{1,t}$. They consider adding this unit, because the revenue they get on execution is one tick higher than on $p_{1,t}$. The equilibrium depths on both sides of the LOB are given by the recursions:

$$q_{+k,t} = \frac{p_{+k,t} - v_t - \gamma}{\alpha} - \sum_{i=+1}^{+k-1} q_{i,t} - \lambda, \quad k = 1, 2, \ldots \quad \text{(ask side)},$$

$$q_{-k,t} = \frac{v_t - p_{-k,t} - \gamma}{\alpha} - \sum_{i=-1}^{-k+1} q_{i,t} - \lambda, \quad k = 1, 2, \ldots \quad \text{(bid side)}. \quad (4)$$

The state of the book is described by the set of bid $(p_{-k,t})$ and ask $(p_{+k,t})$ prices and their associated depths $(q_{-k,t}$ and $q_{+k,t})$. Equation (4) shows that the trade informativeness measure $\alpha$ is a key determinant of book liquidity.

## 3.2 Moment conditions

We follow Sandås (2001) and use three types of moment conditions: two of these are based on Equation (4) where we assume that LOBs have refilled to equilibrium when we take snapshot $t$ (which will be just before the arrival of the next market order $X_{t+1}$). The third condition identifies the expected market order size $\lambda$.

### 3.2.1 Break-even conditions

For the first type of moment conditions, we use information in the book. In order to eliminate the fundamental value, we add the equilibrium depth associated with the $k$th price at the bid side of the book from the corresponding equation at the ask side of the book (see Equation (4)) and assume that the equations hold up to an error term:

$$E\left(p_{+k,t} - p_{-k,t} - 2\gamma - \alpha \left(\sum_{i=+1}^{+k} q_{i,t} + \sum_{i=-1}^{-k} q_{i,t} + 2\lambda\right)\right) = 0. \quad k = 1, 2, \ldots. \quad (5)$$

### 3.2.2 Updating restrictions

For the second type of moment conditions, we use the time dimension and subtract the $k$th price in the book at time $t-1$ from the $k$th price at time $t$. This removes the fundamental asset value $v_t$ of Equation (2), and we obtain:

$$E\left(\Delta p_{+k,t} - \alpha \left(\sum_{i=+1}^{+k} q_{i,t+1} - \sum_{i=+1}^{+k} q_{i,t}\right) - c - \alpha X_t\right) = 0, \quad k = 1, 2, \ldots,$$

$$E\left(\Delta p_{-k,t} + \alpha \left(\sum_{i=-1}^{-k} q_{i,t+1} - \sum_{i=-1}^{-k} q_{i,t}\right) - c - \alpha X_t\right) = 0, \quad k = 1, 2, \ldots, \quad (6)$$

where $\Delta p_{k,t} = p_{k,t} - p_{k,t-1}$.

### 3.2.3 Market order size condition

We use the expected size of the market order to identify $\lambda$ (see Equation (1))via

$$E(|X_t| - \lambda) = 0. \quad (7)$$

## 3.3 GMM estimation results

We use GMM to estimate the structural model based on the four best quotes on both sides of the book. This yields 13 moment conditions: four from the break-even conditions of Equation (5), eight from the updating restrictions of Equation (6), and one from the market order size condition of Equation (7). The estimation is based on event time, where the arrival of a market order marks an event. In the implementation, we take the snapshot of the order book just ahead of the arrival of the next market order, whereby we assume that durations between trades – time between market order arrivals – are long enough so that competitive limit order traders have time to refill the book in between trades. We consider this a credible assumption for our sample, given the high limit order activity. As pointed out above, on average 6.1 limit orders are submitted in between two market order arrivals (see Table 1).

Table 2 reports the GMM estimates of all parameters in the Glosten-model. We estimate on a stock-by-stock basis, but report averages per trade activity quartile (where Q1 contains the most actively traded stocks) in order to conserve space. We standardise the informativeness measure $\alpha$ to enable meaningful comparison across stocks:[2]

$$\alpha^G = \alpha \frac{\text{€50,000}}{P^2}, \tag{8}$$

where $P$ is the average price for the stock throughout the sample period. We use the superscript G to indicate that it is the Glosten-$\alpha$, which we will later compare to an alternative measure, the Hasbrouck-$\alpha$. We interpret $\alpha^G$, in the context of the Glosten-model, as the relative price impact of a €50,000 market order.

Our findings are similar to those reported by Sandås (2001). First, we find that trade informativeness $\alpha^G$ decreases monotonically with trade activity in the cross-section. Market orders seem to be most informative for the least actively traded stocks' quartile (Q4), which contains the smallest stocks in terms of market capitalisation (see Table 1). Second, we find that the transaction cost

Table 2. Estimation results of the Såndas/Glosten model.

| | $\alpha \times 10^3$ | $\gamma$ | $\lambda$ | $c_v \times 10^3$ | $J(9)$ | No reject | $\alpha^G \times 10^3$ |
|---|---|---|---|---|---|---|---|
| All stocks | **0.013** | **−0.010** | **1.380** | **0.030** | 643.7 | 2 | **0.326** |
| | 167.3 | 52.5 | 133.1 | 2.2 | | | |
| Q1 | **0.009** | **−0.006** | **1.600** | **0.029** | 1985.3 | 0 | **0.087** |
| (most active) | 249.6 | 50.5 | 188.8 | 2.5 | | | |
| Q2 | **0.008** | **−0.008** | **1.724** | **0.088** | 539.8 | 0 | **0.189** |
| | 170.3 | 55.7 | 147.1 | 2.0 | | | |
| Q3 | **0.008** | **−0.010** | **1.517** | **−0.063** | 91.9 | 1 | **0.471** |
| | 143.1 | 54.9 | 108.5 | 2.1 | | | |
| Q4 | **0.029** | **−0.018** | **0.610** | **0.071** | 51.6 | 1 | **0.555** |
| (least active) | 109.3 | 48.2 | 89.4 | 2.1 | | | |

Notes: The estimation uses the information from the best four quotes of the visible books to form update and break-even conditions. The table reports in bold face font the first stage GMM estimates of $\alpha$, $\gamma$, $\lambda$ and $c_v$ which are averaged across all stocks as well as across the stocks in the respective trading activity quartile. The values printed in regular font are $t$-values which are also group averages. The $J(9)$ column is the group average of the GMM $J$-statistic (with nine degrees of freedom). Column *no reject* reports the number of stocks for which the model is not rejected at 1% significance level. The last column reports the group averages of the standardised trade informativeness measure $\alpha^G$ (Glosten-$\alpha$, see Equation (8)).

parameter $\gamma$ is significantly negative, which is worrisome in the context of the Glosten-model. Third, and most discomforting, the GMM $J$-test rejects the model for 29 out of the 30 stocks.

We proceed with separate estimation of the break-even conditions and the updating restrictions to analyse why the model is rejected. We find that the $\alpha$ estimates based on the break-even conditions remain significantly positive, whereas those based on the updating restrictions turn insignificant for most of the stocks. It seems that $\alpha$ is identified primarily through snapshots of the book at a single point in time and *not* on updating the value $v_t$ after the arrival of market orders. This evidence is consistent with Sandås' paper which finds that the Glosten-$\alpha$s estimated on the break-even conditions are about nine times higher than those based on the updating restrictions (Sandås 2001, Table 5).

In the second part of our empirical analysis, we deviate from Sandås' (2001) structural approach, and rely on time-series econometrics to study the importance of trade informativeness for book liquidity. We abandon the structural model for two reasons. First, the approach requires strong model assumptions in building the moment conditions (e.g. exponential order size distribution, independence of $X_t$). These assumptions might not be justifiable in real-world markets. Second, the model restricts the same parameter ($\alpha$) to capture the shape of the book *and* the value update based on arriving market orders. The assumption is that the book replenishes and fully reveals the long-term impact (i.e. the informational content) of the trade before the next market order arrives. In the time-series approach, we separate book liquidity from informativeness of market orders to check whether, as the Glosten-model predicts, book liquidity is low during times of highly informative market orders. We rely on Granger causality to identify such effect.

## 4. Time-series econometrics: trade informativeness and book liquidity

In this section, we use the time-series dimension to study trade informativeness and order book liquidity. First, we analyse the time-series properties of the trade informativeness measure proposed by Hasbrouck (1991). Second, we motivate three measures for book liquidity to capture both the spread and the depth of the book. Finally, we analyse the interaction of trade informativeness and book liquidity based on a Granger-causality test including appropriate control variables to isolate the effects of interest.

For our analysis, we aggregate the event-time calendar used for GMM estimation. In particular, we group $N$ subsequent market orders into one time interval $t$. $N$ is chosen in order to retain sufficient observations to estimate Hasbrouck's trade informativeness measure. Our procedure is best explained by the following graph where trade arrivals are denoted by circles and $N = 3$:

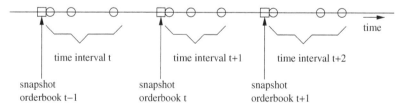

We choose $N$ to trade off too few observations and too little time variation. We therefore set $N$ equal to 250 for the quartile of most actively traded stocks (Q1) yielding an average of 14.9 periods per trading day, each lasting 34 min on average. We take less observations per interval for the three other quartiles by setting $N = 200$ for Q2, $N = 150$ for Q3, and $N = 100$ for Q4. By definition, these quartiles trade less frequently than Q1 so that for equal $N$ we would obtain too few intra-day estimation intervals. Also, these smaller values of $N$ ensure that the average time lengths of the intervals are comparable to Q1. The resulting average interval lengths are 43 min for Q2, 61 min for Q3, and 60 min for Q4. For robustness checks, we try various values for $N$ and find that our main results are not affected.

### 4.1 *Measuring time-varying trade informativeness*

We use the $N$ trades in a time interval to identify trade informativeness closely following Hasbrouck (1991). The approach relies on estimates of the following bivariate vector autoregression (VAR):

$$r_{t,\tau} = a_{1t}r_{t,\tau-1} + a_{2t}r_{t,\tau-2} + \cdots + b_{0t}X_{t,\tau} + b_{1t}X_{t,\tau-1} + b_{2t}X_{t,\tau-2} + \cdots + u_{t,\tau},$$

$$X_{t,\tau} = c_{1t}r_{t,\tau-1} + c_{2t}r_{t,\tau-2} + \cdots + d_{1t}X_{t,\tau-1} + d_{2t}X_{t,\tau-2} + \cdots + w_{t,\tau}, \tag{9}$$

where $\tau \in \{1,\ldots,N\}$ runs over all midquote changes in time interval $t$, $r_{t,\tau}$ is the midquote change from order book snapshot $\tau - 1$ to snapshot $\tau$ in interval $t$, and $X_{t,\tau}$ is the signed order size of trade $\tau$ in interval $t$ (it is zero if there was no transaction at the time of the midquote change). We use the subscript $t$ to indicate the coefficients that belong to time interval $t$. We assume that the innovations $u_{t,\tau}$ and $w_{t,\tau}$ are i.i.d. and contemporaneously uncorrelated.

To identify the long-term impact of a trade, we consider the vector moving average representation of the VAR in Equation (9) (assuming stationarity):

$$r_{t,\tau} = u_{t,\tau} + a_{1t}^{*}u_{t,\tau-1} + a_{2t}^{*}u_{t,\tau-2} + \cdots + b_{0t}^{*}w_{t,\tau} + b_{1t}^{*}w_{t,\tau-1} + \cdots, \tag{10}$$

$$X_{t,\tau} = c_{1t}^{*}u_{t,\tau-1} + c_{2t}^{*}u_{t,\tau-2} + \cdots + w_{t,\tau} + d_{1t}^{*}w_{t,\tau-1} + \cdots, \tag{11}$$

where $b_{0t}^{*}$ identifies the immediate price impact of a market order. The permanent price impact of a market order in time interval $t$ can now be obtained as

$$\alpha_t^{H} = \left(\sum_{i=0}^{\infty} b_{it}^{*}\right) \frac{€50,000}{P^2}, \tag{12}$$

where the second factor on the right-hand side of the equation scales the coefficient in the same way as was done for the Glosten-$\alpha$ (see Equation (8)).

In the VAR estimations, we use 10 lags to ensure uncorrelated residuals. Hasbrouck (1991) chooses five VAR lags, and Dufour and Engle (2000), who extend Hasbrouck's methodology, choose the same lag length. The choice of 10 lags in our sample ensures serially uncorrelated VAR residual series for all stocks. The variation of the lag length within the range indicated by Akaike information criteria does not affect the results of the later stages which make use of the trade informativeness estimates. The increased lag length which is indicated for our recent data supports the view that order splitting/algorithmic trading became more important since the early 1990s.

We follow Hasbrouck (1991) and truncate the infinite sum of Equation (12) at lag 40. As above, we estimate the VAR stock by stock and report the quartile averages.

Table 3 reports the average Hasbrouck-$\alpha$ as well as its time-series characteristics. We find that the average Hasbrouck-$\alpha$ is similar to the average Glosten-$\alpha$. For the quartile of most actively traded stocks (Q1), we find an average $\alpha^{H}$ of 0.08 basis points, which is very close to the average $\alpha^{G}$ of 0.09 basis points reported in Table 2. For the other quartiles, the differences are somewhat larger, and the Hasbrouck-$\alpha$ is consistently smaller than the Glosten-$\alpha$. We interpret the similarity of the Glosten- and Habsrouck-$\alpha$ estimates, which are obtained by very different methodologies,

Table 3. Cross-sectional and time-series properties of estimated trade informativeness measures $\alpha^H$ and immediate impacts $b^H$.

| | $\alpha^H \times 10^3$ | Min | Max | $\rho$ | $\rho_{inter}$ | $\rho_{intra}$ | $b^H \times 10^3$ |
|---|---|---|---|---|---|---|---|
| All stocks | **0.244** | **−0.016** | **0.963** | **0.328** | **0.162** | **0.352** | **0.139** |
| Q1 | **0.076** | **0.005** | **0.279** | **0.365** | **0.158** | **0.387** | **0.042** |
| (most active) | 0.021 | 0.002 | 0.056 | 0.051 | 0.166 | 0.055 | 0.011 |
| Q2 | **0.152** | **−0.011** | **0.649** | **0.355** | **0.168** | **0.380** | **0.089** |
| | 0.041 | 0.034 | 0.260 | 0.114 | 0.181 | 0.113 | 0.025 |
| Q3 | **0.335** | **−0.006** | **1.282** | **0.282** | **0.155** | **0.309** | **0.199** |
| | 0.094 | 0.015 | 0.386 | 0.067 | 0.185 | 0.061 | 0.056 |
| Q4 | **0.412** | **−0.055** | **1.639** | **0.311** | **0.166** | **0.333** | **0.224** |
| (least active) | 0.122 | 0.066 | 0.422 | 0.046 | 0.088 | 0.058 | 0.074 |

Notes: The table reports sample means (bold font) and standard deviations (regular font) of $\alpha^H$ (Hasbrouck-$\alpha$ (see Equation (12)) and the immediate impact computed as $b^H = b_0 50,000/P^2$ (see Equations (10)–(12)). Both $\alpha^H$ and $b^H$ are diurnally adjusted. For that purpose, the trading day is divided into 90 min intervals and the (stock specific) sample mean of $\alpha^H$ and $b^H$ in each interval is computed. Diurnally adjusted variables result from dividing the raw series by the corresponding time-of-day means. To compute sample means and standard deviations reported in the table, the diurnally adjusted series are pooled (overall and by trade size quartile, respectively). The columns labelled min and max report the group averages of the smallest and largest $\alpha^H$ estimate ($\times 10^3$) for each stock. Column $\rho$ reports the autocorrelation of the diurnally adjusted $\alpha^H$ sequence. $\rho_{inter}$ is the inter-day correlation of the diurnally adjusted Hasbrouck-$\alpha$, i.e. the correlation between previous day's last and the next day's first $\alpha^H$ estimate. $\rho_{intra}$ is the intra-day serial correlation of the diurnally adjusted $\alpha^H$. Observations from different trading days are excluded for this computation. Bold (regular) faced numbers are group averages (standard deviations) of the autocorrelations computed in this way.

as further evidence that the updating restrictions are a poor measure of trade informativeness in the GMM test of the Glosten-model. In Section 3.3, we showed that separate estimation of the break-even conditions (based on book depth) and updating restrictions shows that the (overall) Glosten-$\alpha$ estimate largely captures book depth, as it is insignificant in the updating restrictions. Apparently, order book changes in between market orders, captured by these updating restrictions, are not able to identify trade informativeness. The Hasbrouck-$\alpha$ captures the long-term impact of trades and its similarity to the Glosten-$\alpha$ can therefore be interpreted as a support for the Glosten-model.

We further find that trade informativeness is a persistent, mean-reverting process with a distinct intra-day pattern. Figure 1 plots the average $\alpha^H$ for 90-min intervals within the trading day. We generally find that informativeness decreases during the course of the day, which is consistent with the hypothesis that the bulk of price discovery is taking place after the opening of the market. For the quartile of most actively traded stocks (Q1), we find a significant increase of trade informativeness during the interval from 3 to 4.30 pm CET, which contains the NYSE opening time (3.30 pm CET). Not surprisingly, all Q1 shares are cross-listed in New York, whereas few of the stocks in the other quartiles are inter-listed. Menkveld (2008) finds the same pattern for British and Dutch ADRs and argues that some traders prefer to trade during the overlap and split orders in order to benefit from two pools of liquidity.

We remove intra-day seasonality (diurnality) of the $\alpha^H$ estimates by dividing by the time-of-day means, and then compute first-order autocorrelations. We find persistence as first-order autocorrelations are significant for all quartiles, ranging from 0.28 to 0.38 (see Table 3). We also report inter- and intra-day correlations separately, and find that both are positive, although only intra-day autocorrelations are statistically significant.

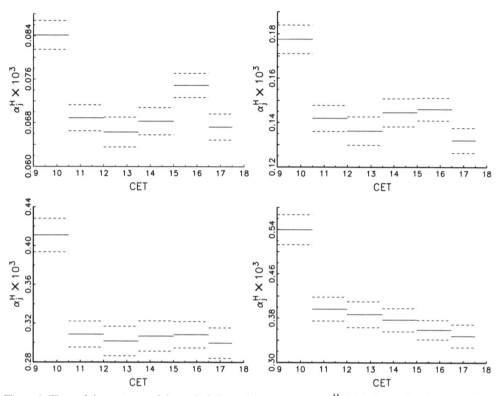

Figure 1. Time-of-day patterns of the trade informativeness measure $\alpha_j^H$. (a) Left panel, Q1 (most active); right panel, Q2; (b) Left panel, Q3; right panel, Q4 (least active). Note: The four panels of the figure show 90 min averages of the estimated trade informativeness measures $\alpha_j^H$. The averages are computed over all $\alpha_j^H$ estimates in the respective 90 min interval and over all stocks belonging to the respective trading activity quartile. The top left panel displays the results for the first quartile (most actively traded), the top right panel for the second quartile, the bottom left panel for the third quartile and the bottom right panel for the fourth quartile (least active). The dashed lines represent bounds of the 95% confidence interval.

The substantial time variation and predictability in trade informativeness is useful to analyse how important trade informativeness is for book liquidity. The persistence suggests that informative trades cluster in time so that we can discriminate times of informative market order trading and times with relatively uninformed market orders. We will study book liquidity at these times to gauge the importance of trade informativeness. Before we turn to this analysis, we first construct appropriate measures of book liquidity.

## 4.2 Measuring time-varying book liquidity

We summarise LOB liquidity at snapshot $t$ (taken at the end of the $t$th estimation window) through three measures: the quoted bid–ask spread and two measures of book depth. In the remainder of the paper, we focus on the results for the ask side of the LOB, and leave out the bid side to conserve space. The results are very similar for both sides.

Our depth measures capture the price concession from the best ask rather than the midquote in order to purge the measure of a quoted spread effect (measured separately). Price concessions are calculated for an average-sized and a large buy value. Price concessions are calculated relative to a book state where the depth at the best ask can fill the total volume of the buy order. Formally, we use

$$\text{ap}(V) = \frac{\sum_{k=0}^{\infty} I_k(V) p_k q_k}{\sum_{k=0}^{\infty} I_k(V) p_1 q_k} - 1 \tag{13}$$

where

$$I_k(V) = \begin{cases} 1 & \text{if } \sum_{i=1}^{k} q_i p_i \leq V, \\ \dfrac{V - \sum_{i=1}^{k-1} q_i p_i}{q_k p_k} & \text{if } \sum_{i=0}^{k-1} q_i p_i \leq V < \sum_{i=1}^{k} q_i p_i, \\ 0 & \text{otherwise.} \end{cases} \tag{14}$$

For ease of notation, we define a summation from $i$ to $j$ with $j < i$ to be zero (as this happens in the second line in Equation (14) for $k = 1$). The depth measure ap($V$) is zero if the market buy order of size $V$ fills at the best ask and becomes strictly positive if it has to walk up the book and consume the depth displayed at higher prices. A large price concession indicated by a large ap($V$) therefore indicates poor book liquidity at and behind the best quote. We compute the depth measure (13) for $V = €50,000$ and €200,000, respectively. In the remainder of the paper, we use ap(50) and ap(200), respectively, to refer to these depth measures.

## 4.3 *Informativeness and liquidity: Granger causality*

We use time-varying trade informativeness and book liquidity to determine whether trade infor-mativeness is an important determinant of book liquidity. We benefit from slow mean-reversion in the trade informativeness process to discriminate highly informative from relatively uninformative trade periods. We also study whether book liquidity predicts next period trade informativeness, which could be the case when limit order submitters know of an oncoming information event that is not predicted by the informativeness of lagged order flow (e.g. a pre-scheduled company news release).

For the remainder of the analysis we standardise all data series – $\alpha$ and the book liquidity measures – in order to be able to compare across intra-day time intervals and across stocks. For that purpose, we divide the trading day into six 90-min time intervals (see also Figure 1). For each stock and each variable, we then remove the diurnality by dividing the time series $x_t$ by its time-of-day mean (i.e. we replace $x_t$ by $x_t/\bar{x}_i$ where $i \in \{1,\ldots,6\}$ is the time interval $t$ falls into and $\bar{x}_i$ is the average of all $x_t$ in that interval). Furthermore, in order to account for heteroskedasticity across stocks, we scale the resulting time series by their stock-specific standard deviation (i.e. we replace the diurnally adjusted $x_t$ by $x_t/\sigma_{x_t}$ where $\sigma_{x_t}$ is the standard deviation of the diurnally adjusted $x_t$). The slope coefficients in the Granger-causality analysis below should therefore be interpreted as the amount of change of the dependent variable (in terms of its standard deviation) on a one standard deviation change of the explanatory variable.

### 4.3.1 *Trade informativeness as a determinant of book liquidity*

Before turning to the Granger causality analysis, we first plot book liquidity against trade infor-mativeness. By construction, the book snapshot $t$ is at the end of time interval $t$, which contains the $N$ trades that are used to calculate $\alpha^H$ (see graph at the start of Section 4). To study whether informativeness matters for subsequent book liquidity, we therefore plot the three book liquidity measures against $\alpha_t^H$ where we group the $\alpha$ into quartiles.

Figure 2 illustrates that book liquidity decreases monotonically in trade informativeness. Panel A illustrates that the bid-ask spread increases linearly in trade informativeness. The spread is 10% higher at times of highest trade informativeness relative to times of lowest trade informativeness. Panels B and C illustrate that trade informativeness has an even stronger effect on the two depth measures (ap(50) and ap(200), respectively) as depth is 20% lower comparing the two tail quartiles. And, the marginal effect seems to be increasing in trade informativeness.

We now turn to Granger-causality regressions to study whether trade informativeness *causes* book liquidity. We propose the following regression:

$$y_t = c + \delta \alpha_t^H + \beta_1 y_{t-1} + \cdots + \beta_p y_{t-p} + \phi_1 z_{1,t} + \cdots + \phi_q z_{q,t} + \varepsilon_t, \tag{15}$$

where $y_t$ is one of the three book liquidity measures (*spread*, ap(50), or ap(200)), $z_{i,t}$ are control variables that are based on the $N$ trades in time interval $t$ to capture market conditions other than trade informativeness. $\varepsilon_t$ is an i.i.d. disturbance. The regression indicates Granger causality if $\delta$ is statistically significant so that trade informativeness explains book liquidity over and above its predicted value based on its own past. By adding control variables, effectively, we consider the component of trade informativeness that is orthogonal to other indicators measuring trading conditions. If, in this case, $\delta$ is significant, we can attribute the effect uniquely to informativeness and not to other correlated trading variables.

Table 4 shows all control variables, their pairwise correlations, and their correlations with $\alpha_t^H$ and the three book liquidity measures. We use evidence from the microstructure literature (see Madhavan 2000 or Biais, Hillion and Spatt 2005 for a survey) to motivate five control variables. First, we include the trade size averaged over the estimation interval (*tsize*). This accounts for a potential size effect driving the significance of the trade informativeness measure if large trades are more informative than small trades. Second, we include the signed trade volume imbalance over the estimation interval (*simb*), in order to account for an asymmetric effect on book liquidity. Third, we add mean inter-trade time duration over the estimation interval (*dura*) to control for fast markets that allegedly indicate more informative trades (see Dufour and Engle 2000). Fourth, we compute *realised volatility* (*rv*) over the estimation interval. Including it as another control variable we aim to differentiate trade informativeness from picking-off risk induced by volatility shocks caused by the arrival of public information. *rv* is computed by summing squared midquote returns within the estimation interval. Midquotes are sampled immediately before the trade events within the interval. The idea to use high frequency sampled midquote changes to estimate and forecast lower frequency fundamental price volatility goes back to Andersen et al. (2003). Fifth, we add the absolute value of trade imbalance (*imb*) to control for trading volume. We prefer this proxy to the conventional volume measure as it better captures the net pressure on liquidity suppliers. The correlations of these five control variables with $\alpha_t^H$ are significantly positive for trade size, duration, realised volatility, and volume. Periods with highly informative trades, therefore, tend to show large trades in slow markets with high volatility and high volume. These correlations are as expected, except maybe for inter-trade duration. Short trade durations in the XETRA LOB setting are associated with relatively uninformative trades. This is in contrast to the findings reported in Dufour and Engle (2000) for the 1991 NYSE market. However, Grammig, Theissen and Wünsche (2007), who propose a structural modelling alternative to Dufour and Engle's (2000) time-series approach, also find that fast trading in the XETRA LOB cannot be associated with informed trading. They refer to the *crowding-out* effect described by Parlour (1998) to explain their finding. Crowding-out means that ample liquidity – a market state that we do not associate

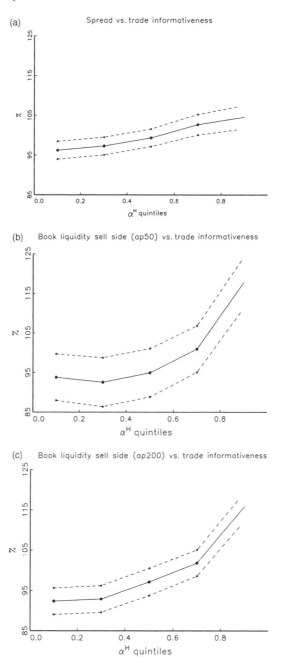

Figure 2. Book liquidity measures versus trade informativeness. (a) Panel A (b) Panel B (c) Panel C. Note: We pool time series of trade informativeness measures $\alpha^H$ (Hasbrouck-$\alpha$) for the 30 stocks and sort them into quintiles. We then compute the quintile means of the book snapshot variables *spread*, ap(50) and ap(200). Quintile means are represented as dots connected with solid lines. The small dots connected with dashed lines are bounds of the 95% confidence intervals. Both $\alpha^H$ and book liquidity measures are diurnally adjusted (division by time-of-day mean) prior to the analysis. Diurnally adjusted book liquidity variables are multiplied by 100 to obtain percentages.

Table 4. Correlation between the trade informativeness, liquidity measures and control variables.

| | $\alpha^H$ | ap(50) | ap(200) | Spread | tsize | simb | dura | rv |
|---|---|---|---|---|---|---|---|---|
| ap(50) | 0.11** | | | | | | | |
| ap(200) | 0.19** | 0.69** | | | | | | |
| spread | 0.11** | −0.04** | 0.00 | | | | | |
| tsize | −0.46** | −0.06** | −0.11** | −0.01 | | | | |
| simb | −0.02* | 0.00 | −0.01 | 0.02* | 0.03** | | | |
| dura | 0.11** | 0.01 | −0.01 | −0.02** | −0.34** | −0.01 | | |
| rv | 0.28** | 0.08** | 0.14** | 0.17** | 0.08** | 0.00 | −0.14** | |
| imb | −0.21** | −0.03** | −0.04** | 0.04** | 0.47** | 0.06** | −0.22** | 0.06** |

Notes: The table reports cross-sectional averages of correlation coefficients for the DAX30 stocks. ap(50) and ap(200) denote the hypothetical ask side price concessions for trades of €50,000 and €200,000, respectively. spread is the quoted spread in basis points. These liquidity measures are sampled just before the first trade occurs after the $\alpha^H$ estimation interval. tsize denotes the trade size and dura the duration between two consecutive trades averaged over the estimation interval. simb is the sum of the signed traded volumes over the estimation interval; imb is the absolute value of simb. Realised volatility (rv) is computed as the sum of the squared midquote returns with midquotes sampled just before a trade event occurs within the estimation interval. All series are diurnally adjusted. For that purpose the trading day is divided into 90 min intervals and the (stock specific) mean of the respective variable in each interval is computed. Diurnally adjusted variables result from dividing the raw series by their corresponding time-of-day means. Computation of the correlations is based on an average (across stocks) of $T = 692$ observations. The standard errors of the mean correlations are approximated by $1/\sqrt{TN}$ where $N = 30$.
*Mean correlation that is significantly different from zero at the 5% level.
**Mean correlation that is significantly different from zero at the 1 % level.

with asymmetric information – causes intense uninformed market order trading. By submitting a market order, an impatient (yet not superiorly informed) trader can jump ahead of a lengthy queue of limit orders at the best quotes.

Panel A of Table 5 summarises the regression results using the quoted spread as dependent variable. Trade informativeness is significant for eight out of 30 stock-specific regressions. The parameter carries the correct sign, since at times of high trade informativeness the book exhibits higher bid–ask spreads. We find that the effect is economically significant as a one standard deviation change of trade informativeness increases the spread by 8% of its standard deviation. The quartile-specific results show that the effect increases monotonically in trade activity. It is strongest for the least actively traded stocks. Regarding the control variables, we find that realised volatility is the only variable more often significant than trade informativeness (for 14 stocks). It also has a stronger economic significance, as a one standard deviation increase in realised volatility increases the spread by 15% of its standard deviation.

Panels B and C of Table 5 report the results for the two depth measures ap(50) and ap(200) which show that trade informativeness is important primarily for a depth further into the book. Using ap(50) as a dependent variable in Equation (15), trade informativeness is statistically significant for six stocks, while it is statistically significant for 17 sample stocks when ap(200) is used as the dependent variable in Equation (15). The estimated coefficients have the correct sign, as high informativeness implies higher price concessions. The effects are economically significant as a one standard deviation change in trade informativeness increases ap(50) by 7% and ap(200) by 12% of the respective standard deviation. Trade informativeness is economically and statistically more important than realised volatility, which is the second-most relevant variable. For ap(200), we again find a monotonic relationship across activity quartiles, where the least active quartile shows the strongest effect.

Table 5. Regression of book liquidity measures on trade informativeness and control variables.

| | $\alpha^H$ | rv | tsize | dura | imb | simb | lag1 | lag2 | $R^2_{adj}$ |
|---|---|---|---|---|---|---|---|---|---|
| | | | | Panel A spread | | | | | |
| All stocks | 0.080 | 0.147 | −0.015 | −0.005 | 0.047 | 0.014 | 0.001 | 0.004 | 0.051 |
| sig_pos (of 30) | 8 | 14 | 0 | 2 | 5 | 0 | 0 | 0 | |
| sig_neg | 0 | 0 | 3 | 3 | 0 | 1 | 1 | 0 | |
| Q1 (most active) | 0.043 | 0.125 | −0.065 | −0.037 | 0.035 | 0.034 | −0.010 | 0.003 | 0.034 |
| Q2 | 0.068 | 0.168 | −0.012 | −0.015 | 0.043 | 0.007 | −0.003 | −0.012 | 0.061 |
| Q3 | 0.089 | 0.192 | 0.002 | 0.005 | 0.036 | −0.007 | −0.007 | 0.024 | 0.067 |
| Q4 (least active) | 0.121 | 0.095 | 0.011 | 0.025 | 0.076 | 0.024 | 0.024 | 0.002 | 0.038 |
| | | | | Panel B ap(50) | | | | | |
| All stocks | 0.068 | 0.063 | −0.041 | −0.008 | 0.004 | 0.003 | 0.009 | 0.005 | 0.015 |
| sigpos (of 30) | 6 | 5 | 0 | 0 | 0 | 1 | 0 | 0 | |
| signeg | 0 | 0 | 4 | 0 | 1 | 1 | 1 | 1 | |
| Q1 (most active) | 0.077 | 0.047 | 0.022 | −0.007 | −0.030 | 0.018 | 0.002 | 0.012 | 0.010 |
| Q2 | 0.060 | 0.041 | −0.069 | −0.010 | 0.034 | 0.013 | 0.014 | −0.015 | 0.010 |
| Q3 | 0.043 | 0.110 | −0.056 | −0.017 | −0.009 | −0.022 | −0.001 | 0.013 | 0.019 |
| Q4 (least active) | 0.097 | 0.050 | −0.055 | 0.004 | 0.017 | 0.006 | 0.021 | 0.011 | 0.022 |
| | | | | Panel C ap(200) | | | | | |
| All stocks | 0.117 | 0.096 | −0.072 | −0.030 | 0.014 | −0.004 | 0.041 | 0.042 | 0.054 |
| sig_pos (of 30) | 17 | 13 | 0 | 0 | 1 | 1 | 1 | 4 | |
| sig_neg | 0 | 0 | 5 | 1 | 1 | 2 | 0 | 1 | |
| Q1 (most active) | 0.108 | 0.099 | −0.035 | −0.036 | 0.005 | 0.001 | −0.010 | 0.018 | 0.034 |
| Q2 | 0.107 | 0.085 | −0.082 | −0.034 | 0.041 | −0.006 | 0.052 | 0.030 | 0.048 |
| Q3 | 0.124 | 0.126 | −0.073 | −0.030 | −0.004 | −0.005 | 0.046 | 0.046 | 0.064 |
| Q4 (least active) | 0.129 | 0.071 | −0.096 | −0.018 | 0.012 | −0.006 | 0.076 | 0.076 | 0.071 |

Notes: The book liquidity indicators spread, ap(50) and ap(200) are regressed on the trade-informativeness indicator $\alpha^H$ and control variables. The liquidity indicators are sampled just before the first trade occurs after the $\alpha^H$ estimation interval. The regression also includes (in addition to a constant and two lags of the dependent variable) the control variables realised volatility (rv), trade size (tsize), trade duration (dura), unsigned trade imbalance (imb) and signed trade imbalance (simb). All variables are diurnally adjusted. See Table 4 for computational details of the procedure. To obtain comparable estimates across stocks dependent variables and regressors are standardised by division by the sample standard deviations. The table reports ordinary least squares (OLS) estimates averaged across stocks. sig_pos (sig_neg) counts the number of significant and positive (negative) coefficients. The significance level is 5%. Adjusted coefficients of determination are averaged across stocks. The regressions use on average 692 observations. Per activity quartile we have 953 (Q1), 744 (Q2), 516 (Q3), 537 (Q4) observations on average.

### 4.3.2 Book liquidity as a determinant of trade informativeness

The Glosten model not only predicts that informativeness Granger-causes book liquidity, but also implies reverse causality. If limit order traders who fill the book at the end of period $t$ know more about the oncoming period than what could be predicted from current and past period informativeness, the book could Granger-cause next period informativeness. For example, traders might know that a company is about to issue a press release, which, of course, leads to an immediate quote update, but also to market orders that are highly informative. This is the case when the public information leads to 'allocational' trades due to portfolio re-balancing based on public news (see Vayanos 2001). The econometrician cannot predict such event based on past trade informativeness.

We test whether book liquidity Granger-causes trade informativeness through the following regression:

$$\alpha_t^H = c + \beta_1 \alpha_{t-1}^H + \cdots + \beta_p \alpha_{t-p}^H + \delta_1 y_{1,t-1} + \cdots + \delta_r y_{r,t-1} + \phi_1 z_{1,t-1} + \cdots + \phi_q z_{q,t-1} + \varepsilon_t,$$

(16)

where the control variables $z_{i,t}$ are the same as in Equation (15). For the measures of book liquidity, $y_{i,t}$, we use quoted spread and our two price concession measures ap(50) and ap(200). We add a book asymmetry measure that is defined as the the ask price concession minus the bid price concession: $dpi50 = $ ap(50)-bp(50) and $dpi200 = $ ap(200)-bp(200). A low value indicates that it is more expensive to sell than to buy, which might foreshadow a downturn. Facing a downturn threat, limit order traders might rely more on the direction of future market orders for price discovery. This would imply increased trade informativeness.

The regression results in Table 6 indicate that book liquidity Granger-causes trade informativeness. We find that a high quoted spread causes trades to be significantly more informative in the oncoming period for 11 out of 30 stocks. In addition, we find that low depth causes increased trade informativeness, albeit primarily for ap(200). We find it to be significant for 22 stocks. Interestingly, the book depth asymmetry measure for large trades is also significant for 15 stocks. The negative sign of the parameter estimate is consistent with the intuition that market orders are more informative when selling is relatively expensive. As for the control variables, we find strong statistical significance only for trade size, as large trades predict lower trade informativeness in the oncoming period for 17 stocks.

## 5. Discussion of the results

Overall, we find evidence that trade informativeness matters for book liquidity in limit order markets. Along with realised volatility it performs better than any other variable that captures trading conditions such as trading intensity, trading volume and order book imbalance. There are, however, some issues that are worthy of discussion.

First, we want to emphasise that book liquidity and trade informativeness are not the same thing. It is true that on poor book liquidity subsequent market orders have a large price concession by definition. However, it is not the immediate price impact that represents the adverse-selection that the Glosten model accounts for. In fact, part of the price concession is temporary and exists to compensate liquidity suppliers for their order-processing cost. In theory, if market orders are not informative (as assumed in most of the dynamic models) all of the price concession would be temporary.

Second, the Granger-causality results warrant some discussion. When constructing the data series for the causality test, we are forced to aggregate across market orders and create time intervals. We do this to estimate the Hasbrouck model and determine the long-term price impact of a trade. In the test, we pursue the Granger causality idea that one should have explanatory power beyond from what can be predicted from a series' own past. One could argue that we have not accurately controlled for book liquidity's own past, as we include only lagged book snapshots from before the trade interval. Ideally, we want to include the snapshot from before the previous market order, but we cannot do this as we need the aggregation to identify the *long-term* price impact. An alternative interpretation of our test is that it does show that trade informativeness is significant in explaining subsequent book liquidity beyond the prediction from its own past from *before* the trade interval.

Table 6. Regression of trade informativeness (Hasbrouck-$\alpha$) on liquidity measures and control variables.

| | Book liquidity indicators | | | | | Control variables | | | | | | | |
|---|---|---|---|---|---|---|---|---|---|---|---|---|---|
| | Spread | ap(50) | ap(200) | dpi50 | dpi200 | rv | tsize | dura | imb | simb | lag1 | lag2 | $R^2_{adj}$ |
| All stocks | 0.043 | −0.070 | 0.204 | 0.030 | −0.098 | 0.023 | −0.096 | 0.045 | 0.004 | 0.005 | 0.189 | 0.130 | 0.164 |
| sig−pos (of 30) | 11 | 0 | 22 | 2 | 0 | 3 | 0 | 7 | 1 | 0 | 27 | 26 | |
| sig−neg | 0 | 6 | 0 | 0 | 15 | 0 | 17 | 0 | 0 | 2 | 0 | 0 | |
| Q1 | 0.064 | −0.064 | 0.152 | 0.044 | −0.081 | 0.048 | −0.097 | 0.019 | 0.022 | 0.026 | 0.226 | 0.155 | 0.184 |
| Q2 | 0.048 | −0.088 | 0.208 | 0.044 | −0.119 | 0.012 | −0.115 | 0.047 | 0.006 | −0.007 | 0.205 | 0.158 | 0.194 |
| Q3 | 0.038 | −0.040 | 0.193 | −0.002 | −0.074 | 0.004 | −0.097 | 0.051 | −0.009 | 0.000 | 0.161 | 0.097 | 0.124 |
| Q4 | 0.020 | −0.089 | 0.266 | 0.038 | −0.118 | 0.033 | −0.073 | 0.061 | −0.003 | 0.005 | 0.167 | 0.111 | 0.156 |

Notes: The trade informativeness measure $\alpha^H$ is regressed on the book liquidity measures spread, ap50, ap200, as well as dpi50 and dpi200 which denote the difference between the ask and the bid price concession for a hypothetical trade of €50,000 and €200,000, respectively. The liquidity indicators are sampled before the first trade occurs after the previous $\alpha^H$ estimation interval. The regression also includes (in addition to a constant and two lags of the dependent variable) the control variables realised volatility (rv), trade size (tsize), trade duration (dura), unsigned trade imbalance (imb) and signed trade imbalance (simb). These variables are computed using data from the previous $\alpha^H$ estimation interval. All variables are diurnally adjusted. See table 4 for computational details of the procedure. To obtain comparable estimates across stocks, the dependent variable and the regressors are standardised by division by the sample standard deviations. The table reports stock group averages of the OLS estimates. sig−pos (sig−neg) counts the number of significant and positive (negative) coefficients. The significance level is 5%. Adjusted coefficients of determination are averaged across stocks. The regressions use on average $T = 692$ observations. Per activity quartile we have 953 (Q1), 744 (Q2), 516 (Q3), 537 (Q4) observations on average.

## 6. Conclusion

We analyse three months of LOB data – January–March 2004 – from the German Stock Exchange for the 30 DAX stocks to test the predictions of the Glosten (1994) model. One of the key predictions is that order books are filled by competitive limit order traders, so that, in equilibrium, the marginal order just earns enough to make up for order-processing cost and the adverse-selection cost of executing against a (potentially) privately informed market order.

First, we follow Sandås (2001) and estimate the parameters of the Glosten model directly using GMM. We reject the model econometrically and diagnose that the key parameter $\alpha$, which measures the level of private information in market orders, is primarily identified on book restrictions and *not* on the updating restrictions that should track the information in the trade. Second, we leave the structural model and exploit the time dimension to study whether trade informativeness matters for book liquidity. We develop measures for book liquidity and use the Hasbrouck (1991) methodology to gauge trade informativeness. We document that trade informativeness Granger-causes book liquidity with the strongest statistical and economical significance for large order price concessions ('behind the market'). To make these results more robust we control for various other determinants of LOB liquidity, such as realised volatility, trading intensity, trade size, and order book imbalance. Among these, we find that only realised volatility rivals trade informativeness in terms of economic and statistical significance. In particular, realised volatility is more relevant for top-of-the-book liquidity, whereas informativeness is more important for beyond-the-best-quote liquidity.

We interpret these results as support for prominent theoretical models of LOB markets. First, our finding that trade informativeness is one of the most important explanatory factors for book liquidity supports Glosten's (1994) model which explains order book equilibrium with order-processing costs and information asymmetry. Second, the finding that realised volatility is more important than trade informativeness for top-of-the-book liquidity supports a key result of dynamic LOB models like that developed by Foucault's (1999). These models start from symmetric information and assume that the key cost to limit orders is picking-off risk. That is, limit orders are costly if they are consumed before cancelling on the arrival of public information. This cost is particularly relevant 'at the market', which explains the result that realised volatility is more important than trade informativeness for top-of-the-book liquidity.

### Acknowledgements

We thank Ekkehart Boehmer, Ruslan Goyenko, Thierry Foucault, and participants of the 2005 European Finance Association Meeting, the 2005 German Finance Association Meeting (where we received the outstanding paper award) and seminars at the University of Copenhagen, University of London, University Louvain-la-Neuve, University Carlos III de Madrid, and the University of Zurich for useful comments. An anonymous referee greatly helped to improve the exposition of the paper. We thank Stefan Frey for his invaluable work on the LOB data, Kerstin Kehrle for research assistance, and the Deutsche Börse Group for data sponsorship, in particular Uwe Schweickert and Miroslav Budomir who shared their knowledge of the XETRA LOB system with us. We further thank the Belgian Fonds National de la Recherche Scientifique, the Center for Financial Research, Cologne, the German Research Foundation, as well as the Netherlands Organization for Scientific Research for financial support. The opinions expressed in this article are those of the authors and do not necessarily reflect the views of Fifth Third Asset Management, Inc. We are responsible for any remaining errors.

### Notes

1. We define 'price concession' as the hypothetical transaction price for a given trade volume relative to a reference price (e.g. the midquote or the best quote). For limit order markets, we prefer price concession to the bid-ask half

spread as a measure of liquidity, since depth at the best quote is often too small to transact the market order, which then runs up the book.

2. Traders seem to transact in terms of value, not in terms of number of shares. That is, we find that the average value per trades is similar across stocks, which is not true for the average number of shares per trade. The reason is that, in the cross-section, stocks trade at different price levels.

## References

Ahn, H., K. Bae, and K. Chan. 2001. Limit orders, depth, and volatility: Evidence from the stock exchange of Hong Kong. *Journal of Finance* 56, no. 2: 767–88.

Andersen, T., T. Bollerslev, F. Diebold, and P. Labys. 2003. Modeling and forecasting realized volatility. *Econometrica* 71, no. 2: 579–625.

Biais, B., P. Hillion, and C. Spatt. 1995. An empirical analysis of the limit order book and the order flow in the Paris Bourse. *Journal of Finance* 50, no. 5: 1655–89.

Biais, B., T. Foucault, and F. Salanié. 1998. Floors, dealer markets, and limit order markets. *Journal of Financial Markets* 1, nos. 3–4: 253–84.

Biais, B., D. Martimort, and J. Rochet. 2000. Competing mechanisms in a common value environment. *Econometrica* 68, no. 4: 799–837.

Biais, B., L. Glosten, and C. Spatt. 2005. A survey of microfoundations, empirical results, and policy implications. *Journal of Financial Markets* 8, no. 2: 217–64.

Bloomfield, R., M. O'Hara, and G. Saar. 2009. How noise trading affects markets: An experimental analysis. *Review of Financial Studies* 22, no. 6: 2275–302.

Dufour, A., and R. Engle. 2000. Time and the price impact of a trade. *Journal of Finance* 55, no. 6: 2467–99.

Easley, D., N. Kiefer, M. O'Hara, and J. Paperman. 1996. Liquidity, information, and less-frequently traded stocks. *Journal of Finance* 51, no. 4: 1405–36.

Easley, D., S. Hvidkjaer, and M. O'Hara. 2002. Is information risk a determinant of asset returns? *Journal of Finance* 57, no. 5: 2185–221.

Foucault, T. 1999. Order flow composition and trading costs in a dynamic limit order market. *Journal of Financial Markets* 2, no. 2: 99–134.

Foucault, T., O. Kadan, and E. Kandel. 2005. Limit order book as a market for liquidity. *Review of Financial Studies* 18, no. 4: 1171–217.

Glosten, L. 1994. Is the electronic limit order book inevitable? *Journal of Finance* 49, no. 4: 1127–61.

Goettler, R., C. Parlour, and U. Rajan. 2005. Equilibrium in a dynamic limit order market. *Journal of Finance* 60, no. 5: 2149–92.

Goettler, R., C. Parlour, and U. Rajan. 2009. Informed traders and limit order markets. *Journal of Financial Economics* 93, no. 1: 67–87.

Grammig, J., E. Theissen, and O. Wünsche. 2007. Time and price impact of a trade: A structural approach. Discussion paper, EFA 2007 Conference Paper, Universities Tübingen and Mannheim.

Griffiths, M., B. Smith, D. Turnbull, and R. White. 2000. The costs and determinants of order aggressiveness. *Journal of Financial Economics* 56, no. 1: 65–88.

Harris, L., and J. Hasbrouck. 1996. Market vs. limit orders: the superDOT evidence on order submission strategy. *Journal of Financial and Quantitative Analysis* 31, no. 2: 213–31.

Hasbrouck, J. 1991. Measuring the information content of stock trades. *Journal of Finance* 46, no. 1: 179–207.

Hasbrouck, J., and G. Saar. 2007. Limit orders and volatility in a hybrid market: the island ECN. Discussion paper, New York University.

Hasbrouck, J., and G. Saar. 2009. Technology and liquidity provision: The blurring of traditional definitions. *Journal of Financial Markets* 12, no. 2: 143–72.

Hollifield, B., R. Miller, and P. Sandås. 2004. Empirical analysis of limit order markets. *Review of Economic Studies* 71, no. 4: 1027–63.

Hollifield, B., R. Miller, and P. Sandås. 2006. Estimating the gains from trade in limit order markets. *Journal of Finance* 61, no. 6: 2753–804.

Huang, R., and H. Stoll. 1997. The components of the bid–ask spread: A general approach. *Review of Financial Studies* 10, no. 4: 995–1034.

Madhavan, A. 2000. Market microstructure: A survey. *Journal of Financial Markets* 3, no. 3: 205–58.

Menkveld, A. 2008. Splitting orders in overlapping markets: A study of cross-listed stocks. *Journal of Financial Intermediation* 17, no. 2: 145–74.

Parlour, C. 1998. Price dynamics in limit order markets. *Review of Financial Studies* 11, no. 4: 789–816.

Parlour, C., and D. Seppi. 2003. Liquidity-based competition for order flow. *Review of Financial Studies* 16, no. 2: 301–43.

Ranaldo, A. 2004. Order aggressiveness in limit order book markets. *Journal of Financial Markets* 7, no. 1: 53–74.

Rosu, I. 2009. A dynamic model of the limit order book. *Review of Financial Studies* 22, no. 11: 4601–4641.

Sandås, P. 2001. Adverse selection and competitive market making: Empirical evidence from a limit order market. *Review of Financial Studies* 14, no. 3 705–734.

Seppi, D. 1997. Liquidity provision with limit orders and a strategic specialist. *Review of Financial Studies* 10, no. 1: 103–150.

Vayanos, D. 2001. Strategic trading in a dynamic noisy market. *Journal of Finance* 56, no. 1: 131–171.

# A forecast-based comparison of restricted Wishart autoregressive models for realized covariance matrices

M. Bonato[a], M. Caporin[b] and A. Ranaldo[c]

[a] Credit Suisse, Zurich, Switzerland; [b] Department of Economics, University of Padova, Padova, Italy; [c] Swiss National Bank, Zurich, Switzerland

Models for realized covariance matrices may suffer from the curse of dimensionality as more traditional multivariate volatility models (such as GARCH and stochastic volatility). Within the class of realized covariance models, we focus on the Wishart specification introduced by C. Gourieroux, J. Jasiak, and R. Sufana [2009. The Wishart autoregressive process of multivariate stochastic volatility. *Journal of Econometrics* 150, no. 2: 167–81] and analyze here the forecasting performances of the parametric restrictions discussed in M. Bonato [2009. Estimating the degrees of freedom of the realized volatility Wishart autoregressive model. Manuscript available at http://ssrn.com/abstract=1357044], which are motivated by asset features such as their economic sector and book-to-market or price-to-earnings ratios, among others. Our purpose is to verify if restricted model forecasts are statistically equivalent to full-model specification, a result that would support the use of restrictions when the problem cross-sectional dimension is large.

## 1.  Introduction

Since the mid-1990s, the availability of high-frequency data attracted considerable interest in the econometric, statistical, and financial literature. On the one side, many authors considered the filtering problems associated with these data, their use for market microstructure studies, or their direct modeling (see Dacorogna et al. 2001 for a survey). On the other side, high-frequency data gave rise to a relevant research area, that of realized volatility, started by the seminal contributions of Andersen et al. (2000), Andersen et al. (2001a), and Andersen et al. (2001b). This strand of the financial econometrics literature could be further divided into two subsets, the first including the theoretical studies dealing with the appropriate measurement of the realized volatility, and the second, more empirical, tackling the problem of modeling realized volatility sequences for their financial applications (see the paper by McAleer and Medeiros 2008 for a survey).

The present paper belongs to the last group and focuses on a specific set of models, the Wishart autoregressive (or WAR) models introduced by Gourieroux, Jasiak, and Sufana (2009) and then analyzed by Bonato, Caporin, and Ranaldo (2009). Realized covariance models, as well as many other covariance models, suffer from the so-called curse of dimensionality, that is, the parameter number increases at an order larger than the model cross-sectional dimension. For this reason, restricted parameterizations have been proposed in many frameworks (see Bauwens, Laurent, and

Rombouts 2006; Billio, Caporin, and Gobbo 2006; Caporin and Paruolo 2009; Silvennoinen and Terasvirta 2009, among others). Within the WAR framework, a set of possible restrictions have been introduced by Bonato, Caporin, and Ranaldo (2009) and motivated by economic and financial features of the analyzed variables. As an example, we may impose that the realized covariance dynamic is constrained to be equal across assets belonging to the same economic sector. When the cross-sectional dimension is small, full models can still be estimated and compared to restricted specifications in order to verify what their effects on model performances are. In this paper, we present an empirical comparison of full and restricted WAR models whose purpose is to verify how close restricted specifications are to the most general model.

We consider a data set of 12 large cap US stocks sampled at a 1 min frequency, which are used to determine the daily realized covariance matrices in the range January 2003 to December 2008. Over these series, we fit a set of alternative WAR specifications and compare them in terms of forecast performances by using statistical criteria. In detail, we consider the (Amisano and Giacomini 2006) weighted-likelihood ratio test, the pairwise model comparison based on two multivariate loss functions similar to those discussed in Patton and Sheppard (2009) and Clements et al. (2009), and the model confidence set (MCS) of Hansen, Lunde, and Nason (2011). Our contribution is characterized by two distinctive features: first, our study uses a data set with a relatively long sample dimension and, more interestingly, with a cross-sectional dimension never considered in previous applications of WAR models; second, it compares models using the most recent and up-to-date approaches.

Our results confirm those obtained by previous studies, suggesting that the choice of the approach used for the comparison could lead to different rankings of alternative models. Nevertheless, we provide evidence showing that restricted model specifications have often forecasting performances better than fully specified models.

The article proceeds as follows. Section 2 describes the model that we have considered, the parametric restrictions driven by economic features of the data, the parameter interpretation, and the model estimation. Section 3 deals with the methods for the forecast evaluation and comparison across multivariate volatility models, while Section 4 presents the empirical results. Section 5 concludes.


## 2. Modeling variance spillovers

We now introduce the model used to analyze and forecast the sequence of realized variance/covariance matrix of the 12 assets in our study. We then describe the set of alternative parametric restrictions to the spillovers between variances that help to reduce the complexity of the model estimation and might be motivated by some economic criterion (e.g. asset classification) or data driven. As we have mentioned in the introduction, we presume that realized covariance sequences are available and we will not tackle the problem of the optimal estimation of realized variances and covariances.


### 2.1 The WAR model

Once we have computed the series of realized variance/covariance matrices from the intra-day returns, it is of fundamental importance for our purpose to adopt a model which is feasible to estimate even with a large set of assets, which guarantees the positive definitiveness of the forecasted covariance matrix, and whose coefficients maintain their interpretability. The last aspect will be even more important if the quality of covariance matrix forecasts would be measured according to an economic criterion (such as the returns on various optimized portfolios).

A model that satisfies the previously itemized requirement is the realized WAR model introduced by Gourieroux, Jasiak, and Sufana (2009). As shown in Bonato, Caporin, and Ranaldo (2009), this model is particularly suitable to test for variance spillover between assets, and in their paper, the authors proposed four specifications to restrict the interaction between past variance/covariances with their contemporaneous values.

Denote by $Y_t$ the time $t$ (realized) covariance for a group of $n$ assets. Following Gourieroux, Jasiak, and Sufana (2009), the WAR(1) process denoted by $W(M, K, \Sigma)$ is defined by mean of the conditional Laplace transformation of $Y_t$

$$\Psi_t(\Gamma) = E[\exp \operatorname{Tr}(\Gamma Y_{t+1})]$$

$$= \exp(\operatorname{Tr}[M'\Gamma(I - 2\Sigma\Gamma)^{-1}MY_t])(\det[I - 2\Sigma\Gamma])^{-K/2}, \qquad (1)$$

where $\Gamma$ is a non-stochastic real symmetric matrix, $K$ denotes the scalar degree of freedom of the process, $M$ is a square matrix of autoregressive parameters, $\Sigma$ is a symmetric and positive definite matrix, Tr denotes the trace operator, and det is the determinant. Gourieroux, Jasiak, and Sufana (2009) showed that the conditional expectation of the WAR(1) process has a simple and interpretable structure highlighting the autoregressive nature of the process. The conditional first-order moment implied by the WAR(1) model reads

$$E[Y_{t+1}|I_t] = MY_tM' + K\Sigma, \qquad (2)$$

where the expectation is made conditionally to the information set at time $t$ ($I_t$). The WAR(1) model states that the covariance matrix forecast for the following day depends on the actual covariance value, the parameter matrix $\Sigma$, and the scalar $K$ that arise from the definition of the WAR(1) model.

This simple formulation resembles in many aspects the classical AR(1) conditional mean widely used in the literature to model and forecast realized volatility. Furthermore, the dynamics in Equation (2) resemble that of well-known multivariate GARCH BEKK specification. However, the WAR strongly differs from BEKK since the dynamic is applied to observed realized covariance matrices, while the BEKK model provides a dynamic for a latent covariance. Parameters in Equations (1) and (2) must satisfy two constraints: first, the degree of freedom must satisfy $K > n - 1$ to ensure model appropriateness (see Bonato 2009 for an in-depth discussion on the topic); secondly, the eigenvalues of matrix $M$ must be in a modulus of less than 1 to ensure stationarity. We refer the interested readers to Gourieroux, Jasiak, and Sufana (2009) for a deeper discussion on the WAR model structure and properties.

The WAR(1) model could be easily generalized, enriching its dynamic. Adding additional lags, we obtain the WAR($p$) model, $p \geq 1$, whose conditional expectation reads

$$E[Y_{t+1}|I^t] = \sum_{j=1}^{p} MjY_{t+1-j}M'_j + K\Sigma. \qquad (3)$$

As discussed in Corsi (2009), agents on the financial markets operate with different time horizons (they are heterogeneous). Such a behavior could generate long-memory patterns. To capture this feature, Corsi (2009) introduced a new univariate realized volatility model named heterogeneous autoregression (HAR) that captures the different agent horizons by making the current day's realized volatility a function of daily, weekly, and monthly past realized volatility component.

Along with the classical WAR model and its restricted specifications described below, we will also test the economic values of the restriction on the HAR–WAR model proposed in Bonato, Caporin, and Ranaldo (2009). Define the $k$-period realized covariance matrix component by the average of the single-period realized covariance matrices:

$$Y_{t-k:t-1} = \frac{1}{k} \sum_{j=1}^{K} Y_{t-j}. \tag{4}$$

Combining a WAR(p) structure with the temporal aggregation induced by the HAR model, the conditional expectation of $Y_t$ becomes

$$E[Y_{t+1}|I^t] = M_1 Y_{t-1} M_1' + M_2 Y_{t-5:t-1} M_2' + M_3 Y_{t-22:t-1} M_3' + K\Sigma. \tag{5}$$

## 2.2 Interpretation of the coefficients

As mentioned previously, one of the advantages of the WAR is that the interpretation of the coefficients in the model is not lost. Bonato, Caporin, and Ranaldo (2009) proposed to restrict the parametric space by setting some parameters to zero according to economic criteria. Such a strategy helps solving the so-called curse of dimensionality, that is, the number of parameters is a power function of the cross-sectional model dimension. The main contribution of this paper is to check whether imposition of these restrictions affects the forecasting performances of the model. Equivalently, by working with a cross-sectional dimension allowing the estimation of a fully parameterized model, we verify if the forecasting performances of a restricted specification are statistically different from those of the fully parameterized model.

In this section, we briefly introduce the four different restricted parameterizations proposed in Bonato, Caporin, and Ranaldo (2009) and discuss their economic interpretation.

Consider the conditional expectation implied by the simple WAR(1) model as in Equation (2):

$$E[Y_{t+1}|I_t] = MY_t M' + K\Sigma. \tag{6}$$

Assume that our portfolio consists of $n$ stocks classified into $N$ groups according to some economic (or data-driven) criterion (for instance, the economic sector, the company market dimension, or the existence of common patterns in realized variances and covariances).

The $N$ groups have dimension $n_i$ with $\sum_i^N n_i = n$. In addition, the assets are ordered following a group rule, that is, assets from 1 to $n_1$ belong to group 1, assets from $n_1 + 1$ to $n_1 + n_2$ belong to group 2, and so on. Given this asset classification, the autoregressive matrix $M$ may be partitioned as follows:

$$M = \begin{pmatrix} M_{11} & \cdots & M_{1N} \\ \vdots & M_{ii} & \vdots \\ M_{N1} & \cdots & M_{NN} \end{pmatrix}, \tag{7}$$

where $M_{ij}$ is a matrix of dimension $n_i \times n_j$.

Bonato, Caporin, and Ranaldo (2009) proposed the following specifications:

(i) $M_{ij} = \mathbf{0} \; \forall i \neq j, \, i,j = 1,\ldots,N$,
(ii) $M_{ij} = \mathbf{0}$ and $M_{ii} = \alpha_i(\mathbf{1}_{n_i} \mathbf{1}'_{n_i})$, $\forall i \neq j, \, i,j = 1,\ldots,N$,
(iii) $M_{ij} = \mathbf{0}$ and $M_{ii} = (\alpha_{i,1},\ldots,\alpha^{i,n_i})(\mathbf{I}_{n_i})$, $\forall i \neq j, \, i,j = 1,\ldots,N$,
(iv) $M_{ij} = \mathbf{0}$ and $M_{ii} = \alpha_i(\mathbf{I}_{n_i})$, $\forall i \neq j, \, i,j = 1,\ldots,N$,

where $\mathbf{1}_{n_i}$ is a $n_i \times 1$ vector of ones and $\mathbf{I}_{n_i}$ is the identity matrix of dimension $n_i$.

If assets belonging to the same group share common reactions to shocks, we can hypothesize, to some extent, that their co-volatilities also have a similar behavior. If the groups are sector specific, model (i) implies that the variances and covariances of each asset are only influenced by the variances and covariances of assets belonging to the same class. Therefore, no volatility spillover exists between assets belonging to different sectors. This model is called *block WAR*. The number of parameters that need to be estimated is $n(n+1)/2 + \sum_{i=1}^{N} n_i^2$, along with the degrees of freedom $K$.

A further reduction of the number of parameters is obtained by imposing a single parameter for each group, as shown in model (ii). In this case, the variance and covariance of each asset belonging to, say, group $j$ depend on its past values, on the past values of the variances of the other assets of the same group, and on the covariances with those assets via a function of the unique parameter $\alpha_j$. We refer to this model as the *restricted block WAR*. This models contains $n(n+1)/2 + N$ parameters in $M$ and $\Sigma$ plus $K$.

Model (iii) relaxes the assumption of spillover between assets belonging to the same sector. It assumes each matrix $M_{ii}$, $i = 1, \ldots, N_i$, to be diagonal, that is, the autoregressive matrix $M$ is diagonal. In this case, grouping the assets according to some criterion does not affect the parametric space. This model is named *diagonal WAR*. For this model, $n$ parameters need to be estimated in the matrix $M$, plus the $n(n+1)/2$ parameters in $\Sigma$ and the degrees of freedom $K$. One of the implications of the diagonal structure for $M$ is that each realized variance is only a function of its past values.

If one assumes again that assets belonging to the same sector have common dynamics for the variance, he or she can find a way to group assets whose volatilities obey the same process, and the number of parameters can be further reduced. This is the case for model (iv). For each group, a single parameter is taken to model the dynamics of the variances for the assets in the considered group, that is, the elements on the diagonal of each $M_{ii}$, $i = 1, \ldots, N$, are all equal. In total, only $N + n(n+1)/2 + 1$ parameters are required in this model. We refer to this model as the *restricted diagonal WAR*.

It is worth mentioning that the specifications (i)–(iv) are only a subset of all the possible specifications of the WAR model. In fact, we set all the off-diagonal blocks to zero. The assumption $M_{ij} = \mathbf{0}$, $\forall i \neq j, i, j = 1, \ldots, N$, can be replaced by the same structure that we imposed on the matrices $M_{ii}$: full, scalar, diagonal, and restricted diagonal. This allows us to consider not only the interactions between assets belonging to the same group but also interactions between a limited set of groups.

## 2.3 *Model estimation*

Under the assumption that $K > n - 1$, Gourieroux, Jasiak, and Sufana (2009) showed that

(i) $K$ and $\Sigma$ are identifiable, while the autoregressive coefficients in $M$ (and thus $M_1, M_2$, and $M_3$) are identifiable up to their sign.

(ii) $\Sigma$ is first-order identifiable up to a scale factor and $M$ is first-order identifiable up to its sign. The degree of freedom $K$ is not first-order identifiable but is second-order identifiable.

Following Gourieroux, Jasiak, and Sufana (2009), the first-order conditional moments can be used to calibrate the parameters in $M$ and $\Sigma$ up to the sign and scale factor, respectively.

We estimate the parameters using nonlinear least squares:

$$(\hat{M}, \hat{\Sigma}^*) = \text{Argmin}_{M, \Sigma^*} S^2(M, \Sigma^*), \tag{8}$$

where

$$S^2(M, \Sigma^*) = \sum_{t=2}^{T} \sum_{i<j} \left( Y_{ij,t} - \sum_{k=1}^{n} \sum_{l=1}^{n} Y_{kl,t-1} m_{ik} m_{lk} - \sigma_{ij}^* \right)^2$$

$$= \sum_{t=2}^{T} \| \text{vech}(Y_t) - \text{vech}(MY_{t-1}M' + \Sigma^*) \|^2 \tag{9}$$

and $\Sigma^* = K\Sigma = KCC'$, where $C$ is a lower triangular matrix of parameters which is introduced to ensure positive definiteness of $\Sigma$. Stationarity constraints could be checked *ex post* or included in the estimation procedure leading to constrained nonlinear least squares.

To estimate the degrees of freedom, we follow the strategy proposed in Bonato (2009), which has been shown to be less sensible to the presence of extreme events in the co-volatility process. Consider a portfolio allocation $\alpha \in R^n$. We know that the unconditional distribution of $Y_t$ is a $W(K, 0, \Sigma(\infty))$, a centered Wishart distribution. We can, therefore, easily show that

$$\alpha' Y_t \alpha \sim \text{Ga}\left( \frac{K}{2}, 2\alpha' \Sigma(\infty)\alpha \right), \tag{10}$$

that is, the distribution of the portfolio with allocation $\alpha$ is a gamma distribution with the degrees of freedom $K$ as shape parameter (see also Meucci 2005). An unbiased estimator of $K$ can be obtained simply via maximum likelihood by fitting a gamma distribution to the process $\alpha' Y_t \alpha$.

The estimation process that we follow does not achieve full efficiency, but it is computationally less intensive than the parameter estimation by maximum-likelihood methods.

## 3. Comparison of realized covariance models

We previously described the various parameter restriction designs that we could use for the WAR and HAR–WAR models. The primary purpose of our work is to compare the forecasts of the realized covariance matrix provided by alternative restricted parameterizations and to compare them to the forecasts of the full model. We denote the alternative specifications by a subscript $i = 1, 2, \ldots m$ and the forecast of time $t$ covariance by $\Sigma_{t,i}^f$. In the following, even if we do not explicitly specify it, all forecasts are conditional to the information set at time $t - 1$. We assume that a set of one-step-ahead forecasts are available in a specific range from time $T + 1$ to $T + W$ for all specifications. Furthermore, the observed time $t$ returns of the assets are included in the vector $R_t$, and the models are estimated with a rolling window approach.

To compare the models, we first consider the weighted-likelihood ratio test of Amisano and Giacomini (2006). The test compares the out-of-sample forecast performances of two models by resorting to a weighed likelihood function comparison. Within this article, we use the normal likelihood based on the realized covariance forecasts and the observed returns

$$f_{i,t} = -\frac{1}{2} \ln \left| \Sigma_{t,i}^f \right| - \frac{1}{2} R_t' \left( \Sigma_{t,i}^f \right)^{-1} R_t. \tag{11}$$

Given two alternative models $i$ and $j$ and following Amisano and Giacomini (2006), we first compute the quantities

$$\text{WLR}_{t,ij} = w(R_t)(f_{i,t} - f_{j,t}),\tag{12}$$

where $w(R_t)$ is a weighting function which could be designed in order to focus on specific regions of the return density. In our setup, we set the weights to 1 without focusing on specific areas of the forecast density, such as the tails. For additional details, see Amisano and Giacomini (2006). The null hypothesis of equal predicting ability of the two models $i$ and $j$ is tested by using the statistic

$$\text{LR}_{ij} = \frac{\overline{\text{WLR}}_{ij}}{\sqrt{\text{Var}(\overline{\text{WLR}}_{ij})}},\tag{13}$$

where $\overline{\text{WLR}}_{ij} = (1/W)\sum_{l=1}^{W} \text{WLR}_{T+l,ij}$ and $\text{Var}(\overline{\text{WLR}}_{ij})$ is obtained by a heteroskedasticity and autocorrelation consistent (HAC) estimator. Under the null hypothesis, $\text{LR}_{ij}$ is asymptotically distributed as a standardized normal and, if the null is rejected, its sign could be used to determine the preferred model.

The second approach that we consider for the comparison of alternative WAR specifications considers two loss functions for multivariate volatility models. Following Patton and Sheppard (2009) and Clements et al. (2009), we define the two following loss functions:

$$L_{i,t}^1 = \frac{1}{k^2} \text{vec}\left(\Sigma_{t,i}^f - \Sigma_t\right)' \text{vec}\left(\Sigma_{t,i}^f - \Sigma_t\right),\tag{14}$$

$$L_{i,t}^2 = \text{trace}\left(\left(\Sigma_{t,i}^f\right)^{-1}\Sigma_t\right) - \log\left(\left|\left(\Sigma_{t,i}^f\right)^{-1}\Sigma_t\right|\right),\tag{15}$$

which are derived from Patton and Sheppard (2009). The function $L_{i,t}^1$ is a multivariate mean-squared error function, while $L_{i,t}^2$ is included in the class of robust loss functions defined in Patton and Sheppard (2009) and similar to a quasi-likelihood loss function.

Then, to verify the null that $E[L_{i,t}^w] = E[L_{j,t}^w]$, $w = 1,2$, we can use a Diebold–Mariano-type test (see Diebold and Mariano 1995; West 1996, 2006), computing the test statistic

$$d_{ij,t}^w = L_{i,t}^w - L_{j,t}^w$$

$$L_{ij}^w = \frac{\bar{d}_{ij}^w}{\sqrt{\text{Var}(\bar{d}_{ij}^w)}},\tag{16}$$

where $\bar{d}_{ij}^w = (1/W)\sum_{l=1}^{W} d_{ij,T+l}^w$, and $\text{Var}(\bar{d}_{ij}^w)$ is obtained by an HAC estimator.

Both the Amisano–Giacomini test and the comparison of models using the Diebold–Mariano tests consider two models only. However, when many alternative models must be considered, other methods are needed. Some popular approaches are the reality check of White (2000), the superior predictive ability test of Hansen (2005), and the MCS of Hansen, Lunde, and Nason (2011). We consider here the last method, which allows creating a set of model whose forecasting performances are statistically equivalent. The MCS uses as inputs all pairwise loss differentials $d_{ij,t}^w$ for a given loss function $w$ and for all $i,j = 1,2,\dots P, i \neq j$, where $P$ is the total number of fitted models. The MCS then proceeds by performing a sequential elimination procedure testing on a set of models $\mathcal{M}_l$ following the null hypothesis $H_0 : E[d_{ij,t}^w] = 0$, with $i > j$ and for all $i,j \in \mathcal{M}_l$. The initial set $\mathcal{M}_1$ contains all models, and if the null hypothesis is rejected, the worst performing model is excluded from the set. The procedure works then iteratively until the null is not rejected. Each step performs thus two operations at a generic iteration $l$: verify the null hypothesis and stop if accepted; if the null is rejected, identify the worst performing model and remove it from the set. To verify the null hypothesis, Hansen, Lunde, and Nason (2011) proposed two distinct test statistics based on the quantity (16) with the difference that the variance is computed using a bootstrap procedure (see Hansen, Lunde, and Nason 2011 for details). The two statistics are as follows:

$$T_R = \max_{i,j \in \mathcal{M}_l} |L_{ij}^w|, \tag{17}$$

$$T_{SQ} = \sum_{i,j \in \mathcal{M}, i>j} (L_{ij}^w)^2. \tag{18}$$

Given that the covariances across the forecasts produced by the models included in a specific set are not null, the test statistics have non-standard and complicated distribution. To determine the $p$-values of the test statistic, a bootstrap approach was proposed by Hansen, Lunde, and Nason (2011). For a specific confidence level $\alpha$, the null hypothesis can thus be verified by determining the bootstrapped $p$-values. If it is rejected, the worst performing model is identified as

$$i = \arg\max_{i \in \mathcal{M}} \sum_{j \in \mathcal{M}} \bar{d}_{ij}^w \left( \mathrm{Var} \left( \sum_{j \in \mathcal{M}} \bar{d}_{ij}^w \right) \right)^{-1}.$$

The MCS method was originally proposed for the comparison of univariate volatility forecasts, but Patton and Sheppard (2009) suggested that it could be of interest also in the multivariate framework, a claim supported by the analysis in Clements et al. (2009). In this paper, the MCS will be used as a tool for comparing nested models with respect to their forecasting performances to verify the null hypothesis that a restricted model provides forecasts statistically equivalent to those produced by an unrestricted model.

## 4. Empirical analysis

### 4.1 *Data set description*

To test whether there is economic value in imposing restriction to the variance spillovers between assets, we used a data set consisting of 12 large cap US stocks quoted at NYSE. These are Boeing Co., Bank of America, Citigroup Inc., Caterpillar Inc., Fedex, Hewlett Packard Co., IBM, JP Morgan Chase Co., Kraft Food Inc., Procter Gamble Co., Time Warner Inc., and Texas Instrument Inc. We then grouped them in four asset classes according to their sector: Financial, Capital Goods, Technology and Consumer Service. In Table 1, the sector-specific clustering of the data set is given.

The data set consists of 1 min intra-day prices over the period ranging from 2 January 2003 to 31 December 2008. The data were provided by TickData.com. After the deletion of holidays and days with no match across the sample, we were left with 1511 trading days. To construct the series of realized covariance matrices, we adopted the classical estimator presented in Andersen et al. (2003) and Barndorff-Nielsen and Shephard (2004) and used, for example, in De Pooter,

Table 1. Grouping of the stocks according to their market sector.

| Stock | Tick symbol | Sector |
|---|---|---|
| Citigroup Inc. | C | |
| Bank of America | BAC | Financial |
| JP Morgan Chase Co. | JPM | |
| Boeing Co. | BA | |
| Caterpillar Inc. | CAT | Capital Goods |
| Fedex | FDX | |
| International Business Machine Corp. | IBM | |
| Hewlett Packard Co. | HPQ | Technology |
| Texas Instrument Inc. | TXN | |
| Kraft Food Inc. | KFT | |
| Procter Gamble Co. | PG | Consumer Service |
| Time Warner Inc. | TWX | |

Martens, and van Dijk (2008):

$$Y_t = \sum_{i=1}^{I} r_{t-1+ih,h} r'_{t-1+ih,h}, \tag{19}$$

where $Y_t$ denotes the realized covariance matrix at time $t$. $r_{t-1+ih,h} \equiv p_{t-1+ih} - p_{t-1+(i-1)/h}$ denotes the $(n \times 1)$ vector of returns for the $i$th intra-day period on day $t$, for $i = 1, \ldots, I$, and with $n = 12$ the number of assets. $I$ is the number of intra-day intervals, each of length $h \equiv 1/I$. In our case, with a frequency of 1 min, $I = 390$.

## 4.2  Forecast-based comparisons

The forecasting period spans the interval from 2 January 2005 until the end of the sample. Following Ait-Sahalia and Mancini (2008) and Gourieroux, Jasiak, and Sufana (2009), we estimated each model with a rolling window approach. The window amplitude was set to 100 days, as in Ait-Sahalia and Mancini (2008), and larger than the 21 days used in Gourieroux, Jasiak, and Sufana (2009). We thus computed 755 1-day-ahead forecasts of the realized variance/covariance matrix for each model estimate. We repeated this operation for all the 10 models as in Table 2 and stored the results to compute the tests described in Section 3: the Amisano–Giacomini and the

Table 2. The different specifications of the WAR models.

| | |
|---|---|
| Full WAR(1) | M1 |
| Block diagonal WAR(1) | M2 |
| Restricted block diagonal WAR(1) | M3 |
| Diagonal WAR(1) | M4 |
| Restricted diagonal WAR(1) | M5 |
| Full HAR–WAR | M6 |
| Block diagonal HAR–WAR | M7 |
| Restricted block diagonal HAR–WAR | M8 |
| Diagonal HAR–WAR | M9 |
| Restricted diagonal HAR–WAR | M10 |

Diebold–Mariano tests for pairwise model comparison and the MCS method for determining the set of models providing statistically equivalent forecasts. Given the purposes of this paper, we are not stating that the WAR is the preferred model to capture the dynamics of realized covariance matrices. We believe that it is an elegant approach to provide positive definite covariance forecasts with limited constraints on model parameters and, at the same time, interpretable coefficients. However, these could be affected by structural breaks which are accounted for by mean of the rolling estimation.

We start by analyzing the outcomes of the Amisano–Giacomini test as reported in Tables 3 and 4. These tables present the test statistic and the corresponding $p$-values, respectively. Several rejections of the null of equal predicting ability are detected and the sign of the test statistics is used to identify the preferred models: positive values indicate a preference for row models, while negative values indicate a preference for column models. We can identify a subset of

Table 3. Results of the Amisano–Giacomini test.

|      | M1 | M2 | M3 | M4 | M5 | M6 | M7 | M8 | M9 | M10 |
|------|----|----|----|----|----|----|----|----|----|-----|
| M1   |    | −3.62 | −4.16 | −0.35 | 0.28 | 0.84 | −2.58 | −3.03 | −0.16 | 0.46 |
| M2   |    |    | −1.85 | 1.97 | 3.83 | 2.87 | 0.47 | −0.02 | 2.33 | 3.44 |
| M3   |    |    |    | 2.22 | 4.33 | 3.08 | 0.93 | 0.56 | 2.55 | 3.76 |
| M4   |    |    |    |    | 0.53 | 0.92 | −1.61 | −1.85 | 0.30 | 0.66 |
| M5   |    |    |    |    |    | 0.57 | −2.58 | −3.03 | −0.32 | 0.38 |
| M6   |    |    |    |    |    |    | −2.85 | −3.05 | −0.92 | −0.44 |
| M7   |    |    |    |    |    |    |    | −1.57 | 2.35 | 2.62 |
| M8   |    |    |    |    |    |    |    |    | 2.59 | 3.00 |
| M9   |    |    |    |    |    |    |    |    |    | 0.47 |
| M10  |    |    |    |    |    |    |    |    |    |     |

Note: Gray cells indicate a 1% preference for the column model or for the row model, according to the sign, negative or positive.

Table 4. $p$-Values of the Amisano–Giacomini test.

|      | M1 | M2 | M3 | M4 | M5 | M6 | M7 | M8 | M9 | M10 |
|------|----|----|----|----|----|----|----|----|----|-----|
| M1   |    | 0.00 | 0.00 | 0.36 | 0.39 | 0.20 | 0.00 | 0.00 | 0.44 | 0.32 |
| M2   |    |    | 0.03 | **0.02** | **0.00** | **0.00** | 0.32 | 0.49 | **0.01** | **0.00** |
| M3   |    |    |    | **0.01** | **0.00** | **0.00** | 0.18 | 0.29 | **0.01** | **0.00** |
| M4   |    |    |    |    | 0.30 | 0.18 | 0.05 | 0.03 | 0.38 | 0.25 |
| M5   |    |    |    |    |    | 0.28 | 0.01 | 0.00 | 0.37 | 0.35 |
| M6   |    |    |    |    |    |    | 0.00 | 0.00 | 0.18 | 0.33 |
| M7   |    |    |    |    |    |    |    | 0.06 | **0.01** | **0.00** |
| M8   |    |    |    |    |    |    |    |    | **0.00** | **0.00** |
| M9   |    |    |    |    |    |    |    |    |    | 0.32 |
| M10  |    |    |    |    |    |    |    |    |    |     |

Note: A gray cell indicates a 1% preference for the column model and a bold value indicates a 1% preference for the row model (test is row model minus column model).

models which are preferred to a number of alternatives. These models are the restricted block diagonal WAR (M3), the block diagonal HAR–WAR (M7), and the restricted block diagonal HAR–WAR (M8). Notably, the full models (both HAR–WAR and WAR) are inferior to several restricted specifications. This result suggests that restricted specifications could be as good as, if not superior to, fully parameterized specifications.

Tables 5 to 8 report the Diebold–Mariano test statistic and the corresponding $p$-values for the loss functions defined in Equations (14) and (15), respectively. If we consider the mean-squared error loss function (14) (Tables 5 and 6), we can observe that all models are statistically equivalent at the 5% level, while some differences are detected only at the 10% level. Differently, moving to the robust loss function in Equation (15), results are sensibly different (Tables 7 and 8). In fact, at the 1% confidence level, fully parameterized models (M1 and M6) are generally statistically preferred to their corresponding restricted specifications (full WAR is preferred to restricted WAR, and full HAR–WAR is preferred to restricted HAR–WAR). There is, however, a common and interesting exception, restricted diagonal models (M5 and M10) are equivalent to fully parameterized specifications. The restricted diagonal models are also preferred to other restricted specifications. Across classes (WAR and HAR–WAR), we observed some common preference for the restricted diagonal HAR–WAR (M10) with respect to many other models.

Finally, Table 9 reports the results of MCS approach for the two loss functions considered: the mean-squared error and the quasi-likelihood loss functions. The table reports, for a given loss function, the MCS results for the two test statistics proposed by Hansen, Lunde, and Nason

Table 5. Values of the Diebold–Mariano test for the comparison of the loss differentials of loss function 1.

| | M1 | M2 | M3 | M4 | M5 | M6 | M7 | M8 | M9 | M10 |
|---|---|---|---|---|---|---|---|---|---|---|
| M1 | | 1.41 | 1.37 | 1.52 | 1.22 | 1.46 | 1.48 | 1.45 | 1.48 | 1.34 |
| M2 | | | 1.17 | −1.20 | 0.33 | −0.84 | 0.64 | 1.27 | −0.74 | 1.00 |
| M3 | | | | −1.19 | −0.88 | −0.93 | −0.21 | 0.70 | −0.88 | 0.33 |
| M4 | | | | | 0.90 | −0.06 | 1.44 | 1.39 | 0.68 | 1.18 |
| M5 | | | | | | −0.70 | 0.15 | 0.79 | −0.60 | 0.69 |
| M6 | | | | | | | 1.20 | 1.19 | 1.08 | 0.98 |
| M7 | | | | | | | | 1.15 | −1.23 | 0.42 |
| M8 | | | | | | | | | −1.21 | −0.91 |
| M9 | | | | | | | | | | 0.94 |
| M10 | | | | | | | | | | |

Table 6. $p$-Values of the Diebold–Mariano test for the comparison of the loss differentials of loss function 1.

| | M1 | M2 | M3 | M4 | M5 | M6 | M7 | M8 | M9 | M10 |
|---|---|---|---|---|---|---|---|---|---|---|
| M1 | | 0.08 | 0.09 | 0.06 | 0.11 | 0.07 | 0.07 | 0.07 | 0.07 | 0.09 |
| M2 | | | 0.12 | 0.12 | 0.37 | 0.2 | 0.26 | 0.1 | 0.23 | 0.16 |
| M3 | | | | 0.12 | 0.19 | 0.18 | 0.42 | 0.24 | 0.19 | 0.37 |
| M4 | | | | | 0.18 | 0.47 | 0.08 | 0.08 | 0.25 | 0.12 |
| M5 | | | | | | 0.24 | 0.44 | 0.22 | 0.27 | 0.25 |
| M6 | | | | | | | 0.12 | 0.12 | 0.14 | 0.16 |
| M7 | | | | | | | | 0.13 | 0.11 | 0.34 |
| M8 | | | | | | | | | 0.11 | 0.18 |
| M9 | | | | | | | | | | 0.17 |
| M10 | | | | | | | | | | |

Table 7. Values of the Diebold–Mariano test for the comparison of the loss differentials of loss function 2.

| | M1 | M2 | M3 | M4 | M5 | M6 | M7 | M8 | M9 | M10 |
|---|---|---|---|---|---|---|---|---|---|---|
| M1 | | 7.22 | 6.99 | 3.37 | −1.40 | −0.13 | 6.41 | 6.44 | 3.85 | −1.70 |
| M2 | | | 1.63 | −5.15 | −4.31 | −4.47 | 2.49 | 2.69 | −0.30 | −4.53 |
| M3 | | | | −4.93 | −4.24 | −4.62 | 2.40 | 2.67 | −0.46 | −4.44 |
| M4 | | | | | −2.89 | −1.23 | 4.43 | 4.48 | 2.26 | −3.16 |
| M5 | | | | | | 0.72 | 4.18 | 4.20 | 3.18 | −2.36 |
| M6 | | | | | | | 5.43 | 5.50 | 3.46 | −0.9 |
| M7 | | | | | | | | 2.24 | −1.51 | −4.39 |
| M8 | | | | | | | | | −1.62 | −4.41 |
| M9 | | | | | | | | | | −3.38 |
| M10 | | | | | | | | | | |

Note: A gray cell indicates preference for the column model (positive sign) or for the row model (negative sign).

Table 8. p-Values of the Diebold–Mariano test for the comparison of the loss differentials of loss function 2.

| | M1 | M2 | M3 | M4 | M5 | M6 | M7 | M8 | M9 | M10 |
|---|---|---|---|---|---|---|---|---|---|---|
| M1 | | **0.00** | **0.00** | **0.00** | 0.08 | 0.45 | **0.00** | **0.00** | **0.00** | 0.04 |
| M2 | | | 0.05 | 0.00 | 0.00 | 0.00 | **0.01** | **0.00** | 0.38 | 0.00 |
| M3 | | | | 0.00 | 0.00 | 0.00 | **0.01** | **0.00** | 0.32 | 0.00 |
| M4 | | | | | 0.00 | 0.11 | **0.00** | **0.00** | **0.01** | 0.00 |
| M5 | | | | | | 0.24 | **0.00** | **0.00** | **0.00** | 0.01 |
| M6 | | | | | | | **0.00** | **0.00** | **0.00** | 0.18 |
| M7 | | | | | | | | **0.01** | 0.07 | 0.00 |
| M8 | | | | | | | | | 0.05 | 0.00 |
| M9 | | | | | | | | | | 0.00 |
| M10 | | | | | | | | | | |

Note: A bold value indicates preference for the row and a gray cell indicates preference for the column.

(2011). In turn, results are composed by a ranking of models and the corresponding $p$-values. Focusing on Table 9 (left panel), first and second columns, mean-squared error loss function (14), test statistic in Equation (17), we observed that for confidence levels higher than 20%, all models are equivalent.

Moving to the loss function in Equation (15), results are different (see the right panel in Table 9). In fact, at the 10% confidence level, only a single model is included in the confidence set, model M8, the restricted block diagonal HAR–WAR. Interestingly, this is also the model with the highest ranking in the right-hand side columns in Table 9 . Lowering the confidence level to 5%, the optimal model set contains also models M2, M9, M3, and M7, all restricted models. Again, the same models have high rankings according to loss function 1. Finally, we observed that the rankings and the $p$-values have similar patterns with respect to the MCS test statistics.

In summary, results are partially influenced by the choice of the loss functions and the approach used. However, our study shows that restricted models have performances similar, if not superior,

Table 9. MCS $p$-values for loss functions 1 and 2.

| Loss function 1 | | | | Loss function 2 | | | |
|---|---|---|---|---|---|---|---|
| MCS test: R | | MCS test: SQ | | MCS test: R | | MCS test: SQ | |
| Model | $p$-Value | Model | $p$-Value | Model | $p$-Value | Model | $p$-Value |
| **1** | 0.276 | **1** | 0.200 | 1 | 0.000 | 1 | 0.000 |
| **4** | 0.290 | **4** | 0.351 | 10 | 0.001 | 10 | 0.001 |
| **6** | 0.417 | **6** | 0.365 | 6 | 0.001 | 6 | 0.001 |
| **2** | 0.417 | **2** | 0.365 | 4 | 0.001 | 4 | 0.005 |
| **9** | 0.417 | **9** | 0.365 | 5 | 0.011 | 5 | 0.008 |
| **5** | 0.417 | **5** | 0.554 | **2** | 0.063 | **2** | 0.031 |
| **7** | 0.417 | **7** | 0.554 | **9** | 0.063 | **9** | 0.031 |
| **10** | 0.546 | **10** | 0.571 | **3** | 0.063 | **3** | 0.031 |
| **3** | 0.546 | **3** | 0.571 | **7** | 0.063 | **7** | 0.031 |
| **8** | 1.000 | **8** | 1.000 | **8** | 1.000 | **8** | 1.000 |

Note: Bold values identify statistically equivalent models at the 1% confidence level.

to those of the fully parameterized models. This outcome is common over different approaches for direct model comparison.

## 5. Conclusion

This article presented an empirical comparison of alternative WAR models differing in their parameterizations. We evaluated the models within a moderate cross-sectional dimension, 12 assets, and by using direct forecast evaluation approaches. We considered a range of model comparison approaches which represent the most recent and up-to-date methods proposed in the literature. The tests provide some evidence on the possible preference of restricted specifications over fully parameterized models. The results suggest the need for further investigations based on indirect model evaluation, in particular, within a portfolio allocation or risk management perspective. These extensions are left to future researches.

## Acknowledgements

This article was written while the second author was visiting the Chiang Mai University, Faculty of Economics, Thailand, whose hospitality is gratefully acknowledged. The views expressed herein are those of the authors and not necessarily those of the Swiss National Bank or of Credit Suisse, which do not accept any responsibility for the contents and opinions expressed in this paper.

## References

Ait-Sahalia, Y., and L. Mancini. 2008. Out of sample forecasts of quadratic variation. *Journal of Econometrics* 147, no. 1: 17–33.
Amisano, G., and R. Giacomini. 2007. Comparing density forecasts via weighted likelihood ratio tests. *Journal of Business and Economic Statistics* 25, no. 2: 177–90.
Andersen, T.G., T. Bollerslev, F.X. Diebold, and H. Ebens. 2001a. The distribution of realized stock return volatility. *Journal of Financial Economics* 61, no. 1: 43–76.
Andersen, T.G., T. Bollerslev, F.X. Diebold, and P. Labys. 2000. Exchange rate return standardized by realized volatility are (nearly) Gaussian. *Multinational Finance Journal* 4–3, no. 4: 159–79.

Andersen, T.G., T. Bollerslev, F.X. Diebold, and P. Labys. 2001b. The distribution of exchange rate volatility. *Journal of the American Statistical Association* 96, no. 453: 42–55.

Andersen, T.G., T. Bollerslev, F.X. Diebold, and P. Labys. 2003. Modeling and forecasting realized volatility. *Econometrica* 71, no. 2: 579–625.

Barndorff-Nielsen, O.E., and N. Shephard. 2004. Econometric analysis of realized covariation: high-frequency based covariance, regressions, and correlation in financial economics. *Econometrica* 72, no. 3: 885–925.

Bauwens, L., S. Laurent, and J.V.K. Rombouts. 2006. Multivariate GARCH models: a survey. *Journal of Applied Econometrics* 21, no. 1: 79–109.

Billio, M., M. Caporin, and M. Gobbo. 2006. Flexible dynamic conditional correlation multivariate GARCH for asset allocation. *Applied Financial Economics Letters* 2, no. 2: 123–30.

Bonato, M. 2009. Estimating the degrees of freedom of the realized volatility Wishart autoregressive model. Manuscript available at http://ssrn.com/abstract=1357044.

Bonato, M., M. Caporin, and A. Ranaldo. 2009. Forecasting realized covariances with a block structure WAR model, Swiss National Bank Working Paper 2009–03.

Caporin, M., and P. Paruolo. 2009. Structured multivariate volatility models. Working Paper 90, Department of Economics 'Marco Fanno', University of Padova.

Clements, A., M. Doolan, S. Hurn, and M. Becker. 2009. On the efficacy of techniques for evaluating multivariate volatility forecasts. Working Paper no. 41, National Centre of Econometric Research (NCER), Australia.

Corsi, F. 2009. A simple approximate long-memory model of realized volatility. *Journal of Financial Econometrics* 7, no. 2: 174–196.

Dacorogna, M., R. Gencay, U.A. Muller, R. Olsen, and O. Pictet. 2001. *An introduction to high-frequency finance.* London: Academic Press.

De Pooter, M., M. Martens, and D. van Dijk. 2008. Predicting the daily covariance matrix for S&P 100 stocks using intraday data – but which frequency to use? *Econometric Reviews* 27, nos. 1–3: 199–229.

Diebold, F.X., and R.S. Mariano. 1995. Comparing predictive accuracy. *Journal of Business and Economic Statistics* 13, no. 3: 253–63.

Gourieroux, C., J. Jasiak, and R. Sufana. 2009. The Wishart autoregressive process of multivariate stochastic volatility. *Journal of Econometrics* 150, no. 2: 167–81.

Hansen, P.R. 2005. A test for superior predictive ability. *Journal of Business and Economic Statistics* 23, no. 4: 365–80.

Hansen, P.R., A. Lunde, and J.M. Nason. 2011. Model confidence sets for forecasting models. *Econometrica* 79, no. 2: 453–97.

McAleer, M., and M. Medeiros. 2008. Realized volatility: a review. *Econometric Reviews* 27, no. (1–3): 10–45.

Meucci, A. 2005. *Risk and asset allocation.* London: Springer.

Patton, A.J., and K. Sheppard. 2009. Evaluating volatility and correlation forecasts. In *Handbook of financial time series,* ed. T.G. Andersen, R.A. Davis, J.P. Kreiß, and T. Mikosch, 801–38. Heidelberg, Berlin: Springer-Verlag.

Silvennoinen, A., and T. Terasvirta. 2009. Multivariate GARCH models. In *Handbook of financial time series,* ed. T.G. Andersen, R.A. Davis, J.P. Kreiß, and T. Mikosch, 201–32. Heidelberg, Berlin: Springer-Verlag.

West, K.D. 1996. Asymptotic inference about predictive ability. *Econometrica* 64, no. 5: 1067–84.

West, K.D. 2006. Forecast evaluation. In *Handbook of economic forecasting,* ed. G. Elliott, C. Granger, and A. Timmermann, chap. 3, 99–134. Amsterdam: North Holland Press.

White, H. 2000. A reality check for data snooping. *Econometrica* 68, no. 5: 1097–126.

# A simple two-component model for the distribution of intraday returns

Laura Coroneo[a] and David Veredas[b]

[a]Economics, School of Social Sciences, University of Manchester, Oxford Road, Manchester, UK; [b]ECARES, Solvay Brussels School of Economics and Management, Université libre de Bruxelles, Brussels, Belgium

We model the conditional distribution of high-frequency financial returns by means of a two-component quantile regression model. Using three years of 30 minute returns, we show that the conditional distribution depends on past returns and on the time of the day. Two practical applications illustrate the usefulness of the model. First, we provide quantile-based measures of conditional volatility, asymmetry and kurtosis that do not depend on the existence of moments. We find seasonal patterns and time dependencies beyond volatility. Second, we estimate and forecast intraday Value at Risk. The two-component model is able to provide good-risk assessments and to outperform GARCH-based Value at Risk evaluations.

## 1.   Introduction

Intraday data have become a major pole of interest for researchers and financial agents who practice intraday trading.[1] For these agents, intraday risk evaluation – through measures such as conditional volatility, kurtosis or Value at Risk – is an important tool to follow the market. The analysis of risk is related to the analysis of probabilities and, therefore, of the conditional probability distribution of asset returns. Any function describing this distribution conveys information about the likelihood that the next realization will take a certain value.

Within the day the distribution of high-frequency financial returns partly depends on a seasonal component and, usually, the focus of intraday seasonality is on volatility. Andersen and Bollerslev (1997) fit a model for the second moment as a function of two components, one for the dynamics and another for the seasonality, and insist on the importance of filtering returns for the time of the day effect prior to fitting a model for volatility. Alternatively, Bollerslev and Ghysels (1996) propose a one-step approach using a periodic volatility model.[2] In either case, if returns are zero-mean Gaussian, the second moment provides enough information to describe the conditional probability law, as all odd moments are zero and even moments are functions of the second moment. This property of the Gaussian distribution is very appealing but, at the same time, this distribution is not able to reproduce the tail behavior present in the data. More flexible distributions, such as the Student-$t$, are needed. However, the drawback of these laws is that moments beyond the second are either zero – e.g. the third moment – or functions of an invariant tail index – e.g. the fourth moment. A possible solution to overcome this problem is to fit conditional models for different moments, similar to Hansen (1994) or Harvey and Siddique (1999) among others, but it is not clear which functional forms these moments should take and/or which regressors to use.

A natural alternative is to model directly the conditional distribution. Among all the functions that characterize it (density, cumulative, characteristic, Laplace, hazard, etc.), the conditional quantile function is suited better due to the existence of quantile regression (QR), introduced by the seminal work of Koenker and Bassett (1978). QR has a number of useful features. First, as said, QR is one of the possible ways to characterize the conditional probability law. Since there is a one-to-one relation with all the other possible characterizations, we can analyze the effect of the time of the day and past information on the density function of asset returns. Second, QR does not assume the existence of any moment. This is a very appealing feature since often, as shown by Mandelbrot (1963) and Fama (1963), the tails of the distribution of high-frequency financial returns are so thick that moments beyond the second may not exist. Third, QR is robust to the presence of outliers in the dependent variable. This is particularly useful in the analysis of high-frequency financial returns since they often present outliers or, at least, observations that are remarkably different from the rest of the process (due to, e.g. lumpy information releases or dramatic liquidity shocks that determine jumps in the price process). Fourth, QR is a distribution-free approach. It does not rely on any distributional specification as it is an estimate of the conditional probability distribution itself. In other words, QR enables to look at slices of the conditional distribution without any reliance on global distributional assumptions.

In finance there is a great deal of interest in quantiles, especially in the context of risk management, as witnessed by the literature on Value at Risk. Since Value at Risk is simply a particular quantile of the distribution, QR is a natural tool for Value at Risk assessments. Engle and Manganelli (2004) introduce the Conditional Autoregressive Value at Risk which extends the traditional linear QR to a nonlinear framework. They also develop a new test of model adequacy, the dynamic quantile test, which is based on the criterion that in each period the probability of exceeding the Value at Risk must be independent of past information. Results suggest that the tails of the distribution of daily returns follow a different behavior than the middle of the distribution, which contradicts the assumption behind the GARCH and RiskMetrics models. Cenesizoglu and Timmermann (2008) explore the predictability of the distribution of monthly stock returns in a QR framework and analyze whether a range of state variables (valuation ratios, bond yield measures, equity risk estimates, corporate finance variables) are helpful in predicting different quantiles. They find that most of the variables have an asymmetric effect on the distribution of returns, affecting lower, central and upper quantiles differently. Bouyé and Salmon (2009) introduce a general approach to nonlinear QR modeling based on the copula function that defines the dependency structure between the variables of interest.

In this article, we depart from the existing literature on Value at Risk modeling (which focuses on monthly, weekly or daily returns) and propose the use of QR to model the distribution of intraday returns. Four reasons are behind this choice. First, QR overcomes most of the problems related to inference for high-frequency financial returns, which still represent a challenge for traditional methods developed for lower frequency data (i.e. existence of moments, outliers, distributional assumptions). Second, intraday returns display a strong intraday seasonality, which could affect in a distinct way each part of their distribution. QR models each conditional quantile without relying on any global assumption. Third, QR allows to construct conditional measures for volatility, asymmetry and kurtosis that do not depend on the existence of moments and are alternatives to the traditional conditional moment-based measures. Fourth, QR delivers straightforwardly intraday Value at Risk, which is relevant for market participants (such as intraday traders and market makers) involved in frequent intraday trades.

Intraday Value at Risk is a useful tool to define risk profiles, monitor risk and measure performance for traders that open and close positions during the day, as it provides a more complete picture than a daily measure, which disregards all the intraday information. Intraday Value at Risk assessments have also been proposed by Giot (2005) and Dionne, Duchesne, and Pacurar (2009). Giot (2005) quantifies intraday Value at Risk using Gaussian GARCH, Student-$t$ GARCH, RiskMetrics and Log-ACD models, and shows that Student-$t$ GARCH model performs best. Dionne, Duchesne, and Pacurar (2009) investigate the use of tick-by-tick data for market risk measurement and estimate intraday Value at Risk at different horizons by intraday Monte Carlo simulations using irregularly time-spaced high-frequency data. To the best of our knowledge, this is the first paper that proposes QR as a valid alternative to traditional methods for high-frequency financial return modeling.

We model the conditional distribution of high-frequency financial returns by means of a QR model with two components: a Fourier series (to account for the intraday seasonality) and lagged absolute returns (to control for the dynamics). We use 30-min returns of the constituents of the Spanish Stock Exchange (SSE) index from January 2001 to December 2003. For all the stocks, we find that at the opening and closing the density flattens and the tails become thicker, while in the middle of the day returns concentrate around the median and the tails are thinner. Results are intuitive, in the sense that they confirm the general perception that, in the opening and closing, the probabilities of finding large price variations are higher than in the middle of the day. The conditional distribution also depends on past observations and the effect is not homogeneous across quantiles, as extreme quantiles are more affected than the middle ones. Past information has a scale effect on the distribution, i.e. the larger the past absolute return, the larger the dispersion.

We use the two-component QR model to compute conditional moment-free measures of volatility, asymmetry and kurtosis. This approach allows us to identify seasonal patterns and time dependencies in the three measures, meaning intraday predictability beyond volatility. These intraday seasonality effects on higher moments cannot be accounted by standard GARCH models. We also perform an out-of-sample forecasting exercise of the Value at Risk at 5%, 2.5% and 1% confidence levels. The maximum expected loss is maximal at the opening and closing and minimal at lunch time. Failure rate tests, based on Christoffersen (1998), confirm that the model is able to provide good-risk assessments for all the stocks. By contrast, the performance of the Gaussian, Student-$t$ and skewed-$t$ GARCH in terms of intraday Value at Risk forecast is deceiving, indicating that these models are unable to explain adequately intraday risk.

The structure of the paper is as follows. Section 2 introduces the data. Section 3 presents the two-component QR model. Section 4 shows the estimation results and specification tests. Section 5 presents the two applications of the two-component QR model. Section 6 concludes and the Appendix contains some technical details.

## 2. Data

Data come from the SSE which holds all the Spanish stocks that achieve pre-determined minimum levels of trading frequency and liquidity. The SSE is organized as an electronic order-driven market with a daily continuous trading session from 9:00 to 17:30 and two call auctions that determine the opening and closing prices.

The official market index of the SSE is the IBEX-35, which includes the 35 most liquid and active stocks of the exchange, weighted by market capitalization. Its composition is regularly revised every semester. The data we use consist of 30-min midpoint returns from January 2001 to December 2003.[3] For each stock, we have 17 intraday observations for a total of 12,733

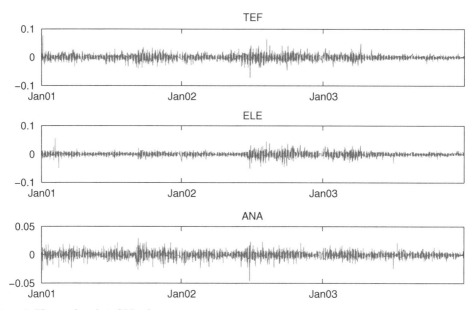

Figure 1. Time series plot of 30-min returns.
Notes: Thirty-minute returns of three stocks: Telefonica (TEF) in the upper plot, Endesa (ELE) in the middle plot and Acciona (ANA) in the bottom plot. Sample period: January 2001– December 2003.

observations over 749 trading days. We consider the 26 stocks that were index constituents for all the sample period and, for ease of exposition, we report the analysis for three representative stocks: Telefonica (TEF), Endesa (ELE) and Acciona (ANA) that are, respectively, a big, a medium and a small company, weighting approximately 20%, 6% and 0.8% in the market index. Results for the other stocks are available on our websites.[4]

A time series plot of the data is presented in Figure 1. Returns have zero mean, exhibit volatility clustering and are characterized by a large number of extreme observations. Summary statistics, reported in Table 1, highlight that the sample medians are zero and the sample skewness indicates a reasonable grade of symmetry. The maximum, the minimum and the volatility increase in magnitude with the liquidity of the stock. The sample kurtosis is well above 3, which clearly indicates that the returns are not Gaussian. This is reflected in the Lilliefors corrected Kolmogorov–Smirnov normality test.[5]

Table 1. Summary statistics.

| Stock | Med | Max | Min | Std | Skew | Kurt | KS |
|---|---|---|---|---|---|---|---|
| TEF | 0.000 | 7.570 | −7.213 | 0.585 | 0.124 | 14.050 | 0.090* |
| ELE | 0.000 | 5.447 | −4.998 | 0.464 | −0.191 | 15.154 | 0.099* |
| ANA | 0.000 | 2.917 | −4.621 | 0.347 | −0.297 | 12.266 | 0.111* |

Notes: Descriptive statistics of 30-min returns of Telefonica (TEF), Endesa (ELE) and Acciona (ANA) over the sample period January 2001– December 2003. Sample medians (Med), maxima (Max), minima (Min) and standard deviations (Std) are reported in percentage. Skew refers to the sample skewness and Kurt to the sample kurtosis. KS refers to the Lilliefors corrected Kolmogorov-Smirnov test of normality and *means statistically significant at 5%.

Table 2. Sample moments at different hours of the day.

| Hour | Med | Std | Skew | Kurt |
|---|---|---|---|---|
| | | *TEF* | | |
| 09:00 | 0.000 | 1.426 | 0.134 | 5.274 |
| 12:00 | 0.000 | 0.395 | −0.037 | 5.799 |
| 14:00 | 0.000 | 0.362 | −0.221 | 7.645 |
| 15:00 | 0.000 | 0.396 | −1.341 | 16.735 |
| 17:00 | 0.000 | 0.563 | −0.394 | 5.589 |
| | | *ELE* | | |
| 09:00 | 0.000 | 1.009 | −0.068 | 7.199 |
| 12:00 | 0.000 | 0.356 | −1.058 | 10.359 |
| 14:00 | 0.000 | 0.299 | −1.568 | 17.956 |
| 15:00 | 0.000 | 0.325 | −0.351 | 8.904 |
| 17:00 | 0.000 | 0.476 | −0.061 | 5.772 |
| | | *ANA* | | |
| 09:00 | 0.000 | 0.673 | −0.524 | 7.210 |
| 12:00 | 0.000 | 0.270 | 0.765 | 11.666 |
| 14:00 | 0.000 | 0.216 | −0.542 | 8.616 |
| 15:00 | 0.000 | 0.250 | −0.235 | 10.167 |
| 17:00 | 0.000 | 0.396 | 0.209 | 5.170 |

Notes: The first column reports the time of the day to which the moments refer. For example, 09:00 denotes the series of 30-min returns from 09:00 to 09:30 for all the 749 trading days in the sample. Sample medians (Med) and standard deviations (Std) are reported in percentages. Skew refers to the sample skewness and Kurt to the sample kurtosis.

Table 2 reports sample moments of the data grouped according to the time of the day. We report the median, the standard deviation, the skewness and the kurtosis for some selected hours (the indicated hour refers to the beginning of the time period). These estimates are proxies of the intraday behavior of the probability law. There is no evidence of an intraday seasonal pattern in the sample median of returns. However, there is a clear U-shaped pattern in the standard deviation, as found in many former studies. In addition to this, the last two columns suggest the presence of an intraday seasonality in the skewness and kurtosis with a significant increase in the thickness of the tails just after 14:00, i.e. prior to the opening of the New York Stock Exchange (NYSE).

## 3. A two-component model for intraday returns

Let $Q_{r_t}(\tau)$ be the $\tau$ quantile of the return $r_t$. It is well known that

$$f(r_t) = \frac{\partial}{\partial r_t} F(r_t)$$

and

$$Q_{r_t}(\tau) = F^{-1}(\tau) = \inf\{z_t : F(z_t) \geq \tau\}, \quad \tau \in (0, 1),$$

where $f$ is the probability density function and $F$ is the cumulative distribution function. QR, introduced by Koenker and Bassett (1978), models the conditional quantiles of the variable of interest as a linear function of a given set of covariates. The fundamental difference of QR with respect to mean regression is that the latter considers the effect of the regressor on the mean of the regressand while QR considers the effect of the regressor on a specific quantile of the regressand. The basic QR model is

$$Q_{r_t}(\tau|\mathbf{x}_t) = \omega(\tau) + \boldsymbol{\beta}(\tau)\mathbf{x}_t, \quad \tau \in (0, 1), \tag{1}$$

where the intercept $\omega(\tau)$ and the vector of slope parameters $\boldsymbol{\beta}(\tau)$ are specific to the quantile.

We decompose the probability law of $\mathbf{x}_t$ into two components, one to account for the intraday seasonality and one for the dispersion clustering. As for the seasonality, we model it using a Fourier series of order three:

$$\text{seas}_d(\tau) = \sum_{j=1}^{3} \alpha_j(\tau) \cos\left(2\pi j \frac{d}{D}\right) + \gamma_j(\tau) \sin\left(2\pi j \frac{d}{D}\right), \tag{2}$$

where $D$ denotes the number of intraday time intervals (17 for the 30-min returns) and $d$ denotes the time of the day in ordinal sense (i.e. the sequence $1, 2, \ldots, D$).[6] Note that the cosine component of the first Fourier series reaches the maximum at the opening and at the closing (the hours of the day in which the dispersion is higher) and has the minimum at lunch time (the time of the day in which the dispersion is minimal). We therefore expect the cosine terms to capture most of the seasonal pattern.

To control for the dynamics, we use one lag of the absolute value of returns $|r_{t-1}|$. Other functions of $r_t$ to capture the dynamics as, for instance, square returns are possible. However, the choice of the lagged absolute value is better suited for two reasons. First, QR is robust to outliers in the dependent variable but not in the independent. Lagged absolute values of returns offer more advantages in terms of robustness, as also pointed out by Koenker and Zhao (1996). Second, autocorrelations of absolute returns are greater than those of squared returns, or other functions of returns, as shown by Taylor (1986).[7]

Putting the elements together, the two-component QR model for intraday returns is

$$Q_{r_t}(\tau|d, |r_{t-1}|) = \omega(\tau) + \beta(\tau)|r_{t-1}| + \text{seas}_d(\tau). \tag{3}$$

Estimation is implemented in Matlab using the interior point method, as described by Portnoy and Koenker (1997). The chosen grid of quantiles is $(0.05, 0.10, \ldots, 0.95)$ and the limiting covariance matrix has been computed using the procedure described in the Appendix.

## 4. Estimation results

Parameters in Equation (3) depend on the considered quantile $\tau$. The number of parameters is therefore equal to the number of quantiles times the number of explanatory variables plus the intercepts $\omega(\tau)$. Since this number is large, we follow the literature, see for instance Koenker (2005), and present all the results graphically. Figure 2 shows the estimated parameters for TEF.[8] Every point is an estimated parameter for a different quantile, with the corresponding 95% confidence interval.

The top left plot shows the estimated intercept parameters $\hat{\omega}(\tau)$ and the top right plot presents the estimated coefficients for past absolute returns $\hat{\beta}(\tau)$. The magnitude of lagged returns is an important source of variation, but its effect is not homogeneous across quantiles. The median return is unaffected by a shock in $|r_{t-1}|$ since $\hat{\beta}(0.5)$ is not statistically different from zero, while any quantile beyond and below 50% is affected. For a given past absolute return, the effect on extreme quantiles is larger than on the ones near the median. Exemplifying, if the return at $t - 1$ was zero, the density, conditional to the time of the day, remains unchanged. If, by contrast, at

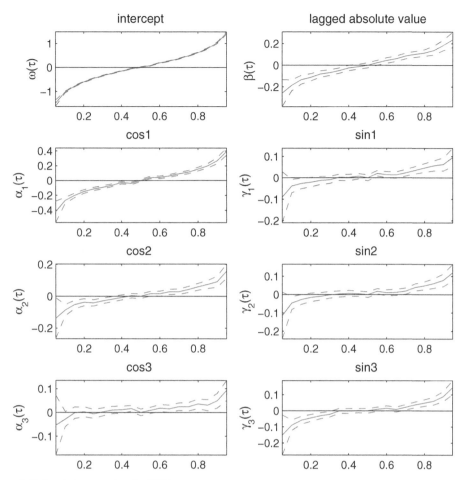

Figure 2. Estimated parameters for TEF.
Notes: Estimated parameters of the two-component QR model in Equation (3). The solid line indicates the estimated parameters for each quantile $\tau$. The dashed lines refer to the 95% confidence intervals. All plots refer to TEF.

$t-1$ there was a large return, the density flattens around the median, pushing out mass to the tails, thus increasing the probability of a large price variation. If the return at $t-1$ was small, the tails of the density shrink, decreasing the probability of large price variations in $t$. Thus, the lagged absolute value of returns has a scale effect on the distribution of returns. The remaining six plots in Figure 2 show the estimated coefficients for the Fourier series. The coefficients for the cosine terms are larger than the ones for the sinus terms. In particular, the coefficients for the first cosine term are the largest, due to the fact that the cosine series peaks at the opening and the closing. None of the coefficients is different from zero at $\tau = 0.5$, meaning that the median is not affected by the time of the day. Consequently, since also the estimated coefficient for $|r_{t-1}|$ at $\tau = 0.5$ is zero, the conditional and the unconditional medians are equal to zero.

To get further insights on the seasonal pattern of the conditional distribution, the upper plot of Figure 3 shows the estimated seasonal component computed as in Equation (2). Each line is the seasonal component at a specific quantile as a function of the time of the day, which is reported

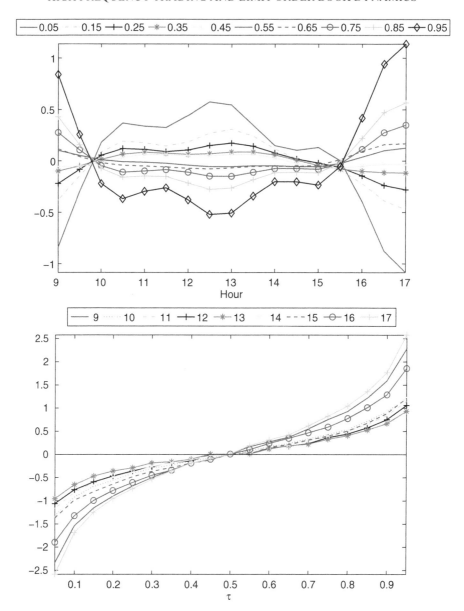

Figure 3. Seasonality.
Notes: The upper plot displays the estimated seasonal component $seas_t(\tau)$ for TEF, for different times of the day. Each line corresponds to a different quantile. The bottom plot displays the conditional quantiles of $r_t$ given $|r_{t-1}| = 0$ for TEF, and for different $\tau$'s. Each line corresponds to a different time of the day.

on the horizontal axis. The estimated seasonal components display different shapes within the day and the following conclusions can be drawn. First, the seasonal component at the median is negligible, but it becomes more important as we move to the tails of the distribution. Second, on the left tail of the distribution the fitted seasonal component is negative till 10:00 then it becomes positive, peaks around 13:00 and then decreases, becoming negative after 15:30. On the other tail of the distribution, the behavior is opposite with a fitted seasonal component positive at the opening, which decreases and becomes negative after 10:00, reaches the minimum at 13:00 and the increases again. In other words, the quantiles to the left and right of the median get further from zero at the opening and closing, and get closer to zero in the middle of the day. This pattern is more pronounced for extreme quantiles, which can be interpreted as an increase in the tails at the opening and closing. Third, for extreme quantiles we can detect a decrease in the fitted seasonal component at 11:00–11:30 and at 14:00–14:30, which can be interpreted as an increase in the tail size at these times of the day.[9]

To better analyze how the conditional distribution of returns moves through the day, the bottom plot of Figure 3 plots the fitted conditional quantiles for different times of the day. Rewriting Equation (3) conditional to a particular value of past absolute return and for different times of the day, we have

$$Q_{r_t}(\tau|d, \overline{|r_{t-1}|}) = \omega(\tau) + \beta(\tau)\overline{|r_{t-1}|} + \text{seas}_d(\tau).$$

The choice of the conditioning value of $|r_{t-1}|$ has a quantitative but not a qualitative effect. For a given $\tau$, $\beta(\tau)\overline{|r_{t-1}|}$ is constant, while the term $\text{seas}_d(\tau)$ changes with the time of the day (as we saw in the upper plot of Figure 3). The only effect of changing $|r_{t-1}|$ is to shift all the $\tau$ conditional quantiles by the same amount along the day. In the plot, we fix $|r_{t-1}|$ to zero. The plot reads as follows: the closer the line is to the horizontal zero line, the more concentrated is the density around the median. And the further it is, the more dispersed it is. The time of the day at which we have the largest seasonal effect is at 17:00, the closure of the market, followed by the effect at 9:00, the opening. At these hours the conditional density becomes more dispersed. In the opposite direction is the seasonal effect at 13:00, which decreases (in absolute value) the conditional quantiles, decreasing the dispersion. This effect can be associated with a reduced trading activity during the lunch break.

## 4.1  Specification tests

An attractive feature of QR is that it enables to look at slices of the conditional distribution without any reliance on global distributional assumptions. However, one potential drawback of independently estimating quantile functions is that it is not possible to impose the monotonicity constraint on the conditional quantiles. This problem, at population level, is know as quantile crossing and it is often considered as a sign of model misspecification. Table 3 reports the number of times that two fitted quantiles cross (not reported quantiles means no crossing). All the crossings are around the median – the 0.45 quantile with the median and the median with the 0.55 quantile – and the percentages of crossings are extremely low. More importantly, the estimates at the median are not statistically different from zero, meaning that population quantile do not cross and hence the few detected quantile crossings are a finite sample artifact.

Specification tests in a quantile framework are based on failure rates, that is the percentage of times that the realizations of the dependent variable are below the conditional quantiles. If a conditional quantile is well specified, its failure rate should be equal to the quantile level $\tau$. The Christoffersen (1998) likelihood ratio test of unconditional coverage is based on this idea. Let $I_t$ be a hit variable that takes value 1 if there is a success, that is if the realized return is larger than the fitted conditional quantile, and 0 otherwise:

$$I_t = \begin{cases} 1 & \text{if } r_t > Q_t(\tau|d, |r_{t-1}|), \\ 0 & \text{otherwise.} \end{cases} \tag{4}$$

Table 3. Model specification – quantile crossings.

| Quantiles | TEF | ELE | ANA |
|---|---|---|---|
| 0.45–0.50 | 136 | 183 | 0 |
| 0.50–0.55 | 402 | 0 | 76 |
| Total | 538 | 183 | 76 |
| % | 0.22 | 0.07 | 0.03 |

Notes: Number of quantile crossings computed as the number of times that a fitted quantile crosses with another fitted quantiles, i.e. 0.45–0.50 counts the number of times that the fitted 45% quantile crosses with the fitted 50% one. Not reported quantiles means no crossing. The row % reports the percentages of crossings over the total number of fitter quantiles, i.e. 12,733 (sample size) × 19 (estimated quantiles) = 241,927.

If $n$ is the sample size, $n_1 = \sum_{t=1}^{n} I_t$ is the number of successes and $n_0 = n - n_1$ the number of failures. The empirical failure rates can be computed as $\hat{f} = n_0/n$ and the test statistic is

$$\text{LR}_{\text{uc}} = -2 \log \left( \frac{(1-\tau)^{n_0} \tau^{n_1}}{(1-\hat{f})^{n_0} \hat{f}^{n_1}} \right) \sim \chi_1^2, \tag{5}$$

where the null of the test is $f = \tau$.

A drawback of the Christoffersen (1998) likelihood ratio test of unconditional coverage is that it just counts the number of successes and failures, testing only for the equality between the failure rates and the quantile level. However, it is also important that the hits are not correlated in time. The likelihood ratio test of independence, Christoffersen (1998), examines serial independence of the hits testing the null of independence of the hits against the alternative of a first-order Markov process.[10] If we denote by $n_{i,j}$ the number of observations in $I_t$ with value $i$ followed by $j$, the likelihood ratio test statistic for independence is

$$\text{LR}_{\text{ind}} = -2 \log \left( \frac{(1-\hat{f})^{n_{0,0}+n_{1,1}} \hat{f}^{n_{0,1}+n_{1,1}}}{(1-\hat{f}_{0,1})^{n_{0,0}} \hat{f}_{0,1}^{n_{0,1}} (1-\hat{f}_{1,1})^{n_{1,0}} \hat{f}_{1,1}^{n_{1,1}}} \right) \sim \chi_1^2, \tag{6}$$

where $\hat{f}_{0,1} = n_{0,1}/n$ is the percentage of successes after a failure and $\hat{f}_{1,1} = n_{1,1}/n$ is the percentage of successes after a success. The null of the test is $f_{0,1} = f_{1,1} = f$.

A joint test of independence and coverage is the Christoffersen (1998) likelihood ratio test of conditional coverage which can be performed using the test statistic

$$\text{LR}_{\text{cc}} = \text{LR}_{\text{uc}} + \text{LR}_{\text{ind}} \sim \chi_2^2, \tag{7}$$

where the null is $f_{0,1} = f_{1,1} = \tau$.

Table 4 reports the likelihood ratio test statistics for the fitted conditional quantiles. The test $\text{LR}_{\text{uc}}$ indicates that all the conditional quantiles are well-specified, as we cannot reject the null that the failure rates are statistically different than the quantile levels. The independence test $\text{LR}_{\text{ind}}$ instead detects some sources of misspecification for ELE, which suggests that it could be useful to include additional covariates on the analysis. However, the conditional coverage test $\text{LR}_{\text{cc}}$ shows that in general the model is well specified, except for some minor violations for ELE at a 5% significance level.

As a robustness check and an investigation of the sources of misspecification, we estimate the model adding $|r_{t-2}|$ in Equation (3). The estimated parameters for $|r_{t-2}|$, not reported here but

Table 4. Model fit – likelihood ratio tests.

| $\tau$ | TEF | | | ELE | | | ANA | | |
|---|---|---|---|---|---|---|---|---|---|
| | $LR_{uc}$ | $LR_{ind}$ | $LR_{cc}$ | $LR_{uc}$ | $LR_{ind}$ | $LR_{cc}$ | $LR_{uc}$ | $LR_{ind}$ | $LR_{cc}$ |
| 0.05 | 0.00 | 0.03 | 0.03 | 0.00 | 6.34* | 6.34* | 0.00 | 0.15 | 0.15 |
| 0.10 | 0.00 | 0.41 | 0.41 | 0.00 | 0.12 | 0.12 | 0.00 | 0.28 | 0.28 |
| 0.15 | 0.00 | 0.90 | 0.90 | 0.00 | 0.00 | 0.00 | 0.00 | 8.58** | 8.58* |
| 0.20 | 0.00 | 1.51 | 1.51 | 0.00 | 1.70 | 1.70 | 0.00 | 5.97* | 5.97 |
| 0.25 | 0.00 | 6.03* | 6.03 | 0.00 | 7.45* | 7.45* | 0.00 | 6.00* | 6.00 |
| 0.30 | 0.00 | 3.50 | 3.50 | 0.00 | 7.06* | 7.06* | 0.00 | 3.40 | 3.40 |
| 0.35 | 0.00 | 1.52 | 1.52 | 0.00 | 6.55* | 6.55* | 0.00 | 2.98 | 2.98 |
| 0.40 | 0.00 | 0.11 | 0.11 | 0.00 | 6.17* | 6.17 | 0.00 | 0.80 | 0.80 |
| 0.45 | 0.12 | 0.08 | 0.20 | 0.01 | 4.74* | 4.74 | 0.00 | 0.80 | 0.80 |
| 0.50 | 0.00 | 0.01 | 0.01 | 0.00 | 9.42** | 9.42* | 0.02 | 0.87 | 0.89 |
| 0.55 | 0.00 | 0.01 | 0.02 | 0.00 | 6.94* | 6.94* | 0.00 | 2.37 | 2.37 |
| 0.60 | 0.00 | 0.04 | 0.04 | 0.00 | 5.28* | 5.28 | 0.00 | 2.51 | 2.51 |
| 0.65 | 0.00 | 0.23 | 0.23 | 0.00 | 4.32* | 4.33 | 0.00 | 2.77 | 2.77 |
| 0.70 | 0.00 | 0.03 | 0.04 | 0.00 | 1.65 | 1.65 | 0.00 | 1.65 | 1.65 |
| 0.75 | 0.00 | 0.03 | 0.03 | 0.00 | 0.93 | 0.93 | 0.00 | 4.13 | 4.13 |
| 0.80 | 0.00 | 0.04 | 0.04 | 0.00 | 1.88 | 1.88 | 0.00 | 3.42 | 3.42 |
| 0.85 | 0.00 | 1.00 | 1.00 | 0.00 | 0.05 | 0.05 | 0.00 | 1.88 | 1.88 |
| 0.90 | 0.00 | 0.07 | 0.07 | 0.00 | 0.94 | 0.94 | 0.00 | 0.20 | 0.20 |
| 0.95 | 0.00 | 0.04 | 0.04 | 0.00 | 2.17 | 2.17 | 0.00 | 1.81 | 1.81 |

Notes: Christoffersen (1998) tests of unconditional coverage ($LR_{uc}$), independence ($LR_{ind}$) and conditional coverage ($LR_{cc}$) of the fitted quantiles obtained from model in Equation (3). *Means statistically significant at 5% significance level, while ** at 1% level.

Table 5. Model fit – two lags of absolute returns.

| $\tau$ | TEF | | | ELE | | | ANA | | |
|---|---|---|---|---|---|---|---|---|---|
| | $LR_{uc}$ | $LR_{ind}$ | $LR_{cc}$ | $LR_{uc}$ | $LR_{ind}$ | $LR_{cc}$ | $LR_{uc}$ | $LR_{ind}$ | $LR_{cc}$ |
| 0.05 | 0.05 | 0.10 | 0.15 | 0.01 | 2.59 | 2.60 | 0.00 | 0.04 | 0.04 |
| 0.10 | 0.01 | 0.04 | 0.05 | 0.01 | 0.27 | 0.28 | 0.00 | 0.05 | 0.05 |
| 0.15 | 0.00 | 1.67 | 1.67 | 0.00 | 0.00 | 0.00 | 0.00 | 4.16* | 4.17 |
| 0.20 | 0.00 | 2.77 | 2.77 | 0.00 | 2.93 | 2.93 | 0.00 | 6.50* | 6.50* |
| 0.25 | 0.00 | 3.84 | 3.84 | 0.00 | 6.95** | 6.95* | 0.00 | 1.15 | 1.15 |
| 0.30 | 0.00 | 4.14* | 4.14 | 0.00 | 6.86** | 6.86* | 0.00 | 2.64 | 2.64 |
| 0.35 | 0.00 | 1.45 | 1.46 | 0.00 | 6.04* | 6.04* | 0.00 | 0.72 | 0.73 |
| 0.40 | 0.00 | 0.16 | 0.17 | 0.00 | 6.31* | 6.31* | 0.00 | 1.01 | 1.01 |
| 0.45 | 0.00 | 0.01 | 0.01 | 0.00 | 5.33* | 5.33 | 0.00 | 0.57 | 0.57 |
| 0.50 | 0.02 | 0.05 | 0.07 | 0.02 | 9.26** | 9.27* | 0.00 | 1.06 | 1.06 |
| 0.55 | 0.01 | 0.36 | 0.37 | 0.00 | 7.37* | 7.37* | 0.00 | 1.83 | 1.83 |
| 0.60 | 0.00 | 0.12 | 0.12 | 0.00 | 6.23* | 6.23* | 0.00 | 1.87 | 1.87 |
| 0.65 | 0.00 | 0.10 | 0.10 | 0.00 | 3.03 | 3.03 | 0.00 | 2.05 | 2.05 |
| 0.70 | 0.00 | 0.05 | 0.05 | 0.00 | 2.18 | 2.18 | 0.00 | 1.12 | 1.12 |
| 0.75 | 0.00 | 0.01 | 0.01 | 0.00 | 0.55 | 0.55 | 0.00 | 1.50 | 1.50 |
| 0.80 | 0.00 | 0.44 | 0.44 | 0.00 | 0.37 | 0.37 | 0.00 | 3.59 | 3.59 |
| 0.85 | 0.00 | 2.29 | 2.29 | 0.00 | 0.09 | 0.09 | 0.00 | 1.28 | 1.28 |
| 0.90 | 0.00 | 0.12 | 0.13 | 0.00 | 0.54 | 0.54 | 0.00 | 0.18 | 0.18 |
| 0.95 | 0.00 | 2.14 | 2.14 | 0.00 | 3.89* | 3.89 | 0.00 | 1.23 | 1.23 |

Notes: Christoffersen (1998) tests of unconditional coverage ($LR_{uc}$), independence ($LR_{ind}$) and conditional coverage ($LR_{cc}$) of the fitted quantiles obtained from model in Equation (3) including a second lag of absolute returns. *Means statistically significant at 5% significance level, while ** at 1% level.

Table 6. Model fit – volume.

| $\tau$ | TEF | | | ELE | | | ANA | | |
|---|---|---|---|---|---|---|---|---|---|
| | $LR_{uc}$ | $LR_{ind}$ | $LR_{cc}$ | $LR_{uc}$ | $LR_{ind}$ | $LR_{cc}$ | $LR_{uc}$ | $LR_{ind}$ | $LR_{cc}$ |
| 0.10 | 0.00 | 0.20 | 0.20 | 0.00 | 0.13 | 0.13 | 0.00 | 0.18 | 0.18 |
| 0.15 | 0.00 | 0.30 | 0.30 | 0.00 | 2.68 | 2.68 | 0.00 | 7.87** | 7.87* |
| 0.20 | 0.00 | 0.00 | 0.01 | 0.00 | 3.65 | 3.65 | 0.00 | 5.43* | 5.43 |
| 0.25 | 0.00 | 0.32 | 0.32 | 0.00 | 7.06** | 7.06* | 0.00 | 4.37* | 4.37 |
| 0.30 | 0.00 | 0.23 | 0.23 | 0.00 | 8.38** | 8.38* | 0.00 | 3.79 | 3.79 |
| 0.35 | 0.00 | 0.03 | 0.03 | 0.00 | 4.82* | 4.82 | 0.00 | 3.40 | 3.40 |
| 0.40 | 0.00 | 0.00 | 0.01 | 0.00 | 5.70* | 5.70 | 0.00 | 0.53 | 0.53 |
| 0.45 | 0.00 | 0.01 | 0.01 | 0.00 | 6.87** | 6.87* | 0.00 | 0.52 | 0.52 |
| 0.50 | 0.85 | 0.34 | 1.19 | 0.00 | 8.99** | 8.99* | 0.00 | 0.80 | 0.80 |
| 0.55 | 0.00 | 0.11 | 0.11 | 0.00 | 8.75** | 8.75* | 0.00 | 2.06 | 2.06 |
| 0.60 | 0.00 | 0.31 | 0.31 | 0.00 | 4.13* | 4.13 | 0.00 | 2.34 | 2.34 |
| 0.65 | 0.00 | 0.47 | 0.47 | 0.00 | 5.27* | 5.27 | 0.00 | 3.09 | 3.09 |
| 0.70 | 0.00 | 2.02 | 2.02 | 0.00 | 4.61* | 4.61 | 0.00 | 3.19 | 3.19 |
| 0.75 | 0.00 | 0.60 | 0.60 | 0.00 | 0.46 | 0.46 | 0.00 | 6.17* | 6.17* |
| 0.80 | 0.00 | 0.81 | 0.81 | 0.00 | 4.04* | 4.04 | 0.00 | 8.32** | 8.32* |
| 0.85 | 0.00 | 0.77 | 0.77 | 0.00 | 1.17 | 1.17 | 0.00 | 2.22 | 2.22 |
| 0.90 | 0.00 | 0.89 | 0.89 | 0.00 | 0.39 | 0.39 | 0.00 | 0.00 | 0.01 |
| 0.95 | 0.00 | 0.30 | 0.30 | 0.00 | 0.37 | 0.37 | 0.00 | 6.73* | 6.74* |

Notes: Christoffersen (1998) tests of unconditional coverage ($LR_{uc}$), independence ($LR_{ind}$) and conditional coverage ($LR_{cc}$) of the fitted quantiles obtained from model in Equation (3) including contemporaneous and lagged total volume. *Means statistically significant at 5% significance level, while ** at 1% level.

available upon request, are small in magnitude and in general not significant. More interestingly, the total number of quantile crossings increases to 663 for TEF, 450 for ELE and 91 for ANA. Table 5 reports the likelihood ratio tests and shows that this extension does not substantially improve the performance of the model.

We also enhance the model with a measure of market activity, namely contemporaneous and lagged total volume of shares traded within the 30-min interval. Estimation results – available upon request – show that contemporaneous total volume has a statistically significant effect on the distribution of returns. It has a scale effect, i.e. the higher the volume, the more dispersed the returns. Lagged total volume does not have any significant effect, while the seasonal component remains an important source of variation of the distribution of high-frequency financial returns. The total number of quantile crossings, 542 for TEF, 214 for ELE and 34 for ANA, is comparable to the ones reported in Table 3 for the baseline model. Table 6 reports the likelihood ratio tests and shows that including total volume does not substantially improve the performance of the model either. Results including only contemporaneous volume are similar.

## 5. Conditional shape measures and intraday Value at Risk

### 5.1 Conditional quantile-based shape measures

Quantiles can be used as the basis for shape measures such as volatility, asymmetry and kurtosis, which are usually computed using averages of second, third and fourth powers of standardized random variables. However, averages are sensitive to outliers and taking second, third or fourth powers greatly amplifies the influence of any outliers. This is particularly harmful in the case of high-frequency financial returns, which are prone to contain outliers, due to jumps in the price processes. To deal with this problem, simple conditional quantile-based measures of volatility, asymmetry and kurtosis can be used.

Correct estimation of the conditional volatility, asymmetry and kurtosis is relevant for portfolio optimization and asset pricing. Under the assumption that investors prefer left-skewed portfolios to right-skewed portfolios, Harvey and Siddique (2000) propose a modified mean-variance asset pricing model where conditional asymmetry is priced. This model has been extended to the case of non-vanishing risk-neutral market variance by Chabi-Yo, Leisen, and Renault (2007). Moreover, Dittmar (2002) and Guidolin and Timmermann (2008) expand the standard mean-variance capital asset pricing model (CAPM) to a four-moment CAPM, including skewness and kurtosis.

A well-known measure of volatility[11] is the interquartile range

$$\text{vol} = Q_{r_t}(0.75) - Q_{r_t}(0.25), \tag{8}$$

which measures the distance between the third and the first quartile of the distribution. The more dispersed the returns, the larger is the volatility. McCulloch (1986), in a context of stable distributions, proposes the following extension of the Bowley (1920) coefficient of asymmetry

$$\text{asym} = \frac{(Q_{r_t}(0.95) - Q_{r_t}(0.5)) - (Q_{r_t}(0.5) - Q_{r_t}(0.05))}{Q_{r_t}(0.75) - Q_{r_t}(0.25)}, \tag{9}$$

which is based on the differences in the distance between the 95% quantile and the median, and the distance between the 0.05% quantile and the median, standardized for the interquartile range. If returns are symmetric, the numerator should be zero and hence asym $= 0$. In the same spirit, Moors (1988) proposes the following measure of kurtosis:

$$\text{kur} = \frac{(Q_{r_t}(0.875) - Q_{r_t}(0.625)) + (Q_{r_t}(0.375) - Q_{r_t}(0.125))}{Q_{r_t}(0.75) - Q_{r_t}(0.25)}, \tag{10}$$

which measures the probability mass around the first and the third quartile of the distribution. This measure is also standardized by the interquartile range to guarantee invariance under linear transformations. If returns are normally distributed kur $= 1.23$.[12]

A limitation of these measures is that they are based on unconditional quantiles and they cannot incorporate useful information contained in the dynamic evolution of quantiles over time. We construct measures of conditional volatility, asymmetry and kurtosis using conditional quantiles in place of the unconditional ones. In practice, we substitute $Q_{r_t}(\tau)$ by $Q_{r_t}(\tau|d, |r_{t-1}|)$ in Equations (8)–(10).

Figure 4 plots the conditional volatility, asymmetry and kurtosis based on the two-component QR model of Equation (3). The first column reports the conditional shape measures for the first week of the sample (85 observations) and the corresponding Gaussian counterparts. The second column reports averages (over the full sample) of the conditional shape measures for different times of the day. For comparison purposes, the plots also show the Gaussian counterparts and the shape measures in Equations (8)–(10) computed using sample quantiles of the standardized residuals of a GARCH model.[13]

As expected, the conditional volatility exhibits a U-shape pattern along the day. The conditional asymmetry and kurtosis also present a strong intraday seasonality. The conditional asymmetry is negative most of the times reaching values near zero an hour prior to the opening of the NYSE and its minimum right after the opening. The conditional kurtosis is uniformly higher than in the Gaussian case and exhibits a U-shape pattern with a pronounced hump at the opening of the

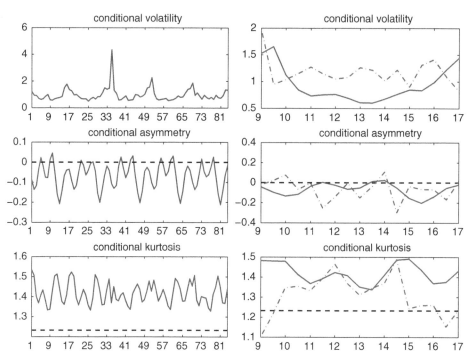

Figure 4. Shape measures.
Notes: The first column reports, in solid lines, the fitted conditional volatility, asymmetry and kurtosis for the first week of the sample (85 observations) using the conditional counterparts of Equations (8)–(10), respectively, and the two-component QR model. The second column reports, in solid lines, the full sample averages of the conditional shape measures for different times of the day. The dash-dotted line refers to Equations (8)–(10) computed using sample quantiles of the standardized residuals of the GARCH model in Section 5.2.1. The dashed black lines refer to the Gaussian distribution. All plots refer to TEF.

NYSE. GARCH-type models take into account the U-shape in the volatility, but do not allow any pattern in higher moments. Indeed, the figure shows that the standardized residuals of a GARCH model may not be independent. Though the volatility of the standardized residuals of the GARCH model is roughly constant through the day, the asymmetry and kurtosis present patterns similar to those of the QR-based shape measures.

## 5.2 Intraday Value at Risk

Risk measures are intimately related with the analysis of the tails of the distribution and, as shown in Figure 3, the density mass at the extremes is way larger around the opening and closing than around lunch. This seasonal tail behavior has to be taken into account in the computation of intraday risk measures, such as intraday Value at Risk. The goal of VaR is to assess the possible loss that can be incurred by a trader or bank, for a given portfolio of assets, over a given time period and for a certain confidence level. For active market participants such as high-frequency traders, trading risk is assessed on very short time intervals. Therefore, a VaR model that characterizes the market risk on intraday basis is useful for market participants involved in frequent intraday trading. Moreover, if traders open and close positions during the day, an intraday VaR measure is a useful tool to define risk profiles, to monitor risk and measure performance.

The VaR at a confidence level $\tau$ for a given portfolio is the loss at the $\tau$ probability level, which can be defined as the $\tau$th quantile of the conditional distribution of returns:

$$P(r_t < \text{VaR}_t(\tau|d, |r_{t-1}|)) = \tau \iff \text{VaR}_t(\tau|d, |r_{t-1}|) = Q_{r_t}(\tau|d, |r_{t-1}|).$$

Our model allows to decompose the intraday VaR into three components: an unconditional component (captured by $\omega(\tau)$), a seasonal component (captured by $\text{seas}_d(\tau)$) and a dynamic component (captured by $\beta(\tau)|r_{t-1}|$). To illustrate this decomposition, Figure 5 reports the fitted intraday VaR at the confidence level 5% for the first week of the sample (this is therefore in-sample VaR). The figure highlights how the intraday VaR is composed of two deterministic components (the unconditional and the seasonal parts), while uncertainty of the estimated intraday VaR is accounted only by the effect of past returns.

To evaluate the intraday VaR forecast capabilities of our model, we perform an out-of-sample analysis. We generate one step ahead out-of-sample intraday VaR forecasts using a rolling window scheme, a method popular among practitioners since Fama (1963) and Gonedes (1973). We fix the window size to 1700 observations, i.e. 100 days, and we estimate the model 11,033 times (number of observations minus window size). After each estimation we forecast the intraday VaR one step ahead.[14] Figure 6 displays the last 500 observations of the 30-min sampled returns for TEF, ELE and ANA with the relative intraday VaR forecasts at the confidence levels of 5%, 2.5% and 1%.[15] The forecasted intraday VaR shows clearly the effects of the two components that we used to model the conditional quantiles. The seasonal component is responsible for the deterministic daily oscillations, while the dynamic one is amplifying or reducing the oscillations. Moreover, as the confidence level of the intraday VaR decreases, the dynamic component becomes more relevant.

Multi-step forecasts are also possible, but forecasts of the absolute value of returns are needed. Granger and Sin (2000) propose a model that is suitable for this task. In the long run, the Value at Risk can be approximated by $\omega(\tau) + \beta(\tau)\rho + \text{seas}_d(\tau)$, where $\rho$ is the long run forecast of the absolute value of returns.

We compute failure rates as in Equation (4), in this case $n$ is equal to the evaluation period (i.e. $11,033$), and the Christoffersen (1998) tests as in Equations (5)–(7). Results are shown in Table 7. Failure rates are fairly close to the theoretical levels. For TEF and ANA, we cannot reject the null hypotheses of unconditional coverage, independence and conditional coverage. In other words, we cannot reject the null of good forecasting performance for all the intraday VaR confidence levels. For ELE, we have some rejections at 5% significance level. However, none of the tests rejects the null of accurate forecast ability at the 1% significance level. In general, results show the ability of the two-component QR to provide good out-of-sample forecasts of the intraday VaR confirming the importance of well specifying the intraday seasonality, which has a crucial role in intraday risk measurement.

### 5.2.1 Comparison with GARCH models

The benchmark models for VaR are the GARCH models, which have been shown, under suitable distributional assumptions, to be able to explain the behavior of returns. To handle the intraday seasonality in the variance of high-frequency returns, we use a multiplicative component GARCH(1,1) model (see, among others, Engle 2002; Engle and Rangel 2008; Hautsch 2008)

$$r_t = \sqrt{g_t \phi_d} \varepsilon_t,$$

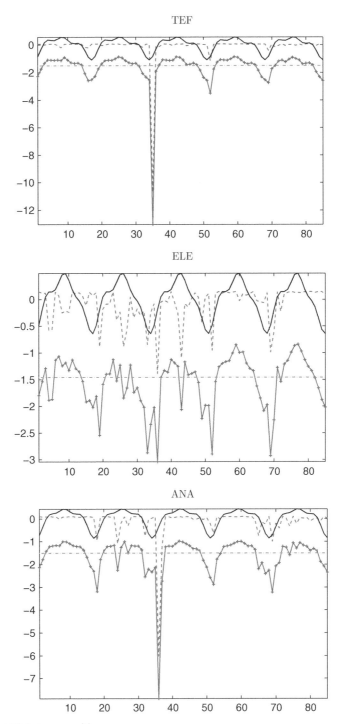

Figure 5. Value at Risk decomposition.
Notes: Decomposition of the fitted Value at Risk at 5% confidence level for the first week of the sample (85 observations). The solid black line is the seasonal component, the dashed line is the dynamic component, the dash-dotted line is the intercept and the solid with crosses is the fitted VaR.

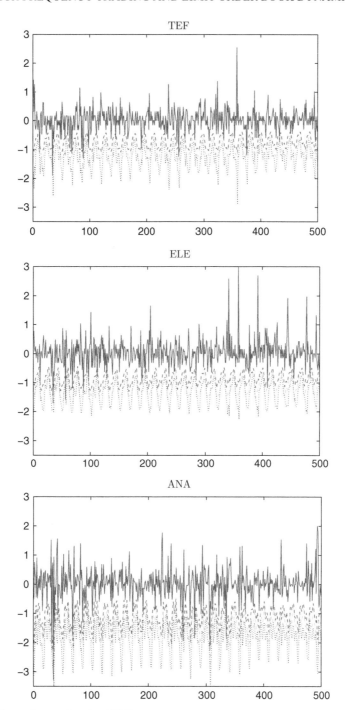

Figure 6. Out-of-sample one-step ahead VaR.
Notes: Last 500 observations of the 30-min returns (solid line) and the corresponding out-of-sample VaR forecast at confidence levels 5% (dashed line), 2.5% (dash-dotted line) and 1% (dotted line).

Table 7. Forecast performance – likelihood ratio tests.

| | VaR (5%) | VaR (2.5%) | VaR (1%) |
|---|---|---|---|
| | *Failure rates* | | |
| TEF | 4.76% | 2.33% | 1.15% |
| ELE | 4.92% | 2.63% | 1.21% |
| ANA | 4.85% | 2.50% | 1.08% |
| | $LR_{uc}$ | | |
| TEF | 1.37 | 1.34 | 2.43 |
| ELE | 0.15 | 0.79 | 4.49* |
| ANA | 0.53 | 0.00 | 0.67 |
| | $LR_{ind}$ | | |
| TEF | 0.00 | 0.64 | 3.08 |
| ELE | 4.76* | 5.92* | 2.60 |
| ANA | 0.16 | 0.17 | 1.71 |
| | $LR_{cc}$ | | |
| TEF | 1.37 | 1.98 | 5.51 |
| ELE | 4.90 | 6.71* | 7.09* |
| ANA | 0.69 | 0.17 | 2.38 |

Notes: Failure rates and Christoffersen (1998) tests for the VaR (5%), VaR (2.5%) and VaR (1%) forecasts from the two-component QR model. The upper panel presents the empirical failure rates. The second panel contains the likelihood ratio test of unconditional coverage ($LR_{uc}$). The third panel presents the likelihood ratio test of independence ($LR_{ind}$). The bottom panel refers to the joint likelihood ratio test of coverage and independence ($LR_{cc}$). *Means statistically significant at 5% level, while ** at 1% level.

where

$$g_t = \omega + \alpha \frac{r_{t-1}^2}{\phi_{d-1}} + \beta g_{t-1}$$

and

$$\phi_d = \exp \left( \sum_{j=1}^{3} \rho_j^c \cos \left( 2\pi j \frac{d}{D} \right) + \rho_j^s \sin \left( 2\pi j \frac{d}{D} \right) \right),$$

where $d$ and $D$ are defined as in the two-component QR model. The innovation $\varepsilon_t$ is an i.i.d. sequence of zero-mean and unit-variance random variables. The intraday VaR of $r_t$ at a confidence level $\tau$ is

$$VaR_t(\tau | \mathcal{F}_{t-1}) = Q_\varepsilon(\tau) \sqrt{g_t \phi_d},$$

where $\mathcal{F}_{t-1}$ denotes the information set available up to time $t - 1$ and $Q_\varepsilon(\tau)$ denotes the $\tau$th quantile of $\varepsilon_t$. We estimate the GARCH(1,1) model under three distributional assumptions: Gaussian, Student-$t$ and the skewed-$t$ distribution of Hansen (1994). The Gaussian distribution is the benchmark widely used in financial practice. The Student-$t$ is often used to account for heavy tails, and the skewed-$t$, less used in practice, features heavy tails and skewness and is the fair competitor of the two-component QR model. Hence, $Q_\varepsilon(\tau)$ denotes the $\tau$ quantile of a standard Gaussian, a standard Student-$t$ or a standard skewed-$t$ distribution.

To compare the predictive accuracy of the two-component QR model with the GARCH models, we perform the same out-of-sample analysis. Table 8 reports the results. Failure rates for the

Table 8. GARCH models forecast performance.

| | Gaussian | | | Student-$t$ | | | Skewed-$t$ | | |
|---|---|---|---|---|---|---|---|---|---|
| | VaR (5%) | VaR (2.5%) | VaR (1%) | VaR (5%) | VaR (2.5%) | VaR (1%) | VaR (5%) | VaR (2.5%) | VaR (1%) |
| | | | | | *Failure rates* | | | | |
| TEF | 4.43% | 2.77% | 1.55% | 2.67% | 1.15% | 0.41% | 2.66% | 1.11% | 0.39% |
| ELE | 4.40% | 2.82% | 1.72% | 2.48% | 1.03% | 0.39% | 2.38% | 1.03% | 0.38% |
| ANA | 4.29% | 2.71% | 1.63% | 0.98% | 0.37% | 0.13% | 1% | 0.38% | 0.12% |
| | | | | | $LR_{uc}$ | | | | |
| TEF | 7.76** | 3.28 | 28.87** | 150.18** | 102.67** | 50.32** | 152.80** | 110.77** | 54.03** |
| ELE | 8.59** | 4.54* | 46.96** | 179.62** | 125.88** | 53.82** | 196.10** | 125.88** | 55.73** |
| ANA | 12.36** | 1.95 | 37.33** | 550.15** | 318.39** | 135.69** | 553.49** | 314.56** | 139.91** |
| | | | | | $LR_{ind}$ | | | | |
| TEF | 0.53 | 0.03 | 0.05 | 0.00 | 1.27 | 0.37 | 0.09 | 0.28 | 0.34 |
| ELE | 11.74** | 19.40** | 9.51** | 15.92** | 7.20** | 0.34 | 18.13** | 10.47** | 0.32 |
| ANA | 0.03 | 2.70 | 1.24 | 2.17 | 0.31 | 0.04 | 2.14 | 0.32 | 0.03 |
| | | | | | $LR_{cc}$ | | | | |
| TEF | 8.30* | 3.31 | 28.91** | 150.18** | 103.95** | 50.69** | 152.88** | 111.05** | 54.36** |
| ELE | 20.34** | 23.94** | 56.46** | 195.54** | 133.09** | 54.15** | 214.23** | 136.36** | 56.06** |
| ANA | 12.39** | 4.65 | 38.57** | 552.33** | 318.70** | 135.72** | 555.62** | 314.88** | 139.94** |

Notes: Failure rates and Christoffersen (1998) tests for the VaR (5%), VaR (2.5%) and VaR (1%) forecasts from the GARCH(1,1) models (Gaussian GARCH on the left, Student-$t$ GARCH in the middle and skewed-$t$ GARCH on the right). The upper panel presents the empirical failure rates. The second panel contains the likelihood ratio test of unconditional coverage ($LR_{uc}$). The third panel presents the likelihood ratio test of independence ($LR_{ind}$). The bottom panel refers to the joint likelihood ratio test of coverage and independence ($LR_{cc}$). *Means statistically significant at 5% significance level, while ** at 1% level.

Gaussian GARCH(1,1) are somehow close to the theoretical levels at 5% and 2.5% confidence levels, but at 1% confidence level they are clearly larger. For the Student-$t$ and the skewed-$t$ GARCH(1,1), the failure rates are systematically below the theoretical values for all levels. This suggests that the Gaussian GARCH(1,1) model underestimates the risk on the far end of the tails, while the Student-$t$ and the skewed-$t$ GARCH(1,1) overestimate it at any point in the tail. The ineffectiveness of these distributions to explain intraday VaR is confirmed by the Christoffersen (1998) tests. Although the tests for independence for the three distributions show that, in most of the cases, we cannot reject the null hypotheses of independence, the distributional assumptions are inadequate. For the heavy-tailed distributions, we reject the null hypotheses of unconditional and conditional coverage for all stocks and for all confidence levels. For the Gaussian distribution, we also reject in most of the cases.

## 6. Conclusion

We propose a simple two-component QR model for intraday returns. Using 30-min returns of stocks traded at the SSE from January 2001 to December 2003, we show that at the opening and closing the density flattens and the tails become thicker, while in the middle of the day returns concentrate around the median and the tails are thinner. Results are intuitive, in the sense that they confirm to the general perception that in the opening and closing the probabilities of finding large price fluctuations are higher than at lunch. The conditional quantiles also depend on past observations and the effect is not homogeneous since more extreme quantiles are more affected than the middle ones. Past information has therefore a scale effect on the distribution of high-frequency returns.

We compute conditional moment-free measures of volatility, asymmetry and kurtosis. We unveil predictability beyond volatility. The two-component QR model also allows straightforward intraday risk evaluations, such as intraday Value at Risk assessments. We perform an out-of-sample forecasting exercise of the maximum expected loss at 5%, 2.5% and 1% confidence levels. The maximum expected loss is maximal at the opening and closing, and minimal at lunch time. Christoffersen (1998) tests confirm that the two-component QR model is able to provide good-risk forecasts and outperforms GARCH-type approaches.

## Acknowledgements

We are grateful to the editor Ingmar Nolte and a referee for the insightful remarks that have improved the paper. We are also grateful to Luc Bauwens, Valentina Corradi, Catherine Dehon, Pierre Giot, Marc Hallin, Peter R. Hansen, Roger Koenker, Francesco Lisi, Simone Manganelli, Alexander McNeil, Maria Pacurar, Roberto Pascual, Sergio Pastorello, and the participants at the ECARES internal seminar, the Zeuthen workshop 2006, the ESEM 2007 and CEF 2007 conferences for the insightful remarks. Any remaining errors and inaccuracies are ours.

## Notes

1. High-frequency trading has received an increasing attention among practitioners and the media press. For instance, Charles Duhigg, from *The New York Times*, published on 23 July 2009, the article 'Stock Traders Find Speed Pays, in Milliseconds'. The second line reads 'It is called high-frequency trading – and it is suddenly one of the most talked-about and mysterious forces in the markets'.
2. For a comparison of the two approaches, see Martens, Chang, and Taylor (2002).
3. A different frequency choice is possible. However, at higher frequencies illiquid stocks present many periods without any trade and thus zero returns. This implies spurious autocorrelations in the return series. Yet, all the estimation results presented in the paper are qualitatively similar at higher frequencies, but the forecast results for the medium liquid and illiquid stocks improve significantly at 30 min, or lower, frequency. An alternative is to choose the frequency as a function of the liquidity of the stock, e.g. 15 min for the most liquid stocks and 30 min for the medium liquid or illiquid stocks.
4. http://personalpages.manchester.ac.uk/staff/laura.coroneo or www.ecares.org/veredas.html
5. The Jarque–Bera and the Shapiro–Wilk normality tests also reject normality.
6. We tried higher orders of the Fourier series, but they turned out not to be statistically significant.
7. To account for possible leverage effects, we have also introduced $r_{t-1}$. It turned out not to be statistically significant. We also included more lags of absolute returns. Results did not improve substantially.
8. For ease of exposition, we omit the graphical results for the other two stocks. They are qualitatively the same as for TEF.
9. This is confirmed in Section 5.1, where we compute quantile-based shape measures. The intuition is as follows. The 50% conditional quantile is zero and the conditional quantiles to the left of the median (i.e. $\tau < 0.5$) are negative, while the ones to the right (i.e. $\tau > 0.5$) are positive. This means that the seasonal component at a $\tau$ smaller than 0.5 will be added to a negative conditional quantile, while the seasonal component at a $\tau$ bigger than 0.5 will be added to a positive conditional quantile. If at a $\tau > 0.5$ we have a positive seasonal component, the $\tau$ conditional quantile increases and hence the dispersion increases. If instead the seasonal component at a $\tau > 0.5$ is negative, the $\tau$ conditional quantile decreases and the dispersion decreases. The same reasoning holds for any $\tau < 0.5$ where a negative seasonal component decreases the $\tau$ conditional quantile (more dispersion), while a positive seasonal component increases the $\tau$ conditional quantile, decreasing the dispersion.
10. Other tests for independence against different alternatives are possible. The duration-based approach in Pelletier and Christoffersen (2004) allows for testing against more general forms of dependence. Candelon et al. (2011) have developed a more robust procedure which does not need a specific distributional assumption for the time intervals

between violations under the alternative. Moreover, Hurlin and Tokpavi (2006) develop a test procedure to jointly test the absence of autocorrelation in the hit variables for various coverage rates.

11. In this article we adopt the terminology that volatility is defined as a measure of dispersion. Likewise, asymmetry is understood as a measure of the difference in the probability mass between both sides of the mode, and kurtosis is defined as a measure of the thickness of the tails of the distribution.

12. For more details about quantile-based skewness and kurtosis measures, see Groeneveld and Meeden (1984), Brys, Hubert, and Struyf (2006) and Dominicy and Veredas (2010).

13. A GARCH model for intraday data (explained at length in Section 5.2.1) is given by $r_t = \sqrt{g_t \phi_d} \varepsilon_t$, where $g_t$ is the conditional volatility and $\phi_d$ is the intraday seasonal component. The conditional quantile of returns is $Q_{r_t}(\tau|\mathcal{F}_{t-1}) = Q_\varepsilon(\tau)\sqrt{g_t \phi_d}$, where $Q_\varepsilon(\tau)$ denotes the $\tau$ quantile of the distribution of $\varepsilon_t$. Substituting $Q_{r_t}(\tau|\mathcal{F}_{t-1})$ in (9) and (10), the term $\sqrt{g_t \phi_d}$ cancels out since it is the same for all the quantiles. Therefore, the theoretical conditional quantile-based asymmetry and kurtosis for a GARCH model are constant. To show that this may not be a tenable assumption, we compute (8)–(10) on the standardized residuals of a GARCH model.

14. We have tried with smaller and larger rolling windows sizes (namely 1000, 1200, 1500, 1600, 1800, 1900 and 2000 observations). Results do not change qualitatively and are available upon request.

15. Note that the confidence levels 2.5% and 1% were not in the grid of quantiles of the in-sample estimation results. We introduce them now since they are two common quantiles in the measurement of downside risk.

# References

Andersen, T.G., and T. Bollerslev. 1997. Intraday periodicity and volatility persistence in financial markets. *Journal of Empirical Finance* 4, no. 2–3: 115–58.

Bofinger, E. 1975. Estimation of a density function using order statistics. *Australian Journal of Statistics* 17, no. 1: 1–7.

Bollerslev, T., and E. Ghysels. 1996. Periodic autoregressive conditional heteroscedasticity. *Journal of Business & Economic Statistics* 14, no. 2: 139–51.

Bouyé, E., and M. Salmon. 2009. Dynamic copula quantile regressions and tail area dynamic dependence in Forex markets. *The European Journal of Finance* 15, no. 7–8: 721–50.

Bowley, A.L. 1920. *Elements of statistics*. New York: Charles Scribner's Sons.

Brys, G., M. Hubert, and A. Struyf. 2006. Robust measures of tail weight. *Computational Statistics and Data Analysis* 50, no. 3: 733–59.

Candelon, B., G. Colletaz, C. Hurlin, and S. Tokpavi. 2011. Backtesting value-at-risk: A GMM duration-based approach. *Journal of Financial Econometrics* 9, no. 2: 314–43.

Cenesizoglu, T., and A.G. Timmermann. 2008. Is the distribution of stock returns predictable? HEC Montreal working paper.

Chabi-Yo, F., D. Leisen, and E. Renault. 2007. Implications of asymmetry risk for portfolio analysis and asset pricing. Bank of Canada working paper.

Christoffersen, P.F. 1998. Evaluating interval forecasts. *International Economic Review* 39, no. 4: 841–62.

Dionne, G., P. Duchesne, and M. Pacurar. 2009. Intraday Value at Risk (IVaR) using tick-by-tick data with application to the Toronto Stock Exchange. *Journal of Empirical Finance* 16, no. 5: 777–92.

Dittmar, R.F. 2002. Nonlinear pricing kernels, kurtosis preference, and evidence from the cross section of equity returns. *Journal of Finance* 57, no. 1: 369–403.

Dominicy, Y., and D. Veredas. 2010. The method of simulated quantiles. ECARES DP 08/2010.

Engle, R.F. 2002. New frontiers for arch models. *Journal of Applied Econometrics* 17, no. 5: 425–46.

Engle, R.F., and S. Manganelli. 2004. CAViaR: Conditional Autoregressive Value at Risk by regression quantiles. *Journal of Business & Economic Statistics* 22, no. 4: 367–82.

Engle, R.F., and J.G. Rangel. 2008. The spline-GARCH model for low-frequency volatility and its global macroeconomic causes. *Review of Financial Studies* 21, no. 3: 1187–223.

Fama, E.F. 1963. Mandelbrot and the stable Paretian hypothesis. *The Journal of Business* 36, no. 4: 420–29.

Giot, P. 2005. Market risk models for intraday data. *The European Journal of Finance* 11, no. 4: 309–24.

Gonedes, N.J. 1973. Evidence on the information content of accounting numbers: Accounting-based and market-based estimates of systematic risk. *The Journal of Financial and Quantitative Analysis* 8, no. 3: 407–43.

Granger, C.W.J., and C.-Y. Sin. 2000. Modelling the absolute returns of different stock indices: Exploring the forecastability of an alternative measure of risk. *Journal of Forecasting* 19, no. 4: 277–98.

Groeneveld, R.A., and G. Meeden. 1984. Measuring skewness and kurtosis. *The Statistician* 33, no. 4: 391–99.

Guidolin, M., and A. Timmermann. 2008. International asset allocation under regime switching, skew and kurtosis preference. *Review of Financial Studies* 21, no. 1: 889–935.

Hansen, B.E. 1994. Autoregressive conditional density estimation. *International Economic Review* 35, no. 3: 705–30.

Harvey, C.R., and A. Siddique. 1999. Autoregressive conditional skewness. *The Journal of Financial and Quantitative Analysis* 34, no. 4: 465–87.

Harvey, C.R., and A. Siddique. 2000. Conditional skewness in asset pricing tests. *Journal of Finance* 55, no. 3: 1263–95.

Hautsch, N. 2008. Capturing common components in high-frequency financial time series: A multivariate stochastic multiplicative error model. *Journal of Economic Dynamics & Control* 32, no. 12: 3978–4009.

Hendricks, W., and R. Koenker. 1992. Hierarchical spline models for conditional quantiles and the demand for electricity. *Journal of the American Statistical Association* 87, no. 417: 58–68.

Hurlin, C., and S. Tokpavi. 2006. Backtesting value-at-risk accuracy: a simple new test. *Journal of Risk* 9, no. 2: 19–37.

Koenker, R. 2005. *Quantile Regression.* Cambridge: Cambridge University Press.

Koenker, R., and G. Bassett. Jr. 1978. Regression quantiles. *Econometrica* 46, no. 1: 33–50.

Koenker, R., and Q. Zhao. 1996. Conditional quantile estimation and inference for Arch models. *Econometric Theory* 12, no. 5: 793–813.

Mandelbrot, B. 1963. The variation of certain speculative prices. *Journal of Business* 36, no. 4: 394–419.

Martens, M., Y.-C. Chang, and S.J. Taylor. 2002. A comparison of seasonal adjustment methods when forecasting intraday volatility. *The Journal of Financial Research* 25, no. 2: 283–99.

McCulloch, J.H. 1986. Simple consistent estimators of stable distribution parameters. *Communications in Statistics-Simulation and Computation* 15, no. 4: 1109–36.

Moors, J.J.A. 1988. A quantile alternative for kurtosis. *The Statistician* 37, no. 11: 25–32.

Pelletier, D., and P. Christoffersen. 2004. Backtesting value-at-risk: A duration-based approach. *Journal of Financial Econometrics* 2, no. 1: 84–108.

Portnoy, S., and R. Koenker. 1997. The Gaussian hare and the Laplacian tortoise: Computability of squared-error versus absolute-error estimators. *Statistical Science* 12, no. 4: 279–96.

Taylor, S.J. 1986. *Modelling financial time series.* New York: John Wiley & Sons.

# Appendix

In the generic linear QR model, the $\tau$ conditional quantile of $r_t$ is linear in the $p$-dimensional covariate vector $\mathbf{x}_t$

$$Q_{r_t}(\tau|\mathbf{x}_t) = \mathbf{x}_t\boldsymbol{\beta}(\tau).$$

From the relation between the conditional distribution function $F_{r_t}(r|\mathbf{x}_t)$ and the conditional quantile function it follows that

$$Q_{r_t}(\tau|\mathbf{x}_t) = F_{r_t}^{-1}(\tau|\mathbf{x}_t) \equiv \xi_t(\tau).$$

The QR estimator is

$$\hat{\boldsymbol{\beta}}_T(\tau) = \arg\min_{b\in\Re^p} \sum_{i=1}^{T} \rho_\tau(r_t - \mathbf{x}_t'\mathbf{b}),$$

where $\rho_\tau(u) = u(\tau - I_{u<0})$ is the so-called check function and its asymptotic distribution, see Koenker (2005) for more details, is given by

$$\sqrt{T}(\hat{\boldsymbol{\beta}}(\tau) - \boldsymbol{\beta}(\tau)) \sim N(0, \tau(1-\tau)\mathbf{H}_T(\tau)^{-1}\mathbf{J}_T\mathbf{H}_T(\tau)^{-1}), \tag{A1}$$

where

$$\mathbf{J}_T = T^{-1}\sum_{t=1}^{T}\mathbf{x}_t\mathbf{x}_t',$$

$$\mathbf{H}_T(\tau) = \lim_{T\to\infty} T^{-1}\sum_{t=1}^{n}\mathbf{x}_t\mathbf{x}_t'f_t(\xi_t(\tau)), \tag{A2}$$

and $f_t(\xi_t(\tau))$ denotes the conditional density of the $r_t$ evaluated at the $\tau$ conditional quantile. In the i.i.d case, these conditional densities are identical for every $t$, i.e. $f_t = f$, and Equation (A1) collapses to $\sqrt{T}(\hat{\boldsymbol{\beta}}(\tau) - \boldsymbol{\beta}(\tau)) \sim N(0, \omega\mathbf{J}_T^{-1})$, where $\omega = \tau(1 - \tau)/f^2(\xi_t(\tau))$. However, the i.i.d assumption is too restrictive in our case, thus we need to estimate the variance–covariance matrix in Equation (A1) where the asymptotic covariance among estimates at different quantiles has blocks

$$\text{Cov}(\sqrt{T}(\hat{\beta}(\tau_r) - \beta(\tau_r)), \sqrt{T}(\hat{\beta}(\tau_s) - \beta(\tau_s))) = [\tau_r \wedge \tau_s - \tau_r \tau_s] \mathbf{H}_T(\tau_r)^{-1} \mathbf{J}_T \mathbf{H}_T(\tau_s)^{-1}.$$

We estimate the conditional density $f_t(\xi_t(\tau))$ in (A2) using the Hendricks and Koenker (1992) sandwich form. This estimation procedure requires at first to compute a bandwidth $h_T$ for each $\tau$. We use the optimal bandwidth suggested by Bofinger (1975)

$$h_T(\tau) = T^{-1/5} \left( \frac{4.5\phi^4(\Phi^{-1}(\tau))}{\left(2\Phi^{-1}(\tau)^2 + 1\right)^2} \right)^{1/5},$$

where $\phi$ is the Gaussian density and $\Phi^{-1}$ is the Gaussian quantile function. Second, we re-estimate the two-component QR model for the grids $\tau^+ = \tau + h_T(\tau)$ and $\tau^- = \tau - h_T(\tau)$ obtaining $\hat{\beta}(\tau^+)$ and $\hat{\beta}(\tau^-)$.

We obtain the distribution function inverting the quantile function, and then the density function by differentiation. Following Hendricks and Koenker (1992), we estimate the conditional density function as

$$\hat{f}_t = \max\left[ 0, \frac{2h_T(\tau)}{\mathbf{x}_t' \hat{\beta}(\tau^+) - \mathbf{x}_t' \hat{\beta}(\tau^-) - \delta} \right],$$

where $\delta$ is a small tolerance parameter that we fix to 0.01 to avoid dividing by zero and the maximum is used to impose positivity on the distribution function.

# Liquidity determination in an order-driven market

Jón Daníelsson[a] and Richard Payne[b]

[a]*Department of Finance and Financial Markets Group, London School of Economics, London, UK;*
[b]*Finance Group, Warwick Business School, University of Warwick, Coventry, UK*

We exploit full order level information from an electronic FX broking system to provide a comprehensive account of the determination of its liquidity. We not only look at bid-ask spreads and trading volumes, but also study the determination of order entry rates and depth measures derived from the entire limit order book. We find strong predictability in the arrival of liquidity supply/demand events. Further, in times of low (high) liquidity, liquidity supply (demand) events are more common. In times of high trading activity and volatility, the ratio of limit to market order arrivals is high but order book spreads and depth deteriorate. These results are consistent with market order traders having better information than limit order traders.

## 1. Introduction

As the recent financial crisis has made clear, the ability to accurately define, measure and explain financial market liquidity is of great importance to academics and market participants alike. Unfortunately, the majority of extant empirical work relies on measures of liquidity that are somewhat narrow in their focus (e.g. bid-ask spreads). The purpose of this article is to add to the academic understanding of liquidity by providing analysis of those aspects of liquidity which are less well understood. Using order level data from a foreign exchange broking system, we empirically analyze various liquidity measures that include spreads, order book depths and order entry rates. Unlike much previous work in this area, we construct depth measures from across the range of open limit orders, rather than focussing only on quantities available at the best prices. Furthermore, we go on to study the joint determination of our liquidity measures, volatility and transaction activity.

Our empirical work is based on analyzing one week of trading in the USD/DEM spot rate on the Reuters D2000-2 system. Thus, our results complement those in much of the extant literature, which are based on analysis of stock market data. FX markets are more fast-paced than stock markets and the evolution of the D2000-2 order book is not interrupted by regular batch auctions caused by daily market opening and closure. The obvious drawback of our data is that they cover only five trading days. However, to give some perspective, these five days see the submission of around 130,000 orders for trade in USD/DEM with over 20,000 of these being market orders.

Conceptually, the task of measuring liquidity is challenging due to the fact that there is no generally accepted definition of a 'liquid market'. However, Kyle's (1985) three component classification of liquidity, covering tightness, depth, and resilience, is well known, and serves as a useful starting point. While empirically implementing Kyle's definition requires the evaluation of multiple characteristics of a given market, many empirical studies fail to do so, focusing solely on tightness (i.e. spreads). Moreover, most extant analysis of liquidity entirely ignores its dynamic aspects and these aspects are key from the perspective of the construction of optimal execution strategies. A trader with a given amount of an asset to buy or sell is usually given a certain horizon over which the trade must be completed and some benchmark against which transaction costs will be judged. Thus, the trader's problem is to work out when to place an order and what type of orders (market versus limit) to place. Clearly, the manner in which the trader expects liquidity to respond to the submission of various order types will be crucial in the formation of his strategy.

The central motivation for our work is to provide a comprehensive look at liquidity determination in a specific order-driven market. We provide analysis of bid-ask spreads, order book depth and dynamic aspects of liquidity supply and demand determination. As such, our work shares features with two seminal papers that focus on dynamics of liquidity, Biais, Hillion and Spatt (1995) and Hasbrouck (1999). More recently, with increased availability of order level data from stock exchanges and other security trading platforms, several papers have emerged which also look at measures of liquidity other than the bid-ask spread and which focus on dependencies in order arrivals. An early example is Sandas (2001), who uses order level data from the Swedish Stock Exchange to test a version of the Glosten (1994) model. Hall and Hautsch (2007) study data on five stocks from the Australian Stock Exchange and model the arrival intensities of limit and market orders. Some of their results overlap with those we derive from the FX data. They, for example, find that market orders are more likely to arrive when liquidity supply to the order book has recently been strong, as do we. Ranaldo (2004) provides similar results for a sample of stocks from the SWX. Gomber, Schweickert and Theissen (2004) study the resilience of the market for German stocks traded on Xetra, using an exchange-constructed measure of order book depth. Large (2007) proposes an intensity model for order arrivals and uses that model to study order book resilience for a single LSE traded stock. Last of all, the data we employ here are used in Lo and Sapp (2008) who study the time between the arrivals of certain types of order in an autoregressive conditional duration (ACD) framework.

We perform a range of empirical exercises based on a variety of techniques. We first characterize the D2000-2 liquidity supply process by measuring where limit orders enter the book, how likely execution is for an order entering the book at a given position, and calculating average lifetimes for orders and average limit order sizes.[1] Results show that the most common entry point for fresh liquidity is precisely at the extant best limit price. Further, while orders entering close to the front of the order book have high execution probabilities, our results show that orders entering the book at relatively poor prices also have reasonable probabilities of executing. For example, limits entering with a price 10 ticks away from the best price, have execution probabilities close to $\frac{1}{4}$. We also show that limit orders placed closer to the front of the book tend to be larger. These results extend similar analysis in Harris and Hasbrouck (1996) and Biais, Hillion and Spatt (1995).

We proceed to investigate the own- and cross-dependence in arrivals of liquidity supply and demand events. To this end, we construct a set of one-step and multi-step Markov transition matrices that give conditional event arrival probabilities. In this case, subsequent to the arrival of a market buy (sell) the supply of fresh liquidity at the front of the limit sell (buy) side of the order book tends to be reduced. This indicates some degree of *dynamic illiquidity*, in the sense that liquidity drained by trading activity is not immediately resupplied on the same terms, and is similar to the result, contained in Hasbrouck (1999), that NYSE market and limit order arrival intensities are negatively correlated at very high frequencies. Further event-time results show that liquidity supply temporally clusters on one side of the market and removal of liquidity at the front of one side of the book implies increased probability of seeing fresh liquidity at the front of the book and lower chances of seeing subsidiary liquidity supply on that side of the book.[2] These effects are persistent, being felt at least over 10 events into the future.

Subsequently, we model order arrival data in calendar time at a 20 s sampling frequency. We characterize the dependence of limit and market order entry rates on volatility, bid ask spreads and extant order book depth. In a calendar-time setting, we obtain a result similar to several studies mentioned above, in that traders respond to low extant liquidity by supplying fresh liquidity. This result dovetails with our event-time result that, subsequent to the removal of liquidity at the front of the book one, is more likely to see fresh liquidity supplied at the front. We observe that limit and market order arrival rates increase with volatility. However, and in line with the theoretical predictions of Foucault (1999), the ratio of limit to market order arrivals also increases with volatility. Unlike previous authors, we demonstrate this result using order arrival data covering the entire limit order book.[3]

Finally, we estimate a joint dynamic model for spreads, depth, transaction activity and volatility.[4] Our depth measures are constructed as counts of the quantity of currency units available for trade at or within $k$ ticks of the best extant limit price. We denote such a measure $d(k)_t^i$ where we allow $k$ to vary between 0 and 10 ticks and $i = b, s$ for the limit buy and sell sides, respectively. Thus, in contrast to many previous studies that have examined factors influencing measures of order book depth (Lee, Mucklow and Ready 1993; Brockman and Chung 1996; Kavajecz 1998; Ahn, Bae and Chan 2001), here depth is calculated from various points along the excess demand and supply curves implied by the order data rather than just at the best quotes. Our results indicate that, while rates of order submission in volatile and high volume intervals are increased, these new orders tend to be at poor prices such that order book spreads rise and depth is reduced. Further results break down activity by the side of the market. We show that market buy activity tends to reduce limit sell side depth but increases limit buy side depth, with corresponding effects following from market sell activity. Thus, the response of buy and sell limit price schedules to transaction activity depends on both the amount and direction of the activity.

Overall, we attempt to provide a comprehensive empirical study of the liquidity of the D2000-2 segment of the USD/DEM market. The main messages of our results are as follows. Liquidity supply and demand exhibit clear self-regulating tendencies. When extant book liquidity is low, limit order entries increase relative to market order arrival. However, this picture is complicated by the responses of book liquidity variables to transaction activity and volatility. In our view, the responses of limit and market order arrivals, and thus spreads and depth, to transactions and volatility suggest an asymmetric information interpretation. We show that transaction activity increases subsequent volatility and reduces book liquidity, both spreads and depth – in response to potentially informed trades, limit orders are re-priced and the order book thins out as liquidity suppliers guard against being picked off by traders with superior information.

Finally, the fact that subsequent to market buy activity we observe a decrease in limit sell side depth and an increase in limit buy depth strengthens our belief that trades are providing information on the likely future direction of exchange rate changes. Corroborating evidence for the existence of asymmetric information in FX markets can be found in the literature linking currency order flows to exchange rate changes. Payne (2003) demonstrates that D2000-2 trades have permanent impacts on exchange rates using the same data that we employ here. Evans and Lyons (2001) demonstrate that a strong relationship between FX order flow and exchange rates is still found at the daily level, lending further credence to the asymmetric information hypothesis.

A final general observation from our analysis is that there is clear inter-dependence of volatility, transaction activity and liquidity. Transaction activity, for example, leads to higher volatility and lower liquidity and, in turn, high volatility and low liquidity tend to reinforce one another – a vicious liquidity/volatility cycle. From a policy perspective, the extent to which liquidity determination might prolong and exacerbate the effects of shocks on markets is an important question. Analysis similar to ours on a lower frequency level using data with a larger time-series dimension might shed light on how liquidity crises and extreme events in financial markets come about.

The rest of the article is structured as follows. In the next section, we give a description of the trading venue under analysis and the basic features of the data set derived from it. We also present our first analysis of the features of the liquidity supply process. In Section 3, we report results on conditional order event probabilities and our calendar time analysis of order arrival rates. Section 4 contains our analysis of the determination of order book depth. Section 5 concludes.

## 2.   The data and basic statistical information

### 2.1   *The data set*

The data employed in this study are drawn from the D2000-2 electronic FX broking system run by Thomson Reuters. D2000-2 is one of the two main electronic brokers in this market, the other being EBS. Since the 1990s these venues have become increasingly important in inter-dealer FX trade. A figure of 15% represents a rough estimate of the portion of total inter-dealer trade in USD/DEM handled by D2000-2 at the time our sample was taken.[5]

The fact that D2000-2 is only one of the electronic brokers operating in the FX market and that we have no information on direct inter-dealer trade or on customer-dealer activity clearly implies that we cannot provide a picture of overall FX market liquidity. Rather, we characterize the order submissions to a particular trading venue in isolation and demonstrate the implications of these submissions for the co-determination of liquidity, volatility and transaction activity on that venue.

D2000-2 operates as a pure limit order market governed by rules of price and time priority.[6] At the time our data were recorded, the D2000-2 screen displayed to users the best limit buy and sell prices, plus quantities available at those prices and a record of recent transaction activity, all for up to six currency pairs. It is important to note that, unlike many order-driven trading systems in equity markets, information on limit buy (sell) orders with prices below (above) the current best price were not disseminated to users. Hence, and importantly for interpreting what follows, order book depth is not observable to D2000-2 users. Another difference between D2000-2 and other venues is that at the time our sample was taken D2000-2 market orders were not allowed to 'walk up the book'. If the size at the extant best limit sell price, for example, was smaller than the quantity required in an incoming market buy, the market order filled the quantity available at the best quote and the excess quantity went unfilled. To the extent that limit order submitters do not monitor their order status on an event-by-event basis, and given that market order traders may input a sequence of orders that effectively 'walk the book', we conjecture that, in practice, D2000-2 operates much like other order books where market orders can 'walk the book'.[7] See Danielsson and Payne (2002) for more detail on the operation of D2000-2 and the processing of this data set. As mentioned earlier, Lo and Sapp (2008) also study the data under analysis here.

Our data set contains order level information on all D2000-2 activity in USD/DEM from the trading week covering the 6–10 October 1997. The entry and exit times of every limit order submitted to D2000-2, plus the timing of every D2000-2 market order are recorded to the one hundredth of a second. As such, we can not only use the data to reconstruct all information displayed to market participants over our trading week, but also see what happened to every limit order submitted to D2000-2, regardless of whether the order was traded or ever displayed to the public. Hence, we can measure the depth of the D2000-2 order book exactly, through reconstructing the excess demand and supply curves for currency implied by the limit order data. As mentioned above, at the time, D2000-2 users got no information on depth outside the best quotes.

Table 1 gives summary information on the frequencies, prices, quantities and fill rates for each order type. Overall, around 130,000 orders were submitted during the sample period with approximately five times as many limit than market orders. Given that all orders must be for an integer number of $M, the average limit order is relatively small at just over $2M. The average market order is somewhat larger at $3M, although still relatively small. Finally, just over one third of limit orders are totally filled while around 60% are not filled at all. About 65% of market orders fill totally with the remainder being partially filled.

Table 2 gives information on the level of activity on D2000-2 and a first look at liquidity. It presents mean bid-ask spreads and transaction activity measures from a 20 s sampling of the data. The smallest price increment for USD/DEM on D2000-2 is one-hundredth of a Pfennig and, from now on, we refer to this increment as one tick. The mean spread from the 20 s data is 2.5 ticks indicating that, at first glance, D2000-2 is a very tight market.[8] Indeed, the modal spread in the data is 1 tick. In the average 20 s period there are between 3 and 4 transactions in USD/DEM with volume totalling $6.15M.

To provide a more detailed (unconditional) picture of D2000-2 liquidity, in Table 3 we give basic statistical information on depth measures derived from the limit buy side of the order book.[9] The depth measure we employ is the total quantity in the book at prices at or within $k$ ticks of the best extant limit price. Again, we generate these data on a 20 s calendar time sampling and

Table 1. Basic summary statistics by order type.

| Order type | Number | $\bar{P}$ | $\bar{Q}$ | $Q_{25}$ | $Q_{75}$ | $\bar{D}$ | Part. fill | Total fill |
|---|---|---|---|---|---|---|---|---|
| Limit buy | 55240 | 1.7512 | 2.09 | 1.00 | 2.00 | 0.68 | 0.036 | 0.339 |
| Limit sell | 53408 | 1.7520 | 2.09 | 1.00 | 2.00 | 0.72 | 0.038 | 0.356 |
| Market buy | 11128 | 1.7515 | 3.29 | 1.00 | 5.00 | 1.82 | 0.356 | 0.644 |
| Market sell | 10655 | 1.7513 | 3.18 | 1.00 | 5.00 | 1.82 | 0.361 | 0.639 |

Notes: $\bar{P}$ is the average price of orders of a given type, $\bar{Q}$ is the average requested quantity and $Q_{25}$ and $Q_{75}$ are the 25th and 75th percentiles of the quantity distribution. $\bar{D}$ is the average traded quantity and the columns headed 'Part. fill' and 'Total fill' give the proportion of all orders which were partially or totally executed.

Table 2. Market activity statistics: 20 s data sampling.

| Variable | Mean | S.D. | $Q_{25}$ | $Q_{50}$ | $Q_{75}$ | $\hat{\rho}_1$ |
|---|---|---|---|---|---|---|
| Spread | 2.54 | 2.09 | 1 | 2 | 3 | 0.46 |
| Trade frequency | 3.35 | 3.70 | 1 | 2 | 5 | 0.51 |
| Gross volume | 6.15 | 7.56 | 1 | 4 | 8 | 0.43 |
| Order flow | 0.06 | 6.94 | −2 | 0 | 2 | 0.18 |

Notes: Spread measurement is in ticks. Gross volume is the sum of market buy and sell volume in each interval. order flow is the difference between market buy and market sell volume. The data are sampled every 20 s and only observations between 6 and 18 GMT are considered. The column headed S.D. gives standard deviations and the following three columns give the 25th, 50th and 75th percentiles of the empirical distributions. The final column gives the estimated autocorrelations at displacement one.

Table 3. Buy side depth statistics: 20 s data.

| Variable | Mean | S.D. | $Q_{25}$ | $Q_{50}$ | $Q_{75}$ | $\hat{\rho}_1$ |
|---|---|---|---|---|---|---|
| $d_t^b(0)$ | 3.55 | 3.14 | 1 | 3 | 5 | 0.19 |
| $d_t^b(2)$ | 9.08 | 6.33 | 4 | 8 | 12 | 0.55 |
| $d_t^b(4)$ | 13.62 | 8.52 | 7 | 12 | 18 | 0.70 |
| $d_t^b(6)$ | 17.61 | 10.17 | 10 | 16 | 23 | 0.76 |
| $d_t^b(8)$ | 21.32 | 11.71 | 12 | 20 | 28 | 0.81 |
| $d_t^b(10)$ | 24.47 | 12.83 | 15 | 23 | 32 | 0.84 |

Notes: $d_t^b(k)$ is the total quantity at limit prices at or within $k$ ticks of the best limit price. The data are sampled every 20 s and only observations between 6 and 18 GMT are considered. The column headed S.D. gives standard deviations and the following three columns give the 25th, 50th and 75th percentiles of the depth distributions. The final column gives the estimated autocorrelations at displacement one.

denote them with $d_t^s(k)$ for the limit sell side and $d_t^b(k)$ for the limit buy side. We record data for $k = 2, 4, 6, 8$ and 10 ticks. We also record the quantity available at the best limit prices, denoting these with $d_t^s(0)$ and $d_t^b(0)$, respectively.

Table 3 indicates that the average depth at the best limit buy price, just over $3M, is only just enough to satisfy one average size market order. Then, there is on average $6M on offer across the two ticks immediately below the best price. From here, each increment of two ticks in limit price adds approximately $4M to depth such that the depth across the limit orders at or within 10 ticks of the best price is between $24M and $25M. The table also demonstrates that, as one would expect, the depth measures for larger $k$ are more strongly autocorrelated than those for small $k$. Hence, the picture of the order book which emerges is that depth appears to cluster just behind the best limit price, but is also significant at prices up to 10 ticks away from the touch.

Finally, in Figures 1 and 2 we use the 20 s data sampling to construct the intra-daily patterns apparent in variables derived from D2000-2. In constructing these plots, we omit data recorded between 16 and 6 GMT due to very light activity in the GMT overnight period.[10] Figure 1 demonstrates that D2000-2 trading volume displays an approximate $M$-shaped pattern over the trading day, with local maxima at around 8 and 13 GMT. The second panel of this figure shows that D2000-2 inside spreads follow the opposite pattern, a $W$-shape. Spreads tend to be lowest between 8 and 10 GMT and 12 and 14 GMT. Figure 2 plots the intra-day activity patterns for limit buy depth

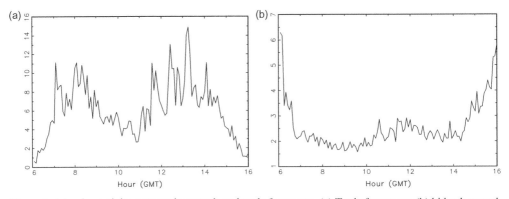

Figure 1. Intra-day activity patterns in spreads and trade frequency. (a) Trade frequency, (b) bid-ask spread.

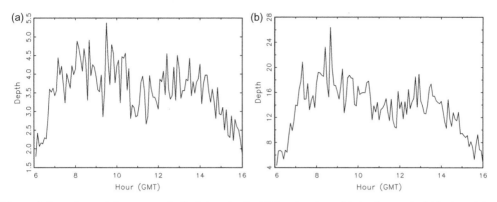

Figure 2. Intra-day activity patterns in limit buy depth. (a) Depth at best, (b) depth at and within four ticks.

measures with $k = 0$ and 4 ticks. It can be seen that, over the course of the trading day, depth follows a fairly similar pattern to trading volume and, as one would expect, the inverse pattern to the bid-ask spread. Hence, as measured by both spreads and depth, D2000-2 is most liquid in the periods from 8 to 10 and 12 to 14 GMT, when trading activity is most intense. The inverse relationship between spreads and depth measures is in line with results from Lee, Mucklow and Ready (1993), Biais, Hillion and Spatt (1995) and Ahn, Bae and Chan (2001).

## 2.2 *D2000-2 order placement*

To give a first insight into the process through which liquidity is supplied to D2000-2, in this section, we provide basic information on the properties of the limit orders submitted.

We begin by breaking down the limit orders by the position at which they entered the order book. We do this in two ways. First, we count the total quantity in $M ahead of the incoming order in the execution queue. Second, we assign each incoming order a price position. If the incoming order is a limit buy then its price position is its price less the extant best limit buy price. If the incoming order is a limit sell then the price position is the extant best sell price less the incoming limit price. As such, all orders with positive price positions improve the prior best limit price.[11] Based on this breakdown of limit orders we examine four-order characteristics; entry probability, fill probability, average lifetime and average size. The results of these breakdowns are given in Figures 3 and 4.

Figure 3 gives information based on the quantity position of orders. The first panel of the figure demonstrates that by far the most common position for order entry is at the front of the execution queue (i.e. a quantity position of zero). Just over 30% of all orders improve upon the best available price in the book. Entry probability declines fairly monotonically with quantity position and, for all positions greater than zero, entry probability is lower than 0.1. Panel (b) presents the obvious result that orders placed at the front of the book are most likely to execute. However, interestingly, it also shows that orders a long way down in the execution queue have fairly good chances of execution. On average, for example, an order with $10M ahead of it in the queue still has a 30% probability of execution. Hence, the expected price improvement from such a limit order is clearly non-negligible. Panel (c) demonstrates that limit order lifetimes increase fairly monotonically with quantity position. Finally, panel (d) shows that those orders entered at the front of the book are for larger quantities on average.

73

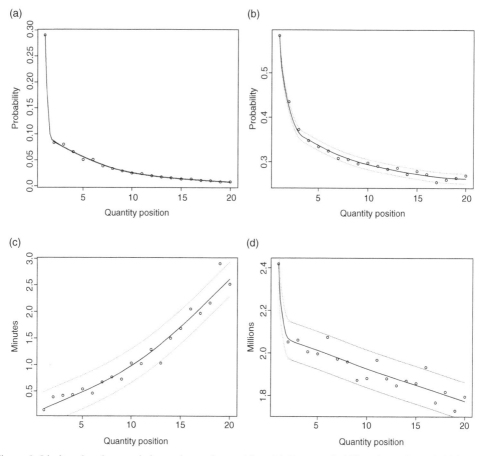

Figure 3. Limit order characteristics and quantity position. (a) Entry probability, (b) trade probability, (c) average lifetime and (d) average size. The x-axes give the quantity position of a limit entry computed as the aggregate quantity ahead of the incoming order in the execution queue. The observations were fitted with a weighted spline, where the weight is the entry probability. The dotted lines are two standard error bands, where the s.e. is computed using the weights.

Figure 4 gives similar results based on the price position of an order at entry. Arguably, the results based on price position are more relevant if we wish to understand the order placement decisions of D2000-2 users. This is because a user can control price position of an order exactly, while in the majority of cases the quantity position of an order will be unknown. From Figure 4, we see that entry probability is most common at the best extant limit price (around 30% of orders enter here). Approximately 20% of orders improve the best price by one tick and just over 5% of orders improve the extant best price by two ticks. Also, over 10% of orders enter at prices one tick worse than the best limit price. Hence, the majority of D2000-2 order placement occurs at or within one tick of the best price. This result conforms with that based on data from the Paris Bourse in Biais, Hillion and Spatt (1995). From Figure 4, we again see that transaction probability increases as the order is positioned closer to the front of the execution queue and that average order lifetime decreases as price position improves. Again, panel (b) demonstrates that execution probabilities for orders a fair way down the execution queue are far from trivial. Finally, the fourth

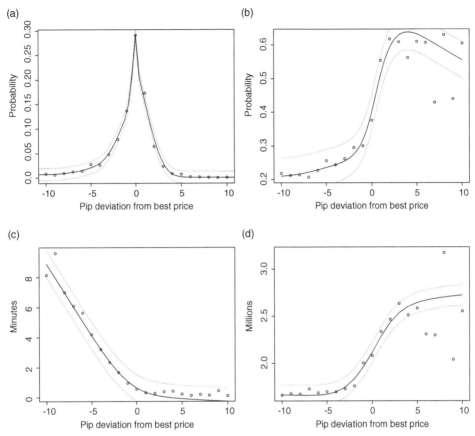

Figure 4. Limit order characteristics and price position. (a) Entry probability, (b) trade probability, (c) average lifetime and (d) average size. The *x*-axes give the price position of a limit entry computed as the difference (in ticks) between the incoming limit price and the previous best price. Price improvements are defined as positive for both limit buys and sells. The observations were fitted with a weighted spline, where the weight is the entry probability. The dotted lines are two standard error bands, where the s.e. is computed using the weights.

panel of the figure gives further evidence that larger orders are placed closer to the front of the book.

Hence, the preceding analysis demonstrates the existence of clear patterns in the order placement decisions of D2000-2 users. D2000-2 liquidity supply is concentrated at the front of the order book, in a range from two ticks below to two ticks above the extant best limit price. A fair amount of limit order flow improving prices by one or two ticks is to be expected at times when revelation of information implies current best prices can be bettered. Concentration of liquidity supply just below the best limit price may exist to make money from uninformed market order traders desiring to deal relatively large amounts.

## 3. Analysis of D2000-2 order flows

Our first set of econometric exercises concentrates on identifying the determinants of and relationship between limit order and market order placement. As such, we hope to shed some light on the dynamics of the D2000-2 liquidity supply and demand processes as discussed in Section 1. On a more practical level, this analysis will reveal how traders' order submission strategies vary with observable market events.

We begin by looking at an event-time data set of order placements and constructing measures of serial and cross dependence for the different types of order arrival. From this analysis, we can empirically evaluate predictions regarding conditional probabilities of order placements contained in Parlour (1998). We then proceed to study a calendar time data set (using a 20 s sampling frequency) which allows us to model the rates of limit and market order arrival. Using these data we can examine the relationship between limit/market order placements and price movements discussed in Foucault (1999).

## 3.1  *Event-time dependence in order arrival*

To begin with, we attempt to characterize how and when liquidity is supplied to D2000-2 and when liquidity is drained from D2000-2 in terms of the recent history of supply/demand events. To accomplish this task we work with an event-time filtration of the D2000-2 data. This data set places each D2000-2 order event into one of 10 categories. These categories are; market buy; market sell; subsidiary limit buy entry; new best limit buy or fresh liquidity at best limit buy; subsidiary limit sell entry; new best limit sell or fresh liquidity at best limit sell; cancellation of subsidiary limit buy; removal of liquidity at best limit buy price; cancellation of subsidiary limit sell; removal of liquidity at best limit sell price. It is important to note that only six of these 10 event types were observable to D2000-2 users. All actions involving subsidiary limit orders were invisible to all D2000-2 participants aside from the agent actually adding or cancelling the order.

We investigate the dependencies in the event-level data through the construction of a number of transition matrices. The typical element of such a matrix gives the conditional probability of observing event type $i$ in $k$ events time, given that one has just observed an event of type $j$. We present results for $k$ equals one and five so as to emphasize the immediate impacts of certain events, while also providing information on the persistence of these effects. Finally, it should also be noted that we only compute probabilities conditional on the group of six order events that were observable to D2000-2 users.[12]

The one- and five-step ahead transition matrices are given in Table 4. The first row of the table gives the unconditional probability of observing the event named in the column head and the remaining rows give probabilities conditional on having observed the event named in the row head.

A number of interesting results emerge upon examination of panel (a) of Table 4. First, there is evidence of positive dependence in all event types represented. The probabilities of market buys/sells conditional on just having observed a market buy/sell are over twice the corresponding unconditional probabilities. A similar observation is true for events based on liquidity removal at the best prices and, to a somewhat smaller extent, for fresh liquidity supply at the front of the order book. The positive dependence in market order arrival might be due to information-based trade generating imbalances in liquidity demand or due to traders wishing a deal a large amount having to repeatedly place small market orders. Positive dependence in liquidity supply at the front of the book is in line with results in Biais, Hillion and Spatt (1995). The dependence in liquidity removal at the front of the book may be due to traders sequentially removing mis-priced orders after the revelation of public information or after informative trading activity.

Table 4. Transition matrices for order data.

| | Market orders | | Limit buy arrivals | | Limit sell arrivals | | Limit buy cancel | | Limit sell cancel | |
|---|---|---|---|---|---|---|---|---|---|---|
| | Mkt. sell | Mkt. buy | New SLB | New BLB | New SLS | New BLS | Cut SLB | Cut BLB | Cut SLS | Cut BLS |
| Uncond. | 0.0540 | 0.0565 | 0.1178 | 0.1571 | 0.1115 | 0.1556 | 0.1129 | 0.0656 | 0.1053 | 0.0638 |
| (a) One-step transitions | | | | | | | | | | |
| Mkt. sell | 0.1135 | 0.0259 | 0.0987 | 0.1010 | 0.0881 | 0.2286 | 0.0730 | 0.0572 | 0.1295 | 0.0845 |
| Mkt. buy | 0.0243 | 0.1228 | 0.0974 | 0.2268 | 0.0866 | 0.1019 | 0.1358 | 0.0870 | 0.0675 | 0.0500 |
| New BLB | 0.0360 | 0.0722 | 0.1479 | 0.1739 | 0.0972 | 0.1326 | 0.1278 | 0.0702 | 0.0847 | 0.0575 |
| New BLS | 0.0708 | 0.0365 | 0.1003 | 0.1359 | 0.1448 | 0.1735 | 0.0890 | 0.0620 | 0.1217 | 0.0654 |
| Cut BLB | 0.0296 | 0.0560 | 0.0821 | 0.1941 | 0.1025 | 0.1596 | 0.1013 | 0.1140 | 0.0965 | 0.0641 |
| Cut BLS | 0.0559 | 0.0396 | 0.1144 | 0.1631 | 0.0795 | 0.1882 | 0.0993 | 0.0599 | 0.0916 | 0.1085 |
| (b) Five-step transitions | | | | | | | | | | |
| Mkt. sell | 0.1010 | 0.0258 | 0.1153 | 0.1257 | 0.1025 | 0.1956 | 0.0747 | 0.0431 | 0.1375 | 0.0788 |
| Mkt. buy | 0.0267 | 0.0975 | 0.1025 | 0.1950 | 0.1106 | 0.1254 | 0.1467 | 0.0816 | 0.0698 | 0.0441 |
| New BLB | 0.0447 | 0.0685 | 0.1202 | 0.1690 | 0.1000 | 0.1354 | 0.1336 | 0.0889 | 0.0869 | 0.0528 |
| New BLS | 0.0636 | 0.0479 | 0.1053 | 0.1397 | 0.1155 | 0.1693 | 0.0930 | 0.0550 | 0.1253 | 0.0855 |
| Cut BLB | 0.0421 | 0.0548 | 0.1131 | 0.1787 | 0.1138 | 0.1676 | 0.1092 | 0.0675 | 0.0918 | 0.0614 |
| Cut BLS | 0.0551 | 0.0407 | 0.1228 | 0.1688 | 0.1023 | 0.1776 | 0.0998 | 0.0638 | 0.1011 | 0.0679 |

The first row of the table gives the unconditional probability of observing the event in the column head. The rest of the table gives the probability of observing the event in the column head subsequent to the event in the row head. Panel (a) gives one-step ahead probabilities and panel (b) five-step ahead probabilities. Probabilities may not sum to unity across rows due to rounding. The results are based on event-time data with all events outside 6–18 GMT omitted. SLB stands for subsidiary limit buy, BLB for best limit buy, SLS for subsidiary limit sell and BLS for best limit sell.

Panel (a) of Table 4 also reveals a number of interesting effects of market orders on conditional limit order arrival probabilities. Arrival of a market buy (sell) at event date $t$ reduces the probability of observing new best limit sell (buy) liquidity at $t + 1$. Conversely, subsequent to a market buy (sell), the chances of seeing new limit buy (sell) liquidity at the front of the book are greatly increased. The fact that market order activity inhibits subsequent liquidity supply at the front of the opposite side of the order book may be generated by concerns regarding asymmetric information in the hands of market order traders. Liquidity suppliers are not (or are less) willing to replace liquidity drained through market order activity at the same price if they believe that market orders convey information. In Section 1, we labeled this phenomenon *dynamic illiquidity*. The effect of market buys (sells) on subsequent best limit buy (sell) entry is also consistent with asymmetric information, in that potentially information revealing buys (sells) lead limit order traders to revise opinions of fair limit buy (sell) prices upwards (downwards).

Finally, the entry and removal of liquidity supply at the best price also have some interesting implications. After liquidity supply at the front of the book there are increased chances of seeing fresh liquidity supply on the same side of the book. Hence traders follow new best prices by supplying extra liquidity behind them (or extra size at the best prices). After observing the removal of liquidity at the best price one is more likely to see that liquidity replaced and less likely to see subsidiary supply on the same side of the book.

The five-step ahead transition matrix in panel (b) of Table 4 demonstrates that the effects of market orders are most persistent over time. Dependence in market order direction is still clearly visible in the table as are the effects of market orders on later liquidity supply decisions. Thus, it would seem that market order activity (i.e. aggressive order placement) has the most long-lasting effects on order book events.

Finally, it is interesting to compare our results to the theoretical predictions regarding order placement probabilities contained in Parlour (1998). Parlour postulates an order-driven market where order live for multiple periods but no limit price variation is permitted. The market is assumed to have symmetric information and traders are distinguished by their degree of patience. Further, traders are exogenously designated as either buyers or sellers. Hence, the basic tradeoff faced by those submitting orders is the cost of market orders versus the execution risk of limit orders. The first result derived is that market order direction is positively autocorrelated. Further, the probability of a limit buy (sell) is lowest if the immediately preceding event was also a limit buy (sell). Finally, the probability of a limit buy (sell) is shown to be maximized after the occurrence of a market sell (buy).

Clearly, only the theoretical prediction regarding serial correlation in market order direction matches our results. In our data, the other two theoretical results are soundly rejected. We show that limit buys are less common than unconditionally after market sells and that the probability of a limit buy after having already observed a limit buy is fairly high. We have argued that asymmetric information might explain these results, an effect which is missing from the analysis of Parlour (1998). Payne (2003) uses the technology developed in Hasbrouck (1991a, 1991b) to demonstrate that market orders in the sample of data studied in the current paper do carry information relevant for exchange rate determination. This may help us explain why Parlour's predictions do not hold in our analysis. It further suggests that models of order-driven markets that allow optimal choice of order type and feature asymmetric information, for example, Handa, Schwartz and Tiwari (2003) and Goettler, Parlour and Rajan (2009), may be more appropriate representations of trade on D2000-2.

### 3.2 *Explaining order arrival rates*

In this section, we focus on evaluating theoretical predictions regarding the effect of price movements on limit and market order *flows* and also on the composition of overall order flow. Further, we empirically relate order flows to prior indicators of book liquidity observable to market participants.

To accomplish this task, we construct a data set sampled every 20 s from the original event time data. For each 20 s interval we record the following variables; the total number of limit orders submitted; the number of market orders submitted; the net number of limit orders submitted (i.e. the number actually submitted less the number cancelled or removed); midquote return volatility; the end-of-interval bid-ask spread; and end of interval size at the best limit prices.[13]

The questions addressed in this section are partially motivated by the work of Foucault (1999), who provides a dynamic model of order placement with variation in asset valuation across agents. The model permits differences in limit prices but restricts limit orders to last for one trading round only. The basic theoretical feature of the model is a Winner's Curse problem for limit order traders. The key empirical prediction from Foucault's analysis is that the proportion of limit orders in total order flow is increasing in return volatility. This is driven by the fact that, with increased volatility, limit orders are placed at less competitive prices. Due to this, market order submission becomes less profitable.

To examine this prediction we regress order entry rates over the interval from $t - 1$ to $t$ on volatility measured as the absolute return over the interval ending at $t - 1$.[14] Denoting the variable to be explained with $z_t$, we run the following linear regression:

$$z_t = \alpha |R_{t-1}| + \sum_{i=1}^{10} \beta_i z_{t-i} + \epsilon_t, \tag{1}$$

where $\epsilon_t$ is a regression residual. We include 10 lags of the dependent variable on the right-hand side of the regression to pick up any own-dependence in arrival rates. A further point to be noted is that, prior to running regressions of the form in Equation (1), we remove the repeated intra-day patterns from all variables involved. This is done so as to ensure that the results derived are not simply due to predictable market activity variation affecting liquidity and volatility variables in similar ways.[15]

Results from the relevant regressions are given in the first panel of Table 5. The table shows that lagged volatility has a significant and positive effect on both limit and market order entry frequency. Moreover, volatility increases subsequent *net* limit order arrivals – faced with price uncertainty the rate at which limit order traders supply liquidity relative to the rate at which liquidity is removed increases. Examination of the final row of this panel also shows that the proportion of limit orders in total order flow increases with volatility. Hence, in line with the contribution of Foucault (1999), greater uncertainty regarding prices translates to less competitive limit prices and this curtails market order placement.

Table 5. Determination of order entry rates.

| Dep. var. | $\lvert R_{t-1}\rvert$ | $t$-stat | $S_{t-1}$ | $t$-stat | $D_{t-1}$ | $t$-stat | $R^2$ |
|---|---|---|---|---|---|---|---|
| | Coefficients and $t$-statistics on the right-hand side variables | | | | | | |
| $LO_t$ | 147.43 | 17.90 | – | – | – | – | 0.54 |
| $MO_t$ | 16.14 | 4.31 | – | – | – | – | 0.22 |
| $NLO_t$ | 25.30 | 2.69 | – | – | – | – | 0.11 |
| $OR_t$ | 0.63 | 4.28 | – | – | – | – | 0.98 |
| $LO_t$ | – | – | 0.35 | 8.91 | – | – | 0.52 |
| $MO_t$ | – | – | −0.10 | −7.89 | – | – | 0.22 |
| $NLO_t$ | – | – | 0.27 | 8.96 | – | – | 0.12 |
| $OR_t$ | – | – | 0.01 | 13.99 | – | – | 0.98 |
| $LO_t$ | – | – | – | – | 0.006 | 0.40 | 0.52 |
| $MO_t$ | – | – | – | – | 0.031 | 5.71 | 0.22 |
| $NLO_t$ | – | – | – | – | −0.075 | −6.01 | 0.12 |
| $OR_t$ | – | – | – | – | −0.001 | −2.64 | 0.98 |
| $LO_t$ | 136.49 | 15.67 | 0.21 | 5.11 | 0.010 | 0.76 | 0.55 |
| $MO_t$ | 21.02 | 5.60 | −0.12 | −8.63 | 0.031 | 5.69 | 0.23 |
| $NLO_t$ | 17.09 | 1.75 | 0.25 | 7.93 | −0.077 | −6.29 | 0.13 |
| $OR_t$ | 0.11 | 0.75 | 0.01 | 13.71 | −0.001 | −2.92 | 0.98 |

The table reports coefficients from regressions of the variables listed on the left-hand column on the variables listed in the heads of the remaining columns plus 10 lags of the dependent variable. All data are calendar time sampled at a 20 s frequency. $t$-values are heteroskedasticity robust. $LO_t$ measures the numbers of limit orders entering in a given interval, $MO_t$ measures the number of market order entering, $NLO_t$ is the number of limit order entries less the number of limits removed and $OR_t$ is the ratio of the number of limits entering to the total number of limits and markets entering. $R_t$ is the midquote return, $S_t$ is the bid–ask spread and $D_t = d(0)_t^b + d(0)_t^s$ is the total size at the best quotes. All variables used in this analysis except $NLO_t$ have had their repeated intra-day patterns removed prior to the analysis. All $t$-statistics are based on Newey–West heteroskedasticity and autocorrelation robust standard errors.

To complement this analysis, in panels 2 and 3 of Table 5 we regress order entry rates on prior measures of liquidity observable to D2000-2 users – bid–ask spreads and size at the best quotes. This regression analysis delivers the nice result that when there are indications of low D2000-2 liquidity, traders tend to supply liquidity via limit orders and, when D2000-2 liquidity is seen to be high, liquidity tends to be demanded. Hence, there appear to be clear self-regulating tendencies in D2000-2 liquidity. A result with a very similar flavour is presented in Hall and Hautsch (2007). It should be noted, though, that our limit order flow variables do not incorporate price information such that we cannot argue that in times of high spreads or low size at the best quotes, the orders entering tend to reduce spreads or increase size.

One might object that the relationship between order flows and observable liquidity indicators are in fact driven by the relationship between volatility and order entries, given that spreads and size are likely to be strongly contemporaneously correlated with volatility. To address such an objection, in the final panel of the table we regress order entry rates on all three variables. In the majority of cases the right-hand side variables retain their significance such that volatility and observable liquidity measures have independent roles to play in explaining subsequent liquidity supply and demand. However, the effect of volatility on the share of limit orders in total order flow now becomes insignificant: it would appear that the composition of D2000-2 order flow is better explained by the prior state of the book rather than prior volatility in the best limit prices.

To summarize, we have derived calendar-time results which complement the event-time analysis of Section 3.1. We show that one can predict liquidity supply and demand based on the sequence of recent order events, but also that one can use liquidity *snapshot* variables plus volatility to explain subsequent rates of liquidity supply and demand.

## 4. Analysis of D2000-2 depth

The analysis of Section 3 focused on the arrivals of limit and market orders to D2000-2 but largely ignored the price and quantity information from incoming limit orders. We now re-involve the price and quantity information and investigate the implications of order arrivals (and removals) for the *slopes of the excess demand and supply curves* implied by the D2000-2 data – i.e. we examine the determination of D2000-2 depth. Based on the analysis of previous sections we attempt to explain depth in terms of three factors; market order activity (the sum of market buy volume and market sell volume, denoted $V_t$), midquote return volatility ($|R_t|$) and spreads ($S_t$). The depth variables we employ, introduced in Section 2, measure the slope of the excess demand and supply curves from the front of the order book to a point $k$ ticks into the order book for $k$ between zero and 10 ticks. As in Section 3.2, all of the variables used in this analysis are sampled every 20 s and have had deterministic intra-day patterns removed.

Prior to our examination of depth determination, in Table 6 we present correlations between depth measures from the buy and sell sides of the order book. This table highlights an interesting result. After accounting for the intra-day patterns in the data, there is essentially no correlation between depth measures on different sides of the book. Hence the quantities available at and around the best bid and ask appear to evolve separately. This implies that D2000-2 liquidity suppliers tend not to mechanically post orders on both sides of the market in the style of a traditional market-maker. Rather, they appear to focus on one side of the market at a given point in time.

Table 6. Correlations between limit buy and sell depth measures.

| Variables | Correlation |
|---|---|
| $d_t^b(0), d_t^a(0)$ | 0.01 |
| $d_t^b(2), d_t^a(2)$ | 0.06 |
| $d_t^b(4), d_t^a(4)$ | 0.01 |
| $d_t^b(6), d_t^a(6)$ | −0.03 |
| $d_t^b(8), d_t^a(8)$ | −0.01 |
| $d_t^b(10), d_t^a(10)$ | −0.01 |

The table reports cross-correlations between limit buy-side and sell-side depth measures where $d_t^b(k)$ is the total quantity at limit prices at or within $k$ ticks of the best limit buy and $d_t^a(k)$ is the total quantity at limit prices within $k$ ticks of the best limit sell. The data used to construct these correlations are based on a 20 s calendar-time sampling and only observations between 6 and 18 GMT are employed. Prior to computing the correlations the repetitive intra-day pattern is filtered from all depth measures.

## 4.1 Depth, spreads, volume and volatility

As noted earlier, the vast majority of academic empirical work on determination of market liquidity looks at bid-ask spreads. Our final piece of analysis extends this research to include investigation the determinants of order book depth.

We employ a general dynamic model for this investigation, adapted to account for the fact that depth is not observable to D2000-2 users. The basis of the empirical model is a sixth-order VAR in total market order volume, midquote return volatility and bid-ask spreads.[16] This VAR is not entirely standard, though, as we allow volume to contemporaneously affect both volatility and spreads and also allow volatility to contemporaneously influence spreads. This causal ordering identifies the VAR. The final piece of the empirical model is a depth equation, where our depth variable is the sum of buy and sell side depth for a given value of $k$ (i.e. the depth measure is $d_t^b(k) + d_t^s(k)$). We regress depth on exactly the same variables that appear on the right-hand side of the spread equation (i.e. current and lagged volume, current and lagged volatility and lagged spreads). Note that depth does not appear on the right-hand side of any equation. Note also that in running this depth regression for several values of $k$ we can investigate how volume, volatility and spreads affect depth close to and further away from the best prices.

The motivation for our model specification is an attempt to capture the dynamic interactions between the four variables under examination while imposing some theory- and microstructure-based restrictions. Hence, depth does not appear on the right-hand side of any equation as it is not observable to D2000-2 users. In the three-variable VAR involving volume, volatility and spreads, the causal ordering is driven by the fact that, in most microstructure models, trading activity is the driving variable, which subsequently affects volatility and both volume and volatility then influence trading costs. However, it should be noted that our results are robust to sensible reorderings of the three variables. The equations we estimate for spreads and depth are similar to those that Bessembinder (1994) specifies for determination of FX spreads, in that we attempt to explain determination of liquidity variables in terms of prior trading volumes and return volatility. Coppejans, Domowitz and Madhavan (2004) also estimate VAR models including volatility and measures of liquidity in their microstructure analysis of the Swedish stock index futures market.

Results from the estimation of this empirical specification are given in Tables 7 and 8. The first of these tables gives results from the VAR estimation in volume, volatility and spreads and the latter gives estimates from the depth equation for $k = 2, 6, 10.$[17] Looking first at Table 7 one sees that all three variables are strongly positively autocorrelated. There is strong evidence that market order volume leads immediately to increased volatility and spreads. Increased volatility leads to significantly increased market order volume and also significantly larger spreads.[18] Finally, larger spreads are associated with lower subsequent trading activity and higher volatility. All of these effects are apparent not only via the $t$-values for individual right-hand side variables, but also from the $\chi^2$ statistics in the final rows of the table which are test statistics for the null that coefficients on all included volume, volatility or spread variables are simultaneously zero. The explanatory power of all three equations is relatively good.

Examination of the estimated coefficients from the depth regressions, presented in Table 8, provides a number of interesting, new results. There is unambiguous evidence that increased volatility leads to a decreased depth. A similar result is reported in the previously mentioned work by Coppejans, Domowitz and Madhavan (2004). Further, increased spreads are associated with

Table 7. VAR coefficients: volume, volatility and spreads.

| Regressor | Volume eqn. | | Volatility eqn. | | Spread eqn. | |
|---|---|---|---|---|---|---|
| | Coeff. | $t$-value | Coeff. | $t$-value | Coeff. | $t$-value |
| $V_t$ | – | – | 0.448 | 17.34 | 0.134 | 8.6 |
| $V_{t-1}$ | 0.214 | 11.42 | 0.015 | 0.9 | 0.002 | 0.12 |
| $V_{t-2}$ | 0.072 | 4.73 | −0.015 | −1.01 | −0.054 | −3.89 |
| $V_{t-3}$ | 0.111 | 6.55 | −0.048 | −3.02 | −0.037 | −2.79 |
| $V_{t-4}$ | 0.079 | 3.53 | −0.014 | −0.99 | −0.025 | −2.05 |
| $V_{t-5}$ | 0.051 | 3.25 | −0.019 | −1.53 | −0.035 | −3.27 |
| $V_{t-6}$ | 0.066 | 3.96 | −0.003 | −0.22 | −0.037 | −3.05 |
| $|R_t|$ | – | – | – | – | 0.086 | 4.15 |
| $|R_{t-1}|$ | 0.067 | 4.73 | 0.108 | 5.06 | 0.027 | 1.54 |
| $|R_{t-2}|$ | 0.041 | 2.31 | 0.057 | 4.03 | 0.048 | 2.52 |
| $|R_{t-3}|$ | 0.035 | 2.2 | 0.063 | 4.63 | 0.000 | 0.02 |
| $|R_{t-4}|$ | 0.014 | 1.15 | 0.022 | 1.46 | 0.002 | 0.12 |
| $|R_{t-5}|$ | 0.003 | 0.27 | 0.018 | 0.83 | 0.018 | 1.37 |
| $|R_{t-6}|$ | 0.02 | 1.79 | 0.034 | 2.85 | 0.004 | 0.25 |
| $S_t$ | – | – | – | – | – | – |
| $S_{t-1}$ | −0.101 | −7.67 | 0.179 | 8.34 | 0.249 | 7.69 |
| $S_{t-2}$ | 0.02 | 1.56 | −0.025 | −1.77 | 0.136 | 7.14 |
| $S_{t-3}$ | −0.019 | −1.69 | −0.006 | −0.46 | 0.063 | 2.85 |
| $S_{t-4}$ | 0.005 | 0.41 | −0.013 | −1.08 | −0.003 | −0.16 |
| $S_{t-5}$ | 0.027 | 2.12 | 0.033 | 2.18 | 0.059 | 3.46 |
| $S_{t-6}$ | −0.005 | −0.49 | 0.009 | 0.74 | 0.079 | 4.71 |
| $R^2$ | – | 0.23 | – | 0.32 | – | 0.23 |
| Volume | – | 643.1 | – | 466.51 | – | 148.81 |
| Volatility | – | 47.47 | – | 130.89 | – | 38.39 |
| Spread | – | 73.27 | – | 89.05 | – | 220.77 |

The table reports coefficients from a 6-lag VAR involving trading volume, absolute returns and spreads. $V_t$ is defined as the sum of market buy and market sell volume in a given interval. The data upon which the VAR is estimated is sampled on a 20 s calendar-time basis and only observations between 6 and 18 GMT are employed. Prior to estimation the repetitive intra-day pattern is filtered from all variables. All $t$-statistics and $\chi^2$-statistics are based on Newey-West heteroskedasticity and autocorrelation robust standard errors.

Table 8. Regressions of depth measures on volume, volatility and spreads.

| Regressor | 2-tick depth eqn. | | 6-tick depth eqn. | | 10-tick depth eqn. | |
|---|---|---|---|---|---|---|
| | Coeff. | $t$-value | Coeff. | $t$-value | Coeff. | $t$-value |
| $V_t$ | −0.049 | −3.34 | −0.073 | −5.61 | −0.074 | −6.15 |
| $V_{t-1}$ | 0.043 | 3.29 | 0.050 | 4.23 | 0.031 | 2.79 |
| $V_{t-2}$ | 0.053 | 3.94 | 0.056 | 4.83 | 0.050 | 4.27 |
| $V_{t-3}$ | 0.071 | 5.79 | 0.070 | 6.58 | 0.060 | 5.25 |
| $V_{t-4}$ | 0.034 | 2.79 | 0.058 | 5.16 | 0.048 | 4.34 |
| $V_{t-5}$ | 0.014 | 1.06 | 0.044 | 3.56 | 0.044 | 3.76 |
| $V_{t-6}$ | 0.032 | 2.51 | 0.042 | 3.14 | 0.046 | 3.48 |
| $|R_t|$ | −0.085 | −5.54 | −0.115 | −8.03 | −0.114 | −8.90 |
| $|R_{t-1}|$ | −0.082 | −6.27 | −0.082 | −6.50 | −0.074 | −6.48 |
| $|R_{t-2}|$ | −0.059 | −4.82 | −0.066 | −5.12 | −0.059 | −4.95 |
| $|R_{t-3}|$ | −0.054 | −4.85 | −0.051 | −4.78 | −0.049 | −4.66 |
| $|R_{t-4}|$ | −0.024 | −2.12 | −0.038 | −3.41 | −0.036 | −3.43 |
| $|R_{t-5}|$ | −0.038 | −3.24 | −0.046 | −3.94 | −0.043 | −3.86 |
| $|R_{t-6}|$ | −0.046 | −4.08 | −0.052 | −4.69 | −0.048 | −4.44 |
| $S_t$ | – | – | – | – | – | – |
| $S_{t-1}$ | −0.059 | −4.7 | −0.069 | −5.55 | −0.068 | −5.49 |
| $S_{t-2}$ | −0.044 | −4.04 | −0.036 | −3.43 | −0.045 | −4.17 |
| $S_{t-3}$ | −0.028 | −2.69 | −0.038 | −4.04 | −0.045 | −4.67 |
| $S_{t-4}$ | −0.005 | −0.47 | −0.020 | −2.22 | −0.031 | −3.14 |
| $S_{t-5}$ | −0.016 | −1.55 | −0.048 | −4.83 | −0.049 | −4.86 |
| $S_{t-6}$ | −0.042 | −3.79 | −0.045 | −4.16 | −0.051 | −5.06 |
| $R^2$ | – | 0.07 | – | 0.11 | – | 0.12 |
| Volume | – | 75.67 | – | 133.50 | – | 122.45 |
| Volatility | – | 67.55 | – | 83.42 | – | 89.44 |
| Spread | – | 35.52 | – | 43.15 | – | 43.63 |

The table reports coefficients from a regression of order book depth on trading volume, absolute returns and spreads. $V_t$ is defined as the sum of market buy and market sell volume in a given interval. Buy/sell depth is measured as the quantity available in the order book at or within $k$ ticks from the best limit buy/sell price. The depth variables used here are sums of buy and sell side depth for $k = 2, 6, 10$. Hence, 2-tick depth is equal to $d^b(2)_t + d^b(2)_t$. The data upon which the VAR is estimated is sampled on a 20 s calendar-time basis and only observations between 6 and 18 GMT are employed. Prior to estimation the repetitive intra-day pattern is filtered from all variables. All $t$-statistics and $\chi^2$-statistics are based on Newey-West heteroskedasticity and autocorrelation robust standard errors. The rows headed volume, volatility and spread give $\chi^2$-statistics relevant to the null that coefficients on all current and lagged values of this variable are zero.

significantly lower subsequent depth. Hence, in times of large price variation those supplying liquidity do so on worse terms and this is reflected in both higher spreads and lower depth. Such a result is consistent with the intuition delivered by a model of liquidity supply based on asymmetric information, as are the results from the VAR estimates. Intuition from a simple asymmetric information model would predict a positive relationship between volume and volatility plus a negative relationship between volatility and subsequent measures of liquidity. The latter relationship could also be driven by risk-aversion on the part of liquidity suppliers.

A more complicated relationship is that between trading volume and depth. Table 8 shows that increased volume tends to immediately decrease the depth, as one might expect, but then leads to significantly a larger depth. This final result would appear to be at odds with any explanation of the inter-relationships between the four variables that is based on private information in the hands of market order traders or risk-aversion.

Table 9. Regressions of buy and sell depth measures on buy and sell volume, volatility and spreads.

| Regressor | 2-tick buy depth | | 2-tick sell depth | | 6-tick buy depth | | 6-tick sell depth | | 10-tick buy depth | | 10-tick sell depth | |
|---|---|---|---|---|---|---|---|---|---|---|---|---|
| | Coeff. | t-value | Coeff. | t-value | Coeff. | t-value | Coeff. | t-value | Coeff. | t-value | Coeff. | t-value |
| $V^B_t$ | -0.019 | -1.31 | -0.026 | -1.78 | -0.075 | -3.53 | -0.017 | -0.84 | -0.105 | -3.88 | -0.012 | -0.51 |
| $V^B_{t-1}$ | 0.082 | 4.93 | -0.028 | -1.98 | 0.181 | 9.47 | -0.058 | -3.05 | 0.187 | 7.86 | -0.082 | -3.71 |
| $V^B_{t-2}$ | 0.065 | 4.31 | 0.016 | 1.20 | 0.128 | 6.70 | -0.005 | -0.29 | 0.147 | 6.08 | -0.013 | -0.6 |
| $V^B_{t-3}$ | 0.084 | 5.91 | 0.009 | 0.70 | 0.170 | 8.98 | -0.025 | -1.46 | 0.215 | 9.01 | -0.023 | -1.19 |
| $V^B_{t-4}$ | 0.051 | 3.35 | -0.018 | -1.39 | 0.138 | 6.77 | -0.043 | -2.46 | 0.16 | 6.81 | -0.054 | -2.68 |
| $V^B_{t-5}$ | 0.055 | 3.40 | -0.015 | -1.13 | 0.140 | 7.11 | -0.036 | -1.87 | 0.171 | 7.81 | -0.054 | -2.3 |
| $V^B_{t-6}$ | 0.043 | 3.01 | -0.025 | -1.83 | 0.118 | 5.71 | -0.075 | -3.69 | 0.168 | 6.81 | -0.096 | -3.96 |
| $V^S_t$ | -0.049 | -3.40 | -0.031 | -1.64 | -0.053 | -2.42 | -0.127 | -4.95 | -0.01 | -0.36 | -0.214 | -7.43 |
| $V^S_{t-1}$ | -0.062 | -4.30 | 0.112 | 6.85 | -0.098 | -5.23 | 0.146 | 6.46 | -0.112 | -4.88 | 0.131 | 5.03 |
| $V^S_{t-2}$ | -0.001 | -0.09 | 0.054 | 3.30 | -0.024 | -1.26 | 0.104 | 4.99 | -0.035 | -1.58 | 0.115 | 4.57 |
| $V^S_{t-3}$ | 0.007 | 0.49 | 0.077 | 4.84 | -0.037 | -2.08 | 0.146 | 7.35 | -0.075 | -3.48 | 0.144 | 5.66 |
| $V^S_{t-4}$ | 0.006 | 0.42 | 0.045 | 2.94 | -0.040 | -2.14 | 0.153 | 7.28 | -0.074 | -3.37 | 0.175 | 6.98 |
| $V^S_{t-5}$ | -0.031 | -2.17 | 0.027 | 1.57 | -0.070 | -3.57 | 0.130 | 5.37 | -0.082 | -3.59 | 0.164 | 5.61 |
| $V^S_{t-6}$ | 0.010 | 0.73 | 0.053 | 3.23 | -0.032 | -1.62 | 0.146 | 5.60 | -0.058 | -2.38 | 0.197 | 6.34 |
| $|R_t|$ | -0.430 | -5.07 | -0.368 | -3.99 | -0.842 | -6.95 | -0.711 | -5.54 | -1.045 | -7.53 | -0.841 | -5.81 |
| $|R_{t-1}|$ | -0.306 | -4.01 | -0.465 | -5.58 | -0.479 | -4.18 | -0.630 | -5.64 | -0.545 | -4.1 | -0.691 | -5.61 |
| $|R_{t-2}|$ | -0.322 | -4.49 | -0.229 | -2.92 | -0.581 | -5.03 | -0.319 | -2.73 | -0.602 | -4.23 | -0.403 | -3.23 |
| $|R_{t-3}|$ | -0.253 | -3.52 | -0.255 | -3.63 | -0.332 | -3.23 | -0.378 | -3.80 | -0.36 | -2.77 | -0.482 | -4.18 |
| $|R_{t-4}|$ | -0.227 | -3.35 | -0.003 | -0.05 | -0.399 | -3.84 | -0.130 | -1.28 | -0.417 | -3.46 | -0.202 | -1.73 |
| $|R_{t-5}|$ | -0.224 | -3.07 | -0.130 | -1.61 | -0.437 | -3.85 | -0.195 | -1.68 | -0.552 | -4.3 | -0.176 | -1.29 |
| $|R_{t-6}|$ | -0.289 | -3.66 | -0.136 | -1.81 | -0.593 | -5.14 | -0.101 | -0.93 | -0.598 | -4.71 | -0.189 | -1.48 |

| | | | | | | | | | | | | |
|---|---|---|---|---|---|---|---|---|---|---|---|---|
| $S_t$ | — | | — | | — | | — | | — | | — | |
| $S_{t-1}$ | −0.171 | −2.67 | −0.310 | −4.89 | −0.361 | −3.79 | −0.444 | −4.93 | −0.455 | −4.04 | −0.512 | −4.73 |
| $S_{t-2}$ | −0.195 | −3.30 | −0.162 | −3.01 | −0.204 | −2.48 | −0.217 | −3.07 | −0.274 | −2.69 | −0.368 | −4.28 |
| $S_{t-3}$ | −0.134 | −2.39 | −0.094 | −1.84 | −0.189 | −2.56 | −0.248 | −3.81 | −0.355 | −3.81 | −0.288 | −3.73 |
| $S_{t-4}$ | −0.009 | −0.18 | −0.024 | −0.44 | −0.066 | −0.91 | −0.165 | −2.35 | −0.224 | −2.36 | −0.215 | −2.65 |
| $S_{t-5}$ | −0.031 | −0.53 | −0.099 | −1.88 | −0.262 | −2.92 | −0.297 | −4.34 | −0.303 | −2.91 | −0.381 | −5.03 |
| $S_{t-6}$ | −0.191 | −2.96 | −0.151 | −2.70 | −0.243 | −2.41 | −0.291 | −3.93 | −0.425 | −3.64 | −0.315 | −3.97 |
| $R^2$ | 0.06 | — | 0.05 | — | 0.11 | — | 0.10 | — | 0.12 | — | 0.1 | — |
| Buy volume | 100.80 | — | 17.20 | — | 287.58 | — | 27.58 | — | 266.7 | — | 33.61 | — |
| Sell volume | 33.25 | — | 96.21 | — | 43.88 | — | 197.64 | — | 44.7 | — | 243.17 | — |
| Volatility | 55.51 | — | 41.03 | — | 74.07 | — | 45.93 | — | 81.14 | — | 47.34 | — |
| Spreads | 20.67 | — | 35.61 | — | 19.44 | — | 50.71 | — | 23.73 | — | 45.46 | — |

The table reports coefficients from a regression of buy/sell depth on buy and sell volume, absolute returns and spreads. Buy/sell depth is measured as the quantity in the order book at or within $k$ ticks from the best limit buy/sell price. The depth variables used here are for $k = 2, 6, 10$. The data upon which the VAR is estimated is sampled every 20 s and only observations between 6 and 18 GMT are employed. Prior to estimation the repetitive intra-day pattern is filtered from each variable. All $t$-statistics and $\chi^2$-statistics are based on Newey-West heteroskedasticity and autocorrelation robust standard errors. The rows headed volume, volatility and spread give $\chi^2$-statistics relevant to the null that coefficients on all current and lagged values of this variable are zero.

However, if one considers the implications of an asymmetric information story more carefully then a complicating factor becomes apparent. One would expect market buys and market sells to have non-symmetric effects on limit buy and sell side depth. Specifically, arrival of a market buy order would signal to liquidity suppliers that the informed market traders have observed news implying that quotes should be higher – a good private signal. A likely response to this is that depth on the limit sell side of the market would be reduced. However, simultaneously one would expect depth on the limit buy side of the market to rise as limit buyers revise downwards their probabilities of the existence of a bad private signal.

Hence, to test this implication, we re-estimate the empirical model with separate equations for market buy volume, market sell volume, limit buy depth and limit sell depth. The results from the market buy volume, market sell volume, volatility and spread equations, respectively, are similar to those for the total volume, volatility and spreads in Table 7 and hence we omit them to save space.[19]

The results from the separate buy and sell side depth equations are contained in Table 9. Again we observe strong evidence that high volatility and large spreads lead to decreases in order book depth, both buy and sell side. However, the separation of market buy and sell volume clarifies the influence of market order activity on depth. We see that limit buy side depth, for example, tends to be negatively affected by market sell activity and positively influenced by market buy activity. A symmetric result holds for limit sell side depth and the significance of these results is greater for depth measures covering a larger number of ticks. These results are entirely consistent with the asymmetric information story outlined above and consistent with the finding, in Payne (2003), that D2000-2 order flow carries information. Further, it is difficult to see how such results could be generated by inventory concerns of limit order traders. The fact that both limit buy and sell curves shift in response to trades on a single, given side of the market is tough to understand if all that matters for depth determination is the distribution of inventory positions across limit order traders.

Finally, these results are consistent with those described in Section 3. There we showed that market buy activity leads to a decreased probability of subsequently seeing aggressively priced limit sells while the converse was true for the probability of seeing aggressively priced limit buys. Also, we showed that volatility leads subsequently to increased shares of limit orders in an overall order flow. We argued that this was due to the fact that the limit orders were repriced to imply poorer execution for market orders. Our depth results confirm this argument – volatility leads to larger spreads and lower depth.

## 5. Conclusion

This article presents a comprehensive examination of liquidity determination on an order-driven FX broking system. We look not only at standard measures of liquidity based on bid-ask spreads and trading activity, but also use the complete order level data available to us to study measures based on order arrival rates (and probabilities) and to examine the determination of order book depth. Our depth measures are based on the slopes of the excess demand and supply curves implied by the limit buy and sell orders. Our study was the first, to our knowledge, to look at such slope-based depth measures rather than simple measures of quantity available at the inside quotes.

A number of interesting results emerge from our analysis. Via event-time transition analysis, we demonstrate that market order activity has strong and relatively persistent effects on subsequent limit order placement. Market buy activity, for example, reduces the likelihood of observing the entry of limit sells orders at the front of the order book. Conversely, after market buy activity one is more likely to observe the placement of limit orders at the front of the buy side of the book.

A calendar time analysis of order arrival rates shows that both limit order and market order arrivals increase in volatile periods. In line with the theoretical results of Foucault (1999), we also provide evidence that the share of limits in total order flow tends to increase with volatility. Further, we demonstrate that when order book liquidity is visibly low (high), limit order entries are more (less) frequent and market order arrivals less (more) frequent.

Our final set of empirical exercises focuses on the determination of limit order book depth. We demonstrate that the magnitudes of the slopes of the excess demand and supply curves implied by outstanding limit orders increase in volatile periods and in periods of high spreads. Thus, liquidity as measured by spreads and depth move in the same direction and both liquidity measures are eroded in times of high volatility. It is likely that this liquidity erosion in volatile times underlies the preceding result whereby volatility increases the share of limit orders in overall order flow – the liquidity reduction makes market orders less attractive. Depth is also related to trading activity. After market buy activity, one sees the slope of the excess demand curve decrease (buy side depth increases) and the slope of the excess supply curve rises (sell side depth is reduced).

We believe that these results are indicative of information asymmetries in inter-dealer FX markets, with the asymmetric information in the hands of market order traders. In such a setting, one would expect trading volume to increase volatility (through the incorporation of information into prices) and one would then expect to see reduced liquidity. Aggressive buy orders would likely signal to liquidity suppliers that prices will rise in future and hence they re-price limit orders upward leading to reduction in limit sell side depth. Similarly upwards re-pricing of limit buy orders will increase buy side depth. On an order-by-order level, asymmetric information will lead to market buys inhibiting subsequent limit sell orders at good prices, exactly as we see in the data. Corroborating evidence for our information-based view can be found in the literature which examines the relationship between FX order flows and exchange rates (Evans and Lyons 2001; Payne 2003).

A final feature of our results is the dynamic interaction between volume, volatility and liquidity variables. In particular, we see that liquidity and volatility are negatively related. This observation squares with much casual empiricism conducted regarding the recent financial crisis as it suggests that the reaction of market liquidity to price shocks may exacerbate and perpetuate price fluctuations. Thus, the behaviour of liquidity can help explain high levels of and persistence in intra-day financial return volatility and may contribute to the observation of extreme return events.

## Acknowledgements

We would like to thank an anonymous referee, Charles Goodhart, Sylvain Friederich, Roberto Pascual, Casper de Vries and seminar participants at LSE, the Bank for International Settlements and the European Finance Association meetings for helpful comments. Thanks also to Thomson-Reuters Group PLC for providing the D2000-2 data. All errors are our own responsibility.

## Notes

1. Harris and Hasbrouck (1996) also track limit order executions and compare implied costs with those of submitting market orders. Lo, Mackinlay and Zhang (2002) provide empirical analysis of the likelihood of limit order executions using survival analysis.
2. By subsidiary liquidity supply we mean submission of limit orders at prices inferior to the extant best limit price.
3. A study using SEHK data on limit arrivals at the best prices only Ahn, Bae and Chan (2001) show that arrival rates of these orders are increasing with volatility.

4. A similar analysis focussing on spread determination only is contained in Bessembinder (1994). Ranaldo (2004) studies how transitory volatility affects order arrival rates, rather than order book depth.

5. This figure is derived from the tri-annual BIS reports on foreign exchange market activity which details the amounts of trade which are brokered versus direct and also on estimates of D2000-2 and EBS penetration in the brokered inter-dealer market.

6. There is an exception to these rules driven by credit relationships between D2000-2 participants. D2000-2 participants must have bilaterally agreed credit relationships if they are to trade together. This means that, at some times, some banks may find the most competitive market prices unavailable. As such, the results derived in this paper should be interpreted from the perspective of an institution with a full set of credit agreements.

7. Under the conditions we have laid out, subsidiary limit orders are still subject to the risk of being picked off by informed traders, for example.

8. This figure of 2.5 ticks corresponds to a percentage spread of around 0.01%.

9. Similar results for the limit sell side are omitted to conserve space.

10. From here on, we refer to the period between 6 GMT and 16 GMT as the trading day. For more detailed information on the basic activity patterns on D2000-2, see Danielsson and Payne (2002).

11. To clarify this procedure, consider the following example. A limit sell enters with price 1.7505. If there are two orders on the book at 1.7502, three at 1.7504, 1 at 1.7505 and 5 at 1.7507 then the incoming order moves to position seven in the execution queue via price and time priority. The price position of the new order is $-3$ ticks. The total quantity ahead of the new order is the sum of the individual quantities for existing orders at 1.7502, 1.7504 and 1.7505.

12. Also, we performed some analysis to investigate the stability of the transition matrices across the trading day. This analysis indicated that time-of-day variation in the conditional probabilities was minor.

13. The midquote is the average of the best, end-of interval bid and ask quotes. The midquote return is the percentage change in this measure from start to end of interval. Volatility is measured as the absolute return. Our size variable is the sum of quantity available at the best limit buy price and quantity available at the best limit sell price.

14. We use lagged volatility as the explanatory variable to avoid picking up a mechanical relationship between order entries and volatility.

15. To remove the intra-day patterns we scale each observation by the mean value of all observations taken at that time of day across all days.

16. The results we present are not at all sensitive to the choice of VAR order. A sixth-order VAR was indicated by the Schwartz Information criterion.

17. It should be noted that all of our inference is based on Newey-West robust standard errors.

18. A similar result to the latter is contained in Bollerslev and Melvin (1994).

19. The only new result here is that market buy and sell volume are effectively unrelated i.e. lagged market buy activity does not affect current market sell activity and vice versa.

# References

Ahn, H.-J., K.-H. Bae, and K. Chan. 2001. Limit orders, depth, and volatility: Evidence from the stock exchange of Hong Kong. *Journal of Finance* 56, no. 2: 767–88.

Bessembinder, H. 1994. Bid–ask spreads in the interbank foreign exchange market. *Journal of Financial Economics* 35, no. 3: 317–48.

Biais, B., P. Hillion, and C. Spatt. 1995. An empirical analysis of the limit order book and the order flow in the Paris Bourse. *Journal of Finance* 50, no. 5: 1655–89.

Bollerslev, T., and M. Melvin. 1994. Bid–ask spreads and volatility in the foreign exchange market: An empirical analysis. *Journal of International Economics* 36, nos. 3–4: 355–72.

Brockman, P., and D. Chung. 1996. An analysis of depth behaviour in an electronic, order-driven environment. *Journal of Banking and Finance* 51, no. 12: 1835–61.

Coppejans, M., I. Domowitz, and A. Madhavan. 2004. Resiliency in an automated auction. Working paper, ITG Group.

Danielsson, J., and R. Payne. 2002. Real trading patterns and prices in spot foreign exchange markets. *Journal of International Money and Finance* 21, no. 2: 203–22.

Evans, M., and R. Lyons. 2001. Order flow and exchange rate dynamics. *Journal of Political Economy* 110, no. 1: 170–80.

Foucault, T. 1999. Order flow composition and trading costs in a dynamic limit order market. *Journal of Financial Markets* 2, no. 2: 99–134.

Glosten, L. 1994. Is the electronic open limit order book inevitable? *Journal of Finance* 49, no. 4: 1127–61.

Goettler, R., C. Parlour, and U. Rajan. 2009. Informed traders and limit order markets. *Journal of Financial Economics*, 93, no. 1: 67–87.

Gomber, P., U. Schweickert, and E. Theissen. 2004. Zooming in on liquidity. Unpublished working paper, University of Bonn.

Hall, A., and N. Hautsch. 2007. Modelling the buy and sell intensity in a limit order book market. *Journal of Financial Markets* 10, no. 3: 249–86.

Handa, P., R. Schwartz, and A. Tiwari. 2003. Quote setting and price formation in an order driven market. *Journal of Financial Markets* 6, no. 4: 461–89.

Harris, L., and J. Hasbrouck. 1996. Market vs. limit orders: The SuperDOT evidence on order submission strategy. The *Journal of Financial and Quantitative Analysis* 31, no. 2: 213–31.

Hasbrouck, J. 1991a. Measuring the information content of stock trades. *Journal of Finance* 46, no. 1: 179–206.

Hasbrouck, J. 1991b. The summary informativeness of stock trades: An econometric analysis. *Review of Financial Studies* 4, no. 3: 571–95.

Hasbrouck, J. 1999. Trading fast and slow: Security market events in real time. Working paper, Stern School of Business, New York University.

Kavajecz, K. 1998. A specialist's quoted depth and the limit order book. *Journal of Finance* 54, no. 2: 747–71.

Kyle, A. 1985. Continuous auctions and insider trading. *Econometrica* 53, no. 6: 1315–35.

Large, J. 2007. Measuring the resiliency of an electronic limit order book. *Journal of Financial Markets* 10, no. 1: 1–25.

Lee, C., B. Mucklow, and M. Ready. 1993. Spreads, depths and the impact of earnings information: An intraday analysis. *Review of Financial Studies* 6, no. 2: 345–74.

Lo, A., A. Mackinlay, and J. Zhang. 2002. Econometric models for limit-order executions. *Journal of Financial Economics* 65, no. 1: 31–71.

Lo, I., and S. Sapp. 2008. The submission of limit orders or market orders: The role of timing and information in the Reuters D2000-2 system. *Journal of International Money and Finance* 27, no. 7: 1056–73.

Parlour, C. 1998. Price dynamics in limit order markets. *Review of Financial Studies* 11, no. 4: 789–816.

Payne, R. 2003. Informed trade in spot foreign exchange markets: An empirical investigation. *Journal of International Economics* 61, no. 2: 307–29.

Ranaldo, A. 2004. Order aggressiveness in limit order book markets. *Journal of Financial Markets* 7, no. 1: 53–74.

Sandas, P. 2001. Adverse selection and competitive market making: Empirical evidence from a limit order market. *Review of Financial Studies* 14, no. 3: 705–34.

# Exchange rate determination and inter-market order flow effects

Jón Daníelsson[a], Jinhui Luo[b] and Richard Payne[c]

[a]Department of Finance and Financial Markets Group, London School of Economics, London, UK; [b]ICBC, Beijing, China; [c]Faculty of Finance, Cass Business School, City University, London, London, UK

The dependence of foreign exchange rates on order flow is investigated for four major exchange rate pairs, EUR/USD, EUR/GBP, GBP/USD and USD/JPY, across sampling frequencies ranging from 5 min to 1 week. Strong explanatory power is discovered for all sampling frequencies. We also uncover cross-market order flow effects, e.g. GBP exchange rates are very strongly influenced by EUR/USD order flow. We proceed to investigate the predictive power of order flow for exchange rate changes, and it is shown that the order flow specifications reduce RMSEs relative to a random walk for all exchange rates at high-frequencies and for EUR/USD and USD/JPY at lower sampling frequencies.

## 1. Introduction

Empirical models of exchange rate determination, especially at intermediate estimation horizons, have frustrated economists at least since the Meese and Rogoff (1983a, 1983b) result that macro-based exchange rate models under-perform a random walk model in predictive ability. In the empirical finance literature there is, however, a long tradition of studying the higher frequency relationship between features of prices of financial assets and measures derived from trading activity.[1] Simple analysis of trading volume, however, does not help resolve the Meese–Rogoff problem, not least because volume is directionless, i.e. a change in volume cannot predict the direction of FX changes.

Recently, though, researchers have investigated the impact of *signed volume*, i.e. the decomposition of volume into transactions initiated by sellers and buyers, separately. The difference between buyer and seller initiated volume is termed *order flow*.[2] Order flow has been shown in empirical market microstructure research to be a key determinant of high frequency asset price changes, with several authors, e.g. Lyons (1995), Evans (2002), and Payne (2003) studying the relationship between order flow and foreign exchange rates.[3]

From the perspective of benchmark rational expectations models of exchange rate determination, the importance of order flow is puzzling. Such models predict that prices should respond to new information without any consistent effect on order flow. Intuitively, when new information arrives each agent immediately revises his estimate of value and there is no reason for trade. Thus, one must look beyond those models to find a rationale for the effects of order flow on prices.

91

Work which can be used to justify the explanatory power of order flow suggests that flows may convey information about asset payoffs or discount factors. Standard private information arguments (e.g. Glosten and Milgrom 1985) imply that order flow carries information about exchange rate payoffs. Alternatively, Evans and Lyons (2002b) suggest that order flow aggregates dispersed information about FX risk premia. Finally, some recent empirical work suggests that public information is partially impounded into exchange rates via order flow (Love and Payne 2008; Rime, Sarno, and Sojli 2010). These arguments also suggest that the relationship between order flow and asset prices persists across sampling frequencies, for example, because information has permanent effects on asset prices. Some empirical work supports this intuition, e.g. Evans and Lyons (2002b) who find strong dependence of daily exchange rate changes on daily order flows, even after accounting for macroeconomic fundamentals.[4] However, Berger et al. (2008) use six years of high-frequency data on EUR/USD and USD/JPY to show that order flows and exchange rate returns are strongly related for sampling frequencies from 1 min to 2 weeks, but the relationship weakens at lower frequencies. They proceed to show that the flow–return relationship is stronger at times of low market liquidity and use this result to argue that liquidity effects are at least a part of the story behind the correlations of flows and returns. Finally, Froot and Ramadorai (2005) use a decomposition for FX returns into permanent, intrinsic value shocks and deviations from intrinsic value (similar to that of Campbell and Shiller 1988), plus a long span of flow data for many currencies (this time from a global custodian bank) to draw conclusions about the long-run effects of flows on exchange rates. They conclude that order flow is related to transitory exchange rate movements and show that positive correlations between returns and flows turn negative at very low frequencies.

The objective of this article is to refine and deepen our understanding of the relationship between FX order flows and exchange rate changes. Our investigation extends prior work in that we have data on four key exchange rates (EUR/USD, EUR/GBP, GBP/USD, USD/JPY) covering between eight and 10 months each. Using these data, we focus on three empirical issues. First, we examine how the flow-return relationship varies across sampling frequencies from 5 min to 1 week. Second, we empirically model cross-market order flow effects, e.g. the effects of EUR/USD order flow on GBP/USD. Last, we evaluate the predictive power of order flows for exchange rate changes using the Meese–Rogoff approach and genuine out-of-sample forecast analysis.

Our data derive from transaction-level information obtained from the Reuters D2000-2 electronic brokerage and we have approximately 10 months of data for EUR/USD and EUR/GBP and eight months of data for GBP/USD and USD/JPY. The sample starts in 1999 and ends in 2000.

Our first set of results shows that contemporaneous order flow significantly explains exchange rates across sampling frequencies. However, we observe considerable differences in the explanatory power of the various regressions. For the EUR/USD rate, $R^2$ hovers around 40% for all frequencies, while for USD/JPY the $R^2$ increases with aggregation, from 6% at 5 min to 67% at one week. These results are comparable to those reported by Evans and Lyons (2002b) and Berger et al. (2008) and, in the latter case, directly corroborate their findings for EUR/USD and USD/JPY using data from a different sample and trading system. In contrast, the $R^2$ for both GBP rates decreases with aggregation from 26% at 5 min to 1% at one week. On first inspection, the inconsistency between the GBP regression results and those for EUR/USD and USD/JPY is somewhat puzzling.

Our analysis of the cross-market flow effects partially resolves the preceding puzzle, however. Including other order flows as explanatory variables in the EUR/USD and USD/JPY regressions makes little difference to their explanatory power. However, for the GBP rates, especially at lower frequencies, order flow from other currencies has a strong and significant impact, greatly increasing the explanatory power. Our results are especially clear in the case of the EUR/GBP rate where EUR/USD order flow is found to be the primary exchange rate driver at low frequencies. Cross-market flow effects similar to these are also reported in Evans and Lyons (2002a) and Lyons and Moore (2009). The former paper studies pre-Euro data and shows that German mark and Swiss franc flows directly affect returns on other European currencies. The latter studies triangular arbitrage in a Yen–Dollar–Euro setting and shows cross-market effects from flow in that context. Our results support theirs in that we derive results from a different triangle i.e. Sterling–Dollar–Euro.

There are several possible explanations for the cross-market order flow effects we find. For example, suppose a currency trader has private information about the future value of the USD, perhaps he expects that it will appreciate. The trader can exploit this information by trading in e.g. GBP/USD or EUR/USD. Since the EUR is more liquid, market impact from trading could be expected to be lower in that market, implying that more profits can be gained by trading in the EUR than in GBP. In this case, EUR/USD order flow would help us to explain the EUR/USD rate. However, liquidity suppliers in GBP/USD who understand the incentives of informed traders will interpret the EUR/USD flow as possibly signalling USD appreciation and will adjust their GBP/USD quotes accordingly. Thus, the EUR/USD flow has an effect on the GBP/USD rate. A similar argument can be made for other cross-market flow effects from liquid to less liquid currency pairs.

In sum, the cross-market flow effects suggest that while the basic own order flow model may be appropriate for the largest currencies, it is less so for less liquid currencies.[5] Information revealed in more liquid pairs spills over to less liquid rates such that flows from liquid pairs significantly contribute to the ability to explain them. These effects persist across our sampling frequencies, and strengthen with aggregation.

Our final results are on the prediction of exchange rates. First, we use the Meese and Rogoff (1983a, 1983b) framework, and find that the order flow model almost always yields a better prediction (in RMSE terms) than does a random walk model. This result is consistent across sampling frequencies and currencies. Therefore, albeit at a somewhat higher sampling frequency than macroeconomists would usually examine, the order flow model passes the Meese–Rogoff test that macroeconomic models have failed so often. We note, however, that the Meese–Rogoff test is not a genuine out-of-sample forecasting test. When we run such a test, albeit with a simple linear specification, we find that order flow does not perform particularly well in forecasting exchange rates except at the highest frequencies. Such results contrast with those from Evans and Lyons (2005) and Rime, Sarno, and Sojli (2010) who suggest that order flows have out-of-sample forecasting power for FX rates at daily and longer horizons. Our findings are supported by Sager and Taylor (2008), who use inter-dealer and customer FX flows. Last of all, we find, as do Sager and Taylor (2008), that order flow itself can be forecasted with own lags and lagged returns.

In sum, our results suggest that order flow contributes strongly to exchange rate determination. Across sampling frequencies from the highest intra-day level to those relevant to macroeconomists, flows help explain exchange rate changes. On this front, our analysis corroborates the work of, inter alia, Evans and Lyons (2002a, 2002b), Payne (2003), Berger et al. (2008) and Lyons and Moore (2009). We go on to show that flow-based forecasts can outperform a random walk model within a Meese–Rogoff setting, although in a genuine out-of-sample setting flow-based forecasts are only helpful at relatively high frequencies. In this area, our results are at odds with those of Evans and Lyons (2005) and Rime, Sarno, and Sojli (2010), although they support the findings of Sager and Taylor (2008).

The rest of the article is structured as follows. Section 2 outlines our data sources and our processing of the data. Section 3 presents our analysis of the explanatory power of order flow for exchange rates and Section 4 presents multi-variate flow analysis. The following section presents our forecasting results. Some discussion of our findings is given in Section 6 and Section 7 concludes.

## 2.  Data description and organization

### 2.1  *The data*

Our data come from the Reuters D2000-2 system, which is a brokered inter-dealer FX trading platform. Thus, our data contain no information on customer-dealer FX trades or on direct (i.e. non-intermediated) trades between dealers. Moreover, it should be noted that the trades occurring on D2000-2 should be regarded as public in the sense that they are published to the D2000-2 screen as they occur.[6]

The raw data set is composed of transaction level information, covering four major floating rates: EUR/USD, EUR/GBP, GBP/USD and USD/JPY. Each transaction record contains a time stamp for the trade, a variable indicating whether the trade was a market buy or sell and the transaction price. Thus, we do not have to use potentially inaccurate, ad hoc algorithms to assign trade direction. The samples for EUR/USD and GBP/USD cover a period of 10 months from 28 September 1999 to 24 July 2000. Samples for EUR/GBP and USD/JPY cover a period of eight months from 1 December 1999 to 24 July 2000. A limitation of the data supplied is a lack of information about the size of each trade. Therefore, we cannot analyze whether the monetary value of order flow matters over and above order flow measured simply in terms of numbers of trades. Nevertheless, this high frequency data set has two valuable characteristics: long sample periods and multiple exchange rates. The long sample period ensures reasonable statistical power for the various econometric tests and the broad currency scope provides a platform to check the robustness of model estimation cross-sectionally on major floating exchange rates.

### 2.2  *Filtering and time aggregation*

We remove sparse trading periods from the data. Such sparse trading periods include the overnight period, weekends, some world-wide public holidays and certain other dates where the feed from D2000-2 failed.[7]

In our analysis, we focus on eight different time aggregation levels: 5 min, 15 min, 30 min, 1 h, 4 h, 6 h, 1 day and 1 week.[8] Note that our definition of one day corresponds to a trading day defined as the interval between 6.00 a.m. and 6.00 p.m. London time. Thus, one day covers 12 rather than 24 h. Similarly, one week covers five trading days. The time aggregation is done as follows. First, we scan along the sample in calendar time minute by minute. At every observation point, the last transaction price is recorded along with the excess of the number of market buys over market sells since the last observation point. From the price data, we construct logarithmic price changes.

After filtering and aggregation, we are left with 32 data sets (eight sampling frequencies × four exchange rates). We summarize their statistical properties in Table 1. At the daily level, we have 201 observations for EUR/USD and GBP/USD and 160 observations for EUR/GBP and USD/JPY. Our sample period covers a time during which there was a depreciation of EUR against USD and GBP, a depreciation of GBP against USD and a depreciation of JPY against USD. These market trends are reflected in the columns of each panel in Table 1 that display mean returns. Comparing

Table 1. Summary statistics for time aggregated data sets.

### (a) EUR/USD

| k | Obs | Trades | Quotes | Buys | $\bar{r}$ | $\sigma$ |
|---|---|---|---|---|---|---|
| 5 min | 29,107 | 16 | 51 | 8 | -0.0006 | 0.06 |
| 15 min | 9701 | 49 | 153 | 25 | -0.0017 | 0.10 |
| 30 min | 4850 | 98 | 306 | 49 | -0.0038 | 0.13 |
| 1 h | 2424 | 196 | 611 | 99 | -0.0050 | 0.20 |
| 4 h | 605 | 782 | 2444 | 395 | -0.0196 | 0.40 |
| 6 h | 404 | 1174 | 3669 | 593 | -0.0313 | 0.47 |
| 12 h | 201 | 2347 | 7317 | 1185 | -0.0676 | 0.62 |
| 1 week | 42 | 11,305 | 35,831 | 5702 | -0.3373 | 1.53 |

### (b) USD/JPY

| k | Obs | Trades | Quotes | Buys | $\bar{r}$ | $\sigma$ |
|---|---|---|---|---|---|---|
| 5 min | 23,148 | 1 | 7 | 1 | 0.0004 | 0.08 |
| 15 min | 7715 | 4 | 21 | 2 | 0.0008 | 0.10 |
| 30 min | 3857 | 7 | 41 | 4 | 0.0022 | 0.13 |
| 1 h | 1928 | 15 | 83 | 8 | 0.0038 | 0.18 |
| 4 h | 481 | 58 | 330 | 30 | 0.0052 | 0.37 |
| 6 h | 321 | 88 | 496 | 45 | 0.0089 | 0.41 |
| 12 h | 160 | 175 | 988 | 90 | 0.0351 | 0.56 |
| 1 week | 33 | 1024 | 5961 | 526 | 0.2785 | 1.22 |

### (c) EUR/GBP

| k | Obs | Trades | Quotes | Buys | $\bar{r}$ | $\sigma$ |
|---|---|---|---|---|---|---|
| 5 min | 23,148 | 14 | 34 | 8 | -0.0002 | 0.05 |
| 15 min | 7715 | 43 | 103 | 23 | -0.0007 | 0.09 |
| 30 min | 3857 | 87 | 206 | 45 | -0.0015 | 0.13 |
| 1 h | 1928 | 174 | 411 | 90 | -0.0025 | 0.18 |
| 4 h | 481 | 694 | 1646 | 362 | -0.0106 | 0.37 |
| 6 h | 321 | 1041 | 2468 | 542 | -0.0160 | 0.45 |
| 12 h | 160 | 2085 | 4944 | 1086 | -0.0384 | 0.61 |
| 1 week | 33 | 10,383 | 25,506 | 5423 | -0.0482 | 1.36 |

### (d) GBP/USD

| k | Obs | Trades | Quotes | Buys | $\bar{r}$ | $\sigma$ |
|---|---|---|---|---|---|---|
| 5 min | 29,107 | 17 | 44 | 9 | -0.0004 | 0.04 |
| 15 min | 9701 | 52 | 131 | 27 | -0.0012 | 0.07 |
| 30 min | 4850 | 104 | 263 | 53 | -0.0029 | 0.09 |
| 1 h | 2424 | 208 | 525 | 106 | -0.0049 | 0.13 |
| 4 h | 605 | 832 | 2098 | 424 | -0.0200 | 0.26 |
| 6 h | 404 | 1249 | 3150 | 636 | -0.0291 | 0.32 |
| 12 h | 201 | 2496 | 6280 | 1271 | -0.0603 | 0.45 |
| 1 week | 42 | 13,245 | 35,328 | 6753 | -0.2299 | 0.92 |

Notes: $k$ is the sampling frequency; Obs. is the total number of observations at sampling frequency $k$; returns are defined as $100 \times (\log(P_t) - \log(P_{t-1}))$ and $\bar{r}$ is the average return for sampling frequency $k$. Columns headed Trades, Quotes, Buys and $\sigma$ give the average number of trades, average number of quotes, average number of buys and standard deviation of returns for that frequency.

panel (b) with the other three panels, we see that the number of trades in USD/JPY is far less than for the other three markets. GBP/USD is the most heavily traded pair with EUR/USD and GBP/USD just behind. These numbers reflect two things. First, Reuters D2000-2 has relatively a poor coverage of JPY markets and, compared to its competitor EBS, has a minority share in EUR/USD trade. In contrast, D2000-2 dominates trade in GBP rates.

## 3. Own order flow and foreign exchange rate determination

The study of the high frequency relationship between price changes and order flow has a long tradition in the microstructure literature. In contrast, it is only fairly recently that such relationships have been studied at lower sampling frequencies, such as daily and weekly.

We first track how the explanatory power of order flow for price changes varies across sampling frequencies and across currencies by running a set of regressions of the following form:

$$\Delta P(k)_{i,t} = \alpha(k)_i + \beta(k)_i F(k)_{i,t} + \varepsilon_{i,t}, \tag{1}$$

where $\Delta P(k)_{i,t}$ is the transaction price change for currency pair $i$ at sampling frequency $k$, and $F(k)_{i,t}$ is order flow in the interval ending at $t$ for currency pair $i$ at sampling frequency $k$. Table 2 contains the estimation results for model (1) for our four exchange rates and over the entire spectrum of time aggregation levels.[9]

At the highest frequencies (less than 1 h), we observe significant effects from order flow for all currencies, with the strongest effects for EUR/USD where $R^2$ ranges from 33% to 45%. These results confirm what microstructure economists have long known – order flow carries information for high-frequency asset price determination. However, there is no immediate reason to believe that these very high frequency results have any bearing on exchange rate determination at lower frequencies. They might simply reflect transitory market liquidity effects, for example.

Thus, we shift focus to a lower frequency. Consider first results at the daily frequency, initially for EUR/USD and USD/JPY in order to provide comparability with Evans and Lyons (2002b).[10] Their daily USD/DEM and USD/JPY regression $R^2$ are just over 60% and 40%, respectively,

Table 2. Explaining exchange rates with order flow.

| | EUR/USD | | | USD/JPY | | | EUR/GBP | | | GBP/USD | | |
|---|---|---|---|---|---|---|---|---|---|---|---|---|
| $k$ | $\hat{\beta}$ | $t$-stats | $R^2$ | $\hat{\beta}$ | $t$-stats | $R^2$ | $\hat{\beta}$ | $t$-stats | $R^2$ | $\hat{\beta}$ | $t$-stats | $R^2$ |
| 5 min | 0.40 | 72.39 | 0.33 | 1.08 | 24.71 | 0.06 | 0.41 | 60.30 | 0.26 | 0.29 | 65.07 | 0.26 |
| 15 min | 0.38 | 53.25 | 0.43 | 1.17 | 26.53 | 0.15 | 0.38 | 32.01 | 0.26 | 0.26 | 36.58 | 0.24 |
| 30 min | 0.36 | 45.30 | 0.45 | 1.19 | 20.96 | 0.25 | 0.33 | 20.51 | 0.21 | 0.23 | 21.30 | 0.21 |
| 1 h | 0.36 | 29.91 | 0.38 | 1.25 | 18.98 | 0.30 | 0.30 | 12.85 | 0.16 | 0.21 | 13.95 | 0.16 |
| 4 h | 0.34 | 17.63 | 0.38 | 1.14 | 9.70 | 0.30 | 0.16 | 3.00 | 0.05 | 0.13 | 3.95 | 0.05 |
| 6 h | 0.34 | 15.35 | 0.38 | 1.21 | 10.59 | 0.42 | 0.10 | 2.00 | 0.02 | 0.11 | 3.66 | 0.05 |
| 12 h | 0.30 | 11.04 | 0.35 | 1.17 | 10.70 | 0.50 | 0.02 | 0.36 | 0.00 | 0.14 | 4.12 | 0.08 |
| 1 week | 0.31 | 5.51 | 0.45 | 0.91 | 11.43 | 0.67 | 0.06 | 0.59 | 0.01 | 0.05 | 0.70 | 0.01 |

Notes: Parameter estimates and inference are obtained from the following model:

$$\Delta P(k)_{i,t} = \alpha(k)_i + \beta(k)_i F(k)_{i,t} + \varepsilon_{i,t},$$

where $\Delta P(k)_{i,t}$ is the price change at sampling frequency $k$ for exchange rate $i$ at time $t$ and $F(k)_{i,t}$ is order flow for the same exchange rate and sampling frequency. All $t$-stats are constructed using the Newey-West estimator of the coefficient variance-covariance matrix. The order flow is scaled by $10^{-2}$.

and these numbers are broadly consistent with our results. Berger et al. (2008) study EUR/USD and USD/JPY and find that daily $R^2$ from the basic order flow specification are at similar levels to those in Evans and Lyons (2002b), although these authors suggest that the $R^2$ drops significantly as one moves to a monthly sampling frequency.

However, our results on the GBP exchange rates are much less supportive of the findings of Evans and Lyons (2002b) and Berger et al. (2008). By looking at the low-frequency regressions in the final two panels of Table 2, we see that the explanatory power of order flow for GBP/EUR and GPB/USD is very poor. At sampling frequencies exceeding 1 h, in no single case does the regression $R^2$ exceed 0.10, although in five of the eight cases the order flow variable is statistically significant. Thus, at least for the GBP, the assertion that order flow matters for exchange rate determination when one moves towards sampling frequencies relevant to international macroeconomics appears less secure than our previous EUR/USD and USD/JPY results suggest.

A graphical representation of these results using a larger set of sampling frequencies is given in Figure 1. The figure clearly demonstrates the importance of order flow regardless of sampling frequency for EUR/USD and USD/JPY but also shows the declining explanatory power of order flow with sampling frequency in the GBP markets.

That the low-frequency GBP results are poor relative to EUR/USD and USD/JPY is puzzling given Reuters dominance in inter-dealer trade in GBP markets. Ex ante, one might have thought that Reuters' GBP flows would thus carry more power than their EUR/USD and USD/JPY counterparts.

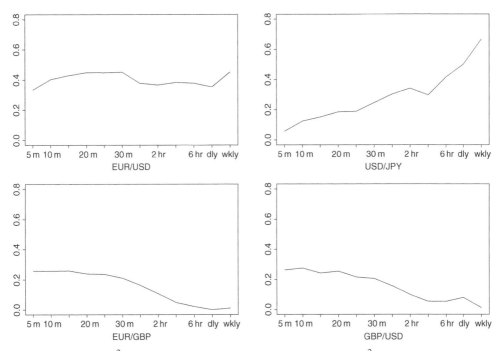

Figure 1. Variation in $R^2$ of order flow model across sampling frequencies. $R^2$ from regression model (1) over sampling frequencies from 5 min to one week for each exchange rate. Labels 'm', 'h', 'dly', 'wkly' represent minute, hour, daily and weekly, respectively.

## 4. Inter-market order flow analysis

Most existing FX order flow research focuses on one asset at a time. However, since exchange rates are relative prices, and three of our exchange rates form a triangular relationship, it is of interest to investigate how order flow in one currency pair might be used to explain the exchange rate of a second currency pair. We denote this as *inter-market order flow* analysis. This issue has been addressed in other papers. Evans and Lyons (2002a) show, using data from before the introduction of the Euro, that order flows in the German mark and Swiss franc spill over to various other European exchange rates. More recently, Lyons and Moore (2009) study information spillovers between currencies that are linked via triangular arbitrage relationships and empirically identify cross-market order flow effects in the EUR–JPY–USD triangle.

The reason for considering inter-market effects is the peculiar nature of exchange rates, in particular, the fact that an informed trader can use any number of currency pairs to exploit his information. Consider, e.g. a trader who has superior information regarding the future value of the USD, perhaps that the USD will appreciate vis-à-vis other currencies. The trader can exploit this information by trading in USD/JPY, EUR/USD, GBP/USD, and so on. The question arising is in which market (if not all of them) will he choose to trade? If he chooses not to trade in all markets but to focus on one, perhaps because it offers small transaction costs and low price impacts, then the possibility exists that order flow in this market might drive price changes in other markets. Rational liquidity suppliers in other markets observe the order flow just traded in the chosen market and revise their valuations of all USD rates.

We incorporate inter-market effects by extending Equation (1) to include order flow from all currency pairs, while still remaining within the linear specification that relates price changes in market $i$ to contemporaneous order flows:

$$\Delta P(k)_{i,t} = \alpha(k)_i + \sum_j \beta(k)_{i,j} F(k)_{j,t} + \epsilon_{i,t}, \tag{2}$$

where both $i$ and $j$ index currency pairs such that $i$ is the rate to be explained and the summation over $j$ gives an explanatory term that is linear in order flow variables from all four markets. The parameter $k$ indexes sampling frequency. Table 3 presents the main results from estimating Equation (2), while the $R^2$ from the multiple-flow regressions are shown in Figure 2 alongside those from the own-market flow models.

Consider first the results for USD/JPY as it is the only JPY rate and because the other three rates form a triangulating relationship. We see that for USD/JPY, aside from the strong own flow effects uncovered in Section 3, there are few other significant flow variables. A couple of the EUR/USD and GBP/USD flows are significant and, as expected given the definition of the rates, they enter with negative signs. In all cases, the improvement in the $R^2$ of the regressions as compared to the univariate specifications in Section 3 is small.

For EUR/USD, the order flow coefficients of EUR/GBP and GBP/USD are, as a triangular arbitrage argument would predict, consistently positive and significant at the 1% level at relatively high frequencies. The significance of the GBP/USD flow persists to the daily level. Also, the USD/JPY flow is significant, with the expected negative coefficient, at very high sampling frequencies. Overall, these effects lead to improvements in the explanatory power over the single flow specification (labelled $\Delta R^2$ in the table) of up to 6%, and for all specifications below the daily level this improvement is significant.

For the GBP rates, the results are interesting. Flows in the other GBP rate (EUR/GBP flow in the GBP/USD price change regressions and vice versa) are strongly significant at higher

Table 3. Inter-market information flow.

### (a) EUR/USD

| k | $\hat{\beta}_{ED}$ | $\hat{\beta}_{DY}$ | $\hat{\beta}_{ES}$ | $\hat{\beta}_{SD}$ | $\Delta R^2$ | p-value |
|---|---|---|---|---|---|---|
| 5 min | 0.32* | -0.05* | 0.18* | 0.14* | 0.054 | 0.01 |
| 15 min | 0.31* | -0.05** | 0.16* | 0.13* | 0.056 | 0.01 |
| 30 min | 0.31* | -0.10* | 0.13* | 0.11* | 0.048 | 0.01 |
| 1 h | 0.32* | -0.01** | 0.11* | 0.12* | 0.039 | 0.01 |
| 4 h | 0.35* | -0.05 | 0.03 | 0.10* | 0.016 | 0.01 |
| 6 h | 0.34* | -0.09 | 0.03 | 0.12* | 0.029 | 0.01 |
| 12 h | 0.33* | -0.03 | -0.05 | 0.08*** | 0.015 | >0.10 |
| 1 week | 0.39* | -0.01 | -0.00 | 0.15 | 0.044 | >0.10 |

### (b) USD/JPY

| k | $\hat{\beta}_{ED}$ | $\hat{\beta}_{DY}$ | $\hat{\beta}_{ES}$ | $\hat{\beta}_{SD}$ | $\Delta R^2$ | p-value |
|---|---|---|---|---|---|---|
| 5 min | -0.02** | 1.07* | -0.01 | -0.01 | 0.001 | 0.01 |
| 15 min | -0.02*** | 1.17* | -0.00 | -0.01 | 0.001 | 0.05 |
| 30 min | -0.01 | 1.19* | 0.00 | -0.01 | 0.001 | >0.10 |
| 1 h | -0.02 | 1.24* | -0.00 | -0.03** | 0.005 | 0.01 |
| 4 h | -0.04*** | 1.13* | 0.05 | -0.03 | 0.010 | 0.10 |
| 6 h | 0.01 | 1.22* | 0.01 | -0.03 | 0.002 | >0.10 |
| 12 h | 0.02 | 1.17* | -0.02 | -0.02 | 0.003 | >0.10 |
| 1 week | 0.04 | 0.89* | 0.06 | -0.12** | 0.057 | >0.10 |

### (c) EUR/GBP

| k | $\hat{\beta}_{ED}$ | $\hat{\beta}_{DY}$ | $\hat{\beta}_{ES}$ | $\hat{\beta}_{SD}$ | $\Delta R^2$ | p-value |
|---|---|---|---|---|---|---|
| 5 min | 0.21* | -0.02 | 0.30* | -0.13* | 0.099 | 0.01 |
| 15 min | 0.23* | -0.02 | 0.26* | -0.13* | 0.130 | 0.01 |
| 30 min | 0.23* | -0.05 | 0.22* | -0.11* | 0.142 | 0.01 |
| 1 h | 0.23* | -0.03 | 0.19* | -0.09* | 0.146 | 0.01 |
| 4 h | 0.26* | -0.05 | 0.07 | -0.02 | 0.220 | 0.01 |
| 6 h | 0.28* | -0.04 | 0.01 | 0.01 | 0.235 | 0.01 |
| 12 h | 0.28* | -0.11 | -0.03 | -0.04 | 0.263 | 0.01 |
| 1 week | 0.29* | -0.07 | 0.01 | 0.08 | 0.335 | 0.01 |

### (d) GBP/USD

| k | $\hat{\beta}_{ED}$ | $\hat{\beta}_{DY}$ | $\hat{\beta}_{ES}$ | $\hat{\beta}_{SD}$ | $\Delta R^2$ | p-value |
|---|---|---|---|---|---|---|
| 5 min | 0.10* | -0.03** | -0.11* | 0.27* | 0.041 | 0.01 |
| 15 min | 0.09* | -0.03 | -0.10* | 0.25* | 0.045 | 0.01 |
| 30 min | 0.08* | -0.03 | -0.10* | 0.22* | 0.048 | 0.01 |
| 1 h | 0.10* | -0.06 | -0.09* | 0.20* | 0.055 | 0.01 |
| 4 h | 0.10* | -0.02 | -0.07** | 0.10* | 0.065 | 0.01 |
| 6 h | 0.09* | -0.09 | -0.01 | 0.09** | 0.053 | 0.01 |
| 12 h | 0.10* | -0.00 | -0.02 | 0.12* | 0.054 | 0.01 |
| 1 week | 0.12** | 0.05 | -0.00 | 0.07 | 0.107 | 0.05 |

Notes: Parameter estimates and inference are obtained from the following model:

$$\Delta P(k)_{i,t} = \alpha(k)_i + \sum_j \beta(k)_{i,j} F(k)_{j,t} + \varepsilon_{i,t},$$

where $k$ indexes sampling frequency, $i$ denotes the rate to be explained and the summation over $j$ gives an explanatory structure that is linear in all four order flow variables. The column headed $\Delta R^2$ gives the change in $R^2$ between the model with and without the order flow from other markets. The last column in each panel is the $p$-value of the $F$-test of the null $H_0 : \beta_j = 0$ for $j \neq i$. The order flow is scaled by a factor of $10^{-2}$. In the column headers, 'ED' is shorthand for EUR/USD, 'SD' is shorthand for GBP/USD, 'ES' is shorthand for EUR/GBP and 'DY' is shorthand for USD/JPY.

*Significance at the 1% level (based on the Newey–West coefficient variance–covariance estimator).

**Significance at the 5% level (based on the Newey–West coefficient variance–covariance estimator).

***Significance at the 10% level (based on the Newey–West coefficient variance–covariance estimator).

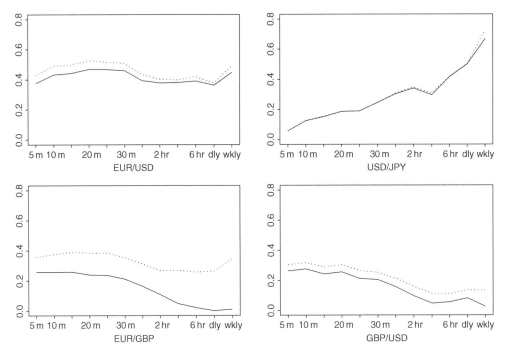

Figure 2. $R^2$ for univariate and multivariate order flow models. The solid and dotted lines are $R^2$s from models (1) and (2), respectively. Each model is estimated over sampling frequencies from 5 min to one week. Labels 'm', 'h', 'dly', 'wkly' represent minute, hour, daily and weekly, respectively.

frequencies while USD/JPY flows have virtually no effects. However, the dominant new right-hand side variable in these regressions is the EUR/USD flow. In each and every case for these two exchange rates, EUR/USD flows are strongly significant with a positive coefficient. The extended specifications show markedly improved explanatory power ($\Delta R^2$) over the univariate models in Section 3, of between 5% and 35% with the largest improvements being at the lowest sampling frequencies. In all cases, the extra right-hand side variables can be shown to significantly improve the explanatory power of the regression. The effect of EUR/USD flow is strongest for the EUR/GBP, providing virtually all the explanatory powers at the lower frequencies.

Thus, our results provide clear evidence of flow information being transmitted across linked exchange rate markets, from more to less liquid markets. Moreover, our results on the GBP–EUR–USD triangle support those of Lyons and Moore (2009) on the JPY–EUR–USD triangle. The EUR/USD exchange rate is the largest and most liquid in the world, and its order flow is shown to contribute strongly to all three currency pairs involved in the GBP triangle at all sampling frequencies. This is especially apparent for the least liquid of these three currency pairs, EUR/GBP. The fact that the order flow from the largest currencies dominates the determination of the smaller currencies suggests that new information flows first to the most liquid markets, i.e. where the new information can be best exploited.

Note that, while EUR/USD is clearly the most liquid of spot exchange rate pairs, only a fraction of its volume is traded on Reuters' D2000-2. Conversely, while the GBP markets are much smaller than EUR/USD, D2000-2 is the venue for the bulk of the electronically brokered trade. If then, Reuters' market in EUR/USD is relatively poor, why do its EUR/USD flows exert such an influence on other exchange rates? Our view is that D2000-2 and its competitor market, EBS, move very tightly together due to the effects of cross market arbitrage. As such, EBS and D2000-2 bid/offer quotes are essentially identical, although EBS is somewhat deeper. Due to this, and to the fact that trades on D2000-2 and EBS tend to be very small on average, an informed (or indeed an uninformed) trader will rationally split his flow across venues. This likely leads to strongly correlated flows on D2000-2 and EBS and thus allows D2000-2 flows to share the information content of those on EBS. While this has not been tested, to our knowledge, given our understanding of how these markets work, it is a plausible argument.

## 5. Forecasting analysis

The order flow models (1) and (2) estimated above used contemporaneous order flow to explain exchange rate changes. However, as argued by Frankel and Rose (1995, p. 1702) 'Fitting exchange rates to contemporary observable variables, in-sample, is one thing. Forecasting out of sample is quite another'. The forecast ability of exchange rate models is examined by Meese and Rogoff (1983a, 1983b) who study the predictive ability of various structural and time series models from 1 to 12 months and conclude that none of these models performed any better than a random walk model at short horizons (one month). We provide investigation of the forecasting performance of the order flow model for exchange rates, across different sampling frequencies using a variety of specifications. We first use the methodology proposed by Meese and Rogoff (1983a, 1983b), and then extend this to genuine out-of-sample forecast testing.

### 5.1 Meese–Rogoff forecast analysis

The Meese and Rogoff (1983a, 1993b) test is based on using data up until time $t$ to estimate the parameters of the relationship between price changes and order flow, and then using the estimated relationship to forecast the price change at $t+1$ based on observed order flow at $t+1$. The root mean squared error (RMSE) from the order flow (OF) model is then compared to the RMSE from a random walk (RW) model with drift. The Meese–Rogoff test is therefore not a genuine out-of-sample forecasting experiment since observed future order flow is used in the forecast construction.

We consider sampling frequency ranging from 5 min to 1 week and for each sampling frequency we evaluate one-step ahead forecasts.[11] The forecasting equation that is equivalent to the regression model (1) is given by

$$\Delta P(k)_{i,t+1} = \alpha(k)_{i,t} + \beta(k)_{i,t} F(k)_{i,t+1} + \varepsilon_{i,t+1}, \tag{3}$$

where $\Delta P(k)_{i,t+1}$ is a one-step ahead return (based on sampling frequency $k$). $\alpha(k)_{i,t}$ and $\beta(k)_{i,t}$ are the estimates of the regression model based on information up to time $t$. $F(k)_{i,t+1}$ is the order flow of the one-step ahead interval.

The benchmark forecasting model is a random walk with drift (RW) for the log price. Under this specification, the one-step ahead forecast for the price change is nothing more than the average exchange rate change from the beginning of the sample until time $t$.

$$\Delta P(k)_{i,t+1} = \mu(k)_{i,t} + \eta_{i,t+1}, \tag{4}$$

where $\mu(k)_{i,t}$ is the estimated drift based on sampling frequency $k$ using information up to time $t$ only and $\eta_{i,t+1}$ is a noise term. For both models and all rates we initiate the estimation using the first four months of data.

Table 4. Meese–Rogoff (1983) forecasting experiments: root mean squared errors (RMSE).

| Freq | EUR/USD | | | USD/JPY | | | EUR/GBP | | | GBP/USD | | |
|---|---|---|---|---|---|---|---|---|---|---|---|---|
| | OF | RW | t-stats | OF | RW | t-stats | OF | RW | t-stats | OF | RW | t-stats |
| 5 min | 0.05 | 0.06 | −6.23 | 0.07 | 0.08 | −0.52 | 0.05 | 0.05 | −4.38 | 0.03 | 0.04 | −4.28 |
| 15 min | 0.07 | 0.10 | −7.82 | 0.09 | 0.10 | −1.30 | 0.08 | 0.09 | −3.44 | 0.06 | 0.07 | −2.99 |
| 30 min | 0.10 | 0.13 | −7.84 | 0.11 | 0.13 | −1.72 | 0.12 | 0.13 | −2.16 | 0.08 | 0.09 | −2.32 |
| 1 h | 0.16 | 0.20 | −4.03 | 0.14 | 0.17 | −2.57 | 0.18 | 0.19 | −1.19 | 0.13 | 0.14 | −1.29 |
| 4 h | 0.33 | 0.42 | −2.50 | 0.32 | 0.37 | −0.94 | 0.36 | 0.37 | −0.25 | 0.27 | 0.27 | −0.04 |
| 6 h | 0.39 | 0.50 | −2.40 | 0.32 | 0.43 | −2.97 | 0.48 | 0.48 | −0.04 | 0.32 | 0.33 | −0.08 |
| 12 h | 0.54 | 0.66 | −2.07 | 0.40 | 0.58 | −2.63 | 0.67 | 0.66 | 0.07 | 0.46 | 0.47 | −0.16 |
| 1 week | 1.28 | 1.62 | −1.10 | 0.76 | 1.20 | −1.86 | 1.68 | 1.63 | 0.12 | 0.97 | 0.94 | 0.15 |

Notes: The first column gives the sampling interval. The columns under OF and RW give the RMSEs of the *1-step-ahead* return forecast for the order flow and random walk models (3) and (4). The t-statistic for forecast improvement of the order flow model over the random walk is as given in Diebold (2001, p. 293).

Our results are reported in Table 4. The columns headed OF and RW are the RMSEs generated by forecast models (3) and (4), respectively. The t-stats comparing forecast accuracy are those given in Diebold (2001, p. 293). The most striking feature of Table 4 is that the RMSEs generated by the order flow model are virtually all lower than those generated by the random walk model. Furthermore, for all exchange rates, this forecast improvement is significant at higher sampling frequencies, while the low-frequency order flow-based forecasts are largely significant for EUR/USD and USD/JPY. Thus, our order flow model outperforms the benchmark models considered by Meese and Rogoff (1983a, 1983b) and, even at the daily and weekly sampling frequency, very heavily traded exchange rates such as EUR/USD and USD/JPY can be predicted using order flow. Furthermore, since these results are generated only by using own order flow, the GBP results would probably improve considerably by using the other order flows as an explanatory variable.

## 5.2 Genuine forecasting

Since the Meese–Rogoff test is not based on an out-of-sample forecast, we extend the results above by moving to a true out-of-sample setting. In this case we only use order flow information available at the forecast date. Thus, we would expect these results to be less strong than those from the Meese–Rogoff test. We concentrate on one-step ahead forecasting for each of our sampling frequencies and exchange rates. Our order flow-based forecasts are derived from the following specification:

$$\Delta P(k)_{i,t+1} = \alpha(k)_{i,t} + \beta(k)_{i,t} F(k)_{i,t} + \varepsilon_{i,t+1}. \tag{5}$$

We compare the ability of specification (5) to forecast price changes with the forecast produced by the random walk model (4). Results are presented in Table 5 for the entire spectrum of sampling frequencies and exchange rates.

The results indicate that if there is any statistical significance in our somewhat naive linear specification then it is concentrated at the highest frequency, i.e. 5 min. For virtually all of the regressions considered here, the RMSE of the order flow forecast model is only marginally below that of the random walk forecast. Thus, the explanatory power of our genuine forecasting regressions is poor and there is little evidence that these simple linear specifications contain true

Table 5. Out-of-sample forecast experiments.

| Freq | (a) EUR/USD | | | | | (b) USD/JPY | | | | |
|------|------|------|------|------|---------|------|------|------|------|---------|
|      | $\hat{\beta}$ | $R^2$ | OF | RW | $t$-stats | $\hat{\beta}$ | $R^2$ | OF | RW | $t$-stats |
| 5 min | 0.03* | 0.002 | 0.06 | 0.06 | −0.02 | 0.09** | 0.000 | 0.09 | 0.09 | 0.00 |
| 15 min | −0.01*** | 0.000 | 0.10 | 0.10 | 0.00 | −0.01 | 0.000 | 0.09 | 0.09 | 0.00 |
| 30 min | −0.00 | 0.000 | 0.13 | 0.13 | 0.01 | −0.12* | 0.003 | 0.13 | 0.13 | 0.03 |
| 1 h | 0.01 | 0.001 | 0.20 | 0.20 | 0.00 | 0.02 | 0.000 | 0.17 | 0.17 | 0.00 |
| 4 h | 0.01 | 0.000 | 0.42 | 0.42 | 0.02 | 0.09 | 0.002 | 0.37 | 0.37 | 0.01 |
| 6 h | 0.00 | 0.000 | 0.50 | 0.50 | 0.02 | 0.03 | 0.000 | 0.43 | 0.43 | 0.04 |
| 12 h | −0.04 | 0.007 | 0.67 | 0.66 | 0.02 | 0.03 | 0.000 | 0.58 | 0.58 | 0.03 |
| 1 week | −0.10** | 0.041 | 1.62 | 1.62 | −0.01 | 0.12 | 0.011 | 1.22 | 1.20 | 0.10 |
|        | (c) EUR/GBP | | | | | (d) GBP/USD | | | | |
| 5 min | 0.05* | 0.004 | 0.05 | 0.05 | −0.04 | 0.02* | 0.001 | 0.04 | 0.04 | 0.00 |
| 15 min | −0.01 | 0.000 | 0.08 | 0.08 | 0.02 | −0.04 | 0.000 | 0.07 | 0.07 | 0.00 |
| 30 min | −0.00 | 0.000 | 0.13 | 0.13 | 0.02 | 0.00 | 0.000 | 0.09 | 0.09 | 0.01 |
| 1 h | −0.00 | 0.000 | 0.19 | 0.19 | 0.02 | 0.00 | 0.000 | 0.14 | 0.14 | 0.01 |
| 4 h | −0.07** | 0.011 | 0.38 | 0.37 | 0.04 | 0.04*** | 0.005 | 0.27 | 0.28 | 0.00 |
| 6 h | 0.01 | 0.000 | 0.48 | 0.48 | 0.03 | 0.01 | 0.001 | 0.33 | 0.33 | 0.02 |
| 12 h | −0.01 | 0.000 | 0.67 | 0.66 | 0.12 | 0.00 | 0.000 | 0.47 | 0.47 | 0.06 |
| 1 week | −0.01 | 0.001 | 1.69 | 1.63 | 0.14 | 0.04 | 0.006 | 1.00 | 0.94 | 0.37 |

Notes: The parameter estimates and inference represented above are obtained from the following model:

$$\Delta P(k)_{i,t+1} = \alpha(k)_{i,t} + \beta(k)_{i,t} F(k)_{i,t} + \varepsilon_{i,t+1},$$

where $\Delta P(k)_{i,t+1}$ is price change at sampling frequency $k$ for exchange rate $i$ at time $t + 1$ and $F(k)_{i,t}$ is order flow for the same exchange rate and sampling frequency at time $t$. The columns under OF and RW give the forecast RMSEs of the model above and a random walk model, respectively, and the $t$-statistic for the forecast improvement of the model above over the random walk is reported in the last column of each panel. The order flow is scaled up by a factor of $10^{-2}$.
*Significance at the 1% level (based on the Newey–West coefficient variance–covariance estimator).
**Significance at the 5% level (based on the Newey–West coefficient variance–covariance estimator).
***Significance at the 10% level (based on the Newey–West coefficient variance–covariance estimator).

forecasting power. Only at the highest frequencies is the relationship between order flow at $t$ and the one-period price change to $t + 1$ positive and significant.

## 5.3 Order flow forecasting

Finally, as in Sager and Taylor (2008), we investigate the predictability of order flow itself, and test whether flows can be forecasted with past information on flows themselves and price changes. If this was the case, then another route to forecasting exchange rate changes might exist. One could combine the strong contemporaneous relationship between price changes and order flows uncovered in Section 3 and an order flow forecast to construct a price forecast.

We consider the following forecasting model for flows:

$$F(k)_{i,t+1} = \alpha(k)_{i,t} + \sum_{j=1}^{J} \beta(k)_{j,i,t} \Delta P(k)_{i,t-j+1} + \sum_{m=1}^{M} \gamma(k)_{m,i,t} F(k)_{i,t-m+1} + \epsilon_{i,t+1}, \qquad (6)$$

i.e. for a given sampling frequency ($k$) and exchange rate ($i$) we regress flow at $t + 1$ on its own first $M$ lags and on $J$ lags of the price change. In the estimations we set both $M$ and $J$ at 2 after some experimentation with alternative lag lengths. The results are presented in Table 6.

Table 6. Forecasting order flow out-of-sample

| | $k$ | $\hat{\beta}_1$ | $\hat{\beta}_2$ | $\hat{\gamma}_1$ | $\hat{\gamma}_2$ | $R^2$ | OF | RW | $t$-stats |
|---|---|---|---|---|---|---|---|---|---|
| EUR/USD | 5 min | 3.15* | 0.22 | 0.13* | 0.01 | 0.020 | 8.45 | 8.49 | −0.10 |
| | 15 min | 2.53 | −4.65*** | 0.05* | 1.55 | 0.005 | 17.01 | 17.01 | 0.00 |
| | 30 min | 1.32 | −2.77 | 0.04*** | 0.72 | 0.002 | 25.97 | 25.95 | 0.01 |
| | 1 h | 4.93 | −3.66 | 0.04 | 5.44*** | 0.003 | 31.39 | 31.34 | 0.03 |
| | 4 h | 4.97 | 13.61 | 0.03 | −7.44 | 0.007 | 70.46 | 70.23 | 0.04 |
| | 6 h | 4.24 | 6.39 | 0.03 | 9.79 | 0.026 | 83.29 | 82.66 | 0.10 |
| | 12 h | 37.13** | 14.59 | 0.01 | −0.16 | 0.048 | 120.40 | 117.32 | 0.24 |
| | 1 week | −32.57 | 51.87 | 0.04 | −27.96 | 0.072 | 331.68 | 278.70 | 1.10 |
| USD/JPY | 5 min | 2.44* | 0.79* | 0.19* | 0.04* | 0.064 | 1.72 | 1.79 | −0.56 |
| | 15 min | 4.21* | 0.22 | 0.10* | 3.41*** | 0.040 | 3.59 | 3.63 | −0.09 |
| | 30 min | 5.25* | 1.29 | 0.03 | 9.20* | 0.032 | 5.96 | 6.03 | −0.09 |
| | 1 h | 5.86* | 0.99 | 0.09** | 0.88 | 0.039 | 8.35 | 8.55 | −0.25 |
| | 4 h | −1.08 | 2.44 | 0.09*** | 0.11 | 0.010 | 18.93 | 18.78 | 0.10 |
| | 6 h | 1.82 | −0.83 | 0.09 | 7.59 | 0.018 | 22.79 | 22.62 | 0.08 |
| | 12 h | 9.59 | 14.30** | −0.04 | −0.11 | 0.050 | 35.25 | 35.39 | −0.03 |
| | 1 week | −4.62 | −50.06** | 0.34 | 0.42*** | 0.161 | 126.06 | 108.08 | 0.71 |
| EUR/GBP | 5 min | −5.70* | −5.55* | 0.12* | 0.04* | 0.013 | 6.53 | 6.57 | −0.11 |
| | 15 min | −14.96* | −10.00* | 0.10* | 0.04** | 0.016 | 12.25 | 12.37 | −0.11 |
| | 30 min | −19.20* | −4.07 | 0.09* | −0.00 | 0.017 | 15.43 | 15.45 | −0.03 |
| | 1 h | −18.91* | −3.56 | 0.05*** | 0.04 | 0.018 | 24.62 | 24.95 | −0.19 |
| | 4 h | −3.39 | −10.91 | 0.09** | −0.04 | 0.017 | 53.35 | 53.09 | 0.06 |
| | 6 h | −8.26 | 3.94 | 0.02 | 0.06 | 0.008 | 68.27 | 67.30 | 0.16 |
| | 12 h | 21.92*** | 9.53 | 0.09 | 0.01 | 0.036 | 104.24 | 97.68 | 0.65 |
| | 1 week | −26.99 | 82.14** | 0.25** | −0.08 | 0.249 | 273.88 | 262.86 | 0.21 |
| GBP/USD | 5 min | −8.12* | −11.83* | 0.07* | 0.04* | 0.007 | 7.03 | 7.08 | −0.18 |
| | 15 min | −23.80* | −10.67* | 0.07* | 0.03** | 0.015 | 12.20 | 12.21 | 0.00 |
| | 30 min | −27.30* | −14.76* | 0.08* | 0.04*** | 0.021 | 17.77 | 18.07 | −0.29 |
| | 1 h | −31.37* | −16.52* | 0.06** | 0.09* | 0.034 | 23.59 | 23.82 | −0.18 |
| | 4 h | −14.35** | 7.23 | 0.13* | 0.03 | 0.021 | 49.42 | 49.46 | −0.01 |
| | 6 h | −10.36 | 24.78** | 0.06 | 0.04 | 0.022 | 67.76 | 67.43 | 0.06 |
| | 12 h | 18.99 | 4.51 | 0.09 | 0.05 | 0.027 | 90.09 | 88.26 | 0.23 |
| | 1 week | −13.88 | 41.59 | 0.09 | 0.05 | 0.044 | 271.59 | 244.34 | 0.80 |

Notes: The parameter estimates and inference represented above are obtained from the following model:

$$F(k)_{i,t+1} = \alpha(k)_{i,t} + \sum_{j=1}^{J} \beta(k)_{j,i,t} \Delta P(k)_{i,t-j+1} + \sum_{m=1}^{M} \gamma(k)_{m,i,t} F(k)_{i,t-m+1} + \varepsilon_{i,t+1},$$

where $\Delta P(k)_{i,t}$ is price change at sampling frequency $k$ for exchange rate $i$ at time $t$ and $F(k)_{i,t+1}$ is order flow for the same exchange rate and sampling frequency at time $t + 1$. The columns under OF and RW give the forecast RMSEs of model (5) and a random walk model, respectively, and the $t$-statistic for the forecast improvement of model (5) over the random walk is reported in the last column. The order flow is scaled up by a factor of $10^{-2}$.
*Significance at the 1% level (based on the Newey–West coefficient variance–covariance estimator).
**Significance at the 5% level (based on the Newey–West coefficient variance–covariance estimator).
***Significance at the 10% level (based on the Newey–West coefficient variance–covariance estimator).

The results indicate that the majority of the statistical significance in the forecasting regressions comes at very high frequencies. Even though there is evidence of high-frequency positive dependence in order flow, in all cases the RMSE from the random walk model and (6) are virtually identical.

For the GBP exchange rates there is also evidence of negative dependence of current flow on past returns. Thus, when prices have been rising in the recent past, order flows tend to become negative – a manifestation of contrarian or negative feedback trading. This causality is reversed for USD/JPY. In this case, there would seem to be evidence of aggressive momentum type trades.

## 6. Discussion

We have presented a number of results on the explanatory power, forecasting ability and multivariate implications of order flow for FX rates. We affirm previous results and demonstrate that order flow has strong explanatory power for exchange rate changes. Furthermore, our results indicate that these patterns persist across sampling frequencies. Indeed, for the major currencies there is no indication that the explanatory power drops off with aggregation. This suggests that the explanatory power of order flow can genuinely be considered of interest to those working in international macroeconomics. We thus confirm the evidence contained in Evans and Lyons (2002b), Payne (2003) and Berger et al. (2008) amongst others.

However, our results contain a very important difference to those in Evans and Lyons (2002b) and Berger et al. (2008). Our univariate regressions of price changes on order flow for GBP exchange rates perform very poorly at lower sampling frequencies (e.g. one day), with explanatory power close to zero. This appears to fly in the face of the preceding discussion – perhaps the USD/JPY and EUR/USD results are anomalous and order flow has no long run effect on exchange rates for the majority of currency pairs. While this is clearly a possibility, we feel that such a conclusion would be unwarranted. Indeed, our multi-flow regressions demonstrate that once one allows for aggressive buying and selling pressure in related markets, order flows have strong effects on all four of the exchange rates at all sampling frequencies. This is a key result. Order flow may carry information that not only affects exchange rate changes in its own market but also in other markets. Empirically, we see information instantly spilling over from market $A$ to prices in market $B$ via order flow. This analysis corroborates the findings of Evans and Lyons (2002a) and Lyons and Moore (2009).

It is interesting to note that the dominant flow variable in our data set is EUR/USD flow. Aggressive buying and selling pressure in this market has clear and persistent effects on both EUR/GBP and GBP/USD rates. This result is intuitive as EUR/USD is the most liquid and heavily traded currency pair in the world and, as such, one would expect any relevant information to hit it first due to its low transaction costs and massive participation. Thus those quoting in related pairs will very likely keep an eye on EUR/USD developments, including order flow, when setting their prices.

A final point to note regarding the inter-market flow analysis carried out in Section 4 is that we see prices for a given exchange rate move in the absence of trade in that exchange rate, as they are affected by flows occurring in *other markets*. One cannot explain away the importance of order flow in an inter-market context by simply asserting that aggressive buying or selling pressure is temporarily moving prices due to low market liquidity and that after such 'digestion effects' have run their course prices would revert – here there is nothing to digest aside from information conveyed by flows in other markets. This, in our view, only serves to reinforce evidence that order flows do carry information and also information that is relevant at macroeconomic sampling frequencies.

Our final area of analysis is the forecasting power of order flows for exchange rates. Here, we have three sets of results. First, the order flow model beats the same random walk benchmark that macroeconomic models of the 1970s and 1980s failed to dominate. This would seem to provide a strong argument in favour of a focus on the order flow approach to exchange rates. Indeed, in a recent paper, Chinn and Moore (2009) embed order flow in a monetary exchange rate model and use this hybrid to forecast monthly exchange rates. Their results indicate that the hybrid model outperforms the random walk and a simple macro model out-of-sample. The second is a true one-step ahead out-of-sample experiment. We show that order flow forecasts can only reduce RMSEs relative to random walks in this experiment at the highest sampling frequencies (i.e. 5 min). It should be noted that this result is weaker than that of Evans and Lyons (2005), who find consistent out-of-sample forecasting power from flows over horizons from 1 to 20 trading days, and also that of Rime, Sarno, and Sojli (2010) who show that order flow can forecast exchange rate returns one day ahead based on economic value criteria. Our return forecasting results do support the findings of Sager and Taylor (2008), however. Last of all, as also reported in Sager and Taylor (2008), order flow itself can be forecasted out-of-sample at high-frequencies using information on its own past and on lagged returns.

## 7.  Conclusion

We study the explanatory and forecasting power of FX order flow for exchange rate changes at sampling frequencies ranging from 5 min to one week using a 10 month span of data for EUR/USD, EUR/GBP, GBP/USD and USD/JPY. We demonstrate that order flow analysis has power both to explain and predict exchange rate changes at virtually all frequencies. Our key results are as follows:

1. The contemporaneous relationship between flows and changes in exchange rates is very strong at intra-day frequencies for all four rates.
2. At the daily and weekly level, there is still strong explanatory power of order flow for exchange rate changes for EUR/USD and USD/JPY. This is not the case for EUR/GBP and GBP/USD.
3. Price changes for EUR/GBP and GBP/USD are strongly affected by EUR/USD order flow. Taking these effects into account, overall flows have strong explanatory power for the GBP rates at all sampling frequencies.
4. An analysis of the forecasting power of order flows, using the technique of Meese and Rogoff (1983a, 1983b), demonstrates that exchange rate regressions based on order flows outperform a naive random walk benchmark across the majority of sampling frequencies for all exchange rates.
5. A true out-of-sample forecasting experiment, however, demonstrates that order flows do not provide very valuable exchange rate forecasts aside from at sampling frequencies below 1 h.
6. Order flow can be forecasted out-of-sample at high frequencies.

These results serve to emphasize the role played by order flow in foreign exchange, and possibly other markets. Order flows can be used to explain and forecast rates at very high frequencies as well as observation intervals relevant to international macroeconomics. The information content of order flow implies that simple symmetric information, rational expectations models of exchange rate determination are not consistent with the data. Further work on modelling exchange rates to take account of these effects as well as further empirical work to clarify the role of order flow in exchange rate determination can only help move exchange rate analysis forward in the coming decades.

## Acknowledgements

Thanks to Charles Goodhart, Richard Lyons, the editors, an anonymous referee and participants in the 2002 Venice Summer Institute for excellent comments. Thanks also to the Bank of England for providing the transactions data used in this study. All remaining errors are our own.

## Notes

1. See e.g. Clark (1973), Epps and Epps (1976), Tauchen and Pitts (1983) and Karpoff (1987).
2. Note that in defining order flow one must distinguish between buyer and seller initiated transactions. Of course every trade consummated in a market has both a buyer and a seller, but from the current perspective the important member of this pair is the aggressive trader, the individual actively wishing to transact at another agent's prices.
3. See also Hasbrouck (1991) and Madhavan and Smidt (1991) who study equity markets, and Cohen and Shin (2002) who study fixed income markets.
4. Similarly, Chordia, Roll, and Subrahmanyam (2001) show that daily changes in US equity market levels are strongly related to market wide order flow measures.
5. To compare the size of these markets, according to the Bank for International Settlements (2002) in April 2001 the EUR/USD represented 30% of all spot FX trading, the JPY/USD 21%, GBP/USD 7% and GBP/EUR 3%. The first three of these are the three largest currency pairs while GBP/EUR is only the eighth.
6. For a full description of the segments of the spot FX market and the data available from each see the excellent descriptions contained in Lyons (2001).
7. In this article we define the overnight period to be 18:00 to 06:00 the following day. It should be noted that this definition is only proper for traders in London and New York, but not for traders in Asian markets. It corresponds to the portion of the day when trade on D2000-2 is least intensive, even for USD/JPY.
8. We have experimented with denser time aggregation levels and the results do not alter the pattern we report in this article.
9. Since the normality of our return data is rejected by the Jarque-Bera test (not reported), we also experimented with a LAD estimator for these regressions, but the results were not qualitatively affected.
10. Note that our definition of the aggregation time interval is slightly different from that in Evans and Lyons (2002b). Whilst their 'daily' aggregation interval is defined as a period from 16:00 to 16:00 next day our definition is a period from 06:00 to 18:00 excluding overnight period. We also experimented with an interval definition that includes the overnight period and find results that do not differ qualitatively from those reported here.
11. We have performed multi-step forecast analysis but it added little new information to the results we present here. Results are available on request.

## References

Bank for International Settlements. 2002. *Foreign exchange markets turnover in April 2001*. Basel: BIS.

Berger, D., A. Chaboud, S. Chernenko, E. Howorka, and J. Wright. 2008. Order flow and exchange rate dynamics in electronic brokerage system data. *Journal of International Economics* 75, no. 1: 93–109.

Campbell, J., and R. Shiller. 1988. The dividend–price ratio and expectations of future dividends and discount factors. *Review of Financial Studies* 1, no. 3: 195–228.

Chinn, M.D., and M.J. Moore. 2009. Private information and a macro model of exchange rates: Evidence from a novel data set. NBER working paper 10434.

Chordia, T., R. Roll, and A. Subrahmanyam. 2001. Order imbalance, liquidity, and market returns. *Journal of Financial Economics* 65, no. 1: 111–30.

Clark, P. 1973. A subordinated stochastic process model with finite variance for speculative prices. *Econometrica* 41, no. 1: 135–55.

Cohen, B.H., and H.S. Shin. 2002. Positive feedback trading under stress: Evidence from the US treasury securities market. Working paper, Bank for International Settlements and the London School of Economics. www.bis.org/cgfs/cgfsconf2002.htm.

Diebold, F. 2001. *Elements of Forecasting*. 2nd ed. Cincinnati, OH: South-Western.

Epps, T., and M. Epps. 1976. The stochastic dependence of security price changes and transaction volumes: Implications for the mixture-of-distributions hypothesis. *Econometrica* 44, no. 2: 305–21.

Evans, M.D. 2002. FX trading and exchange rate dynamics. *Journal of Finance* 57, no. 6: 2405–47.

Evans, M.D., and R.K. Lyons. 2002a. Informational integration and FX trading. *Journal of International Money and Finance* 21, no. 6: 807–31.

Evans, M.D., and R.K. Lyons. 2002b. Order flow and exchange rate dynamics. *Journal of Political Economy* 110, no. 1: 170–80.

Evans, M., and R. Lyons. 2005. Meese–Rogoff redux: Micro-based exchange-rate forecasting. *American Economic Review, Papers and Proceedings* 95, no. 2: 405–14.

Frankel, J., and A. Rose. 1995. Empirical research on nominal exchange rates. In *Handbook of International Economics*, ed. G. Grossman, and K. Rogoff, 1689–729. Amsterdam, The Netherlands: Elsevier Science.

Froot, K., and T. Ramadorai. 2005. Currency returns, intrinsic value and institutional-investor flows. *Journal of Finance* 60, no. 3: 1535–66.

Glosten, L., and P. Milgrom. 1985. Bid, ask and transaction prices in a specialist market with heterogeneously informed traders. *Journal of Financial Economics* 14, no. 1: 71–100.

Hasbrouck, J. 1991. Measuring the information content of stock trades. *Journal of Finance* 46, no. 1: 179–206.

Karpoff, J. 1987. The relation between price changes and trading volume: a survey. *Journal of Financial and Quantitative Analysis* 22, no. 1: 109–26.

Love, R., and R. Payne. 2008. Macroeconomic news, order flows and exchange rates. *Journal of Financial and Quantitative Analysis* 43, no. 2: 467–88.

Lyons, R. 1995. Tests of microstructural hypotheses in the foreign exchange market. *Journal of Financial Economics* 39, nos. 2–3: 321–51.

Lyons, R. 2001. *The Microstructure Approach to Exchange Rates*. Boston, MA: MIT Press.

Lyons, R., and M. Moore. 2009. An information approach to international currencies. *Journal of International Economics* 79, no. 2: 211–21.

Madhavan, A., and S. Smidt. 1991. A Bayesian model of intraday specialist pricing. *Journal of Financial Economics* 30, no. 1: 99–134.

Meese, R., and K. Rogoff. 1983a. Empirical exchange rate models of the seventies. *Journal of International Economics* 14, nos. 1–2: 3–24.

Meese, R., and K. Rogoff. 1983b. The out-of-sample failure of empirical exchange rate models. In *Exchange Rate and International Macroeconomics*, Vol. 14. ed. J. Frenkel, 67–105. Chicago, IL.: University of Chicago Press.

Payne, R. 2003. Informed trade in spot foreign exchange markets: An empirical investigation. *Journal of International Economics* 61, no. 2: 307–29.

Rime, D., L. Sarno, and E. Sojli. 2010. Exchange rate forecasting, order flow and macroeconomic information. *Journal of International Economics* 80, no. 1: 72–88.

Sager, M., and M. Taylor. 2008. Commercially available order flow data and exchange rate movements: caveat emptor. *Journal of Money, Credit and Banking* 40, no. 4: 583–625.

Tauchen, G., and M. Pitts. 1983. The price variability–volume relationship on speculative markets. *Econometrica* 51, no. 2: 485–505.

# Permanent trading impacts and bond yields

Alfonso Dufour[a] and Minh Nguyen[b]

[a]ICMA Centre, Henley Business School, University of Reading, Whiteknights, Reading, UK; [b]Bradford University School of Management, Bradford, West Yorkshire, UK

We analyse four years of transaction data for euro-area sovereign bonds traded on the MTS electronic platforms. In order to measure the informational content of trading activity, we estimate the permanent price response to trades. We not only find strong evidence of information asymmetry in sovereign bond markets, but also show the relevance of information asymmetry in explaining the cross-sectional variations of bond yields across a wide range of bond maturities and countries. Our results confirm that trades of more recently issued bonds and longer maturity bonds have a greater permanent effect on prices. We compare the price impact of trades for bonds across different maturity categories and find that trades of French and German bonds have the highest long-term price impact in the short maturity class, whereas trades of German bonds have the highest permanent price impact in the long maturity class. More importantly, we study the cross-section of bond yields and find that after controlling for conventional factors, investors demand higher yields for bonds with larger permanent trading impact. Interestingly, when investors face increased market uncertainty, they require even higher compensation for information asymmetry.

## 1. Introduction

Recent advances in financial economics have emphasized that market players are asymmetrically informed about asset values and that financial market transactions may convey private information about fundamental values. Moreover, the level of information asymmetry varies across securities (Hasbrouck 1991a, 1991b) and with market conditions (Dufour and Engle 2000). Although most empirical studies examine equity markets, there is a growing consensus on the relevance of asymmetric information in other markets as well. For instance, considering the origin of the 2007 subprime-mortgage market crisis, Calomiris (2009) claims that asymmetric information has crucially affected credit spreads. More importantly for our study, information asymmetry seems to be relevant even when market participants may fully agree on the future notional cash flows of a security, such as in the Treasury market (Brandt and Kavajecz 2004; Pasquariello and Vega 2007).

In this article, we evaluate the empirical relevance of information asymmetry in the euro-area sovereign bond markets. In particular, we examine the significance of information asymmetry across a wide range of bond maturities and countries, assess the impact of information asymmetry on bond yields and study how this impact changes during times of higher market uncertainty. Our focus is on Treasury securities not only due to their traditional role in the investment universe but also due to their use in pricing and hedging other financial instruments.[1]

Empirical research provides evidence consistent with at least two explanations for the existence of asymmetric information in the Treasury markets. The first conjecture is based on the concept of *heterogeneous private information*, namely investors have differential abilities to interpret past economic data or to understand the current state of economy (Balduzzi, Elton and Green 2001; Brandt and Kavajecz 2004; Green 2004). It seems reasonable to assume that sophisticated investors such as hedge funds or proprietary trading desks at investment banks have more sophisticated and powerful models to estimate the effects of changes in economic fundamentals onto the yield curve than a typical investor. The second conjecture assumes that information asymmetry arises because a subset of market participants, such as large banks, privately observe their clients' net order flow and use this information to forecast future prices. This argument closely follows the framework described by Cao, Evans and Lyons (2006) for the foreign exchange market. Peiers (1997) provides evidence that Deutsche Bank is the price leader in the markets for the deutsche mark/US dollar exchange rate prior to the German central bank interventions. Ito, Lyons, and Melvin (1998) show that Japanese banks are perceived as informed traders in the Yen currency markets. In particular, dealers in the foreign exchange markets are convinced that players with large customer bases obtain privileged information about their customers' orders which gives them a competitive advantage (Cheung and Wong 2000).

Market participants are ultimately interested in understanding whether and how information asymmetry affects security prices and returns. Financial theory suggests that risk-sharing limitations may lead to the emergence of asymmetric information risk premia (Wang 1993; O'Hara 2003; Garleanu and Pedersen 2004). On average, uninformed traders lose when trading in markets characterized by the presence of traders with superior information. O'Hara (2003) argues that this information disadvantage cannot be fully diversified away by holding the market portfolio. Consequently, cross-sectional security return differentials arise because uninformed traders require additional compensation for holding securities subject to greater informational asymmetry.

Our analysis is similar to the study by Li et al. (2009), which shows that asymmetric information helps explain the variations in returns across US government bonds. We consider whether the same results hold in the context of the euro-zone Treasury markets. Compared with their US counterpart, the European Treasury markets remain much more heterogeneous in terms of the credit worthiness of the issuers, the maturity spectrum, the issuance amount and the trading mechanism. The data for our empirical analysis are provided by the MTS, which executes a significant share of the wholesale sovereign bond transactions in Europe on its electronic trading platforms.[2] Dealers operating on the MTS markets are required to provide two-sided quotes for a minimum size, a maximum spread and a minimum number of hours during the trading day. Details of quotes and executed trades are recorded and transmitted in real time to the rest of the market or to information providers such as Bloomberg or Reuters. Given the specific institutional features characterizing the euro-zone bond markets, we are interested in investigating whether information asymmetry remains relevant in a transparent electronic market with explicit market making obligations. Since the same monetary policies and interest rate decisions from the European Central Bank (ECB) directly affect all the euro-zone markets, privately informed traders enjoy a greater opportunity set to exploit their information advantages. We study whether information from bond trading activity is eventually incorporated into prices and investigate which sovereign bond market shows greater informational asymmetry.

We employ the methodology developed by Hasbrouck (1991a) to identify and measure the informational impact of order flow on prices. Clearly, the impact of trades on prices is affected by both liquidity and asymmetric information (see also Chordia, Roll and Subrahmanyam 2002).

To separate these liquidity and informational effects of bond trades, we assume that liquidity effects are transient, whereas informational effects are permanent. Hence, we estimate informational effects using the long-term price response to the unexpected component of a bond trade. To facilitate comparability among securities, we construct the series of quotes and transactions sampled with a fixed time interval and measure the persistent price impact over a sufficiently long period of time, which we assume to be 1 h. For the US Treasury market, Green (2004) estimates that it takes less than 15 min for the effect of trade innovations to be fully impounded into prices.

We begin our empirical investigation by estimating the level of asymmetric information in euro-area bond markets and then we study the variations in information asymmetry across bond maturities and across countries. We find that Treasury bond transactions induce permanent price changes. Hence, our evidence is consistent with an informational role of Treasury market trades. When considering bonds within the same maturity group, we find that trades for the most recently issued bonds have larger permanent price effects. Consistent with Admati and Pfleiderer (1988), informed traders facing parallel markets would trade in the most liquid markets, i.e. the on-the-run segment, to disguise their trading and to reduce their execution costs. While trades for both French and German bonds generate the largest permanent changes for the short maturity bond category, the impact of German bond trades clearly dominates in the long maturity bond category. Our findings indicate significant cross-sectional differences among euro-area countries in the information content of bond transactions and therefore in the level of information asymmetry.

Although the above results are obtained after controlling for the average trade size, we recognize that other factors may affect the cross-sectional comparison of permanent trade impacts. Therefore, we propose a cross-sectional model that controls also for the behaviour of the term structure of interest rates, credit quality and microstructure features such as liquidity, tick size and number of market participants. Our analysis strongly supports the conjecture that investors demand compensation for information asymmetry. Bond yields are significantly and positively related to permanent trading impacts after controlling for conventional yield determinants such as the behaviours of the term structure of interest rates, credit quality and liquidity. In addition, this relation between yields and permanent trading impacts varies over time and becomes more pronounced during periods of elevated market uncertainty. Our findings suggest that when volatility in either the equity or bond market increases, investors become significantly more sensitive to adverse selection risk and require much higher returns for holding bonds with higher permanent trading impact.

The remainder of this paper is organized as follows. Section 2 describes the data used for the analysis, while Section 3 discusses the empirical methodology. Section 4 presents the empirical results, and Section 5 provides some conclusions.

## 2. Data

We use transaction data from the MTS Time Series database. MTS is a major wholesale electronic market for trading fixed-income securities in Europe. Details about the data and the institutional characteristics of the MTS markets can be found in Dufour and Skinner (2004) and Dufour and Nguyen (2008).[3] Our sample covers the period from the first available date in the dataset 1 April 2003 to 28 September 2007. We focus on 10 euro-area sovereign bond markets, including Austria, Belgium, Finland, France, Germany, Greece, Italy, the Netherlands, Portugal and Spain. We only select bonds issued by central governments in the euro currency. The bonds must be fixed-rate coupon bonds or zero-coupon bonds with at least 6 months and less than 30 years of remaining time to maturity.[4] We exclude from our sample quasi-government bonds, bonds with special fixed-income features such as floating rate coupons, coupon-stripped, inflation- or index-linked bonds, securities traded prior to issue and when-issued securities. There are up to 375 sovereign bonds in the final sample.

Our data include details of quotes and transactions which are electronically recorded with time stamps precise to the millisecond. For each transaction, we have information on the price, the quantity traded as well as whether the trade was initiated by a buyer or a seller. For each quote revision, our data contain the best three levels of bid and ask prices with their associated quantities. In this study, we focus on the top bid and ask quotes and keep only those posted within the MTS official trading hours (8:15 am–5:30 pm Central European Time).

The MTS dataset also contains daily summary measures of trading activity for bonds traded on the MTS platforms. These measures include the modified duration, the daily average spread and the daily trading volume. In addition, the data provide daily updates on the number of traders enabled to trade a particular bond through a certain platform and on the number of market makers with obligations to post bid and ask quotes on that same platform. Finally, the MTS Time Series database provides the daily yield midpoint computed using the most recent valid quote before 5:00 pm Central European Time and details about the characteristics of the various bonds including coupon rates and tick sizes.

We supplement the MTS data with credit rating data from Markit.[5] The ratings provide an independent assessment of the credit worthiness of the central governments to repay the interest plus the principal. Our bonds are rated by at least one of the rating agencies including Standard & Poor's, Moody's and Fitch. If a bond receives multiple ratings, we keep the lowest rating to be conservative. We have the monthly time series of ratings for each bond in the sample.

Table 1 presents the descriptive statistics of our data. Our bonds can be classified into three credit rating categories: AAA, AA and A. These sovereign ratings remain stable over the whole sample period with two exceptions: Spain was upgraded from AA to AAA in January 2005, while Italy

Table 1. Descriptive statistics.

| Country | Rating | Daily observations | No. of bonds | No. of trades | Total volume | Average trade size | Average duration |
|---|---|---|---|---|---|---|---|
| Austria | AAA | 27,099 | 18 | 21,569 | 188,766 | 8.75 | 5.74 |
| Belgium | AA | 32,778 | 28 | 69,649 | 572,156 | 8.21 | 5.69 |
| Finland | AAA | 14,400 | 9 | 26,995 | 255,433 | 9.46 | 4.26 |
| France | AAA | 66,330 | 60 | 80,138 | 612,652 | 7.64 | 5.37 |
| Germany | AAA | 70,237 | 83 | 88,836 | 600,977 | 6.77 | 4.73 |
| Greece | A | 35,589 | 31 | 77,069 | 581,360 | 7.54 | 5.09 |
| Italy | AA | 68,595 | 68 | 805,902 | 4,474,865 | 5.55 | 5.84 |
| The Netherlands | AAA | 27,744 | 25 | 26,635 | 238,340 | 8.95 | 4.58 |
| Portugal | AA | 34,206 | 19 | 73,795 | 640,548 | 8.68 | 5.09 |
| Spain | AA | 42,716 | 34 | 64,940 | 570,622 | 8.79 | 5.85 |

Note: We consider fixed-rate and zero-coupon bonds issued by 10 euro-area central governments and traded on the MTS markets from 1 April 2003 to 28 September 2007. Rating is the sovereign rating in April 2003. The daily observations are the total number of daily observations contained in our sample for each sovereign bond market. The number of trades is the total number of transactions taking place within MTS trading hours (8:15 am–5:30 pm CET). Total volume is the cumulative transaction quantity measured in million euros. Trade size is the average quantity per transaction in million euros. Duration is the weighted maturity (in years) of bond discounted cash flows.

was downgraded from AA to A in November 2006. Germany accounts for the largest number of bonds in the sample and the highest number of daily observations. However, Italian bonds record the highest number of transactions and account for the majority of the trading volume on the MTS markets. This pattern arises because most of the trading activity for Italian sovereign bonds concentrates on the MTS markets, while transactions of bonds of other countries are more dispersed and fragmented. The average trade size ranges from 5.55 million euro for the Italian bonds to 9.46 million euro for the Finnish bonds. Italy and Spain tend to have longer maturity bonds, while Finland has shorter maturity bonds.

## 3. Empirical methodology

As a measure of asymmetric information, we focus on the permanent trading impact or the persistent price response to an unexpected transaction. Obviously, we need to separate the informational effect of trading activity from the temporary liquidity effect. First, we identify and measure the permanent price effect. Secondly, we compute a number of liquidity measures which are used to control for the microstructure effects in the cross-sectional analysis. Finally, we consider the Nelson-Siegel parametric model to account for the term structure of interest rates.

### 3.1 Permanent trading impacts

Our method closely parallels the framework introduced by Hasbrouck (1991a) to capture trade informativeness. In the market microstructure literature, transactions are important because they convey information about security fundamentals that markets need to aggregate. Hence, the arrival of a trade induces dealers to revise their beliefs on fundamental values, causes their inventory to depart from their desired inventory levels and forces them to adjust prices accordingly. Because the inventory effects are inherently transient, Hasbrouck (1991a) suggests that the information content of a trade should be measured by its long-term, permanent impact on prices.

Let $q_t$ denote the midpoint of the prevailing bid and ask quotes posted by a dealer who stands ready to buy from and sell to other market participants and $t$ is the sampling time indicator. Let $x_t$ denote the net aggregate buy and sell volume for all the trades executed between times $t-1$ and $t$. Thus, the quote return $r_t = \ln(q_t) - \ln(q_{t-1})$ reflects the dealer's response to the net order flow $x_t$. We analyse the dynamics of the quote changes and the net order flows using a vector autoregressive (VAR) model described as:

$$r_t = \sum_{j=1}^{m} a_j r_{t-j} + b_0 x_t + \sum_{i=1}^{m} b_i x_{t-i} + v_{1t}, \tag{1}$$

$$x_t = \sum_{j=1}^{m} c_j r_{t-j} + \sum_{i=1}^{m} d_i x_{t-i} + v_{2t}, \tag{2}$$

where $v_{1t}$ is the quote change innovation, $m$ the order of lags in the autoregression and $a$'s, $b$'s, $c$'s and $d$'s are the coefficients. In this specification, the disturbance $v_{2t}$ is the unexpected component of the order flow or the trade innovation. The dynamics of the order flow can be predicted using Equation (2) above; hence, any private information conveyed by the trades must be captured by $v_{2t}$. The coefficient $b_0$ measures the immediate price response to the trade. Several researchers use this coefficient to estimate the information effects of the transactions (e.g. Brennan and Subrahmanyam 1996; Brandt and Kavajecz 2004). As explained in Chordia, Roll and Subrahmanyam (2002), this coefficient cannot be a good proxy for asymmetric information because it is potentially influenced by both permanent and transitory effects of transactions. Hasbrouck (1991a) suggests measuring asymmetric information by calculating the cumulative impulse response to a shock to the order flow equation. This can be easily computed using the vector moving average representation:

$$\begin{bmatrix} r_t \\ x_t \end{bmatrix} = \begin{bmatrix} \alpha(L)\beta(L) \\ \gamma(L)\delta(L) \end{bmatrix} \begin{bmatrix} v_{1t} \\ v_{2t} \end{bmatrix}, \tag{3}$$

where $L$ is the lag operator. The impact of the unexpected component of a trade on quotes after $k$ periods, $r_{t+k}^x$, is obtained by taking the sum of the coefficients of the impulse response function:

$$r_{t+k}^x = \sum_{i=0}^{k} \beta_i v_{2t}. \tag{4}$$

In the previous literature, the time indicator $t$ is often an event counter, i.e. $t$ is incremented whenever a trade occurs or a quote is revised. However, since trading intensity and the frequency of quote updates typically differ across securities, this indicator becomes less useful when we consider a cross-sectional analysis. To facilitate comparability across securities, Hasbrouck (2007) suggests that the VAR should be estimated in calendar time, i.e. $t$ denotes a fixed time interval. In this study, we choose a sampling interval of 10 s. This choice of sampling time interval balances the need for frequent quote updates in order to carefully track price dynamics and the need of reducing the transitory microstructure effects. For every 10 s interval of the trading day, we save the prevailing quotes and the aggregate order flow and hence obtain time series of quotes and trades. This is repeated for each bond in our sample. We apply VAR models to the time series of quote changes and trades and compute the persistent impact of an average trade shock for each bond over an hour horizon. Our choice of $k$ is consistent with Green (2004) who shows that it takes less than 15 min in the US Treasury markets for new trade-related information to be incorporated into prices. Therefore, by allowing a sufficiently large $k$, we ensure that the cumulative price change fully reflects the revision in the efficient prices caused by the trade innovation.

Bonds have different average trade sizes, and in order to be able to compare estimated permanent trading impacts across bonds, we need to control for these differences in average trade size. Consequently, we scale the signed trade quantity $x_t$ by the average trade size over the estimation window. The VAR estimation also requires the specification of an appropriate number of lags $m$. If the sampling time is small, allowing for lagged effects over even a reasonably short span of clock time leads to an extremely large number of coefficients to be estimated. We follow Hasbrouck (2003) and use polynomial distributed lags to reduce the number of parameters in the VAR.

We estimate the VAR for each bond over a 6-month period. This choice of the estimation window is comparable to the one that Hasbrouck (1991a) uses to analyse NYSE stocks and Li et al. (2009) employ to examine US Treasury securities. To obtain stable estimates, we exclude bonds that have fewer than 30 days with at least one trade over the estimation window. We discard overnight price changes to avoid price contaminations due to overnight news arrival. Due to the complexity of the VAR estimation output, it is easier to study the dynamics of quote changes and order flow by considering the cumulative impulse response functions.

Figure 1 illustrates the price response to a trade innovation for the most recently issued 10-year bonds from Germany, France, Italy and Spain available in April 2003. The impulse response functions are constructed by assuming that at $t = 0$, the system for each bond is in equilibrium

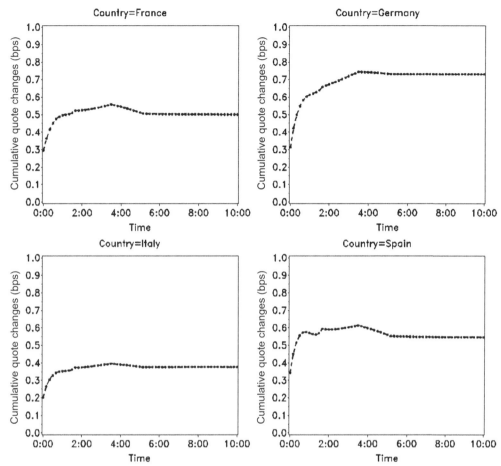

Figure 1. Permanent trading impacts.
Note: This figure exhibits the cumulative midquote price changes in calendar time (minutes: seconds) of the German, French, Italian and Spanish sovereign bonds after an initial unexpected purchase order with an average trade size. Hasbrouck's (1991a) VAR is estimated in calendar time for the most recently issued 10-year bonds over the period from 1 April 2003 to 30 September 2003.

until it is shocked by an unexpected buy order with an average trade size. We track how this shock propagates and compute the cumulative quote change at every subsequent time interval. In general, we observe that quote revisions reach a permanent level within 6 min. More importantly, these persistent levels are greater than zero and differ across securities. For instance, an unexpected buy order leads to a cumulative quote change of 0.7 basis points for the German bond, but for the Italian bond, the cumulative quote change is merely 0.35 basis points. Trades for bonds of different countries have different impacts on prices and hence are differently informative.

## 3.2 Measures of liquidity

For the cross-sectional analysis, we need to further control for non-information components of trading activity by computing measures of liquidity. The most popular liquidity proxy is the bid-ask spread which measures the round-trip cost of executing small trades. Amihud and Mendelson (1991) suggest that the bid-ask spread, the sum of buying cost and selling discount for immediate execution, is the natural measure of transaction costs. Fleming (2001) finds that the bid–ask spread is a good liquidity measure in the Treasury markets because its variations consistently capture the changes in market liquidity.

We use the intraday quote data to compute the bid-ask spread for each bond on a daily basis. In particular, we compute the difference between ask and bid quotes, divide it by the spread midpoint and take the average over all best quote revisions for day $d$. However, rather than treating quote updates equally, we weight each spread by the time it remains valid in order to reduce the effect of extreme intraday quotes which may last very briefly, especially at the opening and at the closing of a trading session. Our time-weighted proportional bid-ask spread is computed as:

$$\mathrm{Spr}_d = \sum_{i=1}^{N_d} \left( \frac{\mathrm{Ask}_i - \mathrm{Bid}_i}{(\mathrm{Ask}_i + \mathrm{Bid}_i)/2} \right) \frac{\mathrm{Duration}_{i+1}}{\mathrm{TotalTime}_d}, \tag{5}$$

where $\mathrm{Bid}_i$ and $\mathrm{Ask}_i$ are the $i$th bid and ask quote revisions; $\mathrm{Duration}_{i+1}$ is the time in seconds that the $i$th quote remains effective, specifically the time between the $i$th and the $(i+1)$th quote revisions; $\mathrm{TotalTime}_d$ is the time from the first quote after the MTS markets open at 8:15 am to the closing time at 5:30 pm for day $d$ and $N_d$ is the total number of revisions to the best quotes for day $d$.

As discussed above, the quoted spread provides a good proxy for the cost of executing small trades (Malz 2003). However, large institutional traders have to execute large size trades and hence are often more concerned with the depth rather than the bid-ask spread of the market. Clearly, this issue is particularly relevant for the inter-dealer Treasury market we study. Therefore, we consider the quoted depth as an additional liquidity measure. The quoted depth indicates the quantity that a market maker is willing to immediately buy from and sell to other market participants. We measure quoted depth as the average of the number of bonds available at the best bid and ask quotes.

More formally, let $\mathrm{BidSize}_i$ and $\mathrm{AskSize}_i$ denote the quantity of bonds available for trading at the best bid and ask quotes, respectively. Our time-weighted average market depth is computed daily for each bond from the intraday quote data as:

$$\mathrm{Dep}_d = \sum_{i=1}^{N_d} \left( \frac{\mathrm{AskSize}_i + \mathrm{BidSize}_i}{2} \right) \frac{\mathrm{Duration}_{i+1}}{\mathrm{TotalTime}_d}, \tag{6}$$

where $\mathrm{BidSize}_i$ and $\mathrm{AskSize}_i$ are the sizes available at the $i$th bid and ask quotes, and $\mathrm{Duration}_{i+1}$, $\mathrm{TotalTime}_d$ and $N_d$ are defined as for the time-weighted bid-ask spread, $\mathrm{Spr}_d$.

Table 2 presents the descriptive statistics for sovereign bonds in the euro area. Instead of pooling all sovereign markets across maturities, we present them separately based on the duration of bonds. In particular, first we classify bonds into 10 sovereign markets based on the nationality of the issuer. For each sovereign market, we divide the sample period into six-month sub-periods. At the beginning of each sub-period, we rank bonds by duration. Bonds in the bottom 30 percentile are classified as short maturity bonds, bonds in the top 30 percentile are classified as long maturity bonds and all remaining bonds are classified as medium maturity bonds. Henceforth, we will refer to this classification procedure as using the 30:40:30 breakpoints of the ranked durations.

This classification provides preliminary evidence consistent with asymmetric information varying with respect to both the nationality of the issuer and the segment of the yield curve to which the bonds belong. A proper test for this issue is presented in Section 4.1. As expected, German bonds tend to post the lowest yields, while Greek bonds tend to have the highest yields. There are

Table 2. Descriptive statistics by maturity.

| Country | Bond yield (%) | Permanent impact (bps) | Bid-ask spread (bps) | Depth (€ million) | Coupon rate (%) | Duration (year) | Participants | Tick size |
|---|---|---|---|---|---|---|---|---|
| Panel A: short maturity group | | | | | | | | |
| Austria | 3.04 | 0.26 | 2.33 | 33.06 | 5.05 | 2.06 | 56 | 0.010 |
| Belgium | 2.91 | 0.20 | 1.94 | 26.02 | 5.42 | 2.03 | 35 | 0.007 |
| Finland | 3.19 | 0.20 | 1.94 | 28.59 | 4.01 | 2.28 | 47 | 0.006 |
| France | 3.06 | 0.25 | 2.29 | 25.36 | 4.36 | 2.03 | 41 | 0.008 |
| Germany | 2.88 | 0.23 | 2.09 | 22.47 | 3.97 | 1.90 | 62 | 0.006 |
| Greece | 3.09 | 0.26 | 2.27 | 23.22 | 4.41 | 2.05 | 42 | 0.007 |
| Italy | 2.96 | 0.17 | 1.54 | 33.80 | 4.40 | 1.94 | 92 | 0.008 |
| The Netherlands | 3.04 | 0.23 | 2.07 | 23.28 | 3.81 | 2.03 | 44 | 0.005 |
| Portugal | 3.01 | 0.22 | 2.09 | 35.87 | 4.17 | 2.08 | 49 | 0.008 |
| Spain | 2.96 | 0.22 | 1.95 | 30.59 | 4.00 | 2.01 | 43 | 0.006 |
| Panel B: medium maturity group | | | | | | | | |
| Austria | 3.44 | 0.41 | 3.24 | 26.23 | 4.76 | 4.87 | 56 | 0.010 |
| Belgium | 3.47 | 0.32 | 2.86 | 26.99 | 5.04 | 4.87 | 36 | 0.010 |
| Finland | 3.35 | 0.38 | 2.69 | 31.52 | 4.59 | 4.77 | 46 | 0.010 |
| France | 3.47 | 0.42 | 3.22 | 23.02 | 4.45 | 4.83 | 41 | 0.010 |
| Germany | 3.43 | 0.50 | 2.86 | 25.95 | 4.31 | 4.74 | 62 | 0.010 |
| Greece | 3.60 | 0.45 | 3.22 | 24.42 | 5.03 | 4.96 | 42 | 0.010 |
| Italy | 3.53 | 0.36 | 2.31 | 36.10 | 4.44 | 4.65 | 90 | 0.010 |
| The Netherlands | 3.46 | 0.44 | 3.04 | 28.71 | 4.25 | 5.01 | 46 | 0.010 |
| Portugal | 3.56 | 0.30 | 3.02 | 33.98 | 4.67 | 5.01 | 47 | 0.010 |
| Spain | 3.55 | 0.37 | 2.83 | 28.66 | 4.73 | 5.00 | 42 | 0.009 |
| Panel C: long maturity group | | | | | | | | |
| Austria | 4.00 | 0.93 | 7.36 | 15.28 | 4.44 | 9.85 | 57 | 0.010 |
| Belgium | 4.04 | 0.67 | 6.07 | 19.64 | 4.93 | 9.96 | 39 | 0.010 |
| Finland | 3.93 | 0.58 | 3.28 | 29.11 | 4.64 | 7.91 | 46 | 0.010 |
| France | 4.00 | 1.04 | 6.58 | 15.72 | 4.57 | 10.13 | 44 | 0.010 |
| Germany | 3.95 | 1.32 | 6.24 | 20.13 | 4.58 | 10.30 | 64 | 0.010 |
| Greece | 4.21 | 0.80 | 5.49 | 16.95 | 5.30 | 9.37 | 42 | 0.010 |
| Italy | 4.31 | 0.88 | 6.33 | 16.24 | 5.17 | 11.10 | 91 | 0.010 |
| The Netherlands | 4.00 | 0.79 | 6.08 | 21.44 | 4.53 | 9.16 | 48 | 0.010 |
| Portugal | 4.05 | 0.65 | 5.65 | 22.84 | 4.32 | 9.40 | 49 | 0.010 |
| Spain | 4.00 | 0.84 | 6.00 | 19.24 | 4.97 | 10.13 | 42 | 0.010 |

Note: We present summary statistics for our sample sovereign bonds grouped by maturity and nationality of the issuer. We first classify bonds based on their nationality. We then split the sample into six-month sub-periods, and at the beginning of each sub-period, we assign bonds to three different maturity groups (short, medium and long) using the 30:40:30 breakpoints of the ranked duration. Permanent price impacts are estimated over each six-month sub-period using VAR models for quote changes and net order flows.

some exceptions with Finnish and Italian bonds showing the highest average yields in the short and long maturity groups, respectively. This can be explained by the fact that these bonds also have the highest average durations in their respective groups. Italian bonds tend to be more liquid with lower bid-ask spreads and higher depths, especially at the short and medium maturities. Austrian, French and Greek bonds register higher average permanent trading impacts for the short maturity group, while German bonds have higher permanent trading impacts in the medium and long maturity groups.

Table 3. Cross-sectional correlation coefficients.

| | Permanent impact | Bid-ask spread | Depth | Duration | Participants | Tick size |
|---|---|---|---|---|---|---|
| Permanent impact | 1 | | | | | |
| Bid-ask spread | 0.3 | 1 | | | | |
| Depth | −0.17 | −0.55 | 1 | | | |
| Duration | 0.33 | 0.88 | −0.53 | 1 | | |
| Participants | 0 | −0.01 | 0.04 | 0.04 | 1 | |
| Tick size | 0.14 | 0.28 | 0.23 | 0.42 | −0.02 | 1 |

Note: This table presents the cross-sectional correlation coefficients between the variables used in our asset pricing tests.

Table 3 illustrates the cross-sectional correlations of the permanent trading impacts and other bond characteristics. Permanent trading impacts are positively related to the bid–ask spread and negatively related to the market depth. In particular, liquidity strongly decreases with bond duration. The correlation coefficients of duration with the bid–ask spread and with the depth are 0.88 and −0.53, respectively. This indicates that longer maturity bonds tend be less liquid. In addition, duration is also positively related to permanent trading impacts and the tick size. The presence of significant correlations between duration and microstructure variables may lead to collinearity problems if duration and liquidity measures are used as explanatory variables in the same regression. This observation is relevant for the asset pricing analysis conducted in Section 4.2.

### 3.3 Nelson and Siegel's yield curve

We aim to control for the behaviour of the term structure of interest rates and hence bond duration in our cross-sectional analysis. Empirical papers (e.g. Dunne, Moore, and Portes 2007; Dufour and Nguyen 2008) indicate that no single sovereign market serves as a benchmark for all maturities in the euro areas. Consequently, we refrain from treating a specific country as a benchmark or analysing the term structure of interest rates for all sovereign countries. Instead, we consider the swap curve as the reference curve, a procedure which has become increasingly common in the recent literature (e.g. Blanco, Brennan and Marsh 2005; Houweling, Mentink and Vorst 2005; Beber, Brandt and Kavajecz 2009). It is argued that although swap rates inherently embed counterparty default risk, the swap curve has several advantages over the government bond yield curve, including the existence of a single swap curve in the euro area and the fact that swap rates are not subject to different tax treatments and repo specialness.

We obtain the euro fixed-leg swap rates from Bloomberg for 15 different constant maturities: 1, 2, 3, 4, 5, 6, 7, 8, 9, 10, 12, 15, 20, 25 and 30 years. To analyse the term structure of the swap rates, we follow Nelson and Siegel's (1987) parametric model that specifies the spot rates $z_{TTM}$ as:

$$ z_{TTM} = \beta_0 + (\beta_1 + \beta_2) \left[ 1 - \frac{1 - e^{-TTM/\tau}}{TTM/\tau} \right] - \beta_2\, e^{-TTM/\tau}, \tag{7} $$

where TTM is the term to maturity, and $\beta_i$ and $\tau$ are the parameters to be estimated. We estimate Nelson and Siegel's model on daily basis by minimizing the squared errors between the predicted and observed swap rates. We then calculate the swap spread defined as the difference between the sovereign bond yield and the corresponding spot rate by matching the duration of the bond with the estimated term structure of the swap rates.

## 4.  Empirical results

We first study the variations in asymmetric information across euro-area Treasury markets by studying the cross-sectional differences in the informational content of bond transactions. We then examine whether information asymmetry matters in explaining the variations of bond yields. We also consider the empirical relevance of credit quality, liquidity and information asymmetry during periods of abnormal market movements. We finally analyse the robustness of our results with respect to the errors-in-variables problems in our estimation.

### 4.1  *The information content of bond trades*

In traditional economic paradigms, transactions have no role in the determination of asset prices. Prices are assumed to fully reflect the economic fundamentals of the assets. The arrival of new information about the aggregate demand or supply leads to instantaneous changes in the prices at which market participants remain indifferent. However, if prices are not fully revealing, privately informed traders transact to exploit their informational advantage. Hence, transactions convey non-public information and cause prices to change. Because these trading impacts are also potentially influenced by transient liquidity effects, we consider the long-term price response to trades in order to capture the informational content of trading activity.

After estimating the level of informational asymmetry for each sample bond, we study the nature of asymmetric information in our sovereign bond markets and investigate whether our data is consistent with previous empirical findings. The previous literature indicates a close relationship between the information content of Treasury securities and their seasonedness or the time since they were first issued. When a new bond is issued, it is called the on-the-run bond, and all the bonds previously issued with the same original maturity become off-the-run bonds. The general consensus (e.g. Amihud and Mendelson 1991; Fleming 2001; Krishnamurthy 2002) is that old bonds tend be less liquid and require higher transaction costs than on-the-run bonds. In addition, lower liquidity is often associated with lack of trading activity and stale quotes. Admati and Pfleiderer (1988) explain this empirical evidence by conjecturing that informed traders facing parallel markets would trade in the more liquid markets to reduce their costs of trading. Consequently, trades of off-the-run bonds tend to be less informative than those of on-the-run bonds. Brandt and Kavajecz (2004) show that price discovery in the Treasury markets occurs in the on-the-run segment. Li et al. (2009) provide evidence that on-the-run bonds exhibit a higher probability of informed trading (PIN) than off-the-run bonds.

We split our sample into six-month windows, and, at the beginning of every window, we sort our sample bonds in terms of how recently they have been issued and form three distinct categories of seasonedness: on-the-run, just-off-the-run and off-the-run. This classification is performed for bonds belonging to various maturity buckets: 2 (1–2 years), 5 (2–5 years), 10 (5–10 years), 15 (10–15 years), 20 (15–20 years) and 30 (20–30 years). For each maturity bucket, the on-the-run group includes bonds that have been classified as the most recently issued bonds within the previous six-month window. Furthermore, just-off-the-run bonds have between six months and two years from the issue date, whereas off-the-run bonds have more than two years from the issue date. The VAR models are estimated over these six-month windows.

Table 4 (panel A) presents the average permanent trading impact for each seasonedness group within each maturity bucket. We observe that the on-the-run group for all maturity buckets tends to register higher trading impacts than the other groups. Figure 2 shows the cumulative distribution of the permanent trading impacts for each of the three seasonedness groups. The trading impacts

Table 4. Permanent trading impacts and seasonedness.

*Panel A: average permanent trading impact by maturity and seasonedness*

| Seasonedness | 2 years | 5 years | 10 years | 15 years | 20 years | 30 years |
|---|---|---|---|---|---|---|
| On-the-run | 0.25 | 0.38 | 0.75 | 0.80 | 1.26 | 1.43 |
| Just-off-the-run | 0.17 | 0.34 | 0.62 | 0.78 | 1.24 | 1.33 |
| Off-the-run | 0.23 | 0.32 | 0.54 | 0.71 | 0.85 | 1.34 |

*Panel B: tests on the cumulative distributions of permanent trading impacts*

| Null hypothesis | Kruskal-Wallis test | Wilcoxon test |
|---|---|---|
| On = just-off = off-the-run | 53.82 (0.001) | |
| On = just-off-the-run | | 2.63 (0.001) |
| On = off-the-run | | 7.20 (0.001) |

Note: We split the sample into six-month sub-periods. On the first day of every sub-period, we sort our sample bonds in terms of how recently they have been issued and form three distinct categories of seasonedness: on-the-run, just-off-the-run and off-the-run. This classification is performed for bonds belonging to various maturity buckets: 2 (1–2 years), 5 (2–5 years), 10 (5–10 years), 15 (10–15 years), 20 (15–20 years) and 30 (20–30 years). For each maturity bucket, the on-the-run group includes bonds that have been classified as the most recently issued bonds within the previous six-month window. Just-off-the-run bonds have between six months and two years from the issue date, whereas off-the-run bonds have more than two years from the issue date. We then examine the significance of the cross-sectional differences in the permanent trading impacts for these groups. The Kruskal-Wallis test examines the null hypothesis that the trading impacts of all of the bond groups are drawn from the same distribution. The Wilcoxon rank-sum test investigates the null hypothesis that the median difference in price impacts between the two sample groups is zero versus the alternative hypothesis that one group has higher price impacts. We report the test statistics and the $p$-values (in parentheses).

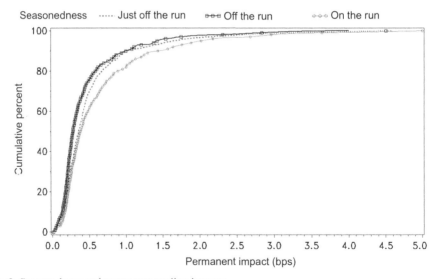

Figure 2. Seasonedness and permanent trading impacts.
Note: This figure presents the cumulative distribution functions of the permanent trading impacts for three seasonedness groups. The on-the-run group includes the bonds that have been classified as the most recently issued bonds within the past six months for each of the maturity buckets: 2 (1–2 year), 5 (2–5 year), 10 (5–10 year), 15 (10–15 year), 20 (15–20 year) and 30 (20–30 year). Furthermore, just-off-the-run bonds have between six months and two years from the issue date, whereas off-the-run bonds have more than two years from the issue date.

generally increase when moving from the off-the-run group to the just-off-the-run group and finally to the on-the-run group.

Similar to Li et al. (2009), we perform the Kruskal-Wallis test and the Wilcoxon rank-sum test to examine the significance of these cross-sectional differences in the permanent trading impacts. The Kruskal-Wallis test examines the null hypothesis that the trading impacts of all bond groups are drawn from the same distribution. The Wilcoxon rank-sum test investigates the null hypothesis that the difference between the median price impacts of two sample groups is zero versus the alternative hypothesis that one group has higher median price impact. Panel B of Table 4 presents the test statistics and the corresponding p-values. The Kruskal-Wallis test statistic suggests that the null hypothesis of identical distribution is strongly rejected. The Wilcoxon test statistics indicate that the on-the-run bonds have significantly higher trading impacts than the just-off-the-run bonds which in turn show significantly higher permanent trading impacts than the off-the-run bonds. These results show that trades for on-the-run bonds are more informative than trades for other bonds and are consistent with evidence provided by Brandt and Kavajecz (2004) and Li et al. (2009).

We then turn our attention to cross-country differences in the permanent trading impacts. Market participants observe that different euro-area countries contribute differently to the price discovery process of the various segments of the euro yield curve. In particular, the International Monetary Fund (IMF 2001) documents that French bonds at short maturities benefit from active French money markets, while the German market prevails at the longer maturities due to the presence of liquid German Bund futures markets. Dufour and Nguyen (2008) provide evidence for the price leadership of the French market in the short maturity bond category and the German market in the medium and long maturity bond categories.

To examine differences in sovereign bond informativeness, we use the same procedure as above and consider six-month sub-periods. At the beginning of every sub-period, first we sort all sample bonds by their durations and then classify them into three maturity groups (short, medium and long) using the usual 30:40:30 breakpoints of the ranked duration. For brevity, we focus on the sovereign bonds from Germany, France, Italy and Spain. The ECB (2004) suggests that these four markets in total account for more than 78% of the outstanding amount in the euro area.

Figure 3(a) illustrates the cumulative distributions of the permanent trading impacts for the short maturity group. While the French bonds fare closely to the German, they tend to exhibit higher trading impacts than the Italian and Spanish bonds. The Kruskal-Wallis test statistic in Panel A of Table 5 significantly rejects the null hypothesis that these countries share the same distribution of the permanent trading impacts. The pair-wise Wilcoxon test statistics show that although the French bonds do not register significantly higher trading impacts than the German bonds, their impacts are strongly larger than those of the Italian and marginally higher than those of the Spanish bonds.

Figure 3(b) exhibits the cumulative distributions of trading impacts for the medium maturity group. We notice that the German market tends to register higher trading impacts. Again, in Panel B of Table 5, the Kruskal-Wallis test statistic rejects the null hypothesis of identical distributions. However, pair-wise comparisons using the Wilcoxon test show that the impacts of German, French and Spanish bonds are not statistically different; whereas Italian bonds have significantly lower trading impacts.

The cross-country differences in permanent trading impacts are most clearly demonstrated in Figure 3(c). In the long maturity group, the trading impacts of the German bonds are clearly larger than those of other euro-area countries. In Panel C of Table 5, the Kruskal-Wallis test statistic also rejects the null hypothesis of identical distributions. The Wilcoxon test statistics

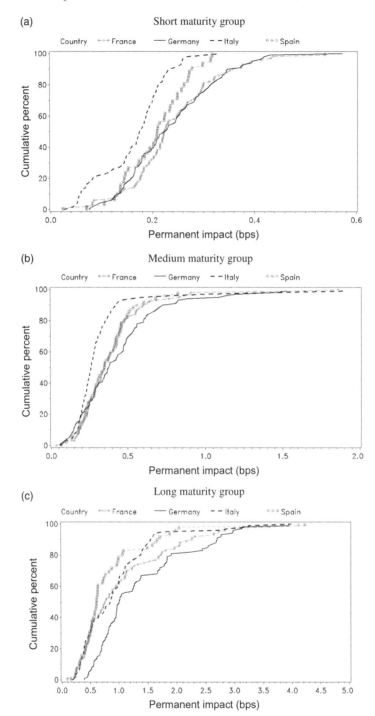

Figure 3. Cross-country differences in permanent trading impacts.
Note: This figure presents the cumulative distribution functions of the permanent trading impacts for the German, French, Italian and Spanish sovereign bonds. We sort these bonds every six months into three maturity groups (short, medium and long) using the 30:40:30 breakpoints of the ranked duration.

Table 5. Cross-country differences in permanent trading impacts.

| Null hypothesis | Kruskal-Wallis test | Wilcoxon test |
|---|---|---|
| *Panel A: short maturity group* | | |
| DE = FR = IT = ES | 51.043 (0.001) | |
| FR = DE | | 0.414 (0.329) |
| FR = IT | | 5.992 (0.001) |
| FR = ES | | 1.668 (0.047) |
| *Panel B: medium maturity group* | | |
| DE = FR = IT = ES | 21.788 (0.001) | |
| FR = DE | | 0.998 (0.160) |
| FR = IT | | 4.037 (0.001) |
| FR = ES | | 1.250 (0.105) |
| *Panel C: long maturity group* | | |
| DE = FR = IT = ES | 21.710 (0.001) | |
| FR = DE | | 2.870 (0.002) |
| FR = IT | | 3.750 (0.001) |
| FR = ES | | 4.568 (0.001) |

Note: We split the sample into six-month sub-periods. On the first day of every sub-period, we sort bonds into three maturity groups (short, medium and long) using the 30:40:30 breakpoints of the ranked duration. We focus on the sovereign bonds from Germany (DE), France (FR), Italy (IT) and Spain (ES) and investigate cross-country differences in the permanent trading impacts for each maturity group. The Kruskal–Wallis test and Wilcoxon rank-sum test are described in Table 4. We provide test statistics and $p$-values (in parentheses).

show that the German bonds have significantly higher trading impacts than the other sovereign bonds. Consistent with past research, these results suggest significant cross-sectional differences between euro-area countries in the informational content of bond transactions.

## 4.2 *Cross-sectional regressions*

Having established the presence of asymmetric information in the euro-area Treasury markets, we examine whether information asymmetry matters in explaining the cross-sectional differences in *expected* bond returns. Similar to Houweling, Mentink and Vorst (2005), we consider bond yields instead of returns because bond yields are a better proxy for the expected returns than *realized* returns. In the presence of asymmetric information, we predict that investors would require an extra compensation for asymmetric information risk. Consequently, bond yields will significantly increase with higher permanent trading impacts.

In our asset pricing tests, we control for other variables that potentially affect bond yields. Gebhardt, Hvidkjaer and Swaminathan (2005) suggest that bond duration and credit quality matter in explaining cross-sectional bond returns. However, because duration is strongly correlated with bond liquidity measures, rather than using duration as one of the explanatory variables, we consider the swap spread as the dependent variable to control for term structure effects and to avoid multicollinearity problems. Credit ratings are used as a proxy for credit quality and are included among the explanatory factors in the regression. In addition, we use the bid-ask spread and the market depth to capture the cross-sectional effects of market liquidity. We also control for tick size because larger tick sizes limit the prices that market makers can quote and, hence, may lead to higher transaction costs and lower market liquidity (for empirical evidence, see Goldstein and Kavajecz (2000) and Bessembinder (2002)). We use the bond coupon rate to account for the effects of different tax regimes, while the number of market participants serves as another control variable. We regress the swap spreads on various explanatory variables in cross-sectional regressions described as:

$$\text{Yield}_{it} - \text{Swap}_{it} = \gamma_{0t} + \gamma_{1t}\text{AA}_{it} + \gamma_{2t}\text{A}_{it} + \gamma_{3t}\text{IMP}_{it-1} + \gamma_{4t}\text{SPR}_{it} + \gamma_{5t}\text{DEP}_{it} + \gamma_{6t}\text{CPN}_{it}$$
$$+ \gamma_{7t}\text{TIC}_{it} + \gamma_{8t}\text{PART}_{it} + \eta_{it}, \tag{8}$$

where $\text{Yield}_{it} - \text{Swap}_{it}$ is the swap spread or the difference between the bond yield and the swap rate of bond $i$ at date $t$. Clearly, we are particularly interested in assessing the role played by the permanent trading impact $\text{IMP}_{t-1}$. To avoid possible endogeneity problems, we use the permanent trading impacts estimated over the previous 6-month window. Additionally, our regressors include the constant, two rating dummies $\text{AA}_{it}$ and $\text{A}_{it}$ (AA equals 1 if the bond has AA rating and 0 otherwise and A equals 1 if the bond is rated A and 0 otherwise), the bid–ask spread $\text{SPR}_{it}$, the market depth $\text{DEP}_{it}$, the number of participants authorized to trade a particular bond on MTS $\text{PART}_{it}$, the tick size of the bond $\text{TIC}_{it}$ and the coupon rate $\text{CPN}_{it}$. The $\gamma$'s are the coefficients, while $\eta_{it}$ is the error term.

Because the initial six-month window is dedicated to the estimation of the first permanent trading impacts, we perform the cross-sectional regressions on a daily basis over the period from 1 October 2003 to 28 September 2007. The time series of the regression estimates are used for the tests of statistical significance. We adopt the Newey-West procedure to correct for heteroscedasticity and auto-correlation in these estimates. Petersen (2009) shows that the Newey-West-adjusted standard errors perform better in asset pricing tests than those derived from ordinary least squares or the traditional Fama and MacBeth (1973) approach.

Table 6 reports the average coefficients and the Newey-West-adjusted $t$-statistics (in parentheses) obtained from the cross-sectional regressions. We initially split the sample into two

Table 6. Cross-sectional regressions.

| Variables | AAA bonds | AA–A bonds | All bonds |
|---|---|---|---|
| AA | | | 0.060 (40.88) |
| A | | 0.074 (49.02) | 0.143 (79.56) |
| Permanent impact | 0.004 (3.96) | 0.042 (7.38) | 0.003 (2.33) |
| Bid-ask spread | 0.006 (21.34) | 0.009 (11.35) | 0.008 (27.42) |
| Depth | −0.007 (−7.59) | −0.032 (−22.72) | −0.023 (−24.29) |
| Coupon rate | 0.006 (23.93) | 0.004 (15.88) | 0.005 (24.28) |
| Tick | 7.939 (14.74) | 20.528 (37.57) | 13.724 (26.29) |
| Participants ($\times 10$) | −0.00 (−1.30) | 0.008 (22.05) | 0.006 (21.59) |
| Adjusted $R^2$ | 0.501 | 0.639 | 0.629 |

Note: This table presents the average of the cross-sectional coefficients and the Newey-West-adjusted $t$-statistics (in parentheses) obtained from the cross-sectional regressions estimated over the period from 1 October 2003 to 28 September 2007. Our dependent variable is the swap spread or the difference between the daily closing sovereign bond yield and the corresponding swap rate estimated from the Nelson and Siegel term structure of the swap rates. The explanatory variables include the intercept, the permanent trading impact, the two rating dummies (AA equals 1 if the bond has AA rating and 0 otherwise, whereas A equals 1 if the bond is rated A and 0 otherwise), the bid–ask spread, the market depth, the daily number of participants for a particular bond, the tick size and the coupon rate. Permanent price impacts are estimated over 6-month sub-periods using VAR models for quote changes and net order flows. Lagged permanent price impacts are used in the cross-sectional regressions.

parts: one includes the AAA-rated bonds and the other includes the AA- and A-rated bonds. We then perform cross-sectional regressions on these two categories of bonds. The regression results are presented in columns 2 and 3, respectively. Next, we pool all the bonds together and show the regression results in column 4. Except for the coefficient of the market participants within the AAA category, all coefficients are significant at the 1% level. The two rating dummies AA and A are used to capture the effects of credit quality differences. In column 4, the coefficients of the credit rating dummies reflect the yield differences of the AA- and A-rated bonds relative to the AAA-rated bonds. The A dummy coefficient in column 3 indicates the yield spread between A- and AA-rated bonds. We find that bonds with higher credit quality require lower yields. On average, the AA-rated bonds register a spread of 6 basis points above the AAA bonds. The yield spread between A-rated and AAA-rated bonds averages 14.3 basis points.

Our tests confirm that liquidity affects bond prices. Bond yield spreads increase with the bid-ask spread and decrease with market depth. For instance, the coefficient of the spread in column 4 implies that a one basis point rise in the bid-ask spread will lead on average to a 0.8 basis point increase in yields, whereas one million euro increase in the tradable quantity results in a 2.3 basis points yield reduction. The coefficient of the market depth is larger and statistically more significant with the AA- and A-rated bonds than with the AAA-rated bonds, suggesting that market depth is more important with the lower-rated bonds. In addition, bond yields are also positively related to the bond tick size. This result indicates that higher tick size imposes higher transaction costs and consequently is associated with higher bond yields.

Surprisingly, bond yields are positively related to the number of market participants trading a particular bond. This relation is mainly relevant to the AA-A category. Therefore, a larger number of market participants is associated with higher bond yields, and hence it does not necessarily mean increased bond liquidity. Nevertheless, this result could simply reflect the Italian bond effect because Italian bonds have a consistently higher number of market participants (see Table 2 and Section 4.4). Additionally, bond yields are positively associated with the coupon rate. Since investors need to pay income taxes for coupon-bearing bonds, they require higher yields for higher coupon bonds.

Most important, we find that bonds with higher trading impacts require higher bond yields. The permanent trading impact variable has positive and significant estimated coefficients across all bond categories. These results are consistent with previous results in the equity market (Easley, Hvidkjaer and O'Hara 2002). The average adjusted $R^2$ values range from 50% for the AAA-rated bonds to 64% for the lower-rated bonds, and this indicates that our variables do well in capturing the cross-sectional variation of Treasury bond yields.

### 4.3 *Asymmetric information and high volatility periods*

After formalizing and estimating the cross-sectional relationship between asymmetric information and Treasury bond yield spreads, we examine how this relationship varies during periods of elevated market uncertainty. Our sample contains a number of extraordinary events often regarded in the financial press as 'flight-to-quality' and 'flight-to-liquidity' events. In particular, we consider the periods surrounding the Madrid bombing in March 2004, the London bombing in July 2005 and the beginning of the sub-prime mortgage crisis in August 2007. Our investigation focuses on the empirical relevance of the information asymmetry variable during these abnormal market movements.

We define the days with abnormal market uncertainty as those days when the implied volatility in the bond or equity markets is one standard deviation above the mean. The periods when this condition does not hold are simply considered as normal. First, we create two sub-samples containing the days with higher equity market volatility and higher bond market volatility, respectively. Then, we run the cross-sectional regressions (8) separately on each of these two sub-samples. We use the pair-wise Wilcoxon test to examine whether the average estimates obtained from the abnormal periods are significantly higher than those derived from the normal periods.

For the definition of high equity volatility periods, we use the volatility implied from equity index options. Specifically, we employ the vStoxx index.[6] This index provides market expectations of the near term volatility in the euro zone, which are embedded in the option prices of the Dow Jones Euro Stoxx 50 equity index. Several researchers have recognized that the equity index-implied volatility is a useful indicator for the level and the uncertainty of future volatility (e.g. Fleming 1998; Veronesi 1999; Blair, Poon and Taylor 2001; Coval and Shumway 2001). Connolly, Stivers and Sun (2005) show that this measure explains return co-movements between equity and bond markets.

For the definition of high bond market volatility periods, we follow Beber, Brandt and Kavajecz (2009) and consider the implied volatility obtained from the prices of swaptions, the one-month option contract on the one-year euro swap rate. From a theoretical viewpoint, volatility is positively related to the price of liquidity. Constantinides (1986) indicates that expected asset returns increase with volatility because higher volatility induces more frequent trading and leads to higher transaction costs. Vayanos (2004) shows that higher volatility amplifies the likelihood that fund managers fail to achieve a certain return target, become subject to fund withdrawals and, subsequently, need to incur higher transaction costs when liquidating assets.

Table 7 presents the regression estimates for each sub-sample. We also report the differences in the estimates between the abnormal and normal sample periods and the test statistics for their significance. While the signs of the coefficients for the high volatility periods remain the same as for the normal periods, the size of the coefficients differs significantly.

Sovereign bond yields are still negatively related to credit quality. Although AAA-rated bonds continue to register lower yields than those of the AA-rated and A-rated bonds, these yield differences are significantly narrowed when volatility increases. In addition, the cross-sectional differences in bond yields are more strongly related to liquidity. During periods of higher uncertainty, bonds with higher bid-ask spread or lower market depth require significantly higher yields. Consistent with Beber, Brandt and Kavajecz (2009), our results indicate that liquidity is more important than credit quality in explaining the behaviour of asset prices during 'flight-to-quality' and 'flight-to-liquidity' events.

We find that information asymmetry has greater impact on cross-sectional bond yields during periods of extreme market uncertainty. For instance, the coefficient of the permanent trading impact variable is four times larger when equity market volatility is abnormally high than during normal periods. Interestingly, when we consider periods with different levels of interest rate volatility, the coefficient of the permanent trading impact variable is only significant for the abnormal volatility period. This result indicates that information asymmetry in the bond market becomes particularly relevant when market participants face increased uncertainty about the future interest rate.

### 4.4 *Country effects and cross-sectional bond yield variations*

Academics and market participants are often interested in exploring how country differences affect the variations in bond yields in the euro zone. To capture the country effects, we create a dummy variable for each issuing country. For example, the Italy dummy variable equals 1 if the

# HIGH FREQUENCY TRADING AND LIMIT ORDER BOOK DYNAMICS

Table 7. Information asymmetry and market uncertainty.

| Variables | Normal | Abnormal | Abnormal–normal |
|---|---|---|---|
| *Panel A: equity market uncertainty* | | | |
| AA | 0.062 (12.03) | 0.061 (14.4) | −0.000 (−10.54) |
| A | 0.150 (19.61) | 0.139 (83.22) | −0.011 (−5.84) |
| Permanent impact | 0.002 (1.87) | 0.008 (4.18) | 0.006 (12.47) |
| Bid-ask spread | 0.008 (20.91) | 0.01 (13.42) | 0.002 (10.05) |
| Depth | −0.021 (−10.74) | −0.023 (−8.04) | −0.002 (−11.65) |
| Coupon rate | 0.007 (22.93) | 0.011 (9.13) | 0.004 (11.50) |
| Tick | 13.452 (24.76) | 11.861 (7.95) | −1.591 |
| Participants ($\times 10$) | 0.006 (11.39) | 0.003 (3.06) | −0.004 (−6.03) |
| Adjusted $R^2$ | 0.621 | 0.579 | |
| *Panel B: interest rate uncertainty* | | | |
| AA | 0.064 (8.84) | 0.061 (60.4) | −0.003 (−3.27) |
| A | 0.142 (72.97) | 0.124 (174.19) | −0.018 (−7.49) |
| Permanent impact | 0.000 (0.26) | 0.016 (9.63) | 0.016 (10.34) |
| Bid-ask spread | 0.008 (62) | 0.014 (8.47) | 0.006 (7.09) |
| Depth | −0.025 (−53.26) | −0.026 (−2.47) | −0.001 |
| Coupon rate | 0.006 (38.57) | 0.01 (29.75) | 0.004 (6.55) |
| Tick | 13.152 (52.86) | 14.077 (37.68) | 0.925 (10.65) |
| Participants ($\times 10$) | 0.006 (49.2) | 0.007 (2.19) | 0.001 (2.32) |
| Adjusted $R^2$ | 0.65 | 0.414 | |

Note: This table presents the average of the cross-sectional coefficients and the Newey–West-adjusted $t$-statistics (in parentheses) obtained for days with different levels of market uncertainty. Equity market uncertainty is captured by the vStoxx index, which indicates the near term volatility embedded in the option prices of the Dow Jones Euro Stoxx 50 equity index. Interest rate uncertainty is measured by the implied volatility obtained from swaption prices (the one-month option contract on one-year Euro swap rate). We define days with abnormal market uncertainty as those days where the implied volatility in the bond or equity markets is one standard deviation above the mean. The days when this condition does not hold are classified as normal. We run the cross-sectional regressions described in Table 6 separately on each of these two sub-samples. We use the pair-wise Wilcoxon test to examine whether the coefficients obtained for the abnormal periods are significantly higher than those estimated for the normal periods.

observation relates to an Italian bond and 0 otherwise. We replace the credit rating variables with these country dummy variables in the cross-sectional regressions. Since the German bonds serve as the benchmark in this model, the variable Italy is expected to capture the average yield spread between the German and Italian bonds. We perform the regressions over the whole sample period from 1 October 2003 to 28 September 2007. In addition, we condition the regressions on high volatility periods in the equity and the bond markets as described in the previous section.

Table 8 shows the estimation results for the regressions with the country dummy variables. German bonds are generally traded with the lowest yields. The spreads between German and Italian bond yields are significantly positive and, normally, average 14 basis points. These yield spreads reflect significant differences in the credit quality of the issuers. Importantly, the coefficients of the permanent impacts, the bid-ask spread and the market depth remain qualitatively unchanged. That is, investors require higher yields for information asymmetry and illiquidity. In addition, the coefficient of the market participants variable becomes economically and statistically insignificant when the country effects are included in the regressions.

The results in this table also show the extent of time variations in the risk premia. All the coefficients of the country dummy variables increase when either equity market or interest rate

Table 8. Cross-sectional regressions with country dummy variables.

| Variables | Whole sample | Abnormal equity market uncertainty | Abnormal interest rate uncertainty |
|---|---|---|---|
| Austria | 0.005 (2.33) | 0.041 (15.53) | 0.056 (42.3) |
| Belgium | 0.027 (11.02) | 0.067 (17.39) | 0.064 (47.51) |
| Finland | 0.029 (11.87) | 0.072 (20.99) | 0.067 (57.92) |
| France | 0.001 (5.13) | 0.022 (9.69) | 0.036 (32.41) |
| Greece | 0.138 (64.3) | 0.178 (41.93) | 0.177 (8.15) |
| Italy | 0.142 (53.36) | 0.166 (32.81) | 0.163 (62.29) |
| The Netherlands | 0.032 (15.42) | 0.065 (28.09) | 0.073 (69.67) |
| Portugal | 0.085 (40.70) | 0.124 (48.19) | 0.110 (65.09) |
| Spain | 0.025 (11.68) | 0.062 (13.93) | 0.042 (18.66) |
| Permanent impact | 0.006 (4.21) | 0.018 (6.86) | 0.037 (16.69) |
| Bid-ask spread | 0.006 (26.21) | 0.008 (21.09) | 0.010 (5.97) |
| Depth | −0.029 (−26.71) | −0.029 (−14.36) | −0.020 (−3.21) |
| Coupon rate | 0.006 (24.20) | 0.008 (23.25) | 0.009 (24.69) |
| Tick | 15.728 (29.38) | 16.632 (20.89) | 18.118 (50.13) |
| Participants ($\times 10$) | −0.000 (−0.99) | −0.000 (−0.49) | 0.003 (0.79) |
| Adjusted $R^2$ | 0.685 | 0.643 | 0.473 |

Note: This table presents the average of the cross-sectional coefficients and the Newey–West-adjusted $t$-statistics (in parentheses) obtained from cross-sectional regressions. To capture the country effects, we use country dummy variables. For instance, the Italy dummy variable equals 1 for Italian bond observations and 0 otherwise. Since the German bonds serve as the benchmark, the Italy dummy variable captures the average yield spread between German and Italian bonds. We perform the cross-sectional regressions over the whole sample period from 1 October 2003 to 28 September 2007. We average the estimated coefficients over the whole sample and over days with abnormal equity and bond market uncertainty. We define days with abnormal market uncertainty as those days where the implied volatility of either the bond or equity market is one standard deviation above the mean.

volatility increases. That is, when facing higher uncertainty, investors prefer high-quality assets such as the German government bonds and, consequently, the yield spreads with respect to the German bonds increase. This is consistent with the 'flight-to-quality' occurrence often described in the financial press. In addition, we also observe significant jumps in the coefficients of the permanent trading impact and the bid-ask spread. These results suggest that investors require much higher compensation for asymmetric information and illiquidity during periods of higher uncertainty.

## 5. Robustness checks

In this section, we examine the robustness of our results by controlling for the errors-in-variables problems caused by permanent trading impacts estimated with errors. Following Black, Jensen and Scholes (1972), we group bonds into portfolios and use the portfolio estimate as the explanatory variable. A portfolio estimate is desirable because it is highly correlated with the estimate of the individual securities and, at the same time, it is less correlated with the estimation errors.

We form bond portfolios with the following procedure. We initially sort bonds into 10 sovereign markets based on the nationality of the issuers. At the beginning of each six-month period, we classify bonds within each sovereign market into three maturity groups (short, medium and long) using the 30:40:30 breakpoints of the ranked duration. As a result, we obtain 30 bond portfolios at the intersection of 10 sovereign markets and three maturity groups. The permanent trading impacts of bond portfolios are the equally weighted averages of the permanent trading impacts

Table 9. Robustness.

| Variables | AAA bonds | AA–A bonds | All bonds |
|---|---|---|---|
| AA | | | 0.068 (40.52) |
| A | | 0.074 (45.6) | 0.143 (83.54) |
| Permanent impact | 0.02 (6.03) | 0.161 (20.22) | 0.028 (7.24) |
| Bid-ask spread | 0.005 (21.71) | 0.006 (12.46) | 0.007 (33.15) |
| Depth | −0.005 (−5.3) | −0.021 (−14.56) | −0.02 (−17.48) |
| Coupon rate | 0.007 (23.09) | 0.006 (20.03) | 0.008 (24.15) |
| Tick | 7.234 (15.66) | 14.706 (24.12) | 12.524 (25.01) |
| Participants ($\times 10$) | −0.000 (−1.24) | 0.006 (31.54) | 0.006 (22.47) |
| Adjusted $R^2$ | 0.533 | 0.694 | 0.629 |

Note: This table presents the average of the cross-sectional coefficients and the Newey-West-adjusted $t$-statistics (in parentheses) obtained from the cross-sectional regressions. Instead of using bond-specific permanent trading impacts as a regressor, we compute the equally weighted portfolio averages of the permanent trading impacts. Bond portfolios are formed by splitting the sample into 6-month sub-periods and by partitioning the data of every sub-period along two dimensions: nationality of the issuer and bond maturity. In particular, we have 10 nationality groups and 3 maturity groups (short, medium and long) computed using the 30:40:30 breakpoints of the ranked duration. Thus, our data are partitioned into 30 portfolios.

estimated for the bonds included in each portfolio. We then assign the average portfolio trading impact to each bond in the bond portfolio. Finally, we use these portfolio trading impacts as a dependent variable in the cross-sectional regressions estimated for each day of the following six-month period. The same process is repeated for every six-month period.

Table 9 presents the estimates of the cross-sectional regressions (8) with the portfolio permanent trading impacts. Note that the coefficients of credit quality, liquidity measures and other bond characteristics remain similar to the coefficients presented in Table 6. Interestingly, the slopes and $t$-statistics of the permanent trading impacts rise significantly, indicating that our original results become even stronger when we use portfolio trading impacts. Hence, after adjusting for errors-in-variable problems, bond yields remain significantly and positively related to the permanent trading impacts.

## 6. Conclusion

We analyse a cross-section of euro-area sovereign bonds traded on the MTS electronic platform from 1 April 2003 to 28 September 2007. We consider the permanent price response to the unexpected component of bond trades to capture the information content of trading activities and to measure adverse selection risk. Our hypothesis is that bond yields increase with larger permanent trading impacts because investors require higher compensations for bonds subject to greater asymmetric information.

The first part of our analysis illustrates the variations of information asymmetry across maturities, across countries and over time. When we consider bonds within the same maturity category, transactions for the most recently issued bonds generate relatively higher long-term price impacts. While trades for French and German bonds seem to induce the largest price revisions for short maturity bonds, the permanent effect of trades for German bonds is clearly the largest for bonds in the long maturity group. This evidence suggests significant cross-sectional differences among euro-areas countries in the information content of bond transactions. However, a proper analysis of the cross-sectional importance of asymmetric information must account for structural differences among the various euro-area Treasury markets in addition to controlling for credit quality and duration.

In the second part of our empirical analysis, we run cross-sectional regressions for the yield spread and find strong evidence supporting our hypothesis that information asymmetry is priced in the Treasury markets. Bond yields are significantly and positively related to the permanent trading impacts even after controlling for the behaviour of the interest rate term structure, credit quality, liquidity and other bond characteristics. In particular, this relation varies over time and depends on market conditions. The impact of information asymmetry on bond yields is stronger during periods of increased market volatility. Our findings indicate that when facing increased uncertainty, investors require higher compensation for information asymmetry.

## Acknowledgements

We are particularly grateful to the editors, Mark Salmon and Ingmar Nolte, to an anonymous referee and to Alan Huang for helpful comments and suggestions. Also, we would like to thank participants of the 41st Annual Conference of the Money, Macro and Finance Research Group, at Bradford University, the 2009 conference on Individual Decision Making, High Frequency Econometrics and Limit Order Book Dynamics at Warwick University and the 2010 Eastern Finance Association Annual Meetings in Miami Beach, Florida.

## Notes

1. Dunne, Moore, and Portes (2007) report that the total outstanding amount of the euro-area government bonds is more than 3.9 trillion euro and that their daily secondary market size averages 30 billion euro. The ECB (2004) indicates that hedging bond positions is commonly developed on the basis of government bond yields.
2. Persaud (2006) estimates that MTS accounts for 71.9% of the electronic trading volume of European cash government bonds.
3. Several other academic studies use data from the MTS markets (see, for example, Codogno, Favero, and Missale 2003; Beber, Brandt, and Kavajecz 2009; Dunne, Moore, and Portes 2007).
4. The ECB (2004) indicates that the fixed-rate coupon bonds alone account for 65% of the euro-area government bonds.
5. These data are available at www.markit.com.
6. The Chicago Board Options Exchange's VIX, a similar US volatility index, is widely known as the 'worry gauge' (see *Financial Times*, 25 August 2007, p. 5).

## References

Admati, A.R., and P.C. Pfleiderer. 1988. A theory of intraday patterns: Volume and price variability. *Review of Financial Studies* 1, no. 1: 3–40.

Amihud, Y., and H. Mendelson 1991. Liquidity, maturity, and the yields on U.S. treasury securities. *Journal of Finance* 46, no. 4: 1411–25.

Balduzzi, P., E.J. Elton, and T.C. Green. 2001. Economic news and bond prices: Evidence from the U.S. treasury market. *Journal of Financial and Quantitative Analysis* 36, no. 4: 523–43.

Beber, A., M.W. Brandt, and K.A. Kavajecz. 2009. Flight-to-quality or flight-to-liquidity? Evidence from the Euro-area bond market. *Review of Financial Studies* 22, no. 3: 925–57.

Bessembinder, H. 2002. Tick size, spreads, and liquidity: An analysis of Nasdaq Securities trading near ten dollars. *Journal of Financial Intermediation* 9, no. 3: 213–39.

Black, F., M. Jensen, and M. Scholes, eds. 1972. *The capital asset pricing model: Some empirical tests*. New York, NY: Praeger.

Blair, B.J., S.-H. Poon, and S.J. Taylor. 2001. Forecasting S&P 100 volatility: The incremental information content of implied volatilities and high-frequency index returns. *Journal of Econometrics* 105, no. 1: 5–26.

Blanco, R., S. Brennan, and I.W. Marsh. 2005. An empirical analysis of the dynamic relation between investment-grade bonds and credit default swaps. *Journal of Finance* 60, no. 5: 2255–81.

Brandt, M.W., and K.A. Kavajecz. 2004. Price discovery in the US treasury market: The impact of orderflow and liquidity on the yield curve. *Journal of Finance* 59, no. 6: 2623–54.

Brennan, M.J., and A. Subrahmanayam. 1996. Market microstructure and asset pricing: On the compensation for illiquidity in stock returns. *Journal of Financial Economics* 41, no. 3: 441–64.

Calomiris, C.W. 2009. The subprime turmoil: What's old, what's new, and what's next. *Journal of Structured Finance* 15, no. 1: 6–52.

Cao, H.H., M.D. Evans, and R.K. Lyons. 2006. Inventory information. *Journal of Business* 79, no. 1: 325–64.

Cheung, Y.-W., and C.Y.-P. Wong. 2000. A survey of market practitioners' views on exchange rate dynamics. *Journal of International Economics* 51, no. 2: 401–19.

Chordia, T., R. Roll, and A. Subrahmanyam. 2002. Order imbalance, liquidity, and market returns. *Journal of Financial Economics* 65, no. 1: 111–30.

Codogno, L., C. Favero, and A. Missale. 2003. Yield spreads on EMU government bonds. *Economic Policy* 18, no. 37: 503–32.

Connolly, R., C.T. Stivers, and L. Sun. 2005. Stock market uncertainty and the stock-bond return relation. *Journal of Financial and Quantitative Analysis* 40, no. 1: 161–94.

Constantinides, G.M. 1986. Capital market equilibrium with transaction costs. *Journal of Political Economy* 94, no. 4: 842–62.

Coval, J.D., and T. Shumway. 2001. Expected option returns. *Journal of Finance* 56, no. 3: 983–1009.

Dufour, A., and R.F. Engle. 2000. Time and the price impact of a trade. *Journal of Finance* 55, no. 6: 2467–98.

Dufour, A., and M. Nguyen. 2008. Time-varying price discovery in the European Treasury markets. Working Paper Series, ICMA Centre, University of Reading.

Dufour, A., and F.S. Skinner. 2004. MTS time series: Market and data description for the European bond and repo database. Working Paper 2004–07, ICMA Centre, University of Reading.

Dunne, P.G., M.J. Moore, and R. Portes. 2007. Benchmark status in fixed-income asset markets. *Journal of Business Finance and Accounting* 34, nos. 9–10: 1615–34.

Easley, D., S. Hvidkjaer, and M. O'Hara. 2002. Is information risk a determinant of asset returns? *Journal of Finance* 57, no. 5: 2185–221.

ECB. 2004. *The Euro bond market study*. Frankfurt: European Central Bank.

Fama, E.F., and J.D. MacBeth. 1973. Risk, return and equilibrium: Empirical tests. *Journal of Political Economy* 81, no. 3: 607–36.

Fleming, J. 1998. The quality of market volatility forecasts implied by S&P 100 index option prices. *Journal of Empirical Finance* 5, no. 4: 317–45.

Fleming, M.J. 2001. Measuring treasury market liquidity. Working paper 133, Federal Reserve Bank of New York.

Garleanu, N., and L.H. Pedersen. 2004. Adverse selection and the required return. *Review of Financial Studies* 17, no. 3: 643–65.

Gebhardt, W.R., S. Hvidkjaer, and B. Swaminathan. 2005. The cross-section of expected corporate bond returns: Betas or characteristics. *Journal of Financial Economics* 75, no. 1: 85–114.

Goldstein, M., and K. Kavajecz. 2000. Eighths, sixteenths and market depth: Changes in tick size and liquidity provision on the NYSE. *Journal of Financial Economics* 56, no. 1: 125–49.

Green, C.T. 2004. Economic news and the impact of trading on bond prices. *Journal of Finance* 59, no. 3: 1201–34.

Hasbrouck, J. 1991a. Measuring the information content of stock trades. *Journal of Finance* 46, no. 1: 179–207.

Hasbrouck, J. 1991b. The summary informativeness of stock trades: An econometric analysis. *Review of Financial Studies* 4, no. 3: 571–95.

Hasbrouck, J. 2003. Intraday price formation in US equity index markets. *Journal of Finance* 58, no. 6: 2375–99.

Hasbrouck, J. 2007. *Empirical market microstructure: The institutions, economics, and econometrics of securities trading.* New York, NY: Oxford University Press.

Houweling, P., A. Mentink, and T. Vorst. 2005. Comparing possible proxies of corporate bond liquidity. *Journal of Banking and Finance* 29, no. 6: 1331–58.

IMF. 2001. The changing structure of major government securities markets: Implications for private financial markets and key policy issues. International Monetary Fund, Washington, DC.

Ito, T., R. Lyons, and M. Melvin. 1998. Is there private information in the foreign exchange market? The Tokyo experiment. *Journal of Finance* 53, no. 3: 1111–30.

Krishnamurthy, A. 2002. The bond/old-bond spread. *Journal of Financial Economics* 66, nos. 2–3: 463–506.

Li, H., J. Wang, C. Wu, and Y. He. 2009. Are liquidity and information risks priced in the Treasury bond market? *Journal of Finance* 64, no. 1: 467–503.

Malz, A.M. 2003. *Liquidity risk: Current research and practice*. New York, NY: Risk Metrics Group.

Nelson, C.R., and A.F. Siegel. 1987. Parsimonious modeling of yield curves. *Journal of Business* 60, no. 4: 473–89.

O'Hara, M. 2003. Presidential address: Liquidity and price discovery. *Journal of Finance* 58, no. 4: 1335–54.

Pasquariello, P., and C. Vega. 2007. Informed and strategic order flow in the bond markets. *Review of Financial Studies* 20, no. 6: 1975–2019.

Peiers, B. 1997. Informed traders, intervention, and price leadership: A deeper view of the microstructure of the foreign exchange market. *Journal of Finance* 52, no. 4: 1589–614.

Persaud, A.D. 2006. Improving efficiency in the European government bond market. ICAP plc.

Petersen, M.A. 2009. Estimating standard errors in finance panel data sets: Comparing approaches. *Review of Financial Studies* 22, no. 1: 435–80.

Vayanos, D. 2004. Flight to quality, flight to liquidity and the pricing of risk. NBER Working Paper 10327.

Veronesi, P. 1999. Stock market overreaction to bad news in good times: A rational expectation equilibrium model. *Review of Financial Studies* 12, no. 5: 975–1007.

Wang, J. 1993. A model of intertemporal asset prices under asymmetric information. *Review of Economic Studies* 60, no. 2: 249–82.

# High-frequency information content in end-user foreign exchange order flows

Ian W. Marsh and Teng Miao

*Cass Business School, City University, London, UK*

This article considers the impact of foreign exchange (FX) order flows on contemporaneous and future stock market returns using a new database of customer order flows in the euro-dollar exchange rate market as seen by a leading European bank. We do not find clear contemporaneous relationships between FX order flows and stock market changes at high frequencies, but FX flows do appear to have significant power to forecast stock index returns over 1–30 min horizons, after controlling for lagged exchange rate and stock market returns. The effects of order flows from financial customers on future stock market changes are negative, while the effects of corporate orders are positive. The latter results are consistent with the premise that corporate order flows contain dispersed, passively acquired information about fundamentals. Thus, purchases of the dollar by corporate customers represent good news about the state of the US economy. Importantly, though, there also appears to be extra information in corporate flows which is directly relevant to equity prices over and above the impact derived from stock prices reacting to (predicted) exchange rate changes. Our findings suggest that financial customer flows only affect stock prices through their impact on the value of the dollar.

## 1. Introduction

This article is an empirical study of cross-market short-run correlations between order flows in the foreign exchange (FX) market and price changes in the US stock market. We argue that evidence of significant cross-market connections inform our understanding of the often observed yet still contentious relationships between FX order flow and FX returns. Specifically, some key hypotheses put forward to explain the correlation of daily order flow and spot exchange rate changes are not consistent with cross-market correlations. The one explanation that is consistent is that order flows contain information and that this is impounded into FX rates through the trading process. We also argue that our results shed some light on the nature of the information in order flow. At its most basic, the results suggest that at least part of the information content in flows relates to fundamentals relevant to both stock and FX markets. While this may not appear to narrow the field much, it does suggest that non-fundamental information in order flow – often thought of in terms of the ability of flows to predict future flows – is not the whole story. Further, we find considerable differences between the impact of order flow from corporate customers and that from financial customers, both in terms of the signs of the correlations and the horizons over which these correlations are significant. This suggests that the information in the flows from these different groups of end-users is radically different.

It is relatively uncontroversial that order flow influences price in equity markets. Theoretical models such as those by Kyle (1985) and Glosten and Milgrom (1985) begin with the observation that customers, from time to time, have private information about the fundamentals that drive an asset's true value that is not available to dealers. Transactions by these informed customers cause prices to change as dealers update their bid and ask quotes. At the same time, other market participants observe these quote changes and update their conditional expectations of the asset's value, adjusting their trades and quotes accordingly. Ultimately, the information conveyed by the trades of the informed becomes fully impounded in the market price of the asset. There is a rich history of empirical work supporting the connection between order flow and equity price changes (see, among many others, Shleifer 1986; Holthausen, Leftwich and Mayers 1990; Chordia, Roll and Subrahmanyam 2002). As data became available, and given the similarities with equity markets, evidence soon emerged that a similar relationship between order flow and prices could be observed in bond markets (Fleming 2003; Brandt and Kavajecz 2005; Pasquariello and Vega 2007).

Given that the exchange rate is just another asset price, it would seem reasonable that the same story should apply in FX markets. While there is plenty of evidence demonstrating a relationship between order flow and spot exchange rate changes, for whatever reason it remains controversial that this reflects the incorporation of private information into the price of FX.[1] In part, this is because, despite years of investigation, there is still no consensus on what the fundamentals are that drive exchange rates. If we do not know what the fundamentals are, it is not easy to convince sceptics that some market participants have private information about them. In part, even if we agree that fundamentals such as interest rates, price levels, and income growth rates matter for FX pricing, it is hard to convince sceptics that anyone could have private information about them. And finally, the scepticism about the information content of FX order flows is due in part to theories and evidence suggesting alternative explanations for the relationship between flows and spot rate changes. Inventory management by FX dealers is very aggressive compared with dealers in other assets, so inventory risk premia ought to be important (Froot and Ramadorai 2005; Breedon and Vitale 2009). Alternatively, the direction of causation between order flow and exchange rate changes comes under question. The empirical evidence may be reflecting the response of flows to exchange rate changes, rather than vice versa.

The FX microstructure literature suggests at least two simple reasons why flows might contain private information. First, the so-called dispersed information approach hypothesises that individual entities might know (and trade FX as a result of) a small part of the macroeconomic picture (Evans and Lyons 2004). The FX market pools these trades and aggregates the dispersed information, learning the bigger picture. Second, the portfolio shifts approach assumes that investors optimally allocate investments across markets (Evans and Lyons 2002). Shifts in preferences or risk appetites of individual investors lead to portfolio rebalancing and the resultant order flows reveal information regarding the private shifts of this subset of investors.

We attempt to shed some light on the nature of the information content of FX order flows using a unique database of end-user transactions as seen by the London FX trading desk of a major European bank. While only covering 25 days, we analyse a total trading volume in excess of €100bn, of which some €52bn are from end-user customers. Unlike almost all other studies using end-user FX flows which are forced to rely on daily aggregated flow measures, our database contains transaction-level detail, allowing us to perform the one of the first intra-day studies of FX end-user flows. In particular, since the data are timed to such a fine degree, we can test the forecasting power of flows over short horizons (up to 30 min). This allows us to minimise the likelihood that correlations between flows and returns are due to momentum or feedback trading. The high-frequency nature of our study also allows us to analyse the simple liquidity explanation. If illiquidity lies behind the widely observed return–flow correlation, we would expect to observe large positive relations between buying pressure and the value of the currency in the short run which reduce as the forecast horizon extends and the market has time to absorb the new inventory. The slightly richer risk premium explanation would in any case suggest that the inventory effect can have very long-lasting effects on returns.

Most innovatively, we examine whether end-user flows in the FX market have forecasting power for equity market returns. Any such evidence would be very hard to explain using feedback trading or inventory effects. They would, however, be consistent with the information content hypothesis since it is quite conceivable that the information contained in FX flows is of value both for FX rates and stock prices.

Moreover, the set of order flow data used in this article is broken into categories based on the orders' initiators: corporate customers, financial institutions, internal units, and inter-bank counterparties. This identification of the source of the orders allows us to examine the heterogeneity in high-frequency order flows, complementing existing studies using lower frequency end-user flows. Heterogeneity is another facet of the flow-return correlation puzzle that is not easily reconciled by liquidity explanations. Trades of a given size ought to have the same impact regardless of their source if that impact is primarily due to the inability of the market to absorb the inventory shock. However, since the information content from different sources is very likely to differ, it is quite reasonable to expect heterogeneity under the information hypothesis.

It is therefore important that we demonstrate that FX order flows have forecasting power for FX and stock market returns and that the impacts from different groups of customers are distinctly different. We see clear patterns in our results: corporate order flows into the US dollar have positive effects on future US stock returns, while order flows into the US dollar from financial institutions have negative effects on future US stock returns. These results as a whole are difficult to reconcile with competing explanations for correlations between flows and asset price changes such as risk premia or feedback trading. While there are still puzzling aspects of our results, we conclude that there is private information conveyed in FX order flows which is valuable for both stock and FX markets. For example, our strongest set of results is the link between corporate customer flows into the dollar and subsequent rises in US stock prices. While this could conceivably be due to portfolio reallocations by corporate, it seems more intuitive to suspect this is driven by the extraction of dispersed macroeconomic information from FX order flow which is also relevant for equity prices. For proponents of this approach, it is not surprising that FX flows contain information that is price relevant for various asset classes.[2]

The remainder of the article is organised as follows. In Section 2, we provide a brief literature review. The high-frequency FX order flows with exchange rates and stock prices data are presented in Section 3. Section 4 outlines the methods used and the hypotheses tested. The empirical findings will be discussed in Section 5, and Section 6 concludes.


## 2. Literature review

Due to space constraints, this review section is particularly brief and we concentrate on papers closely related to ours. The first is Osler and Vandrovych (2009) who examine all the executed price-contingent orders (stop-loss and take-profit orders) placed at the Royal Bank of Scotland from 10 different categories of counterparties (six from customers, four from inter-dealers) over 16 months in 2001 and 2002. The authors document connections between FX order flows triggered by these orders and subsequent exchange rate changes at high frequencies. The heterogeneity across counterparty types observed at low frequencies in the FX market is still present at high frequencies. They also suggest that the leveraged financial institutions such as hedge funds are better informed than other customers, while the inter-dealers are even better placed through observations of orders placed by their customers.

The literature therefore suggests that there should be relationships between disaggregated customer order flows and subsequent exchange rate movements. Our paper is the first to examine a comprehensive order flow data set at such a high frequency since it contains orders triggered by both price-contingent orders and market orders placed by a bank's counterparties. More innovatively, we also consider cross-market effects of such order flows.

A sizable body of the literature investigates the contemporaneous relations between FX and stock markets. Early empirical studies focus on the return spillovers between the two different financial markets with mixed results (Jorion 1991; Bartov and Bodnar 1994; Ajayi and Mougoue 1996; Andersen et al. 2007). Though the evidence in these papers is not unambiguous, there is enough to suggest that the factors driving exchange rates are also relevant for stock prices.

Two studies closely related to our own investigate the relationship between FX and stock markets with order flow data as additional variables.[3] Dunne, Hau, and Moore (2006) obtain a structural relationship between exchange rates, domestic and foreign stock market returns, and the corresponding stock market order flows from a model of heterogeneous belief changes. Their estimated equations regress a stock market return on contemporaneous FX returns and domestic and foreign equity order flow. Recognising the potential endogeneity of the exchange rate in their econometric specification, they instrument exchange rate changes with inter-bank FX order flow for a subsample of their data. Interestingly, they find that an appreciation of the dollar and an inter-bank order flow into the dollar are positively correlated with contemporaneous stock market changes (using daily data).

Francis, Hasan and Hunter (2006) estimate models very close to our own, using lagged equity and FX returns plus FX order flow to explain equity returns in many countries. The key difference is that their order flow data are from the weekly reports of the FX positions of US banks active in the FX markets. As such, they are a low-frequency proxy of the order flows of a select number of participants in the FX market. Francis et al. demonstrate significant correlations between flows and future equity market returns. Interestingly, the sign of the coefficients on order flow differs across countries, with inflows to the dollar from the Deutsche mark and yen being associated with US equity price rises, and inflows from the pound and Canadian dollar associated with US equity falls. They attribute their findings to the information content of FX order flows, and argue that the heterogeneity of coefficients is driven by the heterogeneity of information content.

## 3. High-frequency data

The tick-by-tick high-frequency euro–dollar (denoted as EURUSD afterwards) order flow data used in this paper are provided by the London trading desk of a leading European commercial bank that wishes to remain anonymous. The order flow data records every trade initiated by the bank's counterparties over 25 trading days from 10 October 2005 to 11 November 2005 and includes trades from both customers and banks in the inter-dealer network.[4] Deals smaller than €500,000 are not included in the database but we still have 27,830 transactions over 25 trading days. The period chosen for the study was essentially random and does not appear to have been particularly unusual for either the FX or stock markets. Every deal has a time stamp attached, a bought or sold indicator allowing us to sign the direction of trades, the transaction price, and the contemporaneous inter-bank market price together with the size of each deal. In this paper, we use the inter-bank market price to abstract from the inventory implications of the bank's own customer quotes. Counterparties are identified by a code, allowing us to classify order flows into four categories: financial customers, corporate customers, internal units, and inter-bank counterparties. Flows are signed such that a dollar purchase by a customer (and so a euro sale) is given a positive sign. Flows are measured in euros.

Due to the irregular spacing of trades during the day, we filter the raw data at 1 min intervals. The order flow data for each category are cumulated during each 1 min period, and the transaction exchange rate is the price of the last execution in that 1 min interval. We also use the matched inter-bank rate as the last price in the interval.

An exchange-traded fund (ETF) is an investment vehicle traded on stock exchanges, which is very liquid due to low transactions costs, high tax efficiency, good diversification powers, and pure stock-like features. The first of these, the S&P 500 ETF (denoted as SPY, but more widely known as SPDR), began trading in 1993 and is now the largest ETF in the world. Following SPY's success, the 'Dow Diamond' (denoted as DIA) ETF was introduced tracking the Dow Jones Industrials Average (DOW 30). Since these are traded instruments that accurately track the value of the major US equity indices, we use high-frequency trade and quote prices of these two ETFs as our measure of stock index prices in the USA.

The tick-by-tick stock market data are collected over the 25 trading days sample from 10 October 2005 to 11 November 2005, traded between 9.30 a.m. and 4.00 p.m., New York Time. Since we are examining FX order flows from a London desk and US stock market data, the time difference between USA and UK needs careful attention. When we only need consider FX flows and returns, we have approximately 8.5 h of data each day. After filtering data to 1 min frequencies, we have approximately 510 observations each day or 12,775 observations in total. When considering cross-market effects, the overlap of data between the two markets is from 2.30 p.m. to approximately 5.00 p.m. London time (9.30 a.m. to 12.00 p.m. New York time). We then have approximately 120 observations in the overlapping interval for each day (3025 observations for all 25 days).

## 4. Hypotheses and methodology

The focus of this article is on the cross-market relationships, but we begin with a brief analysis of the correlations between FX flows and FX returns. We begin with contemporaneous analyses by regressing exchange rate returns between time $t - i$ and $t$ on flows from the four different customer groups over the same time interval. We vary the size of the window, given by $i$, from 1 min up to 30 min. The different types of counterparties are denoted by $m$, where $m = 1$ corresponds to financial customers, 2 to commercial corporations, 3 to internal transactions within the bank, and 4 to inter-bank counterparties. Recall that flows are signed such that a positive flow indicates that the counterparty was buying dollars (and so selling euros to the bank). In the regression analysis below, we measure flows in units of €100 m. Exchange rates are defined such that a positive FX return indicates an appreciation of the dollar. A positive coefficient suggests that a flow into the dollar is associated with a strengthening of the dollar.

$$R_{t-i,t}^{FX} = c + \sum_{m=1}^{4} \beta_m OF_{t-i,t}^{FX} + \varepsilon_t. \tag{1}$$

We run these regressions over the full data sample from approximately 7.30 a.m. to 5.00 p.m. over the 25 days of our sample.

In the forecasting model, we test the effects of cumulated order flows over $i$ minutes on exchange rate returns over subsequent $k$-minute intervals, in which $i$ and $k$ both range from 1 to 30 min. In the forecasting regressions, we also include the lagged dependent variable on the right-hand side of the equation. For example, when $i = 3$ and $k = 5$, we use FX order flows over the last 3 min to forecast exchange rate returns over the next 5 min, after controlling for the last 3 min exchange rate return.[5]

$$R^{FX}_{t,t+k} = c + \gamma R^{FX}_{t-i,t} + \sum_{m=1}^{4} \beta_m OF^{FX}_{t-i,t} + \varepsilon_t. \tag{2}$$

Again, the full sample is used for the forecasting regressions. With intervals greater than 1 min, overlapping observations are used, and so all regression models are estimated by using ordinary least squares, correcting the coefficient variance/covariance matrix for autocorrelation and heteroskedasticity using the Newey–West method. These are, of course, in-sample regressions and so not true forecasts. The relatively short data span precludes the use of true out-of-sample forecasting tests.

The main focus of this article is in the cross-market effects from FX order flows to stock market returns at high frequencies. We run corresponding regressions to those described above where the dependent variable is now a stock market return, either from an ETF or from an individual stock. Our analysis is now constrained to the overlapping period from 2.30 p.m. (London) to approximately 5.00 p.m. (London).

We begin with the contemporaneous regression:

$$R^{S}_{t-i,t} = c + \gamma R^{FX}_{t-i,t} + \sum_{m=1}^{4} \beta_m OF^{FX}_{t-i,t} + \varepsilon_t. \tag{3}$$

The stock return between time $t - i$ and $t$ is regressed on the contemporaneous FX return and on the contemporaneous disaggregated end-user FX order flows.

$$R^{S}_{t,t+k} = c + \alpha R^{S}_{t-i,t} + \gamma R^{FX}_{t-i,t} + \sum_{m=1}^{4} \beta_m OF^{FX}_{t-i,t} + \varepsilon_t. \tag{4}$$

In the forecasting model given in equation (4), we regress stock market returns over a $k$-minute interval on lagged stock market returns, lagged exchange rate returns, and the four groups of lagged order flows aggregated over an $i$-minute interval. The four beta coefficients from this model are our focus of interest. Significant coefficients would suggest that lagged end-user FX order flows are useful predictors of future stock returns even when correcting for stock and FX returns contemporaneous with the FX flows.

## 5. Empirical findings

### 5.1 *Contemporaneous relationships between FX flows and FX returns*

We start by investigating the contemporaneous relation between FX end-user order flows and exchange rate returns at frequencies from 1 to 30 min.

From Table 1, we see a clear contemporaneous relationship between FX order flows and exchange rate. Order flows from other inter-bank dealers are significantly negative at all aggregation frequencies from 1 to 30 min. Since the literature finds that inter-dealer orders *in aggregate* are strongly positively correlated with contemporaneous exchange rate changes, our results suggest that the small subset of inter-dealer flows captured by our data (i.e. flows initiated by other banks against our bank's inter-dealer quotes) are negatively correlated with the aggregate inter-dealer flow. Put differently, when our bank passively trades on the inter-bank market, exchange rates contemporaneously move in its favour. Moore and Payne (2009) discuss relative bank informedness, and we return to this issue below when we consider our forecasting results.

Order flows from internal customers within the bank also follow the same pattern, are even more significant, and bear coefficients of larger magnitude. Unfortunately, we have little understanding of the nature of these internal customer flows since the data provider was unwilling (or unable) to clarify the reasons behind internal transactions.

Order flows from end-user customers are not significant until the aggregation window rises to 16 min for corporate and 20 min for financials. Furthermore, it is noticeable that order flows from corporations are positively correlated with exchange rate changes, while order flows from other types of counterparties (financials, internal, and inter-bank) are negatively correlated with exchange rate changes. These are opposite to the correlations typically found at lower frequencies by many other researchers. At daily frequencies, order flows from financial customers are typically positively correlated with contemporaneous exchange rate changes (such that purchases of the dollar by financial sector end-users are typically associated with an appreciation of the dollar) while corporate end-users are more often negatively correlated with changes in the spot rate.

As noted above, the usual explanation for the positive contemporaneous correlation for financials is that their order flows convey useful information to the markets, which is subsequently priced into the spot rate. A contemporaneous negative correlation between flows and rate changes is more difficult to explain within the paradigm that there is information in flows (since it would suggest that buying dollars conveys bad news regarding the value of the dollar). Explanations have been advanced based on the idea that markets cannot discern the source of the end-user flow that causes inter-bank actions by the customer's bank. Thus, the inter-bank price reacts by an average amount before eventually realising the true nature of the information content. For some very informed customers, there will then be an initial positive reaction followed by further positive reactions as the larger-than-average information content of the flow is recognised. For others, there will be an initially positive reaction followed by a reversal once the market learns this was an uninformed (or at least less informed than average) trade. However, these explanations actually imply negative forecasting relationships, not a negative contemporaneous correlation. The negative coefficient between financial customer flows and exchange rate changes is then doubly puzzling, first because it is the opposite of that usually found, and second because it is found contemporaneously in high-frequency data.

One straightforward explanation outside the information paradigm is that financial customers are engaging in negative feedback trading. The contemporaneously negative relationship is because, at very high frequencies, financial customers buy currencies that have just fallen in value. If they are merely feedback trading, we would not expect to see subsequent appreciation in the currency purchased. However, if they are informed about future exchange rate movements and choose to time their trades by buying on temporary falls in the value of a currency, we would expect to see both negative contemporaneous correlation and a positive FX forecasting ability. With this in mind, we now turn to our forecasting results.

Table 1. Impact of order flow on contemporaneous exchange rate changes.

| | Aggregation window | | | | | | | | | | | | | | |
|---|---|---|---|---|---|---|---|---|---|---|---|---|---|---|---|
| | 1 | 2 | 3 | 4 | 5 | 6 | 7 | 8 | 9 | 10 | 11 | 12 | 13 | 14 | 15 |
| Financial | −0.04 | −0.03 | −0.02 | −0.02 | −0.02 | −0.03 | −0.04 | −0.04 | −0.06 | −0.07 | −0.09 | −0.11 | −0.13 | −0.14 | −0.15 |
| Corporate | 0.02 | 0.02 | 0.03 | 0.03 | 0.03 | 0.04 | 0.05 | 0.05 | 0.05 | 0.06 | 0.07 | 0.08 | 0.08 | 0.09 | 0.09 |
| Internal | −0.06 | −0.12 | −0.2 | −0.27 | −0.31 | −0.36 | −0.39 | −0.43 | −0.46 | −0.49 | −0.51 | −0.54 | −0.57 | −0.59 | −0.61 |
| Inter-bank | −0.11 | −0.17 | −0.21 | −0.23 | −0.24 | −0.25 | −0.25 | −0.26 | −0.27 | −0.27 | −0.27 | −0.27 | −0.27 | −0.27 | −0.27 |

| | Aggregation window | | | | | | | | | | | | | | |
|---|---|---|---|---|---|---|---|---|---|---|---|---|---|---|---|
| | 16 | 17 | 18 | 19 | 20 | 21 | 22 | 23 | 24 | 25 | 26 | 27 | 28 | 29 | 30 |
| Financial | −0.15 | −0.15 | −0.16 | −0.17 | −0.17 | −0.18 | −0.18 | −0.18 | −0.18 | −0.18 | −0.17 | −0.17 | −0.17 | −0.17 | −0.17 |
| Corporate | 0.09 | 0.1 | 0.1 | 0.11 | 0.11 | 0.12 | 0.12 | 0.13 | 0.14 | 0.14 | 0.14 | 0.14 | 0.15 | 0.15 | 0.15 |
| Internal | −0.62 | −0.63 | −0.63 | −0.64 | −0.65 | −0.66 | −0.66 | −0.66 | −0.67 | −0.67 | −0.68 | −0.69 | −0.69 | −0.69 | −0.68 |
| Inter-bank | −0.28 | −0.29 | −0.29 | −0.29 | −0.3 | −0.3 | −0.3 | −0.3 | −0.31 | −0.31 | −0.31 | −0.32 | −0.32 | −0.33 | −0.33 |

Notes: Coefficient estimates from the regression $R^{FX}_{t-i,t} = c + \sum_{m=1}^{4} \beta_m OF^{FX}_{t-i,t} + \varepsilon_t$. The column headings give the value of the aggregation window $i$ in the model. Intra-day data from 7.30 a.m. to 5.00 p.m. for 25 days are used. A lightly shaded cell denotes significance at the 10% level using robust standard error estimates. Darker shading denotes significance at the 5% level. Coefficients represent the percentage change in the euro-dollar exchange rate from a €1bn flow into the dollar, expressed such that a positive sign is an appreciation of the dollar.

### 5.2    *Forecasting relationships between FX flows and FX returns*

The beta coefficients from the estimated FX forecasting equation (2) are reported in Tables 2 and 3 for financial and corporate customers, respectively. Results for internal and inter-bank customers are not reported in detail to conserve space but are discussed below. Results are available from the authors on request. Lightly shaded cells denote significance at the 10% level, darker shading denotes significance at the 5% level. The coefficients represent the percentage change in the EURUSD exchange rate from a €1bn flow into the dollar, expressed such that a positive sign is an appreciation of the dollar.

We highlight the following findings:

(1) The effect of financial customer FX order flows on future exchange rate changes follows a clear pattern. Over short horizons and with short aggregation windows (that is, $k$ and $i$, both between 5 and 15 min), flows into the dollar forecast a statistically significant subsequent decline in the dollar. However, as both the aggregation window and forecast horizon increase, the sign of the forecasting correlation reverses. While not becoming significant even when both aggregation and forecasting windows reach half an hour, it is conceivable that for larger values of $i$ and $k$ than we can examine in our data, the forecasting correlation becomes sufficiently positive to generate the positive contemporaneous correlation seen at daily frequencies. As noted above, this pattern would be consistent with financial customers timing their trades by buying (selling) on temporary dips (rises) before the information in their trades is slowly priced into FX rates. There is small positive autocorrelation in FX returns which may also be responsible for the negative short-term forecasting ability of financials' FX orders.

(2) The effect of corporate FX order flows on future exchange rate changes is essentially uniformly positive and statistically significant given appropriate aggregation windows and forecast horizons (that is, $i$ and $k$ both lie between 10 and 20 min). Significance disappears once both the aggregation window and forecast horizon increase to half an hour, and there is no evidence of very short-term forecasting power using small aggregation windows.

(3) The coefficient magnitudes typically suggest a 30 bp change in the exchange rate following a €1bn net flow into the market. This is in line with the findings of other studies. Berger et al. (2006), for example, suggest that a \$1bn flow in the inter-bank market is associated with a 55 bp price impact at the 1 min horizon.

(4) Correlations between order flows from internal and inter-bank counterparties and future exchange rate changes are negative at very short horizons but positive as forecast horizons and aggregation windows expand.

(5) Inter-bank order flows rarely reach significance, suggesting that the data-providing bank cannot learn much about the value of the currency from the flows it receives from inter-bank counterparties. Since the bank is large and active in the currency markets, we can infer that its counterparties are typically less informed than it is. This contrasts with the evidence in Frommel, Mende and Menkhoff (2007) from a smaller European bank which gets much of its information from flows from inter-bank counterparties. See Moore and Payne (2009) for further discussion of relative bank informedness.

(6) $R^2$ figures are low and range from 0.05% for short-horizon/short aggregation window combinations to 0.50% for long-horizon/long aggregation window combinations.

(7) We conduct $F$-tests on the coefficients on order flow terms in equation (2). They show clearly that the four different sources of order flow are jointly significant at almost all aggregation window-forecast horizon combinations. Similarly, the end-user customer flows from

Table 2. Impact of order flow on future exchange rate changes: financial customer order flows.

| Aggregation Window \ Forecast horizon | 1 | 2 | 3 | 4 | 5 | 6 | 7 | 8 | 9 | 10 | 11 | 12 | 13 | 14 | 15 | 16 | 17 | 18 | 19 | 20 | 21 | 22 | 23 | 24 | 25 | 26 | 27 | 28 | 29 | 30 |
|---|---|---|---|---|---|---|---|---|---|---|---|---|---|---|---|---|---|---|---|---|---|---|---|---|---|---|---|---|---|---|
| 1 | 0.04 | 0.00 | 0.03 | -0.01 | -0.08 | -0.09 | -0.13 | -0.15 | -0.17 | -0.19 | -0.22 | -0.22 | -0.26 | -0.23 | -0.17 | -0.17 | -0.20 | -0.18 | -0.21 | -0.22 | -0.17 | -0.20 | -0.16 | -0.16 | -0.15 | -0.15 | -0.09 | -0.08 | -0.08 | -0.09 |
| 2 | 0.00 | -0.04 | -0.04 | -0.07 | -0.10 | -0.13 | -0.16 | -0.17 | -0.20 | -0.22 | -0.23 | -0.26 | -0.26 | -0.21 | -0.19 | -0.20 | -0.20 | -0.20 | -0.22 | -0.21 | -0.19 | -0.19 | -0.17 | -0.16 | -0.16 | -0.13 | -0.10 | -0.09 | -0.09 | -0.09 |
| 3 | -0.01 | -0.03 | -0.05 | -0.07 | -0.11 | -0.13 | -0.16 | -0.18 | -0.20 | -0.22 | -0.24 | -0.25 | -0.23 | -0.20 | -0.18 | -0.19 | -0.20 | -0.20 | -0.20 | -0.20 | -0.18 | -0.17 | -0.16 | -0.15 | -0.13 | -0.11 | -0.08 | -0.08 | -0.08 | -0.08 |
| 4 | 0.00 | -0.03 | -0.05 | -0.08 | -0.11 | -0.13 | -0.16 | -0.18 | -0.20 | -0.22 | -0.23 | -0.22 | -0.21 | -0.19 | -0.18 | -0.19 | -0.19 | -0.19 | -0.19 | -0.18 | -0.17 | -0.16 | -0.14 | -0.14 | -0.12 | -0.10 | -0.08 | -0.08 | -0.07 | -0.07 |
| 5 | -0.02 | -0.04 | -0.07 | -0.09 | -0.12 | -0.14 | -0.16 | -0.18 | -0.21 | -0.22 | -0.21 | -0.21 | -0.20 | -0.18 | -0.18 | -0.17 | -0.18 | -0.19 | -0.18 | -0.17 | -0.16 | -0.16 | -0.14 | -0.13 | -0.11 | -0.10 | -0.08 | -0.07 | -0.07 | -0.08 |
| 6 | -0.02 | -0.04 | -0.07 | -0.09 | -0.12 | -0.14 | -0.16 | -0.18 | -0.19 | -0.19 | -0.19 | -0.19 | -0.18 | -0.18 | -0.16 | -0.18 | -0.18 | -0.17 | -0.16 | -0.15 | -0.15 | -0.13 | -0.12 | -0.10 | -0.09 | -0.08 | -0.06 | -0.06 | -0.06 | -0.07 |
| 7 | -0.02 | -0.07 | -0.07 | -0.09 | -0.12 | -0.14 | -0.15 | -0.17 | -0.18 | -0.18 | -0.17 | -0.17 | -0.17 | -0.17 | -0.16 | -0.17 | -0.16 | -0.15 | -0.15 | -0.14 | -0.12 | -0.11 | -0.10 | -0.09 | -0.07 | -0.06 | -0.05 | -0.06 | -0.05 | -0.06 |
| 8 | -0.02 | -0.04 | -0.07 | -0.09 | -0.12 | -0.13 | -0.15 | -0.17 | -0.18 | -0.16 | -0.18 | -0.15 | -0.16 | -0.15 | -0.15 | -0.13 | -0.14 | -0.13 | -0.13 | -0.12 | -0.10 | -0.09 | -0.08 | -0.07 | -0.05 | -0.04 | -0.03 | -0.04 | -0.04 | -0.05 |
| 9 | -0.02 | -0.04 | -0.07 | -0.08 | -0.11 | -0.13 | -0.15 | -0.14 | -0.14 | -0.16 | -0.15 | -0.15 | -0.14 | -0.14 | -0.13 | -0.13 | -0.12 | -0.12 | -0.13 | -0.12 | -0.10 | -0.09 | -0.08 | -0.07 | -0.05 | -0.04 | -0.03 | -0.04 | -0.04 | -0.05 |
| 10 | -0.02 | -0.04 | -0.06 | -0.08 | -0.10 | -0.11 | -0.12 | -0.13 | -0.16 | -0.16 | -0.14 | -0.13 | -0.13 | -0.12 | -0.11 | -0.11 | -0.11 | -0.10 | -0.09 | -0.10 | -0.08 | -0.07 | -0.06 | -0.05 | -0.04 | -0.03 | -0.01 | -0.02 | -0.03 | -0.04 |
| 11 | -0.02 | -0.04 | -0.06 | -0.08 | -0.09 | -0.10 | -0.11 | -0.11 | -0.12 | -0.12 | -0.12 | -0.12 | -0.11 | -0.11 | -0.10 | -0.10 | -0.09 | -0.08 | -0.07 | -0.06 | -0.04 | -0.03 | -0.02 | -0.01 | -0.01 | -0.01 | 0.01 | 0.00 | 0.00 | 0.00 |
| 12 | -0.02 | -0.04 | -0.06 | -0.07 | -0.08 | -0.09 | -0.09 | -0.10 | -0.11 | -0.11 | -0.11 | -0.10 | -0.10 | -0.09 | -0.08 | -0.08 | -0.07 | -0.06 | -0.05 | -0.05 | -0.02 | -0.02 | 0.00 | 0.00 | 0.00 | 0.01 | 0.01 | 0.03 | 0.02 | 0.01 |
| 13 | -0.02 | -0.04 | -0.06 | -0.07 | -0.07 | -0.08 | -0.08 | -0.09 | -0.09 | -0.10 | -0.09 | -0.08 | -0.08 | -0.08 | -0.07 | -0.04 | -0.05 | -0.04 | -0.03 | -0.02 | -0.01 | 0.00 | 0.00 | 0.01 | 0.01 | 0.02 | 0.02 | 0.03 | 0.03 | 0.03 |
| 14 | -0.01 | -0.03 | -0.04 | -0.05 | -0.06 | -0.07 | -0.08 | -0.08 | -0.08 | -0.08 | -0.08 | -0.07 | -0.07 | -0.06 | -0.05 | -0.04 | -0.04 | -0.02 | -0.01 | 0.00 | 0.01 | 0.01 | 0.02 | 0.02 | 0.03 | 0.03 | 0.04 | 0.04 | 0.05 | 0.04 |
| 15 | -0.01 | -0.02 | -0.03 | -0.04 | -0.06 | -0.06 | -0.07 | -0.07 | -0.07 | -0.07 | -0.07 | -0.06 | -0.06 | -0.05 | -0.04 | -0.03 | -0.02 | -0.01 | 0.00 | -0.01 | 0.02 | 0.02 | 0.03 | 0.03 | 0.04 | 0.04 | 0.05 | 0.05 | 0.06 | 0.05 |
| 16 | -0.01 | -0.02 | -0.03 | -0.04 | -0.05 | -0.05 | -0.06 | -0.06 | -0.05 | -0.05 | -0.05 | -0.06 | -0.05 | -0.04 | -0.03 | -0.02 | -0.01 | 0.00 | 0.01 | 0.01 | 0.02 | 0.03 | 0.03 | 0.04 | 0.04 | 0.05 | 0.06 | 0.06 | 0.06 | 0.06 |
| 17 | -0.01 | -0.02 | -0.03 | -0.04 | -0.05 | -0.05 | -0.05 | -0.06 | -0.05 | -0.05 | -0.05 | -0.05 | -0.04 | -0.03 | -0.02 | -0.01 | 0.00 | 0.01 | 0.02 | 0.02 | 0.02 | 0.03 | 0.04 | 0.04 | 0.05 | 0.06 | 0.07 | 0.07 | 0.07 | 0.07 |
| 18 | -0.01 | -0.02 | -0.03 | -0.04 | -0.05 | -0.05 | -0.05 | -0.06 | -0.05 | -0.04 | -0.05 | -0.04 | -0.03 | -0.02 | -0.01 | 0.00 | 0.00 | 0.01 | 0.02 | 0.02 | 0.03 | 0.03 | 0.04 | 0.04 | 0.05 | 0.06 | 0.07 | 0.07 | 0.07 | 0.07 |
| 19 | -0.01 | -0.02 | -0.03 | -0.04 | -0.04 | -0.05 | -0.05 | -0.05 | -0.05 | -0.04 | -0.03 | -0.03 | -0.02 | -0.01 | 0.00 | 0.00 | 0.01 | 0.01 | 0.03 | 0.03 | 0.03 | 0.04 | 0.05 | 0.05 | 0.06 | 0.06 | 0.07 | 0.07 | 0.08 | 0.07 |
| 20 | -0.01 | -0.02 | -0.03 | -0.04 | -0.04 | -0.04 | -0.04 | -0.05 | -0.04 | -0.03 | -0.02 | -0.01 | 0.00 | 0.00 | 0.01 | 0.01 | 0.01 | 0.02 | 0.03 | 0.04 | 0.04 | 0.05 | 0.05 | 0.05 | 0.06 | 0.07 | 0.07 | 0.08 | 0.08 | 0.08 |
| 21 | -0.01 | -0.02 | -0.02 | -0.03 | -0.03 | -0.04 | -0.04 | -0.03 | -0.02 | -0.02 | -0.01 | -0.01 | 0.00 | 0.01 | 0.01 | 0.02 | 0.02 | 0.03 | 0.03 | 0.04 | 0.05 | 0.05 | 0.05 | 0.06 | 0.06 | 0.07 | 0.08 | 0.08 | 0.08 | 0.08 |
| 22 | -0.01 | -0.01 | -0.02 | -0.02 | -0.03 | -0.03 | -0.03 | -0.03 | -0.02 | -0.01 | -0.01 | 0.00 | 0.00 | 0.01 | 0.02 | 0.02 | 0.02 | 0.03 | 0.03 | 0.04 | 0.05 | 0.05 | 0.06 | 0.06 | 0.07 | 0.08 | 0.08 | 0.09 | 0.08 | 0.08 |
| 23 | -0.01 | -0.01 | -0.02 | -0.02 | -0.03 | -0.03 | -0.02 | -0.03 | -0.02 | -0.01 | -0.01 | 0.00 | 0.00 | 0.01 | 0.02 | 0.03 | 0.03 | 0.04 | 0.04 | 0.05 | 0.06 | 0.06 | 0.07 | 0.07 | 0.08 | 0.08 | 0.09 | 0.09 | 0.09 | 0.08 |
| 24 | -0.01 | -0.01 | -0.02 | -0.02 | -0.02 | -0.02 | -0.02 | -0.02 | -0.01 | -0.01 | 0.00 | 0.00 | 0.01 | 0.01 | 0.02 | 0.03 | 0.03 | 0.04 | 0.04 | 0.05 | 0.06 | 0.07 | 0.07 | 0.08 | 0.08 | 0.08 | 0.09 | 0.09 | 0.09 | 0.08 |
| 25 | 0.00 | -0.01 | -0.01 | -0.02 | -0.02 | -0.02 | -0.01 | -0.01 | -0.01 | -0.01 | 0.00 | 0.00 | 0.01 | 0.02 | 0.02 | 0.03 | 0.03 | 0.04 | 0.05 | 0.05 | 0.06 | 0.07 | 0.08 | 0.08 | 0.08 | 0.08 | 0.09 | 0.09 | 0.09 | 0.09 |
| 26 | 0.00 | -0.01 | -0.01 | -0.01 | -0.01 | -0.01 | -0.01 | -0.01 | -0.01 | 0.00 | 0.00 | 0.00 | 0.01 | 0.02 | 0.03 | 0.03 | 0.04 | 0.05 | 0.05 | 0.06 | 0.06 | 0.07 | 0.08 | 0.08 | 0.08 | 0.08 | 0.09 | 0.09 | 0.09 | 0.08 |
| 27 | 0.00 | -0.01 | -0.01 | -0.01 | -0.01 | -0.01 | -0.01 | -0.01 | 0.00 | 0.00 | 0.00 | 0.01 | 0.01 | 0.02 | 0.03 | 0.04 | 0.04 | 0.05 | 0.06 | 0.06 | 0.07 | 0.07 | 0.08 | 0.08 | 0.08 | 0.09 | 0.09 | 0.09 | 0.09 | 0.09 |
| 28 | 0.00 | -0.01 | -0.01 | -0.01 | -0.01 | -0.01 | -0.01 | -0.01 | 0.00 | 0.00 | 0.01 | 0.01 | 0.01 | 0.02 | 0.03 | 0.04 | 0.04 | 0.05 | 0.06 | 0.06 | 0.07 | 0.07 | 0.08 | 0.08 | 0.08 | 0.09 | 0.09 | 0.09 | 0.09 | 0.09 |
| 29 | 0.00 | -0.01 | -0.01 | -0.01 | -0.01 | -0.01 | -0.01 | 0.00 | 0.00 | 0.00 | 0.01 | 0.01 | 0.02 | 0.03 | 0.03 | 0.04 | 0.05 | 0.05 | 0.06 | 0.06 | 0.07 | 0.07 | 0.08 | 0.08 | 0.08 | 0.09 | 0.09 | 0.09 | 0.09 | 0.08 |
| 30 | 0.00 | 0.00 | -0.01 | -0.01 | -0.01 | -0.01 | -0.01 | 0.00 | 0.00 | 0.00 | 0.01 | 0.01 | 0.02 | 0.03 | 0.03 | 0.04 | 0.05 | 0.05 | 0.06 | 0.06 | 0.07 | 0.07 | 0.08 | 0.08 | 0.08 | 0.09 | 0.09 | 0.09 | 0.09 | 0.08 |

Notes: Coefficient estimates in the regression $R^{FX}_{t+k} = c + \gamma R^{FX}_{t-i,t} + \sum_{m=1}^{4} \beta_m OF^{FX}_{t-i,t} + \varepsilon_t$ for financial end-user customer order flows. The horizontal axis varies over the $k$-minute forecast horizon; the vertical axis varies according to the aggregation window of FX order flows through the $i$-minute period. A lightly shaded cell denotes significance at the 10% level using robust standard error estimates. Darker shading denotes significance at the 5% level. Intra-day data from 7.30 a.m. to 5.00 p.m. for 25 days are used. Coefficients represent the percentage change in the euro-dollar exchange rate from a €1bn flow into the dollar, expressed such that a positive sign is an appreciation of the dollar.

Table 3. Impact of order flow on future exchange rate changes: corporate customer order flows.

| Aggregation Window \ Forecast horizon | 1 | 2 | 3 | 4 | 5 | 6 | 7 | 8 | 9 | 10 | 11 | 12 | 13 | 14 | 15 | 16 | 17 | 18 | 19 | 20 | 21 | 22 | 23 | 24 | 25 | 26 | 27 | 28 | 29 | 30 |
|---|---|---|---|---|---|---|---|---|---|---|---|---|---|---|---|---|---|---|---|---|---|---|---|---|---|---|---|---|---|---|
| 1 | 0.02 | 0.04 | 0.02 | 0.03 | 0.03 | 0.01 | 0.00 | 0.03 | 0.08 | 0.09 | 0.10 | 0.09 | 0.08 | 0.08 | 0.09 | 0.10 | 0.12 | 0.15 | 0.17 | 0.18 | 0.20 | 0.19 | 0.16 | 0.13 | 0.11 | 0.15 | 0.14 | 0.11 | 0.12 | 0.13 |
| 2 | 0.02 | 0.02 | 0.01 | 0.02 | 0.01 | 0.00 | 0.00 | 0.04 | 0.07 | 0.08 | 0.08 | 0.07 | 0.06 | 0.07 | 0.08 | 0.09 | 0.12 | 0.15 | 0.16 | 0.17 | 0.18 | 0.16 | 0.13 | 0.11 | 0.12 | 0.13 | 0.11 | 0.11 | 0.11 | 0.11 |
| 3 | 0.01 | 0.01 | 0.00 | 0.00 | -0.01 | -0.01 | 0.01 | 0.04 | 0.06 | 0.06 | 0.06 | 0.05 | 0.05 | 0.06 | 0.07 | 0.10 | 0.12 | 0.14 | 0.15 | 0.16 | 0.15 | 0.13 | 0.11 | 0.11 | 0.11 | 0.11 | 0.10 | 0.10 | 0.10 | 0.09 |
| 4 | 0.00 | 0.01 | 0.00 | -0.01 | -0.01 | 0.00 | 0.02 | 0.04 | 0.06 | 0.06 | 0.06 | 0.05 | 0.06 | 0.06 | 0.07 | 0.11 | 0.13 | 0.15 | 0.15 | 0.16 | 0.14 | 0.12 | 0.11 | 0.11 | 0.11 | 0.12 | 0.11 | 0.11 | 0.11 | 0.10 |
| 5 | 0.00 | 0.00 | -0.01 | -0.01 | 0.00 | 0.01 | 0.03 | 0.05 | 0.06 | 0.06 | 0.07 | 0.06 | 0.07 | 0.08 | 0.09 | 0.12 | 0.13 | 0.15 | 0.15 | 0.15 | 0.14 | 0.13 | 0.12 | 0.11 | 0.11 | 0.12 | 0.11 | 0.11 | 0.11 | 0.11 |
| 6 | 0.00 | 0.00 | -0.01 | 0.00 | 0.01 | 0.02 | 0.04 | 0.05 | 0.06 | 0.06 | 0.07 | 0.07 | 0.08 | 0.10 | 0.11 | 0.13 | 0.14 | 0.15 | 0.15 | 0.15 | 0.14 | 0.13 | 0.12 | 0.13 | 0.12 | 0.12 | 0.12 | 0.12 | 0.12 | 0.11 |
| 7 | 0.00 | 0.00 | -0.01 | 0.01 | 0.02 | 0.03 | 0.04 | 0.05 | 0.06 | 0.07 | 0.08 | 0.08 | 0.09 | 0.11 | 0.12 | 0.14 | 0.15 | 0.15 | 0.15 | 0.15 | 0.14 | 0.13 | 0.13 | 0.13 | 0.13 | 0.13 | 0.13 | 0.13 | 0.12 | 0.11 |
| 8 | 0.00 | 0.01 | 0.01 | 0.02 | 0.03 | 0.04 | 0.05 | 0.06 | 0.07 | 0.08 | 0.08 | 0.09 | 0.11 | 0.12 | 0.13 | 0.14 | 0.15 | 0.15 | 0.16 | 0.15 | 0.15 | 0.14 | 0.14 | 0.13 | 0.13 | 0.13 | 0.13 | 0.13 | 0.12 | 0.11 |
| 9 | 0.01 | 0.01 | 0.02 | 0.03 | 0.03 | 0.04 | 0.05 | 0.06 | 0.08 | 0.09 | 0.10 | 0.10 | 0.12 | 0.13 | 0.14 | 0.14 | 0.15 | 0.16 | 0.16 | 0.15 | 0.15 | 0.14 | 0.14 | 0.13 | 0.13 | 0.14 | 0.13 | 0.12 | 0.12 | 0.11 |
| 10 | 0.01 | 0.01 | 0.02 | 0.02 | 0.03 | 0.04 | 0.05 | 0.06 | 0.08 | 0.09 | 0.10 | 0.11 | 0.12 | 0.13 | 0.13 | 0.14 | 0.14 | 0.15 | 0.15 | 0.15 | 0.14 | 0.14 | 0.13 | 0.13 | 0.13 | 0.13 | 0.12 | 0.12 | 0.11 | 0.10 |
| 11 | 0.01 | 0.01 | 0.02 | 0.02 | 0.03 | 0.04 | 0.05 | 0.07 | 0.08 | 0.09 | 0.10 | 0.11 | 0.12 | 0.12 | 0.13 | 0.13 | 0.14 | 0.14 | 0.15 | 0.14 | 0.14 | 0.13 | 0.13 | 0.13 | 0.12 | 0.12 | 0.12 | 0.11 | 0.11 | 0.10 |
| 12 | 0.01 | 0.01 | 0.01 | 0.02 | 0.03 | 0.04 | 0.05 | 0.07 | 0.08 | 0.09 | 0.10 | 0.11 | 0.11 | 0.12 | 0.13 | 0.13 | 0.13 | 0.14 | 0.14 | 0.14 | 0.13 | 0.13 | 0.13 | 0.12 | 0.12 | 0.12 | 0.11 | 0.10 | 0.10 | 0.10 |
| 13 | 0.01 | 0.01 | 0.01 | 0.02 | 0.03 | 0.04 | 0.06 | 0.07 | 0.09 | 0.10 | 0.10 | 0.11 | 0.11 | 0.12 | 0.12 | 0.13 | 0.13 | 0.14 | 0.14 | 0.13 | 0.13 | 0.13 | 0.12 | 0.12 | 0.12 | 0.11 | 0.11 | 0.10 | 0.10 | 0.10 |
| 14 | 0.01 | 0.01 | 0.02 | 0.02 | 0.03 | 0.05 | 0.05 | 0.06 | 0.09 | 0.10 | 0.10 | 0.10 | 0.11 | 0.12 | 0.12 | 0.13 | 0.13 | 0.13 | 0.13 | 0.14 | 0.13 | 0.13 | 0.12 | 0.11 | 0.11 | 0.11 | 0.10 | 0.10 | 0.10 | 0.09 |
| 15 | 0.01 | 0.01 | 0.02 | 0.03 | 0.04 | 0.05 | 0.05 | 0.06 | 0.09 | 0.10 | 0.10 | 0.10 | 0.11 | 0.11 | 0.12 | 0.12 | 0.13 | 0.13 | 0.13 | 0.13 | 0.13 | 0.12 | 0.11 | 0.11 | 0.10 | 0.10 | 0.10 | 0.10 | 0.10 | 0.09 |
| 16 | 0.01 | 0.01 | 0.02 | 0.03 | 0.04 | 0.05 | 0.07 | 0.08 | 0.09 | 0.09 | 0.10 | 0.10 | 0.11 | 0.11 | 0.12 | 0.12 | 0.12 | 0.13 | 0.13 | 0.12 | 0.11 | 0.11 | 0.11 | 0.10 | 0.10 | 0.10 | 0.10 | 0.09 | 0.09 | 0.09 |
| 17 | 0.01 | 0.01 | 0.02 | 0.03 | 0.04 | 0.06 | 0.07 | 0.08 | 0.09 | 0.09 | 0.10 | 0.10 | 0.11 | 0.11 | 0.11 | 0.12 | 0.12 | 0.12 | 0.12 | 0.12 | 0.11 | 0.11 | 0.10 | 0.10 | 0.10 | 0.10 | 0.10 | 0.09 | 0.09 | 0.08 |
| 18 | 0.01 | 0.02 | 0.02 | 0.04 | 0.05 | 0.06 | 0.06 | 0.07 | 0.08 | 0.09 | 0.09 | 0.10 | 0.10 | 0.10 | 0.11 | 0.11 | 0.12 | 0.11 | 0.12 | 0.11 | 0.11 | 0.10 | 0.10 | 0.10 | 0.09 | 0.09 | 0.09 | 0.08 | 0.08 | 0.08 |
| 19 | 0.01 | 0.02 | 0.03 | 0.04 | 0.04 | 0.05 | 0.06 | 0.07 | 0.08 | 0.09 | 0.09 | 0.09 | 0.09 | 0.09 | 0.10 | 0.11 | 0.11 | 0.11 | 0.11 | 0.10 | 0.10 | 0.10 | 0.09 | 0.09 | 0.09 | 0.08 | 0.08 | 0.08 | 0.08 | 0.08 |
| 20 | 0.01 | 0.02 | 0.03 | 0.03 | 0.04 | 0.05 | 0.05 | 0.07 | 0.07 | 0.08 | 0.08 | 0.09 | 0.09 | 0.09 | 0.10 | 0.10 | 0.10 | 0.10 | 0.10 | 0.09 | 0.09 | 0.09 | 0.08 | 0.08 | 0.08 | 0.08 | 0.07 | 0.08 | 0.08 | 0.07 |
| 21 | 0.01 | 0.02 | 0.02 | 0.03 | 0.04 | 0.05 | 0.05 | 0.06 | 0.07 | 0.08 | 0.08 | 0.08 | 0.09 | 0.09 | 0.09 | 0.09 | 0.10 | 0.10 | 0.09 | 0.09 | 0.09 | 0.08 | 0.08 | 0.07 | 0.07 | 0.07 | 0.07 | 0.07 | 0.07 | 0.07 |
| 22 | 0.01 | 0.02 | 0.02 | 0.03 | 0.03 | 0.04 | 0.05 | 0.06 | 0.07 | 0.07 | 0.08 | 0.08 | 0.08 | 0.08 | 0.08 | 0.08 | 0.08 | 0.08 | 0.08 | 0.08 | 0.08 | 0.08 | 0.07 | 0.07 | 0.07 | 0.07 | 0.07 | 0.07 | 0.06 | 0.06 |
| 23 | 0.01 | 0.01 | 0.02 | 0.03 | 0.03 | 0.04 | 0.05 | 0.06 | 0.06 | 0.07 | 0.07 | 0.07 | 0.08 | 0.07 | 0.08 | 0.08 | 0.07 | 0.07 | 0.08 | 0.08 | 0.07 | 0.07 | 0.07 | 0.06 | 0.06 | 0.06 | 0.06 | 0.06 | 0.06 | 0.06 |
| 24 | 0.01 | 0.01 | 0.02 | 0.02 | 0.03 | 0.04 | 0.05 | 0.05 | 0.06 | 0.06 | 0.07 | 0.06 | 0.07 | 0.07 | 0.07 | 0.07 | 0.07 | 0.07 | 0.07 | 0.07 | 0.07 | 0.06 | 0.06 | 0.06 | 0.06 | 0.06 | 0.06 | 0.06 | 0.06 | 0.06 |
| 25 | 0.01 | 0.01 | 0.02 | 0.02 | 0.03 | 0.04 | 0.05 | 0.05 | 0.05 | 0.05 | 0.05 | 0.06 | 0.06 | 0.05 | 0.06 | 0.06 | 0.06 | 0.07 | 0.07 | 0.07 | 0.06 | 0.06 | 0.06 | 0.05 | 0.05 | 0.05 | 0.05 | 0.05 | 0.05 | 0.05 |
| 26 | 0.01 | 0.01 | 0.02 | 0.02 | 0.03 | 0.04 | 0.04 | 0.05 | 0.06 | 0.06 | 0.06 | 0.06 | 0.06 | 0.05 | 0.06 | 0.06 | 0.07 | 0.07 | 0.06 | 0.06 | 0.06 | 0.06 | 0.06 | 0.05 | 0.06 | 0.06 | 0.06 | 0.05 | 0.05 | 0.05 |
| 27 | 0.01 | 0.01 | 0.02 | 0.02 | 0.03 | 0.03 | 0.04 | 0.05 | 0.05 | 0.05 | 0.05 | 0.05 | 0.05 | 0.06 | 0.06 | 0.06 | 0.06 | 0.07 | 0.07 | 0.07 | 0.06 | 0.06 | 0.06 | 0.05 | 0.05 | 0.05 | 0.05 | 0.05 | 0.05 | 0.04 |
| 28 | 0.01 | 0.01 | 0.02 | 0.02 | 0.03 | 0.03 | 0.04 | 0.04 | 0.05 | 0.05 | 0.05 | 0.05 | 0.05 | 0.05 | 0.06 | 0.06 | 0.06 | 0.06 | 0.07 | 0.06 | 0.06 | 0.06 | 0.05 | 0.05 | 0.05 | 0.05 | 0.05 | 0.05 | 0.05 | 0.04 |
| 29 | 0.01 | 0.01 | 0.02 | 0.02 | 0.03 | 0.03 | 0.04 | 0.04 | 0.04 | 0.05 | 0.05 | 0.05 | 0.05 | 0.05 | 0.05 | 0.05 | 0.06 | 0.06 | 0.06 | 0.06 | 0.06 | 0.05 | 0.05 | 0.05 | 0.05 | 0.05 | 0.05 | 0.05 | 0.04 | 0.04 |
| 30 | 0.01 | 0.01 | 0.01 | 0.02 | 0.02 | 0.03 | 0.03 | 0.04 | 0.04 | 0.04 | 0.05 | 0.05 | 0.05 | 0.05 | 0.05 | 0.05 | 0.05 | 0.05 | 0.05 | 0.05 | 0.05 | 0.05 | 0.05 | 0.05 | 0.05 | 0.05 | 0.04 | 0.04 | 0.04 | 0.03 |

Notes: Coefficient estimates in the regression $R^{FX}_{t,t+k} = c + \gamma R^{FX}_{t-i,t} + \sum_{m=1}^{4} \beta_m OF^{FX}_{t-i,t} + \varepsilon_t$, for corporate end-user order flows. The horizontal axis varies over the $k$-minute forecast horizon; the vertical axis varies according to the aggregation window of FX order flows through the $i$-minute period. A lightly shaded cell denotes significance at the 10% cent level using robust standard error estimates. Darker shading denotes significance at the 5% level. Intra-day data from 7.30 a.m. to 5.00 p.m. for 25 days are used. Coefficients represent the percentage change in the euro-dollar exchange rate from a €1bn flow into the dollar, expressed such that a positive sign is an appreciation of the dollar.

corporates and financials are jointly significant in the majority of cases. Finally, the coefficients on corporate and financial customer flows are different from each other in most cases. It is clear that customer order flows matter for the pricing of FX rates, and that there is heterogeneity in the flows which matters for FX pricing.

Recall that the order flows used in this article are those seen by a specific bank. As measured, they are not available to the wider FX market. How then do these flows impact on market FX rates? Three explanations suggest themselves[6]:

(i) The customers of this bank are able to forecast high-frequency returns and hence can position themselves accordingly.

(ii) The bank trades upon these customer flows, either by passing these trades directly onto the inter-bank market and/or by actively trading based upon the information content, revealing the information to the wider market.

(iii) The flows seen by the bank are correlated with the flows seen across the wider market.

We have no information to guide us with regard to this issue, but discussions with the bank supplying the data lead us to believe that (iii) is likely for corporate customers, (ii) is likely for corporate, financial, and internal customers, and (i) is possible for a (small) subset of customers.

Previous papers have demonstrated forecasting power from order flows to future exchange rates using both end-user flows (Evans and Lyons 2005) and inter-bank flows (Rime, Sarno, and Sojli 2010). This is the first article, to our knowledge, that demonstrates intra-day forecasting power using end-user flows. Beyond the mere existence of some forecasting power, the main contribution of the analysis has been to highlight the heterogeneity across the different end-user categories. Both signs and horizons over which there is forecasting power differ noticeably between corporate and financial end-users. We return to discuss the FX forecasting results later in the article where we can interpret them with the aid of the cross-market relationship results, to which we now turn.

### 5.3 *Contemporaneous relationships between FX flows and stock market index returns*

Table 4 reports the results of estimating equation (3) using stock index returns for the SPY (S&P 500) contract. Results from the DIA (Dow 30) ETF are very similar and so are not reported. We find essentially no contemporaneous relationship between FX order flows and stock market changes. All but one of the coefficients on order flows are insignificant, and there is no consistency in signs for any category of the bank's counterparties. There is a clear positive contemporaneous relationship between exchange rate returns and stock market returns (over aggregation horizons longer than 10 min), which is consistent with many previous studies on return spillovers between different markets (Ajayi and Mougoue 1996; Andersen et al. 2007).

### 5.4 *Forecasting relationships between FX flows and stock market index returns*

We next investigate the forecasting power of order flows for stock market changes. In Tables 5 and 6, respectively, we report the coefficient estimates on the financial and corporate customer categories of order flow from the forecasting model $R^S_{t,t+k} = c + \alpha R^S_{t-i,t} + \gamma R^{FX}_{t-i,t} + \sum_{m=1}^{4} \beta_m OF^{FX}_{t-i,t} + \varepsilon_t$. The other results are available on request. The horizontal axis varies over the $k$-minute forecast horizon; the vertical axis varies according to the accumulation of foreign

Table 4. SPY regression results in the cross-market contemporaneous model.

| | Aggregation window | | | | | | | | | | | | | | |
|---|---|---|---|---|---|---|---|---|---|---|---|---|---|---|---|
| | 1 | 2 | 3 | 4 | 5 | 6 | 7 | 8 | 9 | 10 | 11 | 12 | 13 | 14 | 15 |
| Financial | 0.05 | 0.08 | 0.09 | 0.07 | 0.05 | 0.04 | 0.04 | 0.04 | 0.04 | 0.04 | 0.04 | 0.05 | 0.05 | 0.04 | 0.05 |
| Corporate | 0.02 | 0.15 | 0.23 | 0.29 | 0.37 | 0.35 | 0.33 | 0.30 | 0.27 | 0.26 | 0.25 | 0.25 | 0.23 | 0.23 | 0.23 |
| Internal | 0.01 | 0.16 | 0.26 | 0.26 | 0.30 | 0.23 | 0.22 | 0.24 | 0.21 | 0.20 | 0.19 | 0.16 | 0.10 | 0.08 | 0.07 |
| Inter-bank | −0.03 | −0.09 | −0.08 | −0.02 | 0.02 | 0.05 | 0.07 | 0.08 | 0.07 | 0.05 | 0.00 | −0.02 | −0.05 | −0.06 | −0.10 |
| Rfx | 0.40 | 0.28 | 0.21 | 0.38 | 0.52 | 0.63 | 0.77 | 0.86 | 0.98 | 1.11 | 1.15 | 1.18 | 1.20 | 1.21 | 1.25 |

| | Aggregation window | | | | | | | | | | | | | | |
|---|---|---|---|---|---|---|---|---|---|---|---|---|---|---|---|
| | 16 | 17 | 18 | 19 | 20 | 21 | 22 | 23 | 24 | 25 | 26 | 27 | 28 | 29 | 30 |
| Financial | 0.05 | 0.05 | 0.05 | 0.06 | 0.06 | 0.06 | 0.07 | 0.07 | 0.07 | 0.07 | 0.08 | 0.09 | 0.10 | 0.11 | 0.12 |
| Corporate | 0.22 | 0.21 | 0.19 | 0.18 | 0.16 | 0.13 | 0.09 | 0.04 | 0.01 | −0.01 | −0.03 | −0.03 | −0.04 | −0.06 | −0.09 |
| Internal | 0.05 | −0.01 | −0.08 | −0.11 | −0.20 | −0.31 | −0.45 | −0.58 | −0.66 | −0.74 | −0.79 | −0.82 | −0.83 | −0.86 | −0.91 |
| Inter-bank | −0.16 | −0.20 | −0.23 | −0.24 | −0.25 | −0.27 | −0.29 | −0.32 | −0.32 | −0.33 | −0.31 | −0.28 | −0.24 | −0.23 | −0.22 |
| Rfx | 1.32 | 1.47 | 1.63 | 1.79 | 1.90 | 2.03 | 2.11 | 2.19 | 2.28 | 2.35 | 2.41 | 2.47 | 2.54 | 2.59 | 2.63 |

Notes: Coefficient estimates from the regression $R_{t,t+i}^{FX} = c + \gamma R_{t,t+i}^{FX} + \beta m \sum_{m=1}^{4} OF_{t,t+i}^{FX} + \varepsilon$. The column headings give the value of the aggregation window $i$ in the model. Intra-day data from 2.30 p.m. to 5.00 p.m. for 25 days are used. A lightly shaded cell denotes significance at the 10% level using robust standard error estimates. Darker shading denotes significance at the 5% level. Coefficients represent the percentage change in the SPY ETF price from a €1bn flow into the dollar.

Table 5. Impact of order flow on future SPY ETF price changes: financial customer order flows.

| Aggregation Window \ Forecast horizon | 1 | 2 | 3 | 4 | 5 | 6 | 7 | 8 | 9 | 10 | 11 | 12 | 13 | 14 | 15 | 16 | 17 | 18 | 19 | 20 | 21 | 22 | 23 | 24 | 25 | 26 | 27 | 28 | 29 | 30 |
|---|---|---|---|---|---|---|---|---|---|---|---|---|---|---|---|---|---|---|---|---|---|---|---|---|---|---|---|---|---|---|
| 1 | 0.04 | 0.08 | 0.03 | -0.03 | -0.03 | -0.03 | 0.02 | 0.04 | 0.10 | 0.05 | 0.09 | 0.00 | -0.02 | 0.12 | 0.04 | 0.01 | 0.00 | 0.04 | -0.01 | 0.04 | 0.04 | 0.05 | -0.01 | -0.02 | -0.08 | -0.05 | -0.06 | -0.09 | -0.10 | -0.06 |
| 2 | 0.04 | 0.04 | -0.02 | -0.04 | -0.04 | -0.02 | 0.02 | 0.03 | 0.06 | 0.05 | 0.02 | -0.03 | 0.03 | 0.06 | 0.01 | -0.01 | 0.00 | 0.00 | 0.00 | 0.03 | 0.03 | 0.01 | -0.03 | -0.06 | -0.08 | -0.06 | -0.08 | -0.10 | -0.09 | 0.00 |
| 3 | 0.01 | -0.01 | -0.05 | -0.06 | -0.05 | -0.02 | 0.02 | 0.01 | 0.04 | 0.00 | -0.02 | -0.01 | 0.00 | 0.01 | -0.03 | -0.03 | -0.04 | -0.02 | -0.02 | 0.01 | -0.01 | -0.03 | -0.07 | -0.09 | -0.10 | -0.10 | -0.12 | -0.12 | -0.06 | -0.04 |
| 4 | 0.00 | -0.02 | -0.05 | -0.05 | -0.03 | 0.00 | 0.02 | 0.03 | 0.02 | -0.01 | 0.00 | -0.01 | -0.01 | -0.01 | -0.03 | -0.04 | -0.03 | -0.02 | -0.03 | -0.01 | -0.03 | -0.06 | -0.08 | -0.09 | -0.11 | -0.11 | -0.11 | -0.08 | -0.07 | -0.02 |
| 5 | -0.01 | -0.02 | -0.03 | 0.00 | 0.00 | 0.01 | 0.03 | 0.02 | 0.01 | 0.01 | 0.00 | -0.02 | -0.02 | -0.01 | -0.04 | -0.04 | -0.03 | -0.03 | -0.03 | -0.02 | -0.05 | -0.06 | -0.09 | -0.10 | -0.12 | -0.11 | -0.09 | -0.08 | -0.05 | -0.03 |
| 6 | 0.00 | 0.00 | -0.01 | 0.00 | 0.01 | 0.02 | 0.02 | 0.21 | 0.02 | 0.00 | -0.01 | -0.02 | -0.02 | -0.03 | -0.04 | -0.04 | -0.03 | -0.04 | -0.05 | -0.04 | -0.06 | -0.07 | -0.10 | -0.11 | -0.11 | -0.11 | -0.09 | -0.07 | -0.05 | -0.04 |
| 7 | 0.00 | 0.00 | 0.00 | 0.01 | 0.02 | 0.02 | 0.02 | 0.31 | 0.01 | -0.01 | -0.02 | -0.03 | -0.04 | -0.04 | -0.03 | -0.04 | -0.03 | -0.05 | -0.06 | -0.05 | -0.06 | -0.08 | -0.10 | -0.12 | -0.11 | -0.10 | -0.08 | -0.07 | -0.05 | -0.06 |
| 8 | 0.01 | 0.01 | 0.00 | 0.01 | 0.02 | 0.02 | 0.01 | 0.32 | 0.00 | -0.02 | -0.03 | -0.03 | -0.04 | -0.04 | -0.04 | -0.04 | -0.05 | -0.05 | -0.06 | -0.06 | -0.08 | -0.10 | -0.12 | -0.11 | -0.09 | -0.09 | -0.08 | -0.07 | -0.08 | -0.08 |
| 9 | 0.01 | 0.01 | 0.01 | 0.00 | -0.01 | 0.01 | 0.01 | 0.31 | 0.00 | -0.02 | -0.03 | -0.04 | -0.05 | -0.05 | -0.06 | -0.06 | -0.07 | -0.07 | -0.06 | -0.08 | -0.10 | -0.12 | -0.11 | -0.11 | -0.10 | -0.09 | -0.09 | -0.10 | -0.10 | -0.10 |
| 10 | 0.00 | 0.00 | -0.01 | -0.01 | -0.01 | 0.01 | 0.01 | 0.00 | -0.02 | -0.03 | -0.05 | -0.06 | -0.07 | -0.06 | -0.07 | -0.08 | -0.08 | -0.09 | -0.10 | -0.08 | -0.12 | -0.12 | -0.12 | -0.12 | -0.11 | -0.10 | -0.10 | -0.10 | -0.12 | -0.12 |
| 11 | 0.01 | 0.00 | -0.01 | 0.00 | -0.01 | 0.01 | 0.01 | -0.03 | -0.02 | -0.05 | -0.06 | -0.07 | -0.07 | -0.07 | -0.08 | -0.09 | -0.10 | -0.11 | -0.11 | -0.12 | -0.12 | -0.11 | -0.12 | -0.13 | -0.12 | -0.12 | -0.13 | -0.13 | -0.12 | -0.13 |
| 12 | 0.00 | -0.01 | -0.01 | -0.02 | -0.02 | -0.03 | -0.03 | -0.05 | -0.06 | -0.07 | -0.07 | -0.08 | -0.08 | -0.08 | -0.09 | -0.10 | -0.10 | -0.11 | -0.11 | -0.12 | -0.12 | -0.13 | -0.13 | -0.13 | -0.13 | -0.13 | -0.14 | -0.13 | -0.12 | -0.13 |
| 13 | 0.00 | -0.01 | -0.01 | -0.02 | -0.03 | -0.03 | -0.04 | -0.06 | -0.05 | -0.06 | -0.07 | -0.08 | -0.09 | -0.10 | -0.09 | -0.11 | -0.11 | -0.11 | -0.11 | -0.11 | -0.12 | -0.13 | -0.14 | -0.13 | -0.13 | -0.13 | -0.14 | -0.14 | -0.15 | -0.17 |
| 14 | 0.01 | 0.00 | -0.01 | -0.02 | -0.03 | -0.03 | -0.04 | -0.04 | -0.05 | -0.07 | -0.07 | -0.08 | -0.08 | -0.10 | -0.10 | -0.11 | -0.11 | -0.11 | -0.11 | -0.11 | -0.11 | -0.12 | -0.13 | -0.13 | -0.14 | -0.14 | -0.14 | -0.16 | -0.15 | -0.18 |
| 15 | 0.00 | -0.01 | -0.02 | -0.03 | -0.04 | -0.04 | -0.04 | -0.05 | -0.05 | -0.07 | -0.08 | -0.09 | -0.09 | -0.10 | -0.10 | -0.12 | -0.12 | -0.12 | -0.11 | -0.11 | -0.12 | -0.13 | -0.14 | -0.14 | -0.15 | -0.15 | -0.16 | -0.14 | -0.15 | -0.17 |
| 16 | 0.00 | -0.01 | -0.02 | -0.03 | -0.04 | -0.04 | -0.04 | -0.05 | -0.06 | -0.07 | -0.08 | -0.09 | -0.10 | -0.11 | -0.11 | -0.12 | -0.12 | -0.11 | -0.12 | -0.12 | -0.13 | -0.13 | -0.14 | -0.15 | -0.15 | -0.16 | -0.18 | -0.16 | -0.17 | -0.18 |
| 17 | -0.01 | -0.01 | -0.02 | -0.03 | -0.03 | -0.04 | -0.04 | -0.05 | -0.06 | -0.07 | -0.08 | -0.09 | -0.10 | -0.11 | -0.11 | -0.12 | -0.11 | -0.11 | -0.11 | -0.12 | -0.13 | -0.14 | -0.15 | -0.16 | -0.17 | -0.18 | -0.19 | -0.18 | -0.19 | -0.19 |
| 18 | 0.00 | -0.01 | -0.02 | -0.03 | -0.03 | -0.04 | -0.04 | -0.07 | -0.07 | -0.08 | -0.09 | -0.10 | -0.10 | -0.11 | -0.12 | -0.13 | -0.13 | -0.13 | -0.14 | -0.15 | -0.16 | -0.17 | -0.18 | -0.19 | -0.20 | -0.20 | -0.20 | -0.21 | -0.21 | -0.21 |
| 19 | -0.01 | -0.01 | -0.02 | -0.03 | -0.03 | -0.04 | -0.05 | -0.05 | -0.07 | -0.09 | -0.10 | -0.10 | -0.10 | -0.11 | -0.13 | -0.13 | -0.13 | -0.14 | -0.15 | -0.16 | -0.17 | -0.18 | -0.19 | -0.19 | -0.19 | -0.20 | -0.21 | -0.21 | -0.21 | -0.21 |
| 20 | 0.00 | -0.01 | -0.02 | -0.03 | -0.04 | -0.05 | -0.05 | -0.08 | -0.08 | -0.09 | -0.10 | -0.10 | -0.11 | -0.11 | -0.12 | -0.13 | -0.13 | -0.13 | -0.14 | -0.15 | -0.16 | -0.16 | -0.18 | -0.19 | -0.20 | -0.20 | -0.20 | -0.20 | -0.21 | -0.21 |
| 21 | 0.00 | -0.01 | -0.02 | -0.03 | -0.04 | -0.05 | -0.05 | -0.06 | -0.09 | -0.09 | -0.10 | -0.11 | -0.11 | -0.12 | -0.12 | -0.13 | -0.14 | -0.15 | -0.16 | -0.17 | -0.17 | -0.18 | -0.19 | -0.20 | -0.20 | -0.21 | -0.21 | -0.21 | -0.21 | -0.20 |
| 22 | 0.00 | -0.01 | -0.02 | -0.03 | -0.04 | -0.05 | -0.06 | -0.07 | -0.08 | -0.10 | -0.10 | -0.11 | -0.11 | -0.12 | -0.12 | -0.13 | -0.14 | -0.16 | -0.16 | -0.17 | -0.17 | -0.18 | -0.19 | -0.20 | -0.20 | -0.21 | -0.21 | -0.20 | -0.21 | -0.20 |
| 23 | 0.00 | -0.01 | -0.03 | -0.04 | -0.04 | -0.05 | -0.06 | -0.07 | -0.08 | -0.10 | -0.10 | -0.11 | -0.11 | -0.12 | -0.13 | -0.13 | -0.13 | -0.18 | -0.18 | -0.18 | -0.18 | -0.18 | -0.19 | -0.20 | -0.20 | -0.20 | -0.20 | -0.20 | -0.21 | -0.21 |
| 24 | -0.01 | -0.02 | -0.03 | -0.04 | -0.04 | -0.05 | -0.06 | -0.07 | -0.08 | -0.09 | -0.09 | -0.10 | -0.11 | -0.11 | -0.12 | -0.13 | -0.14 | -0.14 | -0.15 | -0.16 | -0.17 | -0.17 | -0.18 | -0.19 | -0.20 | -0.20 | -0.20 | -0.20 | -0.20 | -0.19 |
| 25 | -0.01 | -0.01 | -0.03 | -0.04 | -0.04 | -0.05 | -0.06 | -0.07 | -0.08 | -0.09 | -0.10 | -0.10 | -0.11 | -0.11 | -0.11 | -0.12 | -0.15 | -0.16 | -0.15 | -0.16 | -0.16 | -0.17 | -0.18 | -0.18 | -0.18 | -0.18 | -0.19 | -0.19 | -0.19 | -0.19 |
| 26 | -0.01 | -0.01 | -0.03 | -0.04 | -0.05 | -0.06 | -0.07 | -0.07 | -0.08 | -0.09 | -0.10 | -0.10 | -0.11 | -0.11 | -0.10 | -0.12 | -0.13 | -0.16 | -0.16 | -0.16 | -0.17 | -0.17 | -0.18 | -0.18 | -0.18 | -0.18 | -0.18 | -0.18 | -0.18 | -0.18 |
| 27 | -0.01 | -0.02 | -0.03 | -0.05 | -0.05 | -0.06 | -0.07 | -0.08 | -0.09 | -0.10 | -0.10 | -0.11 | -0.11 | -0.11 | -0.12 | -0.13 | -0.13 | -0.17 | -0.17 | -0.17 | -0.17 | -0.17 | -0.18 | -0.18 | -0.18 | -0.17 | -0.17 | -0.18 | -0.18 | -0.18 |
| 28 | -0.01 | -0.02 | -0.04 | -0.05 | -0.06 | -0.07 | -0.08 | -0.09 | -0.09 | -0.10 | -0.11 | -0.11 | -0.12 | -0.11 | -0.13 | -0.13 | -0.14 | -0.17 | -0.17 | -0.17 | -0.17 | -0.17 | -0.17 | -0.17 | -0.17 | -0.17 | -0.17 | -0.17 | -0.18 | -0.18 |
| 29 | -0.01 | -0.02 | -0.04 | -0.06 | -0.07 | -0.08 | -0.08 | -0.09 | -0.10 | -0.10 | -0.11 | -0.11 | -0.13 | -0.11 | -0.12 | -0.13 | -0.13 | -0.14 | -0.15 | -0.15 | -0.16 | -0.16 | -0.16 | -0.17 | -0.17 | -0.17 | -0.17 | -0.17 | -0.18 | -0.18 |
| 30 | -0.01 | -0.03 | -0.04 | -0.06 | -0.07 | -0.08 | -0.08 | -0.09 | -0.10 | -0.10 | -0.11 | -0.11 | -0.11 | -0.11 | -0.12 | -0.12 | -0.13 | -0.14 | -0.15 | -0.15 | -0.15 | -0.16 | -0.16 | -0.16 | -0.16 | -0.17 | -0.17 | -0.17 | -0.18 | -0.18 |

Notes: Coefficient estimates in the regression $R^S_{t,t+k} = c + \alpha R^S_{t-i,t} + \gamma R^{FX}_{t-i,t} + \sum_{m=1}^{4} \beta_m OF^{FX}_{t-i,t} + \varepsilon_t$ for financial end-user customer order flows. The horizontal axis varies over the $k$-minute forecast horizon; the vertical axis varies according to the aggregation window of FX order flows through the $i$-minute period. A lightly shaded cell denotes significance at the 10% level using robust standard error estimates. Darker shading denotes significance at the 5% level. Intra-day data from 2.30 p.m. to 5.00 p.m. for 25 days are used. Coefficients represent the percentage change in the SPY ETF price resulting from a €1bn flow into the dollar.

Table 6. Impact of order flow on future SPY ETF price changes: corporate customer order flows.

| Aggregation Window \ Forecast horizon | 1 | 2 | 3 | 4 | 5 | 6 | 7 | 8 | 9 | 10 | 11 | 12 | 13 | 14 | 15 | 16 | 17 | 18 | 19 | 20 | 21 | 22 | 23 | 24 | 25 | 26 | 27 | 28 | 29 | 30 |
|---|---|---|---|---|---|---|---|---|---|---|---|---|---|---|---|---|---|---|---|---|---|---|---|---|---|---|---|---|---|---|
| 1 | 0.21 | 0.41 | 0.46 | 0.59 | 0.53 | 0.67 | 0.61 | 0.61 | 0.75 | 0.65 | 0.57 | 0.48 | 0.63 | 0.72 | 0.81 | 0.75 | 0.63 | 0.62 | 0.66 | 0.90 | 0.93 | 0.81 | 0.90 | 0.72 | 0.95 | 1.13 | 1.21 | 1.02 | 0.71 | 0.81 |
| 2 | 0.21 | 0.33 | 0.43 | 0.46 | 0.50 | 0.54 | 0.51 | 0.57 | 0.57 | 0.47 | 0.38 | 0.40 | 0.51 | 0.58 | 0.59 | 0.50 | 0.44 | 0.45 | 0.60 | 0.74 | 0.69 | 0.67 | 0.63 | 0.65 | 0.87 | 1.00 | 0.95 | 0.69 | 0.58 | 0.66 |
| 3 | 0.15 | 0.26 | 0.26 | 0.32 | 0.35 | 0.38 | 0.41 | 0.27 | 0.22 | 0.27 | 0.24 | 0.26 | 0.33 | 0.37 | 0.33 | 0.29 | 0.27 | 0.36 | 0.47 | 0.52 | 0.55 | 0.47 | 0.51 | 0.59 | 0.27 | 0.64 | 0.64 | 0.50 | 0.44 | 0.54 |
| 4 | 0.13 | 0.16 | 0.19 | 0.24 | 0.26 | 0.33 | 0.31 | 0.27 | 0.22 | 0.17 | 0.15 | 0.16 | 0.21 | 0.21 | 0.19 | 0.17 | 0.22 | 0.29 | 0.35 | 0.43 | 0.39 | 0.40 | 0.47 | 0.55 | 0.64 | 0.56 | 0.48 | 0.39 | 0.37 | 0.46 |
| 5 | 0.07 | 0.12 | 0.14 | 0.18 | 0.23 | 0.25 | 0.21 | 0.16 | 0.14 | 0.09 | 0.07 | 0.07 | 0.09 | 0.09 | 0.09 | 0.12 | 0.17 | 0.20 | 0.28 | 0.30 | 0.32 | 0.36 | 0.44 | 0.46 | 0.46 | 0.42 | 0.36 | 0.31 | 0.31 | 0.40 |
| 6 | 0.07 | 0.11 | 0.13 | 0.19 | 0.20 | 0.20 | 0.15 | 0.11 | 0.09 | 0.05 | 0.03 | 0.02 | 0.04 | 0.04 | 0.08 | 0.11 | 0.13 | 0.19 | 0.21 | 0.28 | 0.32 | 0.36 | 0.41 | 0.36 | 0.37 | 0.34 | 0.32 | 0.29 | 0.30 | 0.36 |
| 7 | 0.06 | 0.10 | 0.13 | 0.15 | 0.15 | 0.13 | 0.10 | 0.07 | 0.05 | 0.01 | -0.03 | -0.03 | -0.01 | 0.02 | 0.06 | 0.07 | 0.12 | 0.13 | 0.19 | 0.27 | 0.29 | 0.33 | 0.31 | 0.28 | 0.30 | 0.30 | 0.29 | 0.26 | 0.26 | 0.34 |
| 8 | 0.05 | 0.10 | 0.10 | 0.11 | 0.09 | 0.09 | 0.06 | 0.03 | 0.01 | -0.04 | -0.07 | -0.07 | -0.03 | 0.01 | 0.03 | 0.06 | 0.07 | 0.11 | 0.19 | 0.24 | 0.29 | 0.25 | 0.24 | 0.22 | 0.25 | 0.26 | 0.25 | 0.23 | 0.25 | 0.32 |
| 9 | 0.06 | 0.07 | 0.07 | 0.06 | 0.06 | 0.05 | 0.02 | -0.01 | 0.01 | -0.09 | -0.11 | -0.09 | -0.05 | -0.03 | 0.01 | 0.01 | 0.05 | 0.11 | 0.18 | 0.23 | 0.20 | 0.18 | 0.18 | 0.17 | 0.21 | 0.22 | 0.21 | 0.20 | 0.22 | 0.28 |
| 10 | 0.03 | 0.04 | 0.03 | 0.03 | 0.02 | 0.01 | 0.01 | -0.07 | -0.09 | -0.13 | -0.13 | -0.11 | -0.08 | -0.04 | -0.04 | -0.01 | 0.04 | 0.10 | 0.15 | 0.15 | 0.14 | 0.12 | 0.13 | 0.14 | 0.17 | 0.18 | 0.18 | 0.18 | 0.19 | 0.26 |
| 11 | 0.02 | 0.02 | 0.02 | 0.01 | 0.00 | -0.01 | -0.02 | -0.09 | -0.09 | -0.12 | -0.12 | -0.11 | -0.07 | -0.07 | -0.04 | -0.01 | 0.06 | 0.06 | 0.18 | 0.12 | 0.11 | 0.11 | 0.12 | 0.13 | 0.16 | 0.17 | 0.18 | 0.17 | 0.20 | 0.26 |
| 12 | 0.01 | 0.01 | 0.00 | 0.00 | -0.02 | -0.05 | -0.06 | -0.11 | -0.12 | -0.12 | -0.13 | -0.11 | -0.09 | -0.06 | -0.02 | 0.03 | 0.06 | 0.06 | 0.07 | 0.09 | 0.10 | 0.11 | 0.12 | 0.13 | 0.16 | 0.17 | 0.18 | 0.18 | 0.20 | 0.27 |
| 13 | 0.01 | 0.01 | 0.00 | -0.01 | -0.04 | -0.06 | -0.08 | -0.09 | -0.10 | -0.11 | -0.10 | -0.10 | -0.06 | -0.02 | 0.02 | 0.04 | 0.04 | 0.05 | 0.07 | 0.09 | 0.10 | 0.11 | 0.14 | 0.14 | 0.18 | 0.19 | 0.21 | 0.21 | 0.23 | 0.30 |
| 14 | 0.01 | 0.00 | -0.01 | -0.03 | -0.05 | -0.06 | -0.07 | -0.08 | -0.09 | -0.09 | -0.10 | -0.08 | -0.04 | 0.01 | 0.03 | 0.02 | 0.03 | 0.04 | 0.07 | 0.10 | 0.11 | 0.11 | 0.14 | 0.16 | 0.19 | 0.21 | 0.22 | 0.23 | 0.26 | 0.31 |
| 15 | 0.00 | -0.01 | -0.02 | -0.04 | -0.06 | -0.06 | -0.07 | -0.08 | -0.07 | -0.09 | -0.09 | -0.06 | -0.01 | 0.02 | 0.01 | 0.01 | 0.02 | 0.04 | 0.06 | 0.10 | 0.11 | 0.12 | 0.15 | 0.16 | 0.21 | 0.22 | 0.24 | 0.25 | 0.27 | 0.32 |
| 16 | 0.00 | -0.01 | -0.02 | -0.03 | -0.04 | -0.04 | -0.05 | -0.06 | -0.07 | -0.07 | -0.05 | -0.02 | 0.01 | 0.00 | 0.00 | 0.00 | 0.02 | 0.04 | 0.06 | 0.09 | 0.12 | 0.13 | 0.16 | 0.18 | 0.22 | 0.24 | 0.26 | 0.28 | 0.29 | 0.33 |
| 17 | -0.01 | -0.02 | -0.02 | -0.03 | -0.03 | -0.03 | -0.04 | -0.06 | -0.07 | -0.05 | -0.02 | -0.01 | -0.01 | -0.01 | -0.01 | 0.01 | 0.02 | 0.03 | 0.06 | 0.10 | 0.12 | 0.14 | 0.17 | 0.19 | 0.24 | 0.26 | 0.27 | 0.28 | 0.34 | 0.34 |
| 18 | 0.00 | -0.01 | -0.01 | -0.02 | -0.03 | -0.02 | -0.04 | -0.04 | -0.03 | -0.01 | 0.00 | -0.01 | 0.00 | -0.01 | -0.01 | 0.00 | 0.02 | 0.04 | 0.07 | 0.11 | 0.14 | 0.16 | 0.19 | 0.22 | 0.26 | 0.28 | 0.29 | 0.30 | 0.31 | 0.34 |
| 19 | -0.01 | -0.01 | -0.02 | -0.03 | -0.03 | -0.03 | -0.04 | -0.03 | -0.01 | 0.00 | -0.01 | -0.02 | -0.01 | -0.02 | -0.01 | 0.01 | 0.01 | 0.04 | 0.08 | 0.12 | 0.15 | 0.17 | 0.21 | 0.24 | 0.26 | 0.29 | 0.31 | 0.32 | 0.31 | 0.36 |
| 20 | 0.00 | -0.01 | -0.02 | -0.02 | -0.03 | -0.02 | -0.01 | 0.00 | 0.00 | -0.01 | -0.01 | -0.02 | -0.01 | -0.01 | -0.01 | 0.00 | 0.02 | 0.05 | 0.09 | 0.14 | 0.17 | 0.20 | 0.24 | 0.27 | 0.29 | 0.31 | 0.32 | 0.32 | 0.34 | 0.39 |
| 21 | -0.01 | -0.01 | -0.01 | -0.03 | -0.02 | 0.00 | 0.00 | 0.01 | 0.00 | -0.01 | -0.02 | -0.02 | -0.02 | -0.01 | -0.01 | 0.01 | 0.03 | 0.06 | 0.11 | 0.16 | 0.19 | 0.22 | 0.24 | 0.27 | 0.30 | 0.32 | 0.32 | 0.34 | 0.36 | 0.40 |
| 22 | -0.01 | -0.01 | -0.02 | -0.02 | 0.00 | 0.02 | 0.02 | 0.01 | 0.00 | -0.02 | -0.03 | -0.03 | -0.02 | -0.02 | 0.00 | 0.02 | 0.05 | 0.09 | 0.13 | 0.18 | 0.21 | 0.23 | 0.26 | 0.29 | 0.31 | 0.32 | 0.34 | 0.35 | 0.37 | 0.41 |
| 23 | 0.00 | -0.01 | 0.00 | -0.02 | 0.00 | 0.03 | 0.02 | 0.00 | 0.00 | -0.01 | -0.02 | -0.02 | -0.01 | 0.00 | 0.02 | 0.04 | 0.05 | 0.09 | 0.13 | 0.21 | 0.23 | 0.25 | 0.29 | 0.30 | 0.33 | 0.35 | 0.37 | 0.38 | 0.37 | 0.43 |
| 24 | -0.01 | 0.00 | 0.01 | 0.02 | 0.03 | 0.03 | 0.02 | 0.01 | 0.01 | 0.00 | -0.01 | -0.01 | 0.01 | 0.02 | 0.04 | 0.07 | 0.08 | 0.12 | 0.19 | 0.22 | 0.25 | 0.28 | 0.30 | 0.31 | 0.35 | 0.38 | 0.40 | 0.40 | 0.42 | 0.43 |
| 25 | 0.01 | 0.02 | 0.03 | 0.04 | 0.04 | 0.03 | 0.02 | 0.01 | 0.01 | 0.00 | 0.00 | 0.01 | 0.03 | 0.05 | 0.07 | 0.10 | 0.11 | 0.15 | 0.20 | 0.24 | 0.28 | 0.30 | 0.32 | 0.35 | 0.38 | 0.41 | 0.42 | 0.42 | 0.43 | 0.44 |
| 26 | 0.01 | 0.03 | 0.03 | 0.03 | 0.02 | 0.02 | 0.01 | 0.00 | 0.00 | -0.01 | 0.00 | 0.02 | 0.04 | 0.06 | 0.09 | 0.12 | 0.15 | 0.18 | 0.22 | 0.26 | 0.28 | 0.30 | 0.34 | 0.36 | 0.40 | 0.42 | 0.43 | 0.43 | 0.43 | 0.45 |
| 27 | 0.01 | 0.02 | 0.02 | 0.01 | 0.00 | 0.00 | 0.00 | -0.01 | -0.01 | -0.01 | 0.00 | 0.02 | 0.05 | 0.08 | 0.11 | 0.14 | 0.16 | 0.19 | 0.23 | 0.27 | 0.29 | 0.32 | 0.36 | 0.38 | 0.41 | 0.42 | 0.43 | 0.43 | 0.44 | 0.45 |
| 28 | 0.01 | 0.01 | 0.00 | 0.01 | 0.00 | -0.01 | -0.02 | 0.00 | -0.01 | -0.01 | 0.01 | 0.03 | 0.07 | 0.10 | 0.12 | 0.14 | 0.17 | 0.21 | 0.24 | 0.27 | 0.31 | 0.34 | 0.37 | 0.40 | 0.42 | 0.43 | 0.43 | 0.42 | 0.43 | 0.44 |
| 29 | 0.00 | -0.01 | -0.01 | -0.02 | -0.02 | -0.01 | -0.02 | -0.02 | -0.01 | 0.00 | 0.02 | 0.05 | 0.08 | 0.11 | 0.13 | 0.15 | 0.19 | 0.21 | 0.24 | 0.29 | 0.33 | 0.35 | 0.38 | 0.40 | 0.42 | 0.43 | 0.43 | 0.42 | 0.41 | 0.42 |
| 30 | -0.01 | -0.02 | -0.02 | -0.02 | -0.02 | -0.01 | -0.01 | -0.01 | -0.01 | 0.02 | 0.05 | 0.08 | 0.11 | 0.12 | 0.15 | 0.17 | 0.20 | 0.22 | 0.27 | 0.31 | 0.34 | 0.37 | 0.39 | 0.42 | 0.42 | 0.43 | 0.42 | 0.41 | 0.40 | 0.41 |

Notes: Coefficient estimates in the regression $R_{t,t+k}^S = c + \alpha R_{t-i,t}^S + \gamma R_{t-i,t}^{FX} + \sum_{m=1}^{4} \beta_m OF_{t-i,t}^{FX} + \varepsilon_t$ for corporate end-user order flows. The horizontal axis varies over the $k$-minute forecast horizon; the vertical axis varies according to the aggregation window of FX order flows through the $i$-minute period. A lightly shaded cell denotes significance at the 10% level using robust standard error estimates. Darker shading denotes significance at the 5% level. Intra-day data from 2.30 p.m. to 5.00 p.m. for 25 days are used. Coefficients represent the percentage change in the SPY ETF price resulting from a €1bn flow into the dollar.

exchange order flows through the $i$-minute period. The coefficients represent the percentage change in the stock index from a €1bn flow into the dollar, expressed such that a positive sign is a rise in the ETF price. We only report the results for the SPY since those for the DIA are very similar. Light shading denotes significance at the 10% level, dark shading denotes significance at the 5% level.

Once again a clear heterogeneity of relationships between end-user order flows in FX and subsequent stock index movements emerges. The findings are consistent for the two index-tracking ETFs.

(1) Compared with the findings in the contemporaneous regressions, where FX order flows play no role in explaining concurrent stock market changes at the market level, there are strong relationships between FX order flows and future stock market returns in the forecasting model, even after controlling for lagged exchange rate and stock market returns.

(2) There is little evidence of short-horizon forecasting power using financial customer flows. However, financial customer FX order flows have statistically significant forecasting power for longer forecasting horizons, especially when flows are aggregated over long windows. The uniformly negative signs suggest that when financial customers are buying dollars, US stock indices will subsequently fall in value. This rather odd result is addressed further in Section 5.5.

(3) The effect of corporate customer order flows on stock market changes is mainly positive. Statistical significance is less prevalent for this customer class and is confined to relatively short aggregation windows; however, there is statistical forecasting power even over relatively long horizons. The results are stronger for the less liquid DIA than for the SPY. The nature of these results is consistent with the FX forecasting power of corporate customer order flows.

(4) Internal customer forecasting correlations are uniformly negative (like those of financial customers) and highly significant. Given our lack of knowledge of the nature of internal flows, we cannot explore this avenue further. Inter-bank flows have inconsistent forecasting signs but are negative when significant (aggregation windows of around 15 min and forecasting horizons of around 10 min). As such, they are very similar to the findings for financial customers.

(5) The lagged exchange rate has strong forecasting power at high frequencies, suggesting that an appreciation of the dollar is associated with a subsequent rise in US stock indices, again consistent with the previous literature looking at returns spillovers.

(6) Similar to findings in the pure FX environment, the magnitudes of coefficients for financial customer order flows are such that when €1bn flows into the FX market, the forecast percentage change in stock market prices peaks at around 0.3%. Corporate customer flows are much more powerful though, and the maximum coefficient is closer to 1.2%. Internal customer order flows are stronger still with maximal coefficients of close to 2.6%, though negatively signed.

(7) Regression $R^2$ suggest that approximately 6% of variations of market level equity returns can be explained by FX order flows, lagged exchange rate changes, and lagged stock market returns.

(8) Again, unreported $F$-tests suggest that the four classes of customer order flows are jointly significant in explaining future stock returns, corporate and financial end-user flows are jointly significant, and that the coefficient estimates for corporate and financial customers are significantly different at the critical parts of the results tables. FX order flows are important predictors of future stock returns and order flow is heterogeneous.

## 5.5 *Interpretation*

The previous sections have detailed the heterogeneous contemporaneous and forecasting relationships between FX order flows from different end-users and FX and stock returns. In this section, we attempt to interpret these results.

The FX rate results are a puzzle. The contemporaneous correlations between flows from corporate and financial end-users have the opposite sign to that commonly found in the literature. This could simply be due to the intra-day nature of our analysis since the literature is typically based on data sampled at the data frequency. The forecasting results suggest that the significantly negative short-term relationship for financials becomes positive as forecasting horizons and aggregation window extend. Although we are unable to examine this further due to data limitations, it may be that both contemporaneous and forecasting correlations become significantly positive as the aggregation window extends, which would generate results consistent with the data sampled at a daily frequency.

The results are not obviously consistent with the simple liquidity story. None of the patterns suggest an illiquidity-induced peak price impact which gradually declines as the market absorbs the inventory.[7] Of course, the issue is partly obscured by the fact that we are unsure how quickly customer inventory is passed through to the inter-bank market by our source bank. If they hold the inventory on their own books for several minutes before passing it onto the market, we might expect a delayed (positive) reaction in the market price which subsequently declines.[8] This is partially consistent with the results from corporate customers since the price impact of their orders declines both as the aggregation window widens and as the forecast horizon lengthens. However, this cannot explain the financial customer flows where the 'price impact' is actually negative unless we are willing to accept, against what evidence we do have, that the inventory is held for more than 30 min, since it is only over these long horizons that financial customer price-return correlations turn positive.

One possible explanation, as discussed above, is that financial customers time their FX trades to benefit from temporary price moves. If the information on which they are trading is relatively long-lived (in a high-frequency context), they may wait to buy a currency cheap on a short-term dip which would lead to a negative high-frequency contemporaneous correlation between exchange rate returns and their order flows. Since FX returns are slightly positively autocorrelated at high frequencies, buying on dips might also lead to negative short-horizon forecasting correlations. Only as the market slowly prices the (positive) information in their order does the currency appreciate. At longer horizons, this would result in both positive contemporaneous and forecasting correlations, the former consistent with the literature based on daily data and the latter weakly consistent with the longer horizon results in this paper.

The results from the cross-asset regressions are our main interest here, and it is even harder to explain the significant results here without recourse to the information hypothesis. Since corporates are highly unlikely to be trading equities, the ability of their FX flows into the dollar to predict equity price rises is not caused by liquidity effects. When financial customers buy the dollar, equity prices subsequently fall, particularly over relatively long horizons. Both of these are consistent with the idea that their flows predict movements in the dollar (in different directions) and that movements in the dollar are significantly correlated with equity returns. We explore this further by running the following regression:

$$R^S_{t,t+k} = c + \alpha R^S_{t-i,t} + \gamma R^{FX}_{t-i,t} + \delta R^{FX}_{t,t+k} + \sum_{m=1}^{4} \beta_m OF^{FX}_{t-i,t} + \varepsilon_t. \tag{5}$$

149

That is, we augment the equity market forecasting regression with the future FX change. We find that the coefficient on financial customer order flow collapses to zero in all cases in this regression. This suggests that financials' FX order flow (negatively) predicts the dollar, and this subsequent dollar movement is contemporaneously (positively) correlated with equity price movements. There is no information in the FX flow of financial customers which helps predict equity returns over and above the information relevant for exchange rate movements (and recall that we concede the negative short-term relationship between financial flows and exchange rate changes might be due to these customers timing their trades rather than information content).

Conversely, the significance of the corporate flows remains even after including future FX returns in the regression. This suggests that corporate flows are (positively) correlated with future changes in the value of the dollar, and while equities move in response to these exchange rate changes, there is additional information in the flows of corporate customers relevant for equity values.[9]

We are again forced to speculate in explaining this finding, but two scenarios present themselves. First, the dispersed macro-information we hypothesise to be revealed by FX flows may have two components, one relevant for FX rates and another relevant for equities. Lagged order flows would then explain stock returns over and above lagged and current exchange rates. Second, equity and FX markets might price the same information differently. Most straightforwardly, suppose that the information in customer flows suggests that GDP is to rise globally. The simple monetary approach to the exchange rate would not predict any exchange rate change if two countries' income levels were to rise equally. However, we would expect both countries' stock markets to rise on this good news.

## 6. Conclusion

In addition to the daily relationship between order flows in the FX market and exchange rate changes in many well-established papers (see Evans and Lyons 2002, among many others), some studies also give evidence that FX order flows are correlated with exchange rate changes at high frequencies (see Love and Payne 2008 and Osler and Vandrovych 2009, among others). Besides the relationships found in the pure exchange rate market environment, order flows in one market also play an important role in the movements of other markets, and some studies document the evidence of the cross-market effects from currency order flows at a daily frequency (e.g. Francis, Hasan and Hunter 2006; Dunne, Hau and Moore 2006). However, to the best of our knowledge, no one has reported any effects of FX order flows on other market changes at high frequencies. In this paper, we use a unique set of tick-by-tick FX order flow data including end-user orders and inter-dealer orders to test the effects of order flows on stock market changes at frequencies from 1 to 30 min, in addition to the dynamic relationship between currency order flows and exchange rate fluctuations at high frequencies.

We find statistically significant impacts of FX order flows on contemporaneous and future exchange rate changes at high frequencies. Order flows from corporate customers are positively related to exchange rate changes, while order flows from financial customers are negatively signed. We note that these signs contradict results in published studies using daily order flow data, e.g. Evans and Lyons (2006). The high-frequency findings are consistent with Osler and Vandrovych (2009), who also report mixed signs for their 10 groups of counterparties at frequencies less than 30 min, suggesting that this puzzle may be related to the frequency of observation.

This article's main contribution is to consider the impact of FX order flows on contemporaneous and future stock market returns. We do not find clear contemporaneous relationships between FX order flows and stock market changes at high frequencies, but FX flows appear to have significant power to forecast stock index returns over 1–30 min horizons, after controlling for lagged exchange rate and stock market returns. The effects of order flows from financial customers on future stock market changes are negative, while the effects of corporate orders are positive. When financial clients of our data provider are buying dollars, the US stock market subsequently falls in value. This is entirely driven by the positive effect that changes in the value of the dollar have on contemporaneous equity returns. Since financial customer flows (puzzlingly) negatively predict dollar price changes, they also negatively predict US stock returns. We assume that this may in part be due to financial customers attempting to time their trades in the FX market by trading in response to temporary price changes (feedback trading).

Conversely, when corporates are buying dollars, the US stock indices rise in value. These latter results are entirely consistent with one of the most basic premises underlying FX market microstructure modelling – that corporate order flows contain dispersed, passively acquired information about fundamentals. Thus purchases of the dollar by corporate customers represent good news about the state of the US economy. This would be consistent with such orders being associated with subsequent appreciations of the dollar and with rising stock index prices. Importantly, though, there appears to be extra information in corporate flows which is directly relevant to equity prices over and above the impact derived from stock prices reacting to (predicted) exchange rate changes.

## Acknowledgements

We thank Richard Payne, Geoffrey Kendrick, Lucio Sarno, and an anonymous referee for comments, and the anonymous bank for data provision and several explanatory conversations. All errors are our own.

## Notes

1. Osler (2008) surveys this literature in detail.
2. We accept that it is somewhat surprising that it is priced as rapidly as our results suggest. However, our results are limited to very short horizons by data limitations and while they suggest that there is some very high-frequency forecasting power from FX flows to equity returns, they do not rule out the possibility of greater forecasting power over longer horizons. We are investigating this possibility in a separate paper (Marsh and Miao 2010).
3. These two papers explain equity returns using FX order flow. A third paper, Albuquerque, Francisco and Marques (2008), test the relation in the opposite direction, considering the effect of order flows in stock markets on exchange rates.
4. Trades with inter-dealer network banks initiated by the data supplier are unfortunately not available.
5. Below, we forecast stock returns using lagged FX returns, lagged stock returns, and lagged FX order flow. For symmetry, we should include lagged stock returns in equation (2). However, lagged US stock returns are only available for a small portion of the trading day, which dramatically reduces our sample.
6. We thank the referee for clarifying our thinking on this, and other, issues in the article.
7. The only exception to this is in the very short horizon where both of the end-user customer flows show positive point estimates which subsequently decline. However, none of these estimates is significant.
8. Lyons (1998) suggests an inventory half-life from an active dealer of around 10 min. However, the move to electronic inter-bank dealer systems has improved dealers' opportunities to pass inventory into the market faster and cheaper, so this 10 min level might be seen as an upper limit. Discussions with bankers suggest that inventories are now managed over 1–2 min horizons.
9. We note that this is not the case for inter-bank flows, however, which retain negative and significant forecasting power even after accounting for future exchange rate movements.

## References

Ajayi, R.A., and M. Mougoue. 1996. On the dynamic relation between stock prices and exchange rates. *Journal of Financial Research* 19, no. 2: 193–207.

Albuquerque, R., E.D. Francisco, and L. Marques. 2008. Marketwide private information in stocks: Forecasting currency returns. *Journal of Finance* 63, no. 5: 2297–343.

Andersen, T., T. Bollerslev, F.X. Diebold, and C. Vega. 2007. Real-time price discovery in global stock, bond and foreign exchange markets. *Journal of International Economics* 73, no. 2: 251–77.

Bartov, E., and G.M. Bodnar. 1994. Firm valuation, earnings expectations, and the exchange rate exposure effect. *Journal of Finance* 49: 1755–85.

Berger, David, W., Alain P. Chaboud, Sergei V. Chernenko, Edward Howorka, and Jonathan H. Wright (2006). Order flow and exchange rate dynamics in electronic brokerage system data, Board of Governors of the Federal Reserve System, International Finance Discussion Papers No. 830, Washington, DC. http://ideas.repec.org/p/fip/fedgif/830.html#provider.

Brandt, M., and K. Kavajecz. 2005. Price discovery in the US treasury market: The impact of order flow and liquidity on the yield curve. *Journal of Finance* 59: 2623–54.

Breedon, F., and P. Vitale. 2004. An empirical study of liquidity and information effects of order flow on exchange rates. European Central Bank Working Paper 424. http://www.ecb.int/pub/pdf/scpwps/ecbwp424.pdf.

Chordia, T., R. Roll, and A. Subrahmanyam. 2002. Order imbalance, liquidity, and market returns. *Journal of Financial Economics* 65: 111–30.

Dunne, P., H. Hau, and M. Moore. 2006. International order flows: Explaining equity and exchange rate returns. Working paper, SSRN. http://ssrn.com/abstract=890244.

Evans, M.D., and R.K. Lyons. 2002. Order flow and exchange rate dynamics. *Journal of Political Economy* 110, no. 1: 170–80.

Evans, M.D., and R.K. Lyons. 2004. A new micro model of exchange rate dynamics. NBER working paper no. 10379, Cambridge, MA. http://www.nber.org.

Evans, M.D., and R.K. Lyons. 2005. Meese–Rogoff redux: Micro-based exchange rate forecasting. *American Economic Review* 95, no. 2: 405–14.

Evans, M.D., and R.K. Lyons. 2006. Understanding order flow. *International Journal of Finance and Economics* 11, no. 1: 3–23.

Fleming, M. 2003. Measuring treasury market liquidity. *Federal Reserve Bank of New York Economic Policy Review*, 9, no. 3: 83–108.

Francis, B.B., I. Hasan, and D.M. Hunter. 2006. Dynamic relations between international equity and currency markets: The role of currency order flow. *Journal of Business* 79, no. 1: 219–58.

Frommel, M., A. Mende, and L. Menkhoff. 2007. Order flows, news, and exchange rate volatility. Working paper, Ghent University.

Froot, K.A., and T. Ramadorai, 2005. Currency returns, intrinsic value and institutional investor flow. *Journal of Finance* 60, no. 3: 1535–66.

Glosten, L.R., and P.L. Milgrom. 1985. Bid, ask and transaction prices in a specialist market with heterogeneously informed traders. *Journal of Financial Economics* 14, no. 1: 71–100.

Holthausen, R.W., R.W. Leftwich, and D. Mayers. 1990. Large-block transactions, the speed of response, and temporary and permanent stock-price effects. *Journal of Financial Economics* 26: 71–95.

Jorion, P. 1991. The pricing of exchange rate risk in the stock market. *Journal of Financial and Quantitative Analysis* 26, no. 3: 363–76.

Kyle, A.S. 1985. Continuous auctions and insider trading. *Econometrica* 53, no. 6: 1315–35.

Love, R., and R. Payne. 2008. Macroeconomic news, order flows, and exchange rates. *Journal of Financial and Quantitative Analysis* 43, no. 2: 467–88.

Lyons, R. 1998. Profits and position control: A week of FX dealing. *Journal of International Money and Finance* 17, no. 1: 97–115.

Marsh, I.W., and T. Miao. 2010. *Intraday end-user fx order flow*. Mimeo: Cass Business School.

Moore, M., and R. Payne. 2009. Individual trader records on EBS spot: What do they tell us about private information in FX trading? Working paper, Warwick Business School.

Osler, C.L. 2008. Foreign exchange microstructure: A survey of the empirical literature. Working paper, Brandeis University, July 2008.

Osler, C.L., and V. Vandrovych. 2009. Hedge funds and the origins of private information in currency markets. Cass Business School EMG Working Paper, February 2009.

Pasquariello, P., and C. Vega. 2007. Informed and strategic order flow in the bond markets. *Review of Financial Studies*, 16: 385–415.

Rime, D., L. Sarno, and E. Sojli. 2010. Exchange rate forecasting, order flow and macroeconomic information. *Journal of International Economics*, 80: 72–88.

Shleifer, A. 1986. Do demand curves slope down? *Journal of Finance* 41: 579–590.

# A detailed investigation of the disposition effect and individual trading behavior: a panel survival approach

Ingmar Nolte

*Financial Econometric Research Centre, Finance Group, Warwick Business School, University of Warwick, UK*

This article uses a panel survival approach to analyze the trading behavior of foreign exchange traders. We concentrate on a detailed characterization of the shape of the disposition effect over the entire profit and loss regions. In doing so, we investigate the influence of a number of trading characteristics on the impact of the disposition effect. These trading characteristics include: special limit order strategies, trading success, size and the experience of our investors. Our main findings are that (i) the disposition effect has a nonlinear shape. For small profits and losses we find an inverted disposition effect, while for larger ones, the usual positive disposition effect emerges. (ii) The inverted disposition effect is driven to a great extend by patient and cautious investors closing their positions with special limit orders (take-profit and stop-loss). The normal positive disposition effect is found to be intensified for impatient investors closing their positions actively with market orders. (iii) We show that unsuccessful investors reveal a stronger inverse disposition effect. (iv) Evidence that bigger investors are less prone to the disposition effect than smaller investors is also found.

## 1. Introduction

In this article, we investigate investment decisions (open and close) of individual investors. The main focus of the article is the characterization of the shape of the disposition effect over the complete profit and loss region. Our analysis uses detailed transaction data obtained from an electronic trading platform for currencies and we propose to model the investment decision process with a dynamic panel survival model.

A key feature of our model is the definition of investor's roundtrip and inactivity durations. Roundtrip durations are defined as the elapsed time from an initial entry into an investment to its complete exit. This means that we explicitly allow the trading strategy to be complex (e.g. several openings and/or several partial closings) and we do not restrict our attention to simple strategies (open followed by a full close) *a priori*. Inactivity durations are defined as the elapsed time between two roundtrips during which the investor has no exposure to a currency position.

Through our definition of roundtrip durations, we address the problem of how to handle several successive openings and partial closings of an individual investor in a single security. This constitutes one of the key difficulties faced by studies that track individual investors' trading decisions on a high frequency level.[1] The prevalent approach in the literature is to define durations between openings and closings by trying to match every single opening with its corresponding closing. Complications already arise in the case of matching partial closings. Moreover, such a matching procedure automatically introduces overlaps and thus dependencies that would require profound statistical techniques for inference and goodness-of-fit assessments.

Our definition of roundtrip durations is an elegant way to cope with this problem. Within the proposed panel survival model differences in effects for roundtrips relying on simple and complex trading strategies can easily be account for.

Beside this straightforward technical argument for our definition of roundtrip durations, a mental accounting and narrow framing argument (Thaler 1985) implicitly or explicitly invoked in many studies on individual trading behavior and behavioral biases (in particular, the disposition effect) can be related to our setting. It is commonly assumed that especially individual investors consider their investment positions in an isolated form and do not take an overall portfolio view when making an investment decision.[2] In this article, we also follow this point of view and consider therefore periods with exposure (roundtrips) and periods without exposure to a currency position within a dynamic setup. We do, however, believe that the narrow framing argument should not be over-stretched and cannot be used to justify the consideration of *every* single transaction in a single currency pair in isolation. Such an approach ignores problems of overlaps, dynamics spillovers and difficulties of dealing with partial closings.

A main focus of this article is the investigation of individual trading behavior and especially the disposition effect. The disposition effect (Shefrin and Statman 1985) is considered to be the tendency that investors hold losing asset positions longer than corresponding winning asset positions. There is an ongoing debate in the literature whether the disposition effect can be explained within a rational investor framework, with explanations such as informed trading, rebalancing or transaction costs put forward, or whether one should resort to behavioral theories such as the prospect theory[3] of Kahneman and Tversky (1979).

Odean (1998a) shows that the most apparent approaches within a rational investor world seem to be unlikely explanations of the disposition effect. He provides evidence that his traders behave irrationally by selling winning positions too early and holding loosing positions too long which in his analysis implies a real effect on investors' wealth. Locke and Mann (2005) also find that loosing positions are held longer than winning positions, but in contrast to Odean (1998a), they cannot provide conclusive evidence that this trading behavior has significant negative impacts on investors' wealth.

Barberis and Xiong (2009) show that prospect theory preferences can predict a disposition in a rigorous theoretical model framework. They provide evidence in the form of two simulation studies in which preferences are firstly defined over annual gains and losses, and secondly defined over realized gains and looses. In their studies, it also turns out that for specific parameter constellations for expected returns and numbers of trading periods within a year an inverse disposition effect can be observed. Their evidence is based on the comparison of Odean (1998a)'s 'proportion of gains realized (PGR)' and 'proportion of losses realized (PLR)' measures with allow for an assessment of the mean disposition effect only.

Indeed, many of the existing studies use aggregated data to analyze the disposition effect for the mean (representative) investor applying a number of different methodologies. The early studies on investor behavior (Lease, Lewellen, and Schlarbaum 1974; Schlarbaum, Lewellen, and Lease 1978a, 1978b; and Shefrin and Statman 1985) as well as the studies of Badrinath and Lewellen (1991), Shapira and Venezia (2001) and Haigh and List (2005), compare mean durations of profitable and non-profitable investments. The studies of Odean (1998a) and Dhar and Zhu (2006) consider the difference between PGR and PLR measures within a portfolio setting. Grinblatt and

Keloharju (2001) apply Logit models to estimate the probabilities of closing positions conditional on whether the position is traded either in profits or in losses.

The analyses on the disposition effect can furthermore be categorized into studies focusing on individual investors' trading behavior in stock markets (Lease, Lewellen, and Schlarbaum 1974; Schlarbaum, Lewellen, and Lease 1978a, 1978b; Badrinath and Lewellen 1991, Odean 1998a; Feng and Seasholes 2005; Ivkovich, Poterba, and Weisbenner 2005; Chen et al. 2007), on the difference between individual and professional or institutional investors in stock markets (Grinblatt and Keloharju 2001, Shapira and Venezia 2001, Locke and Mann 2005; Brown et al. 2006; Dhar and Zhu 2006; O'Connell and Teo 2009), on investors in options and futures markets (Heisler 1994; Heath, Huddart, and Lang 1999, Locke and Onayev 2005), on investors in the housing market (Genesove and Mayer 2001), and on investors in experimental trading setups (Weber and Camerer 1998, Haigh and List 2005). The studies of Kahneman (1992), Odean (1998a), Weber and Camerer (1998) and Barberis and Thaler (2003) discuss the choice of the correct reference point.

The modeling approach pursued in this article can be seen in the context of survival or holding time approaches.[4] Besides the novel classification of roundtrip and inactivity periods, our approach contributes to this literature by using a sophisticated dynamic intensity model, that accounts for (i) the panel characteristics of the data, (ii) unobserved heterogeneity and (iii) spill-over effects from inactivity to roundtrip periods and vice versa. Our approach allows for (iv) inference on both the inactivity and the roundtrip states and (v) the investigation of specific nonlinearities (and factors driving these) in the disposition effect over the complete profit and loss region. Last but not least, we show that our model is able to explain the underlying data generating process very well by a rigorous econometric assessment of its goodness-of-fit, which strengthens the reliability and the validity of our results.

The data used in this paper is unique and consists of the trading activity record of OANDA FXTrade, which is an internet trading platform for currencies. The set of investors on this platform is quite heterogenous and ranges from retail up to smaller professional investors. From the trading activity record, we construct a dataset of roundtrip and inactivity durations for all active investors during the period from 1 October 2003 to 14 May 2004 (227 days). The analysis presented in this paper focuses on the most actively traded currency pair – EUR/USD – which accounts for 61.5% of the total turnover on OANDA FXTrade during our sample period.

Our dataset is perfectly suited for analyzing individual investors' trading behavior, since in contrast to discount broker datasets, the number of trading instruments is strictly limited. Therefore, we can trace investors' trading strategies separately for every trading instrument (currency pair). By considering these trading strategies, we do not need to account for different risk classes of the underlying instruments. Moreover, since we consider trading in the foreign exchange market, overnight effects are less severe and influences of short sale restrictions do not exist.

Although the trading proportion of OANDA FXTrade is relatively small in comparison to the overall FX market, the results of this study do provide some interesting findings which possess relevance in a broader finance context. It is worth mentioning here that the electronic retail trading segment is becoming more and more important. With advances in computer and internet technologies retail traders, smaller professional investors and institutions have nowadays easy instant access to all sorts of financial instruments. For retails investors, it has been almost impossible to trade currencies or derivatives 20 years ago, without contacting their house bank. The understanding of the trading behavior of retail investors is of utmost importance for banks and markets makers designing and setting up electronic trading platforms. They face the challenge of hedging counterparty risk in the sense of whose investor's position will be kept on the bank's own inventory books and whose position should be hedged away. The design of this hedging algorithm on the basis of individual investors' characteristics and trading behavior is the 'holy grail' of every electronic trading platform acting as a market maker.

Moreover, trading activity records such as the OANDA FXTrade one will become more and more available. They allow to trace all transactions of individual investors over time, thus embody the most valuable form of market microstructure information, and hence provide deeper and more detailed insights into complex trading behavior on the micro level. The development of financial econometric approaches to handle this vast amount of information is still in its infancy.

The article is organized as follows: Section 2 describes the construction of our dataset and provides a brief introduction into the trading mechanism on OANDA FXTrade. Section 3, presents the panel survival model. Section 4 contains the empirical analysis with a detailed interpretation of the results in the light of the disposition effect and further behavioral biases. Section 5 concludes.

## 2. Description of the dataset

The dataset used in our analysis is constructed from the trading activity record of OANDA FXTrade, which ranges from 1 October 2003 to 14 May 2004 (227 days). Therein, all trading activities of 4893 different traders in 30 possible currency pairs is recorded on a second by second basis.[5] OANDA FXTrade is a 24/7 electronic trading platform mainly for retail and smaller professional investors and institutions. OANDA itself acts as a market maker and sets bid and ask quotes based on an external datafeed (crossing network) and a proprietary forecasting algorithm. A trader can submit market orders, limit orders and special limit orders (stop-loss, take profit) to the system. Limit orders are maintained for up to one month, and a trader may change submitted limits at any time without incurring an extra fee. Depending on the transaction type, we receive information on the transaction prices (market orders, limit orders executed, stop-loss, take profit and margin call), on the bid and ask quotes (pending limit orders), on the transaction volume and on the limits of stop-loss and take-profit orders. Moreover, we have information on each traders' invested start position per currency pair on 1 October 2003 00:00:00 (Eastern Standard Time).

For each trader, we compute separately the respective currency pair durations from entering into a position until leaving it, i.e. the time during which he had an exposure to a specific currency

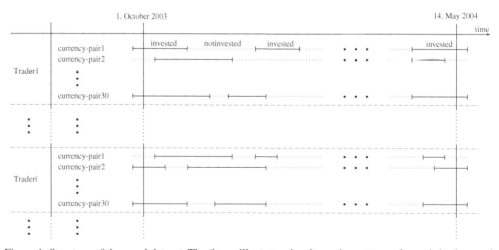

Figure 1. Structure of the panel dataset. The figure illustrates the alternating pattern of roundtrip (invested) and inactivity (not invested) durations.

pair position. We refer henceforth to this duration as the roundtrip (state) duration. Furthermore, we calculate the durations for periods in which the investor has not been invested in the specific currency pair to which we refer as the inactivity (state) duration. Thus, we obtain an alternating series of roundtrip and inactivity durations. Figure 1 clarifies the panel structure of the dataset constructed. We concentrate only on the most actively traded currency pair: EUR/USD which accounts for nearly two-third of all trading activity on OANDA FXTrade.

## 3. The model

We propose a panel survival model with two states: $m = R$ for roundtrips and $m = I$ for inactivity periods. Let $i$, $i = 1, \ldots, N$ denote the $i$th trader. For the $i$th trader, we observe $C_i$ duration cycles, which are either roundtrip or inactivity durations. Let $c$, $c = 1, \ldots, C_i$ denote the $c$th cycle of the $i$th trader. We do not need to distinguish between the origin and the destination state due to the alternating behavior of roundtrip and inactivity states. Thus, transitions from roundtrip to roundtrip as well as from inactivity to inactivity are excluded. We denote the indicator function by $d_{ic}^m$, which takes the value 1 if the $i$th trader is in state $m$ in the $c$th cycle and 0 otherwise. Let $\tau_c^i$ denote the duration of the $c$th cycle of the $i$th trader and let $t_c^i$ denote the calendar time at which the $i$th trader leaves the $c$th cycle. Let

$$f(\tau_c^i | \mathfrak{F}_{t_c^i}) \tag{1}$$

denote the conditional density of the duration $\tau_c^i$ in which we condition on information represented by $\mathfrak{F}_t$ being available at the end of the respective duration at time $t_c^i$. For the ease of notation, we suppress the particular conditioning information and consider $f(\tau_c^i) \equiv f(\tau_c^i | \mathfrak{F}_{t_c^i})$ in the following. We can then decompose $f(\tau_c^i)$ into

$$f(\tau_c^i) = \prod_{m \in \{I,R\}} f^m(\tau_c^i)^{d_{ic}^m}, \tag{2}$$

where $f^m(\tau_c^i)$ denotes the (conditional) $m$th state duration density, which can be further decomposed into

$$f^m(\tau_c^i) = \theta_{ic}^m(t_c^i, \tau_c^i) \bar{F}^m(t_c^i, \tau_c^i). \tag{3}$$

Here $\theta_{ic}^m(t_c^i, \tau_c^i)$, denotes the (conditional) intensity, i.e. the instantaneous probability at time $t_c^i$, of the $i$th trader for leaving the $m$th state in the $c$th cycle and $\bar{F}^m(t_c^i, \tau_c^i)$ the corresponding (conditional) $m$th state survivor function, i.e. the probability that the $i$th trader has not left the $m$th state in the $c$th cycle at time $t_c^i$ and thus survived in that state from $t_c^i - \tau_c^i$ to $t_c^i$. Hence $f(\tau_c^i)$ becomes

$$f(\tau_c^i) = \prod_{m \in \{I,R\}} \left( \theta_{ic}^m(t_c^i, \tau_c^i) \bar{F}^m(t_c^i, \tau_c^i) \right)^{d_{ic}^m}. \tag{4}$$

$\bar{F}^m(t_c^i, \tau_c^i)$ can be expressed in terms of the corresponding integrated intensity given by

$$z_{ic}^m(t_c^i, \tau_c^i) = \int_0^{\tau^i} \theta_{ic}^m(t_c^i, v) \, dv \tag{5}$$

as

$$\bar{F}^m(t_c^i, \tau_c^i) = \exp(-z_{ic}^m(t_c^i, \tau_c^i)), \tag{6}$$

so that the complete log-likelihood of the model is given by

$$\ln \mathcal{L}(W, \beta) = \sum_{i=1}^{N} \sum_{c=1}^{C_i} \sum_{m \in \{I,R\}} d_{ic}^m \left( \ln \theta_{ic}^m(t_c^i, \tau_c^i) - z_{ic}^m(t_c^i, \tau_c^i) \right), \tag{7}$$

where $W$ generically refers to the data and $\beta$ is the generic symbol for all relevant parameters. We propose a parameterization of $\theta_{ic}^m(t_c^i, \tau_c^i)$ consisting of a Burr intensity component being multiplicatively linked to an exponentially transformed flexible Fourier form (FFF) (Gallant 1981) in the following way:

$$\theta_{ic}^m(t_c^i, \tau_c^i) \equiv \frac{\exp(\beta^m x_{ic}^m) \alpha^m (\tau_c^i)^{\alpha^m - 1}}{1 + \sigma^{m2} \exp(\beta^m x_{ic}^m)(\tau_c^i)^{\alpha^m}}$$

$$\cdot \exp\left( \sum_{k=1}^{K} v_{k,s}^m \sin(2k\pi u(\tau_c^i)) + v_{k,c}^m \cos(2k\pi u(\tau_c^i)) \right) \quad \text{for } m = 1, 2, \tag{8}$$

where $x_{ic}^m$ denotes the vector of state-specific explanatory variables of the $i$th trader in the $c$th cycle, and $\beta^m$ denotes the corresponding (state dependent) parameter vector. The variables

Table 1. Description of explanatory variables and associated parameters. All explanatory variables except the constants are trader $i$ and cycle $c$ specific.

| Variable description | Roundtrip parameter | Inactivity parameter |
|---|---|---|
| Constant | $c^R$ | $c^I$ |
| Dummy – if successful | $c_{sc}^R$ | $c_{sc}^I$ |
| Duration of previous roundtrip | $\beta_{dr(-1)}^R$ | $\beta_{dr(-1)}^I$ |
| Duration of previous inactivity period | $\beta_{di(-1)}^R$ | $\beta_{di(-1)}^I$ |
| Maximum invested volume during roundtrip | $\beta_{vol}^R$ | – |
| Dummy – if special limit order close | $c_{sl}^R$ | – |
| Dummy – if complex trading strategy | $c_{cx}^R$ | – |
| Profit over roundtrip | $\beta_p^R$ | – |
| Profit$^2$ over roundtrip | $\beta_{p^2}^R$ | – |
| Profit$^3$ over roundtrip | $\beta_{p^3}^R$ | – |
| Interaction – profit and successful | $\beta_{p*sc}^R$ | – |
| Interaction – profit and special limit order close | $\beta_{p*sl}^R$ | – |
| Interaction – profit and complex trading strategy | $\beta_{p*cx}^R$ | – |
| Loss over roundtrip | $\beta_p^R$ | – |
| Loss$^2$ over roundtrip | $\beta_{l2}^R$ | – |
| Loss$^3$ over roundtrip | $\beta_{l3}^R$ | – |
| Interaction – loss and successful | $\beta_{l*sc}^R$ | – |
| Interaction – loss and special limit order close | $\beta_{l*sl}^R$ | – |
| Interaction – loss and complex trading strategy | $\beta_{l*cx}^R$ | – |

employed in the empirical application are detailed in Table 1. $\alpha^m$ and $\sigma^{m2}$ denote the shape and scaling parameter of the Burr distribution. $K$ denotes the order of the exponential FFF. $v_{k,\cdot}^m$ represent the coefficients associated with the sine and cosine terms, and $u(s) \equiv 1 - \exp(-s)$ is the transformation of $s$ (duration or the backward recurrence time) with the property that $u(s) \in [0, 1]$.

The proposed specification is quite flexible in capturing the shape of the baseline intensity. The model nests the simple Burr specification if all $v_{k,\cdot}^m$ coefficients are equal to zero, the simple Weibull model if $\sigma^{m2} = 0$, the simple Log-Logistic model if additionally $\sigma^{m2} = 1$ and the simple exponential model if $\sigma^{m2} = 0$ and $\alpha^m = 1$ as well as their corresponding exponential FFF extensions for the case where $v_{k,\cdot}^m$ are not equal to zero but the associated parameter restrictions on $\sigma^{m2}$ and $\alpha^m$ are fulfilled. The simple Burr specification can be interpreted as mixed proportional intensity model in which the Weibull density is multiplicatively mixed with a gamma-distributed random variable $v$ with mean 1 and variance $\sigma^{m2}$. The variable $v$ can be interpreted as a random effect capturing unobserved heterogeneity among our investors. Thus, a test of the Burr against the Weibull model can be interpreted as a test for unobserved heterogeneity. Failing to account for unobserved heterogeneity usually results in inconsistent, biased and inefficient parameter estimates.

The desired flexibility of the intensity specification comes at the cost of quasi-maximum likelihood failing to justify parameter consistency and we have to assume that the proposed specification captures the true data generating process so that we can resort to maximum likelihood reasoning for parameter consistency. To this end, under the assumption of the correct specification for $\theta_{ic}^m$, the corresponding integrated intensities $z_{ic}^m$ are unit exponentially distributed and we consider $\hat{z}_{ic}^m$ as generalized model residuals which asymptotically should also be unit exponentially distributed if the model is correctly specified allowing for inference as to whether the proposed intensity specification is correct.

## 4.  Empirical analysis

To address the heterogeneity of our traders, we collect them together according to their total transaction volume over the whole period into 20 groups. The first group contains traders with the smallest transaction volume (0–5% of the transaction volume distribution), and the last group (95–100%) the traders with the largest total volume. This categorization eases the estimation of the proposed intensity-based model and allows us to draw conclusions on the differing trading behavior across groups.

### 4.1  *Descriptive statistics*

The descriptive statistics for all 20 investor groups are presented in Tables A1–A4 in the Appendix. Descriptive statistics on the roundtrip and the inactivity state durations, the durations separately for loss-making and profit-making roundtrips, the profit and loss, the absolute profit and loss and the transaction volume are reported. Furthermore, we construct dummy variables and report the percentages of whether a roundtrip is closed with a special limit order (stop-loss and take profit), whether the roundtrip involved a complex trading strategy and whether the investor has been profitable (successful) over each of the two past roundtrips. Under a complex trading strategy, we understand any trading pattern consisting not just of an initial open followed by a full close.

From the 20 ordered investor groups, we observe that the mean transaction volume involved in a roundtrip ranges from 144€ for the smallest group to around €370,000 for the largest groups. The maximum transaction volume ranges from €4800 to €53 million. These figures highlight the heterogenous composition of the investors on OANDA FXTrade with small retail and private investors up to professional traders. Across all investor groups, we observe that a mean roundtrip duration is roughly half the length of an inactivity period, and that from group 1 to 20, the length of a mean roundtrip duration steadily decreases from 30 to 7 hours. Thus, the small investors do not only trade with smaller volumes they also trade less frequently than the bigger investors. Interestingly, the small investors also trade more complicated strategies than the bigger investors as indicated by the percentages of complex roundtrips, which decline from 50% for group 1 to 25% for group 20. Across all investor groups, we do not observe big differences in the percentages of roundtrips closed with special limit orders (stop-loss or take-profit) – around 20% – and differences in the percentages of successful trading which lie around 45%.

A simple comparison of the mean lengths of loss-making roundtrips with those of profit-making roundtrips suggests a disposition effect for all investor groups, except groups 8 and 14, since the means of the loss-making roundtrips are longer than the means of the profit-making roundtrips. However, comparing the corresponding median values often reveals (except for groups 9, 18, 19 and 20) an inverse disposition effect since the median loss-making roundtrips are shorter than the median profit-making ones. A more detailed look at the higher quantiles shows for all groups an inverse disposition effect up to a certain quantile (for groups 2, 7, 8, 10, 14 and 15 even up to the 95% quantile) and a positive disposition effect from that quantile onwards.

These observations indicate, from a purely descriptive point of view, that mean duration comparisons such as those typically carried out in empirical studies which investigate the disposition effect can be misleading and might yield a distorted and incomplete picture of the true form of the disposition effect. We observe a very clear nonlinearity in the disposition effect over the profit and loss region, which will be further investigated in the proposed intensity framework. Here, we only compared the distributions of the lengths of the roundtrips if the roundtrip has been profitable or not. The estimates of the intensity model, in contrast, will enable us to compare lengths of profitable and loss-making roundtrips at predetermined profit and loss values $\pm 1000$ EUR, say, which will yield a much more detailed picture of the nonlinearity of the disposition effect over the entire profit and loss region, while controlling for the influence and interaction of further explanatory variables describing trading characteristics.

## 4.2  *Estimation results*

The detailed maximum likelihood estimation results of the panel intensity model for all 20 investor groups are presented in Tables A5–A8 in the Appendix. In the following we only present statistics and figures for investor groups 1, 7, 14 and 20.[6] We include the explanatory variables $x_{ic}^m$ described in Table 1 for the roundtrip ($m = R$) and the inactivity state ($m = I$) into the model setup presented in Equations (7) and (8).

The set of variables included in the model motivated the descriptive analysis and intends to capture investor trading characteristics and potential nonlinearities in the shape of the disposition effect over the complete profit and loss region. Before we continue with the interpretation of the estimation results, we need to consider the goodness-of-fit of the estimated model. We clearly observe for all 20 groups that the parameters $v_{k,\cdot}^m$ of the exponential FFF are jointly highly significant for both the roundtrip and inactivity state. The null hypothesis that the scaling parameter $\sigma^{m2} = 0$, which is the test of a Weibull against a Burr specification cannot be rejected for two groups only on the 10% level for the roundtrip component and for eight groups for the inactivity component. Thus, it seems that a Weibull specification alone is not flexible enough to explain the baseline intensity component, which indicates that there is a considerable part of unobserved heterogeneity which is captured by the mixture of the Weibull density with a gamma-distributed random variable with unit mean and variance $\sigma^{m2}$. Unobserved heterogeneity arises because the explanatory variables included into the model are not capable of fully explaining the existing heterogeneity prevalent in the trading behavior of our investors. This is actually not surprising since the groups of investors considered in this study range from small retail up to professional investors. Even within the groups, it turns out that the investors are quite different so that an additional stochastic factor trying to capture these differences seems appropriate. Unobserved heterogeneity can therefore, to a large extent, be associated with an omitted variable problem and failing to account for it usually renders estimation results and model inference invalid.

The estimated baseline intensities (groups 1, 7, 14 and 20) for the roundtrip states are depicted in Figure 2. We observe a very similar pattern across all investor groups: a declining baseline intensity function, with local minima after half-a-day and one-and-a-half days and local maxima after one day and two days. Intuitively, the baseline intensity describes how frequently we observe another opening or closing decision (here in alternating form) for the investor under consideration. Since the pattern depicted in the graphs is very regular with maxima at multiples of full days, we see that it reflects habit persistency in trading behavior and preferences over trading times, which might in part be explained by work schedules, regular office hours and overnight effects.

In Table 2, we report the means and the standard deviations of the raw roundtrip and inactivity duration series (pooled over investors) and their associated residual series. Figures 3 and 4 depict the corresponding QQ-plots for the roundtrip and inactivity residual series for groups 1, 7, 14 and 20. Although we observe a slight underdispersion in the inactivity state residual series, which can be attributed to the higher quantiles, we see that the roundtrip state residual series are very close to

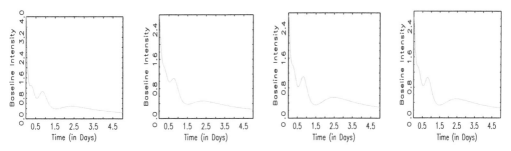

Figure 2. Estimated baseline intensities for investor groups (from left to right) 1, 7, 14 and 20.

Table 2. Mean and standard deviation of the raw and the residual series for the EUR/USD currency pair of the roundtrip and inactivity states for investor groups 1, 7, 14 and 20.

| | Roundtrip | | Inactivity | | Roundtrip | | Inactivity | |
|---|---|---|---|---|---|---|---|---|
| | Raw | Residual | Raw | Residual | Raw | Residual | Raw | Residual |
| | | | 1 | | | | 7 | |
| Mean | 1.29 | 1.00 | 2.46 | 1.00 | 0.46 | 1.00 | 0.83 | 1.00 |
| Standard | 4.62 | 0.98 | 9.00 | 0.93 | 2.65 | 0.98 | 4.42 | 0.95 |
| | | | 14 | | | | 20 | |
| Mean | 0.31 | 1.00 | 0.67 | 1.00 | 0.33 | 1.00 | 0.52 | 1.00 |
| Standard | 1.88 | 0.98 | 3.28 | 0.96 | 2.18 | 0.97 | 2.59 | 0.95 |

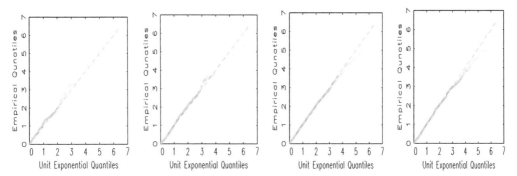

Figure 3. Quantile–quantile plots of the roundtrip residual series against the unit exponential distribution for the EUR/USD currency pair. The plots correspond from left to right to investor groups 1, 7, 14 and 20.

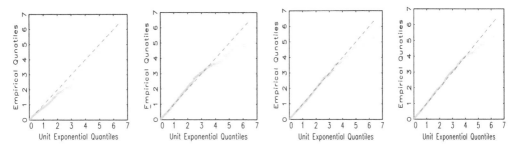

Figure 4. Quantile–quantile plots of the inactivity residual series against the unit exponential distribution for the EUR/USD currency pair. The plots correspond from left to right to investor groups 1, 7, 14 and 20.

a unit exponential distribution. Altogether, the properties of the residual series show an extremely good fit of the proposed Burr baseline intensity model extended by an exponential FFF.[7]

### 4.3   *Interpretation of the estimation results and a detailed look at the disposition effect*

The parameter estimates $\beta^R_{di(-1)}$, $\beta^R_{dr(-1)}$, $\beta^I_{di(-1)}$ and $\beta^R_{dr(-1)}$ (reported in Tables A5–A8 in the Appendix) that capture the influence of the previous roundtrip and inactivity durations on both the current roundtrip and inactivity intensity are for all 20 investor groups always highly (1% level) significantly negative. Thus, we observe a very clear clustering pattern in the trading activity since longer (shorter) durations are followed by lower (higher) intensities for exiting the roundtrip and the inactivity state. This observation clearly shows that there are successive periods in which investors actively trade more frequently and successive periods in which they do not. Such a dynamics pattern cannot simply be ignored and should be addressed in any study concerned with holding times or intensities especially for the disposition effect. Within our proposed modelling framework this is easily achieved.

$c^R_{cx}$ which is the coefficient on the dummy variable, which takes on the value of one if a roundtrip represents a complex trading strategy, is also for all 20 investor groups highly significant and negative. Thus, this coefficient controls for the effect that roundtrips involving a more complex trading strategy are simply longer.

$c_{sl}^R$ is the coefficient on the dummy variable indicating whether a roundtrip is closed by a special limit (stop-loss or take-profit) order. Special limit orders in contrast to standard limit orders are usually submitted on OANDA FXTrade jointly with the opening order for the position. Hence, they reflect extremely cautious and passive trading behavior, since the submitter wants to protect himself from severe losses or wants to realize a profit when a certain threshold is hit right from the very beginning. In both cases, it is less likely that the trader will actively monitor the market and immediately react to new information, than if he had not submitted the special limit order. On the one hand, such behavior can be interpreted either as quite sophisticated and experienced trading since the trader is aware of the fact that he will not be able to follow the market and thus ensures his positions against periods of high risk. On the other hand, it can be interpreted as uniformed and inexperienced trading since the trader does not expect to have access to private information which he could exploit with an active trading strategy. Nevertheless, when a roundtrip is closed by executing a special limit order, the profit and loss region was bounded at least in one direction *a priori*. The sign of $c_{sl}^R$ is always negative and significantly (5% level) negative for 18 investor groups. Thus, $c_{sl}^R$ captures the tendency that roundtrips, which are closed by special limit orders and rely in part on passive trading strategies are longer. This is another important trading characteristic that needs to be account for and whose cross-effects with other variables (especially profit or loss variables) should not be ignored.

$c_{sc}^R$ is the coefficient on the dummy variable, that takes on the value one if the investor has been profitable (successful) in the last two roundtrips. On a 5% significance level, the coefficient $c_{sc}^R$ is significant only for six groups. However, whenever $c_{sc}^R$ is significant it is positive, which shows that successful investors generate higher trading activity. Numerous theoretical models (for instance, Daniel, Hirshleifer, and Subrahmanyam 1998, Odean 1998b, Wang 1998, Gervais and Odean 2001, Scheinkman and Xiong 2003) put overconfidence forward as an explanation for excess trading volumes and empirical evidence is provided by De Bondt and Thaler (1995), Barber and Odean (2001) and Statman, Thorley, and Vorkink (2006) with low frequency data. Self-attribution bias (Wolosin, Sherman, and Till 1973) because of past trading success can be considered as one facet of overconfidence caused by an incorrect interpretation of past investment success. It is usually distinguished from overconfidence caused by biased perceptions of the precision of private information (Alpert and Raiffa 1982, Lichtenstein, Fischhoff, and Phillips 1982). Hence, the above finding can be seen as reflecting the effect of self-attribution bias on trading activity.

The coefficient $\beta_{vol}^R$ which captures the effect of the maximum invested trading volume during a roundtrip is positive at a 1% significance level for all investor groups. It very clearly indicates that higher trading volumes imply shorter roundtrip durations, which reflects an increasing degree of overconfidence given by trading volume also implies more trading activity.

Let us now address the disposition effect directly. In terms of the roundtrip intensity, we consider the following definition of the disposition effect.

DEFINITION 1 (disposition effect) *The tendency to hold losses longer than corresponding profits, reformulated in terms of the roundtrip intensity, is that there is a smaller intensity (instantaneous probability to leave the roundtrip state) for losses than for corresponding profits.*

This definition only requires that for a given loss, there is a smaller intensity than for the corresponding profit. It does not require that the difference between the intensity for losses and the intensity for profits is either constant over the length of the holding period nor constant over the associated monetary amount. Absence of a disposition effect is hence described by a roundtrip

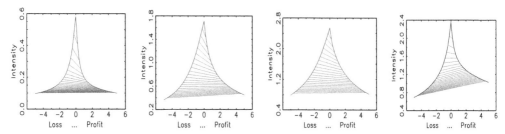

Figure 5. Illustration of the disposition effect for EUR/USD. The plots correspond, from left to right, to investor groups 1, 7, 14 and 20. Each plot shows the intensity to leave the roundtrip state ($y$-axis) over a standardized profit/loss region ($x$-axis). The points $-1$ and $1$ on the $x$-axis correspond to the negative and positive mean absolute profit/loss, respectively, realized in the associated group. The upward (downward) sloping connecting lines indicate a positive (negative) disposition effect in this region.

intensity which is axially symmetric at zero over the profit and loss region. In this case, the probability of leaving the roundtrip state would be exactly the same for a $x > 0$ units-of-the-base-currency-loss as for a $x > 0$ units-of-the-base-currency-profit.

In Figure 5, we show for investor groups 1, 7, 14 and 20 the estimated roundtrip intensity as a function of the profit and loss. All further explanatory variables have been set to their mean values. The graphs are standardized so that the points $-1$ and $1$ on the x-axis correspond to the negative and positive mean absolute profit/loss, respectively, realized in the associated group[8]. The outer values $\pm 5$ appear to roughly correspond to a quantile between the 95% and the 98% quantile of the absolute profit/loss distribution. The upward (downward) sloping lines in the inner region indicate a positive (negative) disposition effect with respect to that particular profit/loss size.

For all groups, we observe, an inverse disposition effect (downward sloping lines) for small profits and losses and especially for the smaller investor groups (1–8), the usual disposition effect for larger profits and losses (upward sloping lines). The bigger investor groups (12–19) seem not to reveal any disposition effect even for larger profits and losses and group 20 – the group with the biggest investors – again shows a disposition effect for larger profits and losses, which might be explained by several extremely high losses with long roundtrip durations within this group.

In general, we observe a highly nonlinear shape to the disposition effect which is inverted for small profit and loss amounts and positive for larger ones. There, is also a tendency for the larger investors to show smaller disposition effects and the inverse relationship also holds.

In the literature several studies (c.f. Odean 1998a, Shapira and Venezia 2001, Grinblatt and Keloharju 2001) document that the 'average investor, exhibits a disposition effect and the studies of Odean (1998a), Ivkovich, Poterba, and Weisbenner (2005), Feng and Seasholes (2005) stress an tax argument (e.g. Stiglitz 1983 and Constantinides 1984) that the disposition effect is diminished, disappears, or is inverted, since in the presence of taxes losses should be immediately realized after they arise. However, Dhar and Zhu (2006) show that even in the absence of tax effects, up to one fifth of their investors exhibit an inverse disposition effect. Barberis and Xiong (2009) show in their simulation studies that even the mean investor can possess an inverse disposition effect for specific parameter constellations of the expected return and monitoring frequencies, but their model assumes full rationality.

Without stressing the tax argument we investigate a straightforward insurance argument as an alternative and/or complementary explanation for the existence of an inverted disposition effect: Investors might want to insure themselves against large losses by submitting limit orders with tight limits which in turn would imply a diminished or an inverse disposition effect for small losses. Stop-loss orders represent the most aggressive form of such limit orders and their effect on the disposition effect is analyzed below. We can compare profit-making roundtrips closed by take-profit orders with loss-making roundtrips closed with stop-loss orders. Osler (2003) also argues that the use of stop-loss orders can be completely rational in a trading scenario in which other traders already use them. Following this line of argument we should observe a diminished disposition effect and therefore less behavioral bias in this case.

A potential counter argument for this point of view is provided by adopting the usual convention of Glosten (1994) and Seppi (1997), that roundtrips closed by special limit orders can be considered as roundtrips being completed by (temporarily) patient or uninformed investors, which accordingly should be more prone to behavioral bias and thus reveal a higher degree of disposition. A large part of the literature on the disposition effect and further behavioral biases in general concentrate on the discrimination between the levels on which investors are affected by behavioral biases. Shapira and Venezia (2001) find that individual (less informed and less sophisticated) investors are more affected by the disposition effect than institutional investors supporting the statement of Ross (1999) that institutional investors are more rational. Dhar and Zhu (2006) find that wealthier, more experienced and professional investors exhibit a smaller disposition effect. Locke and Mann (2005), Brown et al. (2006) and O'Connell and Teo (2009), however, provide evidence that institutional and professional investors are subject to behavioral biases as well. A similar result is found for less sophisticated and experienced Chinese investors by Chen et al. (2007). They find that their investors are contemporaneously subject to several behavioral biases such as the disposition effect, overconfidence, representative biases and narrow framing. The results of our analysis discussed above also provide only mixed evidence for the tendency that more sophisticated and experienced investors, according to their transaction size, possess a smaller disposition effect. We investigate below whether unsuccessful investors possess a stronger form of the disposition effect, which in part would complement the finding that less sophisticated investors are more prone to a disposition effect.

The impact of special limit orders (stop-loss and take-profit) on the disposition effect is depicted in Figure 6. In this figure, we directly plot the difference between the roundtrip intensity for the profit region and the roundtrip intensity for the loss region again for all investor groups. Hence, a positive value describes a positive disposition effect and a negative value an inverse one. The solid line illustrates the shape of the disposition effect if roundtrips are closed by special limit orders and the short dashed line if not. Both lines are the result of the coefficients $\beta_{p*sl}^{R}$ and $\beta_{l*sl}^{R}$ of the corresponding interaction terms. The whiskers at the bottom of the plots represent the absolute

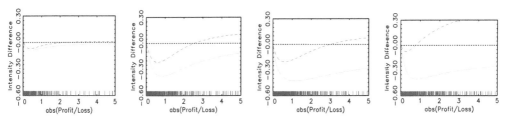

Figure 6. Impact of special limit orders on the disposition effect for the EUR/USD currency pair. The plots correspond from left to right to investor groups 1, 7, 14 and 20. Each plot shows the difference of the roundtrip intensity for profits and the roundtrip intensity for losses. The point 1 on the $x$-axis corresponds to the mean absolute profit/loss realized in the associated group. The solid line represents that a roundtrip is closed by a special limit order and the short dashed line if not. The whiskers at the bottom of the graphs represent the absolute profit/loss distribution.

profit and loss distribution. Again, the graphs are presented in a standardized way across all investor groups, the value 1 on the $x$-axis always represents the mean absolute profit/loss within a group and the value 5 roughly corresponds to a quantile between the 95% and 98% quantiles of the absolute profit/loss distribution. We observe, very clearly and consistently across all investor groups that roundtrips, which are closed by special limit orders, show a less pronounced disposition effect, that is always negative for all investor groups. Thus, we find clear evidence that the general inverse disposition effect for small profit and losses observed above is driven by roundtrips closed with special limit orders, representing the trading behavior of cautious, patient and maybe uniformed investors relying on a passive trading strategy. On the contrary, the general positive disposition effect for larger profits and losses is more pronounced for roundtrips not closed by special limit orders and thus mainly driven by market orders being submitted by traders in periods in which they actively track the market. Moreover, we observe across all investor groups that the distance between the short-dashed and the solid line becomes larger, the larger the investor. This indicates a higher impact of the type of order being used to close a roundtrip on the disposition effect for larger than for smaller investors. This result is highly significant according to the likelihood ratio (LR) tests presented in the first panel of Table 3, which tests whether the two lines are significantly different from each other.

The effect of past trading success on the disposition is presented in Figure 7. The construction of the graphs is the same as for special limit orders. The solid line represents the effect if the roundtrip is closed by an investor who has been profitable in both of the last two roundtrips and the short-dashed line if not. We observe for all investor groups, except groups 3, 4 and 8, the tendency for a more pronounced negative disposition effect over the complete profit/loss region

Table 3. Test statistics and $p$-values for the likelihood ratio test for the full model specification against the restricted model specifications (special limit order close, past trading success and complex trading strategy) for EUR/USD. The test statistics for all tests are $\chi_2^2$-distributed.

| | 1 | 2 | 3 | 4 | 5 | 6 | 7 | 8 | 9 | 10 |
|---|---|---|---|---|---|---|---|---|---|---|
| | | | | Likelihood ratio test: special limit order close | | | | | | |
| LR-Stat | 93.6239 | 6.5816 | 20.8089 | 52.1358 | 49.5902 | 59.4559 | 28.9696 | 23.7222 | 10.4875 | 37.8483 |
| $p$-value | 0.0000 | 0.0372 | 0.0000 | 0.0000 | 0.0000 | 0.0000 | 0.0000 | 0.0000 | 0.0053 | 0.0000 |
| | 11 | 12 | 13 | 14 | 15 | 16 | 17 | 18 | 19 | 20 |
| LR-Stat | 54.4719 | 44.8365 | 103.5667 | 95.0349 | 9.5744 | 174.2150 | 50.0627 | 46.3760 | 42.0606 | 81.4059 |
| $p$-value | 0.0000 | 0.0000 | 0.0000 | 0.0000 | 0.0083 | 0.0000 | 0.0000 | 0.0000 | 0.0000 | 0.0000 |
| | | | | Likelihood ratio test: past trading success | | | | | | |
| | 1 | 2 | 3 | 4 | 5 | 6 | 7 | 8 | 9 | 10 |
| LR-Stat | 2.1367 | 2.9021 | 10.2760 | 1.3454 | 0.8577 | 8.6168 | 63.7331 | 14.7605 | 23.3056 | 2.3655 |
| $p$-value | 0.3436 | 0.2343 | 0.0059 | 0.5103 | 0.6513 | 0.0135 | 0.0000 | 0.0006 | 0.0000 | 0.3064 |
| | 11 | 12 | 13 | 14 | 15 | 16 | 17 | 18 | 19 | 20 |
| LR-Stat | 43.1236 | 23.9128 | 17.5150 | 5.1972 | 10.4448 | 15.9229 | 33.0603 | 21.0800 | 114.9656 | 14.8011 |
| $p$-value | 0.0000 | 0.0000 | 0.0002 | 0.0744 | 0.0054 | 0.0003 | 0.0000 | 0.0000 | 0.0000 | 0.0006 |
| | | | | Likelihood ratio test: complex trading strategy | | | | | | |
| | 1 | 2 | 3 | 4 | 5 | 6 | 7 | 8 | 9 | 10 |
| LR-Stat | 3.2407 | 3.3686 | 5.3949 | 11.4362 | 0.7800 | 2.5850 | 1.5802 | 8.9617 | 23.8882 | 7.6879 |
| $p$-value | 0.1978 | 0.1856 | 0.0674 | 0.0033 | 0.9618 | 0.2746 | 0.4538 | 0.0113 | 0.0000 | 0.0214 |
| | 11 | 12 | 13 | 14 | 15 | 16 | 17 | 18 | 19 | 20 |
| LR-Stat | 0.1195 | 8.3695 | 7.6152 | 2.9698 | 60.0576 | 1.8733 | 4.7229 | 3.3728 | 21.4976 | 2.1144 |
| $p$-value | 0.9420 | 0.0152 | 0.0222 | 0.2265 | 0.0000 | 0.3919 | 0.0943 | 0.1852 | 0.0000 | 0.3474 |

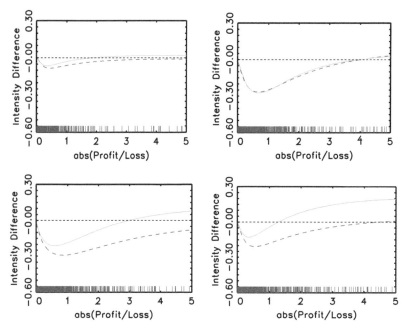

Figure 7. Impact of past trading success on the disposition effect for the EUR/USD currency pair. The plots correspond from left to right to investor groups 1, 7, 14 and 20. Each plot shows the difference of the roundtrip intensity for profits and the roundtrip intensity for losses. The point 1 on the x-axis corresponds to the mean absolute profit/loss realized in the associated group. The solid line represents that a roundtrip is closed by an overconfident investor and the short dashed line if not. The whiskers at the bottom of the graphs represent the absolute profit/loss distribution.

if the roundtrip is closed by an investor who has not been successful (short-dashed line). This tendency also seems to be increasing over the size of investors since the distance between the solid and the short-dashed lines becomes wider, the larger the investors. It is further reflected by the LR-tests in the second panel of Table 3 in which the effect of past trading success on the disposition effect is for smaller investor groups not significant or can be rejected at low significance levels. Thus, we find that unsuccessful investors reveal a stronger inverse disposition effect.

A further interesting question which can be analyzed in our model setup is whether investors with complex trading strategies reveal a different disposition effect than investors trading with simple open-hold-full-close strategies. Figure 8 depicts the corresponding graphs concerning this effect. Although, there is no general effect of complex trading on the disposition effects, the graphs reveal a tendency that for small profit and losses, the inverse disposition effect is intensified if roundtrips rely on a complex trading strategy. For larger profit and losses, this effect is then often reversed strengthening a positive disposition effect in this region. The corresponding LR-tests reveal that this pattern is only significant at the 10% level for 10 out of the 20 groups. Thus, we find only a slight indication that investors who employ complex trading strategies possess a smaller disposition effect. This observation certainly needs deeper investigation, but is generally in line with the finding that more experienced investors, who might apply more complex trading algorithms, possess a less pronounced disposition effect and hence complements the finding on the general distribution of the disposition effect over investor groups and the results on overconfidence.

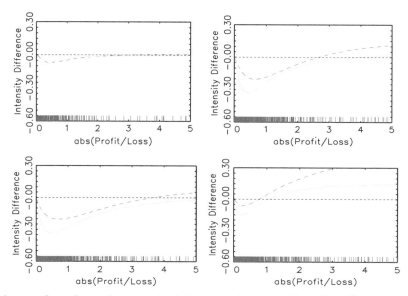

Figure 8. Impact of complex trading strategies during a roundtrip on the disposition effect for the EUR/USD currency pair. The plots correspond from left to right to investor groups 1, 7, 14 and 20. Each plot shows the difference of the roundtrip intensity for profits and the roundtrip intensity for losses. The point 1 on the $x$-axis corresponds to the mean absolute profit/loss realized in the associated group. The solid line represents that a complex trading strategy is applied and the short dashed line if not. The whiskers at the bottom of the graphs represent the absolute profit/loss distribution.

## 5. Conclusion

This paper investigates the high-frequency trading behavior of a heterogenous set of foreign exchange market traders on an electronic trading platform (OANDA FXTrade) by means of a panel survival approach.

Individual trading processes are decomposed into roundtrip periods defined as the time between entering into a position and leaving it, and inactivity periods are defined as the time between two roundtrips. A panel survival model relying on a flexible mixed proportional intensity specification accounting for individual unobserved heterogeneity is used to model the data generating process of these two duration processes. We show that our modeling framework is well suited to characterizing the properties of the data and that the proposed Burr intensity specification extended by an exponentially transformed FFF describes the baseline intensity well.

Time is the central element in our model which we use to investigate individual trading behavior and the disposition effect. We have focussed on the detailed characterization of the shape of the disposition effect over the full profit and loss region, the links between the disposition effect and special limit orders, past trading success and complex trading behavior as well as assessing the disposition effect across the size and the degree of experience of our investors.

Our main findings are that:

(i) the general disposition effect has a nonlinear shape. For small profits and losses, we find an inverted disposition effect and for larger profit and losses, the usual positive disposition effect.

(ii) the inverted disposition effect is to a great extent driven by patient and cautious investors closing their positions with special limit orders (take-profit and stop-loss), whereas the positive disposition effect is found to be intensified for impatient investors closing their positions actively with market orders

(iii) in addition, we find that unsuccessful investors display a stronger inverted disposition effect

(iv) evidence that bigger investors are less prone to the disposition effect than smaller ones is provided and

(v) we find indication that investors relying on complex trading strategies are less affected by the disposition effect.

The approach presented in this article can be extended in several dimensions: A multivariate specification in which the duration processes of several currency pairs are modelled jointly could provide a better characterization of the individual trading behavior and perhaps deeper insights into individual trading preferences and the motivation to open and close positions taking the cross effects with further currency pairs into account. Although the proposed intensity specification is very flexible, a semi-parametric approach could be an alternative. The dynamics within this panel survival model are modelled in a rudimentary way including only the previous lagged durations. A specification relying on the autoregressive conditional intensity model of Russell (1999) could also be a reasonable alternative. A time dependent factor capturing unobservable heterogeneity might help to improve the goodness-of-fit of the model. From an application point of view, a better categorization of large and small, experienced and inexperienced, patient and impatient as well as cautious and not-cautious investors would be desirable to obtain a better discrimination of behavioral biases across the investor groups. However, all of these tasks are left for further research on individual trading behavior and trading activity datasets.

## Acknowledgements

This work has been supported in part by the European Community's Human Potential Program under contract HPRN-CT-2002-00232, Microstructure of Financial Markets in Europe; and by the Fritz Thyssen Foundation through the project 'Dealer-Behavior and Price-Dynamics on the Foreign Exchange Market'. I wish to thank Richard Olsen for helpful comments and for providing me with the data. The article benefited from several discussions with Günter Franke, Sandra Nolte, Mark Salmon and Winfried Pohlmeier. Previous versions of the article circulated under the title 'Retail Investors' Trading Behavior in the Foreign Exchange Market: A Panel Duration Approach'. The article has been presented at the 61st European Meeting of the Econometric Society, Vienna 2006, International Conference on High Frequency Finance, Konstanz 2006 and faculty seminars at the Universities of Tuebingen, Aarhus and Bruxells.

## Notes

1. See for example Odean (1998a), Grinblatt and Keloharju (2001), Feng and Seasholes (2005), Locke and Onayev (2005), Dhar and Zhu (2006), O'Connell and Teo (2009).
2. See Nolte and Voev (2011) for a deeper discussion and relaxation of this assumption.
3. A key concept in prospect theory is that investors assess profits and losses relative to a reference point, which is usually considered to be a function of the assets' purchase prices. It is assumed that investors behave risk-averse when their asset position has established a paper profit, and risk-seeking when their position suffers from a paper loss.
4. c.f. Feng and Seasholes (2005), Ivkovich et al. (2005), Locke and Mann (2005), Locke and Onayev (2005) and Shumway and Wu (2005).
5. A more elaborate description of the trading mechanism on OANDA FXTrade and an analysis of the relationship between the order flow and price changes can be found in (Nolte and Nolte 2011).
6. The full set of statistics and figures for all 20 investor groups are available from the author upon request.

7. In particular, when being compared with the residual series of standard baseline intensity specifications without FFF augmentation that were used as benchmark specifications in a previous version of the paper.
8. See also the descriptive statistics in Table A1.

# References

Alpert, M., and H. Raiffa. 1982. A progress report on the training of probability assessors. In *Judgment under uncertainty: heuristics and biases*, ed. D. Kahneman, P. Slovic, and A. Tversky, 294–305. Cambridge: Cambridge University Press.

Badrinath, S.G., and W.G. Lewellen. 1991. Evidence on tax-motivated securities trading behavior. *Journal of Finance* 46, no. 1: 369–82.

Barber, B.M., and T. Odean. 2001. Boys will be boys: gender, overconfidence, and common stock investment. *The Quarterly Journal of Economics* 116, no. 1: 261–92.

Barberis, N., and R. Thaler. 2003. A survey of behavioral finance. In *Handbook of the economics of finance*, ed. G. Constantinides, M. Harris, and R. Stulz, 1052–121. Amsterdam: Elsevier Science B.V.

Barberis, N., and W. Xiong. 2009. What drives the disposition effect? An analysis of a long-standing preference-based explanation. *Journal of Finance* 64, no. 2: 751–84.

Brown, P.R., N. Chappel, R. da Silva Rosa, and T.S. Walter. 2006. The reach of the disposition effect: large sample evidence across investor classes. *International Review of Finance* 6, nos. 1–2: 43–78.

Chen, G.-M., K.A. Kim, J.R. Nofsinger, and O.M. Rui. 2007. Trading performance, disposition effect, overconfidence, representativeness bias, and experience of emerging market investors. *Journal of Behavioral Decision Making* 20, no. 4: 425–51.

Constantinides, G.M. 1984. Optimal stock trading with personal taxes: implications for prices and the abnormal January returns. *Journal of Financial Economics* 13, no. 1: 65–89.

Daniel, K., D. Hirshleifer, and A. Subrahmanyam. 1998. Investor psychology and security market under- and overreactions. *Journal of Finance* 53, no. 6: 1839–85.

De Bondt, W.F.M., and R.H. Thaler. 1995. Financial decision making in markets and firms: a behavioral perspective. In *Handbooks in operations research and management science*, ed. R.A. Jarrow, V. Maksimovic and W.T. Ziemba, Vol. 9, 385–410. Amsterdam: North-Holland Elsevier.

Dhar, R., and N. Zhu. 2006. Up close and personal: an individual level analysis of the disposition effect. *Managment Science* 52, no. 5: 726–40.

Feng, L., and M. Seasholes. 2005. Do investor sophistication and trading experience eliminate behavioral biases in finance markets? *Review of Finance* 9, no. 3: 305–51.

Gallant, R.A. 1981. On the bias in flexible functional forms and an essential unbiased form: the Fourier flexible form. *Journal of Econometrics* 15, no. 2: 211–45.

Genesove, D., and C. Mayer. 2001. Loss aversion and seller behaviour: evidence from the housing market. *Quarterly Journal of Economics* 116, no. 4: 1233–60.

Gervais, S., and T. Odean. 2001. Learning to be overconfident. *Review of Financial Studies* 14, no. 1: 1–27.

Glosten, L.R. 1994. Is the electronic open limit order book inevitable? *The Journal of Finance* 49, no. 4: 1127–61.

Grinblatt, M., and M. Keloharju. 2001. What makes investors trade? *Journal of Finance* 56, no. 2: 1053–73.

Haigh, M.S., and J.A. List. 2005. Do professional trades exhibit myopic loss realization aversion? An experimental analysis. *Journal of Finance* 60, no. 1: 523–34.

Heath, C., S., Huddart, and M. Lang. 1999. Psychological factors and stock option exercise. *The Quarterly Journal of Economics* 114, no. 2: 601–27.

Heisler, J. 1994. Loss aversion in a futures market: an empirical test. *The Review of Futures Markets* 13, no. 3: 793–822.

Ivkovich, Z., J., Poterba, and S. Weisbenner. 2005. Tax-motivated trading by individual investors. *American Economic Review* 95, no. 5: 1605–30.

Kahneman, D. 1992. Reference points, anchors, norms, and mixed feelings. *Organizational Behavior and Human Decision Processes* 51, no. 2: 296–312.

Kahneman, D., and A. Tversky. 1979. Prospect theory: an analysis of decision under risk. *Econometrica* 47, no. 2: 263–92.

Lease, R.C., W.G., Lewellen, and G.G. Schlarbaum. 1974. The individual investor: attributes and attitudes. *Journal of Finance* 29, no. 2: 413–33.

Lichtenstein, S., B. Fischhoff, and L. Phillips. 1982. Calibration of probabilities: the state of the art to 1980. In *Judgment under uncertainty: heuristics and biases*, ed. D. Kahneman, P. Slovic, and A. Tversky, 306–34. Cambridge: Cambridge University Press.

Locke, P.R., and S.C. Mann. 2005. Professional trader discipline and trade disposition. *Journal of Financial Economics* 76, no. 1: 401–44.

Locke, P.R., and Z. Onayev. 2005. Trade duration: information and trade disposition. *The Financial Review* 40, no. 1: 113–29.

Nolte, I., and S. Nolte. 2011. How do individual investors trade? *The European Journal of Finance*, Forthcoming.

Nolte, I., and V. Voev. 2011. Trading dynamics in the foreign exchange market: a latent factor panel intensity approach. *Journal of Financial Econometrics*, Forthcoming, http://dx.doi.org/10.1093/jjfinec/nbq033.

O'Connell, P.G.J., and M. Teo. 2009. Institutional investors, past performance, and dynamic loss aversion. *Journal of Financial and Quantitative Analysis* 44, no. 1: 155–88.

Odean, T. (1998a). Are investors reluctant to realize their losses? *Journal of Finance* 53, no. 5: 1775–98.

Odean, T. (1998b). Volume, volatility, price, and profit when all traders are above average. *Journal of Finance* 53, no. 6: 1887–934.

Osler, C.L. 2003. Currency orders and exchange rate dynamics: an explanation for the predictive success of technical analysis. *Journal of Finance* 58, no. 5: 1791–820.

Ross, S.A. 1999. Adding risks: Samuelson's fallacy of large numbers revisited. *Journal of Financial and Quantitative Analysis* 34, no. 3: 323–39.

Russell, J.R. 1999. Econometric modeling of multivariate irregularly-spaced high-frequency data, working paper, University of Chicago.

Scheinkman, J.A., and W. Xiong. 2003. Overconfidence and speculative bubbles. *Journal of Political Economy* 111, no. 6: 1183–219.

Schlarbaum, G.G., W.G. Lewellen, and R.C. Lease. 1978a. The common-stock-portfolio performance record of individual investors: 1964–70. *Journal of Finance* 33, no. 2: 429–41.

Schlarbaum, G.G., W.G., Lewellen, and R.C. Lease. 1978b. Realized returns on common stock investments: the experience of individual investors. *Journal of Business* 51, no. 2: 299–325.

Seppi, D.J. 1997. Liquidity provision with limit orders and a strategic specialist. *Review of Financial Studies* 10, no. 1: 103–50.

Shapira, Z., and I. Venezia. 2001. Patterns of behavior of professionally managed and independent investors. *Journal of Banking & Finance* 25, no. 8: 1573–87.

Shefrin, H., and M. Statman. 1985. The disposition to sell winners too early and ride losers too long: theory and evidence. *Journal of Finance* 40, no. 3: 770–90.

Shumway, T., and G. Wu. 2005. Does disposition drive momentum? Working paper, University of Michigan.

Statman, M., S. Thorley, and K. Vorkink. 2006. Investor overconfidence and trading volume. *Review of Financial Studies* 19, no. 4: 1531–65.

Stiglitz, J.E. 1983. Some aspects of the taxation of capital gains. *Journal of Public Economics* 21, no. 2: 257–94.

Thaler, R. 1985. Mental accounting and consumer choice. *Marketing Science* 4, no. 3: 199–214.

Wang, F.A. 1998. Strategic trading, asymmetric information and heterogeneous prior beliefs. *Journal of Financial Markets* 1, nos. 3–4: 321–52.

Weber, M., and C.F. Camerer. 1998. The disposition effect in securities trading: an experimental analysis. *Journal of Economic Behavior & Organization* 33, no. 2: 167–84.

Wolosin, R., S. Sherman, and A. Till. 1973. Effects of cooperation and competition on responsibility attribution after success and failure. *Journal of Experimental and Social Psychology* 9, no. 3: 220–35.

# Appendix

## A.1 Descriptive statistics

Table A1. Descriptive statistics of the roundtrip, inactivity durations and explanatory variables for the EUR/USD currency pair.

| EUR/USD | Durations in hours | | | Profit | Profit/loss | Absolute profit/loss | Volume | Dummy variable | Mean |
|---|---|---|---|---|---|---|---|---|---|
| | Roundtrip | Inactivity | Loss | | | | | | |
| | | | | Group 1: (0–5%), # investors 138 | | | | | |
| Observations | 4348.00 | 4283.00 | 1723.00 | 2518.00 | 4348.00 | 4348.00 | 4348.00 | Complex trading strategy | 0.50 |
| Mean | 30.88 | 58.97 | 33.22 | 30.49 | -0.05 | 0.64 | 144.18 | | |
| Standard deviation | 110.89 | 216.12 | 127.47 | 100.40 | 2.53 | 2.45 | 244.20 | Close special limit order | 0.21 |
| Minimum | 0.00 | 0.00 | 0.00 | 0.00 | -67.32 | 0.00 | 1.00 | | |
| 5% quantile | 0.02 | 0.00 | 0.01 | 0.03 | -1.11 | 0.00 | 1.00 | | |
| 25% quantile | 0.25 | 0.05 | 0.17 | 0.34 | -0.07 | 0.01 | 17.00 | | |
| 50% quantile | 1.99 | 2.73 | 1.80 | 2.31 | 0.01 | 0.10 | 81.00 | | |
| 75% quantile | 17.27 | 26.31 | 15.87 | 19.27 | 0.13 | 0.42 | 170.00 | | |
| 95% quantile | 137.84 | 237.67 | 146.65 | 136.86 | 1.35 | 2.19 | 500.00 | Successful investor | 0.41 |
| Maximum | 2545.21 | 3722.03 | 2545.21 | 1989.13 | 27.43 | 67.32 | 4800.00 | | |
| | | | | Group 2: (5–10%), # investors 142 | | | | | |
| Observations | 6374.00 | 6297.00 | 2566.00 | 3604.00 | 6374.00 | 6374.00 | 6374.00 | Complex trading strategy | 0.50 |
| Mean | 22.92 | 42.51 | 24.79 | 22.63 | -0.09 | 0.96 | 299.12 | | |
| Standard deviation | 121.53 | 193.55 | 158.93 | 90.03 | 4.37 | 4.26 | 409.72 | Close special limit order | 0.20 |
| Minimum | 0.00 | 0.00 | 0.00 | 0.00 | -235.76 | 0.00 | 1.00 | | |
| 5% quantile | 0.02 | 0.00 | 0.01 | 0.02 | -1.92 | 0.00 | 5.00 | | |
| 25% quantile | 0.15 | 0.06 | 0.12 | 0.21 | -0.12 | 0.03 | 60.00 | | |
| 50% quantile | 0.87 | 1.03 | 0.62 | 1.25 | 0.01 | 0.18 | 180.00 | | |
| 75% quantile | 6.51 | 17.08 | 3.74 | 10.10 | 0.23 | 0.72 | 420.00 | | |
| 95% quantile | 96.18 | 166.01 | 92.71 | 101.90 | 2.04 | 3.80 | 1000.00 | Successful investor | 0.40 |
| Maximum | 4233.81 | 4266.44 | 4233.81 | 1980.54 | 51.91 | 235.76 | 7000.00 | | |
| | | | | Group 3: (10–15%), # investors 147 | | | | | |
| Observations | 6318.00 | 6234.00 | 2611.00 | 3545.00 | 6318.00 | 6318.00 | 6318.00 | Complex trading strategy | 0.44 |
| Mean | 21.42 | 41.22 | 24.98 | 19.69 | -0.30 | 2.46 | 713.61 | | |
| Standard deviation | 116.04 | 189.90 | 137.88 | 99.85 | 19.27 | 19.11 | 889.89 | | |

| | | | | | | | | | |
|---|---|---|---|---|---|---|---|---|---|
| Minimum | 0.00 | 0.00 | 0.00 | 0.00 | −686.46 | 0.00 | 1.00 | Close special limit order | 0.19 |
| 5% quantile | 0.02 | 0.01 | 0.02 | 0.02 | −3.78 | 0.01 | 40.00 | | |
| 25% quantile | 0.13 | 0.04 | 0.11 | 0.16 | −0.39 | 0.12 | 200.00 | | |
| 50% quantile | 0.74 | 0.89 | 0.60 | 0.91 | 0.04 | 0.47 | 500.00 | | |
| 75% quantile | 6.08 | 15.49 | 4.51 | 8.41 | 0.52 | 1.60 | 1000.00 | | |
| 95% quantile | 86.10 | 155.84 | 98.46 | 82.28 | 4.16 | 7.80 | 2000.00 | Successful investor | 0.34 |
| Maximum | 3389.15 | 4858.68 | 3389.15 | 2907.46 | 974.18 | 974.18 | 23000.00 | | |
| Group 4: (15 –20%), # investors 137 | | | | | | | | | |
| Observations | 8308.00 | 8235.00 | 3320.00 | 4725.00 | 8308.00 | 8308.00 | 8308.00 | Complex trading strategy | 0.48 |
| Mean | 16.11 | 33.11 | 20.67 | 13.74 | −0.48 | 2.57 | 933.77 | | |
| Standard deviation | 93.06 | 163.21 | 125.28 | 64.56 | 14.44 | 14.22 | 1083.03 | | |
| Minimum | 0.00 | 0.00 | 0.00 | 0.00 | −839.95 | 0.00 | 1.00 | Close special limit order | 0.18 |
| 5% quantile | 0.02 | 0.00 | 0.02 | 0.03 | −5.43 | 0.01 | 25.00 | | |
| 25% quantile | 0.14 | 0.03 | 0.13 | 0.16 | −0.48 | 0.13 | 211.00 | | |
| 50% quantile | 0.64 | 0.52 | 0.63 | 0.71 | 0.04 | 0.50 | 575.00 | | |
| 75% quantile | 4.06 | 10.31 | 3.57 | 4.94 | 0.51 | 1.80 | 1032.00 | | |
| 95% quantile | 67.25 | 130.52 | 72.36 | 64.56 | 4.40 | 8.98 | 3000.00 | Successful investor | 0.41 |
| Maximum | 4056.95 | 4568.80 | 4056.95 | 2517.26 | 634.25 | 839.95 | 16000.00 | | |
| Group 5: (20–25%), # investors 142 | | | | | | | | | |
| Observations | 9649.00 | 9563.00 | 3635.00 | 5666.00 | 9649.00 | 9649.00 | 9649.00 | Complex trading strategy | 0.44 |
| Mean | 16.29 | 27.46 | 21.63 | 13.75 | −0.95 | 4.00 | 1295.80 | | |
| Standard deviation | 89.11 | 133.62 | 104.48 | 80.50 | 21.20 | 20.84 | 1813.66 | | |
| Minimum | 0.00 | 0.00 | 0.00 | 0.00 | −1169.60 | 0.00 | 1.00 | Close special limit order | 0.19 |
| 5% quantile | 0.02 | 0.00 | 0.02 | 0.03 | −7.83 | 0.01 | 40.00 | | |
| 25% quantile | 0.16 | 0.04 | 0.16 | 0.17 | −0.52 | 0.12 | 200.00 | | |
| 50% quantile | 0.69 | 0.78 | 0.72 | 0.74 | 0.06 | 0.60 | 900.00 | | |
| 75% quantile | 4.54 | 12.60 | 5.00 | 4.88 | 0.70 | 2.40 | 1698.50 | | |
| 95% quantile | 70.44 | 104.34 | 96.22 | 64.83 | 6.76 | 14.60 | 4094.15 | Successful investor | 0.42 |
| Maximum | 4031.26 | 4528.48 | 2595.92 | 4031.26 | 260.42 | 1169.60 | 50000.00 | | |

Note: The sample ranges from 1 October 2003 00:00:00 (EST) to 14 May 2004 23:59:59 (EST), which are 227 full days (5448 h).

Table A2. Descriptive statistics of the roundtrip, inactivity durations and explanatory variables for the EUR/USD currency pair.

| EUR/USD | Durations in hours | | Loss | Profit | Profit/loss | Absolute profit/loss | Volume | Dummy variable | Mean |
|---|---|---|---|---|---|---|---|---|---|
| | Roundtrip | Inactivity | | | | | | | |
| | | | | Group 6: (25–30%), # investors 146 | | | | | |
| Observations | 10669.00 | 10579.00 | 4330.00 | 5855.00 | 10669.00 | 10669.00 | 10669.00 | Complex trading strategy | 0.42 |
| Mean | 13.98 | 26.08 | 17.24 | 12.60 | −1.27 | 5.21 | 1821.73 | | |
| Standard deviation | 71.33 | 115.00 | 81.24 | 66.08 | 23.49 | 22.94 | 2557.32 | Close special limit order | 0.18 |
| Minimum | 0.00 | 0.00 | 0.00 | 0.00 | −765.85 | 0.00 | 1.00 | | |
| 5% quantile | 0.02 | 0.00 | 0.01 | 0.02 | −11.50 | 0.00 | 25.00 | | |
| 25% quantile | 0.13 | 0.05 | 0.11 | 0.14 | −0.78 | 0.16 | 400.00 | | |
| 50% quantile | 0.54 | 0.69 | 0.50 | 0.64 | 0.03 | 0.80 | 1000.00 | Successful investor | 0.39 |
| 75% quantile | 3.28 | 10.54 | 3.12 | 3.87 | 0.80 | 3.00 | 2191.50 | | |
| 95% quantile | 64.77 | 117.77 | 75.48 | 59.00 | 9.00 | 19.83 | 6000.00 | | |
| Maximum | 3067.68 | 3771.70 | 1850.84 | 3067.68 | 549.30 | 765.85 | 100000.00 | | |
| | | | | Group 7: (30–35%), # investors 141 | | | | | |
| Observations | 13067.00 | 12986.00 | 5318.00 | 7284.00 | 13067.00 | 13067.00 | 13067.00 | Complex trading strategy | 0.39 |
| Mean | 11.14 | 19.89 | 12.20 | 10.83 | −0.64 | 5.70 | 2076.74 | | |
| Standard deviation | 63.69 | 106.03 | 77.85 | 52.88 | 35.23 | 34.78 | 2841.86 | Close special limit order | 0.19 |
| Minimum | 0.00 | 0.00 | 0.00 | 0.00 | −1517.50 | 0.00 | 1.00 | | |
| 5% quantile | 0.02 | 0.00 | 0.01 | 0.02 | −10.00 | 0.00 | 90.00 | | |
| 25% quantile | 0.11 | 0.04 | 0.10 | 0.13 | −0.92 | 0.25 | 500.00 | | |
| 50% quantile | 0.48 | 0.47 | 0.44 | 0.58 | 0.06 | 1.00 | 1000.00 | Successful investor | 0.39 |
| 75% quantile | 2.66 | 7.85 | 2.32 | 3.16 | 1.00 | 3.20 | 2500.00 | | |
| 95% quantile | 46.44 | 81.66 | 44.65 | 48.76 | 8.80 | 18.28 | 7000.00 | | |
| Maximum | 2325.87 | 4201.72 | 2325.87 | 2035.47 | 1771.67 | 1771.67 | 50000.00 | | |
| | | | | Group 8: (35–40%), # investors 141 | | | | | |
| Observations | 13083.00 | 12994.00 | 5392.00 | 7116.00 | 13083.00 | 13083.00 | 13083.00 | Complex trading strategy | 0.42 |
| Mean | 9.97 | 20.99 | 10.27 | 10.40 | −1.27 | 8.36 | 3001.59 | | |
| Standard deviation | 64.88 | 106.93 | 67.87 | 65.07 | 54.31 | 53.68 | 4166.86 | Close special limit order | 0.16 |
| Minimum | 0.00 | 0.00 | 0.00 | 0.00 | −3798.30 | 0.00 | 1.00 | | |

| | | | | | | | | |
|---|---|---|---|---|---|---|---|---|
| 5% quantile | 0.02 | 0.00 | 0.01 | 0.02 | -15.00 | 0.00 | 40.00 | |
| 25% quantile | 0.11 | 0.04 | 0.10 | 0.12 | -0.90 | 0.20 | 500.00 | |
| 50% quantile | 0.42 | 0.54 | 0.38 | 0.47 | 0.04 | 1.00 | 1240.00 | Successful investor 0.38 |
| 75% quantile | 2.06 | 8.73 | 1.75 | 2.62 | 1.20 | 4.40 | 4000.00 | |
| 95% quantile | 34.97 | 90.83 | 34.41 | 40.28 | 13.80 | 29.05 | 10000.00 | |
| Maximum | 3166.38 | 4024.91 | 2011.06 | 3166.38 | 1877.60 | 3798.30 | 60000.00 | |

**Group 9: (40–45%), # investors 149**

| | | | | | | | | |
|---|---|---|---|---|---|---|---|---|
| Observations | 14464.00 | 14369.00 | 5343.00 | 8614.00 | 14464.00 | 14464.00 | 14464.00 | Complex trading strategy 0.43 |
| Mean | 9.34 | 19.37 | 11.05 | -1.44 | 9.14 | | 3806.51 | |
| Standard deviation | 51.15 | 103.64 | 63.36 | 50.85 | 50.05 | | 5673.49 | Close special limit order 0.18 |
| Minimum | 0.00 | 0.00 | 0.00 | -2397.20 | 0.00 | | 1.00 | |
| 5% quantile | 0.02 | 0.01 | 0.02 | -17.39 | 0.00 | | 50.00 | |
| 25% quantile | 0.13 | 0.05 | 0.13 | -0.84 | 0.30 | | 575.00 | |
| 50% quantile | 0.50 | 0.42 | 0.54 | 0.12 | 1.30 | | 2000.00 | Successful investor 0.44 |
| 75% quantile | 2.52 | 6.03 | 2.74 | 1.65 | 5.60 | | 5000.00 | |
| 95% quantile | 38.39 | 85.45 | 44.83 | 17.00 | 32.00 | | 12000.00 | |
| Maximum | 1677.39 | 5025.12 | 1677.39 | 691.00 | 2397.20 | | 120000.00 | |

**Group 10: (45–50%), # investors 146**

| | | | | | | | | |
|---|---|---|---|---|---|---|---|---|
| Observations | 14678.00 | 14596.00 | 5795.00 | 8253.00 | 14678.00 | 14678.00 | 14678.00 | Complex trading strategy 0.36 |
| Mean | 10.77 | 19.54 | 13.20 | -1.79 | 11.75 | | 4630.25 | |
| Standard deviation | 65.76 | 105.01 | 85.06 | 56.35 | 55.14 | | 6923.37 | Close special limit order 0.18 |
| Minimum | 0.00 | 0.00 | 0.00 | -2598.16 | 0.00 | | 1.00 | |
| 5% quantile | 0.02 | 0.01 | 0.02 | -22.82 | 0.00 | | 71.00 | |
| 25% quantile | 0.13 | 0.05 | 0.13 | -1.04 | 0.32 | | 798.50 | |
| 50% quantile | 0.52 | 0.50 | 0.54 | 0.12 | 1.60 | | 2280.00 | Successful investor 0.40 |
| 75% quantile | 2.88 | 7.23 | 2.95 | 2.00 | 7.00 | | 5148.50 | |
| 95% quantile | 45.54 | 77.61 | 46.27 | 21.00 | 43.00 | | 19010.00 | |
| Maximum | 2225.20 | 4650.45 | 2225.20 | 1040.64 | 2598.16 | | 125027.00 | |

Note: The sample ranges from 1 October 2003 00:00:00 (EST) to 14 May 2004 23:59:59 (EST), which are 227 full days (5448 h).

Table A3. Descriptive statistics of the roundtrip, inactivity durations and explanatory variables for the EUR/USD currency pair.

| EUR/USD | Durations in hours | | Loss | Profit | Profit/ loss | Absolute profit/loss | Volume | Dummy variable | Mean |
|---|---|---|---|---|---|---|---|---|---|
| | Roundtrip | Inactivity | | | | | | | |
| | | | Group 11: (50–55%), # investors 146 | | | | | | |
| Observations | 14824.00 | 14749.00 | 5881.00 | 8349.00 | 14824.00 | 14824.00 | 14824.00 | Complex trading strategy | 0.40 |
| Mean | 10.72 | 20.51 | 12.58 | 10.06 | −2.38 | 15.20 | 6017.88 | | |
| Standard deviation | 62.17 | 102.80 | 73.33 | 55.35 | 80.69 | 79.28 | 8732.65 | | |
| Minimum | 0.00 | 0.00 | 0.00 | 0.00 | −3027.00 | 0.00 | 1.00 | Close special limit order | 0.20 |
| 5% quantile | 0.02 | 0.01 | 0.01 | 0.02 | −28.00 | 0.00 | 65.00 | | |
| 25% quantile | 0.12 | 0.05 | 0.11 | 0.14 | −1.90 | 0.50 | 1000.00 | | |
| 50% quantile | 0.49 | 0.46 | 0.44 | 0.57 | 0.11 | 2.30 | 1000.00 | | |
| 75% quantile | 2.70 | 6.80 | 2.49 | 3.12 | 2.73 | 9.00 | 3000.00 | | |
| 95% quantile | 43.11 | 90.84 | 47.76 | 42.23 | 26.29 | 55.00 | 20000.00 | Successful investor | 0.40 |
| Maximum | 2185.84 | 3359.36 | 2185.84 | 1858.51 | 2760.20 | 3027.00 | 310000.00 | | |
| | | | Group 12: (55–60%), # investors 144 | | | | | | |
| Observations | 14845.00 | 14759.00 | 5706.00 | 8453.00 | 14845.00 | 14845.00 | 14845.00 | Complex trading strategy | 0.37 |
| Mean | 10.84 | 20.77 | 14.47 | 9.10 | −3.85 | 18.92 | 7169.12 | | |
| Standard deviation | 65.68 | 97.34 | 80.90 | 55.89 | 98.18 | 96.42 | 10436.24 | | |
| Minimum | 0.00 | 0.00 | 0.00 | 0.00 | −3421.40 | 0.00 | 1.00 | Close special limit order | 0.22 |
| 5% quantile | 0.02 | 0.01 | 0.02 | 0.03 | −33.00 | 0.00 | 180.00 | | |
| 25% quantile | 0.12 | 0.07 | 0.12 | 0.13 | −2.00 | 0.50 | 1000.00 | | |
| 50% quantile | 0.43 | 0.50 | 0.44 | 0.45 | 0.20 | 2.40 | 3250.00 | | |
| 75% quantile | 2.18 | 7.51 | 2.29 | 2.31 | 2.88 | 9.79 | 10000.00 | | |
| 95% quantile | 46.26 | 91.57 | 64.50 | 38.82 | 30.18 | 66.50 | 27000.00 | Successful investor | 0.41 |
| Maximum | 2373.72 | 3034.45 | 2137.58 | 2373.72 | 2552.80 | 3421.40 | 300000.00 | | |
| | | | Group 13: (60–65%), # investors 147 | | | | | | |
| Observations | 18939.00 | 18842.00 | 8053.00 | 10103.00 | 18939.00 | 18939.00 | 18939.00 | Complex trading strategy | 0.31 |
| Mean | 8.42 | 15.26 | 9.57 | 8.05 | −2.99 | 18.95 | 8350.72 | | |
| Standard deviation | 54.63 | 78.73 | 66.33 | 45.59 | 123.18 | 121.75 | 14026.45 | | |
| Minimum | 0.00 | 0.00 | 0.00 | 0.00 | −5893.00 | 0.00 | 1.00 | Close special limit order | 0.18 |

## (continued)

|  | | | | | | |
|---|---|---|---|---|---|---|
| 5% quantile | 0.02 | 0.00 | 0.02 | 0.02 | −35.20 | 0.00 | 100.00 |
| 25% quantile | 0.11 | 0.04 | 0.10 | 0.12 | −2.80 | 0.60 | 1047.75 |
| 50% quantile | 0.41 | 0.28 | 0.40 | 0.45 | 0.10 | 3.00 | 5000.00 |
| 75% quantile | 1.94 | 3.99 | 1.83 | 2.24 | 3.30 | 11.00 | 10000.00 |
| 95% quantile | 27.28 | 67.58 | 31.05 | 28.20 | 29.00 | 62.00 | 30000.00 |
| Maximum | 2661.71 | 2342.16 | 2661.71 | 1914.52 | 7395.00 | 7395.00 | 450000.00 |

Successful investor 0.36

### Group 14: (65–70%), # investors 147

|  | | | | | | |
|---|---|---|---|---|---|---|
| Observations | 18462.00 | 18366.00 | 7809.00 | 9782.00 | 18462.00 | 18462.00 | 18462.00 |
| Mean | 7.41 | 16.13 | 7.38 | 7.95 | −3.32 | 26.72 | 11921.28 |
| Standard deviation | 45.15 | 78.60 | 44.65 | 47.41 | 159.78 | 157.56 | 17266.69 |
| Minimum | 0.00 | 0.00 | 0.00 | 0.00 | −9412.50 | 0.00 | 1.00 |
| 5% quantile | 0.02 | 0.01 | 0.01 | 0.03 | −45.00 | 0.00 | 360.20 |
| 25% quantile | 0.10 | 0.05 | 0.09 | 0.12 | −4.20 | 1.09 | 2700.00 |
| 50% quantile | 0.34 | 0.37 | 0.30 | 0.41 | 0.20 | 4.72 | 7000.00 |
| 75% quantile | 1.53 | 5.30 | 1.35 | 1.88 | 5.00 | 15.00 | 14050.00 |
| 95% quantile | 25.65 | 71.58 | 26.31 | 27.85 | 45.00 | 92.00 | 40021.20 |
| Maximum | 1895.68 | 3005.62 | 1895.68 | 1831.42 | 9162.00 | 9412.50 | 400000.00 |

Complex trading strategy 0.37
Close special limit order 0.17
Over-confident investor 0.36

### Group 15: (70–75%), # investors 146

|  | | | | | | |
|---|---|---|---|---|---|---|
| Observations | 21653.00 | 21574.00 | 8818.00 | 11878.00 | 21653.00 | 21653.00 | 21653.00 |
| Mean | 7.23 | 13.78 | 8.23 | 6.96 | −5.15 | 28.35 | 12325.48 |
| Standard deviation | 47.60 | 73.51 | 58.54 | 39.74 | 234.58 | 232.91 | 19915.76 |
| Minimum | 0.00 | 0.00 | 0.00 | 0.00 | −24175.85 | 0.00 | 1.00 |
| 5% quantile | 0.02 | 0.00 | 0.01 | 0.02 | −50.57 | 0.00 | 100.00 |
| 25% quantile | 0.09 | 0.03 | 0.08 | 0.11 | −3.00 | 0.66 | 1200.00 |
| 50% quantile | 0.35 | 0.23 | 0.33 | 0.40 | 0.14 | 4.00 | 6000.00 |
| 75% quantile | 1.56 | 3.51 | 1.45 | 1.81 | 4.50 | 16.20 | 15000.00 |
| 95% quantile | 23.36 | 65.74 | 23.37 | 24.75 | 46.00 | 95.00 | 50000.00 |
| Maximum | 1869.31 | 2396.31 | 1869.31 | 1544.82 | 4196.34 | 24175.85 | 1000000.00 |

Complex trading strategy 0.39
Close special limit order 0.18
Successful investor 0.38

Note: The sample ranges from 1 October 2003 00:00:00 (EST) to 14 May 2004 23:59:59 (EST), which are 227 full days (5448 h).

Table A4. Descriptive statistics of the roundtrip, inactivity durations and explanatory variables for the EUR/USD currency pair.

| EUR/USD | Durations in hours | | | | Profit/ loss | Absolute profit/loss | Volume | Dummy variable | Mean |
|---|---|---|---|---|---|---|---|---|---|
| | Roundtrip | Inactivity | Loss | Profit | | | | | |
| | | | | Group 16: (75–80%), # investors 146 | | | | | |
| Observations | 23314.00 | 23224.00 | 9502.00 | 12798.00 | 23314.00 | 23314.00 | 23314.00 | Complex trading strategy | 0.29 |
| Mean | 6.93 | 13.93 | 7.54 | 6.89 | −8.25 | 37.19 | 17838.46 | | |
| Standard deviation | 39.39 | 73.25 | 45.28 | 35.99 | 175.54 | 171.75 | 26604.71 | Close special limit order | 0.17 |
| Minimum | 0.00 | 0.00 | 0.00 | 0.00 | −6623.00 | 0.00 | 1.00 | | |
| 5% quantile | 0.02 | 0.00 | 0.01 | 0.02 | −79.82 | 0.00 | 432.70 | | |
| 25% quantile | 0.11 | 0.03 | 0.10 | 0.12 | −6.00 | 1.54 | 3144.00 | | |
| 50% quantile | 0.38 | 0.23 | 0.38 | 0.41 | 0.35 | 6.50 | 10000.00 | | |
| 75% quantile | 1.88 | 3.14 | 1.79 | 2.12 | 7.10 | 22.66 | 20000.00 | | |
| 95% quantile | 25.49 | 66.99 | 26.93 | 26.15 | 63.00 | 137.03 | 60000.00 | Successful investor | 0.38 |
| Maximum | 1682.17 | 2374.48 | 1682.17 | 1488.00 | 2421.40 | 6623.00 | 500000.00 | | |
| | | | | Group 17: (80–85%), # investors 147 | | | | | |
| Observations | 23522.00 | 23412.00 | 8917.00 | 13508.00 | 23522.00 | 23522.00 | 23522.00 | Complex trading strategy | 0.39 |
| Mean | 6.39 | 13.85 | 7.74 | 5.93 | −7.20 | 46.77 | 24291.91 | | |
| Standard deviation | 33.96 | 74.53 | 43.38 | 27.58 | 196.01 | 190.49 | 32220.84 | Close special limit order | 0.24 |
| Minimum | 0.00 | 0.00 | 0.00 | 0.00 | −10151.60 | 0.00 | 1.00 | | |
| 5% quantile | 0.02 | 0.01 | 0.01 | 0.02 | −100.00 | 0.01 | 1000.00 | | |
| 25% quantile | 0.11 | 0.04 | 0.10 | 0.12 | −7.60 | 2.04 | 5000.00 | | |
| 50% quantile | 0.39 | 0.28 | 0.38 | 0.43 | 0.90 | 10.00 | 13500.00 | | |
| 75% quantile | 1.78 | 4.29 | 1.73 | 1.96 | 11.00 | 33.00 | 30000.00 | | |
| 95% quantile | 23.78 | 68.00 | 27.99 | 23.86 | 85.00 | 179.87 | 100000.00 | Successful investor | 0.42 |
| Maximum | 1534.95 | 3447.64 | 1534.95 | 886.31 | 3590.00 | 10151.60 | 1040400.00 | | |
| | | | | Group 18: (85–90%), # investors 145 | | | | | |
| Observations | 20982.00 | 20884.00 | 8117.00 | 11823.00 | 20982.00 | 20982.00 | 20982.00 | Complex trading strategy | 0.36 |
| Mean | 6.82 | 14.48 | 8.42 | 6.21 | −15.48 | 85.08 | 40069.26 | | |
| Standard deviation | 45.85 | 72.50 | 58.38 | 37.18 | 543.92 | 537.45 | 52697.31 | Close special limit order | 0.19 |
| Minimum | 0.00 | 0.00 | 0.00 | 0.00 | −45935.70 | 0.00 | 1.00 | | |

|  | | | | | | | |
|---|---|---|---|---|---|---|---|
| 5% quantile | 0.02 | 0.01 | 0.02 | 0.02 | −166.50 | 0.00 | 1161.10 | Successful investor 0.40 |
| 25% quantile | 0.10 | 0.05 | 0.10 | 0.10 | −16.69 | 4.02 | 10000.00 | |
| 50% quantile | 0.36 | 0.41 | 0.38 | 0.37 | 1.30 | 18.00 | 23329.00 | |
| 75% quantile | 1.68 | 5.36 | 1.70 | 1.81 | 18.18 | 56.12 | 50000.00 | |
| 95% quantile | 23.23 | 69.43 | 26.45 | 22.56 | 140.00 | 279.00 | 125000.00 | |
| Maximum | 2232.12 | 3465.18 | 2232.12 | 1555.09 | 15169.50 | 45935.70 | 1200000.00 | |

**Group 19: (90–95%), # investors 146**

|  | | | | | | | |
|---|---|---|---|---|---|---|---|
| Observations | 23261.00 | 23180.00 | 8378.00 | 13910.00 | 23261.00 | 23261.00 | 23261.00 | Complex trading strategy 0.25 |
| Mean | 7.41 | 12.91 | 9.04 | 6.82 | −12.93 | 126.84 | 62529.85 | |
| Standard deviation | 41.42 | 72.74 | 49.41 | 37.28 | 575.81 | 561.81 | 85607.01 | Close special limit order 0.26 |
| Minimum | 0.00 | 0.00 | 0.00 | 0.00 | −18630.00 | 0.00 | 1.00 | |
| 5% quantile | 0.02 | 0.01 | 0.02 | 0.02 | −250.00 | 0.02 | 1000.00 | |
| 25% quantile | 0.11 | 0.04 | 0.11 | 0.12 | −12.50 | 4.60 | 10000.00 | |
| 50% quantile | 0.40 | 0.29 | 0.42 | 0.41 | 2.05 | 20.00 | 30000.00 | |
| 75% quantile | 1.93 | 3.26 | 2.18 | 1.95 | 28.00 | 80.00 | 90462.00 | |
| 95% quantile | 27.68 | 62.76 | 35.91 | 26.72 | 240.00 | 478.39 | 200000.00 | Successful investor 0.45 |
| Maximum | 1824.01 | 2480.13 | 1698.30 | 1824.01 | 34727.50 | 34727.50 | 1200000.00 | |

**Group 20: (95–100%), # investors 149**

|  | | | | | | | |
|---|---|---|---|---|---|---|---|
| Observations | 26325.00 | 26237.00 | 9172.00 | 15910.00 | 26325.00 | 26325.00 | 26325.00 | Complex trading strategy 0.26 |
| Mean | 7.81 | 12.37 | 10.14 | 7.00 | −53.40 | 880.21 | 366229.32 | |
| Standard deviation | 52.41 | 62.10 | 67.75 | 43.46 | 10674.13 | 10637.91 | 1047316.73 | Close special limit order 0.25 |
| Minimum | 0.00 | 0.00 | 0.00 | 0.00 | −809400.00 | 0.00 | 1.00 | |
| 5% quantile | 0.02 | 0.01 | 0.01 | 0.02 | −858.75 | 0.05 | 6000.00 | |
| 25% quantile | 0.09 | 0.04 | 0.10 | 0.10 | −41.42 | 16.50 | 45000.00 | |
| 50% quantile | 0.35 | 0.30 | 0.41 | 0.34 | 10.00 | 76.62 | 100000.00 | |
| 75% quantile | 1.69 | 3.75 | 2.12 | 1.66 | 100.00 | 295.00 | 300000.00 | |
| 95% quantile | 26.86 | 63.28 | 41.78 | 24.37 | 1140.00 | 2350.00 | 1400000.00 | Successful investor 0.46 |
| Maximum | 3284.07 | 3485.18 | 3284.07 | 1296.50 | 688400.00 | 809400.00 | 53000000.00 | |

Note: The sample ranges from 1 October 2003 00:00:00 (EST) to 14 May 2004 23:59:59 (EST), which are 227 full days (5448 h).

## A.2 *Estimation results*

Table A5. Estimation results for investor groups 1–5 for EUR/USD. Quasi-maximum likelihood standard errors reported.

| Parameters | 1 Estimate | 1 Standard error | 2 Estimate | 2 Standard error | 3 Estimate | 3 Standard error | 4 Estimate | 4 Standard error | 5 Estimate | 5 Standard error |
|---|---|---|---|---|---|---|---|---|---|---|
| | | | | Roundtrip intensity Baseline intensity | | | | | | |
| $\alpha^R$ | 0.9541 | 0.0460 | 1.0078 | 0.0316 | 1.1047 | 0.0358 | 1.0614 | 0.0177 | 1.0782 | 0.0176 |
| $\sigma^{2,R}$ | 0.0557 | 0.1126 | 0.1874 | 0.0682 | 0.2908 | 0.0578 | 0.1542 | 0.0507 | 0.2285 | 0.0463 |
| $\nu^R_{s,1}$ | -0.1735 | 0.0458 | -0.1321 | 0.0445 | -0.1063 | 0.0525 | 0.0035 | 0.0512 | -0.0708 | 0.0329 |
| $\nu^R_{s,2}$ | -0.0002 | 0.1312 | 0.1181 | 0.0412 | 0.0038 | 0.1794 | 0.0154 | 0.0344 | 0.0386 | 0.0324 |
| $\nu^R_{s,3}$ | -0.2197 | 0.0377 | -0.1825 | 0.0311 | -0.2034 | 0.0593 | -0.2144 | 0.0410 | -0.1589 | 0.0260 |
| $\nu^R_{c,1}$ | 0.0364 | 0.0381 | 0.0466 | 0.0326 | 0.0664 | 0.0338 | 0.0510 | 0.0451 | -0.0060 | 0.0274 |
| $\nu^R_{c,2}$ | 0.1780 | 0.0324 | 0.1963 | 0.0308 | 0.1753 | 0.0392 | 0.2010 | 0.0461 | 0.2401 | 0.0304 |
| $\nu^R_{c,3}$ | 0.0956 | 0.0417 | 0.0924 | 0.0316 | 0.1263 | 0.0704 | 0.0888 | 0.0312 | 0.1271 | 0.0249 |
| | | | | Explanatory variables | | | | | | |
| $c^R$ | 2.6288 | 0.6426 | 2.3556 | 0.3248 | 1.2231 | 0.4646 | 1.0073 | 0.1035 | 1.3277 | 0.0831 |
| $c^R_{sl}$ | -0.7485 | 0.3105 | -0.2360 | 0.1141 | -0.2728 | 0.3491 | -0.5841 | 0.0527 | -0.5697 | 0.0340 |
| $c^R_{sc}$ | -0.1559 | 0.1996 | -0.0541 | 0.1319 | 0.1935 | 0.1518 | -0.0634 | 0.0611 | -0.0073 | 0.0579 |
| $\beta^R_p$ | -3.3570 | 0.4153 | -2.8717 | 0.3019 | -2.7995 | 0.2447 | -2.0900 | 0.1053 | -2.5563 | 0.1063 |
| $\beta^R_{p*sl}$ | 0.4062 | 0.1478 | 0.0180 | 0.0308 | 0.0204 | 0.2916 | 0.1654 | 0.0398 | 0.1173 | 0.0391 |
| $\beta^R_{psov}$ | 0.0541 | 0.1032 | -0.0262 | 0.0749 | -0.1609 | 0.0874 | -0.0512 | 0.0517 | -0.0071 | 0.0456 |
| $\beta^R_l$ | 2.3996 | 0.3372 | 1.4166 | 0.2659 | 1.6355 | 0.1908 | 0.9926 | 0.1043 | 1.4372 | 0.0860 |
| $\beta^R_{l*sl}$ | -0.4813 | 0.1359 | -0.1168 | 0.0629 | -0.2301 | 0.1515 | -0.3119 | 0.0365 | -0.2785 | 0.0329 |
| $\beta^R_{lsov}$ | 0.0389 | 0.0929 | 0.0847 | 0.0656 | 0.1225 | 0.0767 | 0.0361 | 0.0465 | 0.0341 | 0.0431 |
| $\beta^R_{p^2}$ | 0.7994 | 0.1706 | 0.8554 | 0.1589 | 0.5869 | 0.1097 | 0.3530 | 0.0468 | 0.6003 | 0.0627 |
| $\beta^R_{l^2}$ | 0.2993 | 0.1218 | 0.1099 | 0.1145 | 0.0225 | 0.0791 | -0.1540 | 0.0554 | 0.0231 | 0.0399 |

| | | | | | | | | | |
|---|---|---|---|---|---|---|---|---|---|
| $\beta_{p^3}^R$ | -0.0808 | 0.0218 | -0.1068 | 0.0232 | -0.0556 | 0.0136 | -0.0398 | 0.0060 | -0.0720 | 0.0110 |
| $\beta_{f^3}^R$ | 0.0162 | 0.0141 | 0.0150 | 0.0126 | 0.0003 | 0.0079 | -0.0122 | 0.0082 | 0.0021 | 0.0054 |
| $\beta_{pscx}^R$ | 0.0657 | 0.0879 | -0.0366 | 0.1064 | 0.0589 | 0.1047 | 0.0201 | 0.0513 | 0.0005 | 0.0576 |
| $\beta_{l*cx}^R$ | -0.1092 | 0.0742 | -0.0713 | 0.0824 | -0.1366 | 0.0856 | -0.1529 | 0.0514 | -0.0012 | 0.0385 |
| $\beta_{dr(-1)}^R$ | -0.2493 | 0.0344 | -0.2536 | 0.0233 | -0.2502 | 0.0236 | -0.1860 | 0.0087 | -0.2190 | 0.0085 |
| $\beta_{di(-1)}^R$ | -0.0840 | 0.0198 | -0.0739 | 0.0111 | -0.0735 | 0.0133 | -0.0614 | 0.0070 | -0.0437 | 0.0053 |
| $\beta_{vol}^R$ | 0.4157 | 0.0819 | 0.3854 | 0.0634 | 0.6209 | 0.0805 | 0.6159 | 0.0219 | 0.5423 | 0.0122 |
| $c_{cx}^R$ | -1.5016 | 0.1833 | -1.4318 | 0.1554 | -1.5252 | 0.1815 | -1.6460 | 0.0901 | -1.1892 | 0.0635 |

Inactivity intensity
Baseline intensity

| | | | | | | | | | |
|---|---|---|---|---|---|---|---|---|---|
| $\alpha^2$ | 0.4453 | 0.0279 | 0.5163 | 0.0397 | 0.5230 | 0.0359 | 0.5114 | 0.0084 | 0.4917 | 0.0085 |
| $\sigma^{2,I}$ | -0.5886 | 0.2043 | -0.2719 | 0.2074 | -0.2368 | 0.1614 | -0.2402 | 0.0546 | -0.4379 | 0.0599 |
| $\nu_{s,1}^I$ | -0.1005 | 0.0589 | -0.1276 | 0.0567 | -0.1361 | 0.0482 | -0.0536 | 0.0388 | -0.1616 | 0.0320 |
| $\nu_{s,2}^I$ | -0.1673 | 0.0428 | 0.0147 | 0.0816 | -0.0665 | 0.0418 | -0.1114 | 0.0283 | -0.0803 | 0.0276 |
| $\nu_{s,3}^I$ | -0.3750 | 0.0394 | -0.4202 | 0.0410 | -0.4099 | 0.0396 | -0.4367 | 0.0345 | -0.4858 | 0.0257 |
| $\nu_{c,1}^I$ | -0.0652 | 0.0315 | -0.0644 | 0.0324 | -0.0793 | 0.0263 | -0.1105 | 0.0281 | -0.0659 | 0.0237 |
| $\nu_{c,2}^I$ | 0.2576 | 0.0433 | 0.3854 | 0.0374 | 0.3758 | 0.0412 | 0.3533 | 0.0293 | 0.3244 | 0.0260 |
| $\nu_{c,3}^I$ | 0.1608 | 0.0346 | 0.1148 | 0.0360 | 0.0541 | 0.0374 | 0.0893 | 0.0252 | 0.0330 | 0.0258 |

Explanatory variables

| | | | | | | | | | |
|---|---|---|---|---|---|---|---|---|---|
| $c^I$ | -0.0059 | 0.0375 | 0.2169 | 0.1691 | 0.2677 | 0.1069 | 0.3237 | 0.0573 | 0.3365 | 0.0462 |
| $c_{sc}^I$ | 0.1988 | 0.0945 | -0.0121 | 0.1733 | 0.0093 | 0.0747 | 0.1476 | 0.0354 | 0.0618 | 0.0211 |
| $\beta_{dr(-1)}^I$ | -0.1818 | 0.0262 | -0.1778 | 0.0261 | -0.2184 | 0.0306 | -0.2044 | 0.0064 | -0.1717 | 0.0055 |
| $\beta_{di(-1)}^I$ | -0.1371 | 0.0218 | -0.1555 | 0.0228 | -0.1462 | 0.0160 | -0.1551 | 0.0051 | -0.1544 | 0.0046 |

Notes: Subindexes: $p$, profit; $l$, loss; $sl$, special limit order; $sc$, successful; $cx$, complex trading strategy; $dr(-1)$, lagged roundtrip duration; $di(-1)$, lagged inactivity duration; $vol$, transaction volume; $*$, respective interaction term. All other parameters are detailed in the main text.

Table A6. Estimation results for investor groups 6–10 for EUR/USD. Quasi-maximum likelihood standard errors reported.

| Parameters | 6 Estimate | 6 Standard error | 7 Estimate | 7 Standard error | 8 Estimate | 8 Standard error | 9 Estimate | 9 Standard error | 10 Estimate | 10 Standard error |
|---|---|---|---|---|---|---|---|---|---|---|
| **Roundtrip intensity** | | | | | | | | | | |
| **Baseline intensity** | | | | | | | | | | |
| $\alpha^R$ | 0.9972 | 0.0354 | 1.0559 | 0.0167 | 1.0501 | 0.0241 | 1.1202 | 0.0150 | 1.0328 | 0.0141 |
| $\sigma^{2,R}$ | 0.0841 | 0.0687 | 0.1103 | 0.0434 | 0.1114 | 0.0587 | 0.2108 | 0.0328 | 0.0839 | 0.0355 |
| $v^R_{s,1}$ | −0.0904 | 0.0396 | −0.0262 | 0.0317 | −0.0965 | 0.0424 | −0.1208 | 0.0356 | −0.0372 | 0.0351 |
| $v^R_{s,2}$ | 0.0270 | 0.0321 | −0.0084 | 0.0299 | 0.0481 | 0.0286 | 0.0202 | 0.0301 | 0.0065 | 0.0303 |
| $v^R_{s,3}$ | −0.1561 | 0.0287 | −0.1558 | 0.0280 | −0.1815 | 0.0279 | −0.2106 | 0.0300 | −0.2505 | 0.0268 |
| $v^R_{c,1}$ | 0.0652 | 0.0308 | 0.0399 | 0.0311 | 0.0546 | 0.0325 | 0.0623 | 0.0228 | 0.0928 | 0.0235 |
| $v^R_{c,2}$ | 0.2673 | 0.0305 | 0.2118 | 0.0266 | 0.1770 | 0.0366 | 0.2141 | 0.0291 | 0.2155 | 0.0300 |
| $v^R_{c,3}$ | 0.1060 | 0.0280 | 0.0306 | 0.0279 | 0.1099 | 0.0295 | 0.0058 | 0.0267 | −0.0156 | 0.0286 |
| **Explanatory variables** | | | | | | | | | | |
| $c^R$ | 1.7223 | 0.4811 | 0.9290 | 0.0533 | 1.9464 | 0.4244 | 1.6318 | 0.0571 | 1.1997 | 0.0593 |
| $c^R_{sl}$ | −0.5079 | 0.1329 | −0.3105 | 0.0278 | −0.2726 | 0.1418 | −0.3259 | 0.0247 | −0.5697 | 0.0286 |
| $c^R_{sl}$ | −0.0558 | 0.1316 | 0.3303 | 0.0458 | 0.1045 | 0.0636 | 0.1127 | 0.0373 | −0.0333 | 0.0466 |
| $c^R_{sc}$ | −1.7693 | 0.2289 | −1.7124 | 0.0642 | −1.4313 | 0.1860 | −1.7335 | 0.0640 | −1.7625 | 0.0565 |
| $\beta^R_p$ | 0.1740 | 0.0666 | −0.0257 | 0.0282 | −0.0669 | 0.0628 | −0.0185 | 0.0270 | 0.0824 | 0.0267 |
| $\beta^R_{p*sl}$ | 0.0300 | 0.0809 | −0.2293 | 0.0453 | −0.1161 | 0.0412 | −0.0448 | 0.0341 | 0.0465 | 0.0361 |
| $\beta^R_{p*ov}$ | 0.8816 | 0.1855 | 0.6402 | 0.0521 | 0.7167 | 0.1721 | 0.7886 | 0.0701 | 0.9082 | 0.0685 |
| $\beta^R_l$ | −0.2537 | 0.0626 | −0.1581 | 0.0273 | −0.1176 | 0.0745 | −0.0910 | 0.0236 | −0.1893 | 0.0219 |
| $\beta^R_{l*sl}$ | 0.0828 | 0.0577 | 0.2316 | 0.0413 | 0.0963 | 0.0379 | 0.1567 | 0.0338 | −0.0062 | 0.0382 |
| $\beta^R_{l*ov}$ | 0.2980 | 0.0876 | 0.3264 | 0.0301 | 0.2854 | 0.0782 | 0.3493 | 0.0388 | 0.3548 | 0.0310 |

| | | | | | | | | | | |
|---|---|---|---|---|---|---|---|---|---|---|
| $\beta_{l2}^R$ | -0.0688 | 0.0811 | -0.1858 | 0.0266 | -0.0591 | 0.0707 | -0.0589 | 0.0382 | -0.0304 | 0.0377 |
| $\beta_{p3}^R$ | -0.0344 | 0.0114 | -0.0351 | 0.0036 | -0.0374 | 0.0102 | -0.0463 | 0.0064 | -0.0419 | 0.0050 |
| $\beta_{l3}^R$ | -0.0062 | 0.0094 | -0.0190 | 0.0037 | 0.0004 | 0.0078 | 0.0001 | 0.0054 | 0.0021 | 0.0056 |
| $\beta_{p*cx}^R$ | 0.0259 | 0.0630 | -0.0522 | 0.0314 | -0.0239 | 0.0443 | 0.1533 | 0.0345 | -0.0958 | 0.0309 |
| $\beta_{l*cx}^R$ | 0.0429 | 0.0560 | -0.0030 | 0.0349 | -0.0973 | 0.0491 | -0.1567 | 0.0294 | 0.0572 | 0.0323 |
| $\beta_{dr(-1)}^R$ | -0.2328 | 0.0201 | -0.2469 | 0.0058 | -0.2352 | 0.0166 | -0.2547 | 0.0067 | -0.2451 | 0.0063 |
| $\beta_{di(-1)}^R$ | -0.0543 | 0.0094 | -0.0995 | 0.0046 | -0.0857 | 0.0114 | -0.0514 | 0.0039 | -0.0622 | 0.0045 |
| $\beta_{vol}^R$ | 0.3250 | 0.0943 | 0.4508 | 0.0104 | 0.2802 | 0.0584 | 0.4062 | 0.0077 | 0.3889 | 0.0089 |
| $c_{cx}^R$ | -1.1377 | 0.1373 | -1.1857 | 0.0404 | -1.2873 | 0.1014 | -1.6842 | 0.0590 | -1.0183 | 0.0389 |

Inactivity intensity
Baseline intensity

| | | | | | | | | | | |
|---|---|---|---|---|---|---|---|---|---|---|
| $\alpha^2$ | 0.5334 | 0.0231 | 0.6470 | 0.0102 | 0.5504 | 0.0319 | 0.6032 | 0.0053 | 0.5949 | 0.0069 |
| $\sigma^2 J$ | -0.2904 | 0.1062 | 0.0161 | 0.0434 | -0.2725 | 0.1509 | -0.1332 | 0.0283 | -0.1896 | 0.0387 |
| $v_{s,1}^I$ | -0.1003 | 0.0544 | -0.1223 | 0.0362 | -0.1344 | 0.0544 | -0.0538 | 0.0321 | -0.0688 | 0.0290 |
| $v_{s,2}^I$ | -0.0351 | 0.0373 | -0.1396 | 0.0220 | -0.0404 | 0.0407 | -0.0647 | 0.0224 | -0.0912 | 0.0222 |
| $v_{s,3}^I$ | -0.3650 | 0.0337 | -0.4836 | 0.0251 | -0.4738 | 0.0393 | -0.4093 | 0.0182 | -0.4630 | 0.0259 |
| $v_{c,1}^I$ | -0.1047 | 0.0240 | -0.1072 | 0.0287 | -0.0873 | 0.0286 | -0.0365 | 0.0241 | -0.0646 | 0.0228 |
| $v_{c,2}^I$ | 0.3578 | 0.0349 | 0.3658 | 0.0266 | 0.3792 | 0.0302 | 0.3876 | 0.0288 | 0.4580 | 0.0233 |
| $v_{c,3}^I$ | 0.1121 | 0.0318 | 0.0258 | 0.0181 | 0.0573 | 0.0393 | 0.0649 | 0.0206 | -0.0061 | 0.0188 |

Explanatory variables

| | | | | | | | | | | |
|---|---|---|---|---|---|---|---|---|---|---|
| $c^I$ | 0.4580 | 0.1021 | 0.6843 | 0.0591 | 0.3655 | 0.0974 | 0.5761 | 0.0449 | 0.5684 | 0.0417 |
| $c_{sc}^I$ | -0.1461 | 0.0612 | -0.0272 | 0.0320 | 0.0123 | 0.0579 | 0.0011 | 0.0205 | 0.0013 | 0.0264 |
| $\beta_{dr(-1)}^I$ | -0.1559 | 0.0174 | -0.2427 | 0.0049 | -0.1992 | 0.0213 | -0.2003 | 0.0049 | -0.1787 | 0.0047 |
| $\beta_{di(-1)}^I$ | -0.1679 | 0.0159 | -0.2065 | 0.0049 | -0.1656 | 0.0227 | -0.1634 | 0.0031 | -0.1787 | 0.0038 |

Notes: Subindexes: $p$, profit; $l$, loss; $sl$, special limit order; $sc$, successful; $cx$, complex trading strategy; $dr(-1)$, lagged roundtrip duration; $di(-1)$, lagged inactivity duration; $vol$, transaction volume; $*$, respective interaction term. All other parameters are detailed in the main text.

Table A7. Estimation results for investor groups 11–15 for EUR/USD. Quasi-maximum likelihood standard errors reported.

| Parameters | 11 Estimate | 11 Standard error | 12 Estimate | 12 Standard error | 13 Estimate | 13 Standard error | 14 Estimate | 14 Standard error | 15 Estimate | 15 Standard error |
|---|---|---|---|---|---|---|---|---|---|---|
| | | | | | **Roundtrip intensity** | | | | | |
| | | | | | **Baseline intensity** | | | | | |
| $\alpha^R$ | 1.0615 | 0.0122 | 1.0927 | 0.0310 | 1.1246 | 0.0137 | 1.1018 | 0.0138 | 1.0880 | 0.0092 |
| $\sigma^{2,R}$ | 0.1075 | 0.0322 | 0.2001 | 0.0560 | 0.2360 | 0.0335 | 0.1573 | 0.0347 | 0.1170 | 0.0271 |
| $v_{s,1}^R$ | −0.0750 | 0.0289 | −0.0513 | 0.0337 | 0.0288 | 0.0339 | −0.0562 | 0.0303 | −0.0331 | 0.0319 |
| $v_{s,2}^R$ | −0.0152 | 0.0306 | 0.0307 | 0.0288 | −0.0095 | 0.0300 | 0.0224 | 0.0260 | 0.0444 | 0.0258 |
| $v_{s,3}^R$ | −0.1854 | 0.0280 | −0.2335 | 0.0260 | −0.2426 | 0.0240 | −0.2336 | 0.0268 | −0.2224 | 0.0225 |
| $v_{c,1}^R$ | 0.0462 | 0.0260 | 0.1119 | 0.0288 | 0.0588 | 0.0285 | 0.1270 | 0.0305 | 0.0955 | 0.0272 |
| $v_{c,2}^R$ | 0.1815 | 0.0290 | 0.2719 | 0.0317 | 0.2595 | 0.0352 | 0.2593 | 0.0282 | 0.2121 | 0.0316 |
| $v_{c,3}^R$ | 0.0744 | 0.0254 | 0.1121 | 0.0266 | 0.0200 | 0.0275 | 0.0575 | 0.0231 | 0.0147 | 0.0261 |
| | | | | | **Explanatory variables** | | | | | |
| $c^R$ | 1.6324 | 0.0559 | 1.7587 | 0.4326 | 2.1036 | 0.0685 | 2.6214 | 0.0714 | 2.3337 | 0.0653 |
| $c_{sl}^R$ | −0.6105 | 0.0251 | −0.3817 | 0.1280 | −0.7768 | 0.0346 | −0.5720 | 0.0285 | −0.4129 | 0.0222 |
| $c_{sc}^R$ | 0.1410 | 0.0387 | 0.0996 | 0.0722 | 0.0827 | 0.0383 | −0.0035 | 0.0455 | 0.0108 | 0.0300 |
| $\beta_p^R$ | −1.3000 | 0.0585 | −1.5209 | 0.1948 | −1.2849 | 0.0485 | −0.9109 | 0.0468 | −1.1166 | 0.0540 |
| $\beta_{p*sl}^R$ | 0.0849 | 0.0249 | −0.0321 | 0.0693 | 0.1964 | 0.0269 | 0.1132 | 0.0201 | 0.0097 | 0.0229 |
| $\beta_{p*ov}^R$ | −0.1541 | 0.0344 | −0.0906 | 0.0474 | −0.0015 | 0.0306 | 0.0208 | 0.0294 | −0.0151 | 0.0248 |
| $\beta_l^R$ | 0.4675 | 0.0527 | 0.6431 | 0.1888 | 0.5831 | 0.0514 | 0.2378 | 0.0502 | 0.4741 | 0.0470 |
| $\beta_{l*sl}^R$ | −0.2347 | 0.0229 | −0.1802 | 0.0651 | −0.2845 | 0.0279 | −0.2707 | 0.0199 | −0.0840 | 0.0219 |
| $\beta_{l*ov}^R$ | 0.1833 | 0.0306 | 0.1459 | 0.0413 | 0.1121 | 0.0318 | 0.0504 | 0.0339 | 0.0923 | 0.0243 |
| $\beta_{p^2}^R$ | 0.2230 | 0.0359 | 0.3313 | 0.0881 | 0.1577 | 0.0253 | 0.0659 | 0.0257 | 0.1866 | 0.0317 |
| $\beta_{l^2}^R$ | −0.1567 | 0.0298 | −0.0818 | 0.0940 | −0.1102 | 0.0250 | −0.2405 | 0.0276 | −0.0644 | 0.0215 |
| $\beta_{p^3}^R$ | −0.0297 | 0.0053 | −0.0415 | 0.0113 | −0.0197 | 0.0036 | −0.0127 | 0.0039 | −0.0262 | 0.0047 |
| $\beta_{l^3}^R$ | −0.0111 | 0.0040 | −0.0020 | 0.0110 | −0.0041 | 0.0033 | −0.0200 | 0.0040 | 0.0005 | 0.0025 |

| | | | | | | | | | | |
|---|---|---|---|---|---|---|---|---|---|---|
| $\beta_{p*cx}^R$ | −0.0191 | 0.0317 | −0.0961 | 0.0729 | 0.0062 | 0.0282 | −0.0517 | 0.0224 | −0.0623 | 0.0224 |
| $\beta_{l*cx}^R$ | 0.0132 | 0.0337 | 0.0689 | 0.0749 | −0.0844 | 0.0287 | 0.0130 | 0.0268 | 0.0272 | 0.0270 |
| $\beta_{dr(-1)}^R$ | −0.2410 | 0.0052 | −0.2107 | 0.0148 | −0.2752 | 0.0045 | −0.2642 | 0.0051 | −0.3078 | 0.0050 |
| $\beta_{di(-1)}^R$ | −0.1010 | 0.0041 | −0.0818 | 0.0090 | −0.0630 | 0.0034 | −0.0876 | 0.0032 | −0.0582 | 0.0031 |
| $\beta_{vol}^R$ | 0.2997 | 0.0039 | 0.2898 | 0.0567 | 0.2809 | 0.0040 | 0.1437 | 0.0030 | 0.1883 | 0.0047 |
| $c_{cx}^R$ | −1.3427 | 0.0538 | −1.2024 | 0.1578 | −1.5603 | 0.0499 | −1.1052 | 0.0308 | −1.3336 | 0.0297 |
| | | | | | Inactivity intensity | | | | | |
| | | | | | Baseline intensity | | | | | |
| $\alpha^2$ | 0.6427 | 0.0067 | 0.6623 | 0.0244 | 0.6582 | 0.0074 | 0.6798 | 0.0060 | 0.6441 | 0.0068 |
| $\sigma^{2,I}$ | 0.0030 | 0.0293 | 0.0200 | 0.0308 | 0.0483 | 0.0300 | 0.0742 | 0.0250 | 0.0689 | 0.0287 |
| $v_{s,1}^I$ | −0.0053 | 0.0265 | −0.1695 | 0.0379 | −0.0855 | 0.0257 | −0.1341 | 0.0267 | −0.1854 | 0.0254 |
| $v_{s,2}^I$ | −0.1212 | 0.0226 | −0.0404 | 0.0291 | −0.1306 | 0.0195 | −0.0652 | 0.0192 | −0.0232 | 0.0188 |
| $v_{s,3}^I$ | −0.4246 | 0.0226 | −0.4040 | 0.0280 | −0.4380 | 0.0214 | −0.4544 | 0.0177 | −0.5296 | 0.0200 |
| $v_{c,1}^I$ | −0.0452 | 0.0204 | −0.0326 | 0.0232 | −0.0720 | 0.0224 | −0.0982 | 0.0249 | −0.1016 | 0.0195 |
| $v_{c,2}^I$ | 0.3873 | 0.0221 | 0.4092 | 0.0347 | 0.3919 | 0.0232 | 0.5056 | 0.0211 | 0.4370 | 0.0234 |
| $v_{c,3}^I$ | 0.0785 | 0.0194 | 0.0919 | 0.0289 | 0.0203 | 0.0190 | 0.0124 | 0.0171 | −0.0439 | 0.0165 |
| | | | | | Explanatory variables | | | | | |
| $c^I$ | 0.6284 | 0.0412 | 0.6489 | 0.0936 | 0.9503 | 0.0519 | 0.7517 | 0.0433 | 1.0667 | 0.0505 |
| $c_{sc}^I$ | −0.1059 | 0.0207 | −0.0385 | 0.0437 | −0.0017 | 0.0167 | −0.0550 | 0.0122 | −0.1267 | 0.0146 |
| $\beta_{dr(-1)}^I$ | −0.2411 | 0.0050 | −0.2223 | 0.0161 | −0.1899 | 0.0043 | −0.2408 | 0.0043 | −0.1735 | 0.0035 |
| $\beta_{di(-1)}^I$ | −0.1692 | 0.0040 | −0.1599 | 0.0125 | −0.2063 | 0.0036 | −0.1738 | 0.0030 | −0.2209 | 0.0038 |

Notes: Subindexes: $p$, profit; $l$, loss; $sl$, special limit order; $sc$, successful; $cx$, complex trading strategy; $dr(-1)$, lagged roundtrip duration; $di(-1)$, lagged inactivity duration; $vol$, transaction volume; $*$, respective interaction term. All other parameters are detailed in the main text.

Table A8. Estimation results for investor groups 16–20 for EUR/USD. Quasi-maximum likelihood standard errors reported.

| Parameters | 16 | | 17 | | 18 | | 19 | | 20 | |
|---|---|---|---|---|---|---|---|---|---|---|
| | Estimate | Standard error | Estimate | Standard error | Estimate | Standard error | Estimate | Standard error | Estimate | Standard error |
| | | | | | Roundtrip intensity | | | | | |
| | | | | | Baseline intensity | | | | | |
| $\alpha^R$ | 1.0871 | 0.0086 | 1.1260 | 0.0138 | 1.1662 | 0.0126 | 1.1294 | 0.0094 | 1.0980 | 0.0099 |
| $\sigma^{2,R}$ | 0.0887 | 0.0245 | 0.1818 | 0.0313 | 0.2351 | 0.0297 | 0.1979 | 0.0213 | 0.2292 | 0.0231 |
| $\nu_{s,1}^R$ | −0.0806 | 0.0274 | −0.0157 | 0.0292 | −0.0832 | 0.0329 | −0.0981 | 0.0290 | −0.0510 | 0.0287 |
| $\nu_{s,2}^R$ | 0.0263 | 0.0222 | −0.0203 | 0.0256 | −0.0273 | 0.0280 | 0.0587 | 0.0199 | 0.0065 | 0.0240 |
| $\nu_{s,3}^R$ | −0.2601 | 0.0196 | −0.1915 | 0.0203 | −0.2058 | 0.0233 | −0.2773 | 0.0215 | −0.2265 | 0.0243 |
| $\nu_{c,1}^R$ | 0.0838 | 0.0251 | 0.0913 | 0.0228 | 0.0773 | 0.0275 | 0.0978 | 0.0204 | 0.0886 | 0.0200 |
| $\nu_{c,2}^R$ | 0.2223 | 0.0272 | 0.2009 | 0.0227 | 0.2118 | 0.0273 | 0.2154 | 0.0237 | 0.2547 | 0.0274 |
| $\nu_{c,3}^R$ | 0.0854 | 0.0231 | 0.0262 | 0.0190 | −0.0106 | 0.0198 | 0.0705 | 0.0212 | 0.0558 | 0.0182 |
| | | | | | Explanatory variables | | | | | |
| $c^R$ | 1.9495 | 0.0567 | 1.8576 | 0.0595 | 2.0001 | 0.0630 | 1.9345 | 0.0486 | −0.1432 | 0.0412 |
| $c_{sl}^R$ | −0.7639 | 0.0240 | −0.4868 | 0.0155 | −0.5107 | 0.0182 | −0.5809 | 0.0258 | −0.4074 | 0.0155 |
| $c_{sc}^R$ | −0.0264 | 0.0342 | 0.2175 | 0.0317 | 0.1357 | 0.0328 | 0.2760 | 0.0254 | 0.0191 | 0.0186 |
| $\beta_p^R$ | −1.2518 | 0.0363 | −1.5617 | 0.0516 | −1.2907 | 0.0543 | −1.1904 | 0.0384 | −1.8799 | 0.0392 |
| $\beta_{p*sl}^R$ | 0.2481 | 0.0207 | 0.1174 | 0.0170 | 0.1241 | 0.0215 | 0.0803 | 0.0207 | −0.2098 | 0.0226 |
| $\beta_{p*ov}^R$ | 0.0147 | 0.0256 | −0.0728 | 0.0223 | −0.0653 | 0.0287 | −0.1604 | 0.0214 | −0.0068 | 0.0220 |
| $\beta_l^R$ | 0.5688 | 0.0411 | 0.7747 | 0.0449 | 0.6587 | 0.0470 | 0.6672 | 0.0494 | 1.3744 | 0.0404 |
| $\beta_{l*sl}^R$ | −0.3078 | 0.0161 | −0.1669 | 0.0138 | −0.1753 | 0.0192 | −0.1676 | 0.0169 | −0.1132 | 0.0204 |
| $\beta_{l*ov}^R$ | 0.0841 | 0.0254 | 0.1443 | 0.0242 | 0.1229 | 0.0276 | 0.2571 | 0.0251 | 0.1060 | 0.0289 |
| $\beta_{p^2}^R$ | 0.2554 | 0.0244 | 0.2947 | 0.0300 | 0.1688 | 0.0318 | 0.2217 | 0.0218 | 0.4546 | 0.0188 |
| $\beta_{l^2}^R$ | −0.0431 | 0.0225 | −0.0201 | 0.0240 | −0.0521 | 0.0243 | 0.0186 | 0.0265 | 0.1490 | 0.0210 |
| $\beta_{p^3}^R$ | −0.0384 | 0.0040 | −0.0394 | 0.0053 | −0.0232 | 0.0052 | −0.0324 | 0.0034 | −0.0481 | 0.0024 |
| $\beta_{l^3}^R$ | 0.0025 | 0.0033 | 0.0046 | 0.0035 | 0.0018 | 0.0034 | 0.0087 | 0.0038 | 0.0125 | 0.0029 |

| | | | | | | | | | |
|---|---|---|---|---|---|---|---|---|---|
| $\beta^R_{p*cx}$ | −0.0338 | 0.0259 | −0.0193 | 0.0197 | 0.0329 | 0.0300 | −0.0982 | 0.0199 | −0.0446 | 0.0206 |
| $\beta^R_{l*cx}$ | 0.0274 | 0.0250 | 0.0574 | 0.0198 | 0.0245 | 0.0246 | 0.1041 | 0.0184 | 0.0021 | 0.0227 |
| $\beta^R_{dr(-1)}$ | −0.3345 | 0.0041 | −0.2372 | 0.0051 | −0.2789 | 0.0050 | −0.2308 | 0.0040 | −0.2219 | 0.0037 |
| $\beta^R_{di(-1)}$ | −0.0481 | 0.0024 | −0.0861 | 0.0036 | −0.1037 | 0.0038 | −0.0876 | 0.0029 | −0.0905 | 0.0024 |
| $\beta^R_{vol}$ | 0.2040 | 0.0038 | 0.2990 | 0.0066 | 0.2645 | 0.0046 | 0.2319 | 0.0040 | 0.4010 | 0.0054 |
| $c^R_{cx}$ | −1.2162 | 0.0495 | −1.2305 | 0.0357 | −1.4532 | 0.0453 | −1.2298 | 0.0296 | −1.5042 | 0.0267 |

Inactivity intensity
Baseline intensity

| | | | | | | | | | |
|---|---|---|---|---|---|---|---|---|---|
| $\alpha^2$ | 0.6316 | 0.0071 | 0.6682 | 0.0053 | 0.6392 | 0.0064 | 0.7061 | 0.0063 | 0.6737 | 0.0052 |
| $\sigma^{2,I}$ | 0.0162 | 0.0315 | 0.0608 | 0.0223 | −0.0812 | 0.0306 | 0.0932 | 0.0235 | −0.0090 | 0.0224 |
| $v^I_{s,1}$ | −0.1198 | 0.0254 | −0.0726 | 0.0254 | −0.1575 | 0.0274 | −0.0279 | 0.0254 | −0.1010 | 0.0197 |
| $v^I_{s,2}$ | −0.0834 | 0.0163 | −0.1457 | 0.0186 | −0.0072 | 0.0144 | −0.1596 | 0.0177 | −0.1473 | 0.0191 |
| $v^I_{s,3}$ | −0.4569 | 0.0211 | −0.4984 | 0.0177 | −0.4530 | 0.0210 | −0.4349 | 0.0203 | −0.4289 | 0.0149 |
| $v^I_{c,1}$ | −0.0528 | 0.0188 | −0.0803 | 0.0193 | −0.1299 | 0.0159 | −0.0772 | 0.0196 | −0.0533 | 0.0180 |
| $v^I_{c,2}$ | 0.4609 | 0.0171 | 0.4661 | 0.0206 | 0.4049 | 0.0213 | 0.4762 | 0.0197 | 0.3502 | 0.0193 |
| $v^I_{c,3}$ | −0.0043 | 0.0170 | 0.0451 | 0.0159 | 0.0802 | 0.0135 | −0.0162 | 0.0159 | 0.0334 | 0.0146 |

Explanatory variables

| | | | | | | | | | |
|---|---|---|---|---|---|---|---|---|---|
| $c^I$ | 0.8642 | 0.0467 | 0.8225 | 0.0416 | 0.7242 | 0.0362 | 1.0549 | 0.0392 | 1.0136 | 0.0433 |
| $c^I_{sc}$ | −0.0150 | 0.0152 | −0.0525 | 0.0119 | −0.0155 | 0.0149 | 0.0067 | 0.0120 | −0.0059 | 0.0113 |
| $\beta^I_{dr(-1)}$ | −0.1723 | 0.0031 | −0.2349 | 0.0038 | −0.1995 | 0.0048 | −0.1968 | 0.0042 | −0.1705 | 0.0025 |
| $\beta^I_{di(-1)}$ | −0.2073 | 0.0037 | −0.1812 | 0.0022 | −0.1845 | 0.0032 | −0.2100 | 0.0030 | −0.2110 | 0.0028 |

Notes: Subindexes: $p$, profit; $l$, loss; $sl$, special limit order; $sc$, successful; $cx$, complex trading strategy; $dr(-1)$, lagged roundtrip duration; $di(-1)$, lagged inactivity duration; $vol$, transaction volume; $*$, respective interaction term. All other parameters are detailed in the main text.

# How do individual investors trade?

Ingmar Nolte[a] and Sandra Nolte[b]

[a] Financial Econometric Research Centre, Finance Group, Warwick Business School, University of Warwick, Coventry, UK; [b] School of Management, University of Leicester, Leicester, UK

This paper examines how high-frequency trading decisions of individual investors are influenced by past price changes. Specifically, we address the question as to whether decisions to open or close a position are different when investors already hold a position compared with when they do not. Based on a unique data set from an electronic foreign exchange trading platform, OANDA FXTrade, we find that investors' future order flow is (significantly) driven by past price movements and that these predictive patterns last up to several hours. This observation clearly shows that for high-frequency trading, investors rely on previous price movements in making future investment decisions. We provide clear evidence that market and limit orders flows are much more predictable if those orders are submitted to close an existing position than if they are used to open one. We interpret this finding as evidence for the existence of a monitoring effect, which has implications for theoretical market microstructure models and behavioral finance phenomena, such as the endowment effect.

## 1.  Introduction

In this paper, we study how investors trade on a high-frequency time scale. We investigate how information on the past price process is fed back into the investors' trading decisions. Specifically, we examine whether investors' decisions to open or close a position are different if they already hold a position compared with when they do not. We also investigate whether stop-loss orders contribute to self-reinforcing price movements and whether take-profit orders impede them (Osler 2005).

Our study concentrates on a large set of individual investors over a period of 8 months who trade currencies on an electronic trading platform: OANDA FXTrade. Most of the traders are small retail investors without access to private information such as own customer order flow or to news networks such as Reuters or Bloomberg. Electronic trading platforms such as OANDA FXTrade have become very popular during the last decade, since they provide immediate access to trading a large range of securities such as currencies, stocks and options for retail investors by bypassing traditional trading venues including banks and brokers.[1] It is not surprising, therefore, that consortiums of banks have started to set up their own electronic trading platforms. Understanding the trading behavior of these investors is therefore of major importance for these companies when creating trading protocols and their own hedging algorithms.

The data set analyzed in this paper is unique. It can be considered as field data on individual investors trading behavior in a real trading environment. Therefore, it naturally complements many studies in the behavioral economics and finance literature based on experimental designs.

Through in-sample and out-of-sample forecasting analyses, we find that investors' future order flow is significantly affected by past price movements and that these predictive patterns last for several hours. This observation clearly shows that investors try to learn from previous price movements and exploit this knowledge for future high-frequency trading decisions, especially in the absence of private information and news.[2] Our study does not permit us to analyze the extent to which this might be explained by the use of technical analysis or simply eyeball assessment of potential price trends. We note, however, that Taylor and Allen (1992) report that about 90% of professional currency traders consider technical analysis as a valuable tool when designing their trading strategies. Our observations shed some light on the mechanisms of how market efficiency (within the retail trader segment) is actually obtained at a high-frequency level while past prices seem to influence traders' decisions significantly for up to several hours. It turns out that market orders are easier to predict than limit orders.

We provide very clear evidence that prior price changes forecast order flows related to position closures better than order flows related to position initiations. We also show through in-sample investigations that the explanatory power of past price changes is about three to five times higher for position closures than position initiations. We interpret this finding as evidence for the existence of a monitoring effect. Such a monitoring effect can be related to the literature on reference-based decision-making and endowment effects (cf. Thaler 1980; Kahneman, Knetsch, and Thaler 1990). The endowment effect argues that an individual attributes a higher than its true value to a good once it becomes part of the individual's own endowment. In a situation where costs are related to the possession of a good for which the investor requires compensation, an endowment effect might be diminished and explained in a more rational way. Monitoring costs are exactly such costs, especially in the context of security trading. Our observations can also be related to an asymmetric learning effect in the sense that the learning process is more intense, when investors already have a certain risk exposure through an open position.

The existence of a monitoring effect has implications for a large body of the market microstructure literature. A relatively recent branch of this literature focusses on optimal order placement strategy and on the question of the optimal mix at the equilibrium between market and limit orders. Parlour (1998) considers a dynamic model with strategic traders, explaining various patterns observed in order placement strategies and transaction prices. Hollifield, Miller, and Sandas (2004) provide a model of optimal order submission, in which traders' optimal order placements depend on the valuation of the asset and the trade-offs between prices, execution probabilities and the risk of being picked off. Foucault (1999) derives the equilibrium in a trading game where traders arrive sequentially and choose to submit either a market or a limit order with a one-period life. He provides a complete closed-form characterization of traders order placement strategies, which allows him to analyze the order flow composition (mix between market and limit orders) and trading costs. In his model, he explicitly incorporates the risk of price mis-specification into traders strategies. He also finds that the proportion of limit orders in order flow is positively related to asset return volatility. A cross-sectional analysis of order flow composition and trading costs in limit order markets allows him to test whether the proportion of limit orders in order flow is positively related to volatility or to the average size of the spread.

Foucault, Kadan, and Kandel (2005) develop dynamic models of a limit order market populated by strategic liquidity traders. They analyze the question of how a trader's impatience affects order placement strategies and show that at the equilibrium patient traders tend to provide liquidity to the impatient. They also address the question of waiting costs implied by limit orders, which is particularly important for traders who choose between limit and market orders (Demsetz 1968) and show that liquidity suppliers tend to submit more aggressive limit orders to reduce their waiting time, and therefore their waiting costs. The idea of waiting costs is not new, Demsetz (1968, 41) addressed this question: 'Waiting costs are relatively important for trading in organized markets, and would seem to dominate the determination of spreads'. Rosu (2010) observes that the waiting cost of a patient trader is lesser than that of an impatient trader. He shows that the price impact of a market order is about four times higher than the price impact of a limit order.

While many of the studies mentioned above ignore the presence of information asymmetry, another branch of the theoretical literature considers such models in which informed traders and uninformed investors consider the trade-off between the use of market and limit orders in a dynamic setting. Among others, Anand, Chakravarty, and Martell (2005), Bloomfield, O'Hara, and Saar (2005) and Kaniel and Liu (2006) show that limit orders play an important role in the order submission strategies of informed traders and therefore might convey information about future price movement and volatility. Chakravarty and Holden (1995) and Harris (1998) provide theoretical models in which informed investors are allowed to place both market and limit orders. A combined strategy of market and limit orders seems to be more profitable than only submitting market orders.

Neither this part of the literature nor that which ignores the asymmetry of information addresses the question of whether order submission strategies are affected by reference mechanisms such as holding an open position or the current inventory of the traders or by managing of active risk. Do traders exhibit different strategies when they hold an open position? The existence of a monitoring effect suggests that this question should be answered in the affirmative and that such effects should be addressed in theoretical market microstructure models.

Traditional studies on order flow (Evans and Lyons 2002a, 2002b, 2005, 2006; Rime 2003; Payne 2003; Bjønnes and Rime 2005; Berger et al. 2008; Daníelsson, Payne, and Luo 2011) focus on agents in the interbank market and consider the relationship between prices and order flow obtained either from direct (e.g. Reuters dealing 2000-1) or brokeraged (e.g. Reuters dealing 2000-2, Electronic Broking Services (EBS)) interdealer trading. The studies of Osler (2005) and Marsh and O'Rourke (2005) use a data set of customer trades collected by the Royal Bank of Scotland. They investigate how customer-trading order flow, which is the primary source of private information for a player in the interbank market, is related to currency prices. In these studies, order flow is usually measured by the standard net order flow measure of Lyons (1995), who suggests aggregating all the dispersed information into one single measure: the difference between the number of buyer- and seller-initiated trades for a given sampling frequency. Using standard instrumental variable techniques to estimate a vector autoregressive model that allows for contemporaneous feedback trading. Daníelsson and Love (2006) show that when data are sampled at the 1 and 5 min frequencies, the price impact of order flow is underestimated when feedback trading is not incorporated into the model, implying that trades carry more information than previous estimates suggest. All these studies concentrate on the question of how order flow can be used to predict future prices changes, but *not* in which way price changes affect order flow.

The paper is organized as follows. Section 2 explains the trading mechanism and the different order types on the OANDA FXTrade platform. Section 3 presents our economic hypotheses. Section 4 presents the empirical results and evidence toward the verification of the hypotheses, while Section 5 concludes.

## 2. OANDA FXTrade

OANDA FXTrade is an electronic trading platform for currencies, without limits on trade size, operating 24 hours, 7 days per week. This platform is a market making system that executes orders using the exchange rate prevalent in the market determined either by their own inventory book and/or by predicted prices relying on a proprietary forecasting algorithm based on an external data-feed. OANDA FXTrade offers immediate settlement of trades and tight spreads as low as two to three pips for all transaction sizes. Given various boundary conditions, such as sufficient margin requirements, orders are always executed. The legal counterparty of a trade, however, is always OANDA FXTrade. The OANDA FXTrade platform is based on the concept of margin trading. This means that a trader can enter into positions larger than his/her available funds. The platform requires a minimum initial margin of 2% on positions in the major currency pairs and 4% in all other currency pairs, which correspond to a leverage of 50:1 and 25:1, respectively. In other words, for each dollar margin available, the trader can make a 50 (25) dollar trade. The trader receives a margin call when the net asset value (i.e. the current value of all open positions plus the value of the remaining deposited funds) becomes half the margin requirement. Thus, if the trader does not have sufficient margin to cover twice the losses on an open position, an automatic margin call order is used to close all open positions using the prevalent market rates at the current time.

Market orders (buy or sell) are executed immediately and affect existing open positions. Limit orders are maintained in the system for up to 1 month. A server manages the inventory book, the current exchange rates and the current market orders to match existing limit orders. A limit order can therefore be matched either against a market order, or against a bid or an ask price obtained from the external data-feed. Stop-loss orders and take-profit orders are special limit orders in the sense that they can be set for existing open positions. They can be specified directly while entering a market or a limit order, but they can also be specified later for existing open positions. Stop-loss and take-profit orders are automatically erased from the system whenever a position is closed as a result of further trading activity. Take-profit orders are typically set to close an existing position after a certain profit has been realized. Stop-loss orders, in contrast, specify that the position should be closed after the realization of a certain loss to avoid further losses. Table 1 provides an overview of the transactions and further activities of traders on OANDA FXTrade, which are recorded in an activity record file. We get detailed information on whether an order is submitted to open (close) an existing position and thus reflects an increase (or decrease) in risk exposure.

The group of traders on OANDA is quite heterogeneous, varying from small retail investors, to small professional traders and smaller institutions and businesses.[3] The attractiveness of OANDA FXTrade is that it provides instant access to currency trading without the involvement of banks, brokers or other intermediaries and thus without additional trading costs.

## 3. Motivation

We construct order flow using the standard definition given by Lyons (1995). He defines aggregated net order flow as the difference between buyer- and seller-initiated trades (within a given period) or, stated differently, as the cumulative sum of signed trades where buyer-initiated and seller-initiated trades receive positive and negative signs, respectively (See Table 2). Focussing on the initiating party of a trade, this definition aims to capture changes in the expectations of future prices that may arise because of new (private) information. For example, an executed buy limit order is treated as a seller-initiated trade since it has to be merged with a sell market order. Therefore, the seller is treated as being more important than the buyer, who might not have the

Table 1. Activity record entries of OANDA FXTrade.

| | |
|---|---|
| Buy/sell[a] market open (close) | Immediately executed to open or close a position in a specific currency pair |
| Buy/sell limit order | The trader posted a buy or sell limit order to the system, which is then pending |
| Buy/sell limit order executed open (close) | Pending limit order is executed to open or close a certain position |
| Buy/sell take-profit close | Closes an open position by buying or selling the currency pair when the exchange rate reaches a predetermined level, in order to make a profit |
| Buy/sell stop-loss close | Closes an open position by buying or selling the currency pair when the exchange rate reaches a predetermined level in order to avoid further losses |
| Buy/sell margin call close | Closes automatically all open positions using the current market rates. This happens if the trader does not have sufficient margin to cover two times the losses of all open positions |
| Change order | Change of a pending limit order (limits for take-profit or stop-loss, the value of the upper or lower bounds, the quote as well as the number of units) |
| Change stop-loss or take-profit on open trade | Change stop-loss or take-profit limit on an open position. |
| Cancel order by hand | Cancel a pending limit order by hand |
| Cancel order: insufficient funds | Automatically recorded when the trader does not have enough funds to open a new position |
| Cancel order: bound violation | Market order or limit order is cancelled because the applied exchange rate is not located inside the specified bounds. |
| Order expired | A pending limit order is expired |

[a]On the OANDA FXTrade platform, buying EUR/USD means that one buys the base currency (EUR) and sells the quote currency (USD). Recorded units always refer to the base currency.

latest information. This standard measure of order flow has been used by Daníelsson, Payne, and Luo (2011) to predict future prices in the interbank market. Chordia and Subrahmanyam (2004) show that daily US equity order flow is helpful in predicting one period ahead price returns.

In this standard order flow measure, buy and sell orders are treated symmetrically (opposite signs), and following the same logic, we compute, in addition, order flow imbalances for every order category. For example, we can compute the order flow of the market order (open) category as the difference between the number of buy market orders (open) and sell market orders (open) over a specific sampling period. Altogether, we obtain eight category-specific order flow measures which are summarized in Table 3.

The category-specific order flow measures allow insight into several aspects of a trader's preference structure. In particular, we are able to exploit the information of whether trades are executed to open or close a position, which allows us to analyze the existence of a monitoring effect. We claim that there is a monitoring effect in the sense that traders react faster when they fear losing something (i.e. when they already hold a position) than when they are only planning to take a position. Within a fully rational setup, such fear should not exist or at least there should be no difference between entering the market at the wrong price (thereby implying subsequent losses) and leaving the market at the wrong price (thereby realizing losses). Differences in both types of fear are related to the existence of endowment effects (Thaler 1980), which ultimately can be seen as a manifestation of loss aversion (Kahneman and Tversky 1979) and reference-based

Table 2. Standard order flow signs.

| Transaction record | Standard order flow signs |
|---|---|
| Buy market (open) | + |
| Sell market (open) | − |
| Buy market (close) | + |
| Sell market (close) | − |
| Limit order: buy | not used |
| Limit order: sell | not used |
| Buy limit order executed (open) | − |
| Sell limit order executed (open) | + |
| Buy limit order executed (close) | − |
| Sell limit order executed (close) | + |
| Buy take-profit (close) | − |
| Sell take-profit (close) | + |
| Buy stop-loss (close) | − |
| Sell stop-loss (close) | + |
| Buy margin call (close) | not used |
| Sell margin call (close) | not used |
| Change order | not used |
| Change stop-loss or take-profit | not used |
| Cancel order by hand | not used |
| Cancel order: insufficient funds | not used |
| Cancel order: bound violation | not used |
| Order expired | not used |

Note: Column 1 states the record entries and column 2 contains the signs for the construction of the standard net order flow measure.

Table 3. Description of the category order flow.

| Category | Description |
|---|---|
| 1 | Limit orders |
| 2 | Limit orders executed (open) |
| 3 | Limit orders executed (close) |
| 4 | Market orders (open) |
| 5 | Market orders (close) |
| 6 | Stop-loss orders (close) |
| 7 | Take-profit orders (close) |
| 8 | Margin call orders (close) |

Note: Column 1 states the number of the category and column 2 gives the category description.

decision-making. On the contrary, continuous monitoring of the market is costly, for which the investor expects to be compensated by realizing a higher profit through picking a potentially better execution opportunity. The existence of a costly monitoring effect might partially explain the existence of endowment effects within a rational trading strategy.

Provided that such a monitoring effect exists, we should observe that the order flow in the (*close*) categories is easier to predict (based on the information contained in the price process) than order flow in the (*open*) categories. On the one hand, one could argue that this effect should be even more pronounced for market orders than for limit orders since market orders are usually submitted by active and impatient investors who trade for liquidity reasons and watch the market more closely, whereas limit orders are thought to be submitted by passive traders who might not monitor the market continuously (cf. Glosten 1994, Seppi 1997), even if they have an open position. On the other hand, one could argue that limit order traders might also be very keen to monitor the price process, when their limit orders are outstanding. After placing their limit orders, they may monitor the market and so hark back to stop-loss or take-profit orders, either by placing such orders or by changing their outstanding stop-loss or take-profit orders.

With the category-specific order flow measures, we can furthermore investigate whether we observe self-reinforcing price movements as reported by Osler (2005) on OANDA FXTrade, in the sense that executed stop-loss orders contribute to self-reinforcing price movements, whereas executed take-profit orders impede them. Provided that there exists a self-reinforcing price movements, then

(i) based on their own histories, order flow in the stop-loss order category should lend itself more readily to prediction than order flow in the take-profit order category,
(ii) if stop-loss orders induce self-reinforcing price movements and take-profit orders do not, then (in addition to their own histories) information on the price process itself should be more valuable, for predicting order flow of take-profit orders than for predicting order flow of stop-loss orders.

The idea behind this is that there are local downward or upward trends in the price process. Those trends are accelerated by the execution of stop-loss orders, which generate positive feedback trading (De Long et al. 1990), and are decelerated by the execution of take-profit orders, which generate negative feedback trading or resistance barriers. For illustration of the argument, let us assume that the price is decreasing, which in the first case may cause an execution of a sell stop-loss order and induces further selling pressure, which leads to further executions of sell stop-loss orders. Thus, we get an accelerated downward moving price process (price cascades). In the second case, a downward moving price may cause an execution of a buy take-profit order, which does not induce further selling pressure and therefore neither execution of further stop-loss nor take-profit orders, which yields a decelerated downward movement or even an upward moving price process (bounce back).

## 4. Empirical findings

### 4.1 *Description of the data set*

The data set used in our analysis is constructed from the trading activity record of OANDA FXTrade from 1 October 2003 to 14 May 2004 (227 days). This record contains the complete trading activities for 30 currency pairs on a second by second basis and allows us to distinguish the transaction types listed in Table 1. In addition, depending on the order type, we receive information on transaction prices (market orders, limit orders executed, stop-loss, take-profit, margin call), bid and ask quotes (limit orders pending), additional transaction units and the limits of stop-loss and take-profit orders.

In our analysis, we focus on the most actively traded currency pair EUR/USD, which accounts for nearly 39% of all records with an average inter-record duration of 8.5 s. Table 4 contains the descriptive statistics for the data set and the transaction volumes for each order category. All figures are daily averages computed over the whole data set containing 227 days. The average number of different traders per day amounts to 744 for the EUR/USD currency pair.

Table 4. Descriptive statistics for the OANDA FXTrade trading activity data set for the EUR/USD currency pair.

| Transaction record | % | Obs | Trading volume in EUR per day | | | | | | | | |
|---|---|---|---|---|---|---|---|---|---|---|---|
| | | | Total | Mean | Min | 5% Qtl | 25% Qtl | 50% Qtl | 75% Qtl | 95% Qtl | Max |
| Buy market (open) | 13.10 | 1322 | 37,930,860 | 25,854 | 82 | 113 | 515 | 2065 | 9240 | 85,854 | 2,220,414 |
| Sell market (open) | 10.61 | 1072 | 30,816,226 | 27,218 | 44 | 89 | 592 | 2138 | 9861 | 96,214 | 1,759,412 |
| Buy market (close) | 8.27 | 835 | 25,074,760 | 27,468 | 163 | 201 | 672 | 2326 | 9553 | 95,940 | 1,630,034 |
| Sell market (close) | 10.27 | 1037 | 31,839,764 | 29,534 | 29 | 66 | 564 | 2164 | 10,063 | 97,248 | 1,930,846 |
| Limit order: buy | 5.41 | 546 | 14,041,270 | 28,876 | 24 | 63 | 549 | 2053 | 9469 | 95,436 | 1,934,417 |
| Limit order: sell | 4.76 | 482 | 11,080,825 | 34,283 | 237 | 267 | 515 | 1662 | 7509 | 117,914 | 1,511,133 |
| Buy limit order executed (open) | 3.22 | 325 | 5,416,146 | 17,484 | 41 | 79 | 422 | 1410 | 6267 | 67,127 | 735,479 |
| Sell limit order executed (open) | 2.92 | 295 | 3,231,307 | 10,554 | 58 | 84 | 242 | 824 | 3652 | 34,607 | 584,303 |
| Buy limit order executed (close) | 0.46 | 46 | 1,382,690 | 32,718 | 4800 | 4824 | 5313 | 7020 | 17,994 | 80,426 | 506,182 |
| Sell limit order executed (close) | 0.46 | 46 | 1,470,630 | 32,287 | 407 | 436 | 927 | 3440 | 16,816 | 93,447 | 452,512 |
| Buy take-profit (close) | 3.14 | 317 | 2,918,779 | 9779 | 144 | 170 | 310 | 704 | 2724 | 30,314 | 583,296 |
| Sell take-profit (close) | 3.49 | 352 | 4,404,025 | 12,857 | 61 | 75 | 256 | 796 | 3960 | 43,028 | 820,876 |
| Buy stop-loss (close) | 2.18 | 220 | 4,488,496 | 16,433 | 126 | 175 | 667 | 2535 | 9837 | 70,968 | 513,989 |
| Sell stop-loss (close) | 2.55 | 258 | 5,309,807 | 16,667 | 23 | 59 | 503 | 2255 | 9424 | 66,743 | 650,061 |
| Buy margin call (close) | 0.12 | 12 | 166,375 | 7263 | 1006 | 1010 | 1185 | 1817 | 3718 | 14,211 | 71,133 |
| Sell margin call (close) | 0.17 | 17 | 275,282 | 6381 | 1369 | 1372 | 1440 | 2351 | 4409 | 17,266 | 77,231 |
| Change order | 3.01 | 305 | 13,898,910 | 49,771 | 105 | 203 | 1295 | 4888 | 18,181 | 162,927 | 1,622,712 |
| Change stop-loss or take-profit | 22.36 | 2260 | 60,965,013 | 26,748 | 10 | 79 | 867 | 3694 | 14,163 | 95,983 | 1,703,030 |
| Cancel by hand | 2.41 | 243 | 10,043,949 | 42,295 | 211 | 272 | 1031 | 4186 | 16,003 | 148,571 | 1,662,224 |
| Cancel: insufficient funds | 0.28 | 28 | 2,439,586 | 67,905 | 4938 | 4953 | 5431 | 7354 | 66,280 | 186,280 | 622,650 |
| Cancel bound violation | 0.20 | 20 | 195,118 | 14,803 | 571 | 571 | 627 | 2650 | 6860 | 29,909 | 98,308 |
| Order expired | 0.65 | 66 | 1,063,061 | 19,942 | 44 | 54 | 443 | 1682 | 7204 | 68,648 | 355,982 |

Note: All numbers are daily averages over 227 days and all transaction volume statistics are denominated in EUR.

One observation, which is striking when considering the descriptive statistics, is that the traders on OANDA FXTrade submit more market orders than limit orders. This characteristic might well be explained by the fact that most traders on this platform are small retail investors who are more impatient and more willing to submit market orders which are executed immediately than limit orders which can be pending for up to 1 month.[4] Another interesting observation in Table 4 is that on average more than 22% of all actions are changes of stop-loss or take-profit limit orders. This figure provides evidence from a descriptive point of view that not only market order traders but also limit order traders do monitor the market closely, when they have an outstanding limit order. This is also in support of the existence of the monitoring effect.

From a series of quotes from the interbank market, we construct the corresponding mid-quotes series for 12 frequencies (1, 2, 5, 10, 15, 20, 25, 30 and 45 min and 1, 2 and 4 hours). The quotes from the interbank market are provided by Olsen Financial Technologies and represent tradeable quotes stemming from different electronic brokerage systems including Reuters dealing 3000 and EBS. These quote series do not coincide with the bid and ask quotes on OANDA FXTrade. The bid and ask quotes on OANDA FXTrade are generated by a proprietary forecasting algorithm based on an external data feed which also includes tradeable quotes from Reuters dealing 3000 and EBS. In addition to the price series, we construct the order flow measures (standard and category-specific) defined in the previous section for the corresponding 12 frequencies.

Figure 1 depicts the empirical bivariate autocorrelation functions for lags up to 20 periods between price changes and standard order flow for a 1 min frequency. The analysis of the bivariate autocorrelation functions sheds light on the dynamic interaction of order flow and price change.

- In the upper left panel, we observe the autocorrelation function of the order flow measure itself. We see a very clear slowly declining pattern of the autocorrelation function, showing that order flow itself is persistent.
- The lower left panel depicts the cross-correlation function of lagged order flow with price changes. We observe that only the first-order cross-correlation coefficient is significantly positive, which shows that future price changes are driven by current order flow. This supports the literature concentrated on predicting/explaining price changes with order flow (e.g. Evans and Lyons 2002a, 2002b, 2005, 2006; Danielsson, Payne, and Luo 2011).
- The upper right panel depicts the cross-correlation function of lagged price changes with order flow.[5] We observe significant cross-correlation coefficients, which show that future order flow is driven by current price changes. This observation supports heuristically the idea that investors update their beliefs and place their orders based on the past development of the price process, and hence is another indication for the existence of a learning effect (cf. Bikhchandani, Hirshleifer, and Welch 1992; Avery and Zemsky 1998). From this observation, this effect seems to be a short-run effect, since the cross-correlation coefficients between future order flow and current price changes are significant for only up to five lags.
- In the lower right panel, we observe the autocorrelation function of the price changes themselves. The price changes are positively first-order auto-correlated. Thus, we observe a kind of short-term positive feedback trading pattern for the price process itself, and we do not observe a traditional bid–ask bounce effect, since we consider mid-quotes on a 1 min frequency.

## 4.2 *Estimation framework*

Although the above analysis provides some insight into the dynamic relationship between order flows and price changes, giving for a first impression of the validity of the hypotheses stated at the

## Standard order flow versus price changes

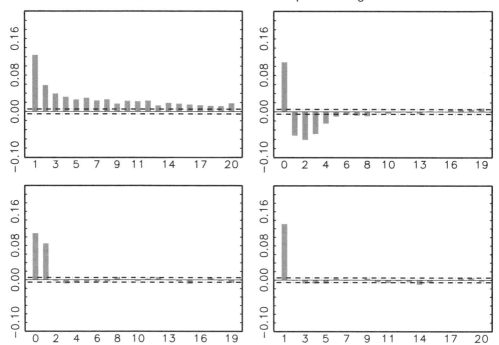

Figure 1. Empirical bivariate autocorrelation functions of price changes and standard order flow for an aggregation level of 1 min. The upper left panel depicts the autocorrelation function (lag: 1–20) of the order flow measure and the lower right panel depicts the autocorrelation function (lag: 1–20) for price changes. The lower left panel depicts the cross-correlation function (lag: 0–19) of lagged order flow with price changes and the upper right panel depicts the cross-correlation function (lag: 0–19) of lagged price changes with order flow. The dotted lines mark the approximate 99% confidence bounds, computed as $\pm 2.58/\sqrt{T}$, where $T$ denotes the particular number of observations.

outset, we now investigate them in detail with the help of in-sample and out-of-sample forecasting analyses.

Based on the results of the descriptive analysis,[6] we now consider AR($p$) benchmark models (BMs) in which only the history of the order flow measures themselves serve to explain and to predict future order flows. These predictions are then compared, using the modified Diebold–Mariano (mDM) test of Harvey, Leybourne, and Newbold (1997), with the predictions based on including the history of price changes. This enables us to identify whether the inclusion of *additional* information contained in past prices improves order flow forecasts significantly.

The AR($p$) benchmark specification is given by

$$(1 - B_p^x(L))x_t^k = c + \varepsilon_t, \qquad \text{(AR-}k)$$

where $B_p^x(L)$ denotes the associated lag-polynomial of order $p$, $\varepsilon_t$ a white noise process and $x_t^k$ denotes the value of the order flow measured at $t$. The forecasting study is implemented for the standard order flow measure ($k = \text{SOF}$), and the eight category-specific order flow measures ($k = 1, \ldots, 8$) listed in Table 3. The forecasting models containing additional information on the

Table 5. In-sample and out-of-sample periods of the forecasting study.

| Period | In-sample | Out-of-sample |
|---|---|---|
| 1 | 6–24 October 2003 | 27–31 October 2003 |
| 2 | 3–21 November 2003 | 24–28 November 2003 |
| 3 | 1–19 December 2003 | 22–26 December 2003 |
| 4 | 29 December 2003–26 January 2004 | 19–23 January 2004 |
| 5 | 26 January–13 February 2004 | 16–20 February 2004 |
| 6 | 23 February–12 March 2004 | 15–19 March 2004 |
| 7 | 22 March–9 April 2004 | 12–19 April 2004 |
| 8 | 19 April–7 May 2004 | 10–14 May 2004 |

history of the price change process are given by

$$(1 - B_p^x(L))x_t^k = c + B_q^y(L)\Delta y_t + \varepsilon_t, \qquad \text{(IP-}k\text{)}$$

where $\Delta y_t$ denotes the interbank price change process and $B_q^y(L)$ the lag-polynomial of order $q$.

The forecasting study is executed in the following ways. Altogether we consider a period of 32 weeks starting on Monday the 6th of October 2003 and ending on Friday the 14th of May 2004. We divide these 32 weeks into 8 periods of 4 weeks each where the first 3 weeks are considered as the in-sample estimation period and the last week is considered as the out-of-sample forecasting period. Table 5 summarizes the setup of the in-sample and out-of-sample periods. We choose this forecasting setup with alternating in-sample and out-of-sample periods in order to guarantee robust forecasting results when compared with studies with only one estimation and one forecasting period. Our forecasting setup is particularly conservative in the sense that we estimate the model parameters only once for every in-sample period and do not use a rolling window regression technique with continuous updating of model parameter estimates. Holidays and weekends are excluded from the sample.

The results we are going to present are very robust to the choice of the in-sample estimation and out-of-sample prediction periods. Moreover, the same conclusions can be drawn if the hypotheses are evaluated separately with respect to the eight individual forecasting setups presented in Table 5. The results are furthermore robust to the inclusion or exclusion of the overnight periods. In our analysis, we have chosen to include the overnight periods.

## 4.3 In-sample estimation results

Let us first consider the in-sample estimation results. In order to be able to compare the results, we choose to present them for a lag-polynomial of order one, implying that equation (IP-$k$) simplifies to

$$x_t^k = c + \rho x_{t-1}^k + \phi \Delta y_{t-1} + \varepsilon_t, \quad \text{for } k = 1, \ldots, 8,$$

and we are going to interpret the magnitude of the estimated coefficients.

Tables 6–8 present the estimated coefficients of the in-sample estimations of the category-specific order flow measures for each period on the 1, 2 and 5 min sampling frequencies, respectively. We observe that the estimated coefficients on lagged price changes and lagged order flows have the expected signs, for each order flow category and each period. Let us consider, for example, the stop-loss order flow category. We see that the estimated coefficients for the price change are positive. Assume for the moment that the price change is positive and remember that

199

Table 6. In-sample coefficients (1 min frequency).

| Periods/coefficients | | Standard order flow | Limit order | Limit order executed open | Limit order executed close | Market order open | Market order close | Stop-loss order | Take-profit order | Margin call order |
|---|---|---|---|---|---|---|---|---|---|---|
| 1 | $c$ | -0.0669 | 0.0443 | 0.0183 | 0.0094 | 0.0887 | -0.1282 | -0.0128 | 0.0054 | 0.0018 |
| | $\rho$ | 0.0799 | 0.2431 | 0.1432 | 0.1014 | 0.1553 | 0.1747 | 0.1615 | 0.2471 | 0.0396 |
| | $\phi$ | -0.5212 | -0.2208 | -0.2839 | -0.0785 | -0.0186 | -1.4091 | 0.6460 | -0.8058 | 0.0135 |
| | $R^2$ | 0.0069 | 0.0625 | 0.0307 | 0.0011 | 0.0240 | 0.0559 | 0.0478 | 0.0894 | 0.0021 |
| 2 | $c$ | 0.0960 | 0.0241 | 0.0141 | 0.0027 | 0.0789 | -0.0602 | 0.0169 | -0.0853 | 0.0038 |
| | $\rho$ | 0.1035 | 0.1721 | 0.1002 | 0.0004 | 0.1968 | 0.1188 | 0.1383 | 0.2367 | 0.0761 |
| | $\phi$ | -1.8104 | -0.1135 | -0.3830 | -0.0573 | -0.6455 | -2.3909 | 0.8272 | -1.0846 | 0.0952 |
| | $R^2$ | 0.0178 | 0.0305 | 0.0245 | 0.0005 | 0.0430 | 0.0455 | 0.0409 | 0.0742 | 0.0103 |
| 3 | $c$ | 0.1166 | 0.0270 | 0.0030 | -0.0074 | 0.2324 | -0.1876 | -0.0060 | -0.0245 | 0.0264 |
| | $\rho$ | 0.0901 | 0.3776 | 0.1327 | 0.0693 | 0.1886 | 0.1727 | 0.1672 | 0.1846 | 0.0312 |
| | $\phi$ | -1.4268 | -0.0894 | -0.5164 | -0.1553 | -0.8601 | -2.3096 | 0.6273 | -1.2807 | 0.3071 |
| | $R^2$ | 0.0122 | 0.1428 | 0.0326 | 0.0094 | 0.0432 | 0.0708 | 0.0453 | 0.0646 | 0.0042 |
| 4 | $c$ | 0.2078 | 0.0833 | 0.0678 | 0.0036 | 0.3556 | -0.2200 | -0.0807 | -0.0344 | -0.0020 |
| | $\rho$ | 0.1217 | 0.4167 | 0.0781 | -0.0018 | 0.2188 | 0.2375 | 0.2028 | 0.2827 | 0.1071 |
| | $\phi$ | -1.4371 | -0.2959 | -0.3396 | -0.1561 | -0.8523 | -2.0128 | 0.7321 | -1.2813 | 0.3159 |
| | $R^2$ | 0.0190 | 0.2681 | 0.0120 | 0.0015 | 0.0534 | 0.1066 | 0.0590 | 0.1252 | 0.0199 |
| 5 | $c$ | 0.1828 | 0.0043 | -0.0049 | 0.0032 | 0.2657 | -0.1936 | -0.0493 | -0.0306 | 0.0020 |
| | $\rho$ | 0.1323 | 0.3899 | 0.1694 | 0.0189 | 0.2763 | 0.2598 | 0.1665 | 0.2667 | 0.1132 |
| | $\phi$ | -1.3272 | -0.1742 | -0.0318 | -0.0801 | -0.1310 | -2.7899 | 0.7590 | -1.2043 | 0.2026 |
| | $R^2$ | 0.0189 | 0.1527 | 0.0287 | 0.0016 | 0.0552 | 0.1249 | 0.0471 | 0.0977 | 0.0397 |
| 6 | $c$ | 0.1358 | 0.0929 | 0.0939 | -0.0020 | 0.2663 | -0.2048 | -0.0736 | -0.0917 | -0.0255 |
| | $\rho$ | 0.1619 | 0.4201 | 0.1833 | 0.0570 | 0.2821 | 0.1630 | 0.1169 | 0.2260 | 0.5365 |
| | $\phi$ | -1.6794 | -0.1937 | 0.0913 | -0.0999 | -0.7343 | -3.8426 | 1.5667 | -2.5881 | 0.2685 |
| | $R^2$ | 0.0275 | 0.1775 | 0.0339 | 0.0046 | 0.0739 | 0.1016 | 0.0520 | 0.1140 | 0.2946 |
| 7 | $c$ | 0.2039 | 0.0276 | 0.0425 | -0.0096 | 0.1955 | -0.1185 | -0.0356 | -0.1154 | -0.0115 |
| | $\rho$ | 0.1564 | 0.5497 | 0.2329 | 0.0172 | 0.2288 | 0.1764 | 0.1230 | 0.2293 | 0.1397 |
| | $\phi$ | -1.2569 | -0.2079 | 0.2041 | -0.1799 | -0.9590 | -3.0670 | 1.6381 | -3.1767 | 0.3999 |
| | $R^2$ | 0.0013 | 0.3032 | 0.0553 | 0.0005 | 0.0552 | 0.0883 | 0.0489 | 0.1093 | 0.0511 |

(Continued)

Table 6. Continued.

| Periods/coefficients | Standard order flow | Limit order | Limit order executed open | Limit order executed close | Market order open | Market order close | Stop-loss order | Take-profit order | Margin call order |
|---|---|---|---|---|---|---|---|---|---|
| 8 | | | | | | | | | |
| $c$ | 0.0105 | −0.0447 | −0.1118 | 0.0117 | 0.0367 | −0.0459 | −0.0023 | 0.0864 | −0.0012 |
| $\rho$ | 0.1029 | 0.5178 | 0.2210 | 0.0776 | 0.2505 | 0.1865 | 0.1248 | 0.2419 | 0.1789 |
| $\phi$ | −0.9889 | −0.1914 | 2.3429 | −0.3399 | −0.7982 | −3.5646 | 0.8586 | −4.4995 | 0.2493 |
| $R^2$ | 0.0107 | 0.2681 | 0.0820 | 0.0126 | 0.0650 | 0.1066 | 0.0304 | 0.1162 | 0.0505 |

Notes: Estimated coefficients of the in-sample estimations of the standard order flow and the category-specific order flow measures on the 1 min sampling frequency for each forecasting period. $c$, the estimated constant; $\rho$, the estimated coefficient of the lagged order flow and $\phi$, the estimates coefficient of the price change. The estimated coefficients in bold are significant at the 5% level.

Table 7. In-sample coefficients (2 min frequency).

| Periods/coefficients | | Standard order flow | Limit order | Limit order executed open | Limit order executed close | Market order open | Market order close | Stop-loss order | Take-profit order | Margin call order |
|---|---|---|---|---|---|---|---|---|---|---|
| 1 | $c$ | −0.1337 | 0.0880 | 0.0378 | 0.0185 | 0.1720 | −0.2442 | −0.0272 | 0.0123 | 0.0034 |
| | $\rho$ | 0.0646 | 0.2501 | 0.1211 | 0.1251 | 0.1854 | 0.2059 | 0.1104 | 0.1943 | 0.1230 |
| | $\phi$ | −1.6515 | −0.3798 | −0.3681 | −0.1185 | −0.5498 | −2.5280 | 0.7220 | −1.1802 | 0.0400 |
| | $R^2$ | 0.0140 | 0.0713 | 0.0296 | 0.0180 | 0.0348 | 0.1138 | 0.0339 | 0.0787 | 0.0200 |
| 2 | $c$ | 0.1850 | 0.0470 | 0.0277 | 0.0054 | 0.1465 | −0.1127 | 0.0365 | −0.1753 | 0.0064 |
| | $\rho$ | 0.1576 | 0.1973 | 0.1278 | −0.0003 | 0.2660 | 0.1531 | 0.0577 | 0.2170 | 0.2255 |
| | $\phi$ | −3.0206 | −0.1795 | −0.4880 | −0.0547 | −1.2523 | −3.2364 | 1.0380 | −1.0574 | 0.1024 |
| | $R^2$ | 0.0447 | 0.0411 | 0.0413 | 0.0005 | 0.0862 | 0.0820 | 0.0248 | 0.0644 | 0.0587 |
| 3 | $c$ | 0.2450 | 0.0094 | 0.0064 | −0.0152 | 0.4628 | −0.3610 | −0.0132 | −0.0486 | 0.0525 |
| | $\rho$ | 0.0556 | 0.3388 | 0.1246 | 0.0133 | 0.1951 | 0.1970 | 0.1147 | 0.1805 | 0.0359 |
| | $\phi$ | −2.4092 | −0.2329 | −0.6470 | −0.3357 | −1.4253 | −3.2542 | 0.7633 | −1.4940 | 0.3231 |
| | $R^2$ | 0.0162 | 0.1572 | 0.0367 | 0.0159 | 0.0584 | 0.1158 | 0.0321 | 0.0722 | 0.0048 |
| 4 | $c$ | 0.3913 | 0.1679 | 0.1259 | 0.0070 | 0.6386 | −0.3864 | −0.1861 | −0.0766 | −0.0040 |
| | $\rho$ | 0.1724 | 0.4121 | 0.1449 | 0.0083 | 0.2982 | 0.3314 | 0.0809 | 0.2075 | 0.0846 |
| | $\phi$ | −1.6346 | −0.2597 | −0.2126 | −0.4436 | −1.1155 | −2.6758 | 1.1846 | −2.1920 | 0.4119 |
| | $R^2$ | 0.0353 | 0.1725 | 0.0254 | 0.0145 | 0.0985 | 0.1598 | 0.0283 | 0.1243 | 0.0208 |
| 5 | $c$ | 0.2715 | 0.0094 | −0.0104 | 0.0061 | 0.4859 | −0.3752 | −0.1029 | −0.0669 | 0.0039 |
| | $\rho$ | 0.1498 | 0.3388 | 0.1617 | 0.0635 | 0.3396 | 0.2808 | 0.1288 | 0.1971 | 0.1607 |
| | $\phi$ | −2.9081 | −0.2329 | 0.1108 | −0.0390 | −0.7715 | −3.5961 | 0.5452 | −1.3821 | 0.1658 |
| | $R^2$ | 0.0265 | 0.1157 | 0.0262 | 0.0045 | 0.1072 | 0.1723 | 0.0283 | 0.0650 | 0.0478 |
| 6 | $c$ | 0.2715 | 0.1665 | 0.1953 | −0.0044 | 0.5170 | −0.3938 | −0.1514 | −0.1994 | −0.0586 |
| | $\rho$ | 0.1498 | 0.4796 | 0.1513 | 0.0265 | 0.3010 | 0.1978 | 0.1049 | 0.1453 | 0.4703 |
| | $\phi$ | −2.9081 | −0.2666 | 0.0914 | −0.1608 | −1.1733 | −3.9745 | 0.7991 | −1.7344 | 0.1879 |
| | $R^2$ | 0.0323 | 0.2320 | 0.0232 | 0.0047 | 0.0810 | 0.1392 | 0.0272 | 0.0509 | 0.2258 |
| 7 | $c$ | 0.4128 | 0.0455 | 0.0878 | −0.0196 | 0.3650 | −0.2386 | −0.0747 | −0.2528 | −0.0262 |
| | $\rho$ | 0.1477 | 0.6263 | 0.2088 | 0.0002 | 0.2806 | 0.1711 | 0.0821 | 0.1592 | 0.0227 |
| | $\phi$ | −0.8253 | −0.4406 | 0.3284 | −0.1714 | −0.7977 | −3.1338 | 1.6239 | −4.0912 | 0.3815 |
| | $R^2$ | 0.0353 | 0.3954 | 0.0457 | 0.0040 | 0.0796 | 0.0978 | 0.0378 | 0.0965 | 0.0233 |

(Continued)

Table 7. Continued.

| Periods/coefficients | Standard order flow | Limit order | Limit order executed open | Limit order executed close | Market order open | Market order close | Stop-loss order | Take-profit order | Margin call order |
|---|---|---|---|---|---|---|---|---|---|
| 8 | | | | | | | | | |
| $c$ | 0.0191 | -0.0878 | -0.2259 | 0.0227 | 0.0729 | -0.0909 | -0.0053 | 0.1893 | -0.0028 |
| $\rho$ | 0.1217 | 0.5283 | 0.2156 | 0.1021 | 0.2522 | 0.1993 | -0.0022 | 0.1740 | 0.1003 |
| $\phi$ | -1.6207 | -0.5594 | 1.8946 | -0.3719 | -0.9890 | -3.6624 | 1.0755 | -4.2999 | 0.2081 |
| $R^2$ | 0.0162 | 0.2799 | 0.0744 | 0.0211 | 0.0681 | 0.1289 | 0.0098 | 0.0802 | 0.0230 |

Notes: Estimated coefficients of the in-sample estimations of the standard order flow and the category-specific order flow measures on the 2 min sampling frequency for each forecasting period. $c$, the estimated constant; $\rho$, the estimated coefficient of the lagged order flow and $\phi$, the estimates coefficient of the price change. The estimated coefficients in bold are significant at the 5% level.

Table 8. In-sample coefficients (5 min frequency).

| Periods/coefficients | | Standard order flow | Limit order | Limit order executed open | Limit order executed close | Market order open | Market order close | Stop-loss order | Take-profit order | Margin call order |
|---|---|---|---|---|---|---|---|---|---|---|
| 1 | $c$ | −0.3258 | 0.2263 | 0.0872 | 0.0483 | 0.3848 | −0.5615 | −0.0749 | 0.0339 | 0.0076 |
| | $\rho$ | 0.0783 | 0.2284 | 0.1802 | 0.0921 | 0.2729 | 0.2638 | 0.0399 | 0.1650 | 0.1879 |
| | $\phi$ | −2.0463 | −0.2974 | −0.2012 | −0.1774 | −0.5175 | −3.1197 | 1.0414 | −1.6232 | 0.0935 |
| | $R^2$ | 0.0216 | 0.0584 | 0.0408 | 0.0128 | 0.0732 | 0.1782 | 0.0262 | 0.0808 | 0.0560 |
| 2 | $c$ | 0.4630 | 0.1252 | 0.0673 | 0.0135 | 0.3217 | −0.2910 | 0.0895 | −0.4655 | 0.0166 |
| | $\rho$ | 0.1509 | 0.1473 | 0.1399 | −0.0037 | 0.3555 | 0.1216 | 0.1031 | 0.1603 | 0.1766 |
| | $\phi$ | −2.6838 | −0.2317 | −0.3450 | −0.0347 | −1.1251 | −3.5067 | 0.6781 | −1.6963 | 0.1552 |
| | $R^2$ | 0.0381 | 0.0246 | 0.0359 | 0.0002 | 0.1393 | 0.0771 | 0.0261 | 0.0513 | 0.0443 |
| 3 | $c$ | 0.6305 | 0.1391 | 0.0126 | −0.0392 | 1.1215 | −0.8945 | 0.0895 | −0.1312 | 0.1307 |
| | $\rho$ | 0.0435 | 0.3761 | 0.2135 | 0.0027 | 0.2207 | 0.2020 | 0.1031 | 0.1349 | 0.0464 |
| | $\phi$ | −3.6552 | −0.4762 | −0.3444 | −0.2567 | −1.4583 | −3.5703 | 0.6781 | −1.2263 | 0.2030 |
| | $R^2$ | 0.0322 | 0.1436 | 0.0583 | 0.0084 | 0.0675 | 0.1205 | 0.0184 | 0.0404 | 0.0037 |
| 4 | $c$ | 0.9889 | 0.4863 | 0.3176 | 0.0173 | 1.4171 | −1.0935 | −0.4569 | −0.1875 | −0.0101 |
| | $\rho$ | 0.1637 | 0.3197 | 0.1373 | 0.0412 | 0.3776 | 0.2436 | 0.0978 | 0.2213 | 0.0850 |
| | $\phi$ | −2.0823 | −0.2437 | −0.1944 | −0.2745 | −0.6348 | −3.3677 | 0.9881 | −1.7302 | 0.4784 |
| | $R^2$ | 0.0363 | 0.1042 | 0.0225 | 0.0091 | 0.1454 | 0.1184 | 0.0269 | 0.1108 | 0.0263 |
| 5 | $c$ | 0.9039 | 0.0217 | −0.0236 | 0.0155 | 1.0724 | −0.9821 | −0.2799 | −0.1722 | 0.0090 |
| | $\rho$ | 0.1455 | 0.3946 | 0.2268 | 0.0686 | 0.4170 | 0.2463 | 0.0585 | 0.1603 | 0.2223 |
| | $\phi$ | −1.7444 | −0.1504 | −0.0539 | −0.1535 | −0.6012 | −3.8549 | 1.0151 | −2.2359 | 0.1913 |
| | $R^2$ | 0.1560 | 0.0713 | 0.0514 | 0.0048 | 0.1659 | 0.1451 | 0.0197 | 0.0622 | 0.0797 |
| 6 | $c$ | 0.6953 | 0.4200 | 0.4439 | −0.0103 | 1.1955 | −0.9952 | −0.3777 | −0.4956 | −0.2269 |
| | $\rho$ | 0.1501 | 0.4782 | 0.2281 | 0.0531 | 0.3593 | 0.1930 | 0.1089 | 0.1562 | 0.1529 |
| | $\phi$ | −0.5469 | 0.1770 | 0.3988 | −0.0666 | 0.6281 | −4.6819 | 0.6560 | −2.3292 | 1.4470 |
| | $R^2$ | 0.0223 | 0.2281 | 0.0556 | 0.0039 | 0.1389 | 0.1631 | 0.0247 | 0.0664 | 0.0492 |
| 7 | $c$ | 1.0280 | 0.1204 | 0.2157 | −0.0484 | 0.8050 | −0.5818 | −0.1876 | −0.6327 | −0.0584 |
| | $\rho$ | 0.1491 | 0.5907 | 0.2184 | 0.0178 | 0.3661 | 0.1993 | 0.0794 | 0.1583 | 0.1287 |
| | $\phi$ | −1.6289 | −0.4199 | 0.4697 | −0.1730 | −0.5313 | −4.2164 | 1.9232 | −4.6241 | 0.3723 |
| | $R^2$ | 0.0256 | 0.3509 | 0.0514 | 0.0048 | 0.1344 | 0.1448 | 0.0438 | 0.0991 | 0.0457 |

(Continued)

Table 8. Continued.

| Periods/coefficients | | Standard order flow | Limit order | Limit order executed open | Limit order executed close | Market order open | Market order close | Stop-loss order | Take-profit order | Margin call order |
|---|---|---|---|---|---|---|---|---|---|---|
| 8 | $c$ | 0.0496 | −0.2703 | **−0.6011** | 0.0616 | 0.2001 | −0.2357 | −0.0143 | 0.5409 | −0.0073 |
| | $\rho$ | 0.0426 | **0.4253** | **0.1727** | **0.0398** | **0.1754** | **0.1676** | −0.0980 | 0.0619 | **0.1234** |
| | $\phi$ | **−2.1192** | **−1.6292** | 0.3279 | **−0.1811** | **−1.2644** | **−3.2275** | **1.2247** | **−3.7611** | 0.0964 |
| | $R^2$ | 0.0074 | 0.1892 | 0.0325 | 0.0042 | 0.0387 | 0.0946 | 0.0074 | 0.0254 | 0.0199 |

Notes: Estimated coefficients of the in-sample estimations of the standard order flow and the category-specific order flow measures on the min sampling frequency for each forecasting period. $c$, the estimated constant; $\rho$, the estimated coefficient of the lagged order flow and $\phi$, the estimates coefficient of the price change. The estimated coefficients in bold are significant at the 5% level.

we defined the dependent variable in our regression as the difference between the number of buy and sell stop-loss orders. A positive price change leads in this case to an increase in the dependent variable, meaning that we have an increase in the execution of buy stop-loss orders. On the contrary, if the price change is negative, the dependent variable decreases inducing a larger execution of sell stop-loss orders. The reverse is true if we consider the take-profit order flow category.

Moreover, we see that the impact of price changes on limit order flows (executed open and close) is always lower than the impact of price changes on the market order flows (open and close). Specifically, the estimated coefficients of the price changes on *market (open)* order flow is roughly three to four times larger than the estimated coefficients for the *limit* executed (*open*) order flow category. In addition, if we only have a look at the market order flow categories, we note that the price impact is always about three to five times larger for the *market (close)* order flow category than for the market (open) category. This is another observation in support of the existence of a monitoring effect, in the sense that traders monitor the market more closely when they already hold an open position. We also observe that the impact of the price process is larger for take-profit order flow than for stop-loss order flow for all three sampling frequencies. This shows that prices are more valuable for the explanation of take-profit orders than stop-loss orders, which supports our hypothesis that take-profit orders seem to impede price movements and stop-loss orders seem to self-reinforce them.

Altogether, these effects are relatively stable over all periods and over all order flow categories and confirm within an in-sample analysis our hypotheses. Our analysis, furthermore, sheds light on the discussion whether prices already reflect all relevant information and can be considered as sufficient statistics. Our results show that they are not. If the price series were a sufficient statistic, one should observe a significant coefficient only for the lagged price changes.[7] Below we are going to discuss the results of our out-of-sample forecasting study which provides stronger evidence in support of our hypotheses.

## 4.4 *Forecasting study*

To validate our claims, we compare the Root Mean-Squared Prediction Errors (RMSPE) of the $AR(p)$ BMs with those of the corresponding forecasting models for the in-sample and out-of-sample forecasting studies.

The results over all eight periods of the in-sample and out-of-sample studies using the standard order flow measure are presented in Table 9. The in-sample results based on the category-based order flow are given in Tables 10 and 11 and the corresponding out-of-sample results can be found in Tables 12 and 13. The first cell entry in Table 9 as well as in all other following tables is the RMSPE of the associated forecasting model. The second cell entries in parenthesis are the $p$-values from the mDM-test with the null hypothesis that the RMSPE of the associated forecasting model is not smaller than the RMSPE of the corresponding $AR(p)$ BM. $p$-Values in bold correspond to those cases where the RMSPE of the associated forecasting model is smaller than the RMSPE of the BM.

We clearly observe that the information contained in the history of the price process in addition to the information contained in the order flow measures themselves is helpful in predicting the aggregated standard order flow as well as the eight category-specific order flow measures. This statement is based on the following observations.

(i)  For the in-sample prediction of the standard order flow measure (Table 9, columns 2 and 3), we observe that on all frequencies, the forecasting models containing the additional information

Table 9. Results for the standard order flow measure's in-sample and out-of-sample predictions.

| Frequency | In-sample | | Out-of-sample | |
|---|---|---|---|---|
| | BM | Historical prices | BM | Historical prices |
| 1 min | 4.3485 | 4.3275 (**0.0000**) | 4.2978 | 4.2726 (**0.0000**) |
| 2 min | 6.5269 | 6.4809 (**0.0000**) | 6.5110 | 6.4540 (**0.0000**) |
| 5 min | 11.1317 | 11.0924 (**0.0005**) | 11.2270 | 11.2066 (**0.1451**) |
| 10 min | 16.6981 | 16.6804 (**0.1550**) | 16.8088 | 16.9430 (0.9996) |
| 15 min | 20.9063 | 20.8962 (**0.3847**) | 21.5097 | 21.6271 (0.9888) |
| 20 min | 25.0626 | 25.0171 (**0.0958**) | 25.8728 | 26.0218 (0.9914) |
| 25 min | 28.7239 | 28.7046 (**0.3424**) | 29.8577 | 29.9160 (0.7327) |
| 30 min | 32.0495 | 31.8593 (**0.0141**) | 33.4052 | 33.5240 (0.8807) |
| 45 min | 41.4252 | 41.2203 (**0.1617**) | 44.6980 | 44.9230 (0.7714) |
| 1 h | 48.3953 | 48.0999 (**0.1627**) | 52.1271 | 52.8020 (0.9685) |
| 2 h | 72.2455 | 71.5105 (**0.0333**) | 85.9340 | 86.3036 (0.6968) |
| 4 h | 116.3498 | 115.7275 (**0.0704**) | 143.6758 | 144.5649 (0.7909) |

Notes: The forecasting study is conducted over a period of 32 weeks starting on 6 October 2003 and ending on 14 May 2004. These 32 weeks are divided into 8 periods of 4 weeks each, where the first 3 weeks are always considered as the in-sample estimation periods and the last weeks are always considered as the out-of-sample forecasting periods. Weekends and holidays are excluded from the analysis. The BM column contains the RMSPEs of the AR($p$) benchmark model. The RMSPEs of the forecasting model with historical prices are shown in the first entry of the historical prices column, the second entry in parenthesis are the $p$-value of the mDM test with the null hypothesis that the RMSPEs of the associated forecasting model is not smaller than the RMSPEs of the AR($p$) BMs. $p$-Values in bold correspond to those cases where the RMSPE of the associated forecasting model is smaller than the RMSPE of the AR($p$) BM.

on the historical interbank price changes are able to beat the benchmark specification (AR) in terms of smaller RMSPEs (bold cell entries). Considering the $p$-values of the mDM-tests, we see that these models outperform the AR BM, with five exceptions, always at the 10% significance level.

(ii) For the out-of-sample prediction of the standard order flow measure (Table 9, columns 4 and 5), the RMSPEs are for the three forecasting horizons up to 5 min smaller than those of the AR($p$) BMs, when additional information on the interbank price change process is incorporated in the forecasting models. We see that the RMSPEs for 1 and 2 min forecasting horizons are significantly smaller using a 1% significance level in the mDM-test.

(iii) For the in-sample prediction of the category-specific order flow measures (Tables 10 and 11), we find that the RMSPEs of the AR($p$) BMs are, except for 10 cases, always higher than those of the forecasting models with the historical prices, and 67 are significant at the 10% level.

(iv) For the out-of-sample prediction of the category-specific order flow measures (Tables 12 and 13), we observe that over all eight categories 59 RMSPEs are smaller than those of the AR($p$) BMs; 19 of them are significantly smaller at the 1% level, 25 of them are significantly smaller at the 5% level and even 31 at the 10% level.

These results enable an interesting interpretation: the aggregated standard order flow as well as the category-specific order flow measures can generally be easily predicted with the help of historical price information being, in particular in the absence of macroeconomic news and private (customer order flow) information, the only source of information available to the traders. This might indicate that traders update their beliefs and place orders based on their interpretation of recent historical price movements, and therefore might rely on either technical analysis as pointed out by Taylor and Allen (1992)[8] or simply attempt to intuitively extrapolate recent price movements information. Especially on OANDA FXTrade, such information is more valuable than

Table 10. Results of the *in-sample* predictions of the category-specific order flow measures.

| Frequency | Limit orders | | Limit orders executed open | | Limit orders executed close | | Market orders open | |
|---|---|---|---|---|---|---|---|---|
| | BM | Historical prices | BM | Historical prices | BM | Historical prices | BM | Historical prices |
| 1 min (AR) | 1.4454 | 1.4445 (**0.0000**) | 1.6270 | 1.6175 (**0.0976**) | 0.6330 | 0.6315 (**0.0010**) | 1.9857 | 1.9770 (**0.0000**) |
| 2 min (AR) | 2.4518 | 2.4484 (**0.0002**) | 2.5267 | 2.5158 (**0.0726**) | 0.9106 | 0.9073 (**0.0019**) | 3.0876 | 3.0700 (**0.0000**) |
| 5 min (AR) | 5.1312 | 5.1219 (**0.0599**) | 4.5255 | 4.5236 (**0.2658**) | 1.4973 | 1.4948 (**0.0011**) | 5.5784 | 5.5518 (**0.0000**) |
| 10 min (AR) | 9.0484 | 9.0444 (**0.3588**) | 7.1240 | 7.1464 (0.9509) | 2.1762 | 2.1722 (**0.0010**) | 9.1244 | 9.0985 (**0.0019**) |
| 15 min (AR) | 12.2393 | 12.2766 (0.8578) | 9.1686 | 9.1475 (**0.1799**) | 2.7164 | 2.7143 (**0.3744**) | 12.1184 | 12.1397 (0.7651) |
| 20 min (AR) | 15.1778 | 15.1480 (**0.1501**) | 10.7343 | 10.7400 (0.6278) | 3.1611 | 3.1526 (**0.0032**) | 14.5709 | 14.4889 (**0.0335**) |
| 25 min (AR) | 17.9797 | 17.9766 (**0.4771**) | 12.1639 | 12.2353 (0.8521) | 3.5789 | 3.5638 (**0.0105**) | 17.4819 | 17.3621 (**0.0088**) |
| 30 min (AR) | 19.8530 | 19.8267 (**0.2631**) | 14.5193 | 14.5874 (0.8520) | 3.9716 | 3.9339 (**0.0237**) | 20.1194 | 19.9743 (**0.0061**) |
| 45 min (AR) | 26.7754 | 26.8938 (0.7577) | 18.8809 | 18.8847 (0.5364) | 4.9625 | 4.9513 (**0.0902**) | 26.7991 | 26.5359 (**0.0112**) |
| 1 hr (AR) | 32.6755 | 32.6807 (0.5225) | 22.3827 | 22.3710 (**0.3974**) | 5.8760 | 5.8693 (**0.2387**) | 33.6136 | 33.3265 (**0.0318**) |
| 2 hr (AR) | 52.3839 | 52.2478 (**0.1935**) | 36.2961 | 36.3494 (0.6072) | 8.3189 | 8.2904 (**0.1125**) | 57.5232 | 56.8558 (**0.0050**) |
| 4 hr (AR) | 83.9541 | 83.7328 (**0.2998**) | 66.0293 | 65.9525 (**0.3041**) | 11.9968 | 11.9914 (**0.4525**) | 102.0218 | 101.0879 (**0.0485**) |

Notes: The forecasting study is conducted over a period of 32 weeks starting on 6 October 2003 and ending on 14 May 2004. These 32 weeks are divided into 8 periods of 4 weeks each, where the first 3 weeks are always considered as the in-sample estimation periods and the last week is always considered as the out-of-sample forecasting periods. Weekends and holidays are excluded from the analysis. The BM column contains the RMSPEs of the AR($p$) benchmark model. The RMSPEs of the forecasting model with historical prices are shown in the first entry of the historical prices column, the second entry in parenthesis are the $p$-value of the mDM test with the null hypothesis that the RMSPEs of the associated forecasting model is not smaller than the RMSPEs of the AR($p$) BMs. $p$-Values in bold correspond to those cases where the RMSPE of the associated forecasting model is smaller than the RMSPE of the AR($p$) BM.

Table 11. Results of the *in-sample* predictions of the category-specific order flow measures.

| Frequency | Market orders close | | Stop-loss orders close | | Take-profit orders close | | Margin call orders close | |
|---|---|---|---|---|---|---|---|---|
| | BM | Historical prices | BM | Historical prices | BM | Historical prices | BM | Historical prices |
| 1 min (AR) | 2.7454 | 2.6613 (**0.0000**) | 1.9344 | 1.9238 (**0.0000**) | 3.2039 | 3.1693 (**0.0000**) | 0.7265 | 0.7239 (**0.0002**) |
| 2 min (AR) | 4.2203 | 4.0575 (**0.0000**) | 3.0333 | 3.0210 (**0.0000**) | 5.2630 | 5.2056 (**0.0000**) | 1.2003 | 1.1954 (**0.0022**) |
| 5 min (AR) | 7.8304 | 7.5485 (**0.0000**) | 5.2662 | 5.2454 (**0.0000**) | 9.8193 | 9.7153 (**0.0000**) | 2.6045 | 2.5830 (**0.0779**) |
| 10 min (AR) | 12.5372 | 12.1819 (**0.0000**) | 7.9106 | 7.8903 (**0.0002**) | 15.3615 | 15.3124 (**0.0667**) | 3.8643 | 3.8418 (**0.0347**) |
| 15 min (AR) | 16.5733 | 16.2111 (**0.0000**) | 9.9829 | 9.9745 (**0.0798**) | 19.8503 | 19.8464 (**0.4749**) | 4.9016 | 4.8678 (**0.0371**) |
| 20 min (AR) | 20.1138 | 19.6528 (**0.0000**) | 11.7201 | 11.6999 (**0.0208**) | 23.0231 | 22.8464 (**0.0001**) | 6.0462 | 5.9750 (**0.0642**) |
| 25 min (AR) | 23.3486 | 22.9671 (**0.0000**) | 13.2341 | 13.2237 (0.2025) | 27.0023 | 26.9249 (**0.0567**) | 6.4416 | 6.3820 (**0.0544**) |
| 30 min (AR) | 27.4590 | 27.1266 (**0.0000**) | 15.1372 | 15.1554 (0.6431) | 32.6134 | 32.4378 (**0.0015**) | 7.0998 | 7.0261 (**0.0401**) |
| 45 min (AR) | 35.8041 | 35.3963 (**0.0014**) | 19.0306 | 19.0036 (**0.0917**) | 41.8647 | 41.7748 (**0.0203**) | 9.5666 | 9.4286 (**0.0681**) |
| 1 hr (AR) | 44.7921 | 44.2294 (**0.0007**) | 22.0938 | 21.9956 (**0.0693**) | 50.5215 | 50.3161 (**0.0214**) | 10.9656 | 10.8131 (**0.0540**) |
| 2 hr (AR) | 73.2669 | 72.8933 (**0.0425**) | 32.0076 | 31.6867 (**0.0437**) | 83.8739 | 83.6420 (**0.1951**) | 16.1938 | 16.0723 (**0.1540**) |
| 4 hr (AR) | 115.5674 | 114.7439 (**0.0385**) | 47.2952 | 46.6408 (**0.0262**) | 137.1682 | 136.1951 (**0.1650**) | 22.9814 | 22.8589 (**0.1321**) |

Notes: The forecasting study is conducted over a period of 32 weeks starting on 6 October 2003 and ending on 14 May 2004. These 32 weeks are divided into 8 periods of 4 weeks each, where the first 3 weeks are always considered as the in-sample estimation periods and the last week is always considered as the out-of-sample forecasting periods. Weekends and holidays are excluded from the analysis. The BM column contains the RMSPEs of the AR($p$) benchmark model. The RMSPEs of the forecasting model with historical prices are shown in the first entry of the historical prices column, the second entry in parenthesis are the $p$-value of the mDM test with the null hypothesis that the RMSPEs of the associated forecasting model is not smaller than the RMSPEs of the AR($p$) BMs. $p$-Values in bold correspond to those cases where the RMSPE of the associated forecasting model is smaller than the RMSPE of the AR($p$) BM.

Table 12. Results of the *out-of-sample* predictions of the category-specific order flow measures.

| Frequency | Limit orders | | Limit orders executed open | | Limit orders executed close | | Market orders open | |
|---|---|---|---|---|---|---|---|---|
| | BM | Historical prices | BM | Historical prices | BM | Historical prices | BM | Historical prices |
| 1 min (AR) | 1.5059 | 1.5050 (**0.0031**) | 1.8412 | 1.8370 (**0.1212**) | 0.7415 | 0.7409 (**0.1797**) | 1.8765 | 1.8708 (**0.0000**) |
| 2 min (AR) | 2.5477 | 2.5435 (**0.0002**) | 2.8676 | 2.8699 (0.6597) | 1.1982 | 1.1969 (**0.2627**) | 2.8995 | 2.8844 (**0.0000**) |
| 5 min (AR) | 5.5135 | 5.4916 (**0.0118**) | 5.1697 | 5.1626 (**0.0662**) | 1.7648 | 1.7621 (**0.0305**) | 5.2898 | 5.2926 (0.6315) |
| 10 min (AR) | 9.8622 | 9.8526 (**0.3319**) | 8.3812 | 8.4009 (0.9185) | 2.8620 | 2.8594 (**0.1706**) | 8.7090 | 8.7002 (**0.2641**) |
| 15 min (AR) | 13.5125 | 13.4816 (**0.3837**) | 11.7627 | 11.7542 (**0.3281**) | 3.5404 | 3.5243 (**0.1543**) | 11.6636 | 11.7545 (0.9845) |
| 20 min (AR) | 16.5926 | 16.4909 (**0.0745**) | 12.8240 | 12.8136 (**0.4148**) | 4.1443 | 4.1438 (**0.4413**) | 14.1298 | 14.1836 (0.7615) |
| 25 min (AR) | 19.9732 | 19.8155 (**0.1639**) | 16.1600 | 16.2733 (0.9573) | 4.6501 | 4.6562 (0.8752) | 16.7700 | 16.9292 (0.9079) |
| 30 min (AR) | 22.2530 | 22.1888 (**0.2247**) | 17.6244 | 17.8720 (0.9036) | 5.3137 | 5.2601 (**0.1672**) | 19.5854 | 19.7348 (0.9072) |
| 45 min (AR) | 30.3289 | 30.2350 (**0.2603**) | 23.3965 | 23.5171 (0.9981) | 6.5633 | 6.5685 (0.7099) | 25.6376 | 25.9390 (0.9258) |
| 1 h (AR) | 36.3297 | 36.1042 (**0.1467**) | 27.4002 | 27.5341 (0.9314) | 7.4748 | 7.4618 (**0.2858**) | 31.2881 | 31.9349 (0.9688) |
| 2 h (AR) | 58.4704 | 58.5918 (0.6544) | 49.5621 | 49.8873 (0.9539) | 10.9815 | 10.8932 (**0.0080**) | 53.8287 | 55.6411 (**0.9771**) |
| 4 h (AR) | 107.3412 | 105.0585 (**0.0482**) | 81.5804 | 80.6359 (**0.0775**) | 17.0937 | 17.0386 (**0.1817**) | 101.5470 | 103.8547 (0.8717) |

Notes: The forecasting study is conducted over a period of 32 weeks starting on 6 October 2003 and ending on 14 May 2004. These 32 weeks are divided into 8 periods of 4 weeks each, where the first 3 weeks are always considered as the in-sample estimation periods and the last week is always considered as the out-of-sample forecasting periods. Weekends and holidays are excluded from the analysis. The BM column contains the RMSPEs of the AR($p$) benchmark model. The RMSPEs of the forecasting model with historical prices are shown in the first entry of the historical prices column, the second entry in parenthesis are the $p$-value of the mDM test with the null hypothesis that the RMSPEs of the associated forecasting model is not smaller than the RMSPEs of the AR($p$) BMs (RW, AR). $p$-Values in bold correspond to those cases where the RMSPE of the associated forecasting model is smaller than the RMSPE of the AR($p$) BM.

Table 13. Results of the out-of-sample predictions of the category-specific order flow measures.

| Frequency | Market orders close | | Stop-loss orders close | | Take-profit orders close | | Margin call orders close | |
|---|---|---|---|---|---|---|---|---|
| | BM | Historical prices | BM | Historical prices | BM | Historical prices | BM | Historical prices |
| 1 min (AR) | 2.6810 | **2.6100 (0.0000)** | 1.8428 | **1.8324 (0.0000)** | 3.5039 | **3.4894 (0.0091)** | 0.7707 | **0.7687 (0.0693)** |
| 2 min (AR) | 4.1646 | **4.0264 (0.0000)** | 2.8420 | **2.8272 (0.0000)** | 5.8825 | **5.8311 (0.0004)** | 1.1404 | **1.1373 (0.1203)** |
| 5 min (AR) | 7.9576 | **7.6980 (0.0000)** | 4.9441 | **4.9223 (0.0000)** | 10.8902 | **10.7474 (0.0001)** | 2.1087 | **2.0974 (0.2095)** |
| 10 min (AR) | 12.9142 | **12.6485 (0.0000)** | 7.4257 | **7.4011 (0.0002)** | 17.3042 | **17.2111 (0.0217)** | 3.1301 | **3.1080 (0.1991)** |
| 15 min (AR) | 17.3679 | **17.1217 (0.0000)** | 9.4822 | **9.4698 (0.1016)** | 23.7763 | 23.8357 (0.6523) | 3.9560 | **3.9300 (0.1594)** |
| 20 min (AR) | 21.1034 | **21.0014 (0.1051)** | 11.0635 | 11.0712 (0.7544) | 26.5161 | 26.6077 (0.7757) | 4.5620 | 4.6193 (0.9044) |
| 25 min (AR) | 25.6057 | **25.4827 (0.1614)** | 12.7121 | **12.6941 (0.2426)** | 32.6157 | 32.7224 (0.7022) | 5.6977 | **5.6005 (0.0596)** |
| 30 min (AR) | 28.3720 | **28.2159 (0.0538)** | 14.0931 | **14.0252 (0.0062)** | 36.6937 | **36.4566 (0.0071)** | 5.7202 | 5.7616 (0.7729) |
| 45 min (AR) | 37.7322 | 37.9234 (0.8651) | 17.6807 | 17.6993 (0.8152) | 47.9815 | **47.8084 (0.0373)** | 7.0983 | 7.2341 (0.9954) |
| 1 h (AR) | 44.0571 | 44.2877 (0.8383) | 20.3353 | 20.4799 (0.9346) | 55.7560 | 55.8053 (0.5955) | 9.0440 | 9.1169 (0.8867) |
| 2 h (AR) | 77.4225 | 77.4581 (0.5472) | 30.9472 | 30.8688 (0.2532) | 98.1701 | 98.2703 (0.5990) | 13.4674 | 13.8434 (0.8713) |
| 4 h (AR) | 23.6795 | 125.0778 (0.7443) | 43.0342 | **42.0985 (0.0150)** | 145.2135 | **144.3137 (0.3253)** | 20.6128 | 21.4649 (0.8248) |

Notes: The forecasting study is conducted over a period of 32 weeks starting on 6 October 2003 and ending on 14 May 2004. These 32 weeks are divided into 8 periods of 4 weeks each, where the first 3 weeks are always considered as the in-sample estimation periods and the last week is always considered as the out-of-sample forecasting periods. Weekends and holidays are excluded from the analysis. The BM column contains the RMSPEs of the AR($p$) benchmark model. The RMSPEs of the forecasting model with historical prices are shown in the first entry of the historical prices column, the second entry in parenthesis are the $p$-value of the mDM test with the null hypothesis that the RMSPEs of the associated forecasting model is not smaller than the RMSPEs of the AR($p$) BMs. $p$-Values in bold correspond to those cases where the RMSPE of the associated forecasting model is smaller than the RMSPE of the AR($p$) BM.

on the interbank market, since most of the traders do not have own customer order flow, which can serve as private information. Our observation also shows that it might take up to several hours to process new information and gain market efficiency.

Moreover, regardless of whether traders hold an open position or not, we find that the price process contributes more to the prediction of market order flow than to the prediction of limit order flow, in both in-sample and out-of-sample periods. Following Foucault (1999), who shows that in equilibrium impatient traders tend to submit market orders and patient traders limit orders, and taking the descriptive statistics into account, a likely interpretation is that traders on OANDA FXTrade are very impatient. The evidence supports the view that small, not sophisticated traders, who place their orders based on their interpretation of recent price movements, and thus react quickly to recent price changes, prefer to submit market orders which are executed immediately, instead of limit orders. This is reflected at the end of the day by the fact that market orders are more predictable than limit orders. This finding is also consistent with the results of Rosu (2010).

Our postulate of the existence of a monitoring effect is clearly supported. Indeed, we see, in Tables 12 and 13, that the price process contributes more to the prediction of market (close) order flow than to the prediction of market (open) order flow.[9] Thus, we find evidence that traders employ different strategies when they hold an open position. In detail, we observe that only the RMSPEs for the 1 and 2 min frequencies of the price changes for the market order (open) forecasting models are significantly smaller (1% level) than those of the corresponding AR($p$) BMs, but that the first five RMSPEs corresponding to frequencies up to 15 min are significantly smaller than those of the BMs for the market order (close) flow category at the 1% level. From the remaining (lower) frequencies only one is significant on the 10% level of the mDM-test for price changes for the market order (close) forecasting models. A similar observation, but not as pronounced, can be made for limit order executed (close) flow and limit order executed (open) flow as well. The reason why this effect is not as clear as for market orders is that limit orders are posted to the system before market orders, and their execution is later then simply implied by the price process. Market orders, however, reflect changes in price preferences directly since they are executed immediately.

Our results complete the work of Feng and Seasholes (2005), who investigate the question of whether investors sophistication and trading experience attenuate behavioral biases in financial markets. They analyze if investors actively monitor stocks they have sold, and their results provide indirect evidence that they do. Our analysis is more focussed on a small set of securities and not a large universe of stocks, but we also provide evidence that the investors monitor the price process closer when they already hold an open position.

Let us now consider the hypothesis that executed stop-loss orders contribute whereas executed take-profit orders impede, self-reinforcing price movements. Table 13 shows that at all forecasting frequencies, the RMSPEs of the BMs for the stop-loss order flow category are smaller than those of BMs for the take-profit order flow category. This observation supports the existence of price cascades since stop-loss order flow, based on its own historical order flow, is better predictable (in terms of smaller RMSPEs) than take-profit order flow. This is foreseen if stop-loss orders contribute to self-reinforcing price movements causing a sequence of further stop-loss order executions. Comparing the RMSPE pattern of the stop-loss and take-profit order flow categories, forecasting models containing additional information on the history of the price change process, we observe that there is essentially no difference in the value of the history of the price process in predicting take-profit or stop-loss order flow. This observation thus provides little additional evidence for the validity of our statement, since we expected that the information on the direction of the price change process should already be included in the historical stop-loss order flow.

It therefore should be of less importance in predicting future stop-loss order flow in contrast to the case when take-profit order flow is considered. Taking also the results of the in-sample analysis into account, altogether, we find weak evidence that stop-loss orders self-reinforce price movements, but we cannot draw a clear cut conclusion here.

## 5. Conclusion

We have investigated the predictive power of past price changes for the aggregated order flow measure Lyons (1995) and eight transaction category-specific order flows, based on a unique data set from the currency trading platform, OANDA FXTrade. Our data contain detailed information on generally small retail investors' trading characteristics, currency positions and detailed information on order flows of several different order types. The main focus of this paper lies in investigating whether investors behave differently when they already hold a position compared with when they do not. The key question asked is: does the current inventory matter? Answer: yes!

We conduct forecasting studies on 12 intraday frequencies and find that those forecasting models incorporating information on order flow and price changes provide significantly better forecasts than BMs using only information on past order flow through AR specifications. Our in-sample and out-of-sample forecasting analyzes show that investors' future order flow is affected by past price movements, and that market and limit order flows are much better predictable if those orders are submitted to close an existing position than if they are used to open one. This suggests evidence for the existence of a monitoring effect stating that investors value price information with respect to their current inventory. Monitoring effects are generally ignored in theoretical market microstructure models in which decisions regarding the submission of market and limit orders are modeled regardless of the inventory of the investor. Our study shows that monitoring effects play an important role, and that theoretical market microstructure models can be improved by the incorporation of monitoring or inventory effects. Furthermore, we find some evidence that stop-loss orders contribute to and take-profit impede self-reinforcing price movements, results which support the hypothesis of Osler (2005).

## Acknowledgements

The work is supported by the Fritz Thyssen Foundation through the project 'Measurement Error in Nonlinear Regression Models and Business Tendency Data'. The authors wish to thank Günter Franke, Richard Olsen, Carol Osler, Richard Payne, Winfried Pohlmeier, Mark Salmon and an anonymous referee for helpful comments and constructive discussions. Special thanks go to Olsen Financial Technologies for providing us with the data. The usual disclaimer applies.

## Notes

1. Lyons (2002) has already pointed out that there has been a shift in the interdealer market from direct trading toward electronic brokerage trading. This shift is partially explained by more transparency on electronic brokerage systems. In the customer market, a similar argument applies to explain the shift from customer-to-dealer-bank trading toward electronic internet trading platforms. These platforms are also more transparent and try to offer small (interbank) spreads to all of their customers independently of their transaction volume and thus order handling costs.
2. The relationship between learning, feedback effects, information cascades, technical analysis and price bubbles is discussed for instance in De Long et al. (1990), Bikhchandani, Hirshleifer, and Welch (1992), Avery and Zemsky (1998), Lee (1998) and Shiller (2002).
3. A description of who uses OANDA FXTrade can be found on their webpage http://fxtrade.oanda.com/.
4. After 1 month, the order expires on OANDA FXTrade.

5. For both cross-correlation functions, we plot lag 0 through 19. The value at lag 0 is the same in both cross-panels and represents the contemporaneous correlation between order flow and price changes.

6. We observed that the order flow process is persistent.

7. See Caplin and Leahy (1996).

8. The survey study of Taylor and Allen (1992) shows that at least 90% of the London-based dealers rely, in addition to private and fundamental information, on information from technical analyzes to design their trading strategies.

9. The same conclusion can be drawn from the in-sample forecasting studies.

# References

Anand, A., S. Chakravarty, and T. Martell. 2005. Empirical evidence on the evolution of liquidity: Choice of market versus limit orders by informed and uninformed traders. *Journal of Financial Markets* 8, no. 3: 288–308.

Avery, C., and P. Zemsky. 1998. Multidimensional uncertainty and herd behavior in financial markets. *American Economic Review* 88, no. 4: 724–48.

Berger, D., A. Chaboud, S. Chernenko, E. Howorka, and J. Wright. 2008. Order flow and exchange rate dynamics in electronic brokerage system data. *Journal of International Economics* 75, no. 1: 93–109.

Bikhchandani, S., D. Hirshleifer, and I. Welch. 1992. A theory of fads, fashion, custom, and cultural change in informational cascades. *Journal of Political Economy* 100, no. 5: 992–1026.

Bjønnes, G.H., and D. Rime. 2005. Dealer behavior and trading systems in foreign exchange markets. *Journal of Financial Economics* 75, no. 3: 571–605.

Bloomfield, R., M. O'Hara, and G. Saar. 2005. The 'make or take' decision in an electronic market: Evidence on the evolution of liquidity. *Journal of Financial Economics* 75, no. 1: 165–99.

Caplin, A., and J. Leahy. 1996. Trading costs, price, and volume in asset markets. *The American Economic Review* 86, no. 2: 192–6.

Chakravarty, S., and C. Holden. 1995. An integrated model of market and limit orders. *Journal of Financial Intermediation* 4, no. 3: 213–41.

Chordia, T., and A. Subrahmanyam. 2004. Order imbalance and individual stock returns. *Journal of Financial Economics* 72, no. 3: 485–518.

Daníelsson, J., and R. Love. 2006. Feedback trading. *International Journal of Finance and Economics* 11, no. 1: 35–53.

Daníelsson, J., R. Payne, and J. Luo. 2011. Exchange rate determination and inter-market order flow effects. *The European Journal of Finance* XX: XXX, DOI: 10.1080/1351847X.2011.601655.

De Long, J.B., A. Shleifer, L.H. Summers, and R.J. Waldmann. 1990. Positive feedback investment strategies and destabilizing rational speculation. *Journal of Finance* 45, no. 2: 379–95.

Demsetz, H. 1968. The cost of transacting. *Quarterly Journal of Economics* 82, no. 1: 33–53.

Evans, M.D., and R.K. Lyons. 2002a. Informational integration and FX trading. *Journal of International Money and Finance* 21, no. 6: 807–31.

Evans, M.D., and R.K. Lyons. 2002b. Order flow and exchange rate dynamics. *Journal of Political Economy* 110, no. 1: 170–80.

Evans, M.D., and R.K. Lyons. 2005. Meese–Rogoff redux: Micro-based exchange-rate forecasting. *American Economic Review* 95, no. 2: 405–14.

Evans, M.D., and R.K. Lyons. 2006. Understanding order flow. *International Journal of Finance and Economics* 11, no. 1: 2–23.

Feng, L., and M. Seasholes. 2005. Do investor sophistication and trading experience eliminate behavioral biases in financial markets? *Review of Finance* 9, no. 3: 305–51.

Foucault, T. 1999. Order flow composition and trading costs in a dynamic limit order market. *Journal of Financial Markets* 2, no. 2: 99–134.

Foucault, T., O. Kadan, and E. Kandel. 2005. Limit order book as a market for liquidity. *Review of Financial Studies* 18, no. 4: 1171–217.

Glosten, L.R. 1994. Is the electronic open limit order book inevitable? *The Journal of Finance* 49, no. 4: 1127–61.

Harris, L.E. 1998. Optimal dynamic order submission strategies in some stylized trading problems. *Financial Markets, Institutions & Instruments* 7, no. 2: 1–76.

Harvey, D., S. Leybourne, and P. Newbold. 1997. Testing the equality of prediction mean squared errors. *International Journal of Forecasting* 13, no. 2: 281–91.

Hollifield, B., R. Miller, and P. Sandas. 2004. Empirical analysis of limit order markets. *Review of Economic Studies* 71, no. 4: 1027–63.

Kahneman, D., J.L. Knetsch, and R.H. Thaler. 1990. Experimental tests of the endowment effect and the coase theorem. *Journal of Political Economy* 98, no. 6: 1325–48.

Kahneman, D., and A. Tversky. 1979. Prospect theory: An analysis of decision under risk. *Econometrica* 47, no. 2: 263–92.

Kaniel, R., and H. Liu. 2006. So what orders do informed traders use? *Journal of Business* 79, no. 4: 1867–913.

Lee, I.H. 1998. Market crashes and informational avalanches. *Review of Economic Studies* 65, no. 4: 741–59.

Lyons, R.K. 1995. Tests of microstructural hypothesis in the foreign exchange market. *Journal of Financial Economics* 39, nos. 2–3: 321–51.

Lyons, R.K. 2002. The future of the foreign exchange market. In *Brookings–Wharton papers on financial services*, eds. R. Litan and R. Herring, 253–80. Washington, DC: Brookings Institution Press.

Marsh, I.W., and C. O'Rourke. 2005. Customer order flow and exchange rate movements: Is there really information content? Working paper, Cass Business School, London.

Osler, C.L. 2005. Stop-loss orders and price cascades in currency markets. *Journal of International Money and Finance* 24, no. 2: 219–41.

Parlour, C. 1998. Price dynamics in limit order markets. *Review of Financial Studies* 11, no. 4: 789–816.

Payne, R. 2003. Informed trade in spot foreign exchange markets: An empirical investigation. *Journal of International Economics* 61, no. 2: 307–29.

Rime, D. 2003. New electronic trading systems in the foreign exchange markets. In *New Economy Handbook*, ed. Derek C. Jones, 469–504. USA: Elsevier, Academic Press.

Rosu, I. 2010. Liquidity and information in order driven markets. Working paper, Booth School of Business, University of Chicago.

Seppi, D.J. 1997. Liquidity provision with limit orders and a strategic specialist. *Review of Financial Studies* 10, no. 1: 103–50.

Shiller, R.J. 2002. Bubbles, human judgment, and expert opinion. *Financial Analysts Journal* 58, no. 3: 18–26.

Taylor, M.P., and H. Allen. 1992. The use of technical analysis in the foreign exchange market. *Journal of International Money and Finance* 11, no. 3: 304–14.

Thaler, R. 1980. Toward a positive theory of consumer choice. *Journal of Economic Behavior & Organization* 1, no. 1: 39–60.

# On the hidden side of liquidity

Angel Pardo[a] and Roberto Pascual[b]

[a]Department of Financial Economics, Universidad de Valencia, Valencia, Spain; [b]Department of Business Economics, Universidad de las Islas Baleares, Palma, Spain

This article deals with the informativeness of iceberg orders, also known as hidden limit orders (HLOs). Namely, we analyze how the market reacts when the presence of hidden volume in the limit order book is revealed by the trading process. We use high-frequency book and transaction data from the Spanish Stock Exchange, including a large sample of *executed* HLOs. We show that just when hidden volume is detected, traders on the opposite side of the market become more aggressive, exploiting the opportunity to consume more than expected at the best quotes. However, neither illiquidity nor volatility increases in the short term. Furthermore, the detection of hidden volume has no relevant price impact. Overall, our results suggest that market participants do not attribute any relevant information content to the hidden side of liquidity.

## 1. Introduction

Market transparency refers to the quantity, quality, and promptness of the information that market participants receive about the trading process. The pros and cons of transparent venues lie at the heart of a debate that has deserved a significant empirical and theoretical research effort in the last few years (e.g. Madhavan 2000). Part of this literature focuses on pre-trade transparency, that is to say, the open dissemination of limit order book (LOB) information (e.g. Boehmer, Saar, and Yu 2005; Madhavan, Porter, and Weaver 2005). Other researchers look at post-trade transparency, the free and real-time disclosure of information about transactions (e.g. Pagano and Roëll 1996; Naik, Neuberger, and Viswanathan 1999). Finally, the public availability of information about the identity of liquidity providers (e.g. Simaan, Weaver, and Whitcomb 2003; Foucault, Moinas, and Theissen 2007) and trade participants (e.g. Garfinkel and Nimalendran 2003) has also been analyzed. All these studies compare the impact of more or less opaque trading systems on market quality as defined by liquidity, volatility, trading costs, price efficiency, etc. This paper deals with a dimension of pre-trade transparency that has produced a more limited theoretical and empirical research so far, the use of the so-called iceberg orders in order-driven markets.

Electronic order-driven markets are usually held up as the paradigm of a highly pre-trade transparent market since LOB information is disseminated in real time to all market participants. Many of these markets, however, provide facilities that allow traders to submit partially or totally undisclosed limit orders, also known as iceberg orders or hidden limit orders (henceforth HLOs).[1] By submitting an HLO, the trader displays only a small fraction of the total amount of shares he or she wishes to buy or sell. As in an iceberg, the rest of the order remains hidden. Because of these orders, market participants do not know the exact depth offered or demanded at the posted quotes.

From a market design point of view, HLOs represent a real trade-off between liquidity and pre-trade transparency. By allowing HLOs, regulators encourage traders to provide liquidity when they might be reluctant to disclose their trading interests. At the same time, regulators impose a certain degree of opacity in the trading mechanism. HLOs may, therefore, diminish the presumed benefits of a transparent LOB, such as low costs of market monitoring, real-time assessment of liquidity, less significant information asymmetries, and enhanced price efficiency.[2]

Two basic tentative arguments have been proposed regarding the rationale for HLOs. The first widespread belief is that HLOs are used by large liquidity traders to reduce the option value of the limit orders, that is, their exposure risk (Copeland and Galai 1983). Thus, these traders use HLOs as a self-protective strategy against either informed traders or parasitic traders, who profit from trading ahead of other traders they anticipate will have an impact on prices (e.g., Harris 2003). On the one hand, a limit order executing against an informed agent does it in the money, and the amount of the loss increases with the limit order size. Therefore, large traders facing adverse selection costs may choose to partially hide the size of their limit orders. If informed traders knew only the displayed depth at prices where they can profitably trade, they might submit smaller market orders than they would if they could also see the hidden volume. On the other hand, parasitic traders seek to infer the security's ultimate value from the exposed liquidity. These traders use front-running and quote-matching strategies, jumping in front of the heavy side of the LOB and stealing price priority from the exposed limit orders (e.g. Harris and Panchapagesan 2005). This activity benefits from a highly pre-trade transparent venue. HLO placement increases the trading risk borne by parasitic traders by creating uncertainty over the total available depth in the LOB.[3]

As a second argument, some researchers postulate that HLOs are submitted by informed traders so as to obscure their positions and minimize the price impact of their trades. Informed traders are habitually characterized as impatient because, by assumption, their information advantage is perishable in the very short term. Thus, it is typically assumed that these traders make use of orders that guarantee an immediate execution. Despite this, recent theoretical and empirical papers have shown that informed traders may use limit orders under certain circumstances. Thus, Harris (1998) concluded that informed traders facing wide spreads and distant deadlines, such as a market closure, are more likely to submit limit orders. Kaniel and Liu (2006) showed that informed traders prefer to use limit orders when their information is long-lived or their valuation is close to the current market quotes. In an experimental setting, Bloomfield, O'Hara, and Saar (2005) even showed that informed traders use more limit orders than liquidity traders do. Finally, Anand, Chakravarty, and Martell (2005) complemented previous studies providing evidence that institutional investors use limit orders, particularly toward the end of the day. Intuitively, if the private information is substantial and it will not become public soon, informed traders may choose to trade less aggressively. In this case, they may prefer undisclosed instead of disclosed limit orders. Indeed, in a first theoretical development about the choice between disclosed and undisclosed limit orders, Moinas (2005) showed that, in equilibrium, submitting hidden orders may be part of informed traders' camouflage strategy. The submission of an HLO allows informed traders to get a large transaction volume without signaling their presence.

The question of whether HLO traders are predominantly liquidity- or information-motivated has been empirically analyzed in several markets, providing contradictory conclusions. Aitken, Berkman, and Mak (2001) observed HLO traders in the Australian Stock Exchange (ASX) concentrating on the less frequently traded stocks, which they interpreted as being supportive of the liquidity-motivated hypothesis. Anand and Weaver (2004), however, found the opposite pattern in the Toronto Stock Exchange (TSX). Moreover, while Aitken, Berkman, and Mak (2001) concluded that a more restrictive undisclosed order regulation discourages liquidity-motivated HLO traders, Anand and Weaver (2004) determined that more permissive rules foster information-motivated HLO traders. It could be argued that these mixed findings might be due to microstructure disparities between markets.[4] Nonetheless, it seems more reasonable to presume that, in practice, both large liquidity and informed traders use HLOs to conceal their trading interests.

In this paper, we study the informativeness of hidden volume by analyzing how the market responds when the presence of non-displayed depth in the LOB is revealed by the trading process. Therefore, instead of looking for indirect evidence on the motivation of HLO traders, we look at partially or totally executed iceberg orders, which are the only ones that, at last, are publicly known.

We use data from the electronic order-driven market of the Spanish Stock Exchange (SSE). In the SSE, traders are allowed to place HLOs with a minimum displayed size of only 250 shares. Consequently, HLOs may be submitted more frequently than in the ASX and TSX markets. These orders are not marked when submitted. Therefore, the presence of undisclosed volume is only revealed when the undisclosed part of the HLO is totally or partially executed. Hence, the SSE is well suited for our purposes.

We use six months of displayed LOB and transaction data on a representative sample of 70 SSE-listed stocks. Among them, 35 stocks are index constituents, frequently traded; the other 35 stocks are thinly traded. We do not have information on HLO submissions. However, we develop a reliable algorithm that identifies an HLO as soon as it is picked up by a market order or a marketable limit order. With this information on *executed* HLOs, we study the incidence of detecting hidden volume on posterior stock returns and volatility. We also examine the influence of HLO detection on the traders' strategies by analyzing its impact on the composition of the order flow.

We find that HLOs temporally increase the aggressiveness of traders when they are discovered, but only on the opposite side of the market, suggesting that traders exploit the opportunity to consume more than displayed at the best quotes. Neither liquidity nor volatility deteriorates when hidden volume is unconcealed. Moreover, hidden volume revelation has no relevant price impact. We do not find remarkable differences when we control for variations in the trading frequency of the stock. These findings suggest that market participants do not attribute any relevant information content to the hidden side of liquidity.

Our findings and conclusions have been recently corroborated by posteriors, but already published, papers that try to answer similar questions but using alternative methodological approaches and databases. On the one hand, De Winne and D'Hondt (2007) used Euronext data to analyze how traders respond to the detection of hidden depth. They used a traditional probit model for order aggressiveness to show that the detection of hidden volume increases order aggressiveness. Their findings also suggest that traders use HLOs to manage exposure risk and picking-off risk. Although the authors have a richer database that includes information on HLO submissions, so as to analyze the response of the market to the revelation of hidden volume, only the information about executed orders is required. Since the submission of an HLO is not publicly known, the presence of hidden volume is only revealed through HLO execution. Our algorithm detects all HLO executions. On the other hand, Bessembinder, Panayides, and Venkataraman (2009) used Euronext data to show that HLOs are associated with lower probability of full execution, more time to completion, and lower average execution costs than fully displayed limit orders. Moreover, HLO exposure does not cause defensive traders to withdraw from the market. These authors concluded that the option to hide order size is most valuable to patient traders. The findings reported by Bessembinder, Panayides, and Venkataraman (2009) are, therefore, in line with our main conclusions.

The paper proceeds as follows. Section 2 reviews former empirical studies on HLOs. Section 3 details the microstructure of the SSE. Section 4 describes the database and provides some statistics. Section 5 evaluates the information content of HLOs. Finally, Section 6 concludes.

## 2. Literature review

A recent group of papers make the relevance of HLOs in electronic order-driven systems plain. HLOs account for about 16% of the entire LOB of the Brussels CATS system (Degryse 1999); 14% of all the limit orders submitted and 45% of the quoted depth at the Paris Euro-NM (D'Hondt, De Winne, and François-Heude 2001); almost 12% of all order executions and shares transacted through the Island electronic communication network (ECN) (Hasbrouck and Saar 2002); 22% of the inside depth of NASDAQ stocks following the Super SOES implementation (Tuttle 2006); and 50% of the book depth (five best levels) of the Euronext (D'Hondt, De Winne, and François-Heude 2004).

The cross-sectional evidence at hand provides some insights into the motives for submitting HLOs. Harris (1996); Aitken, Berkman, and Mak (2001); and D'Hondt, De Winne, and François-Heude (2001) reported that HLO submissions decrease with the relative tick size. Since larger tick sizes make front-running strategies more difficult and expensive, this finding supports the view that HLO traders manage the exposure costs of their limit orders. As well, Aitken, Berkman, and Mak (2001) found that HLOs are more common among the more volatile stocks. Since the option value of a limit order increases with volatility, this finding also supports the view that HLO traders are liquidity motivated.

In some other cases, however, the empirical evidence is not conclusive. Aitken, Berkman, and Mak (2001) found that the use of HLOs decreases with trading activity. Given that a higher non-execution risk enhances the option value of limit orders, the authors concluded that ASX HLOs are liquidity motivated. Anand and Weaver (2004), however, reported a positive relationship between HLO submissions and trading intensity. They argued that if informed traders were to make use of limit orders, they would probably choose stocks with a low non-execution risk. Hence, they concluded that TSX HLOs are information driven.

Aitken, Berkman, and Mak (2001) and Anand and Weaver (2004) also studied the impact of disclosure regulation changes on market liquidity and activity. Once more, their conclusions are quite opposed. In October 1994, ASX regulators decided to enhance pre-trade transparency by increasing the minimum disclosed volume. Aitken, Berkman, and Mak (2001) found that this decision caused a significant decline in trading volume. They concluded that by tightening the undisclosed order regulation, ASX regulators discouraged primary liquidity suppliers. Similarly, Anand and Weaver (2004) analyzed the decision made by the TSX of abolishing HLOs in 1996 and then reintroducing them in 2002. These authors did not find a significant effect on trading activity. Nonetheless, they reported an increase in the number of quote updates and an increase in total depth, both disclosed and undisclosed, after the 2002 reintroduction. Since this effect is particularly important among the active stocks, they concluded that the 2002 reintroduction encouraged informed traders to submit more HLOs. Anand and Weaver's (2004) standpoint is that informed traders are the most impatient type of traders. Hence, these traders balance the inherent non-execution risk of their limit orders by choosing stocks with the smallest non-execution risk. Harris (1998) and Bloomfield, O'Hara, and Saar (2005), however, illustrated that aggressiveness is also agreeable with large liquidity traders facing a deadline to fulfill a target, such as rebalancing a portfolio. If these traders were to focus on frequently traded stocks, Anand and Weaver's findings would also be compatible with liquidity-motivated traders using HLOs aggressively to mitigate the risk of non-execution and, simultaneously, reducing the option value of their limit orders.

Taken as a whole, this exposition suggests that making inference about the motivation of HLO traders based exclusively on cross-sectional statistics on HLO usage may be misleading, and it makes the need for a direct test of the information content of HLOs prominent.[5]

## 3. Institutional background

The SSE Interconnection System (SIBE) is a computer-assisted trading platform that holds all the SSE-listed stocks that achieve certain minimum levels of liquidity and trading activity.[6] The SIBE is a pure order-driven market. By 'pure', we mean that there are no market makers, and liquidity is provided by an open LOB. Trading is continuous from 9.00 a.m. to 5.30 p.m. and is governed by a strict price–time priority rule. There is no floor trading and price improvements are impossible. Hence, all the orders are submitted through vendor feeds and stored or matched electronically.[7] During the continuous trading session, orders are submitted, modified, or cancelled, and a trade takes place whenever a counterpart order hits the quotes. Stocks are quoted in euros (€) and the tick equals €0.01 for prices up to €50 and €0.05 for prices above €50. The SIBE is highly transparent, with information on both book and trade data provided in real time to all market participants.

There are three basic types of orders: market, market-to-limit, and limit orders. Market orders are executed against the best prices on the opposite side of the book. They walk up or down the book until they are fulfilled. Market-to-limit orders are limited to the best opposite-side price in the book at the time of entry; the non-executed part is stored in the book as a limit order at that price. Limit orders are to be executed at the limit price or better. By default, orders expire at the end of the session. The maximum validity period is 90 calendar days and the minimum order size is one share. For every basic order type, special conditions are allowed, like 'fill or kill', 'execute or eliminate', 'minimum execution', or 'hidden volume'.

The SIBE allows the submission of partially undisclosed limit orders. No mark indicates the condition of 'hidden volume'; consequently, only the supervisor of the SIBE and the broker that submits the order know of its presence. The investor chooses the 'displayed volume unit' of the order, with a minimum of 250 shares. A new displayed volume unit emerges as soon as the current one is executed. That is, when a market order hits an HLO in the book and the size of the market order is larger than or equal to the displayed volume unit, a new peak of an iceberg order comes to the surface. The hidden part of the order loses, however, its time precedence, meaning that the displayed volume, either from the HLO or from other limit orders with the same limit price, must be filled before the hidden volume.[8]

## 4. Data

The database consists of six months of book and trade files, from July to December 2000 (124 trading days), on the 70 SSE-listed common stocks. We will distinguish between two subsets of stocks: the 35 stocks' constituents of the official market index (henceforth, IDX stocks), the IBEX-35, and the remaining 35 stocks (hereafter, NIDX stocks).[9] In 2000, IBEX-35 stocks represented 72.68% of the market capitalization and 84.83% of the trading activity. IDX stocks include six stocks cross-listed (as ADRs) in US markets. Most of the NIDX stocks should be considered as thinly traded.

Table 1 provides some descriptive statistics on our sample. All the statistics are computed over 30 minute intervals, averaged first per stock and, after that, across stocks. We provide separate statistics for the IDX and NIDX stocks. It could be observed that there are striking differences between both subsamples in terms of liquidity and trading activity. In average terms, the quoted bid–ask spread is three times smaller for the IDX stocks than for the NIDX stocks. Moreover, order flow, as measured by limit order and market order submissions (trades), is 7 times and 12 times larger, respectively, for the IDX stocks. Finally, volume (in shares) is 19 times larger for the IDX, implying that the average trade size is also larger for these stocks.

The database includes the information disseminated in real time to every market member. LOB files contain the five best buy and sell positions, including quotes, (displayed) depth, and number of orders. These files are updated each time the book changes and are time-stamped at the nearest hundredth of a second. The trade files are updated each time the first level of the LOB changes. For each trade, they provide information about the marginal price of the last share traded, the trade size, and the broker/dealer codes.

Since HLOs are not marked as such on the SIBE screens, we cannot directly identify all iceberg order submissions and cancellations. Nonetheless, we have developed a reliable algorithm that detects an HLO when it is totally or partially executed and its presence is then revealed to the whole marketplace. The algorithm works in the following way. First, we match the book and the trade files. After that, it is straightforward to classify all the updates of the LOB into cancellations, modifications, market (or marketable limit) orders (trades), market-to-limit orders, and limit orders.[10] The classification of trades as buyer- or seller-initiated is straightforward since there are neither reporting lags nor price improvements like those in the NYSE data. All trades involve a market or marketable limit order that matches with a limit order previously stored in the LOB. Therefore, a trade that consumes liquidity on the bid (ask) side of the LOB is classified as a seller (buyer)-initiated trade.

Table 1. Sample: descriptive statistics.

| Stocks | Volume/100 | Trades | Volatility | Spread × 100 | Limit orders |
|---|---|---|---|---|---|
| All | | | | | |
| Mean | 1062.35 | 493.82 | 0.0274 | 0.64 | 360.07 |
| Std. | (3220.28) | (1038.78) | (0.0104) | (0.43) | (598.74) |
| IDX | | | | | |
| Mean | 2045.41 | 923.37 | 0.0314 | 0.33 | 645.44 |
| Std. | (4400.31) | (1335.68) | (0.0104) | (0.15) | (750.29) |
| NIDX | | | | | |
| Mean | 107.38 | 76.54 | 0.0236 | 0.95 | 82.86 |
| Std. | (204.76) | (102.68) | (0.0090) | (0.39) | (100.25) |

Notes: Some cross-sectional average daily statistics on the 70 SSE-listed stocks in our sample, covering from July to December 2000, are reported. We provide separate statistics for the 35 index constituents (IDX) and for the 35 remaining stocks (NIDX). 'Volume' is the number of shares traded. 'Trades' is the number of trades completed. 'Volatility' is the high–low ratio of the quote midpoint minus one. 'Spread' is the relative bid–ask spread weighted by time. 'Limit orders' is the number of limit orders submitted during the interval. The tick is €0.01 for all the stocks, the displayed depth per level is one share, as it is the minimum trade size.

To infer about the presence of hidden volume, we compare the reported trade sizes (changes in the accumulated volume) with the corresponding updates in the LOB. In the SIBE, a deviation between these two quantities can only be explained by the presence of hidden volume.[11] We illustrate this procedure in Table 2. It provides four typical examples of HLO detection.

Table 2. Examples of HLO detection.

| | Before the trade | | | After the trade | |
|---|---|---|---|---|---|
| Quote | Depth | Orders | Quote | Depth | Orders |
| Case #1 | | | | | |
| 9.79 | 1700 | 2 | 9.8 | 3400 | 3 |
| 9.78 | 1300 | 2 | 9.79 | 1700 | 2 |
| 9.75 | 1931 | 3 | 9.78 | 1300 | 2 |
| 9.72 | 1833 | 2 | 9.75 | 2937 | 1 |
| 9.71 | 588 | 3 | 9.72 | 1833 | 2 |
| 9.7 | 10,833 | 14 | 9.71 | 588 | 3 |
| Case #2 | | | | | |
| 9.84 | 2300 | 2 | 9.84 | 2300 | 2 |
| 9.83 | 2219 | 2 | 9.83 | 2219 | 2 |
| 9.82 | 847 | 1 | 9.82 | 847 | 1 |
| 9.8 | 3152 | 3 | 9.8 | 1299 | 2 |
| 9.79 | 3000 | 2 | 9.79 | 3000 | 2 |
| 9.77 | 1000 | 1 | 9.77 | 1000 | 1 |
| Case #3 | | | | | |
| 22.68 | 2696 | 1 | 22.68 | 2696 | 1 |
| 22.67 | 145 | 1 | 22.67 | 145 | 1 |
| 22.65 | 2718 | 2 | 22.65 | 2718 | 2 |
| 22.63 | 4391 | 2 | 22.61 | 3443 | 3 |
| 22.61 | 3443 | 3 | 22.6 | 4626 | 13 |
| 22.6 | 4626 | 13 | 22.56 | 500 | 1 |
| Case #4 | | | | | |
| 22.67 | 145 | 1 | 22.67 | 145 | 1 |
| 22.66 | 1500 | 1 | 22.66 | 1500 | 1 |
| 22.65 | 5578 | 2 | 22.65 | 5578 | 2 |
| 22.64 | 824 | 1 | 22.64 | 367 | 1 |
| 22.63 | 4000 | 2 | 22.63 | 4000 | 2 |
| 22.61 | 3443 | 3 | 22.61 | 3443 | 3 |

Notes: Four illustrative examples of HLO detection are reported. For each case, the three best levels of the LOB before and after a trade took place are reported. The upper three quote levels represent the ask side of the book, while the lower three quote levels represent the bid side of the book. Case #1: it seems that a market-to-limit order consumes the 1931 shares available at the best ask (€9.75). The unexecuted part of the order is stored at that price on the bid side of the book. The trade file, however, reports a trade size of 3063 shares. Thus, the algorithm reveals that the actual size of the market-to-limit order was 6000 (2937 + 3063) shares and that the limit order supporting the best ask was an HLO (Stock: ACR, 4 July 2000, 1.53.11 p.m.). Case #2: it seems that a market order (or equivalent) consumes 1853 shares at the best bid (€9.8) and, as a consequence, one limit order is totally executed. The trade file reports a trade size of 3000 shares. In this case, the algorithm reveals that at least one of the three orders supporting the best bid was an HLO (Stock: ACR, 4 July 2000, 2.56.12 p.m.). Case #3: apparently, a market order (or equivalent) consumes the best bid (€22.63), 4391 shares. The trade file, however, reports a trade size of 26,391 shares. The algorithm reveals an HLO at €22.63 with 22,000 shares hidden. The arriving order is, probably, a market order with an 'execute or eliminate' condition for a size larger than 26,391 shares (Stock: TEF, 3 July 2000, 9.16.44 a.m.). Case #4: it seems that a market order (or equivalent) of 457 shares reduces the quoted depth at €22.64 from 824 shares to 367 shares. The trade file, however, reports a trade size of 5457 shares. The algorithm reveals an HLO at €22.64 with displayed volume unit 5000 shares: 824(displayed) − 5457(demanded) + 5000(displayed volume unit) = 367 (Stock: TEF, 3 July 2000, 9.13.46 a.m.).

With this algorithm, we identify *executed* HLOs while we ignore unexecuted HLOs, either because they expire or because they are cancelled. In average terms, we find that 16% of the trades executed in the SSE during our sample period involve hidden volume, 18% for the IDX stocks, and 14% among the NIDX stocks. Roughly 60% of all trades involving hidden volume were fulfilled when there was only the HLO supporting the best quote. Following the evolution of these orders backwards, it is possible to find the exact time of submission of 104,452 orders. Around 93% of these orders were placed inside the bid–ask spread, and the median time to execution was three minutes.

## 5. Empirical analysis

In the SSE, hidden volume is only exposed to the marketplace when an incoming market or marketable limit order is executed against an HLO. Moreover, the size of the incoming order must exceed the available displayed depth. We, therefore, evaluate the informativeness of the hidden volume by examining the reaction of stock returns and price volatility when hidden volume is discovered. If the market were to regard hidden volume as a signal of information-motivated trading, we would expect prices to move in the direction of the disclosed HLO. Namely, prices would tend to increase (decrease) when hidden volume is detected on the bid (ask) side of the LOB. In addition, the disclosure of these orders would increase volatility in the short term, as prices would adjust to the new information.

We look for additional insights into the informativeness of HLOs by studying their influence on other traders' behavior. In particular, we assess the effect of disclosing hidden volume on the liquidity provision and the order flow composition. If the market were to believe that hidden volume conceals informed traders, we would expect liquidity to deteriorate once the presence of hidden volume has been revealed because of the increase in adverse selection costs. Moreover, if HLO traders were to provide new information, we would expect other traders to mimic them. Namely, we would predict more buyer (seller)-initiated activity when hidden volume is exposed on the bid (ask) side of the market. Moreover, we would expect imitators to trade aggressively so as to make profits before the new information is totally incorporated into prices.

The experiment is designed as follows. We construct two samples of matched trades. The first sample includes trades revealing the presence of HLOs on either side of the LOB (henceforth, TH trades). Note that a TH order does not necessarily reveal the whole size of the HLO. The second sample includes matched 'ordinary' trades, that is, trades that do not involve hidden volume (henceforth, TO trades). A TH trade and a TO trade match if both are either buyer- or seller-initiated, equally sized, and executed under similar market conditions. We use these matched samples to test for statistically significant differences in terms of post-trade stock returns, volatility, liquidity, trading activity, and order flow composition. Since TH and TO trades are equivalent in every aspect but the hidden volume, any post-trade difference should be attributed to the revelation by TH trades of hidden liquidity in the LOB. Note that buyer (seller)-initiated TH trades expose hidden volume on the ask (bid) side of the LOB. We eliminate any TH trade preceded by some other TH trade within a five minute interval. In this manner, we aim to pick up those TH trades that were the first in revealing the presence of undisclosed volume on a given quote. Similarly, we discard every TO trade preceded or followed by a TH trade within a five minute interval. With this filter, we aspire to minimize the risk of market conditions near ordinary trades being contaminated by TH trades.

For each trade remaining, we compute the post-trade quote midpoint returns $(QR_t)$ and volatility $(QV_t)$ as

$$QR_t = \log\left(\frac{Q_\tau}{Q_t}\right),\tag{1}$$

$$QV_t = \left(\frac{\log(\bar{Q}_t^\tau)}{\log(\underline{Q}_t^\tau)}\right) - 1,\tag{2}$$

where $\tau > t$ defines four different time intervals $(\tau - t)$: 5, 10, 30 min, and until the end of the trading session; $Q$ is the quote midpoint; $\bar{Q}_t^\tau$ $(\underline{Q}_t^\tau)$ is the maximum (minimum) of $Q$ in the interval $(t, \tau)$; $Q_\tau$ is the value at the end of the interval; and $Q_t$ is the value at the beginning of the interval.

In addition, for each minute $(m)$ in a 5 min window before and after each trade, we compute the following variables:

- Quote midpoint returns $(R_m)$: as in Equation (1), but taking the value of $Q$ at the end $(Q_\tau)$ and at the beginning $(Q_t)$ of each 1 min interval.
- Quote midpoint volatility $(VLT_m)$: as in Equation (2), but using the maximum $(\bar{Q}_t^\tau)$ and minimum $(\underline{Q}_t^\tau)$ of $Q$ in each interval.
- Bid–ask spread $(SPR_m)$: average number of ticks between the best offer and bid quotes. Each spread in the interval is weighted by time:

$$SPR_m = \sum_{i=1}^{k} \frac{SPR_{m,i} \times t_i}{\sum_{i=1}^{k} t_i},\tag{3}$$

where $t_i$ is the time (in seconds) the quoted spread $SPR_{m,i}$ lasts in the 1 min interval.
- Net depth $(ND_m)$: average difference between the displayed shares on the ask side of the book minus the displayed shares on the bid side of the book, weighted by time as in Equation (3). We consider the five best quotes on each side of the book.
- Net trades $(NT_m)$: difference between the number of buyer-initiated and seller-initiated trades.
- Net volume $(NV_m)$: difference between the buyer-initiated volume and the seller-initiated volume, in shares.
- Net limit orders $(NLO_m)$: difference between number of limit orders to buy and limit orders to sell submitted during the interval.

We standardize the former variables per stock and half-hour interval:

$$\tilde{X}_{s,d,j,i} = \frac{(X_{s,d,j,i} - \bar{X}_{s,j})}{std(X_{s,j})},$$

where $\tilde{X}_{s,d,j,i}$ is the $i$th standardized observation of the variable $X$ for stock $s$, on day $d$, and in the half-hour interval $j$ of the trading session; $X_{s,d,j,i}$ is the corresponding non-standardized observation; $\bar{X}_{s,j}$ is the average of $X$ for stock $s$ across all days and all the observations in the half-hour interval $j$, and $std(X_{s,j})$ is the corresponding standard deviation.

For each stock, we separate buyer-initiated trades from seller-initiated trades (henceforth, BITs and SITs, respectively). BITs and SITs are further partitioned into six trade-size categories each, from S1 to S6. These categories are defined by the stock-specific percentiles of the empirical distribution of trade sizes: (0%, 25%), (25%, 50%), (50%, 75%), (75%, 90%), (90%, 95%), and

(95%, 99%).[12] We group all trades across stocks by size category. Then, for each category, we compute the 10%, 30%, 50%, 70%, and 90% percentiles of the pre-trade empirical distribution of the control variables: $R_t$, $VLT_t$, $SPR_t$, $ND_t$, $NT_t$, $NV_t$, and $NLO_t$. These percentiles are used as thresholds to define six value intervals, henceforth L1 to L6, which will typify the level of each control variable in the pre-trade matching period. Different matching periods have been considered, from 1 to 5 min. Our main findings are independent of the matching interval considered. Thus, we will only report the results for the five minute pre-trade matching interval.

For each TH trade, we look for a TO trade with the same sign, the same size category, and perfectly matching pre-trade market conditions, that is, the same level in each control variable. When no matching occurs, the TH trade is eliminated. When multiple matching occurs, we choose the TO trade that minimizes the sum of the absolute deviations in prior market conditions with respect to the TH trade of reference.[13]

After all this process, we end up with 12 matched samples, two for each of the six trade-size categories, six for BITs, and six for SITs. Table 3 provides some details on the resulting matched samples. The percentage of matched TH trades is quite successful from S1 to S4 trade-size categories, with an average percentage of matched trades of 84.2% for BITs and 85.85% for SITs. For larger size categories, however, it becomes more difficult to find matched TO trades, and the percentage of success decreases to an average 41% for BITs and about 46% for SITs. There are no remarkable differences in the matching attainment between IDX and NIDX trades. Table 3 also shows that there are no remarkable trade size differences between the matched pairs of trades.

We check for differences in post-trade market conditions between TH and TO trades using the non-parametric Wilcoxon test of equality of medians ($H_0$: TH = TO).[14] We consider different alternative hypotheses for this test: the medians are different ($H_1$: TH $\neq$ TO); the median for TH trades is larger than the median for TO trades ($H_1$: TH > TO); and the median for TH trades is smaller than the median for TO trades ($H_1$: TH < TO).[15] To get more robust findings, tests are performed over 1000 subsamples of 1000 trades each, randomly selected with replacement from the S1 to S6 samples described above.

Tables 4 and 5 summarize our main findings. For each particular variable, we report the percentage of cases for which the null ($H_0$: TH = TO) is rejected at the 1% level. We distinguish between TH trades revealing hidden volume on the ask side of the LOB and TH trades revealing hidden volume on the bid side of the LOB.

Table 4 focuses on short-run impact of hidden volume disclosure on liquidity and order flow. We consider the five minute interval following the time stamp of each trade ($t$ in Table 4). Due to space limitations, we only report the findings for the medium-sized (S4) category of TH trades. The results for the other trade-size categories are similar and available upon request from the authors.

Panel A in Table 4 shows our findings using the 70 stocks in our sample. The first noticeable finding is that liquidity does not deteriorate with the detection of hidden volume. Theoretical research claims for the existence of an adverse selection component in the bid–ask spread.[16] According to these models, we should expect the bid–ask spread to widen when the presence of informed traders is revealed to the marketplace. Table 4 shows that the null of equal bid–ask spreads is rejected in 30.4% (19.9%) of the subsamples when hidden volume is detected on the ask (bid) side of the book, but always against the alternative of narrower bid–ask spreads after the TH trade. Regarding quoted depth, the literature has suggested that liquidity providers use both quoted spreads and depth to manage adverse selection costs (e.g. Kavajecz 1999; Caglio and Kavajecz 2006). In Table 4, however, the null hypothesis of equality of medians for the LOB depth ($ND_t$) is strongly supported. Furthermore, no remarkable change in the sum of the quoted depth

Table 3. Matched samples.

| | | Size catagory | | | | | |
|---|---|---|---|---|---|---|---|
| | | S1 | S2 | S3 | S4 | S5 | S6 |
| | | Buyer-initiated trades | | | | | |
| **All 70 stocks** | | | | | | | |
| Hidden | Avg. size | 117.87 | 355.53 | 971.80 | 2572.91 | 5007.30 | 10329.20 |
| | | (71.54) | (233.52) | (809.41) | (2237.21) | (3665.68) | (8722.65) |
| No hidden | Avg. size | 97.02 | 318.25 | 860.23 | 2371.95 | 5119.36 | 10773.02 |
| | | (75.22) | (234.86) | (773.29) | (2164.91) | (3870.18) | (9655.67) |
| | Obs. | 6207 | 15,806 | 34,874 | 41,952 | 19,237 | 20,718 |
| | % matches | 87.76% | 87.32% | 85.96% | 75.77% | 44.72% | 36.78% |
| **35 IDX stocks** | | | | | | | |
| Hidden | Avg. size | 116.07 | 355.77 | 1001.51 | 2669.94 | 5185.81 | 10614.49 |
| | | (67.39) | (233.62) | (838.92) | (2302.85) | (3751.06) | (8722.08) |
| No hidden | Avg. size | 93.97 | 313.92 | 872.75 | 2446.70 | 5300.80 | 11020.52 |
| | | (64.68) | (224.39) | (777.53) | (2202.75) | (3873.11) | (9139.59) |
| | Obs. | 5576 | 14,181 | 31,272 | 37,955 | 17,337 | 18,891 |
| | % matches | 87.84% | 87.26% | 85.84% | 75.70% | 44.74% | 36.81% |
| **35 NIDX stocks** | | | | | | | |
| Hidden | Avg. size | 133.94 | 351.57 | 717.21 | 1660.96 | 3368.58 | 7359.65 |
| | | (99.95) | (232.71) | (407.55) | (1133.31) | (2157.09) | (8162.30) |
| No hidden | Avg. size | 118.18 | 351.18 | 774.29 | 1872.90 | 4055.20 | 9376.08 |
| | | (124.12) | (300.87) | (737.95) | (1816.01) | (3678.35) | (12074.90) |
| | Obs. | 631 | 1625 | 3602 | 3997 | 1900 | 1827 |
| | % matches | 87.00% | 87.82% | 86.98% | 76.48% | 44.47% | 36.56% |
| | | Seller-initiated trades | | | | | |
| **All 70 stocks** | | | | | | | |
| Hidden | Avg. size | 100.49 | 262.48 | 664.35 | 1958.01 | 4406.02 | 9628.53 |
| | | (60.53) | (140.21) | (425.23) | (1462.54) | (2943.84) | (7245.96) |
| No hidden | Avg. size | 82.05 | 239.66 | 627.91 | 1997.43 | 4752.94 | 9921.26 |
| | | (60.55) | (153.93) | (449.34) | (1537.33) | (3268.40) | (7720.23) |
| | Obs. | 6384 | 12,734 | 30,299 | 40,134 | 20,895 | 22,071 |
| | % matches | 89.00% | 88.17% | 87.59% | 78.65% | 51.74% | 40.52% |
| **35 IDX stocks** | | | | | | | |
| Hidden | Avg. size | 100.03 | 263.24 | 683.28 | 2065.90 | 4631.06 | 10224.60 |
| | | (59.19) | (134.68) | (426.73) | (1489.15) | (2993.15) | (7383.30) |
| No hidden | Avg. size | 81.81 | 234.54 | 635.07 | 2100.38 | 5046.98 | 10600.23 |
| | | (56.81) | (127.05) | (411.15) | (1498.02) | (3150.41) | (7442.02) |
| | Obs. | 5643 | 10,917 | 26,111 | 35,486 | 18,763 | 19,700 |
| | % matches | 88.59% | 87.74% | 87.31% | 78.14% | 51.40% | 40.09% |
| **35 NIDX stocks** | | | | | | | |
| Hidden | Avg. size | 103.81 | 258.06 | 548.98 | 1178.11 | 2546.10 | 5127.86 |
| | | (68.81) | (168.75) | (396.96) | (937.68) | (1539.77) | (3796.18) |
| No hidden | Avg. size | 83.49 | 266.12 | 590.10 | 1450.46 | 3271.89 | 6985.55 |
| | | (79.60) | (248.94) | (611.33) | (1625.55) | (3445.92) | (8201.66) |
| | Obs. | 741 | 1817 | 4188 | 4648 | 2132 | 2371 |
| | % matches | 92.17% | 90.75% | 89.30% | 82.53% | 54.74% | 44.12% |

Notes: The descriptive statistics on matched samples of ordinary trades or TO trades (reported as 'No Hidden') and trades involving hidden volume or TH trades (reported as 'Hidden') are provided. We construct separate subsamples for BITs and for SITs. We further separate BITs and SITs into six trade-size categories, S1–S6. S1 includes the smallest trades and S6 the largest ones. These six categories are defined using the 25, 50, 75, 90, 95, and 99% percentiles of the empirical distribution of the trade size per stock and trade sign (BITs versus SITs). The market conditions preceding each trade are characterized in terms of liquidity (bid–ask spread, depth, and limit orders submitted), volatility of the quote midpoint, activity (share volume and number of trades), and midpoint returns. For each of these variables, we define six value levels (L1–L6) using as thresholds the 10, 30, 50, 70, and 90% percentiles of the pre-trade empirical distribution. We consider a 5 min pre-trade matching interval. Two trades are matched if they are both either BIT or SIT, belong to the same trade-size category (from S1 to S6), and are preceded by similar market conditions (L1–L6), for every dimension, in the pre-trade matching interval. For each sample, the average trade size (standard deviation in the parentheses) and the number of TH trades finally matched, both in absolute terms and in relative terms (in the parentheses), are reported. We report separate findings for IDX stocks (index constituents) and NIDX stocks (thinly traded).

Table 4. Liquidity and order flow.

| | | Percentage of rejections at the 1% level ($H_0$: equality of medians) | | | | | | | | | |
| | | Ask side of the book | | | | | Bid side of the book | | | | |
| Variable | Test ($H_1$) | $t+1$ | $t+2$ | $t+3$ | $t+4$ | $t+5$ | $t+1$ | $t+2$ | $t+3$ | $t+4$ | $t+5$ |
|---|---|---|---|---|---|---|---|---|---|---|---|
| Panel A: all stocks | | | | | | | | | | | |
| $SPR_t$ | TH ≠ TO | 30.40 | 6.90 | 6.60 | 3.80 | 2.50 | 19.90 | 10.90 | 4.80 | 1.90 | 2.50 |
| | TH > TO | 0.00 | 0.00 | 0.00 | 0.10 | 0.00 | 0.00 | 0.00 | 0.00 | 0.00 | 0.00 |
| $ND_t$ | TH ≠ TO | 0.10 | 0.20 | 0.90 | 0.70 | 0.90 | 0.00 | 0.90 | 0.20 | 0.40 | 0.30 |
| | TH > TO | 0.00 | 0.00 | 0.00 | 0.00 | 0.00 | 0.00 | 0.90 | 0.20 | 0.40 | 0.30 |
| $NV_t$ | TH ≠ TO | 81.50 | 1.60 | 1.10 | 1.00 | 2.20 | 75.80 | 3.20 | 2.80 | 1.50 | 0.90 |
| | TH > TO | 81.50 | 1.50 | 1.10 | 1.00 | 2.20 | 0.00 | 0.00 | 0.00 | 0.00 | 0.10 |
| $NT_t$ | TH ≠ TO | 21.70 | 4.60 | 3.60 | 5.90 | 6.31 | 29.80 | 2.30 | 1.20 | 0.30 | 1.30 |
| | TH > TO | 21.70 | 4.60 | 3.60 | 5.90 | 6.31 | 0.00 | 0.00 | 0.10 | 0.10 | 0.30 |
| $NLO_t$ | TH ≠ TO | 18.88 | 4.21 | 4.41 | 2.60 | 1.91 | 8.52 | 0.71 | 0.70 | 0.90 | 0.90 |
| | TH > TO | 0.00 | 0.00 | 0.10 | 0.00 | 0.00 | 8.52 | 0.10 | 0.10 | 0.20 | 0.60 |
| Panel B: IDX stocks | | | | | | | | | | | |
| $SPR_t$ | TH ≠ TO | 28.30 | 7.50 | 6.50 | 4.20 | 2.90 | 27.20 | 13.30 | 6.31 | 4.60 | 3.80 |
| | TH > TO | 0.00 | 0.00 | 0.00 | 0.00 | 0.00 | 0.00 | 0.10 | 0.00 | 0.00 | 0.00 |
| $ND_t$ | TH ≠ TO | 0.10 | 0.60 | 1.10 | 1.10 | 0.60 | 0.00 | 0.20 | 0.30 | 0.50 | 0.60 |
| | TH > TO | 0.00 | 0.00 | 0.00 | 0.00 | 0.00 | 0.00 | 0.20 | 0.30 | 0.50 | 0.60 |
| $NV_t$ | TH ≠ TO | 78.40 | 1.80 | 2.10 | 3.40 | 2.40 | 67.60 | 4.60 | 4.60 | 2.30 | 1.90 |
| | TH > TO | 78.40 | 1.80 | 2.10 | 3.30 | 2.30 | 0.00 | 0.00 | 0.00 | 0.10 | 0.00 |
| $NT_t$ | TH ≠ TO | 20.04 | 4.11 | 2.80 | 3.41 | 4.40 | 24.90 | 1.81 | 1.10 | 0.40 | 0.70 |
| | TH > TO | 20.04 | 4.11 | 2.80 | 3.41 | 4.40 | 0.00 | 0.00 | 0.10 | 0.10 | 0.20 |
| $NLO_t$ | TH ≠ TO | 21.40 | 6.41 | 6.51 | 2.80 | 2.82 | 9.50 | 0.60 | 1.80 | 1.31 | 1.01 |
| | TH > TO | 0.00 | 0.00 | 0.00 | 0.00 | 0.10 | 9.50 | 0.20 | 0.30 | 0.20 | 0.40 |
| Panel C: NIDX stocks | | | | | | | | | | | |
| $SPR_t$ | TH ≠ TO | 45.80 | 14.00 | 3.10 | 2.00 | 1.30 | 0.60 | 0.50 | 1.60 | 1.30 | 1.30 |
| | TH > TO | 0.00 | 0.00 | 0.00 | 0.00 | 0.00 | 0.00 | 0.00 | 0.00 | 0.00 | 0.30 |
| $ND_t$ | TH ≠ TO | 0.00 | 1.30 | 1.30 | 1.20 | 0.60 | 0.00 | 4.00 | 0.90 | 1.30 | 2.30 |
| | TH > TO | 0.00 | 1.30 | 0.10 | 0.20 | 0.30 | 0.00 | 4.00 | 0.10 | 1.30 | 2.30 |
| $NV_t$ | TH ≠ TO | 98.20 | 0.40 | 22.30 | 35.10 | 1.81 | 100.00 | 4.12 | 0.40 | 0.50 | 6.05 |
| | TH > TO | 98.20 | 0.00 | 0.00 | 0.00 | 0.20 | 0.00 | 4.12 | 0.30 | 0.50 | 6.05 |
| $NT_t$ | TH ≠ TO | 51.36 | 16.60 | 34.27 | 27.53 | 68.57 | 71.47 | 11.70 | 14.50 | 8.63 | 18.84 |
| | TH > TO | 51.26 | 16.60 | 34.27 | 27.53 | 68.57 | 0.00 | 0.00 | 0.00 | 0.00 | 0.00 |
| $NLO_t$ | TH ≠ TO | 1.01 | 16.20 | 12.40 | 5.02 | 17.42 | 1.11 | 3.73 | 8.96 | 1.33 | 0.71 |
| | TH > TO | 1.01 | 16.20 | 12.40 | 5.02 | 17.42 | 0.70 | 0.00 | 8.96 | 1.23 | 0.00 |

Notes: The evidence on the impact of the hidden volume disclosure on both liquidity and order flow is provided. Liquidity is measured by the bid–ask spread (SPR) and the net (ask minus bid) quoted book depth (ND). The net (buyer- minus seller-initiated) share volume (NV), the net number of trades (NT), and the net number of limit orders submitted (NLO) stand for order flow composition. All these variables are standardized per stock and intraday time interval. TH trades reveal the presence of hidden volume on a given side of the LOB. TO trades are ordinary trades. All trades are separated into buyer-initiated and seller-initiated trades and further split into six trade-size categories (S1–S6). We report the results for the medium-sized (S4) trades only, that is, those with size between the 75% and 90% percentiles of the trade-size empirical distribution of the corresponding stock. We construct 1000 subsamples with 1000 matched TH and TO trades each. Two trades are matched if they have a similar size and the same sign (buyer/seller initiated) and are preceded by similar market conditions. To test the null of equal medians (TH = TO), we use the non-parametric Wilcoxon test. We provide the percentage of subsamples for which the null is rejected against (a) medians are different (TH ≠ TO) or (b) the median for the TH trades is bigger than the median for the matched TO trades (TH > TO). We consider the 5 min interval following the time stamp of each trade ($t$ in the table), and we apply the test minute by minute from $t+1$ to $t+5$ (with $t-5$ to $t-1$ being the matching interval). We report separate findings for IDX stocks (index constituents) and NIDX stocks (thinly traded).

Table 5. Returns and volatility.

| | | | Percentage of rejections at the 1% level ($H_0$: equality of medians) | | | | | | | |
| | | | Ask side of the book | | | | Bid side of the book | | | |
| Stocks | Trade-size category | Test (H1) | $t+5$ | $t+10$ | $t+30$ | Closing | $t+5$ | $t+10$ | $t+30$ | Closing |
|---|---|---|---|---|---|---|---|---|---|---|
| **Panel A: returns** | | | | | | | | | | |
| ALL | S2 (small) | TH $\neq$ TO | 6.81 | 6.11 | 4.60 | 2.00 | 11.41 | 7.21 | 2.00 | 5.40 |
| | | TH $>$ TO | 0.00 | 0.00 | 0.00 | 0.00 | 11.41 | 7.21 | 2.00 | 5.40 |
| | S4 (medium-sized) | TH $\neq$ TO | 7.01 | 5.42 | 5.00 | 6.60 | 5.30 | 3.50 | 6.10 | 8.20 |
| | | TH $>$ TO | 0.00 | 0.10 | 0.10 | 0.00 | 5.30 | 3.50 | 6.10 | 8.20 |
| | S6 (large) | TH $\neq$ TO | 14.93 | 10.80 | 15.40 | 18.50 | 11.10 | 13.30 | 24.70 | 6.70 |
| | | TH $>$ TO | 0.00 | 0.10 | 0.00 | 0.00 | 11.10 | 13.30 | 24.70 | 6.60 |
| IDX | S2 (small) | TH $\neq$ TO | 6.01 | 3.80 | 4.30 | 2.30 | 14.80 | 8.60 | 1.60 | 9.00 |
| | | TH $>$ TO | 0.00 | 0.00 | 0.00 | 0.20 | 14.80 | 8.60 | 1.40 | 9.00 |
| | S4 (medium-sized) | TH $\neq$ TO | 6.91 | 6.01 | 4.20 | 6.30 | 8.80 | 7.51 | 8.50 | 6.60 |
| | | TH $>$ TO | 0.00 | 0.00 | 0.00 | 0.00 | 8.80 | 7.51 | 8.50 | 6.60 |
| | S6 (large) | TH $\neq$ TO | 14.80 | 9.90 | 15.40 | 19.80 | 12.84 | 19.20 | 29.10 | 8.30 |
| | | TH $>$ TO | 0.00 | 0.00 | 0.00 | 0.00 | 12.84 | 19.20 | 29.10 | 8.30 |
| NIDX | S2 (small) | TH $\neq$ TO | 5.21 | 15.23 | 7.91 | 0.90 | 1.32 | 1.70 | 7.23 | 1.80 |
| | | TH $>$ TO | 0.00 | 0.00 | 0.00 | 0.70 | 0.91 | 1.20 | 7.23 | 0.00 |
| | S4 (medium-sized) | TH $\neq$ TO | 1.01 | 1.81 | 0.90 | 13.20 | 11.41 | 2.64 | 1.13 | 18.92 |
| | | TH $>$ TO | 0.90 | 0.10 | 0.40 | 0.00 | 0.00 | 0.10 | 1.03 | 18.92 |
| | S6 (large) | TH $\neq$ TO | 89.70 | 90.10 | 81.30 | 61.00 | 93.30 | 89.10 | 77.20 | 61.70 |
| | | TH $>$ TO | 30.20 | 18.80 | 19.30 | 24.00 | 31.50 | 25.20 | 17.20 | 50.30 |
| **Panel B: volatility** | | | | | | | | | | |
| ALL | S2 (small) | TH $\neq$ TO | 32.60 | 19.40 | 4.90 | 2.80 | 39.40 | 18.50 | 3.20 | 6.30 |
| | | TH $>$ TO | 0.00 | 0.00 | 0.00 | 2.80 | 0.00 | 0.00 | 0.00 | 6.30 |
| | S4 (medium-sized) | TH $\neq$ TO | 52.90 | 35.80 | 10.20 | 0.40 | 44.00 | 21.50 | 8.80 | 1.30 |
| | | TH $>$ TO | 0.00 | 0.00 | 0.00 | 0.20 | 0.00 | 0.00 | 0.00 | 1.30 |
| | S6 (large) | TH $\neq$ TO | 44.20 | 32.30 | 13.00 | 1.10 | 18.80 | 8.10 | 12.60 | 1.80 |
| | | TH $>$ TO | 0.00 | 0.00 | 0.00 | 0.80 | 0.00 | 0.00 | 0.00 | 1.80 |
| IDX | S2 (small) | TH $\neq$ TO | 30.20 | 11.20 | 2.70 | 1.50 | 35.40 | 18.00 | 2.40 | 6.70 |
| | | TH $>$ TO | 0.00 | 0.00 | 0.00 | 1.50 | 0.00 | 0.00 | 0.00 | 6.70 |
| | S4 (medium-sized) | TH $\neq$ TO | 52.60 | 34.10 | 8.00 | 0.20 | 49.40 | 23.20 | 10.80 | 1.00 |
| | | TH $>$ TO | 0.00 | 0.00 | 0.00 | 0.10 | 0.00 | 0.00 | 0.00 | 0.90 |
| | S6 (large) | TH $\neq$ TO | 54.50 | 39.30 | 15.20 | 1.60 | 25.00 | 10.20 | 11.60 | 3.00 |
| | | TH $>$ TO | 0.00 | 0.00 | 0.00 | 1.50 | 0.00 | 0.00 | 0.00 | 3.00 |
| NIDX | S2 (small) | TH $\neq$ TO | 44.00 | 84.10 | 49.70 | 6.40 | 78.30 | 39.00 | 38.18 | 0.30 |
| | | TH $>$ TO | 0.00 | 0.00 | 0.00 | 6.40 | 0.00 | 0.00 | 0.00 | 0.20 |
| | S4 (medium-sized) | TH $\neq$ TO | 58.30 | 74.20 | 67.90 | 6.20 | 19.10 | 22.02 | 6.80 | 2.10 |
| | | TH $>$ TO | 0.00 | 0.00 | 0.00 | 0.00 | 0.00 | 0.00 | 0.00 | 2.00 |
| | S6 (large) | TH $\neq$ TO | 7.50 | 6.40 | 7.50 | 13.60 | 1.40 | 1.60 | 27.20 | 1.00 |
| | | TH $>$ TO | 0.00 | 0.00 | 0.00 | 0.00 | 1.30 | 0.00 | 0.00 | 0.10 |

Notes: The impact of hidden volume on stock returns (Panel A) and volatility (Panel B) when it is revealed is summarized. For each trade, we compute the post-trade mid-quote returns ($QR_t$) and the mid-quote volatility ($QV_t$) as

$$QR_t = \log\left(\frac{Q_\tau}{Q_t}\right) \quad \text{and} \quad QV_t = \left(\frac{\log(\bar{Q}_t^\tau)}{\log(\underline{Q}_t^\tau)}\right) - 1,$$

where $\tau > t$ defines four different time intervals ($\tau - t$): 5, 10, 30 min and until the end of the trading session; $Q$ is the quote midpoint; and $\bar{Q}_t^\tau$ ($\underline{Q}_t^\tau$) is the maximum (minimum) of $Q$ in the interval $(t, \tau)$. We standardize these variables per stock and half-hour interval of the trading session. We consider the same trade-size categories that have been considered in Table 4. We report the results for the small (S2), medium-sized (S4), and large (S6) trades. We construct 1000 subsamples with 1000 matched TH and TO trades each. Two trades are matched if they have a similar size and the same sign (buyer/seller initiated) and are preceded by similar market conditions in a 5 min window before their time stamp. To test the null of equality of medians (TH = TO), we use the non-parametric Wilcoxon test. We provide the percentage of subsamples for which the null is rejected at the 1% level against the alternative (a) the medians are different (TH $\neq$ TO) or (b) the median for the TH trades is bigger than the median for the matched TO trades (TH $>$ TO). We report separate findings for IDX stocks (index constituents) and NIDX stocks (thinly traded).

on ask and bid sides of the LOB is found either (not reported). In conclusion, our findings do not agree with the market perceiving an increase in adverse selection costs when hidden volume is detected.

The strongest effect reported in Table 4 is the sudden increase in the aggressiveness of traders after an HLO is exposed. In 81.5% (75.8%) of the subsamples, we reject the null of equal $NV_t$ one minute after hidden volume is revealed on the offer (bid) side of the book. Incoming traders, however, do not mimic HLO traders. We observe a negative (positive) $NV_t$ when iceberg orders to buy (sell) are exposed. A similar, though weaker, pattern is observed for the net number of trades ($NT_t$), with percentages of rejection of 21.7% and 29.8%, respectively. Regarding limit order submissions, the equality of $NLO_t$ is infrequently rejected, with percentages of only 18.88% and 8.52%, respectively. The direction of the rejection is, however, consistent with traders reacting when hidden volume has been disclosed on the opposite side of the market. Once more, our findings are at odds with market participants assigning information content to the hidden side of liquidity: the revelation of hidden volume on the ask (bid) side of the book is not interpreted as a negative (positive) signal about the true value of the asset. Instead, traders react immediately to seize the hidden side of liquidity as soon as it is revealed. Therefore, the revelation of hidden volume fosters order aggressiveness by those traders that closely monitor the market.

Order aggressiveness has been the subject of many previous empirical studies, such as Biais, Hillion, and Spatt (1995); Ranaldo (2004); and Pascual and Veredas (2009). These papers used ordered probit models to analyze the relationship between the state of the LOB and the choice between market and limit orders. All these papers, however, ignored hidden volume. Our findings qualify previous papers by showing that hidden volume revelation is a relevant determinant of order choice by incoming traders. In a recent paper, De Winne and D'Hondt (2007) built on our empirical analysis and findings to justify the inclusion of hidden volume detection in the usual ordered probit model for order aggressiveness. They concluded that (a) hidden volume can be detected; (b) traders respond to the detection of hidden volume on the opposite side of the market by adjusting their order submission strategies; and (c) traders do not link hidden orders to informed trading. Their conclusions can be inferred from our empirical findings.

Panels B and C in Table 4 provide the findings for the subsamples of IDX and NIDX stocks, respectively. In general, the findings for the two subsamples do not differ from those reported in Panel A. For IDX (NIDX) stocks, the null of equal $NV_t$ 1 min after hidden volume is revealed on the ask side of the book is rejected for 78.4% (98.2%) of the subsamples against the alternative that $NV_t$ is unusually high and positive; the null of equal $NT_t$ after hidden volume is disclosed on the ask side of the book is rejected for 20.4% (51.36%) of the subsamples against the same alternative. When hidden volume is revealed on the bid side, in 67.6% (24.9%) of the IDX subsamples, the null of equality is rejected, with $NV_t$ ($NT_t$) being unusually negative. For NIDX stocks, the percentage of rejection in the same direction is even higher, 100% (71.47%) Therefore, our evidence shows that the effect of hidden volume revelation on order aggressiveness is more pronounced among NIDX stocks. The latter conclusion is remarkable because it indicates that even among the less frequently traded stocks in the SSE, we can find traders that closely monitor the evolution of the LOB. In a recent paper, Liu (2009) argued that because of the higher costs of monitoring limit orders, small cap traders tend to place less aggressive limit orders (resulting in wider bid–ask spreads) and revise them less frequently than large cap traders. In contrast, our findings suggest that small cap traders still keep an eye on the market in search for depth improvement opportunities. Intuitively, the possibility of buying or selling larger quantities than displayed at the same immediacy cost induces traders to submit more aggressive orders. This effect, however, dissipates quickly, since from $t + 2$ onwards, the null hypothesis is rarely rejected.

Table 5 summarizes our findings regarding post-trade mid-quote returns ($QR_t$) and mid-quote volatility ($QV_t$). We report findings for three trade-size categories: S2 (small-sized trades), S4 (medium-sized trades), and S6 (large-sized trades). In seminal adverse selection models, such as those proposed by Kyle (1985) and Glosten and Milgrom (1985), informed traders exploit their information advantage through trading, whereas uninformed traders learn from observing the trading process. Moreover, the existence of a positive connection between the direction of trades and the subsequent price changes is one of the most corroborated empirical findings (see Glosten and Harris 1988; Hasbrouck 1991, among many others). Likewise, if undisclosed depth were information motivated, we would expect uninformed traders to revise downwards (upwards) their expectation about the true value of the asset in response to the detection of hidden volume on the ask (bid) side of the LOB. As a result, we would expect to find a positive (negative) price impact ($QR_t$) immediately after hidden volume is revealed on the bid (ask) side of the LOB. Table 5 (Panel A), however, reports weak differences in stock returns after TH and TO trades. Among the S2 and S4 trade-size categories, percentages of rejection are generally below 15%, independently of the time horizon considered. When rejected, however, they are in the expected direction: when hidden volume comes into view on the ask (bid) side, the null is rejected against the alternative TH < TO (TH > TO), suggesting that prices move in the direction of the hidden volume. For the S6 category, the percentage of rejection slightly increases, suggesting that the inferences drawn by market participants about the information content of hidden volume may depend on the size of the TH trade exposing the HLO. In any case, the percentage of rejection is never above the 25% in the 30 minute interval following the detection of hidden volume and never above the 20% at the end of the trading session.

Panel A in Table 5 also provides separate findings for IDX stocks and NIDX stocks. For the IDX stocks, the findings are similar to those discussed above for the complete sample. With regard to NIDX stocks, we find low percentages of rejection for the S2 and S4 categories, but a high percentage of rejection for the S6 category, around 60% at the end of the trading session. Nonetheless, the results concerning the sign of the difference in median returns are inconclusive. Thus, when hidden volume is detected on the ask side of the book, the null is rejected more frequently against the alternative TH < TO, consistent with our prediction. However, when hidden volume is exposed on the bid side, the null is usually rejected against the same alternative (TH < TO), which is inconsistent with the claim that exposing hidden depth on the bid side is always a positive signal for the marketplace.

Regarding volatility, previous empirical literature reports a positive connection between information asymmetry risk and volatility (e.g. Lee, Mucklow, and Ready 1993). If hidden volume were informative, we would expect volatility to increase as soon as it is exposed. Moreover, exposing an HLO could cause other traders to withdraw liquidity if they infer that it is information motivated, causing subsequent trades to have a larger temporary price impact. Panel B in Table 5 shows that the null of equal volatility after matched TH and TO trades is only rejected with remarkable strength in the 5 min interval that follows the trades. Across trade-size categories, the average percentage of rejection is 43.23% (34.07%) when hidden volume is revealed on the offer (bid) side of the LOB. Unexpectedly, however, volatility tends to be lower after TH trades than after TO trades. This finding is robust across trade-size categories (S1–S6) and across market capitalization subsamples (IDX and NIDX stocks). In any case, the volatility effect of hidden volume disclosure dissipates quickly.[17]

In summary, our findings suggest that HLOs induce traders on the opposite side of the market to act more aggressively in the very short term, probably fostered by the depth improvement opportunity. Hidden volume exposure tends to reduce short-term volatility and has very limited impact on daily returns, which is inconsistent with the hidden side of liquidity conveying information about the true value of the stock. Although the null of equal stock returns is sometimes rejected in the expected direction, our findings are more favorable to the assumption that hidden volume is liquidity motivated. Recently, Bessembinder, Panayides, and Venkataraman (2009) have shown that HLOs are associated with lower execution costs but more time to completion, a trade-off that seems more consistent with the reasoning that HLOs tend to be used by uninformed traders. Our findings are totally consistent.

## 6. Summary and conclusions

In this article, we studied the market reaction to the exposure of hidden depth in the LOB. We used high-frequency data from an electronic order-driven market, the SSE. In the SSE, iceberg orders have a relatively small displayed volume unit and are less exposed than those in other markets. Hidden volume is only detected when an iceberg order is totally or partially executed and the transaction consumes more liquidity than is displayed at the best quotes.

We found that when hidden volume is detected, traders in the market do not mimic HLO traders. Instead, we observed that traders on the opposite side of the market that closely follow the evolution of the trading process turn out to be more aggressive immediately after they become aware of the presence of hidden volume. These traders exploit the opportunity to buy or sell more than expected at the best quotes. This effect vanishes as soon as the hidden volume is finally consumed. We also showed that volatility decreases but also in the very short run. Finally, no remarkable daily price impact arises from the detection of hidden volume.

Certainly, iceberg orders could be used by both informed and uninformed traders. Our findings do not necessarily discard informed traders choosing iceberg orders sometimes. However, considering the big picture, our evidence suggests that market participants do not attribute relevant information content to the hidden volume in the LOB. Our findings are consistent with recent empirical evidence from other order-driven markets, such as Euronext.

## Acknowledgements

We thank Yakov Amihud, Ingmar Nolte, Bruce N. Lehmann, Julio J. Lucia, Gideon Saar, Mikel Tapia, Daniel G. Weaver, an anonymous referee, seminar participants at ECARES (Université Libre de Bruxelles, Belgium), and conference participants in the XII *Foro de Finanzas* (Barcelona, Spain), MICFINMA Conference in Tilburg (The Netherlands), and VII Spanish–Italian Conference on Financial Mathematics (Cuenca, Spain) for their suggestions and comments. We gratefully acknowledge helpful discussions with 10 practitioners from Spanish fund managers and financial services organizations (Bancaja, CAM, Fibanc, Gesamed, Inverseguros, and Morgan Stanley). Roberto Pascual also acknowledges the financial sponsorship of the Fulbright Grant and the Spanish Ministry of Education, Culture and Sports and the financial support of the Spanish DGICYT project ECO2010-18567. We thank *Sociedad de Bolsas* for providing the database. Financial support for this project was also obtained from the *Instituto Valenciano de Investigaciones Económicas* (IVIE) and the *Cátedra Finanzas Internacionales – Banco Santander*. A former version of this article was awarded with the 2004 Joseph de La Vega Prize by the Federation of European Securities Exchanges (FESE). The first version of this article was finished while Roberto Pascual was a visiting scholar at the New York University Salomon Center.

## Notes

1. To name a few: ASX, Copenhagen Stock Exchange, Deutsche Börse (XETRA), Euronext, NASDAQ ECNs, Milan Stock Exchange, Oslo Stock Exchange, SSE, Stockholm Stock Exchange, SWX Swiss Exchange, TSX, and Warsaw Stock Exchange.
2. Baruch (2005) theoretically concluded that higher pre-trade transparency must increase market efficiency and liquidity. Empirical and experimental evidence, however, is very inconclusive as to whether market quality is enhanced by

increased pre-trade transparency. Thus, Hendershott and Jones (2005) showed that when the Island ECN stopped displaying the LOB of exchange-traded funds in 2002, Island's share of trading activity and price discovery fell. Flood et al. (1999) provided experimental evidence of less transparent venues being less efficient and less liquid. In contrast, Simaan, Weaver, and Whitcomb (2003) concluded that making the level of pre-trade transparency on NASDAQ more opaque could improve price competition and narrow spreads further. Madhavan, Porter, and Weaver (2005) also reported reduced liquidity, increased volatility, and higher execution costs after the LOB of the TSX was publicly displayed.

3. Certainly, limit order traders might protect themselves from an elevated exposure risk using other strategies rather than submitting HLOs. For example, by breaking up their large orders into small ones and spreading them over time, the limit order traders may reduce both the probability of being front-run and the price impact of their orders. They can also cancel and modify orders more frequently or simply switch to market orders. These alternative strategies, however, might increase the traders' transaction costs.

4. To name a few, HLOs are remarkably more important in the ASX than in the TSX: 28% and 7% of the share volume submitted and less than 4% and 1% of all orders submitted, respectively. ASX and TSX differ in the minimum displayed volume requirements for HLOs. In the ASX, the minimum displayed volume unit was \$10,000 before October 1994, \$25,000 between October 1994 and October 1996, and \$100,000 afterwards. In the TSX, the displayed threshold for stock trading for more than \$1/share was set to 2000 shares when HLOs were reintroduced in April 2002 (5000 shares before 1996). This means that for a stock trading at \$5, the ASX regulation was as permissive as the TSX regulation in 1996, but after 2002, the ASX regulation became more restrictive. Finally, HLOs lose time precedence in the TSX, but not in the ASX.

5. Aitken, Berkman, and Mak (2001) also studied the stock price behavior around HLO submissions by comparing matched samples of HLOs and disclosed limit orders (DLOs). They concluded that HLOs are not more informative than DLOs. In the ASX, however, HLOs are exposed to the market since the quantity field on the ASX-SEATS displays a 'U' for undisclosed, visible for all market participants. In this context, informed traders may be less willing to submit HLOs since the mark would signal the stock being wrongly priced, increasing the non-execution risk of the HLO. Therefore, the microstructure of these markets may not be appropriate for evaluating the attractiveness of HLOs for liquidity and informed traders in a more general context.

6. Those stocks that do not comply with these requirements are assigned to a single-auction-based market called 'Fixing' where trades are only possible twice a day.

7. Pre-arranged trades are possible, but only at the so-called Block Market and Off-Hours Market. The Block Market opens from 9.00 a.m. to 5.30 p.m. and the Off-Hours Market opens from 5.40 to 8.00 p.m. These segments allow market members to manage large volume orders, but under very rigid price and minimum size conditions. Data about these particular sections of the market are excluded from our database. There are also two daily call auctions that determine the official opening and closing prices that we do not consider either. In this paper, we concentrate exclusively on the continuous trading session.

8. For more complete and detailed information on the SSE regulation, organization, and trading procedures, please visit http://www.sbolsas.es.

9. The IBEX-35 is composed of the 35 most liquid and active SSE-listed stocks during the most recent 6-month control period. The composition is ordinarily revised twice a year, but extraordinary revisions are possible due to major events, like mergers or new stock issues.

10. Briefly, a cancellation produces no increase in the accumulated trading volume and cuts the number of orders in the LOB by 1 unit. A modification causes neither an increase in the accumulated trading volume nor a decrease in the number of orders in the LOB, but it changes the available depth. A limit order augments the accumulated depth in the LOB and the number of orders supporting the limit order price (by 1 unit), but it does not have an effect on the accumulated trading volume. In this case, the increase in the accumulated depth is equal to the size of the limit order except when it is an HLO. Like the cancellation case, a market order may also reduce the number of orders stored in the LOB, but it increases the accumulated trading volume. The change in the accumulated trading volume is equal to the size of the market order. Finally, a market-to-limit order that demands fewer shares than available on the best opposite quote is undistinguishable from a market order. However, an aggressive market-to-limit order consumes the best opposite quote and the unexecuted part is stored in the LOB at the limit price.

11. We have discussed the output of the algorithm with market members and supervisors, and all of them agree with us on this assertion. Other possible explanations are discarded. For example, two market orders cannot interact with each other except when the book is empty on one side (a very rare event). Besides, each update in the LOB corresponds to a single order, that is, two or more orders cannot be registered in the book simultaneously (recall that LOB updates are recorded at the nearest hundredth of a second). Therefore, a limit order and a market order cannot interact with each other before the limit order is stored in the LOB.

12. We discard the largest trades because they are so unusual that they become very difficult to match.
13. Following the suggestion of an anonymous referee, we have replicated all our empirical analyses by using a more complex and restrictive matching algorithm. We have imposed that any TO trade to be matched with a given TH trade must be executed in a different session and that it must be time-stamped within a 1 h window around the TH trade. We have extended the set of variables defining the pre-trade market conditions by including the total (buys plus sells) number of trades, the total volume traded in shares, the number of limit orders submitted, and the LOB depth (ask plus bid side). The findings obtained with this alternative matching algorithm do not remarkably differ from those reported in this paper. These additional analyses are available upon request from the authors.
14. For details on the non-parametric Wilcoxon rank-sum test, see Gibbons and Chakraborti (2003, 298–307).
15. We only report the findings for the first two alternatives. The third alternative ($H_1$: TH < TO) is redundant, given the results for the other two. In any case, the results are available upon request from the authors.
16. Copeland and Galai (1983) and Glosten and Milgrom (1985), for price-driven markets, and more recently Glosten (1994); Handa, Schwartz, and Tiwari (2003); and Goettler, Parlour, and Rajan (2005), for order-driven markets, emphasized the role of adverse selection costs.
17. As noted by an anonymous referee, the analysis summarized in Table 5 can be distorted by TH trades that occur within the 10 and 30 min intervals considered after each trade or until the end of the continuous trading session. Unfortunately, it is very difficult to find in our sample TH trades that are not followed by other TH trades with time windows like those we considered in the later analysis.

# References

Aitken, M.J., H. Berkman, and D. Mak. 2001. The use of undisclosed limit orders on the Australian Stock Exchange. *Journal of Banking and Finance* 25, no. 8: 1589–603.

Anand, A., and D.G. Weaver. 2004. Can order exposure be mandated? *Journal of Financial Markets* 7, no. 4: 405–26.

Anand, A., S. Chakravarty, and T. Martell. 2005. Empirical evidence on the evolution of liquidity: choice of market versus limit orders by informed and uninformed traders. *Journal of Financial Markets* 8, no. 3: 288–309.

Baruch, S. 2005. Who benefits from an open limit order book? *Journal of Business* 78, no. 4: 1267–306.

Bessembinder, H., M. Panayides, and K. Venkataraman. 2009. Hidden liquidity: an analysis of order exposure strategies in electronic stock markets. *Journal of Financial Economics* 94, no. 3: 361–83.

Biais, B., P. Hillion, and C. Spatt. 1995. An empirical analysis of the limit order book and the order flow in the Paris Bourse. *Journal of Finance* 50, no. 5: 1655–89.

Bloomfield, R., M. O'Hara, and G. Saar. 2005. The 'make or take' decision in an electronic market: evidence on the evolution of liquidity. *Journal of Financial Economics* 75, no. 1: 165–99.

Boehmer, E., G. Saar, and L. Yu. 2005. Lifting the veil: an analysis of pre-trade transparency at the NYSE. *Journal of Finance* 60, no. 2: 783–815.

Caglio, C., and K.A. Kavajecz. 2006. A specialist's quoted depth as a strategic choice: an application to spread decomposition models. *Journal of Financial Research* 29, no. 3: 367–82.

Copeland, T.E., and D. Galai. 1983. Information effects on the bid-ask spread. *Journal of Finance* 38, no. 5: 1457–69.

Degryse, H. 1999. The total costs of trading Belgian shares: Brussels versus London. *Journal of Banking and Finance* 23, no. 9: 1331–55.

De Winne, R., and C. D'Hondt. 2007. Hide-and-seek in the market: placing and detecting hidden orders. *Review of Finance* 11, no. 4: 663–92.

D'Hondt, C., R. De Winne, and A. François-Heude. 2001. Hidden orders: an empirical study on the French segment of Euro. NM. University of Perpignan and FUCaM working paper.

D'Hondt, C., R. De Winne, and A. François-Heude. 2004. Hidden orders on Euronext: nothing is quite as it seems. University of Perpignan and FUCaM working paper.

Flood, M.D., R. Huisman, K.G. Koedijk, and R.J. Mahieu. 1999. Quote disclosure and price discovery in multiple-dealer financial markets. *Review of Financial Studies* 12, no. 1: 37–59.

Foucault, T., S. Moinas, and E. Theissen. 2007. Does anonymity matter in electronic limit order markets? *Review of Financial Markets* 20, no. 5: 1707–47.

Garfinkel, J.A., and M. Nimalendran. 2003. Market structure and trader anonymity: an analysis of insider trading. *Journal of Financial and Quantitative Analysis* 38, no. 3: 591–610.

Gibbons, J.D., and S. Chakraborti. 2003. *Nonparametric statistical inference*. 4th edn. New York: Marcel Dekker.

Glosten, L.R. 1994. Is the electronic limit order book inevitable? *Journal of Finance* 49, no. 4: 1127–61.

Glosten, L.R., and L.E. Harris. 1988. Estimating the components of the bid/ask spread. *Journal of Financial Economics* 21, no. 1: 123–42.

Glosten, L.R., and P.R. Milgrom. 1985. Bid, ask and transaction prices in a specialist market with heterogeneously informed traders. *Journal of Financial Economics* 14, no. 1: 71–100.

Goettler, R.L., C.A. Parlour, and U. Rajan. 2005. Equilibrium in a dynamic limit order market. *Journal of Finance* 60, no. 5: 2149–92.

Handa, P., R.A. Schwartz, and A. Tiwari. 2003. Quote setting and price formation in an order driven market. *Journal of Financial Markets* 6, no. 4: 461–89.

Harris, L.E. 1996. Does a minimum price variation encourage order exposure? Marshall School of Business working paper.

Harris, L.E. 1998. Optimal dynamic order submission strategies in some stylized trading problems. *Financial Markets, Institutions, and Instruments* 7, no. 2: 26–74.

Harris, L. 2003. *Trading & exchanges. Market microstructure for practitioners.* Financial Management Association Survey and Synthesis Series. New York: Oxford University Press.

Harris, L.E., and V. Panchapagesan. 2005. The information content of the limit order book: evidence from NYSE specialist trading decisions. *Journal of Financial Markets* 8, no. 1: 25–67.

Hasbrouck, J. 1991. Measuring the information content of stock trades. *Journal of Finance* 46, no. 1: 179–207.

Hasbrouck, J., and G. Saar. 2002. Limit orders and volatility in a hybrid market: The Island ECN. Stern School of Business, New York University working paper.

Hendershott, T., and C.M. Jones. 2005. Island goes dark: transparency, fragmentation, and regulation. *Review of Financial Studies* 18, no. 3: 743–93.

Kaniel, R., and H. Liu. 2006. So what orders do informed traders use? *Journal of Business* 79, no. 4: 1867–913.

Kavajecz, K.A. 1999. A specialist's quoted depth and the limit order book. *Journal of Finance* 54, no. 2: 747–71.

Kyle, A.S. 1985. Continuous auctions and insider trading. *Econometrica* 53, no. 6: 1315–35.

Lee, C.M.C., B. Mucklow, and M.J. Ready. 1993. Spreads, depths, and the impact of earnings information: an intraday analysis. *Review of Financial Studies* 6, no. 2: 345–74.

Liu, W.M. 2009. Monitoring and limit order submission risks. *Journal of Financial Markets* 12, no. 1: 107–41.

Madhavan, A. 2000. Market microstructure: a survey. *Journal of Financial Markets* 3, no. 3: 205–58.

Madhavan, A., D. Porter, and D. Weaver. 2005. Should security markets be transparent? *Journal of Financial Markets* 8, no. 3: 265–88.

Moinas, S. 2005. Hidden limit orders and liquidity in limit order markets. HEC School of Management working paper.

Naik, N.Y., A. Neuberger, and S. Viswanathan. 1999. Trade disclosure regulation in market with negotiated trades. *Review of Financial Studies* 12, no. 4: 873–900.

Pagano, M., and A. Roëll. 1996. Transparency and liquidity: a comparison of auction and dealer markets with informed trading. *Journal of Finance* 51, no. 2: 579–611.

Pascual, R., and D. Veredas. 2009. What pieces of limit order book information matter in explaining order choice by patient and impatient traders? *Quantitative Finance* 9, no. 5: 527–45.

Ranaldo, A. 2004. Order aggressiveness in limit order book markets. *Journal of Financial Markets* 7, no. 1: 53–74.

Simaan, Y., D.G. Weaver, and D.K. Whitcomb. 2003. Market maker quotation behavior and pretrade transparency. *Journal of Finance* 58, no. 3: 1247–67.

Tuttle, L. 2006. Hidden orders, trading costs and information. Fisher College of Business working paper.

# Price discovery in spot and futures markets: a reconsideration

Erik Theissen

*Finance Area, University of Mannheim, Mannheim, Germany*

We reconsider the issue of price discovery in spot and futures markets. We use a threshold error correction model to allow for arbitrage opportunities to have an impact on the return dynamics. We estimate the model using quote midpoints, and we modify the model to account for time-varying transaction costs. We find that (a) the futures market leads in the process of price discovery and (b) the presence of arbitrage opportunities has a strong impact on the dynamics of the price discovery process.

## 1. Introduction

Which market impounds new information faster into prices, the index futures market or the spot market? Transaction costs are lower in the futures market. Given that the magnitude of the transaction costs determines whether a trader can profitably trade on a given piece of information, the adjustment of prices to market-wide information (e.g. announcements of macroeconomic variables) should be faster in the futures market. In contrast, traders possessing information about the value of individual stocks will most likely trade that stock rather than the whole index.[1] Consequently, stock-specific information should be reflected in the spot market first.

The issue of the relative contributions of spot and futures markets to the process of price discovery is of obvious importance and consequently has received considerable attention in the literature. Most previous studies (to be surveyed briefly in Section 2) have compared index values computed from the prices of the component stocks to index futures prices. However, investors nowadays can also trade in shares of exchange-traded funds (ETFs) which replicate the index. ETF shares are a close substitute for the index portfolio, and their bid-ask spreads are low. Consequently, ETF shares should allow for low-cost index arbitrage.

The standard methodology to analyse price discovery is to estimate an error correction model (ECM). Applying this methodology to data on equity index values and futures prices is fraught with several problems which make straight estimation of the model troublesome. First, the constituent stocks of the index trade infrequently. Consequently, index values are partially based on stale prices. The infrequent trading effect together with bid–ask bounce introduces distinct serial correlation patterns into the time series of index returns, which may induce a spurious lead of the futures market. Although Stoll and Whaley (1990) have proposed a method to purge the return data of the infrequent trading effects, it is much less clear how the index level data needed in the estimation of the ECM can be purged of those effects. Second, the cointegrating relation between index levels and index futures prices implied by the cost-of-carry model is not constant over time but rather changes daily. Third, the standard ECM implies that the speed of adjustment of prices to deviations from the long-run equilibrium relation is independent of the size of the deviation. This is not necessarily the case, however, because arbitrageurs will start trading when the deviation is larger than the expected round-trip transaction cost. Their trading activity is likely to speed the adjustment. ETF prices do not suffer from an infrequent trading problem. All other problems alluded to above, however, are also relevant in analyses using ETF data instead of equity index values.

One potential solution to the infrequent trading (and bid-ask bounce) problem, first proposed by Shyy, Vijayraghavan, and Scott-Quinn (1996), is to use quote midpoints rather than prices. The time variability of the cointegrating relationship can be accounted for by either demeaning the log price series as proposed by Dwyer, Locke, and Yu (1996) or by using discounted futures prices as is done by Kempf and Korn (1996) and Martens, Kofman, and Vorst (1998). Finally, a threshold ECM (TECM) allows the adjustment coefficients to depend on the magnitude of the deviation from the long-run equilibrium relation and is thus able to account for the presence of arbitrageurs (Dwyer, Locke, and Yu 1996).

The present article contributes to this line of research. We use data from the German blue chip index DAX, the most liquid ETF replicating the DAX, and the DAX futures contract traded on the EUREX to assess the contributions to price discovery of the spot and futures markets. As suggested above, we use quote midpoint data, demeaned log price series, and a TECM. The contribution of our article is twofold. First, we modify the TECM to allow for time-varying transaction costs. Previous papers (Dwyer, Locke, and Yu 1996; Martens, Kofman, and Vorst 1998) have estimated the threshold transaction costs (i.e. the size of the deviation of prices from their long-run equilibrium that allows arbitrageurs to break even) and implicitly assumed the costs to be constant. It is, however, well established that bid-ask spreads follow a distinct intraday pattern. In our data set, the third quartile of the spread distribution is between 1.5 and 2 times larger than the first quartile, and the 95% quantile is between 2 and 6 times larger than the 5% quantile. Consequently, the price deviation that allows for profitable arbitrage varies substantially. Our article is the first to allow for this time variation by making the threshold dependent on the bid-ask spreads in the two markets. Second, this is the first article to estimate a TECM using midquote data. This is potentially important because arbitrage signals should be based on tradable prices (i.e. bid and ask quotes) rather than on past transaction prices. Another distinctive feature of our article is that all markets under scrutiny are electronic limit order markets. Consequently, the results are unlikely to be caused by differences in market microstructure.

Our results can be summarized as follows. The futures market dominates the price discovery process. Returns in the spot market depend much more heavily on lagged returns in the futures market than vice versa. When measuring the contributions to price discovery, we also find that the futures market leads. We further find that the dynamics of the adjustment process is different when arbitrage opportunities exist. This finding underpins the importance of taking the existence of arbitrage opportunities explicitly into account.

The article is structured as follows. Section 2 provides a brief survey of the literature. Section 3 describes the data set and presents some descriptive statistics. Methodology and results of our empirical analysis are presented in Section 4. Section 5 concludes.

## 2. A brief review of the literature

Empirical analysis of the relation between stock index values and index futures prices is complicated by methodological problems. Stocks in the spot market are not traded simultaneously. Consequently, the index is partially calculated from stale prices.[2] This introduces positive serial correlation in the index returns, which, in turn, may introduce a spurious lead-lag relation. Further, bid-ask bounce may induce negative serial correlation in the return series. Stoll and Whaley (1990) propose to estimate an autoregressive moving average (ARMA) model for the index returns and to use the innovations from the model rather than the index returns to analyse the lead-lag relation between the spot and the futures markets. Using a vector autoregressive (VAR) model, they find that the futures market leads the stock market by about 5 min. The general result that the futures market leads the spot market has, despite all methodological differences, been confirmed in subsequent research. A notable exception is Shyy, Vijayraghavan, and Scott-Quinn (1996). These authors confirm the result of a lead of the futures markets when basing their estimates on price data. Estimation based on quote midpoints, on the other hand, leads to the reverse conclusion that the spot market leads.

The VAR approach does not take into account that index values and futures prices are cointegrated. What is required instead is an ECM. Different approaches at estimating an ECM have been proposed. Some authors have estimated the cointegrating relationship (e.g. Shyy, Vijayraghavan, and Scott-Quinn 1996; Bose 2007), but the more common approach is to use a pre-specified cointegrating vector based on the theoretical cost-of-carry relation (e.g. Dwyer, Locke, and Yu 1996; Fleming, Ostdiek, and Whaley 1996; Kempf and Korn 1996; Martens, Kofman, and Vorst 1998; Booth, So, and Tse 1999; Tse 2001; Schlusche 2009).

Two issues deserve attention. First, the cost-of-carry relation $F_t = S_t e^{r(T-t)}$ implies that the cointegrating relation is not constant over time but rather changes daily.[3] Many previous papers do not take that into account. There are, however, some notable exceptions. Dwyer, Locke, and Yu (1996) subtract the daily mean from the time series of log prices before estimating the ECM. Kempf and Korn (1996), Martens, Kofman, and Vorst (1998), and, more recently, Schlusche (2009) use discounted futures prices. These should, according to the cost-of-carry relation, be equal to the spot prices.

The second issue is related to the infrequent trading problem. The ECM is usually estimated using simple log returns. These returns do, however, suffer from the infrequent trading problem addressed above. Some authors (e.g. Fleming, Ostdiek, and Whaley 1996; Kempf and Korn 1996; Pizzi, Economopoulos, and O'Neill 1998) have used ARMA residuals rather than log returns when estimating the ECM. The problem with this approach is that it combines an error correction term directly derived from the index and futures price levels with the ARMA residuals in one model, thereby introducing a sort of inconsistency into the model. A convenient way to circumvent this problem[4] is to use quote midpoints rather than transaction prices (e.g. Shyy, Vijayraghavan, and Scott-Quinn 1996). Midpoints are based on firm quotes and thus should not suffer from an infrequent trading problem. Further, there is no bid-ask bounce in quote data.

The standard ECM specification implies that whenever prices deviate from the long-run equilibrium relation (which, in turn, is given by the cost-of-carry relation), there is a tendency for prices to adjust. The size of the adjustment coefficient is independent of the magnitude of the deviation. Several authors have argued that this is likely to be an incomplete description of the adjustment process. When deviations from the long-run equilibrium are larger than the round-trip transaction costs, arbitrageurs step in, thereby speeding the adjustment process. The resulting dynamics can be captured by a TECM. This approach was pioneered by Yadav, Pope, and Paudyal (1994) and subsequently adopted by Dwyer, Locke, and Yu (1996), Kempf and Korn (1996), and Martens, Kofman, and Vorst (1998).

In these papers, the TECM is estimated using transaction price data. Thus, it is assumed that a sufficiently large deviation between lagged futures prices and lagged spot index values triggers an arbitrage signal. However, arbitrageurs cannot trade at these prices. This is particularly true for the spot index because the calculation of the index value is partially based on stale prices. It would be preferable to construct the arbitrage signal from quote data because trades can actually be executed at these prices. Data on bid and ask quotes are, however, not usually available from open outcry futures markets.

A second implicit assumption made in previous papers is that the transaction cost and, consequently, the price difference triggering an arbitrage signal is constant. This is not necessarily the case, though. The most important determinant of the transaction cost is the bid–ask spread. The spread, however, is time-varying. Some of the variation is caused by distinct intraday patterns. Consequently, a model that assumes constant round-trip transaction costs may fail to fully capture the dynamics of the adjustment process. The methodology used in the present paper takes the time-varying nature of transaction costs explicitly into account.

Analysing the relation between index ETF prices and index futures prices poses less problems because ETF prices do not suffer from an infrequent trading problem. The other issues addressed above – the specification of the cointegrating relationship and the implications of the (potentially time-varying) transaction costs for the adjustment process – are, however, still relevant. We are aware of four papers that analyse price discovery in ETF and futures markets. None of these papers has estimated a TECM. Hasbrouck (2003) and Schlusche (2009) find that the futures market dominates price discovery. Tse, Bandyopadhyay, and Shen (2006) report more differentiated results. The contribution of the ETF market to price discovery is negligible when ETF prices from a floor-based trading system (the Amex) are used. When prices from an electronic trading system (Archipelago) are used instead, the estimated contribution to price discovery of the ETF market increases substantially. Hendershott and Jones (2005) find that ETF prices from the Island ECN dominated price discovery until, in 2002, Island stopped displaying quotes on its trading screens.

## 3. Data

We use data from three different markets: the German stock market, the index ETF market, and the index futures market. From these data, we compile two data sets. The first one combines DAX index values from the spot equity market with DAX index futures data, while the second data set combines data for the most liquid DAX ETF with index futures data.

### 3.1 Data set 1

The sample period for data set 1 is the first quarter of 1999 and covers 61 trading days. All data were obtained from Bloomberg. We use data for the German blue chip index DAX and the DAX futures contract. The DAX is a value-weighted index calculated from the prices of the 30 most liquid German stocks. The index is calculated from share prices in Xetra.[5] Index values are given with a precision of two digits after the decimal point. The DAX is a performance index, i.e. the calculation of the index is based on the presumption that dividends are reinvested. Consequently, the expected dividend yield does not enter the cost-of-carry relation.

During our sample period, Deutsche Börse AG (2000) also calculated an index from the current best ask prices (ADAX) and an index from the current best bid prices (BDAX).[6] These indices are value-weighted averages of the inside quotes, and the difference between them is equivalent to a value-weighted average bid-ask spread.

Futures contracts on the DAX are traded on the EUREX. The contracts are cash-settled and mature on the third Friday of the months March, June, September and December. The DAX futures contract is a highly liquid instrument. In the first quarter of 1999, more than 3.6 million contracts were traded. The open interest at the end of the quarter was more than 290,000 contracts.[7] The minimum tick size in the futures market corresponds to 1/2 index point.

Both Xetra and EUREX are electronic open limit order books. Therefore, the results of our empirical analysis are unlikely to be affected by differences in the microstructure of the markets.[8] The trading hours in the two markets differ. Trading in Xetra starts with a call auction held between 8.25 am and 8:30 am. After the opening auction, continuous trading starts and extends until 5 pm, interrupted by an intraday auction which takes place between 1:00 pm and 1:02 pm. Trading of the DAX futures contract starts at 9 am and extends until 5 pm.

Our data set comprises the values of the DAX index and the two quote-based indices ADAX and BDAX at a frequency of 15 s. The values in our data set correspond to the last observation in each interval. From the quote-based indices, we calculate a midquote index, denoted $MQDAX_t$, and a time series of percentage bid–ask spreads, denoted $S_t$. The data set further comprises a time series of all bid and ask quotes and all transaction prices of the nearby DAX futures contract.

We only use data for the period of simultaneous operation of both markets. We further discard all observations before 9 am and from 4:55 pm onwards. We also discard all observations within 5 min of the time of the intraday call auction (held between 1:00 pm and 1:02 pm). When estimating the ECM, we assure that all lagged returns are from the same trading day.

In order to synchronize the data from the spot and the futures markets, we proceeded as follows. For each index level observation, we identify the most recent transaction price and the most recent quote midpoint from the DAX futures data. Thus, in each pair of observations, the observation from the futures market is older (though by some seconds only) than the matched observation from the spot market. This procedure clearly works to the disadvantage of the futures market.

The cost-of-carry relation implies that the spot index and the futures contract are cointegrated. In order to eliminate the time variation of the cointegrating relation, we follow the procedure introduced by Dwyer, Locke, and Yu (1996). We calculate the mean of the log price series for each trading day and subtract the mean from the original series. This procedure leaves the intraday returns unaffected but eliminates the average daily level difference between the futures prices and the spot index level.[9] All ECMs are estimated using these demeaned series.

Panel A of Table 1 shows descriptive statistics for data set 1. The first line displays the frequency of zero return observations. Zero returns for the DAX are observed in 5% of the return intervals. For the midquote returns, this frequency is substantially lower, amounting to only 0.53%. These low values are not too surprising because a transaction or a quote change, respectively, will be observed whenever there is a transaction or a quote change in at least one of the 30 constituent stocks of the index. Things look different for the futures market. Here, we observe zero returns in 21.1% of the cases when we consider returns calculated from prices and in 16.7% of the cases when considering midquote returns. These figures, also being considerably higher than those for the DAX, are still low enough to suggest that our data frequency is adequate.

Besides the frequency of zero returns, Table 1 provides a variety of further descriptive statistics. The return standard deviation is higher in the futures market, and in both markets, it is higher for the price returns than for the midquote returns. This is most likely due to the fact that price returns

Table 1. Descriptive statistics.

|  | DAX | DAX midquote | FDAX price | FDAX midquote |
|---|---|---|---|---|
| *Panel A: data set 1* | | | | |
| Percentage of zero returns (%) | 5.00 | 0.53 | 21.05 | 16.7 |
| Return standard deviation | 0.000298 | 0.000223 | 0.000404 | 0.000340 |
| First-order serial correlation | 0.120 | 0.129 | −0.079 | 0.040 |
| Average bid-ask spread (%) | | 0.2846 | | 0.0292 |

|  | DAX EX price | DAX EX midquote | FDAX price | FDAX midquote |
|---|---|---|---|---|
| *Panel B: data set 2* | | | | |
| Percentage of zero returns (%) | 63.65 | 18.63 | 13.55 | 7.91 |
| Return standard deviation | 0.000396 | 0.000362 | 0.000368 | 0.000362 |
| First-order serial correlation | −0.027 | −0.011 | −0.017 | −0.005 |
| Average bid-ask spread (%) | | 0.0382 | | 0.0105 |

Notes: Panel A displays descriptive statistics for data set 1 (the index sample). It shows statistics for four return series: DAX returns, DAX midquote returns, DAX futures returns, and DAX futures midquote returns. The returns are calculated over intervals of 15 s. The last line shows the average quoted bid–ask spread. For the spot market, this is the value-weighted average of the spreads of the constituent stocks. Panel B displays similar statistics for data set 2 (the ETF sample). There are again four return series: DAX EX returns, DAX EX midquote returns, DAX futures returns, and DAX futures midquote returns. The returns are calculated over intervals of 1 min. The last line shows the average quoted bid-ask spread.

are affected by bid-ask bounce, whereas midquote returns are not. The DAX returns exhibit positive serial correlation ($\rho = 0.12$). This comes as no surprise given that the constituent stocks of the index trade infrequently and non-synchronously. What is a surprise, however, is the observation that the first-order serial correlation of the midquote returns is even higher, amounting to 12.9%. This contrasts with the negative serial correlation at the individual stock level documented by Hasbrouck (1991) and others. A possible explanation for the positive serial correlation is that a quote change in one stock may trigger a quote change in other stocks. This would induce positive serial correlation in the returns of the midquote index. This correlation, then, would be a characteristic feature of the modus operandi of the spot market. We therefore did not attempt to remove the serial correlation by applying an ARMA filter to the data.

The autocorrelation pattern for the futures market is in line with what one would expect. The returns calculated from prices are negatively correlated, most likely because of bid-ask bounce. The midquote returns are weakly positively correlated ($\rho = 0.04$).

The last line of Panel A of Table 1 shows the average bid-ask spreads. They amount to 0.28% for the DAX but to only 0.03% for the DAX futures contract. These figures are consistent with results for the UK reported in Berkmann, Brailsford, and Frino (2005) and substantiate our earlier claim that transaction costs are lower in the DAX futures market.

As a prerequisite for our empirical analysis, we have to establish that the time series are $I(1)$ and are cointegrated. Panel A of Table 2 presents the results of augmented Dickey-Fuller tests and Phillips-Perron tests applied to the log of the levels and their first differences. Four time series are considered: the DAX index itself, the DAX midquote index and the prices, and the quote midpoints of the DAX futures. The results of the stationarity tests clearly suggest that all series are $I(1)$. Results of Johansen tests (not shown) applied to pairs of log time series (DAX level and DAX futures prices, DAX midquote index, and DAX futures midquotes) provide clear evidence that the time series are cointegrated.

Table 2. Stationarity tests.

| | Level | | First difference | |
|---|---|---|---|---|
| | Augmented DF | Phillips–Perron | Augmented DF | Phillips–Perron |
| *Panel A: data set 1* | | | | |
| Log(DAX) | 0.349 | 0.412 | 0.000 | 0.000 |
| Log(MQ DAX) | 0.401 | 0.519 | 0.000 | 0.000 |
| Log(FDAX) | 0.439 | 0.399 | 0.000 | 0.000 |
| Log(MQ FDAX) | 0.370 | 0.396 | 0.000 | 0.000 |
| *Panel B: data set 2* | | | | |
| Log(DAX EX) | 0.510 | 0.405 | 0.000 | 0.000 |
| Log(MQ DAX EX) | 0.501 | 0.397 | 0.000 | 0.000 |
| Log(FDAX) | 0.349 | 0.330 | 0.000 | 0.000 |
| Log(MQ FDAX) | 0.373 | 0.360 | 0.000 | 0.000 |

Notes: The table presents the *p*-values from augmented Dickey-Fuller tests and Phillips-Perron tests applied to both the levels and to the first differences of the time series. Panel A (Panel B) shows the results for data set 1 (data set 2).

## 3.2 Data set 2

Our second data set covers 61 trading days in the last quarter of 2010. It combines data for the most liquid ETF (the DAX EX) and data for the DAX futures contract. The data were obtained from Bloomberg.

The iShares DAX (DAX EX) is an ETF issued by BlackRock Asset Management.[10] It tracks the blue chip index DAX. The fund exists since December 2000 and is the largest ETF replicating the DAX. Its net asset value at year-end 2010 was more than €4.3 billion. The average monthly trading volume in the fourth quarter of 2010 was more than €1.3 billion. Trades by institutional investors account for 90–95% of the total volume (Schlusche 2009). The DAX EX is traded on Xetra. The price of a fund certificate corresponds to 1/100 of the index value. We therefore multiplied all ETF prices and quotes by 100. The minimum tick size corresponds to one index point. It is thus twice as large as the minimum tick size in the futures market.

The DAX futures market was already described in the previous section. It was even more liquid in 2010 than it was in 1999. The number of contracts traded in the last quarter of 2010 was 9.2 million (as compared to 3.6 million in Q1 1999), and the average percentage spread declined from 0.029% to 0.011% (Table 1).

The data set comprises a complete record of all transaction prices, bid and ask quotes for the DAX EX, and the nearby DAX futures contract. We only use data for the period of simultaneous operation of both markets. We discard all observations before 9:05 am and from 5:30 pm onwards. We also discard all observations around the intraday call auction in the DAX EX market, which is held at a randomly chosen point in time between 1:10 pm and 1:12 pm. We construct a simultaneous data set by recording the last transaction price and the last bid and ask quote at the end of each minute.[11] As in data set 1, we eliminate the time variation in the cointegrating vector by demeaning the log price series. Further, we again use the pre-specified cointegrating vector (1; −1). When estimating the ECM, we assure that all lagged returns are from the same trading day.

Panel B of Table 1 shows descriptive statistics for data set 2. The zero return frequencies reflect the differing liquidity of the DAX EX and the DAX futures contract. While we observe 63.7% zero returns for the DAX EX, the corresponding figure for the DAX future is much lower, at 13.6%. Quote changes are much more frequent in both markets. The percentage of intervals with no quote change is 18.6% for the DAX EX and 7.9% for the DAX future. Our main conclusions are obtained from ECMs estimated on quote midpoint data.

In both markets, the standard deviation of price returns is higher than the standard deviation of midquote returns. This may be due to the presence of bid-ask bounce in the time series of transaction prices. All four time series display negative serial correlation. It is more pronounced for the price returns than for the midquote returns ($-0.027$ versus $-0.011$ for the DAX EX and $-0.017$ versus $-0.005$ for the DAX future). This may, again, be due to bid-ask bounce. The last line of Panel B of Table 1 shows the average bid-ask spreads. They amount to 0.038% for the DAX EX and to 0.011% for the DAX futures contract. The spread difference between the two markets under scrutiny is thus much lower in data set 2 than in data set 1.

Panel B of Table 2 presents the results of unit root tests applied to the log of the levels and their first differences. The results clearly suggest that all series are $I(1)$. Results of Johansen tests (not shown) applied to pairs of log time series (DAX EX level and DAX futures prices, DAX EX quote midpoints, and DAX futures quote midpoints) provide clear evidence that the time series are cointegrated.

## 4. Methodology and results

### 4.1 Base model

Having established that the time series are $I(1)$ and cointegrated, we can proceed by estimating the ECM:

$$r_t^X = \alpha^X + \sum_{\tau=1}^{k} \beta_\tau^X r_{t-\tau}^X + \sum_{\tau=1}^{k} \gamma_\tau^X r_{t-\tau}^F + \delta^X \left( p_{t-1}^X - p_{t-1}^F \right) + \varepsilon_t^X$$

$$r_t^F = \alpha^F + \sum_{\tau=1}^{k} \beta_\tau^F r_{t-\tau}^F + \sum_{\tau=1}^{k} \gamma_\tau^F r_{t-\tau}^X + \delta^F \left( p_{t-1}^X - p_{t-1}^F \right) + \varepsilon_t^F,$$

(1)

where $p$ denotes a demeaned log price series and $r$ denotes a log return. The indices X and F identify observations and coefficients relating to the spot market (the stock market in data set 1 and the ETF market in data set 2, denoted X for Xetra in both cases) and the futures market (F). We follow the literature (e.g. Dwyer, Locke, and Yu 1996; Fleming, Ostdiek, and Whaley 1996; Kempf and Korn 1996; Martens, Kofman, and Vorst 1998; Booth, So, and Tse 1999; Tse 2001; Schlusche 2009) by using the pre-specified cointegrating vector $(1; -1)$.[12]

We estimate model (1) using ordinary least squares (OLS), for both prices and quote midpoints. This allows us to check whether we can replicate the result obtained by Shyy, Vijayraghavan, and Scott-Quinn (1996), i.e. to check whether prices and quote midpoints yield different conclusions as to which market leads in the process of price discovery. Because there is evidence of heteroscedasticity and serial correlation of the residuals, all $t$-statistics are based on Newey–West standard errors. The number of lags is (based on the Schwartz information criterion (SIC)) set to 16 for data set 1 and to 10 for data set 2.[13]

We measure both markets' contributions to price discovery using the common factor weight (CFW) measure.[14] It has first been proposed by Schwarz and Szakmary (1994) on intuitive grounds. A formal justification, based on the work of Gonzalo and Granger (1995), has been provided by Booth et al. (2002), deB Harris, McInish, and Wood (2002), and Theissen (2002). The CFWs are easily obtained from the coefficients on the error correction terms in Equation (1):

$$\text{CFW}^{\text{X}} = \frac{\delta^{\text{F}}}{\delta^{\text{F}} - \delta^{\text{X}}}, \quad \text{CFW}^{F} = \frac{-\delta^{\text{X}}}{\delta^{\text{F}} - \delta^{\text{X}}}. \tag{2}$$

The results are presented in Table 3. To conserve space, we only report coefficients for the first four lags.

We discuss the results obtained from data set 1 (shown in Panel A of Table 3) first. Starting with the model estimated from transaction price data, we note that the independent variables have considerable explanatory power for the spot market returns, as is evidenced by an adjusted $R^2$ of 0.18. They have much less explanatory power for the returns in the futures markets. The adjusted $R^2$ for the futures market equation is a mere 0.01. Returns in both markets depend negatively on their own lagged values. This may be due to bid-ask bounce. We further find that returns in both markets depend positively on lagged returns in the other market. The $F$-statistic indicates bi-directional Granger causality. A look at the values of the $F$-statistics and at the coefficient values and their $t$-statistics reveals, however, that the impact of lagged futures returns on the spot market is far stronger than the impact of spot market returns on the futures market.

In both equations, the coefficient on the error correction term has the expected sign and is significant. Thus, both markets contribute to price discovery. Apparently, however, the futures market dominates the process of price discovery. According to the CFWs, the futures market contributes 71.7% to price discovery, while the contribution of the spot market is only 28.3%. The results thus imply that the futures market is the clear leader in the process of price discovery.

The results obtained when estimating Equation (1) with quote midpoint data are comparable. The $R^2$ for the spot market equation is higher at 0.23, whereas the $R^2$ for the futures market equation drops to 0.007. Midquote returns in the spot market depend negatively on their own lagged values. We do not observe a similar pattern for the futures market. Returns in both markets depend positively on lagged returns in the other market. Although the $F$-statistic again indicates bi-directional Granger causality, it is obvious from the estimation results that the futures market dominates.

The CFWs assign the spot market a slightly higher contribution to price discovery than in the transaction price model (40.2% as compared to 28.3%). Still, the results indicate that the futures market leads in the process of price discovery. This contrasts with the results of Shyy, Vijayraghavan, and Scott-Quinn (1996) who find that the spot market leads in the process of price discovery when the estimation is based on quote midpoints. When interpreting our results, it should be kept in mind that the construction of our data set puts the futures market at a disadvantage. Thus our results are likely to even understate the role of the futures market in the process of price discovery.

The results for data set 2 are shown in Panel B of Table 3. They share several similarities with those from data set 1. The explanatory variables again have much higher explanatory power for the spot market returns than for the futures market returns. The futures market clearly dominates the process of price discovery. The significant $F$-statistic implies that the futures returns Granger-cause the returns in the ETF market. Evidence for Granger causality in the opposite direction is much weaker; the corresponding $F$-statistic is insignificant when the estimation is based on transaction prices and significant only at the 10% level when the estimation is based on midquote returns. The coefficient estimate for the error correction term is insignificant in the futures market equation, which already indicates that the futures market does not adjust to deviations from the long-run relation given by the cost-of-carry model. This is confirmed by the CFWs which also indicate that the futures market dominates price discovery. Its share is estimated to be 98.5% and

Table 3. Results of ECMs.

| | Transaction prices | | Quote midpoints | |
| --- | --- | --- | --- | --- |
| | XDAX | FDAX | XDAX | FDAX |
| *Panel A: data set 1* | | | | |
| Constant | $-4.26 \times 10^{-6a}$ | $-7.96 \times 10^{-7}$ | $-2.65 \times 10^{-6a}$ | $-7.04 \times 10^{-7}$ |
| EC | $-0.056556^a$ | $0.022349^a$ | $-0.029377^a$ | $0.019736^a$ |
| XDAX(−1) | $-0.007426$ | $0.064078^a$ | $-0.071744^a$ | $0.043607^a$ |
| XDAX(−2) | $-0.034063^a$ | $0.048440^a$ | $-0.062804^a$ | $0.042332^a$ |
| XDAX(−3) | $-0.031447^a$ | $0.042881^a$ | $-0.048973^a$ | $0.047461^a$ |
| XDAX(−4) | $-0.036544^a$ | $0.024176^a$ | $-0.038622^a$ | $0.038573^a$ |
| FDAX(−1) | $0.150425^a$ | $-0.073297^a$ | $0.191583^a$ | $0.048087^a$ |
| FDAX(−2) | $0.123504^a$ | $-0.030181^a$ | $0.139903^a$ | $-0.003362$ |
| FDAX(−3) | $0.107591^a$ | $-0.017890^a$ | $0.104424^a$ | $-0.005091$ |
| FDAX(−4) | $0.084878^a$ | $-0.006991$ | $0.082565^a$ | $0.003325$ |
| $R^2$ | 0.180021 | 0.014389 | 0.227733 | 0.007471 |
| $F$-statistic | $143.77^a$ | $14.22^a$ | $291.24^a$ | $8.32^a$ |
| Lags included | | 16 | | 16 |
| CFW | 0.283 | 0.717 | 0.402 | 0.598 |

| | Transaction prices | | Quote midpoints | |
| --- | --- | --- | --- | --- |
| | DAX EX | FDAX | DAX EX | FDAX |
| *Panel B: data set 2* | | | | |
| Constant | $9.03 \times 10^{-7}$ | $1.58 \times 10^{-6}$ | $7.05 \times 10^{-7}$ | $1.55 \times 10^{-6}$ |
| EC | $-0.404736^a$ | $0.006068$ | $-0.522558^a$ | $0.051058$ |
| XDAX(−1) | $-0.047799^a$ | $0.019743$ | $-0.291539^a$ | $0.039016$ |
| XDAX(−2) | $-0.003253$ | $-0.007547$ | $-0.277453^a$ | $-0.006837$ |
| XDAX(−3) | $-0.002759$ | $0.002917$ | $-0.314209^a$ | $-0.108706$ |
| XDAX(−4) | $0.005678$ | $0.007943$ | $-0.059857$ | $0.093721^b$ |
| FDAX(−1) | $0.113850^a$ | $-0.028950^b$ | $0.287857^a$ | $-0.041466$ |
| FDAX(−2) | $0.048352^a$ | $-0.020270$ | $0.260817^a$ | $-0.011556$ |
| FDAX(−3) | $0.032030^a$ | $-0.005183$ | $0.299833^a$ | $0.096120$ |
| FDAX(−4) | $-0.013971$ | $-0.024223$ | $0.051562$ | $-0.101816^b$ |
| $R^2$ | 0.239293 | 0.002502 | 0.044766 | 0.005020 |
| $F$-statistic | $8.91^a$ | 1.21 | $4.69^a$ | $1.80^b$ |
| Lags included | | 10 | | 10 |
| CFW | 0.015 | 0.985 | 0.089 | 0.911 |

Notes: The table presents the results of the ECM

$$r_t^X = \alpha^X + \sum_{\tau=1}^{k} \beta_\tau^X r_{t-\tau}^X + \sum_{\tau=1}^{k} \gamma_\tau^X r_{t-\tau}^F + \delta^X \left(p_{t-1}^X - p_{t-1}^F\right) + \varepsilon_t^X$$

$$r_t^F = \alpha^F + \sum_{\tau=1}^{k} \beta_\tau^F r_{t-\tau}^F + \sum_{\tau=1}^{k} \gamma_\tau^F r_{t-\tau}^X + \delta^F \left(p_{t-1}^X - p_{t-1}^F\right) + \varepsilon_t^F,$$

where $p$ denotes a demeaned log price series and $r$ denotes a log return. The indices X and F identify observations and coefficients relating to the spot market (the DAX index in data set 1 and the DAX EX in data set 2) and the futures market (F). We use a pre-specified cointegrating vector. The models are estimated by OLS with Newey–West standard errors. Only the coefficients for lags 1–4 are shown. At the bottom of the table, we report $R^2$ and the $F$-statistic for a test of the null hypothesis that the coefficients for the lagged returns of the other markets (i.e., the spot market in the futures equation and vice versa) are jointly zero. We further report the lag order of the models. The last line reports the CFWs. Results for data set 1 are shown in Panel A and those for data set 2 in Panel B.
[a] Significance at the 5% level. [b] Significance at the 10% level.

91.1% in the transaction price and quote midpoint model, respectively. These values are much higher than the corresponding value of 74.7% reported by Schlusche (2009) for data from 2005.

## 4.2 Threshold ECM

As noted previously, Model (1) assumes that the speed of adjustment to deviations of the price levels from their long-run equilibrium relation is independent of the size of these deviations. This is unlikely to be the case, however, as arbitrageurs stand ready to take opportunity of any profits available. Thus, when the deviations are large enough to make arbitrage profitable (i.e. when they are larger than the transaction costs), we should expect faster adjustment.

In order to pursue this issue further, we first have to define an arbitrage signal. Previous papers assumed that arbitrage will set in when the price deviation exceeds a constant threshold level. However, it is well known that transaction costs are time-varying. Table 4 provides evidence on the variation of percentage bid–ask spreads. In the DAX futures market, the 75% quantile of the spread distribution is about twice as large as the 25% quantile. The corresponding ratio for the spreads on the spot market is about 1.5. This holds for both data sets. When we consider the 95% and 5% quantiles instead, we obtain (of course) larger differences. The ratios range from 2.2 for the Xetra DAX to more than 6 for the DAX futures contract in the first quarter of 1999.

In order to take advantage of profit opportunities, arbitrageurs have to trade fast. They are thus likely to use market orders and consequently have to pay the spread. An arbitrage trade consists of selling at the bid price in one market and buying at the ask price in the other market. In both cases, the total transaction cost is the half spread in the spot market plus the half spread in the futures market.[15] We assume that arbitrage is profitable when the price deviation exceeds this threshold. We thereby assume that there are no other relevant transaction costs besides the spread, and we assume that the position is either held until maturity or can be unwound at zero cost.[16] This corresponds to the conjecture by Dwyer, Locke, and Yu (1996, p. 312) that 'the trigger for index arbitrage is about one-half of the round-trip transaction costs'.

As both markets under scrutiny are fully automated, arbitrage trades may be executed as programme trades. We therefore do not consider the possibility of delays between the occurrence of price deviations and the onset of arbitrage.[17] We thereby implicitly assume that the reaction time is no more than our data frequency.

Table 5 takes a closer look at the arbitrage opportunities. In data set 1, the deviation between the (demeaned) spot and futures market quote midpoints exceeds the transaction costs in about

Table 4. Distribution of bid–ask spreads.

|  | 5% | 25% | 50% (Median) | 75% | 95% |
|---|---|---|---|---|---|
| *Panel A: data set 1* | | | | | |
| XDAX | 0.1877 | 0.2347 | 0.2740 | 0.3225 | 0.4194 |
| FDAX | 0.0097 | 0.0189 | 0.0211 | 0.0396 | 0.0622 |
| *Panel B: data set 2* | | | | | |
| DAX EX | 0.0159 | 0.0311 | 0.0325 | 0.0480 | 0.0641 |
| FDAX | 0.0071 | 0.0073 | 0.0077 | 0.0147 | 0.0158 |

Notes: The table shows the 5%, 25%, 50%, 75%, and 95% percentiles of the distribution of percentage bid–ask spreads. Figures for data set 1 (data set 2) are provided in Panel A (Panel B).

Table 5. Arbitrage opportunities.

|  | DAX>FDAX | FDAX>DAX | Both |
|---|---|---|---|
| *Panel A: data set 1* |  |  |  |
| Number of cases | 2658 (2.42%) | 3331 (3.03%) | 5989 (5.46%) |
| Mean arbitrage profit | 1.4788 | 2.1086 | 1.8291 |
| Median arbitrage profit | 1.0751 | 1.2503 | 1.1559 |
| Maximum arbitrage profit | 16.9659 | 18.9944 | 18.9944 |
| Lowest daily number of observations | 1 | 1 | 9 |
|  | DAX EX>FDAX | FDAX>DAX EX | Both |
| *Panel B: data set 2* |  |  |  |
| Number of cases | 3542 (12.01%) | 3936 (13.34%) | 7478 (25.35%) |
| Mean arbitrage profit | 1.2078 | 0.9441 | 1.0690 |
| Median arbitrage profit | 0.8292 | 0.6165 | 0.7221 |
| Maximum arbitrage profit | 37.9671 | 7.6698 | 37.9671 |
| Lowest daily number of observations | 0 | 0 | 0 |

Notes: An arbitrage signal, in our definition, occurs when the absolute difference between the demeaned spot and futures prices is larger than the transaction cost (the sum of the half-spread in the spot market and the half-spread in the futures market). The table shows the number of arbitrage opportunities, the mean and median arbitrage profit, and the maximum profit. Profits are measured in index points. The last line shows the lowest number of arbitrage opportunities observed on any individual day of the sample period. Columns 1 and 2 show separate figures for arbitrage opportunities in which the spot index value (data set 1) and the value of the DAX EX (data set 2), respectively, are larger [smaller] than the futures price.

5.46% of the cases. In 2.42% of the observations, the spot index is larger than the futures price, whereas in 3.03% the reverse is true.[18] In most cases, the price deviation exceeds the transaction cost only by a small amount. The average value is 1.83 index points. Larger deviations do occur, however, as is evidenced by a maximum value of almost 19 points. We observe more arbitrage opportunities in data set 2. The deviation between the quote midpoints exceeds the transaction costs in more than 25% of the cases. The higher percentage of arbitrage opportunities is due to the very low bid–ask spreads in data set 2. Remember from Table 1 that the average percentage spread is 0.038% for the DAX EX and 0.011% for the DAX futures contract. In most cases, the arbitrage profits are small. The mean profit is about 1.1 index points. Large deviations occur occasionally, as is evidenced by a maximum value of 38 index points.[19]

We define a dummy variable $D_t$ taking on the value 1 if there is an arbitrage opportunity as defined above and zero otherwise. We then augment Model (1) to obtain

$$r_t^X = \alpha^X + \sum_{\tau=1}^k \beta_\tau^X r_{t-\tau}^X + \sum_{\tau=1}^k \gamma_\tau^X r_{t-\tau}^F + \delta_1^X \left(p_{t-1}^X - p_{t-1}^F\right) + \delta_2^X D_{t-1}\left(p_{t-1}^X - p_{t-1}^F\right) + \varepsilon_t^X$$

$$(3)$$

$$r_t^F = \alpha^F + \sum_{\tau=1}^k \beta_\tau^F r_{t-\tau}^F + \sum_{\tau=1}^k \gamma_\tau^F r_{t-\tau}^X + \delta_1^F \left(p_{t-1}^X - p_{t-1}^F\right) + \delta_2^F D_{t-1}\left(p_{t-1}^X - p_{t-1}^F\right) + \varepsilon_t^F.$$

The coefficients $\delta_2^X$ and $\delta_2^F$ measure whether the adjustment to price deviations is different in the presence of arbitrage opportunities. We expect these coefficients to have the same sign as $\delta_1^X$ and $\delta_1^F$, respectively.

As already noted, arbitrage either requires to sell in the spot market and buy in the futures market or to do the reverse. The price dynamics in the two cases may be different because selling in the spot market may require short sales. We therefore estimate an additional model in which we allow the coefficient on the error correction term to be different in the two cases alluded to above. The model is

$$
\begin{aligned}
r_t^X = \alpha^X &+ \sum_{\tau=1}^{k} \beta_\tau^X r_{t-\tau}^X + \sum_{\tau=1}^{k} \gamma_\tau^X r_{t-\tau}^F + \delta_1^X \left( p_{t-1}^X - p_{t-1}^F \right) + \delta_2^X D_{t-1}^1 \left( p_{t-1}^X - p_{t-1}^F \right) \\
&+ \delta_3^X D_{t-1}^2 \left( p_{t-1}^X - p_{t-1}^F \right) + \varepsilon_t^X
\end{aligned}
$$

$$
\begin{aligned}
r_t^F = \alpha^F &+ \sum_{\tau=1}^{k} \beta_\tau^F r_{t-\tau}^F + \sum_{\tau=1}^{k} \gamma_\tau^F r_{t-\tau}^X + \delta_1^F \left( p_{t-1}^X - p_{t-1}^F \right) + \delta_2^F D_{t-1}^1 \left( p_{t-1}^X - p_{t-1}^F \right) \\
&+ \delta_3^F D_{t-1}^2 \left( p_{t-1}^X - p_{t-1}^F \right) + \varepsilon_t^F,
\end{aligned}
$$

(4)

where $D_t^1$ and $D_t^2$ are dummy variables identifying those arbitrage opportunities that require selling in the spot market $(D_t^1)$ and selling in the futures market $(D_t^2)$.

We can construct suitable extensions of the CFWs as follows:

$$
\mathrm{CFW}_2^X = \frac{(\delta_1^F + \delta_2^F)}{(\delta_1^F + \delta_2^F) - (\delta_1^X + \delta_2^X)}, \quad \mathrm{CFW}_2^F = \frac{-(\delta_1^X + \delta_2^X)}{(\delta_1^F + \delta_2^F) - (\delta_1^X + \delta_2^X)}.
$$

(5)

$\mathrm{CFW}_2^X$ and $\mathrm{CFW}_2^F$ measure the contribution to price discovery in the presence of arbitrage opportunities. Analogous to Equation (5), we can also define CFW measures for the two 'arbitrage regimes' in Model (4).

We have argued earlier that the identification of arbitrage opportunities should be based on quote data rather than on transaction price data. Consequently, we estimate Models (3) and (3) using quote midpoint data. To enhance comparability with our previous results, we include the same number of lags (16 for data set 1 and 10 for data set 2).

The results for data set 1 are presented in Panel A of Table 6. They are comparable to those shown in Table 3. The spot market returns depend negatively on their own lagged values and depend strongly and positively on lagged futures returns. Futures returns, on the other hand, depend positively on lagged spot market returns but depend on their own lagged values significantly only at lag 1. As before we find bi-directional Granger causality, and as before we can conclude from the magnitude of the coefficient estimates and the test statistics that the dependence of the spot market on the futures market is much stronger than the reverse dependence. These results hold for Model (3) as well as for Model (4).

The estimates of the coefficient on the error correction term in the 'no-arbitrage regime' have the same sign but are smaller in magnitude than those presented before. Based on these estimates, the CFW measure attributes both markets almost equal contributions to price discovery (47.1% for the spot market and 52.9% for the futures market). It should be kept in mind, though, that we are likely to understate the contribution of the futures market. The coefficients $\mathrm{CFW}_2^X$ and $\mathrm{CFW}_2^F$ have the expected sign and are significant. The contributions to price discovery in the arbitrage regime, measured using Equation (4), reveal that the share of the spot market drops to 36.3% in the presence of arbitrage opportunities, whereas the share of the futures market rises to 63.7%. The results thus suggest that the leading role of the futures market in the price discovery process is particularly pronounced when price deviations are large (i.e. when arbitrage opportunities exist).

Table 6. Results of TECMs.

| | Arbitrage signals pooled (Equation (3)) | | Separate arbitrage signals (Equation (4)) | |
|---|---|---|---|---|
| | XDAX | FDAX | XDAX | FDAX |
| *Panel A: data set 1* | | | | |
| Constant | $-2.83 \times 10^{-6}$ | $-6.20 \times 10^{-7}$ | $4.26\times10^{-7}$ | $-1.44 \times 10^{-6}$ |
| EC/no arbitrage | $-0.013674^a$ | $0.012159^a$ | $-0.014775^a$ | $0.012437^a$ |
| EC/arbitrage | $-0.050915^a$ | $0.024569^a$ | | |
| EC/arb. X-F | | | $-0.091940^a$ | $0.034925^a$ |
| EC/arb. F-X | | | $-0.026632^a$ | $0.018439^a$ |
| XDAX(-1) | $-0.073381^a$ | $0.044397^a$ | $-0.071992^a$ | $0.044047^a$ |
| XDAX(-2) | $-0.063698^a$ | $0.042763^a$ | $-0.062631^a$ | $0.042494^a$ |
| XDAX(-3) | $-0.049866^a$ | $0.047892^a$ | $-0.048698^a$ | $0.047598^a$ |
| XDAX(-4) | $-0.039288^a$ | $0.038894^a$ | $-0.038021^a$ | $0.038574^a$ |
| FDAX(-1) | $0.187369^a$ | $0.050121^a$ | $0.183106^a$ | $0.051197^a$ |
| FDAX(-2) | $0.139643^a$ | $-0.003237$ | $0.137180^a$ | $-0.002615$ |
| FDAX(-3) | $0.105444^a$ | $-0.005583$ | $0.103422^a$ | $-0.005073$ |
| FDAX(-4) | $0.084098^a$ | $0.002586$ | $0.082477^a$ | $0.002995$ |
| $R^2$ | 0.235761 | 0.008265 | 0.240010 | 0.008372 |
| *F*-statistic | $265.90^a$ | $8.44^a$ | $291.14^a$ | $8.39^a$ |
| Lags included | 16 | | 16 | |
| CFW/no arbitrage | 0.471 | 0.529 | 0.457 | 0.543 |
| CFW/arbitrage | 0.363 | 0.637 | | |
| CFW/arb. X-F | | | 0.307 | 0.693 |
| CFW/arb. F-X | | | 0.427 | 0.573 |

| | Arbitrage signals pooled (Equation (3)) | | Separate arbitrage signals (Equation (4)) | |
|---|---|---|---|---|
| | DAX EX | FDAX | DAX EX | FDAX |
| *Panel B: data set 2* | | | | |
| Constant | $7.56 \times 10^{-7}$ | $1.61 \times 10^{-6}$ | $1.29 \times 10^{-6}$ | $2.13 \times 10^{-6}$ |
| EC/no arbitrage | $-0.648522^a$ | $-0.095461$ | $-0.650214^a$ | $-0.097114$ |
| EC/arbitrage | $0.292950^a$ | $0.340754^a$ | | |
| EC/arb. X-F | | | $0.240208^a$ | $0.289217^a$ |
| EC/arb. F-X | | | $0.382039^a$ | $0.427808^a$ |
| XDAX($-1$) | $-0.305934^a$ | $0.022272$ | $-0.304022^a$ | $0.024141$ |
| XDAX($-2$) | $-0.287087^a$ | $-0.018042$ | $-0.285533^a$ | $-0.016524$ |
| XDAX($-3$) | $-0.321308^a$ | $-0.116964$ | $-0.320338^a$ | $-0.116016$ |
| XDAX($-4$) | $-0.065216$ | $0.087487^b$ | $-0.065020$ | $0.087679^b$ |
| FDAX($-1$) | $0.304588^a$ | $-0.022005$ | $0.302479^a$ | $-0.024066$ |
| FDAX($-2$) | $0.270784^a$ | $0.000037$ | $0.269360^a$ | $-0.001354$ |
| FDAX($-3$) | $0.307254^a$ | $0.104752$ | $0.306279^a$ | $0.103799$ |
| FDAX($-4$) | $0.057405$ | $-0.095020^b$ | $0.057220$ | $-0.095201^b$ |
| $R^2$ | 0.046096 | 0.006821 | 0.046204 | 0.006921 |
| *F*-statistic | $4.97^a$ | $1.79^b$ | $4.90^a$ | $1.79^b$ |
| Lags included | 10 | | 10 | |
| CFW/no arbitrage | 0 | 1 | 0 | 1 |
| CFW/arbitrage | 0.408 | 0.592 | | |

*(Continued)*

Table 6. Continued

| | Arbitrage signals pooled (Equation (3)) | | Separate arbitrage signals (Equation (4)) | |
|---|---|---|---|---|
| | DAX EX | FDAX | DAX EX | FDAX |
| CFW/arb. X-F | | | 0.319 | 0.681 |
| CFW/arb. F-X | | | 0.552 | 0.448 |

Notes: The table presents the results of the ECMs

$$r_t^X = \alpha^X + \sum_{\tau=1}^{k} \beta_\tau^X r_{t-\tau}^X + \sum_{\tau=1}^{k} \gamma_\tau^X r_{t-\tau}^F + \delta_1^X \left(p_{t-1}^X - p_{t-1}^F\right) + \delta_2^X D_{t-1} \left(p_{t-1}^X - p_{t-1}^F\right) + \varepsilon_t^X$$

$$r_t^F = \alpha^F + \sum_{\tau=1}^{k} \beta_\tau^F r_{t-\tau}^F + \sum_{\tau=1}^{k} \gamma_\tau^F r_{t-\tau}^X + \delta_1^F \left(p_{t-1}^X - p_{t-1}^F\right) + \delta_2^F D_{t-1} \left(p_{t-1}^X - p_{t-1}^F\right) + \varepsilon_t^F$$

(columns 1 and 2) and

$$r_t^X = \alpha^X + \sum_{\tau=1}^{k} \beta_\tau^X r_{t-\tau}^X + \sum_{\tau=1}^{k} \gamma_\tau^X r_{t-\tau}^F + \delta_1^X \left(p_{t-1}^X - p_{t-1}^F\right) + \delta_2^X D_{t-1}^1 \left(p_{t-1}^X - p_{t-1}^F\right) + \delta_3^X D_{t-1}^2 \left(p_{t-1}^X - p_{t-1}^F\right) + \varepsilon_t^X$$

$$r_t^F = \alpha^F + \sum_{\tau=1}^{k} \beta_\tau^F r_{t-\tau}^F + \sum_{\tau=1}^{k} \gamma_\tau^F r_{t-\tau}^X + \delta_1^F \left(p_{t-1}^X - p_{t-1}^F\right) + \delta_2^F D_{t-1}^1 \left(p_{t-1}^X - p_{t-1}^F\right) + \delta_3^F D_{t-1}^2 \left(p_{t-1}^X - p_{t-1}^F\right) + \varepsilon_t^F$$

(columns 3 and 4). $p$ denotes a demeaned log price series and $r$ denotes a log return. The indices X and F identify observations and coefficients relating to the spot market (the DAX in data set 1 and the DAX EX in data set 2) and the futures market (F). We use a pre-specified cointegrating vector. The dummy variable $D_t$ identifies all arbitrage signals. The dummy variables $D_t^1$ [$D_t^2$] identify those arbitrage signals where the spot market midquote index is larger [smaller] than the midquote in the futures market. The models are estimated by OLS with Newey–West standard errors. Only the coefficients for lags 1–4 are shown. At the bottom of the table, we report $R^2$ and the $F$-statistic for a test of the null hypothesis that the coefficients for the lagged returns of the other markets (i.e., the spot market in the futures equation and vice versa) are jointly zero. We further report the lag order of the models. The last lines report the CFWs. Results for data set 1 are shown in Panel A and those for data set 2 in Panel B.
[a] Significance at the 5% level. [b] Significance at the 10% level.

The estimates of the parameters $\delta_2^X$, $\delta_3^X$, $\delta_2^F$, and $\delta_3^F$ in Model (4) have the expected sign and are significant. The result that the contribution of the futures market to the price discovery process is higher when price deviations are large is confirmed. Additionally, we observe that the share of the spot market is lowest when there are arbitrage opportunities and the spot market index is larger than the futures price. This is the case in which arbitrage requires selling in the spot market.

The results for data set 2, shown in Panel B of Table 5, resemble those shown in Table 3. There is clear evidence that returns in the futures market Granger-cause returns in the ETF market. Evidence of causality in the reverse direction is much weaker; the corresponding $F$-statistics are significant only at the 10% level. In the absence of arbitrage opportunities, prices in the futures market do not adjust to deviations from the cost-of-carry relation. The coefficient of the error correction term is insignificant and even has the wrong sign. As a consequence, Equation (2) would yield a CFW for the futures market in excess of 100% and a negative weight for the spot market. We therefore set the weights to 100% and 0%, respectively. All these results indicate that, absent arbitrage signals, only the futures market contributes to price discovery.

The contributions to price discovery change considerably in the presence of arbitrage signals. The CFW for the spot market jumps to 40.8% in the presence of arbitrage signals. Model (4) implies that the spot market contributes 31.9% when arbitrage involves selling in the spot market and contributes 55.2% when arbitrage involves buying in the spot market. Taken together, the results imply that under normal market conditions, price discovery occurs only in the futures market. In the presence of arbitrage signals, the spot market catches up and contributes significantly to price discovery. The latter finding is at odds with the results obtained using data set 1. There, we concluded that the lead of the futures market becomes stronger in the presence of arbitrage opportunities. The most likely reason for these apparently contradictory findings is the difference in the spot market instruments considered in the two data sets. In data set 1, we considered an index (which cannot be traded), while in data set 2 we consider an ETF.

In summary, our results imply that (a) the futures market leads in the process of price discovery and (b) the presence of arbitrage opportunities has a strong impact on the nature of the price discovery process.

## 5. Summary and conclusion

In this article, we reconsider the issue of price discovery in spot and futures markets. Its contribution is twofold. First, we modify the TECM to allow for time-varying transaction costs. Second, we estimate a TECM using midquote data whereas previous papers used price data. Midquote data are conceptually superior because arbitrage signals should be based on tradable prices (i.e. bid and ask quotes) rather than on past transaction prices.

Our basic finding that the futures market leads in the process of price discovery is consistent with most previous results. We do not confirm the finding of Shyy, Vijayraghavan, and Scott-Quinn (1996) that the spot market leads when the estimation is based on quote midpoints rather than on transaction prices. We further document that the presence of arbitrage opportunities has a strong impact on the nature of the price discovery process.

Our results imply that the futures market generally impounds new information faster than the spot market. As a consequence, researchers investigating into the market response to macro-economic news, or into informational linkages between markets in different countries, should consider using futures market data rather than spot market data.

## Acknowledgements

I thank Bloomberg for providing the data. I thank an anonymous referee, Alexander Kempf, Olaf Korn, Mark Salmon (the editor), seminar participants at the University of Cologne, and participants of the 8th Asia-Pacific Futures Research Symposium in Bangkok for valuable comments.

## Notes

1. Alternatively, investors could trade in single stock futures. However, the market for single stock futures is rather illiquid. The monthly statistics for December 2010 available on the EUREX website (see http://www.eurexchange.com/market/statistics/monthly/2010_en.html) reveals that the number of traded contracts is very low for most constituent stocks of the DAX; there is even one DAX member firm (Heidelberger Zement AG) for which there was no trade in the entire month.
2. Trading activity in today's markets is, of course, much higher than it used to be when the first papers addressing the infrequent trading problem were written. However, since then, not only the trading intensity but also the data resolution used in empirical studies has increased tremendously. Relative to the frequency of observations, there are still stale prices today. This is evidenced by significant positive serial correlation in index returns at high data frequencies. Using data (obtained from Bloomberg) at the 1 s frequency (a resolution used in several recent papers,

e.g., Tse, Bandyopadhyay, and Shen 2006), we found that the serial correlation of DAX returns exceeded 0.1 in 6 out of the 10 trading days (7–18 March 2011) we considered.

3. If, as is usual, the model is estimated using logs, the relation becomes $\ln(F_t) = \ln(S_t) + r(T - t)$. This implies that, in a regression of $\ln(F_t)$ on $\ln(S_t)$, the slope is constant and equal to 1, whereas the intercept changes daily. Note that we do not include the expected dividend yield in the cost-of-carry relation. The reason is that the DAX is a performance index, i.e. calculation of the index is based on the presumption that dividends are reinvested.

4. There is an alternative. Jokivuolle (1995) developed a procedure (based on the Beveridge–Nelson decomposition) that allows estimation of the true index level. Using these estimates rather than the observed index levels allows us to formulate an ECM in which both the error correction term and the lagged returns are purged of infrequent trading effects. To the best of our knowledge, this procedure has not yet been applied to test the lead-lag relation between spot and futures markets.

5. During our sample period, Xetra accounted for 79.9% of the total order book turnover in the constituent stocks of the DAX on all German exchanges. See the fact book 1999 of Deutsche Börse AG (2000), p. 33. Note that, during our sample period, Deutsche Börse AG also calculated DAX values based on the prices of the Frankfurt Stock Exchange.

6. The calculation of these quote-based indices was discontinued in 2005. Bloomberg did provide intraday data, but deleted it after 30 trading days. Consequently, intraday data on the quote-based indices are no longer available. We therefore had to rely on data that we had collected for a different research project (Freihube and Theissen 2001). It is for this reason that we use data from 1999 in this article.

7. See the fact book 1999 of Deutsche Börse AG (2000), p. 88.

8. Some previous papers, most notably Grünbichler, Longstaff, and Schwartz (1994), Kempf and Korn (1998), and Frino and McKenzie (2002), analyse spot and futures markets with different trading protocols. The focus of these papers is to assess the implications of the trading protocol for price discovery.

9. As noted previously, an alternative procedure would be to use discounted futures prices (as in Martens, Kofman, and Vorst 1998). However, futures prices appear to deviate systematically from the values implied by the cost-of-carry relation (see e.g. Bühler and Kempf (1995) for the German market), most likely because of different tax treatments of dividends in spot and futures markets. In this case, discounting futures prices will produce biased arbitrage signals. Demeaning, on the other hand, removes any systematic deviation of futures prices from the cost-of-carry relation.

10. BlackRock bought the investment unit from Barclays plc in 2009.

11. We opted for 1 min intervals because the trading frequency of the DAX EX is not high enough to sustain a data frequency of 15 s. As can be seen from Panel B of Table 1, even at the 1 min frequency, the probability of observing no transaction in an interval is above 0.6. The probability of observing no quote change is much lower, at 18.6%. Our main conclusions are derived from ECMs estimated on quote midpoint data.

12. We use this pre-specified cointegrating vector because the cost-of-carry relation gives us a strong theoretical reason to believe that the demeaned log prices from the spot and futures markets should be equal.

13. To enhance the comparability of the results, we decided to use the same number of lags in the models based on transaction prices and quote midpoints. The SIC suggests to include 16 (12) lags in the price (midquote) model for data set 1 and 2 (10) lags in the price (midquote) model for data set 2.

14. A very popular alternative is the Hasbrouck (1995) information share. We decided against this measure for two reasons. First, the measure cannot be calculated for our extended models which take the existence of arbitrage opportunities into account. Second, Grammig and Peter (2008) and Yan and Zivot (2010) have pointed out that the information shares have limitations when the estimates are based on high sampling frequencies.

15. We note that this measure may overstate the true transaction costs in data set 1. Arbitrageurs do not necessarily have to trade all 30 DAX stocks. They can instead trade a tracking portfolio consisting of fewer stocks (thereby, of course, introducing tracking error). As this portfolio is likely to be tilted towards liquid stocks, the average spread will be lower than the average spread of all DAX stocks. This argument does obviously not apply to data set 2 because the DAX EX is a basket.

16. There is a positive probability that an arbitrageur will be able to unwind her position early at a profit. The value of the early unwinding option (Brennan and Schwartz 1988, 1990) reduces the price differential necessary to make arbitrage profitable.

17. In contrast, Dwyer, Locke, and Yu (1996) use data from open outcry markets. In such an environment, delays are likely. They address the issue empirically and estimate delays ranging from 1 to 5 min.

18. These figures are clearly lower than the corresponding values in Dwyer, Locke, and Yu (1996, p. 324). They report that slightly less than 9% of their observations are in each of the two tail regimes that are associated with arbitrage opportunities.

19. The extreme values were observed on one day on which the DAX lost more than 1% shortly after the opening. As a robustness check, we re-estimated all our models excluding this day. The results were very similar.

## References

Berkmann, H., T. Brailsford, and A. Frino. 2005. A note on execution costs for stock index futures: Information versus liquidity effects. *Journal of Banking and Finance* 29, no. 3: 565–77.

Booth, G., R. So, and Y. Tse. 1999. Price discovery in the German equity index derivatives markets. *Journal of Futures Markets* 19, no. 6: 619–43.

Booth, G., J.-Ch. Lin, T. Martikainen, and Y. Tse. 2002. Trading and pricing in upstairs and downstairs stock markets. *Review of Financial Studies* 15, no. 4: 1111–35.

Bose, S. 2007. Contribution of Indian index futures to price formation in the stock market. *Money and Finance* 3, no. 1: 39–56.

Brennan, M., and E. Schwartz. 1988. Optimal arbitrage strategies under basis variability. *Studies in Banking and Finance* 5: 167–80.

Brennan, M., and E. Schwartz. 1990. Arbitrage in stock index futures. *Journal of Business* 63, no. 1 part 2: S7–31.

Bühler, W., and A. Kempf. 1995. DAX index futures: Mispricing and arbitrage in German markets. *Journal of Futures Markets* 15, no. 7: 833–59.

Deutsche Börse AG. 2000. *Fact book 1999*, Frankfurt.

Dwyer, G. Jr., P. Locke, and W. Yu. 1996. Index arbitrage and nonlinear dynamics between the S&P 500 futures and cash. *Review of Financial Studies* 9, no. 1: 301–32.

Fleming, J., B. Ostdiek, and R. Whaley. 1996. Trading costs and the relative rates of price discovery in stock, futures and option markets. *Journal of Futures Markets* 16, no. 4: 353–87.

Freihube, Th., and E. Theissen. 2001. An index is an index is an index? *Schmalenbach Business Review* 53, no. 4: 295–320.

Frino, A., and M. McKenzie. 2002. The impact of screen trading on the link between stock index and stock index futures prices: Evidence from UK Markets. Working Paper, University of Sydney.

Gonzalo, J., and C. Granger. 1995. Estimation of common long-memory components in cointegrated systems. *Journal of Business and Economic Statistics* 13, no. 1: 27–35.

Grammig, J., and F. Peter. 2008. International price discovery in the presence of market microstructure effects. CFR Working Paper 08-10, Centre for Financial Research, Cologne.

Grünbichler, A., F. Longstaff, and E. Schwartz. 1994. Electronic screen trading and the transmission of information: An empirical examination. *Journal of Financial Intermediation* 3, no. 2: 166–87.

Harris, F. H. deB., T. McInish, and R. Wood. 2002. Common factor components versus information shares: A reply. *Journal of Financial Markets* 5, no. 3: 341–8.

Hasbrouck, J. 1991. Measuring the information content of stock prices. *Journal of Finance* 46, no. 1: 179–207.

Hasbrouck, J. 1995. One security, many markets: Determining the contributions to price discovery. *Journal of Finance* 50, no. 4: 1175–99.

Hasbrouck, J. 2003. Intraday price formation in US equity index markets. *Journal of Finance* 58, no. 6: 2375–400.

Hendershott, T., and C. Jones. 2005. Island goes dark: Transparency, fragmentation, and regulation. *Review of Financial Studies* 18, no. 3: 743–93.

Jokivuolle, E. 1995. Measuring true stock index value in the presence of infrequent trading. *Journal of Financial and Quantitative Analysis* 30, no. 3: 455–64.

Kempf, A., and O. Korn. 1996. Preisführerschaft und imperfekte Arbitrage. *Zeitschrift für Betriebswirtschaft* 66, no. 7: 837–59.

Kempf, A., and O. Korn. 1998. Trading system and market integration. *Journal of Financial Intermediation* 7, no. 3: 220–39.

Martens, M., P. Kofman, and T. Vorst. 1998. A threshold error correction model for intraday futures and index returns. *Journal of Applied Econometrics* 13, no. 3: 245–63.

Pizzi, M., A. Economopoulos, and H. O'Neill. 1998. An estimation of the relationship between stock index cash and futures markets: A cointegration approach. *Journal of Futures Markets* 18, no. 3: 297–305.

Schlusche, B. 2009. Price formation in spot and futures markets: Exchange traded funds versus index funds. *Journal of Derivatives* 17, no. 2: 26–40.

Schwarz, T., and A. Szakmary. 1994. Price discovery in petroleum markets: Arbitrage, cointegration, and the time interval of analysis. *Journal of Futures Markets* 14, no. 2: 147–67.

Shyy, G., V. Vijayraghavan, and B. Scott-Quinn. 1996. A further investigation of the lead–lag relationship between the cash market and stock index futures market with the use of bid/ask quotes: The case of France. *Journal of Futures Markets* 16, no. 4: 405–20.

Stoll, H., and R. Whaley. 1990. The dynamics of stock index and stock index futures returns. *Journal of Financial and Quantitative Analysis* 25, no. 4: 441–68.

Theissen, E. 2002. Price discovery in floor and screen trading systems. *Journal of Empirical Finance* 9, no. 4: 455–74.

Tse, Y. 2001. Index arbitrage with heterogeneous investors: A smooth transition error correction analysis. *Journal of Banking and Finance* 25, no. 10: 1829–55.

Tse, Y., P. Bandyopadhyay, and Y.-P. Shen. 2006. Intraday price discovery in the DJIA index markets. *Journal of Business Finance and Accounting* 33, nos. 9–10: 1572–85.

Yadav, P., P. Pope, and K. Paudyal. 1994. Threshold autoregressive modeling in finance: The price differences of equivalent assets. *Mathematical Finance* 4, no. 2: 205–21.

Yan, B., and E. Zivot. 2010. A structural analysis of price discovery measures. *Journal of Financial Markets* 13, no. 1: 1–19.

# Optimal informed trading in the foreign exchange market

Paolo Vitale

*Faculty of Economics, Università d'Annunzio, Pescara, Italy*

We formulate a market microstructure model of exchange determination that we employ to investigate the impact of informed trading on exchange rates and on foreign exchange (FX) market conditions. With our formulation, we show how strategic informed agents influence exchange rates via both the portfolio-balance and information effects. We outline the connection which exists between the private value of information, market efficiency, liquidity and exchange rate volatility. Our model is also consistent with recent empirical research on the micro-structure of FX markets.

## 1. Introduction

A recent strand of research in exchange rate economics investigates the microstructure of foreign exchange (FX) markets and the impact of trading activity on exchange-rate dynamics. The principal result of this new strand is that *order flow* is an important determinant of exchange-rate dynamics in the short-term and possibly even in the medium-term.[1] Theoretical underpinnings of this empirical result link the explanatory power of order flow to two different channels of transmission, due respectively to portfolio-balance and information effects. With respect to the former channel, it has simply been suggested that trade innovations perturb the inventories of FX investors which need to be compensated with a shift in expected returns.

With respect to the latter, it has been claimed that the empirical failure of the traditional models of exchange-rate determination lies with the particular forward-looking nature of exchange rates and with the impact that news arrivals have on the value of currencies. Thus, when news arrivals condition market expectations of future values of exchange-rate fundamental variables, currency values immediately react anticipating the effect of these fundamental shifts. Since news is hard to observe, it is difficult to control for news effects in the empirical investigation of exchange rate dynamics and hence it is difficult to conduct any meaningful analysis of the traditional models of exchange-rate determination.

However, the analysis of the relation between fundamental variables and exchange rates can be bypassed by analyzing buying/selling pressure in FX markets. Indeed, it has been argued that the imbalance between buyer-initiated and seller-initiated trades in FX markets, i.e. *signed* order flow, represents the transmission link between information and exchange rates, in that it conveys information on deeper determinants of exchange rates, which FX markets need to aggregate and impound in currency values. More specifically, according to this thesis, FX traders collect from various sources information on the fundamental value of foreign currencies and trade accordingly. A general consensus and equilibrium exchange rates are then reached via the trading process, in that information contained in the order flow is progressively shared among market participants and incorporated into exchange rates.

Empirical studies suggest that in FX markets, order flow possesses an information content. Thus, Lyons (1995), Evans and Lyons (2002), and Berger et al. (2008) find that trade imbalance possesses *large* explanatory power for exchange-rate returns. Moreover, Payne (2003), Biønnes and Rime (2005), Daníelsson and Love (2006), and Killeen, Lyons, and Moore (2006) provide evidence that order flow has a *significant*, *large* and *persistent* impact on exchange-rate returns. Finally, Evans and Lyons (2005a), Froot and Ramadorai (2005), and Evans and Lyons (2008) show how order flow *anticipates* movements in exchange rate fundamentals, while King, Sarno, and Sojli (2010) and Rime, Sarno, and Sojli (2010) find that order flow is a powerful predictor of exchange-rate returns.[2]

Recently, several attempts to model the microstructure of FX markets have been made. Thus, Hau and Rey (2006) consider a model in which exchange-rate dynamics is linked to equity returns and portfolio flows. In particular, in the face of constant risk-free interest rates, dividend innovations influence the portfolio holdings of international investors and hence affect capital flows and exchange returns. Carlson and Osler (2005), on the other hand, develop a model where exchange-rate dynamics is linked to shifts in interest rates and current account flows. Specifically, according to their formulation, the demand for foreign currency of risk-averse speculators meets the supply of non-speculative traders. While the former reflects shifts in the interest rate differential, which modify expected currency returns, the latter is price sensitive and reflects current account transactions.

Importantly, in these models, there exists *no* asymmetric information between FX traders, so that order flow cannot have any information content. On the contrary, Evans and Lyons (2005b) and Bacchetta and van Wincoop (2006) propose market microstructure models of exchange-rate determination which assign an informative role to order flow. The former contribution combines a general equilibrium set-up, derived from the recent new open macroeconomics literature, with a microstructure framework, originally proposed by Lyons (1997), in which spot contracts are traded on a decentralized dealership market. Bacchetta and van Wincoop instead combine a standard monetary model of exchange-rate determination with a microstructure framework in which trading takes place on a centralized platform. Given the recent increasing consolidation of FX markets, in the model we formulate we follow the lead of Bacchetta and van Wincoop.

In both models, there is no asymmetric information between FX dealers and their customers. Nevertheless, Froot and Ramadorai (2005) and Evans and Lyons (2005a, 2008) find that *customer* order flow possesses an information content, as end-users' transactions in FX markets anticipate movements in exchange rates and other macro-variables. Consequently, in our formulation, private information on exchange-rate fundamentals reaches FX markets via the trading activity of FX customers. By focusing on short-lived private information, we are then able to derive the optimal trading strategies for the privately informed customers and the risk-averse FX dealers, and hence find closed form solutions for the equilibrium value of the spot rate. Studying the market equilibrium, we then isolate the portfolio-balance and information effects of the customer order flow on exchange rates, identifying a clear *link* between trade imbalance, FX dealers' expectations and exchange dynamics, and on FX market characteristics. In addition, we derive testable implications which are consistent with a large body of empirical evidence concerning the statistical relations between trade innovations, exchange rates and macroeconomic innovations.

Through our formulation, we show how the market orders of privately informed customers are linearly dependent on their private signals. Thus, by trading in the FX market, privately informed customers reveal part of their private information on exchange-rate fundamentals and increase the efficiency of the FX market, while gaining speculative profits. Amid such informed trading activity, risk-averse FX dealers impose transaction costs to their customers for the liquidity they provide. In this way, they are able to unwind the losses incurred when trading with superiorly informed customers onto the rest of their customer base.

While privately informed customers improve the efficiency of the FX market, they can also make it more unstable. In fact, an important feature of our formulation is that when the informational asymmetry between market participants is particularly severe and the FX dealers are extremely risk-averse, an equilibrium for the FX market does not exist, as transaction costs increase dramatically and liquidity dries up to the point that the FX market crashes. In this respect, another important feature of our formulation is that the characteristics of the monetary markets also influence the equilibrium of the FX market. Indeed, the smaller the semi-elasticity of money demand to the interest rate, the smaller the sensitivity of the exchange rate to order flow and the more aggressively the privately informed customers trade. Then, in the limit, when such semi-elasticity is particularly small, the privately informed customers are willing to trade infinite amounts and the FX market crashes.

This article is organized as follows. In Section 2, we develop our analytical framework: we first describe how spot FX contracts are traded in the FX market and set out the corresponding equilibrium conditions; we then discuss the properties of the fundamental process which governs exchange rate dynamics. In Section 3, we introduce privately informed customers and characterize the rational expectations (RE) equilibria of the model. In Section 4, we analyze the impact of private information on the FX market and consider an extensive comparative statics exercise. Specifically, we investigate the interplay between the trading activity of the privately informed customers, their speculative profits, the efficiency and liquidity of the FX market. In Section 5, we study the effect of private information on the volatility of exchange rates. In Section 6, we propose some final remarks and suggest further lines of research. An appendix provides the proofs of the main analytical results proposed in the article.

## 2.  A market microstructure model

Here, we present a market microstructure model of exchange rate determination which replicates the specific features of the spot FX markets. Inspired by the market microstructure model of exchange-rate determination proposed by Bacchetta and van Wincoop (2006), it is based on the formulation put forward by Breedon and Vitale (2010).

In this formulation, the FX market operates as an auction market, in which FX dealers and their customers simultaneously submit their limit and market orders and then a clearing spot price for a foreign currency is found. FX dealers are short-sighted, risk-averse agents which provide liquidity to the market, charging transaction costs which cover their inventory risk and adverse selection cost. Customers are either unsophisticated traders, which trade for liquidity reasons, or informed traders, which have access to private signals on impending shifts in the real fundamental value of the foreign currency and trade strategically to gain speculative profits.

We now set to describe the structure of the FX market, deriving a modified uncovered interest rate parity which reflects the risk-aversion of the FX dealers. This parity, alongside a standard equilibrium condition for the monetary markets, allows to obtain a forward looking equation for the spot exchange rate, linking the price of the foreign currency to the expectations of the

FX dealers over its fundamentals. We finally describe our assumptions pertaining to the process governing the fundamental value and customer order flow, characterizing the linear RE equilibria of our model.

## 2.1 The FX market and FX dealers' trading

We assume that a single foreign currency is traded for the currency of a large domestic economy in the spot FX market by a population of FX dealers and their clients. Trading takes place according to a sequence of Walrasian auctions. This sequence of auctions represents the trading activity over the two centralized electronic trading platforms, Reuters D2 and EBS, which dominate FX markets. In any day $t$, a single auction is completed. When an auction is called customers enter market orders while FX dealers submit limit orders into the centralized platform. Hence, a clearing price (exchange rate) for the foreign currency is established.

At the beginning of trading day $t$, before trading starts on the centralized platform, a generic FX dealer $d$ owns $w_t^d$ units of the foreign currency and $g_t^d$ units of a domestic bond. By trading in the bond and FX markets, he can liquidate his initial endowment and invest into a portfolio of domestic bonds, $b_t^d$, foreign bonds, $f_t^d$, and real balances, $\underline{M}_t^d \equiv (M_t^d/P_t)$. Domestic bonds pay day-by-day interest rate $i_t$, foreign bonds pay day-by-day interest rate $i_t^*$, whereas real balances return total output $h(\underline{M}_t^d)$ at the end of the day, as they are employed into a given production technology. This last assumption is introduced for tractability, as it is the simplest way to obtain demand functions for domestic real balances.

Therefore, dealer $d$'s budget constraint is

$$g_t^d + S_t w_t^d = b_t^d + S_t f_t^d + \underline{M}_t^d,$$

where $S_t$ is the spot rate, i.e. the number of units of domestic currency required to purchase one unit of the foreign one. A log-linearization of the end-of-day wealth for dealer $d$ allows us to write his end-of-day wealth as follows:

$$W_{t+1}^d = (1+i_t)g_t^d - (1+i_t)\underline{M}_t^d + h(\underline{M}_t^d) + (1+i_t^*+s_{t+1})w_t^d + (i_t^* - i_t + s_{t+1} - s_t)x_t^d,$$

where $s_t = \ln(S_t)$, i.e. the log of the spot rate, and $x_t^d = f_t^d - w_t^d$, i.e. the quantity of the foreign currency dealer $d$ will purchase (sell) in the FX market.

Our dealers are supposed to be short-sighted in that their investment horizon is just one day long. This assumption is introduced for tractability, but also captures a quite a well known feature of the behavior of FX dealers, which usually attempt to unwind their FX exposure by the end of any trading day. Indeed, empirical evidence by Lyons (1995) and Biønnes and Rime (2005) shows how inventory effects are particularly strong in FX markets, in that FX dealers move quotes to manage their inventories of foreign currencies and typically conclude a daily trading session with very limited FX exposure. This clearly indicates that FX dealers are risk-averse agents. Then, dealer $d$ selects his optimal portfolio of domestic and foreign assets in order to maximize the expected utility of his end-of-day wealth, where his utility is given by a CARA utility function with coefficient of absolute risk-aversion $\gamma_d$ (and coefficient of risk-tolerance $\tau_d = 1/\gamma_d$).[3]

Assuming that dealer $d$ is the price-taker and that the log spot rate is normally distributed, the optimal quantity of the foreign currency he will trade corresponds to a linear excess demand function, i.e. a *limit order*, in the log of the spot rate,

$$x_t^d(s_t) = v_t^d(E_t^d[s_{t+1}] - s_t + (i_t^* - i_t)) - w_t^d,$$

where $E_t^d[s_{t+1}]$ denotes the conditional expectation of the next day spot rate, given the information dealer $d$ possesses in day $t$ ($E_t^d[s_{t+1}] \equiv E[s_{t+1} \mid \Omega_t^d]$), $v_t^d$ is dealer's $d$ *trading intensity* and is equal to $\tau_d \pi_{s,t}^d$, while $\pi_{s,t}^d$ represents the conditional precision of the next day spot rate, given the information dealer $d$ possesses in day $t$ ($\pi_{s,t}^d \equiv (\mathrm{Var}[s_{t+1} \mid \Omega_t^d])^{-1}$).

## 2.2 *The FX market equilibrium*

Given the demands of the individual FX dealers, through aggregation we can obtain the total demand for the foreign currency on the part of the population of FX dealers. In particular, we assume that the FX dealers form a continuum of agents of mass 1, uniformly distributed in the interval $[0, 1]$.[4] Thus, in day $t$

$$x_t \equiv \int_0^1 x_t^{d'} dd' = v_t(\bar{E}_t^1[s_{t+1}] - s_t + (i_t^* - i_t)) - w_t, \tag{1}$$

where $v_t \equiv \int_0^1 \tau_d' \pi_{s+,t}^{d'} dd'$ is the *aggregate* trading intensity of the population of FX dealers, $w_t \equiv \int_0^1 w_t^{d'} dd'$ is the corresponding *aggregate* initial endowment of the foreign bond they hold, and $\bar{E}_t^1[s_{t+1}]$ is the weighted *average* of the expected value of next day spot rate across all FX dealers, where the individual FX dealers' weights are given by their trading intensities ($\bar{E}_t^1[s_{t+1}] = (1/v_t)\int_0^1 v_t^{d'} E_t^{d'}[s_{t+1}] dd'$).

In equilibrium, the total demand for the foreign currency on the part of the population of FX dealers, $x_t$, equals the total amount of foreign currency supplied by their customers, $-o_t$.

$$x_t = -o_t. \tag{2}$$

The supply of foreign currency corresponds to the opposite of order flow, $o_t$, i.e. the imbalance between buy and sell orders submitted by customers in the FX market.[5]

## 2.3 *The uncovered interest rate parity*

Considering Equations (1) and (2) and the definition of order flow, one finds that

$$i_t - i_t^* = (\bar{E}_t^1[s_{t+1}] - s_t) + \frac{1}{v_t} z_t, \tag{3}$$

where $z_t$ corresponds to *the cumulative*-order flow, $z_t = z_{t-1} + o_t$.

Equation (3) implies that, thanks to the FX-dealers' risk-aversion, the *uncovered interest rate parity* does not hold. Indeed, the interest rate differential, $i_t - i_t^*$, is equal to the difference between the average expected devaluation of the domestic currency in day $t$, $\bar{E}_t^1[s_{t+1}] - s_t$, and a risk-premium on the foreign currency the FX dealers collectively require to hold foreign assets. This is a *time-varying* risk-premium, given by the product of the total amount of foreign assets the FX dealers have to share, $-z_t$, and the inverse of their aggregate trading intensity, $v_t$. This aggregate trading intensity is a measure of the FX dealers' capacity to hold risky assets in their portfolios.

Given Equation (3), one can show that dealer $d$'s holding of foreign currency in day $t$ can be decomposed in two parts: the former, due to a speculative motive for investment, is proportional to the difference between his individual expectation and the average expectation of the future spot rate, $\bar{E}_t^d[s_{t+1}] - \bar{E}_t^1[s_{t+1}]$; the latter associated with risk-sharing. Thus, if dealer $d$ expects a larger value for the next period spot rate than the rest of the population of FX dealers, he will be willing to bet on his *belief* and *ceteris paribus* purchase the foreign currency. If instead all FX dealers possess symmetric information, then the amount of foreign currency absorbed by the dealer $d$ for risk-sharing is proportional to his risk-tolerance.

Equation (3) also implies that the forward rate is not the unbiased estimator of the future exchange rate. Importantly, such an equation can be used to provide an explanation for the bias of the forward discount, as found for the EBS inter-dealer market by Rime, Breedon, and Vitale (2010).[6]

## 2.4 The spot rate fundamental equation

Given the production technology for real balances introduced by Bacchetta and van Wincoop (2006), $h(\underline{M}_t^d) \equiv \underline{M}_t^d - (1/\alpha)\underline{M}_t^d(\ln(\underline{M}_t^d) - 1)$, maximizing the expected utility of the log-linearized, end-of-day wealth of FX dealer $d$ with respect to $\underline{M}_t^d$ and taking logs, we find that his demand for real balances is given by

$$m_t^d = p_t - \alpha i_t,$$

where $p_t$ is the log of the price level, $p_t = \ln(P_t)$, $m_t^d$ is the log of the demand for money of dealer $d$, $m_t^d = \ln(M_t^d)$, and $\alpha$ corresponds to the semi-elasticity of money demand to the interest rate. Hence, aggregating the individual demand functions for real balances and imposing a market clearing condition, we find that in equilibrium, the domestic money market respects the condition

$$m_t = p_t - \alpha i_t, \tag{4}$$

where $m_t$ is the log of the total money supply. Assuming that a similar equilibrium condition holds for the foreign monetary, we have that

$$m_t^* = p_t^* - \alpha i_t^*, \tag{5}$$

where the asterisk $(*)$ refers to the foreign country variables.

By definition, we can write the spot rate as follows:

$$s_t \equiv p_t - p_t^* + q_t, \tag{6}$$

where $q_t$ is the log of the *real* exchange rate, $q_t \equiv \ln(S_t P_t^*/P_t)$. Combining Equation (6) with Equations (4) and (5), we conclude that

$$s_t = \alpha(i_t - i_t^*) + v_t, \tag{7}$$

where $v_t$ denotes the exchange-rate *fundamental* variable, $v_t \equiv m_t - m_t^* + q_t$.

Hence, substituting the expression for the interest rate differential presented in Equation (3) into Equation (7), we obtain the following forward-looking equilibrium condition for the spot rate

$$s_t = v_t + \alpha(\bar{E}_t^1[s_{t+1}] - s_t) + \frac{\alpha}{v_t}z_t. \tag{8}$$

In a stationary equilibrium, the conditional precision of $s_{t+1}$ of our dealers is time invariant ($\forall t$ $\pi_{s,t}^d = \pi_s^d$) and so is the aggregate trading intensity of the FX dealers ($\forall t$ $v_t = v = \int_0^1 \tau_{d'}\pi_s^d dd'$). Assuming the FX dealers possess symmetric information, proceeding via iterated substitutions, we find from Equation (8) that[7]

$$
s_t = \frac{1}{1+\alpha} \left( v_t + \frac{\alpha}{v} z_t + \sum_{k=1}^{\infty} \left( \frac{\alpha}{1+\alpha} \right)^k \left( E_t[v_{t+k}] + \frac{\alpha}{v} E_t[z_{t+k}] \right) \right),
\tag{9}
$$

where $E_t[v_{t+k}]$ $(E_t[z_{t+k}])$ is the FX dealers' conditional expectation of period $t+k$ fundamental variable, $v_{t+k}$ (cumulative demand of the foreign currency, $z_{t+k}$).

Equation (9) emphasizes two important features of our formulation. First, besides the traditional fundamental variable of the monetary approach $v_t$, pertaining to standard nominal, $m_t - m_t^*$, and real, $q_t$, macroeconomic factors, a new fundamental value $z_t$, representing the total supply of the foreign currency in the FX market, underpins the equilibrium value of the spot rate. Thus, in the presence of risk-averse FX dealers the impact of order flow on exchange rates is not only via its informative content, but also via a portfolio-balance effect. Indeed, in the next section, we will see how the FX dealers' risk-aversion heavily conditions the way private information is impounded in the spot rate. Secondly, differently from traditional microstructure models of equity markets, the impact of order flow on exchange rates is magnified by the forward looking nature of the spot rate, as a trade innovation in day $t$ will condition the FX dealers' expectations of future values of the fundamental variables, $v_{t+k}$ and $z_{t+k}$ for $k \geq 1$.

To determine a closed-form solution for the equilibrium spot rate, we now need to investigate the processes governing the dynamics of the fundamental variable $v_t$ and the cumulative demand $z_t$, alongside the information the FX dealers possess on such processes.

## 2.5 The fundamental process and customer order flow

Employing the definition of the fundamental variable, $v_t \equiv m_t - m_t^* + q_t$, we can decompose it into two terms, $v_{m,t}$ and $v_{q,t}$ $(v_t \equiv v_{m,t} + v_{q,t})$, respectively, function of the difference in the money supply in the home and foreign countries and the real exchange rate. The former, $v_{m,t}$, reflects domestic and foreign monetary policies, while the latter, $v_{q,t}$, is subject to real perturbations associated with demand and supply shocks, such as technological innovations, fiscal stimuli, taste changes and so on.

In the formulation we study, we assume that the *monetary* fundamental component $v_{m,t}$ follows a white noise process $(v_{m,t} \sim \text{NID}(0, \sigma_m^2))$, whereas the *(real)* fundamental component $v_{q,t}$ is generated by a random walk process $(v_{q,t} = v_{q,t-1} + \epsilon_{q,t}$, with $\epsilon_{q,t} \sim \text{NID}(0, \sigma_q^2))$. Indeed, several studies suggest that the real exchange rate presents a very high level of persistence,[8] which provides support for our choice for the specification of the real fundamental process. Similarly, monetary shocks present some degree of persistence. This would suggest a specification where the monetary component $v_{m,t}$ follows an AR(1) process. We have abstracted from such a broader specification, as it would greatly complicate our analysis without providing more insights on the role of private information in FX markets.

The FX dealers' customers are mostly formed by the financial arms of industrial corporations and by other unsophisticated commercial and financial traders, whose FX transactions are mostly due to liquidity needs. Their orders may be associated with current account transactions, such as trade in goods and services, transfers of capital income, public and private unilateral transfers of funds, or with capital movements, such as foreign direct and portfolio investment. We suppose that these customers correspond to *liquidity* traders and that their orders are neither price-sensitive, nor linked to innovations in the fundamental variable $v_t$. In synthesis, we assume that their aggregate market order in day $t$ will amount to pure *noise trading*, $u_t$ (where $u_t \sim \text{NID}(0, \sigma_u^2)$).[9]

Besides this population of unsophisticated customers, we assume that some sophisticated traders, *hedge funds*, may have access in day $t$ to some fundamental information, i.e. some signal on future realizations of the fundamental variable, $v_{t+k}$, or of its components, $v_{m,t+k}$ and $v_{q,t+k}$. These informed traders will act rationally and trade in the FX market on their private information in order to gain speculative profits.[10] This means that in day $t$ order flow, $o_t$, is the sum of noise, $u_t$, and informed trading, $I_t$.

## 3. Private information on fundamental innovations

In their empirical investigations, Froot and Ramadorai (2005) and Evans and Lyons (2008) find that end-users' flows in FX markets anticipates shifts in exchange-rate fundamentals. Thus, Froot and Ramadorai, using data on 6 years of FX transactions obtained from State Street Corporation, show that the end-user order flow is positively correlated with future changes in interest rates. While Evans and Lyons, using 6 years of data on Citigroup proprietary trading, show that the customer order flow helps predicting surprises in several macro-economic variables such as output growth, inflation and money supply growth.

In line with this empirical evidence, we then suppose that in day $t$, before an auction is called, $1 + L$ sophisticated traders (*hedge funds*) observe *individual* noisy signals on next day innovation, $\epsilon_{q,t+1}$, in the *real* fundamental component, $v_{q,t}$. Thus, on day $t$ hedge fund $l$ observes the private signal $\xi_{q,t}^l \equiv \epsilon_{q,t+1} + \eta_{q,t}^l$ (with $\eta_{q,t}^l \sim \text{NID}(0, \sigma_n^2)$ and $\eta_{q,t}^l \perp \eta_{q,t}^{l'}$).

The signals $\xi_{q,t}^l$ can be considered as the result of the investigation of sophisticated agents, such as currency strategists at hedge funds, which continuously search for any sort of information on future shifts in exchange-rate fundamentals. Such information mostly falls in the public domain, as it can be readily obtained from various sources, such official publications, newswire services, newsletters, and so on. However, only few sophisticated agents possess enough resources to process the considerable amount of economic data which continuously reaches financial markets and to derive the implications of such a stream of data for the dynamics of currency values. Thus, we can legitimately claim that even if they only have access to public sources of information, such sophisticated agents maintain an informational hedge, which we represent via the private signal $\xi_{q,t}^l$.[11]

We could consider a different specification in which private information pertains to the *monetary* fundamental component, $v_{m,t}$. However, we deem more likely that asymmetric information between the FX dealers and some of their customers concerns real shocks to the fundamental variable, so that we assume that informed traders observe a signal on $\epsilon_{q,t+1}$ rather than on $v_{m,t+1}$. In effect, FX dealers typically pay great attention to the liquidity conditions of the monetary markets and to shifts in interest rates. In addition, FX dealers have close-hand access to detailed high-frequency data on monetary aggregates and interest rates. In synthesis, we argue that it is less likely that other traders in FX markets have either access to more accurate data on monetary variables or a better understanding of the implications for exchange-rate dynamics of publicly available information on monetary data.

The informed traders act strategically and can only submit market orders to the centralized trading platform.[12] In addition, as typically hedge funds have a large appetite for risk-exposure, the informed traders are risk-neutral and trade in order to maximize the profits they expect to obtain from their trading activity. Finally, notice that since the economic value of their informational advantage is limited to one day, the horizon of their optimal trading strategy corresponds to one period (day).

In equilibrium, the market orders of the hedge funds possess an information content. Such information content is partially revealed through the trading process. As market orders are submitted anonymously on the centralized platform, the FX dealers are not able to observe the individual orders of the privately informed traders. Rather, they observe total order flow, that is the *sum* of the orders of the informed traders and those of the noise traders. This has a twofold implication.

On the one hand, given that hedge funds can conceal their trades within the flow of orders of other customers, they maintain an incentive to trade and can expect to gain speculative profits. On the other hand, while not revealing the exact amount of the foreign currency traded by the informed traders, order flow reflects the information content of the hedge funds' market orders and hence will be employed by the FX dealers to update their beliefs on future shifts in the fundamental value of foreign currency.

## 3.1 *RE equilibria with private information on fundamental innovations*

In our analysis, we concentrate on steady-state REs equilibria. Then, in the Appendix, we give a brief proof of the following Proposition which characterizes stationary, linear equilibria.

PROPOSITION 1 *In a symmetric and stationary, linear RE equilibrium in day t the spot rate is*

$$s_t = \lambda_m v_{m,t} + \lambda_o o_t + v_{q,t} + \frac{\alpha}{\nu} z_t, \tag{10}$$

*while the market order of a generic informed trader, l, is*

$$I_t^l = \theta_m v_{m,t} + \theta_q \xi_{q,t}^l. \tag{11}$$

*Explicit formulae for the positive coefficients $\lambda_m$, $\lambda_o$, $\theta_m$, and $\theta_q$ are derived in the Appendix.*

Proposition 1 confirms our claim that: (i) the market orders of the privately informed traders will possess an information content, as in Equation (11) $I_t^l$ is linearly dependent on the signal, $\xi_{q,t}$, hedge fund $l$ receives in day $t$; and (ii) the FX dealers will extract information on future changes in fundamentals from order flow, $o_t$, so that the trade imbalance will affect the current value of the foreign currency.

## 3.2 *The existence of stationary, linear RE equilibria*

Before we can analyze the properties of these RE equilibria, and the impact of private information on the FX market, we need to investigate the issue of their existence. The statement of Proposition 1 characterizes symmetric and stationary, linear RE equilibria, but does not establish their existence. Then, from the proof of Proposition 1, one obtains the following:

COROLLARY 1 *Stationary, linear RE equilibria exist only if $\alpha > 1 + \phi L$, with $\phi = \sigma_q^2/(\sigma_q^2 + \sigma_n^2)$.*

Corollary 1 indicates that symmetric and stationary, linear equilibria may exist *only* when the semi-elasticity of money demand to the interest rate is large enough. Technically this ensures that the second-order condition of the maximization problem for the informed traders is met. The semi-elasticity of money demand, $\alpha$, determines the sensitivity of the spot rate to order flow. This means that for $\alpha$ small, an informed trader can place large market orders in the centralized trading platform without moving much the spot rate against which she trades. Then, if $\alpha \leq 1 + \phi L$ the hedge fund finds it optimal to place infinite market orders destabilizing the FX market, which consequently crashes. A possible interpretation of this result is that when $\alpha$ is close to zero, the money demand function which pins down the dependence of the spot rate on macro fundamentals virtually breaks down and hence the order flow becomes ineffective in that it does not affect exchange-rate returns.

One should, however, notice that the condition $\alpha > 1 + \phi L$, while *necessary*, is not *sufficient* to ensure the existence of stationary, linear RE equilibria. To see this, we now turn to the analysis of the conditional variance of the spot rate.

The coefficients $\lambda_m$ and $\lambda_o$ in the symmetric and stationary, linear RE equilibria depend on the average trading intensity of the population of FX dealers, $\nu$. This in turn depends on the conditional variance of the spot rate of our population of FX dealers, which in a stationary equilibrium is time invariant, so that we can write $\mathrm{Var}[s_{t+1} \mid \Omega_t^d] = \sigma_{s+}^2, \forall t$. This conditional variance, $\sigma_{s+}^2$, depends on the coefficients $\lambda_m$ and $\lambda_o$ of the symmetric and stationary, linear RE equilibria. In other words, proving the existence of linear RE equilibria entails solving a fixed-point problem.

To solve such a fixed-point problem, we define a mapping. Thus, one can *conjecture* that a given conditional variance for the spot rate, $\sigma_{s+}^2$, applies to all FX dealers, since they share symmetric information. Given this value, one can derive the corresponding average trading intensity $\nu$ and the coefficients $\lambda_m$ and $\lambda_o$. These allow to derive the *actual* conditional variance of the average dealer, $\sigma_{s+}^{2\prime}$. In synthesis, we have the following mapping $\sigma_{s+}^{2\prime} = G(\sigma_{s+}^2)$. Fixed points for this mapping, $\sigma_{s+}^{2*} = G(\sigma_{s+}^{2*})$, identify RE equilibria for the FX market.

As a benchmark formulation, consider the scenario in which in any day $t$ a *single* hedge fund observes the real fundamental innovation $\epsilon_{q,t+1}$. We denote such formulation, where $L = 0$ and $\sigma_n^2 = 0$, as the *monopolistic* scenario. In Figure 1, we plot in the $(\sigma_{s+}, \sigma_{s+}')$ space the corresponding mapping between the conjectured and implied conditional standard deviation of next day spot rate, alongside the 45 degree straight line, for two different sets of parameter values. The intersections

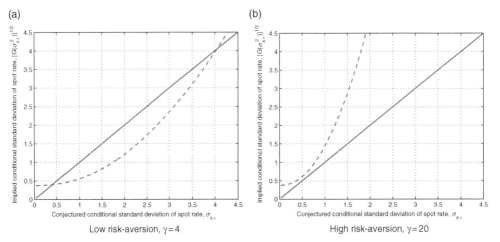

Low risk-aversion, $\gamma = 4$    High risk-aversion, $\gamma = 20$

Figure 1. Steady-state values of the conditional standard deviation. (a) Low risk-aversion, $\gamma = 4$ and (b) high risk-aversion, $\gamma = 20$.
Notes: The continuous line represents the conjectured conditional standard deviation for the generic FX dealer, $\sigma_{s+}$. The dashed line represents the implied conditional standard deviation, $\sigma_{s+}'$. This implied conditional standard deviation is obtained from the mapping $\sigma_{s+}' = [G(\sigma_{s+}^2)]^{1/2}$. In the plots an intersection between the continuous and dashed lines identifies a fixed point for the conditional standard deviation of the spot rate. Parameter values are $\alpha = 1.5$, $L = 0$, $\sigma_n^2 = 0$, $\sigma_m^2 = \sigma_q^2 = 0.15$, $\sigma_u^2 = 0.0002$. The values for $\alpha$, $\sigma_m^2$ and $\sigma_q^2$ are drawn from Breedon and Vitale (2010), that for $\sigma_u^2$ from Vitale (2006).

between the two lines identify fixed points for the mapping $G$. Thus, the right panel of Figure 1 shows that the stationary, linear RE equilibrium may not exist, as no intersection is found between the continuous and dashed lines. Moreover, the left panel of Figure 1 shows that when intersections between the continuous and the dashed lines exist they usually come in couples, suggesting potential indeterminacy of the equilibrium. However, a graphical investigation indicates that when two different RE equilibria exist only one (that is characterized by a smaller value for the conditional variance) is dynamically stable, so that the issue of multiplicity of the equilibria may be less severe than it appears at *prime facie*.

Numerical analysis shows that typically in the monopolistic scenario RE equilibria do *not* exist when: (i) as shown in Figure 1, the FX dealers are particularly risk-averse ($\gamma$ large); (ii) severe adverse selection conditions prevail in the FX market, in that the hedge fund possesses a large informational advantage (as $\sigma_q^2$, the variance of the real fundamental innovation, is large); and (iii) the signal the FX dealers receive from order flow is particulary noisy (as $\sigma_u^2$, the volume of noise trading of order flow, is large).

In Figure 2, we investigate the role that the number of informed traders, $1+L$, and the precision of the signals received by the hedge funds, $\xi_{q,t}^l$, play in determining the existence of symmetric and stationary, linear RE equilibria. Thus, in the left panel, we plot the mapping $G$ alongside the 45 degree straight line for three different values of $1+L$. Then, by focusing on dynamically stable RE equilibria, we notice a clear dependence between the number of informed traders and the conditional variance of the spot rate: the larger the number of hedge funds, the larger the conditional standard deviation of the next day spot rate, $\sigma_{s+}$, as the adverse selection mechanism

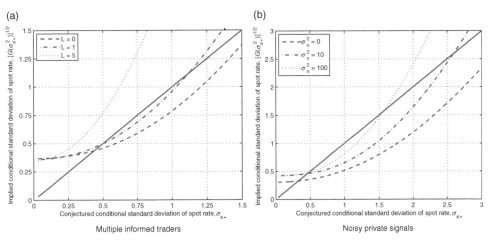

Figure 2. Steady-state values of the conditional standard deviation. (a) Multiple informed traders and (b) noisy private signals.
Notes: In the two panels, the continuous line represents the conjectured conditional standard deviation for the generic FX dealer, $\sigma_{s+}$. The dashed lines represent the implied conditional standard deviation, $\sigma_{s+}'$, obtained for different values of respectively: (i) the number of informed traders, $1+L$; and (ii) the amount of noise in the signal on the impending real fundamental shock observed by the informed trader(s), $\sigma_n^2$. This implied conditional standard deviation is obtained from the mapping $\sigma_{s+}' = [G(\sigma_{s+}^2)]^{1/2}$. In the plots, an intersection between the continuous and dashed lines identifies a fixed point for the conditional standard deviation of the spot rate. In the left panel $\alpha = 8$, $\sigma_n^2 = 0$ and $\sigma_u^2 = 0.0001$; in the right panel, instead, $\alpha = 1.5$, $L = 0$ and $\sigma_u^2 = 0.0002$. In both panels, the other parameter values are $\sigma_m^2 = \sigma_q^2 = 0.15$ and $\gamma = 4$.

which makes the spot rate react to trade innovations is more severe. The left panel also indicates that for $1 + L$ large and close to $\alpha$ (for $1 + L = 6$ versus $\alpha = 8$) no RE equilibrium exists. This is consistent with Corollary 1, as the necessary condition for the existence of symmetric and stationary, the linear RE becomes more stringent, the larger the number of informed traders.

In the right panel of Figure 2, we plot, under the assumption that only one informed trader observes the signal $\xi^l_{q,t}$ (i.e. for $L = 0$), the mapping $G$ for three different values of $\sigma^2_n$. Even in this case, we are able to outline a clear dependence between the quality of private signals and the conditional variance of the spot rate. In fact, we see that the poorer the quality of the signal observed by the informed trader (i.e. the larger $\sigma^2_n$), the larger the conditional standard deviation of the next day spot rate, $\sigma_{s+}$. This is because the FX dealers will be able to extract less precise information from the order flow they observe.

In brief, we conclude that the FX market may crash as consequence of the interplay between the risk-aversion of the FX dealers and the adverse selection mechanism induced by the presence of superiorly informed clients. In fact, from our analysis, we see that a market crash is more likely when the FX dealers are particularly risk-averse and the adverse selection mechanism is severe (because either the hedge funds possess a large informational advantage or they are numerous or the signal in the order flow is noisy).

## 3.3  The characteristics of the linear RE equilibria

From Equation (10), we derive interesting empirical implications which are borne out by recent empirical research on the microstructure of FX markets. Thus, order flow possesses a large and persistent impact on currency values as confirmed among others by Lyons (1995), Evans and Lyons (2002), Payne (2003), and Berger et al. (2008). In addition, Equation (10) implies that the spot rate and *cumulative* order flow are cointegrated, as suggested empirically by Biønnes and Rime (2005). Finally, the spot rate turns out to be a weak predictor of future fundamental values, as found by Engel and West (2005) and Froot and Ramadorai (2005).

The coefficients in Equation (10) also offer some useful insights into the properties of the equilibrium relation. Thus, the coefficients for the components of the fundamental variable are positive. This is not surprising. Indeed, an increase in $v_{m,t}$ corresponds to a rise in the relative money supply, $m_t - m_t^*$, or equivalently in the interest-rate differential, $i_t^* - i_t$. Since a rise in the interest-rate differential corresponds to an increase in the excess return on the foreign currency, the spot rate, $s_t$, appreciates when the monetary fundamental variable, $v_{m,t}$, augments. Similarly, an increase in $v_{q,t}$ corresponds to an increase in the real value of the foreign currency, whose nominal value then rises by an equal amount.

Both the cumulative order flow coefficient, $\alpha/v$, and the order flow coefficient, $\lambda_o$, are positive. This is because order flow affects the spot rate via both the portfolio-balance and information effects. According to the former, an increase in the supply of the foreign currency (i.e. a smaller $z_t$) depresses its value since the FX dealers will be willing to hold a larger quantity of the foreign currency only if they are compensated for the increased risk they bear. Thus, a smaller $z_t$ forces a depreciation of the foreign currency as this corresponds to a larger excess return the FX dealers expect from holding foreign bonds.

According to the latter effect, a positive order flow might correspond to an impending positive fundamental shock, $\epsilon_{q,t+1} > 0$, and hence it induces the FX dealers to expect an exchange-rate appreciation. Consequently, amid a positive order flow, they will be willing to hold the same amount of the foreign currency only if an increase in $s_t$ re-establishes the expected excess return foreign bonds yield.

Interestingly, Breedon and Vitale (2010) estimate a simple structural model of the exchange-rate determination closely linked to the current one, using data from EBS and Reuters' trading platforms. They find that both the portfolio-balance and information effects are at work in FX markets.

Having identified and characterized the symmetric and stationary, linear RE equilibria of the model, we are now in the position to study the impact of private information on the FX market.

## 4. Efficiency, liquidity and the value of private information

### 4.1 *Market efficiency*

By exploiting their informational advantage, the hedge funds gain speculative profits, while at the same time affecting the efficiency of the FX market, given that their market orders present an information content. By observing the flow of orders in the FX market, the FX dealers extract part of the information contained into the hedge funds' market orders. The information they are able to extract allows to reduce their uncertainty over future fundamental innovations and hence increases the overall efficiency of the FX market. The following proposition reveals how much of the private information hedge funds own is impounded into the exchange rate.

PROPOSITION 2    *When symmetric and stationary, linear RE equilibria exist, the conditional precision of the generic FX dealer, d, of next day real fundamental innovation, $\epsilon_{q,t+1}$, is*

$$\pi_{q,1} \equiv Var(\epsilon_{q,t+1} \mid \Omega_t^d)^{-1} = \left(1 + \frac{(1+\alpha)(1+L)\pi_n/\pi_q}{(2\alpha - \phi L) + (\alpha - 1 - \phi L)\pi_n/\pi_q}\right)\pi_q,$$

*where*

$$\pi_n = \frac{1}{\sigma_n^2}, \quad \pi_q = \frac{1}{\sigma_q^2}, \quad and \quad \phi = \frac{\pi_n/\pi_q}{1 + \pi_n/\pi_q}.$$

Proposition 2 suggests that the information the FX dealers extract from order flow depends on the precision of the real fundamental innovation, $\pi_q$, the precision of the private signals hedge funds observe $\pi_n$, their number, $1 + L$, and the semi-elasticity of money demand, $\alpha$.

In particular, consider the *monopolistic* scenario, where $L = 0$ and $\sigma_n^2 = 0$ ($\pi_n \uparrow \infty$). In this scenario, the informed trader is well aware that her market order presents and information content. She realizes that the FX dealers will be able to extract some information from the order flow they observe. Then, in selecting her optimal trading strategy, she balances the trade-off between two different forces. On the one hand, a larger market order on her part yields, *ceteris paribus*, larger speculative profits. On the other hand, a larger market order reveals more information on next day fundamental innovation. Thus, the price at which she will trade will be less convenient. Since the informed trader acts strategically, she will balance these two forces.

In equilibrium, she selects the optimal trading strategy given by Equation (11). From Proposition 2, we see that for $L = 0$ and $\sigma_n^2 = 0$, this leads to the following conditional precision for the FX dealers:

$$\pi_{q,1} = \frac{2\alpha}{\alpha - 1}\pi_q,$$

which is more than twice the *ex ante* value, $\pi_q$. This shows that in such a scenario, the uncertainty of the generic FX dealer on next day real fundamental innovation *more than halves* as consequence of the information he extracts from order flow. This means that the informed trader finds it optimal to consume a large part of her informational advantage.

With multiple perfectly informed traders instead, i.e. for $L > 0$ and $\sigma_n^2 = 0$, we find that

$$\pi_{q,1} = \frac{\alpha(2+L)}{\alpha - (1+L)}\pi_q$$

concluding that the Cournot competition among the informed traders forces them to consume even more of their informational advantage. On the other hand, with noisy private signals, i.e. for $L = 0$ and $\sigma_n^2 > 0$, we find that

$$\pi_{q,1} = \frac{2\alpha(\pi_n + \pi_q)}{(\alpha - 1)\pi_n + 2\alpha\pi_q}\pi_q,$$

indicating that in this scenario, the FX dealers may not extract much information from order flow.

## 4.2 Market liquidity

By exploiting their informational advantage, the hedge funds also affect the liquidity conditions prevailing in the FX market. From Equation (10), we see that transaction costs are measured by the sum of the order flow coefficient, $\lambda_o$, and the cumulative order flow coefficient, $\alpha/\nu$, in that the impact of a buy order of size one, $o_t = 1$, on the spot rate is given by $\lambda_o + \alpha/\nu$.[13] This reflects the fact that the transaction costs in the FX market are due to both an information effect and portfolio-balance one.

In this respect, notice that in the proof of Proposition 1, we derive the following corollary:

COROLLARY 2  *When symmetric and stationary, linear RE equilibria exist, the order flow coefficient is given by*

$$\lambda_o = \left(\frac{\phi(1+L)(\alpha - 1 - \phi L)}{(2 + \phi L)^2(1+\alpha)}\right)^{1/2}\left(\frac{\sigma_q^2}{\sigma_u^2}\right)^{1/2}, \quad \text{where } \pi_u = \frac{1}{\sigma_u^2}.$$

From this result, we see that when no asymmetric information exists between the hedge funds and the FX dealers, as the former does not observe any signal on $\epsilon_{q,t+1}$ (or equivalently observe a signal $\xi_{q,t}$ of no precision, so that $\pi_n = 0$ and $\phi = 0$), the order flow coefficient $\lambda_o$ vanishes. Then, transaction costs in the FX market are entirely due to the FX dealers' risk-aversion. As the FX dealers are uncertain on the final payoff associated with foreign bonds, and given that customers' trades perturb the FX dealers' inventories, they charge customers for the liquidity they provide.

On the other hand, when the FX dealers are risk-neutral, so that cumulative order flow coefficient, $\alpha/\nu$,[14] vanishes, transaction costs are entirely due to an adverse selection mechanism. In fact, in order to recoup the losses they incur when trading against superiorly informed clients, the FX dealers impose transaction costs to all their customers. In this way, they are able to unload these losses onto their unsophisticated clients.

## 4.3 The value of private information

Simple algebra yields the expected profits the hedge funds gain from their informational advantage.

PROPOSITION 3  *When symmetric and stationary, linear RE equilibria exist, the unconditional expected profits of hedge fund l are*

$$E[\Pi_t^l] = \left( \frac{\phi}{(2 + \phi L)^2} \sigma_q^2 + \frac{1}{\alpha^2(1 + \alpha)^2} \sigma_m^2 \right) \frac{1}{\lambda_o}.$$

This proposition shows how the unconditional expected profits of the hedge funds depend, via $\phi$, on their informational advantage, given by the ratio between their precision $\pi_q + \pi_n$ and the corresponding ex ante value for the FX dealers, $\pi_q$. This ratio, equal to $1 + \pi_n/\pi_q$, is increasing in $\pi_n/\pi_q$. Then, either more precise signals (a larger $\pi_n$) for the informed traders or a larger volatility of the innovation in the real fundamental component (a smaller $\pi_q$) corresponds to a bigger informational advantage for the hedge funds.

In addition, we see that the volume of noise trading, $\sigma_u^2$, which jams the signal observed by the FX dealers in the FX market and influences the slope of the price function against which the hedge funds trade, $\lambda_o$, and the semi-elasticity of money demand to the interest rate, $\alpha$, affect their unconditional expected profits $E[\Pi_t^l]$.

## 4.4  Comparative statics

To shed more light on the impact of private information on the FX market, we derive, from Propositions 2 and 3 and from Corollary 2, a series of comparative static results with respect to the informational advantage of the hedge funds, measured by the ratio $\pi_n/\pi_q$, the number of informed traders, $1 + L$, the volume of noise trading in the FX market, $\sigma_u^2$, and the semi-elasticity of money demand, $\alpha$.

### 4.4.1  The informational advantage of the hedge funds

COROLLARY 3  *When symmetric and stationary, linear RE equilibria exist, the conditional precision, $\pi_{q,1}$, of the generic FX dealer of next day real fundamental innovation, $\epsilon_{q,t+1}$, is increasing in the informational advantage of the hedge funds, $\pi_n/\pi_q$. The unconditional expected profits of hedge fund l, $E[\Pi_t^l]$ and the order flow coefficient, $\lambda_o$, are not monotonic functions of $\pi_n/\pi_q$.*

The result pertaining to the conditional precision, $\pi_{q,1}$, is not surprising, as it indicates that when the hedge funds possess a larger informational advantage, order flow will be more informative and hence that FX dealers will receive a more precise signal on the impending real fundamental innovation. However, to have a better understanding of the dependence of the efficiency of the market on the informational advantage of the hedge funds, consider that $\pi_{q,1}$ can be written as

$$\pi_q + \kappa_n(1 + L)\pi_n, \quad \text{where } \kappa_n = \frac{(1 + \alpha)}{(2\alpha - \phi L) + (\alpha - 1 - \phi L)\pi_n/\pi_q}.$$

The coefficient $\kappa_n$ can be interpreted as the proportion of the informational advantage the hedge funds release by trading in the FX market. If this value were null, the FX dealers would obtain no information on $\epsilon_{q,t+1}$ from order flow and their uncertainty over the impending fundamental innovation would not change, $\pi_{q,1} = \pi_q$. If instead $\kappa_n$ were equal to 1, the hedge funds would relinquish completely their collective informational advantage, $\pi_{q,1} = \pi_q + (1 + L)\pi_n$. For $\alpha > 1 + \phi L$, the coefficient $\kappa_n$ is decreasing in $\pi_n/\pi_q$, our measure of the hedge funds' informational advantage. Thus, we conclude that the hedge funds consume a large proportion of their informational

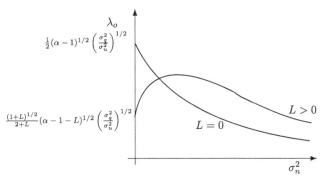

Figure 3. The dependence of $\lambda_o$ on $\sigma_n^2$.

advantage exactly when either $\pi_n$ is small or $\pi_q$ is large, i.e. exactly when their informational advantage is small.

Corollary 3 also indicates that we do not have monotonic dependence of the order flow coefficient, $\lambda_o$, and the unconditional expected profits of hedge fund $l$, $E[\Pi_l^l]$, on her informational advantage, $\pi_n/\pi_q$. Indeed, the dependence of these characteristics of the FX market on the quality of private information is complex and influenced by the monetary market conditions. Interestingly, differently from basic intuition, a larger informational advantage, $\pi_n/\pi_q$, does not *necessarily* bring about larger profits for the hedge funds. Thus, it can be shown that the unconditional expected profits of the informed trader, $E[\Pi_l^l]$, are increasing in $\pi_n/\pi_q$ insofar the semi-elasticity of the money supply, $\alpha$, is large enough.

Similarly, the dependence of the order flow coefficient, $\lambda_o$, on $\pi_n/\pi_q$ is influenced by $\alpha$.[15] To see this, consider that when only one informed trader exists, i.e. for $L = 0$, $\lambda_o$ decreases with $\sigma_n^2$ (the inverse of $\pi_n$). Hence, in this scenario, the coefficient $\lambda_o$ is an increasing function of $\pi_n/\pi_q$. This is not the case for $L \geq 1$. In fact, in this scenario $\lambda_o$ is first increasing and then decreasing in $\sigma_n^2$ as represented in Figure 3. The maximum for $\lambda_o$ is found for $\pi_n/\pi_q = 2(\alpha - 1)/[4 + (L - 2)(\alpha - 1)]$, a value which depends on the semi-elasticity of money demand, $\alpha$.

### 4.4.2 The number of informed traders

COROLLARY 4 *When symmetric and stationary, linear RE equilibria exist, the conditional precision $\pi_{q,1}$ is increasing in the number of informed traders, $1 + L$. The unconditional expected profits $E[\Pi_l^l]$ and the order flow coefficient $\lambda_o$ are not monotonic functions of $1 + L$.*

Corollary 4 indicates that with a greater number of informed traders, when RE equilibria exist, more information is revealed to the FX dealers. This is because with more informed traders, these trade collectively more aggressively on their private signals. Indeed, with more informed traders, while Cournot competition induces individual hedge funds to restrict the informative component of their market orders (for $L$ larger $\theta_q$ in Equation (11) is smaller), collectively this component is larger $((1 + L)\theta_q$ is instead bigger). In brief, order flow presents a more precise information content so that the conditional precision $\pi_{q,1}$ is larger.

This proposes an intriguing result. In fact, with a larger number of informed traders which compete on their private information, while the equilibrium of the FX market becomes more fragile (for $\alpha \leq 1 + \phi L$ no equilibrium exists and the FX market crashes), when a RE equilibrium emerges this is more efficient (the larger $1 + L$ the larger the conditional precision $\pi_{q,1}$). In other words, more informed traders increase the risk the market crashes, but at the same time, when the market

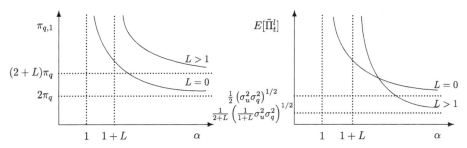

Figure 4. The dependence of $\pi_{q,1}$ and $E[\tilde{\Pi}_t^l]$ on $L$ for $\sigma_n^2 = 0$.

operates, competition among hedge funds induces them to reveal more of their informational advantage ($\kappa_n$ is increasing in $L$).

Strikingly, a greater number of informed traders does not *necessarily* imply that individually the hedge funds gain smaller unconditional expected profits. In fact, consider Figure 4, where we represent the conditional precision $\pi_{q,1}$ and the unconditional expected profits $E[\Pi_t^l]$ against $\alpha$ for different values of $L$ when $\sigma_n^2 = 0$. In the right panel, we see that for $\alpha$ small (but greater than $1 + L$) the unconditional expected profits $E[\Pi_t^l]$ are larger when $L > 1$ than when $L = 0$. At *prime facie*, this seems counter-intuitive, as common presumption is that competition among informed traders should reduce the private value of information. However, when $1 + \phi L$ approaches $\alpha$, the order flow coefficient $\lambda_o$ diminishes. The smaller $\lambda_o$ the flatter the price function against which the hedge funds trade, so that they are able to submit larger market orders and gain larger profits. Once again, these results emphasize the influence of the monetary markets in determining the impact of private information on the performance of the FX market.

Finally, one can show that $\partial \lambda_o / \partial L > 0$ if $\pi_n / \pi_q$ is large enough. This means that liquidity conditions deteriorate with a larger number of informed traders if they possess a large informative advantage. However, if their signals are unprecise, the opposite result holds. Once again, this outlines the complexity of the impact of private information on the characteristics of the FX market.

### 4.4.3 *The volume of noise trading*

COROLLARY 5 *When symmetric and stationary, linear RE equilibria exist, the unconditional expected profits $E[\Pi_t^l]$ are increasing in the volume of noise trading in the FX market, $\sigma_u^2$, while the order flow coefficient $\lambda_o$ is decreasing in $\sigma_u^2$. The conditional precision $\pi_{q,1}$ is constant in $\sigma_u^2$.*

Corollary 5 shows that a larger volume of noise trading in the FX market brings about more favorable profit opportunities for the hedge funds. Indeed, the larger $\sigma_u^2$ the more aggressively the hedge funds can trade, as their market orders are better concealed in the flow of orders, and the larger the expected profits they gain. To see this, consider that with a larger volume of noise trading, the hedge funds will be able to trade larger quantities, while relinquishing the same proportion of their informational advantage to the FX dealers, and gain larger profits on their private information.

In fact, the hedge funds find it optimal to accommodate a larger volume of noise trading by increasing proportionally the informative component of their market orders, $\theta_q \xi_{q,t}^l$, and consequently by maintaining unaltered the signal-to-noise ratio in the flow of orders the FX dealers observe. In this way, the information content of order flow is unmodified and the conditional precision, $\pi_{q,1}$, is independent of the volume of noise trading in order flow, $\sigma_u^2$, while the expected profits $E[\Pi_t^l]$ of hedge fund $l$ are bigger. This also implies that with a larger volume of noise trading, the losses the FX dealers incur from trading with the hedge funds can be diluted with a larger population of noise traders, so that the FX dealers will be able to charge less their clients for the liquidity they provide, reducing the order flow coefficient $\lambda_o$.

Since we have seen how the monetary conditions influence the equilibrium of the FX market and its characteristics, as a final comparative static exercise, we consider the impact of changes in the semi-elasticity of money demand, $\alpha$.

### 4.4.4 The semi-elasticity of money demand

COROLLARY 6 *When symmetric and stationary, linear RE equilibria exist, the conditional precision $\pi_{q,1}$ and the unconditional expected profits $E[\Pi_t^l]$ are decreasing in the semi-elasticity of money demand, $\alpha$, while the order flow coefficient $\lambda_o$ is increasing in $\alpha$.*

Corollary 6 shows a negative dependence of the conditional precision $\pi_{q,1}$ and the unconditional profits $E[\Pi_t^l]$ on $\alpha$. This is because the smaller the semi-elasticity of money demand, $\alpha$, the smaller the order flow coefficient, $\lambda_o$, and hence the slope of the price function against which the hedge funds trade. The informed traders are then induced to trade more aggressively. In doing so, they reveal more of their informational advantage (as witnessed by larger values for $\kappa_n$ and $\pi_{q,1}$) and gain larger expected profits.

In the limit, as $\alpha$ approaches the area of non-existence of RE equilibria, that is as $\alpha \downarrow 1 + \phi L$, the slope of the price function, $\lambda_o$, against which the hedge funds trade becomes so low as to bring about infinite expected profits for the informed trader, $E[\Pi_t^l] \uparrow \infty$, and a fully revealing RE equilibrium, $\pi_{q,1} \uparrow \pi_q + (1 + L)\pi_n$. In other words, under these extreme circumstances, the informed traders find it optimal to consume all their informational advantage ($\kappa_n \uparrow 1$) as this generates infinite expected profits.

## 5. Exchange rate volatility

We conclude our analysis by investigating the impact of private information on the volatility of exchange rates. Private information in the FX market conditions the second moment of exchange rate returns via two distinct channels of transmission which affect the exchange-rate volatility in opposite directions. Thus, on the one hand, because of adverse selection market orders from superiorly informed traders induce FX dealers to impose transaction costs which make exchange rates more volatile. On the other hand, market orders from privately informed traders convey information and reduce FX dealers' uncertainty on future values of the foreign currency. This reduces exchange rate volatility.

### 5.1 Comparative statics

To see how these two different channels combine, we conduct a comparative statics exercise. While an analytical expression for the unconditional variance of the spot rate innovation, $\text{Var}[s_{t+1} - s_t]$, can be obtained from Equation (10), this expression is so convoluted that its dependence on the parameters of the model is best analyzed numerically. Thus, the upper panels in Figure 5 reproduce the dependence of the unconditional standard deviation of the spot-rate innovation, $\text{Var}[s_{t+1} - s_t]^{1/2}$, on the risk-aversion of the FX dealers, $\gamma$, and the volume of noise trading in order flow, $\sigma_u^2$, for three different values of the semi-elasticity of money demand, $\alpha$, in the monopolistic scenario (where $L = 0$ and $\sigma_n^2 = 0$).

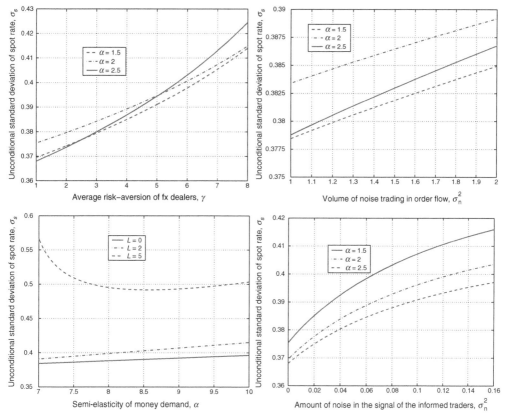

Figure 5. Comparative statics: exchange-rate volatility.
Notes: In the upper panels, we plot the unconditional standard deviation of the spot rate, $\mathrm{Var}(s_{t+1} - s_t)^{1/2}$, against the average risk-aversion of the FX dealers, $\gamma$ (left panel), and the volume of noise trading, $\sigma_u^2$ (right panel), for different values of the semi-elasticity of money demand, $\alpha$, and for $L = 0$ and $\sigma_u^2 = 0$. In the lower panels, we plot $\mathrm{Var}(s_{t+1} - s_t)^{1/2}$ against: (i) the semi-elasticity of money demand, $\alpha$, for different values of the number of hedge funds, $1 + L$, and for $\sigma_n^2 = 0$ (left panel); and (ii) the volume of noise in the signal observed by an informed trader, $\sigma_n^2$, for different values of $\alpha$ (right panel). Benchmark values for the parameters are $L = 0$, $\sigma_n^2 = 0$, $\gamma = 4$, $\sigma_m^2 = \sigma_q^2 = 0.15$ and $\sigma_u^2 = 0.0002$.

From the upper panels of Figure 5, we conclude that the volatility of the exchange rate is increasing in the risk aversion of the FX dealers, $\gamma$ (left-upper panel), and the volume of noise trading in the order flow, $\sigma_u^2$ (right-upper panel). The portfolio-balance effect explains the dependence of the exchange-rate volatility on $\gamma$ and $\sigma_u^2$. Thus, more risk-averse FX dealers will move the spot rate more to accommodate a given portfolio shift. Likewise, a larger volume of noise trading in the FX market induces a more volatile exchange rate, in that the FX dealers will accommodate ampler portfolio-shifts with larger movements in the price of foreign currency.

In the remaining panels of Figure 5, we investigate the role that the number of informed traders, $1 + L$, and the precision of their signal, $\pi_n$, plays in determining exchange-rate volatility. Thus, in the left-bottom panel, we reproduce the dependence of the unconditional standard deviation of the spot rate innovation, $\mathrm{Var}(s_{t+1} - s_t)^{1/2}$, on the semi-elasticity of money demand, $\alpha$, for different values of the number of hedge funds, $1 + L$, under the assumption that the informed traders observe the innovation in the real fundamental, $\epsilon_{q,t+1}$, while in the right panel we reproduce the dependence of $\mathrm{Var}(s_{t+1} - s_t)^{1/2}$ on the amount of noise in the signal observed by a single-informed trader, $\sigma_n^2$, for three values of the semi-elasticity of money demand, $\alpha$.

The left-bottom panel shows a clear positive dependence of the exchange-rate volatility on the number of hedge funds, as a larger $L$ exacerbates the adverse selection mechanism faced by the FX dealers and induces a more volatile exchange rate for all levels of the semi-elasticity of money demand, $\alpha$. From the right-bottom panel, we conclude that a larger $\sigma_n^2$ also determines a more volatile exchange rate. Indeed, we know that a larger $\sigma_n^2$ implies that the informational advantage of the hedge fund is smaller. Then, the adverse selection mechanism is less severe. This should reduce exchange-rate volatility. On the other hand, a less informative order flow implies that future fundamental innovations are more uncertain. As the foreign currency is then perceived to be riskier, the exchange rate should be more volatile. Figure 5 indicates that the latter effect prevails. Finally, notice that no clear pattern emerges with respect to the semi-elasticity of money demand, $\alpha$.

## 6. Concluding remarks

We have formulated a microstructure model of exchange-rate determination, where private information reaches the FX market via the trading activity of some FX dealers' customers (hedge funds) which observe signals on impending fundamental shifts and where order flow conditions the equilibrium value of a foreign currency via the portfolio-balance and information effects.

### 6.1 *A summary of our results*

Our analysis provides several results. First, our model generates empirical implications which are consistent with some recent empirical research on FX market microstructure. Thus, we find that the order flow possesses a persistent impact on the value of the foreign currency, that the cumulative order flow and the exchange rate are cointegrated and that the spot rate is a weak predictor of future fundamental values. Secondly, we clarify the impact that private information has on the characteristics of the FX market. In particular, we uncover the close link which exists between the trading activity of privately informed traders, the information that order flow signals and exchange rate dynamics. We also see how such a link influences the efficiency and liquidity of the FX market.

In our formulation, order flow possesses an information content, in that hedge funds submit market orders which are linear in their private signals. In addition, risk-averse FX dealers accommodate shifts in their portfolios by imposing a risk premium on the foreign currency. In this context, stationary RE equilibria for the FX market may not exist. This is exactly the consequence of: (i) the informational asymmetry which exists between market participants; and (ii) the risk-aversion of the FX dealers. We find that the non-existence of stationary RE is more likely when FX dealers: (i) are extremely risk-averse; (ii) face a severely uncertain environment (in that either their uncertainty over impending fundamental innovations is substantial, or the hedge funds observe private signals of very poor quality, or a large volume of noise trading in the FX market makes order flow particularly noisy); and (iii) deal with a large number of informed traders.

By trading in the FX market, the hedge funds reveal part of their private information, while on average gaining speculative profits. Then, in order to recoup the losses, the FX dealers incur dealing with such superiorly informed customers, they charge their clients for the liquidity they provide. By doing so the FX dealers manage to unwind these losses onto their non-informed customers.

Through comparative statics exercises, we see how the impact of private information on exchange-rate dynamics and on the characteristics of the FX market crucially hinges on its quality and on its dispersion among sophisticated traders. In particular, we find that the larger the informational advantage of the hedge funds, either due to a greater uncertainty of the FX dealers over the impending fundamental innovations or more accurate private signals received by the informed traders, the larger the proportion of such an advantage they preserve.

As mentioned, the larger the number of informed traders, the less likely the existence of the stationary RE equilibria. However, when these equilibria exist a larger number of hedge funds imply that a larger proportion of their informational advantage is relinquished by the informed traders. This means that with more hedge funds while the FX market is more fragile, it is also more efficient.

Finally, we outline the influence of the monetary markets over the performance of the FX market. As the slope of the price function against which the hedge funds trade depends on the semi-elasticity of money demand, the characteristics of the monetary markets condition the speculative profits of the informed traders and their optimal-trading strategy. For a larger semi-elasticity of money demand forces the hedge funds to trade less aggressively, less information is impounded in order flow. This reduces the proportion of private information released by the informed traders and their speculative profits, while the transaction costs imposed by the FX dealers are augmented.

## 6.2  *Future research*

An important assumption we have made is that private information is short-lived, so that the informed traders are forced to exploit immediately and in full their informational advantage. However, more insight into the impact of private information on the FX market would be derived from a formulation in which informed traders have access to signals on fundamental innovations which enter into the public domain in the distant future. With long-lived private information, an informed trader can decide how optimally consumed her informational advantage over time is. This modifies and enriches the transmission link between private information, order flow and exchange rate dynamics. Analyzing the impact of long-lived private information on the FX market is however a very challenging task that we leave to future research.

Similarly, we leave to future research the analysis of three alternative formulations of the model. First, we could allow for time-varying risk aversion among FX dealers, as this may vary endogenously according to the prevailing market conditions. Secondly, we could consider the possibility that some privately informed traders gain access to signals on impending shocks to the monetary component of the fundamental variable. Finally, we could assume that private information concerns order flow, in that some rational traders may possess some information on the future transactions of noise traders. Such a formulation would be particularly interesting, as within the academic debate some have argued that private information in FX markets may only concern trade imbalance.

In our formulation, noise traders correspond to unsophisticated traders, whose FX transactions are due to liquidity needs and are not motivated by movements in exchange rates, but are rather associated with the current account and capital movements. Some knowledge of the future dynamics of the FX transactions of these agents could be potentially profitable. Then, it would be fairly interesting to investigate what optimal use a rational trader could make of any information pertaining to noise trading in the FX market.

## Acknowledgements

I would like to thank the editor and the referee for valuable comments and suggestions. Hospitality by the Imperial College, where part of this research was undertaken, is gratefully acknowledged. Any errors remain my responsibility.

## Notes

1. See Lyons (2001) and Vitale (2007) for presentations of this literature.
2. One should, however, mention that such results are controversial. In particular, Sager and Taylor (2008) question the predictive power of order flow in FX markets.
3. In practice, in our multi-period setting, FX dealers maximize the end of period expected utility. While such myopic behavior contrasts with the prescriptions of standard asset allocation, and only guarantees conditional efficiency rather than unconditional efficiency, it can be justified on two grounds: first, FX dealers are indeed myopic; secondly, period-by-period maximization is now common place in the FX literature (Della Corte, Sarno, and Tsiakas 2009; King, Sarno, and Sojli, 2010; Rime, Sarno, and Sojli 2010).
4. This assumption is reasonable given that according to the Bank of International Settlements (BIS 2004) there are more than 2000 dealers operating in FX markets. Clearly this implies that all FX dealers are price-takers.
5. Consistently with the usual convention a positive $o_t$ indicates a net purchase of foreign currency. If instead $o_t$ is negative, FX customers collectively place an order to sell the foreign currency.
6. Several contributions, including among others Bilson (1981), Fama (1984), Froot and Frankel (1989), Frankel and Chinn (1993), Cavaglia, Verschoor, and Wolff (1994), Chinn and Frankel (2002), Burnside, Eichenbaum, and Rebelo (2007), Bacchetta, Mertens, and van Wincoop (2008), and Burnside, Eichenbaum, and Rebelo (2009), indicate that when running a regression of the exchange rate return on the forward discount the slope coefficient is significantly smaller than 1, the value consistent with the forward rate unbiased hypothesis. Using Equation (3) Rime, Breedon, and Vitale (2010) derive a decomposition of this slope coefficient which links its value to a time-varying risk premium related to order flow. Using EBS data they find that order flow contributes significantly to the negative bias of the forward discount.
7. In their formulation Bacchetta and van Wincoop (2006) allow for heterogeneous information among FX dealers, so that in Equation (9) the conditional expectation of future values of the exchange rate fundamentals, $E_t[\Xi_{t+k}]$, is replaced by the order $k$ average RE across all FX dealers, $\bar{E}_t^k(\Xi_{t+k}) = \bar{E}_t\bar{E}_{t+1}, \ldots, \bar{E}_{t+k-1}(\Xi_{t+k})$. In this way, a complicated infinite regress problem needs to be solved to find the equilibrium spot rate. Importantly, the computational complexity of such formulation leads to a trade off. Thus, while it allows to show that rational confusion induces a magnification effect for the impact of order flow on the spot rate, it also imposes an approximated equilibrium solution rather than the exact one we establish in the current formulation.
8. Even the most conservative estimations (Imbs et al. 2005) put its half-life at around 1 year.
9. This assumption implies that cumulative order flow, $z_t$, is not stationary. This is born out by data, as shown for instance by Rime, Breedon, and Vitale (2010) for the inter-dealer market operated via EBS.
10. Indeed, recently some financial institutions, mainly hedge and currency funds, have been allowed to complete transactions directly on the EBS trading platform. In addition, these financial institutions may access these centralized trading platforms via FX brokers.
11. In addition, in our formulation we could integrate the private signal $\xi_{q,t}^l$ with a public one. We abstract from such public signal as it would not improve our understanding of the role of private information in FX markets.
12. In a different specification, the informed traders could submit limit orders. However, limit orders are subject to execution risk. With short-lived private information informed traders will still privilege market orders as these are immediately executed.
13. The inverse of $\lambda_o + \alpha/\nu$, the market depth, is a very common measure of liquidity. The larger the market depth the larger the trade size required to move the transaction price by one and hence the larger the liquidity of the FX market.
14. Recall that the average trading intensity $\nu$ of the population of FX dealers is equal to the product of their average risk tolerance, $\tau$, and the precision on next day spot rate, $\pi_s \equiv (\mathrm{Var}[s_{t+1} \mid \Omega_t^d])^{-1}$, $\nu = \tau\pi_s$.
15. One should notice that to appreciate the overall impact of changes in the parameters of the model on the liquidity conditions of the FX market we need to investigate also their effect on the cumulative order flow coefficient, $\alpha/\nu$. Since we do not have a closed-form expression for such a value we rely on numerical analysis. The results of such analysis suggest that typically the impact of a parameter change on the order flow coefficient $\lambda_o$ tends to dominate that on $\alpha/\nu$.

## References

Bacchetta, P., E. Mertens, and E. van Wincoop. 2008. Predictability in financial markets: What do survey expectations tell us? *Journal of International Money and Finance* 28, no. 3: 406–26.

Bacchetta, P., and E. van Wincoop. 2006. Can information heterogeneity explain the exchange rate determination puzzle? *American Economic Review* 96, no. 3: 552–76.

Berger, D.W., A.P. Chaboud, S.V. Chernenko, E. Howorka, and J.H. Wright. 2008. Order flow and exchange rate dynamics in electronic brokerage system data. *Journal of International Economics* 75, no. 1: 93–109.

Bilson, J.F.O. 1981. The 'Speculative Efficiency' hypothesis. *Journal of Business* 54, no. 3: 435–51.

Biønnes, G.H., and D. Rime. 2005. Dealer behavior and trading systems in foreign exchange markets. *Journal of Financial Economics* 75, no. 3: 571–605.

BIS. 2004. *Triennal central bank survey: foreign exchange and derivatives market activity in 2004*. Basel: Bank of International Settlement.

Breedon, F., and P. Vitale. 2010. An empirical study of information and liquidity effects of order flow on exchange rates. *Journal of International Money and Finance* 29, no. 3: 504–24.

Burnside, C., M. Eichenbaum, and S. Rebelo. 2007. The returns to currency speculation in emerging markets. *American Economic Review Papers and Proceedings* 97, no. 2: 333–38.

Burnside, C., M.S. Eichenbaum, and S. Rebelo. 2009. Understanding the forward premium puzzle: a microstructure approach. *American Economic Journal: Macroeconomics* 1, no. 2: 127–54.

Carlson, A.J., and C.L. Osler. 2005. *Short-run exchange rate dynamics: evidence, theory, and evidence*. mimeo.

Cavaglia, S.M.F.G., W.F.C. Verschoor, and C.C.P. Wolff. 1994. On the biasedness of forward foreign exchange rates: irrationality or risk premia? *Journal of Business* 67, no. 3: 321–43.

Chinn, M., and J.A. Frankel. 2002. Survey data on exchange rate expectations: more currencies, more horizons, more tests. In *Monetary policy, capital flows and financial market developments in the era of financial globalization: essays in honor of Max Fry*, ed. W. Allen and D. Dickinson. London: Routledge.

Daníelsson, J., and R. Love. 2006. Feedback trading. *International Journal of Finance and Economics* 11, no. 1: 35–53.

Della Corte, P., L. Sarno, and L. Tsiakas. 2009. An economic evaluation of empirical exchange rate models. *Review of Financial Studies* 22, no. 9: 3491–3520.

Engel, C., and K.D. West. 2005. Exchange rates and fundamentals. *Journal of Political Economy* 113, no. 3: 485–517.

Evans, M.D., and R.K. Lyons. 2002. Order flow and exchange rate dynamics. *Journal of Political Economy* 110, no. 1: 170–80.

Evans, M.D., and R.K. Lyons. 2005a. Meese–Rogoff Redux: Micro-based exchange rate forecasting. *American Economics Review: Papers and Proceedings* 95, no. 2: 405–14.

Evans, M.D., and R.K. Lyons. 2005b. A new micro model of exchange rate dynamics. NBER working paper 10379, Boston.

Evans, M.D., and R.K. Lyons. 2008. *Forecasting exchange rates and fundamentals with order flow*. University of California at Berkeley, mimeo.

Fama, E.F. 1984. Forward and spot exchange rates. *Journal of Monetary Economics* 14, no. 3: 319–38.

Frankel, J.A., and M.D. Chinn. 1993. Exchange rate expectations and the risk premium: tests for a cross section of 17 countries. *Review of International Economics* 1, no. 2: 136–44.

Froot, K., and T. Ramadorai. 2005. Currency returns, intrinsic value, and institutional investor flows. *Journal of Finance* 60, no. 3: 1535–66.

Froot, K.A., and J.A. Frankel. 1989. Forward discount bias: is it an exchange risk premium? *Quarterly Journal of Economics* 104, no. 1: 139–61.

Hau, H., and H. Rey. 2006. Exchange rates, equity prices and capital flows. *Review of Financial Studies* 19, no. 1: 273–317.

Imbs, J., H. Mumtaz, M.O. Ravn, and H. Rey. 2005. PPP strikes back: aggregation and the real exchange rate. *Quarterly Journal of Economics* 120, no. 1: 1–43.

Killeen, W.P., R.K. Lyons, and M.J. Moore. 2006. Fixed versus flexible: lessons from EMS order flow. *Journal of International Money and Finance* 25, no. 4: 551–79.

King, M., L. Sarno, and E. Sojli. 2010. Timing exchange rates using order flow: the case of the Loonie. *Journal of Banking and Finance* 34, no. 12: 2917–28.

Lyons, R.K. 1995. Tests of microstructural hypotheses in the foreign exchange market. *Journal of Financial Economics* 39, nos. 2–3: 321–51.

Lyons, R.K. 1997. A simultaneous trade model of the foreign exchange hot potato. *Journal of International Economics*, 42, nos. 3–4: 275–98.

Lyons, R.K. 2001. *The microstructure approach to exchange rates*. Cambridge, MA: MIT Press.

Payne, R. 2003. Informed trade in spot foreign exchange markets: an empirical investigation. *Journal of International Economics* 61, no. 2: 307–29.

Rime, D., F. Breedon, and P. Vitale. 2010. A transaction data study of the forward discount puzzle. CEPR discussion paper 7791, London.

Rime, D., L. Sarno, and E. Sojli. 2010. Exchange rate forecasting, order flow and macroeconomic information. *Journal of Internationl Economics* 80, no. 1, 72–88.

Sager, M.J., and M.P. Taylor. 2008. Commercially available order flow data and exchange rate movements: caveat emptor. *Journal of Money Credit and Banking* 40, no. 4: 583–625.

Vitale, P. 2006. A market microstructure analysis of foreign exchange intervention. CEPR discussion paper 5468, London.

Vitale, P. 2007. A guided tour of the market microstructure approach to exchange rate determination. *Journal of Economic Surveys* 21, no. 5: 903–34.

# Appendix

*Proof of Proposition* 1   All FX dealers possess the same information sets, which in day $t$ include current and past observations of order flow $(o_t, o_{t-1}, \ldots)$ and of the fundamental components $(v_{m,t}, v_{q,t}, v_{m,t-1}, v_{q,t-1}, \ldots)$. Then, in a RE equilibrium all FX dealers will formulate the same conjecture on the trading strategy of the informed traders. In particular, assume that according to such a conjecture in any day $t$ any informed trader $l$ submits market order, $I_t^l$ (where if $I_t^l$ is positive (negative) the informed trader actually buys (sells) the foreign currency) according to the formulation given in Equation (11) where $\theta_m$ and $\theta_q$ are two generic constants.

Under these assumptions for $k > 0$, $E_t[v_{m,t+k}] = 0$, $E_t[v_{t+k}^q] = v_{q,t} + E_t[\epsilon_{q,t+1}]$ and $E_t[z_{t+k}] = z_t$, so that Equation (9) reduces to

$$s_t = \frac{1}{1+\alpha} v_{m,t} + v_{q,t} + \frac{\alpha}{1+\alpha} E_t[\epsilon_{q,t+1}] + \frac{\alpha}{v} z_t. \tag{A1}$$

To calculate $E_t[\epsilon_{q,t+1}]$ we apply the projection theorem for normal distributions,

$$E_t[\epsilon_{q,t+1}] = \frac{\pi_o}{\pi_o + \pi_{q'}} \frac{1}{(1+L)\theta_q} (o_t - (1+L)\theta_m v_{m,t}), \tag{A2}$$

where $\pi_o = (1+L)^2 \theta_q^2 \pi_u$, with $\pi_u = 1/\sigma_u^2$ and $\pi_q = 1/\sigma_q^2$, while $\pi_{q'} = \pi_q (1 + \pi_o/\pi_{n'})$ and $\pi_{n'} = (1+L)\pi_n$. Therefore, inserting Equation (A2) into Equation (A1) we find that the exchange rate respects Equation (10) where

$$\lambda_m = \frac{1}{1+\alpha} - \frac{\alpha}{1+\alpha} \frac{\pi_o}{\pi_o + \pi_{q'}} \frac{\theta_m}{\theta_q} = \frac{1}{1+\alpha} - \lambda_o(1+L)\theta_m,$$

$$\lambda_o = \frac{\alpha}{1+\alpha} \frac{\pi_o}{\pi_o + \pi_{q'}} \frac{1}{(1+L)\theta_q}.$$

Suppose now that the informed trader $l$ conjectures that: (i) the spot rate respects Equation (10); and (ii) that any other informed trader, $l'$ (with $l' \neq l$), submits a market order, $I_t^{l'}$, equal to $I_t^{l'} = \theta_m^L v_{m,t} + \theta_q^L \xi_{q,t}^{l'}$. Thus, in day $t$, informed trader $l$ will maximize the expected value of her end-of-day profits, $\Pi_t^l$, which is given by $\Pi_t^l = I_t^l(s_{t+1} - s_t + i_t^* - i_t) = I_t^l r_t$, where $r_t$ denotes the excess return on the foreign currency. The information set of the informed trader in day $t$, $\Omega_t^l$, contains past observations of the spot rate, $(s_{t-1}, s_{t-2}, \ldots)$, current and past observations of the fundamental components, $(v_{m,t}, v_{q,t}, v_{m,t-1}, v_{q,t-1}, \ldots)$, and the observation of the signal $\xi_{q,t}^l$ on next day innovation to the real fundamental component, $\epsilon_{q,t+1}$. Assuming that the spot rate respects Equation (10), informed trader $l$ can *ex-post* back-out the order flow variable $o_t$ from the spot rate, $s_t$, as long as we assume that in the distant past the order flow variable was observed or announced. Then, we can claim that $E[r_t|\Omega_t^l] = \phi(1 - \lambda_o L \theta_q^L)\xi_{q,t}^l + (\frac{1}{\alpha} - \lambda_m - \lambda_o L \theta_m^L) v_{m,t} - \lambda_o I_t^l$. The first-order condition of her optimization problem is

$$I_t = \frac{1}{2\lambda_o} \left( \frac{1}{\alpha} - \lambda_m - \lambda_o L \theta_m^L \right) v_{m,t} + \frac{\phi}{2\lambda_o} (1 - \lambda_o L \theta_q^L) \xi_{q,t}^l = \theta_m^l v_{m,t} + \theta_q^l \xi_{q,t}^l, \tag{A3}$$

while the second-order condition requires that $\lambda_o > 0$. By imposing the symmetry conditions $\forall l\ \theta_m^l = \theta_m^L = \theta_m$ and $\theta_q^l = \theta_q^L = \theta_q$, we find that

$$\theta_m = \left( \frac{1}{\alpha} - \lambda_m \right) \frac{1}{\lambda_o}, \quad \theta_q = \frac{\phi}{2 + \phi L} \frac{1}{\lambda_o}.$$

Solving simultaneously for $\theta_q$ and $\lambda_o$ we have that

$$\lambda_o = \frac{(1+L)}{(2+\phi L)} \left(\phi \frac{[\alpha - (1+\phi L)]}{(1+\alpha)(1+L)}\right)^{1/2} \left(\frac{\sigma_q^2}{\sigma_u^2}\right)^{1/2},$$

$$\theta_q = \left(\phi \frac{1+\alpha}{(1+L)[\alpha - (1+\phi L)]}\right)^{1/2} \left(\frac{\sigma_u^2}{\sigma_q^2}\right)^{1/2}.$$

For $\alpha > 1 + \phi L$, $\lambda_o > 0$ and the second-order condition of the optimization problem of the informed trader is met. Notice that employing the definition of $\lambda_m$ we find that

$$\theta_m = \frac{2+\phi L}{\alpha(1+\alpha)} \frac{1}{\phi} \theta_q = \frac{2+\phi L}{\alpha(1+\alpha)} \left(\frac{1}{\phi} \frac{1+\alpha}{(1+L)[\alpha - (1+\phi L)]}\right)^{1/2} \left(\frac{\sigma_u^2}{\sigma_q^2}\right)^{1/2},$$

$$\lambda_m = \frac{\alpha - (1+L)}{\alpha(1+\alpha)}.$$

∎

*Proof of Proposition 2*   The result is immediate. From the projection theorem for normal distributions we find that $\mathrm{Var}(\epsilon_{q,t+1} \mid \Omega_t^d)^{-1} = \pi_q + 1/(1/\pi_{n'} + 1/\pi_o)$. Substituting in $\pi_o$ the optimal trading intensity $\theta_q$ we find the expression for the conditional precision in the statement of the proposition. ∎

*Proof of Proposition 3*   Similarly, consider that $E[\Pi_t^l \mid \Omega_t^l] = E[r_t|\Omega_t^l] \times I_t^l$, where $E[r_t|\Omega_t^l] = \phi(1 - \lambda_o L\theta_q^L)\xi_{q,t}^l + (\frac{1}{\alpha} - \lambda_m - \lambda_o L\theta_m^L)v_{m,t} - \lambda_o I_t^l$. Then, by substituting into this expression the optimal trading strategy of informed trader $l$ in Equation (11), and taking expectations of the random variables, her unconditional expected profits are found. ∎

# The impact of aggressive orders in an order-driven market: a simulation approach

Gunther Wuyts

*Faculty of Business and Economics, Department of Accountancy, Finance and Insurance, Katholieke Universiteit Leuven, Leuven, Belgium*

This article investigates resiliency in an order-driven market. On basis of a vector autoregressive model capturing various dimensions of liquidity and their interactions, I simulate the effect of a large liquidity shock, measured by a very aggressive market order. I show that, despite the absence of market makers, the market is resilient. All dimensions of liquidity (spread, depth at the best prices and order book imbalances) revert to their steady-state values within 15 orders after the shock. For prices, a long run effect is found. Furthermore, different dimensions of liquidity interact. Immediately after a liquidity shock, the spread becomes wider than in the steady state, implying that one dimension of liquidity deteriorates, while at the same time, depth at the best prices increases, meaning an improvement of another liquidity dimension. In subsequent periods, the spread reverts back to the steady-state level but also depth decreases. Also, I find evidence for asymmetries in the impact of shocks on the ask and bid side. Shocks on the ask side have a stronger impact than shocks on the bid side. Finally, resiliency is higher for less-frequently traded stocks and stocks with a larger relative tick size.

## 1. Introduction

This article analyzes resiliency in an order-driven market. Resiliency refers to how fast dimensions of liquidity, such as best prices, depths or duration, recover to their normal (i.e. steady state) level after the market has been hit by a liquidity shock. Recovery of liquidity following liquidity shocks is especially crucial in order-driven markets since no market makers are present with an obligation to maintain an orderly market by providing liquidity. Can order-driven markets be resilient without their presence?

To answer this question, I develop a vector autoregressive (VAR) model that incorporates the different dimensions of liquidity (prices, depths and duration between orders). The VAR model allows for analyzing jointly these various dimensions of liquidity and capturing the interactions between them. Models such as Rosu (2009) and Parlour (1998) show that the bid and ask side of the market do not evolve independently. Also, the ask price cannot move arbitrarily far away from the bid price: Engle and Patton (2004) find that they are co-integrated. Moreover, prices and depths at these prices could interact. If an arriving trader is faced with a long queue of limit orders at the ask, she might prefer to undercut the ask to obtain price priority and probably faster execution. Based on my VAR model, I analyze resiliency by simulating a liquidity shock. In the literature, such shock is typically implemented via the innovation process of the VAR model (e.g. Beltran, Durré and Giot 2009). The disadvantage of this is that little is said about the specific origins of such 'general' shock. Therefore, I use an alternative approach by analyzing a well-defined liquidity shock having a very specific source. More specifically, I measure a liquidity shock by a very aggressive order. In particular, a liquidity shock on the ask (bid) side is defined as a very aggressive buy (sell) order that consumes at least all the depth at the three first ask (bid) prices in the book and part of the depth at the next price. It is natural to specify a liquidity shock in terms of a specific type of order (see also Degryse et al. 2005; or Large 2007), since in a limit order market, liquidity (and resiliency) is determined by the interaction between limit orders, which supply liquidity, and market orders, which consume it. Ultimately, it is the mix between both types of orders that shapes the liquidity of a limit order market. While VAR models are regularly used in market microstructure research to model resiliency, other methods have been used as well. They include the intensity model of Large (2007), copula techniques applied to multivariate transaction processes (see e.g. Nolte 2008; or Bien, Nolte and Pohlmeier 2011) and event studies (see Degryse et al. 2005). These methods all are alternatives to the VAR approach, that is used in my paper. My choice for a VAR model is economically motivated by the theoretical framework of Foucault, Kadan, and Kandel (2005) (henceforth FKK05), one of the very few theoretical contributions explicitly focussing on resiliency. Their theoretical model defines resiliency as the 'probability that the spread reverts to its competitive level before the next transaction occurs'. I measure the competitive level of variables, including the spread, by their steady-state value, i.e. their average value over time. Furthermore, FKK05 define a liquidity shock as 'a succession of market orders that enlarges the spread'. My measure of a liquidity shock – a very aggressive market order that uses several levels in the limit order book – is very close to this concept of a series of market orders that enlarges the spread. Moreover, given that FKK05 'have checked numerically that all our implications regarding our measure of market resiliency (for instance, Corollary 1) hold for the order-based measure of resiliency as well' (see p. 1185 of FKK05), I estimate my VAR model and compute the impulse responses to a liquidity shock in order time. In sum, I favor a VAR approach over the other approaches because it offers a convenient framework for analyzing resiliency in a way that is closely linked to and motivated by theory, and therefore allows an intuitive economic interpretation.

I apply my model and simulation framework to a sample of 35 Spanish index stocks over the period July–December 2000 (124 trading days). The Spanish stock market operates as an order-driven market. My key results can be summarized as follows. First, I show that, in general, the Spanish stock market is resilient, even though no market makers are present to provide liquidity at all times. The bid-ask spread, depth at the best prices and the duration between order submissions all recover to their steady-state levels within 15 orders after the liquidity shock. For the best bid and ask prices, as well as for the mid-price, a long-run effect is documented. Secondly, I find an interaction and complementarity between different dimensions of liquidity. After a liquidity shock, there is a long-run effect on prices as a result of which the spread becomes wider than in the steady state, implying that one dimension of liquidity (spread) deteriorates. However, at the same time, depth at the best prices increases which implies an improvement of another dimension of liquidity. In subsequent periods, I observe the opposite evolution: the spread reverts (declines) back to the steady-state level but also depth declines. Thirdly, after a liquidity shock, the limit order book becomes imbalanced. Following a shock on the ask side, depth at the ask side becomes considerably larger than the depth at the bid side. It takes around 15 orders for the order book to become balanced again. A similar picture is found after a shock on the bid side. Fourth, I find evidence for asymmetries in the impact of shocks on the ask and bid side. Shocks on the ask side have a larger impact and – depending on the liquidity measure though – it may take longer for the liquidity measure to recover, compared with shocks on the bid side. Finally, I find that resiliency is higher for stocks which are less frequently traded and stocks with a larger relative tick size (i.e. tick size/mid-price). These findings thus confirm the theoretical predictions in FKK05.

The remainder of this article is organized as follows. In Section 2, I relate my work to the existing literature and elaborate on the differences with and contributions to previous studies. In Section 3, the econometric model is developed. Also, I explain the simulation methodology for studying resiliency. Section 4 presents the data set used. In Section 5, first the estimation results of the VAR model are presented. Subsequently, I discuss in detail my results for resiliency. Section 6 concludes.

## 2.   Related literature and contributions

In empirical market microstructure research, the use of VAR models has been pioneered by Hasbrouck (1991). He finds that the full impact of a trade innovation is not realized instantaneously but with a lag. Moreover, the impact is higher if the stock is more infrequently traded, if the trade size is larger and if there exists a wide spread at the moment of the trade. Since this seminal paper, numerous variants and extensions have been developed. Dufour and Engle (2000) investigate the informational role of market activity and show how the dynamics in prices and trades are affected by the information revealed by the time between transactions. In the model of Easley and O'Hara (1992), the time between trades is an indication whether or not a news event has occurred. Uninformed traders use this signal to revise their beliefs about the arrival of news about which some traders might be informed. Dufour and Engle find that both the larger quote revisions and the stronger positive autocorrelation of trades are linked to a higher trading activity. In this case, prices converge faster to the full information value after an unexpected trade. When combining their results with those of Hasbrouck, they conclude that high-trading activity goes together with large spreads, high volume and a high price impact of trades. Active markets are then illiquid in the sense that the price impact of trades is higher. Both Hasbrouck (1991) and Dufour and Engle (2000) include the change in the quote mid-point (and the trade direction) as endogenous variables in their VAR models. Two more recent papers, Engle and Patton (2004) and Escribano and Pascual (2006), include both bid and ask quotes in their model and in this way allow trades to have an asymmetric impact on bid and ask prices. They also correct for co-integration between bid and ask. The motivation of Engle and Patton (2004) for including both bid and ask quotes lies in a study by Jang and Venkatesh (1991). The latter show that the most common response by liquidity suppliers to news is no adjustment, but the second preferred response is that only one of both quotes is changed. After a buy, it is more likely for the ask to be changed than for the bid. This means that the dynamics of ask and bid quotes will be different after a buy order than after a sell order. Engle and Patton (2004) find evidence for a strong asymmetric impact on bid and ask prices of buyer- and seller-initiated trades in the short run. Short-duration and medium-volume trades have the largest impact. The order of magnitude of the effects is, in general, larger in the lower trade frequency deciles. Also Escribano and Pascual (2006) find that the responses of bid and ask quotes to a trade are not necessarily symmetric. They show that the mean impact of an unexpected buy on the ask quote differs from the mean impact of an unexpected sell on the bid quote. Moreover, the sensitivity of the response of the ask to a trade innovation when market conditions are changed, differs from that of the bid quote. The impact of a buy on the ask quote depends e.g. more on the time since the previous trade than the impact of the corresponding sell on the bid quote. However, symmetry is more likely the more informative the trades are.

Coppejans, Domowitz and Madhavan (2006) also address the issue of liquidity in a limit order market, although they use five-minute intervals, instead of order time as I do. They use market depth at the buy and sell side as a measure of liquidity and the change in the mid-price as a return. With data from the limit order book of the market for Swedish stock index futures, they show that a liquidity shock on the ask (bid) side of the market lowers (increases) returns. The effects are short-lived since almost all the impact occurs during the 10 min following the shock. Moreover, they find evidence of liquidity clustering since if there is an increase in liquidity[1] on one side of the market, this leads to an increase in liquidity at the other side of the market as well. The study most related to ours is Degryse et al. (2005). They also analyze resiliency, but employ an event study instead of a simulation based on a VAR model. They find that depths stay around their mean before and after aggressive orders, whereas spreads return to their mean after about 20 best limit updates. Aggressive orders induce a long-term price effect. To conclude this paragraph, I would like to remark that my article does not aim to explain *why* a trader chooses a certain order type. Ranaldo (2004) discusses the complementary issue of the determinants of the choice of an order type by a trader. I do not model this choice, but take the submission of the order as given and analyze its aftermath. In this sense, Ranaldo focuses on the period *before* the submission of an order while I investigate the period *thereafter*. In this way, I shed some light on the consequences of the order choices and how the market responds to them. Note, however, that I do correct in the regression models for past order flow.

How does my article differ from and aim to contribute to the above-mentioned literature? First, most papers in the literature employing VAR models only focus on spreads or prices as measures for liquidity, in this way ignoring depth in the market, another important dimension of liquidity. I therefore make a contribution to Dufour and Engle (2000), Engle and Patton (2004) and Escribano and Pascual (2006) by analyzing prices, depth and duration in a unifying VAR framework (in alternative specifications I also look at spreads, depth imbalances and mid-prices), in this way disentangling spread/price effects and depth effects of shocks. Recall from the introduction that other approaches exist, next to VAR models (see e.g. Large 2007; or Bien, Nolte and Pohlmeier 2011). As argued, I opt for the VAR approach because of its close relation with theory, given the research question of my article. Further, Engle and Patton (2004) focus on the estimation results of a VAR (in error correction form) model, and do not consider the impact of liquidity shock over time as I do. Also, these authors consider the New York Stock Exchange, which is a hybrid market, while I study a pure order-driven market without market makers that have an obligation to provide liquidity, providing thus a more clear picture of a pure order-driven market. Secondly, my study differs from Coppejans, Domowitz and Madhavan (2006) since I investigate effects in order time, and thus offer a more high-frequency, less aggregate analysis. Moreover, I use a clearly identifiable liquidity shock (a very aggressive order) instead of an innovation in the error terms of the VAR model, which is harder to interpret from an economic point of view. Furthermore, my paper also differs from Degryse et al. (2005) in a number of ways. Compared with Degryse et al. (2005), my shock is a much more extreme event, since very aggressive orders are rare (less than 1% of buy or sell orders, see Table 3) but have a large price impact. Moreover, given that order types are clustered over time,[2] an event study, while having the advantage of looking directly at what happens in the limit order book around aggressive orders, has the potential drawback that multiple events (i.e. liquidity shocks) can occur within the event window. I can isolate one individual shock in my simulation framework. Furthermore, their descriptive approach does not allow for disentangling the effects of the order type and order size. Therefore, my article complements the event study in Degryse et al. (2005) by developing a formal econometric analysis of liquidity, allowing for the accommodation of some drawbacks of the descriptive approach.

I am able to correct for the problem of confounding events and can account for the state of the limit order book around aggressive orders. Moreover, I can separate the impact of an aggressive order in itself from other elements such as order size or market environment. Also interactions between dimensions of liquidity are captured in my econometric model, in contrast with an event study. Finally, I motivate the definition of my model explicitly by the theoretical literature and, in particular, Foucault, Kadan, and Kandel (2005). I also contribute to the above literature by empirically testing a number of theoretical predictions about the determinants of resiliency that emerge from their model.

## 3. Econometric methodology

### 3.1 *Modeling prices, depths and duration*

As argued in the introduction, prices and depths at the bid and ask side of the market may not move independently, but rather interact with each other. The same holds for prices and duration between updates of the limit order book. Therefore, I develop in this section an empirical model which is able to capture these elements. In empirical research, VAR models are a popular and convenient methodology for analyzing the interaction between variables of interest and their behavior around shocks. In my study, which makes use of a VAR model, the variables of interest are the best bid and ask prices in the limit order book, the depths at these best prices and duration between orders. By explicitly modeling both sides of the market, I allow for potential asymmetries between them. This approach is also in line with existing work, for example, by Engle and Patton (2004) and Escribano and Pascual (2006) who consider both bid and ask prices. When analyzing a limit order market, also depth at the best prices needs to be incorporated in the model. Parlour (1998) shows that in an order-driven market, the choice between limit and market orders depends on the depth at both sides of the book. Recall that it is precisely the mix between market and limit orders which determines liquidity in a limit order market, since they determine liquidity demand and supply, respectively. I also include duration in my model. Theory shows that the time between trades is informative. In the model of Easley and O'Hara (1992), the lack of trades (or in other words, the duration since the last trade) provides a signal about the existence of new information in the market.[3] As a result, spreads are shown to decrease as the time between trades increases. Foucault, Kadan, and Kandel (2005) show that the resiliency of a limit order market is decreasing in the order arrival rate, i.e. a market having a lower order arrival rate, is more resilient than a fast market. The reasoning is that, when the order arrival rate increases, limit order traders become less aggressive in their price improvements. As a consequence, more orders are needed to bring down the spread to its competitive level, implying resiliency declines. Empirically, Engle and Patton (2004) confirm that the impact of a trade is different depending on the time elapsed since the previous trade. They find that short-duration and medium-volume trades have the largest impacts on quote prices. Hence, I define the vector of endogenous variables $y_t$ as follows:

$$y_t = \{\Delta \ln(A_t), \Delta \ln(B_t), \ln(AD_t), \ln(BD_t), \ln(Dur_t)\} \tag{1}$$

with $A_t(B_t)$ the best ask (bid) price at time $t$, $AD_t(BD_t)$ the depth at the best ask (bid) at time $t$, $Dur_t$ the duration since the previous order and ln the natural logarithm (in Section 4.2, I provide the details how these variables are measured in my empirical implementation). In this specification, I follow Harris (1990) who considers prices and depths as two separate aspects of liquidity. I take first differences of the price series because the null hypothesis of a unit root in both the best bid and ask series cannot be rejected. These first differences of log prices can be interpreted as the return on the best bid (or ask). The time index $t$ refers to order time, i.e. I record a new observation each time when a new order occurs in the market. This means that the VAR model is specified in event time (as opposed to calendar time). If there are multiple orders at the same $1/100$ s, I take the values after the last order.

When modeling prices, depths and duration, I account for the characteristics of the order flow. Order flow is modeled by including three sets of exogenous variables. The first set describes the degree of *aggressiveness* of the submitted orders and consists of dummy variables for each order type $i = 1, \ldots, 18$. I classify each order according to a scheme which is inspired by the one proposed in Biais, Hillion and Spatt (1995) and also used in other papers, see e.g. Griffiths et al. (2000) or Ranaldo (2004). A definition of each order type is provided in Table 1. From this table, it can be seen that I use nine different types of buy order, and nine types of sell order. The orders are presented in descending aggressiveness: MO_B1 can be interpreted as the most aggressive buy order type, Canc_B3 is the least aggressive buy order. The main distinction in my classification is based on the fact whether an order is a market order or marketable limit order (MO), a (non-marketable) limit order (LO) or a cancellation or modification (Canc). From the table, it can be seen that I use a slightly more elaborate version of the Biais, Hillion and Spatt (1995) scheme. First, I add one category of market order – the most aggressive – because I want to measure a liquidity shock by a very aggressive market order $MO\_B1_t$ and $MO\_S1_t$ (and my data set allows doing so, see Section 3.2). Secondly, I also add cancellations and modifications. The reason is that, in principle, a cancellation can have the same impact as the submission of a market order. For instance, the cancellation of an order at the best ask may cause the best ask to increase, just as an aggressive market order. To make a distinction between market orders and cancellations, I added both in the classification scheme.

The second set of order flow variables is related to *order size*. For market orders, orders with a higher degree of aggressiveness have a larger order size (as can be expected from definition), see Table 3. For other order types (limit orders or modifications/cancellations), the relation

Table 1. Definition of order types.

| Notation | Definition |
|---|---|
| | Panel A: buy orders |
| MO_B1 | Market buy order that consumes at least all depth until the 3rd ask price (or a further price) and part of the subsequent level |
| MO_B2 | Market buy order that consumes minimum all depth at the best ask price and maximum part of the depth at the 3rd ask price |
| MO_B3 | Market buy order that consumes part of the depth at the best ask price |
| LO_B1 | Limit buy order that improves the best bid price |
| LO_B2 | Limit buy order that increases depth at the best bid price |
| LO_B3 | Limit buy order that queues in the book beyond the best bid price |
| Canc_B1 | Cancellation or modification of buy order that consumes all depth at the best bid price |
| Canc_B2 | Cancellation or modification of buy order that consumes part of the depth at the best bid price |
| Canc_B3 | Cancellation or modification of buy order beyond the best bid |
| | Panel B: sell orders |
| | Sell orders are classified symmetrically in the same way as buy orders from MO_S1 to Canc_S3. |

Note: This table gives an overview of the various order types. Panel A (Panel B) presents the various buy (sell) order types. The notation is given in the first column, the definition of the type in the second column.

between aggressiveness and order size is not monotonic. Therefore, by including both the degree of aggressiveness and size, I am able to disentangle aggressiveness in itself and order size. Moreover, Easley and O'Hara (1987) show that order size is important in determining price impacts. Hence, Size_MO_B1$_t$ represents the order size of an order of type MO_B1; more specifically, the variable is equal to the order size if order $t$ is of type MO_B1, and zero otherwise. For all other order types, the order size variables are defined in a similar way.

Third, to account for possible intraday patterns in returns and depth,[4] I include *time of day* dummies. I take a separate dummy for the first and last 15 min of trading because of the more pronounced trading activity during these intervals. Hence, $T01_t$ ($T18_t$) equals 1 if the order takes place between 9:00 and 9:15 a.m. (5:15 and 5:30 p.m.). The remainder of the trading day is divided in intervals of 30 min: $T02_t$ is 1 if the order is between 9:15 and 9:30 a.m., ..., $T17_t$ is 1 if the order is between 4:45 and 5:15 p.m. and zero otherwise. It needs to be remarked that other frequently used techniques for diurnal adjustments are piecewise linear splines (from the duration literature) or trigonometric functions (from the volatility literature). I have performed a robustness check and diurnally adjusted the endogenous variables and order sizes using piecewise linear splines. Re-estimating the VAR and plotting impulse responses with the adjusted variables does not change my results. I therefore use time of day dummies, because they allow for a more intuitive interpretation. This approach is also in line with other market microstructure papers using VAR models, such as Dufour and Engle (2000), Engle and Patton (2004) or Escribano and Pascual (2006).

Hence, the vector of exogenous variables $x_t$ is

$$x_t = \{MO\_B1_t, \ldots, Canc\_S2_t, \ln(Size\_MO\_B1_t), \ldots, \ln(Size\_Canc\_S2_t), T01_t, \ldots, T17_t\}, \tag{2}$$

where I left out Canc_S3$_t$ (which is then the reference category for order types) and the dummy for the last interval of the trading day $T18_t$ to avoid perfect multicollinearity in estimation.

A final point concerns the econometric properties of the series used. Best ask and bid prices not only have a unit root, but can also be expected to be *cointegrated*. Engle and Patton (2004) find empirical evidence of the presence of cointegration. In my model, the cointegrating term has a simple interpretation, being the log spread, hence: $LSpread_t = \ln(A_t) - \ln(B_t)$. This means that the VAR model is specified in error correction form. I do not impose other cointegrating relations since only bid and ask prices are found to be integrated of order 1 or $I(1)$. Depths and duration are $I(0)$.

Bringing all of the above together, my VAR model is specified as follows:

$$y_t = \sum_{l=1}^{L} A_l y_{t-l} + A_0 \sum_{m=0}^{M} B_m x_{t-m} + \Phi LSpread_{t-1} + u_t, \tag{3}$$

with $u_t$ the error term which is assumed to be white noise and $A_0$, $A_l$, $B_m$ and $\Phi$ the coefficient matrices to be estimated. Note that for the endogenous variables, only lags are included, while for the vector of exogenous variables, also the contemporaneous values are considered.

## 3.2 Resiliency

Resiliency, a crucial aspect of liquidity in order-driven markets, refers to the ability of a trading system to cope with liquidity shocks hitting the market. Earlier, I defined resiliency as 'the speed of recovery to their steady-state levels of different measures of liquidity (i.e. prices, depths and duration) after a liquidity shock hits the market'. It then remains to be specified what comprises such liquidity shock. Most of the market microstructure literature uses a 'general' shock, implemented via the error terms in a VAR model (in my case, this would be $u_t$ in Equation (3)). In contrast, my article proposes an alternative approach by using a clearly identifiable and concrete event. More specifically, I measure a *liquidity shock* on the ask (bid) side as a type MO_B1 (type MO_S1) order. From Table 1, it is clear that such orders are the most aggressive market buy (sell) orders. Such shock widens the bid-ask spread and consumes all the depth at the first three prices and some of the depth behind the third price. Note that a distinction is made between a shock on the buy and sell side of the market to investigate potential asymmetries. This measure is also in line with the one in the model of Foucault, Kadan, and Kandel (2005), who define a liquidity shock as 'a succession of market orders that enlarges the spread'. My measure of a liquidity shock – a very aggressive market order that uses several levels in the limit order book – is very close to this concept of a series of market orders that enlarge the spread.

To investigate resiliency, I start from the estimation results of the VAR model in Equation (3). I then implement a simulation of the impact of a liquidity shock (a type MO_B1 or MO_S1 order) on each of the endogenous variables. I am able to study the resiliency by comparing these impulse responses of the endogenous variables with their steady-state values, and more in particular, how fast – expressed in number of orders – variables return to their steady-state level after the shock. This methodology is also in line with the theory. Given that Foucault, Kadan, and Kandel (2005) 'have checked numerically that all our implications regarding our measure of market resiliency (for instance Corollary 1) hold for the order-based measure of resiliency as well' (see p. 1185 of their paper), I follow their theoretical model and estimate our VAR model and compute the impulse responses to a liquidity shock in order time. For the full technical discussion of my simulation methodology, I refer to the Appendix. Finally, it should be noted that I can only compute steady-state levels in a meaningful way for variables that are stationary (hence not for prices).

## 4. Data

### 4.1 *Sample*

This article uses data from the Spanish Stock Exchange SIBE, an exchange which operates essentially as a pure order-driven market. For the institutional details of SIBE and a description of its main features, I refer to Pardo and Pascual (2007). The sample contains 35 stocks that were part of the IBEX35 stock index during the sample period. The IBEX35 is composed by the 35 most liquid and active stocks, traded on the exchange. My sample period ranges from July–December 2000 and thus spans 124 trading days. The data on the limit order book contain the five best bid and ask prices and the displayed depth at each of these 10 prices. Moreover, I have data on all trades that were executed during the continuous trading session. Pre-opening or post-closing orders are not included since the trading mechanism during this period is different from the one during the trading day. All changes in the book (i.e. submitted orders) are time-stamped to 100th of a second. The trading data show price and size of each trade. The index numbers and time-stamps allow for a perfect matching of trade and limit order book data. Since the sample period is before 2001, I do not have to take into account the presence of volatility auctions (see Pardo and Pascual 2007). These auctions were only introduced on 14 May 2001. Finally, I filtered the database to exclude items that contain errors (e.g. registers out of sequence, increases in the accumulated volume over the day that are negative . . .).

Table 2 presents the summary statistics of each of the stocks in my sample. The first column shows the code of the stock. Columns 2 and 3 present the market capitalization (expressed in

Table 2. Sample: descriptive statistics.

| | Market cap | Annual trading | # Trades | Trade size | Duration | Spread | Mid-price |
|---|---|---|---|---|---|---|---|
| ACE | 2,590,264 | 1,362,467 | 342 | 1751 | 48.93 | 3.02 | 8.99 |
| ACR | 1,153,006 | 866,086 | 370 | 802 | 41.62 | 3.17 | 9.3 |
| ACS | 1,607,952 | 1,801,030 | 249 | 664 | 51.61 | 13.7 | 27.11 |
| ACX | 1,925,285 | 2,518,999 | 329 | 650 | 40.52 | 13.07 | 32.09 |
| AGS | 1,818,759 | 887,916 | 233 | 875 | 59.01 | 6.63 | 14.19 |
| ALB | 1,969,448 | 1,288,164 | 189 | 910 | 58.35 | 19.03 | 27.55 |
| ALT | 5,040,279 | 7,958,527 | 773 | 1832 | 20.93 | 4.05 | 16.31 |
| AMS | 4,663,754 | 6,940,124 | 925 | 1552 | 16.58 | 2.84 | 10.23 |
| ANA | 2,583,331 | 2,135,196 | 288 | 531 | 45.54 | 14.68 | 38.48 |
| BBVA | 50,654,255 | 61,753,870 | 2024 | 3944 | 8.58 | 1.71 | 16.07 |
| BKT | 2,709,682 | 5,406,253 | 559 | 490 | 26.33 | 11.73 | 44.19 |
| CAN | 2,252,616 | 2,861,239 | 148 | 1191 | 79.40 | 12.06 | 20.97 |
| CTG | 600,639 | 782,829 | 369 | 1316 | 34.48 | 7.29 | 18.94 |
| DRC | 1,999,276 | 1,979,024 | 440 | 1853 | 33.82 | 3.6 | 9.94 |
| ELE | 19,216,351 | 28,783,198 | 1496 | 2549 | 11.52 | 2.45 | 20.8 |
| FCC | 2,426,060 | 1,637,996 | 323 | 695 | 41.43 | 8.63 | 19.56 |
| FER | 1,907,601 | 1,144,835 | 397 | 538 | 40.02 | 4.96 | 13.92 |
| IBE | 12,035,682 | 12,600,314 | 758 | 3451 | 21.08 | 2.57 | 13.8 |
| IDR | 1,486,405 | 2,358,084 | 531 | 654 | 28.35 | 5.87 | 17.81 |
| MAP | 1,228,587 | 921,525 | 117 | 1493 | 101.95 | 12.12 | 18.27 |
| NHH | 1,565,881 | 1,780,277 | 232 | 2022 | 57.40 | 6.26 | 13.09 |
| POP | 8,056,418 | 6,826,078 | 464 | 1092 | 29.63 | 8.57 | 34.72 |
| PRS | 3,851,100 | 3,369,875 | 555 | 883 | 27.40 | 7.95 | 23.68 |
| REE | 1,359,464 | 1,075,761 | 280 | 662 | 51.85 | 4.49 | 10.66 |
| REP | 20,779,096 | 30,377,832 | 1655 | 2655 | 10.45 | 2.41 | 20.32 |
| SCH | 51,476,555 | 52,786,425 | 2962 | 3804 | 6.24 | 1.34 | 11.45 |
| SGC | 2,037,499 | 4,146,904 | 546 | 451 | 23.93 | 12.24 | 33.37 |
| SOL | 2,034,392 | 1,309,640 | 293 | 1199 | 49.64 | 4.7 | 10.92 |
| TEF | 76,396,509 | 152,323,837 | 6609 | 3505 | 2.70 | 1.56 | 21.9 |
| TPI | 2,098,936 | 5,192,664 | 1009 | 1384 | 15.35 | 2.41 | 8.83 |
| TPZ | 563,465 | 3,708,955 | 848 | 1915 | 19.48 | 1.6 | 4.92 |
| TRR | 7,206,684 | 32,774,256 | 4597 | 814 | 3.52 | 4.75 | 34.53 |
| UNF | 5,956,481 | 6,864,353 | 414 | 2159 | 36.33 | 4.4 | 20.47 |
| VAL | 836,328 | 914,042 | 254 | 1580 | 59.31 | 3.01 | 6.71 |
| ZEL | 1,989,150 | 5,817,857 | 1776 | 594 | 8.35 | 4.25 | 34.95 |

Note: This table presents the descriptive statistics of the sample. The first column gives the code of the stock, while columns 2 and 3 in the table present the market capitalization (in 1000 euro) at the end of the year 2000 and the total trading volume (in 1000 euro) during 2000. The next four columns show the average daily number of trades, the average trade size (in shares), the average duration (in seconds) between orders, the average bid-ask spread and the average mid-price, where averages are computed over the sample period. For all stocks, the tick size is equal to 0.01 euro.

1000 euro) at the end of the year 2000, and the total trading volume (in 1000 euro) during 2000, respectively. The next four columns show the average daily number of trades, the average trade size (in shares), the average duration (in seconds) between orders, the average bid-ask spread and the average mid-price. All these averages are computed over the whole sample period. From this table, it can be seen that there is substantial variation between the stocks with respect to market capitalization, trading volume and spreads. As a final remark, it should be noted that the tick size for all stocks is 1 cent (0.01 euro). Hence, bid-ask spreads expressed in cents give the same results as when expressed in the number of ticks.

## 4.2 Definition and summary statistics of endogenous and exogenous variables

Table 3 presents the summary statistics for the endogenous and exogenous variables that are used in my VAR model, specified in Section 3.1. I now provide their empirical definition and the unit of measurement. All endogenous variables, as well as log order sizes and log durations are winsorized at the 99.5% level to account for extreme outliers. In Panel A, I first show the mean, median and standard deviation for the five endogenous variables. For all stocks, the *returns* on the best ask and bid, expressed in % and denoted $\Delta \ln(A_t)$, $\Delta \ln(B_t)$, are small on average. This is due to the fact that for a majority of the orders, there is no change in the best price (see the definitions in Table 1), hence the return is zero for these observations. Subsequently, the log of *depths* at the best bid and ask, $\ln(AD_t)$ and $\ln(BD_t)$, are shown. Depths $AD_t(BD_t)$ are measured in euros and obtained by multiplying depth in shares at the best ask (bid) with the prevailing best ask (bid price). Note that the average depth at the best ask is larger than the average depth at the best bid. The average log of *duration* $\ln(Dur_t)$ is the next variable, $Dur_t$ is computed as the time in seconds between order $t-1$ and order $t$.

The second part of Panel A contains summary statistics of variables that will be used in transformations of my main model (see Sections 5.2.2 and 5.2.3). Spread is the bid-ask spread in cents, it is on average 6.36 cents. The second variable, $\ln(BADR)$ is the log of the ratio of depth at the

Table 3. Model variables: descriptive statistics.

| | Panel A: endogenous variables | | | | | | | | |
|---|---|---|---|---|---|---|---|---|---|
| | $\Delta \ln(A_t)$ | $\Delta \ln(B_t)$ | $\ln(AD_t)$ | $\ln(BD_t)$ | $\ln(Dur_t)$ | $Spread_t$ | $\ln(BADR_t)$ | $\Delta \ln(M_t)$ | $\ln(BAD\_Avg_t)$ |
| Mean | −0.0004 | 0.0002 | 9.4985 | 9.5134 | 1.7706 | 6.3600 | 0.0150 | −0.0001 | 9.5060 |
| Median | 0.0000 | 0.0000 | 9.6060 | 9.6235 | 2.3428 | 4.9100 | 0.0103 | 0.0000 | 9.6147 |
| S.d. | 0.0945 | 0.0943 | 1.2895 | 1.2684 | 2.5158 | 4.4200 | 1.7770 | 0.0772 | 1.2790 |

| | Panel B: exogenous variables | | | | | | | |
|---|---|---|---|---|---|---|---|---|
| | Buy orders | | | | Sell orders | | | |
| Notation | Frequency | Size | ln (Size) | Notation | Frequency | Size | ln (Size) |
| $MO\_B1_t$ | 0.06% | 11069 | 8.423 | $MO\_S1_t$ | 0.08% | 10845 | 8.455 |
| $MO\_B2_t$ | 5.76% | 2687 | 6.514 | $MO\_S2_t$ | 6.00% | 2836 | 6.534 |
| $MO\_B3_t$ | 15.17% | 1050 | 5.773 | $MO\_S3_t$ | 17.10% | 833 | 5.543 |
| $LO\_B1_t$ | 8.24% | 2104 | 6.582 | $LO\_S1_t$ | 7.14% | 1956 | 6.516 |
| $LO\_B2_t$ | 5.55% | 1789 | 6.618 | $LO\_S2_t$ | 4.98% | 1795 | 6.555 |
| $LO\_B3_t$ | 6.32% | 1487 | 6.468 | $LO\_S3_t$ | 6.08% | 1381 | 6.371 |
| $Canc\_B1_t$ | 2.12% | 1494 | 6.400 | $Canc\_S1_t$ | 1.87% | 1451 | 6.316 |
| $Canc\_B2_t$ | 1.07% | 1557 | 6.485 | $Canc\_S2_t$ | 0.90% | 1530 | 6.403 |
| $Canc\_B3_t$ | 6.10% | 1541 | 6.582 | $Canc\_S3_t$ | 5.47% | 1572 | 6.543 |

Note: Panel A presents the descriptive statistics of the endogenous variables, i.e. their mean, median and standard deviation across the stocks in the sample. $\Delta \ln(A)$ and $\Delta \ln(B)$ are the returns of the best ask and bid price in %, $\ln(AD)$ and $\ln(BD)$ are the log of depth in euro at the best ask (bid), $\ln(Dur)$ is the log of duration in seconds since the previous order. Spread is the bid-ask spread in cents, $\ln(BADR)$ is the log of the ratio of depth at the best bid and ask price, $\Delta \ln(M)$ is the return on the mid-price in % and $\ln(BAD\_Avg)$ is the log of the average of depth in euro at the best bid and ask price. Panel B shows the frequency of occurring, in % of the total number of orders, of the different order types, and the average order size (in shares and in logs) of each order type. The definition of the order types can be found in Table 1. In both panels, all statistics are computed after winsorizing at the 99.5% level.

best bid and ask (in euro) and can be interpreted as a measure for the imbalance of the limit order book. Its value is close to zero, implying on average a balanced book. Next, $\Delta \ln(M)$ is the return on the mid-price in % and $\ln(\text{BAD\_Avg})$ is the log of the average of depth (in euro) at the best bid and ask.

Panel B presents the frequency (in %) of occurring of the different *order types*, the average order size in shares and the log of order size per type (which are the size variables in my VAR model), the left part of the table for the buy order, the right part for sell orders. The results reveal that the most aggressive buy and sell orders (type MO_B1 and MO_S1) have the smallest frequency of occurring across order types. So when these two types are used as measures for a liquidity shock, I am looking at relatively rare events but with a large impact as they consume depth at at least the first three price levels in the order book. The most frequent order type are the market orders that are filled completely and have no price impact (type MO_B3 and MO_S3). All frequencies are in line with the findings of Biais, Hillion and Spatt (1995) or Degryse et al. (2005) for the Paris Bourse and of Griffiths et al. (2000) for the Toronto stock exchange.[5] Furthermore, it can be seen that, in general, more aggressive market orders are also larger, with the largest orders being types MO_B1 and MO_S1. At first sight, this finding may seen to be expected from their definition since these are the most aggressive orders, consuming all depth at one or more prices. However, *a priori*, it could also be true that orders are classified as aggressive because they are submitted at times when depths in the book are small. The fact that the average order size of aggressive market orders is large and moreover considerably larger than the average depth shows that this is not the case. For limit order types and cancellations/modifications, the relation between aggressiveness and order size is not monotonic, but there are no theoretical reasons to a priori expect such a monotonic relation (e.g. there is no reason why a cancellation should be smaller than a limit order). This is my motivation for including both the type and size of an order in the econometric model, in this way I distinguish both effects.

## 5. Empirical results

### 5.1 *Model estimation*

Before estimating the model, I verify the econometric properties of the series. Augmented Dickey-Fuller tests (not reported) reveal that log best prices $\ln(A_t)$ and $\ln(B_t)$ contain a unit root, while log depth at the best ask and bid and log duration between orders are stationary. As stated in Section 3, I take this into account in the model specification. During the estimation of the model in Equation (3), I include five lags of the endogenous variables ($L = 5$) and zero lags of the exogenous variables ($M = 0$). I aim to make the specification of the VAR as concise as possible, while on the other hand also optimizing the Akaike information criterion. My choice of $L = 5$ and $M = 0$ balances both points and it is also in line with the literature, see e.g. Engle and Patton (2004). The VAR model is estimated for each of the 35 stocks separately with least squares and Newey-West standard errors are computed. Recall that the definition of the variables is explained in Section 3 and the units of measurement are shown in Section 4.2, I do not repeat them here. All endogenous variables, as well as log-order sizes and log durations are winsorized at the 99.5% level to account for extreme outliers. Finally, it should be noted that all results for resiliency (see the next section), are robust to alternative specifications of the VAR model (3). Neither adding more lags of endogenous and/or exogenous variables, nor leaving out certain exogenous variables (e.g. estimating the VAR only with order-type dummies, or leaving out order sizes) changes the main conclusions obtained in the resiliency section.

Table 4 present the estimation results of the VAR model in Equation (3) with the vector of endogenous variables $y_t = \{\Delta \ln(A_t), \Delta \ln(B_t), \ln(AD_t), \ln(BD_t), \ln(Dur_t)\}$ and the vector of exogenous variables $x_t = \{MO\_B1_t, \dots, Canc\_S2_t, \ln(Size\_MO\_B1_t), \dots, \ln(Size\_Canc\_S2_t),$ $T01_t, \dots, T17_t\}$. The first column in the table gives the right-hand-side variables, the next columns are the five equations in the VAR, the header shows the endogenous variable. For each coefficient, I give the unweighted average value of the coefficient across the 35 stocks, followed – between brackets – by the number of stocks out of 35 for which the coefficient is significantly positive (first element) and negative (second element) at the 5% level. For instance, the first element in the table, $-0.0980$ (0,35), should be interpreted as follows: the average coefficient across the 35 stocks of the variable $\Delta \ln(A_{t-1})$ in the equation for $\Delta \ln(A_t)$ is $-0.0980$. For zero stocks, the coefficient is significantly positive, for 35 stocks it is significantly negative. For 0 stocks (the difference between the 35 stocks in my sample and the sum of the two elements 0+35), it is insignificant. To save space, I do not report results in the table for the log-order size variables and time-of-day dummies, but they are included in the estimation (and later in the simulation). Below the table, the average adjusted $R^2$ across stocks are reported for the different equations.

As the main interest of my analysis is in resiliency (see next subsection), I discuss the estimation results in a relatively concise way and just highlight the main points. I consider coefficients to be significant if they are so for a majority of the stocks (see the numbers between brackets). Table 4 clearly provides evidence for the existence of a number of relationships between the *endogenous variables*. First, the estimates show a relation between both sides of the market. Ask returns are significant in the bid return equation and the other way around. Depth at the ask (bid) side of the market is positively related to lagged depth at the bid (ask) side, in line with the theory in Parlour (1998) who shows that traders look at both sides of the market when determining their order choice between market and limit orders (and this choice determines liquidity in a limit order market). Secondly, my results also demonstrate an interaction between the dimensions of liquidity, as argued by Harris (1990). This can be seen by noting that $\ln(AD)$ has a negative sign in the ask and bid return equations, while $\ln(BD)$ has a positive sign. The intuition is as follows. Suppose depth at the best ask is high and a seller arrives. Since the execution probability of an additional sell limit order joining the queue at the best ask is small, she will not submit such an order. She will either improve the best ask (implying a negative return on the ask) or submit a market order. If in the latter case, all depth at the best bid is consumed, this implies a negative return on the bid. Similarly, if depth at the best bid is higher, *ceteris paribus*, a buyer will cither submit a market order (increasing the best ask if all depth at the best ask is consumed), or improve the best bid, implying a positive return on the best bid. Furthermore, I find significant coefficients of returns in the equations for depth, positive for the ask return, negative for the bid return. The intuition is that an undercutting of the best ask by a limit order, implying a negative return on the best ask, will lower depth at the best ask (since the size of the order becomes the new depth and this is most likely smaller than the depth that was present before the order). This in turn leads to a positive correlation between $\Delta \ln(A)$ and $\Delta \ln(AD)$. Turning to duration, I find a no relation between lagged duration and returns or depth. This is in line with Engle and Patton (2004) and the predictions in Easley and O'Hara (1992) that long durations do not reveal information. In the duration equation, I find significant coefficients for returns, and for the first lag of depth. Finally, in line with the literature, all endogenous variables are autocorrelated, the coefficients of their own five lags are significant. However, their magnitude quickly decreases. For returns, the autocorrelations are negative, while for depths and duration they are positive.

Table 4. Estimation results of the VAR-model.

| | $\Delta \ln(A_t)$ | $\Delta \ln(B_t)$ | $\ln(AD_t)$ | $\ln(BD_t)$ | $\ln(Dur_t)$ |
|---|---|---|---|---|---|
| $\Delta \ln(A_{t-1})$ | −0.0980 (0,35) | 0.0220 (35,0) | 0.4030 (35,0) | 0.0510 (16,0) | −1.0560 (0,35) |
| $\Delta \ln(A_{t-2})$ | −0.0540 (0,35) | 0.0110 (33,0) | 0.2730 (35,0) | 0.0630 (16,0) | 0.6410 (35,0) |
| $\Delta \ln(A_{t-3})$ | −0.0370 (0,35) | 0.0060 (23,0) | 0.1960 (35,0) | 0.0530 (12,0) | 0.4310 (30,0) |
| $\Delta \ln(A_{t-4})$ | −0.0250 (0,35) | 0.0050 (18,0) | 0.1470 (33,0) | 0.0500 (18,0) | 0.3520 (28,0) |
| $\Delta \ln(A_{t-5})$ | −0.0170 (0,35) | 0.0040 (20,1) | 0.0650 (24,0) | 0.0290 (10,0) | 0.2130 (21,0) |
| $\Delta \ln(B_{t-1})$ | 0.0220 (35,0) | −0.0990 (0,35) | −0.0600 (0,17) | −0.3970 (0,35) | 0.9840 (35,0) |
| $\Delta \ln(B_{t-2})$ | 0.0110 (32,0) | −0.0530 (0,35) | −0.0840 (0,18) | −0.2660 (0,34) | −0.6750 (0,34) |
| $\Delta \ln(B_{t-3})$ | 0.0070 (28,0) | −0.0360 (0,35) | −0.0690 (0,15) | −0.1830 (0,33) | −0.4680 (0,31) |
| $\Delta \ln(B_{t-5})$ | 0.0030 (15,1) | −0.0230 (0,35) | −0.0530 (0,13) | −0.1350 (0,33) | −0.4130 (0,35) |
| $\Delta \ln(B_{t-5})$ | 0.0020 (14,0) | −0.0160 (0,35) | −0.0380 (0,9) | −0.0500 (0,13) | −0.2710 (0,29) |
| $\ln(AD_{t-1})$ | 0.0020 (35,0) | 0.0010 (29,1) | 0.7680 (35,0) | −0.0080 (0,27) | −0.0400 (0,31) |
| $\ln(AD_{t-2})$ | −0.0010 (0,28) | 0.0000 (0,4) | 0.0430 (35,0) | 0.0040 (11,0) | 0.0080 (5,6) |
| $\ln(AD_{t-3})$ | 0.0000 (0,16) | 0.0000 (1,2) | 0.0170 (35,0) | 0.0020 (7,0) | 0.0100 (8,2) |
| $\ln(AD_{t-4})$ | 0.0000 (0,10) | 0.0000 (1,3) | 0.0140 (35,0) | 0.0020 (6,0) | 0.0070 (2,1) |
| $\ln(AD_{t-5})$ | −0.0010 (0,24) | 0.0000 (0,2) | 0.0230 (35,0) | 0.0040 (16,0) | 0.0020 (3,2) |
| $\ln(BD_{t-1})$ | −0.0010 (0,28) | −0.0020 (0,35) | −0.0080 (0,27) | 0.7530 (35,0) | −0.0530 (0,32) |
| $\ln(BD_{t-2})$ | 0.0000 (3,4) | 0.0010 (26,0) | 0.0040 (12,0) | 0.0450 (35,0) | 0.0170 (11,4) |
| $\ln(BD_{t-3})$ | 0.0000 (3,3) | 0.0000 (11,0) | 0.0020 (7,1) | 0.0170 (34,0) | 0.0100 (5,0) |
| $\ln(BD_{t-4})$ | 0.0000 (2,4) | 0.0000 (9,0) | 0.0020 (8,0) | 0.0150 (35,0) | 0.0040 (4,1) |
| $\ln(BD_{t-5})$ | 0.0000 (5,0) | 0.0000 (17,0) | 0.0040 (18,0) | 0.0230 (35,0) | 0.0080 (7,1) |
| $\ln(Dur_{t-1})$ | 0.0000 (2,7) | 0.0000 (11,1) | −0.0010 (1,11) | 0.0000 (0,6) | 0.0170 (23,6) |
| $\ln(Dur_{t-2})$ | 0.0000 (1,12) | 0.0000 (16,0) | 0.0000 (1,5) | 0.0000 (3,2) | 0.1080 (35,0) |
| $\ln(Dur_{t-3})$ | 0.0000 (0,11) | 0.0000 (10,0) | 0.0000 (0,7) | 0.0000 (2,1) | 0.0700 (35,0) |
| $\ln(Dur_{t-4})$ | 0.0000 (0,10) | 0.0000 (15,1) | 0.0000 (2,4) | 0.0000 (2,3) | 0.0700 (35,0) |
| $\ln(Dur_{t-5})$ | 0.0000 (0,4) | 0.0000 (7,1) | 0.0000 (2,5) | 0.0000 (2,4) | 0.0560 (35,0) |
| C | 0.0140 (34,0) | −0.0160 (0,33) | 1.2550 (35,0) | 1.3770 (35,0) | 1.9090 (35,0) |
| $MO\_B1_t$ | 0.4339 (35,0) | −0.0002 (0,0) | 1.3310 (34,0) | −0.0230 (0,0) | −0.3433 (0,6) |
| $MO\_B2_t$ | 0.1734 (35,0) | 0.1071 (35,0) | 0.5631 (29,6) | −0.2867 (0,34) | −0.8168 (0,35) |
| $MO\_B3_t$ | −0.0005 (0,0) | 0.0020 (7,0) | −0.5087 (0,35) | 0.0188 (11,0) | −0.5793 (0,35) |
| $LO\_B1_t$ | 0.0068 (35,0) | 0.1004 (35,0) | −0.0012 (0,2) | −0.0288 (20,14) | −1.0720 (0,35) |
| $LO\_B2_t$ | 0.0032 (28,0) | 0.0005 (0,0) | 0.0009 (2,0) | 1.0883 (35,0) | −1.3744 (0,35) |
| $LO\_B3_t$ | 0.0019 (6,0) | 0.0029 (22,0) | 0.0032 (2,0) | −0.0235 (0,18) | −0.7196 (0,35) |
| $Canc\_B1_t$ | 0.0017 (0,0) | −0.1502 (0,35) | 0.0142 (0,0) | 0.0145 (14,20) | −0.0318 (3,4) |
| $Canc\_B2_t$ | 0.0018 (0,0) | 0.0006 (0,0) | 0.0126 (0,0) | −0.7161 (0,35) | 0.0234 (2,2) |
| $Canc\_B3_t$ | 0.0024 (15,0) | 0.0022 (8,0) | 0.0026 (0,0) | 0.0049 (3,0) | −0.0366 (0,6) |
| $MO\_S1_t$ | −0.0005 (0,0) | −0.4078 (0,35) | 0.0018 (0,0) | 1.2596 (34,0) | −0.4278 (0,6) |
| $MO\_S2_t$ | −0.1061 (0,35) | −0.1664 (0,35) | −0.2856 (0,35) | 0.5306 (29,5) | −0.8299 (0,35) |
| $MO\_S3_t$ | 0.0007 (3,0) | 0.0024 (12,0) | 0.0104 (6,0) | −0.5284 (0,35) | −0.4818 (0,35) |
| $LO\_S1_t$ | −0.1027 (0,35) | −0.0046 (0,31) | −0.0204 (20,14) | −0.0036 (0,2) | −1.2030 (0,35) |
| $LO\_S2_t$ | 0.0019 (5,0) | −0.0007 (0,0) | 1.1220 (35,0) | 0.0006 (2,1) | −1.3410 (0,35) |
| $LO\_S3_t$ | −0.0005 (0,1) | 0.0006 (0,0) | −0.0233 (0,16) | 0.0053 (2,0) | −0.5815 (0,35) |
| $Canc\_S1_t$ | 0.1604 (35,0) | 0.0008 (1,0) | −0.0029 (15,20) | 0.0188 (1,0) | −0.0143 (8,2) |
| $Canc\_S2_t$ | 0.0013 (2,0) | 0.0009 (0,0) | −0.7542 (0,35) | 0.0161 (0,0) | 0.0461 (3,0) |

(*Continued*)

Table 4. (*Continued*)

| | $\Delta \ln(A_t)$ | $\Delta \ln(B_t)$ | $\ln(AD_t)$ | $\ln(BD_t)$ | $\ln(Dur_t)$ |
|---|---|---|---|---|---|
| $\ln(Size\_MO\_B1_t)$ ... | Yes | Yes | Yes | Yes | Yes |
| $\ln(Size\_Canc\_S2_t)$ $T01_t \ldots T17_t$ | Yes | Yes | Yes | Yes | Yes |
| $LSpread_{t-1}$ | $-1.7336\ (0,35)$ | $1.7459\ (35,0)$ | $-2.1463\ (0,18)$ | $-0.6536\ (5,7)$ | $-51.6209\ (1,34)$ |
| Adj $R^2$ | 0.50543 | 0.50961 | 0.71097 | 0.69507 | 0.10115 |

Note: This table presents the estimation results of equation (1): $y_t = A_0 + \sum_{l=1}^{5} A_l y_{t-l} + B_0 x_t + \Phi LSpread_{t-1} + u_t$. The vector of endogenous variables is $y_t = \{\Delta \ln(A_t), \Delta \ln(B_t), \ln(AD_t), \ln(BD_t), \ln(Dur_t)\}$ with $\Delta \ln(A_t)(\Delta \ln(B_t))$ the return on the best ask (bid) price in % at time $t$, $\ln(AD_t)(\ln(BD_t))$ the log of depth in euro at the best ask (bid) at time $t$, $\ln(Dur_t)$ the log of duration in seconds since the previous order and ln the natural logarithm. The vector of exogenous variables is $x_t = \{MO\_B1_t, \ldots, Canc\_S2_t, \ln(Size\_MO\_B1_t), \ldots, \ln(Size\_Canc\_S2_t), T01_t, \ldots T17_t\}$. The definition of the order types $MO\_B1_t, \ldots, Canc\_S2_t$ can be found in Table 1; the next set of variables in $x_t$ is the corresponding log of order sizes (in number of shares); $T01_t, \ldots T17_t$ are time of day dummies, equal to one if the order is in period $1 \ldots 17$ of the day, respectively, and zero otherwise. $LSpread_{t-1} = \ln(A_t) - \ln(B_t)$. $A_i, B_i$ and $\Phi$ are the coefficient matrices to be estimated. Estimations are done per stock using least squares. Newey-West standard errors are computed. The first column shows the right-hand-side variables, the next columns the VAR equations (endogenous variables are shown in the header). For each variable, we show the unweighted average value of the coefficient across stocks, followed – between brackets – by the number of stocks out of 35 for which the coefficient is significantly positive (first element) and negative (second element) at the 5% level. All endogenous variables, log order sizes and log durations are winsorized at the 99.5% level.

Secondly, as in Engle and Patton (2004), I find evidence of *cointegrating* behavior, since the lagged log spread $LSpread_{t-1}$ is significant in the return equations. Its sign is as expected. If the spread after the previous period was large, the ask can be expected to decrease and/or the bid to increase at the next order. This causes the spread to become narrower and revert to its equilibrium value. Also, if the spread is larger, it is easier to undercut the best prices in the limit order book. My results confirm this intuition since the lagged spread has a negative sign in the ask return equation and a positive sign in the bid return. In the duration equation, the spread has a negative sign, meaning that when the lagged spread was larger, the duration between orders will become smaller.

The signs of the *order type variables* in the return equations are as can be expected from their definition. Focusing on the types that will be used as measures for shocks, I find that type MO_B1 orders have a positive sign in the ask return equation, implying a large positive ask return of 0.4339% (recall this is on an order by order basis), while type MO_S1 orders have a negative sign in the bid return equation, i.e. a decrease in the best bid by 0.4078%. Now turning the effect of different order types on the depth at the best prices, I find that type MO_B1 orders have a positive sign in the $\ln(AD)$ equation, while type MO_S1 orders have a positive sign in the $\ln(BD)$ equation. This can be interpreted as evidence that the limit order book behind the three first prices is deep. Finally, the type of the order has only a limited impact on the duration since only few coefficients of order types are significant in the duration equation.

## 5.2 Resiliency

In this section, I discuss the results for resiliency. As explained in Section 3.2, resiliency is analyzed by simulating the paths of different dimensions of liquidity after a liquidity shock. This simulation is performed on the basis of the estimated VAR model in Equation (3). I do the simulation separately for each stock and then compute the median, and 5% and 95% percentile across the 35 stocks in my sample. In the discussion, I make a distinction between a shock occurring on the ask side of the market and one occurring on the bid side. Such shock is measured by a type MO_B1 order on the ask side and a type MO_S1 order on the bid side. I first discuss results for my main model. Next, I transform the model to analyze the behavior of the bid-ask spread and depth imbalance after a liquidity shock. A third subsection investigates mid-price returns and the average depth. In a final subsection, I make a distinction between more and less frequently traded stocks, and stocks with a large and small relative tick size.

### 5.2.1 Responses a liquidity shock

Figure 1 presents the impulse responses of different variables after a liquidity shock, during a period of 15 orders (x-axis) after the shock. I define a liquidity shock as an order of type MO_B1 in Panel A (which measures a shock on the ask side), and as an order of type MO_S1 in Panel B (measuring a shock on the bid side). The first graph in each panel draws the impact of such shock on the return (in %) on the best ask price $\Delta \ln(A)$, the second graph the impact on the return (in %) on the best bid price $\Delta \ln(B)$. The third and fourth graph display the impact of the shock on the log depth in euro at the best ask and best bid price, $\ln(AD)$ and $\ln(BD)$, respectively. The fifth graph shows the impact on log duration (in seconds) $\ln(Dur)$. The simulation for the impulse responses is done for each stock separately according to the procedure outlined in the Appendix, full lines in the graphs represent the median value of the responses across the 35 stocks in my sample, the upper (lower) dashed lines are the 95% (5%) percentile across stocks. The dotted straight lines are the steady-state levels, measured as the average value of the variable over the sample period. In my discussion below, I focus mainly on the median value (full line), if not stated explicitly otherwise, all statements should be interpreted in this way.

The return graphs demonstrate that a liquidity shock has a long-term effect on the best *prices* in the book. This effect is, however, realized very quickly. More specifically, after a type MO_B1 order, there is a positive return on the best ask, but in the periods after this initial impact of the shock, there is a small reversal: in subsequent periods, returns on the best ask are slightly negative. A similar response is found for a shock at the bid side MO_S1: a negative return on the best bid immediately after the shock, followed by a small reversal. One interpretation for this long-run effect on prices is the presence in the market of informed traders that are trading on perishable information. I further find some evidence that the impact of a shock also affects the other side of the market than where the shock occurred. There is a small positive return on the best bid following a type MO_B1 order, while after an aggressive sell order (type MO_S1) a small negative return on the best ask is found. These small effects disappear after some periods. They offset part of the effect on the own side of the market on the spread.[6] The effect on the other side of the market is confirming the empirical predictions of the model of Rosu (2009).

The impact of a liquidity shock on log *depths* is found mainly at the side of the market at which the shock occurs. More specifically, depth increases at that side of the market: after an MO_B1 order, $\ln(AD)$ increases. After this initial increase, however, $\ln(AD)$ moves gradually back to its steady state, which it achieves around 15 orders after the shock. A symmetric result applies for $\ln(BD)$ after a MO_S1 order. An interpretation can be given to this result. At first, just after the shock, the limit order book behind the best prices is deep. In subsequent periods, new liquidity (in the form of new limit orders) is provided to the market after it has been consumed by the aggressive order. These orders slightly improve the best prices, while the depth of these orders becomes the new depth at the best prices. At the other side of the market, depth remains more flat

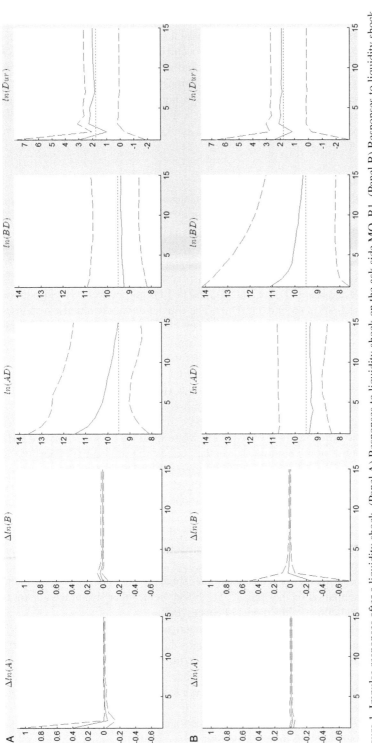

Figure 1. Impulse responses after a liquidity shock. (Panel A) Responses to liquidity shock on the ask side MO_B1. (Panel B) Responses to liquidity shock on the bid side MO_S1.

Note: This figure presents the impulse responses of a number of variables after a liquidity shock, during a period of 15 orders (x-axis) after the shock. This shock is defined as an order of type MO_B1 in Panel A (measuring a shock on the ask side), and as an order of type MO_S1 in Panel B (measuring a shock on the bid side). The definition of the order types can be found in Table 1. The first graph in each panel draws the impact of such shock on the return on the best ask price $\Delta \ln(A)$, the second graph the impact on the return on the best bid price $\Delta \ln(B)$. The third and fourth graph display the impact of the shock on the log of depth in euro at the best ask and best bid price, $\ln(AD)$ and $\ln(BD)$, respectively. The fifth graph shows the impact on log of duration (in seconds) $\ln(Dur)$. The simulation for the impulse responses is done for each stock separately, full lines in the graphs represent the median value of the responses across stocks, the upper (lower) dashed lines are the 95% (5%) percentile across stocks. The dotted straight lines are the steady-state values, measured as the average value of the variable over the sample period. The computational details for the impulse responses can be found in the Appendix.

and the impact of the shock is small since median log depths do not move far away from their steady state.

The last graphs in Figure 1 show that the duration between orders declines in the periods immediately after the shock. However, very quickly duration increases and stabilizes again around its steady-state value.

Furthermore, my results demonstrate the interaction and complementarity between different dimensions of liquidity. Immediately after the shock, there is a long-run effect on prices as a result of which the spread becomes wider than in the steady state, such that one aspect of liquidity (spread) deteriorates. However, at the same time, the depth increases which implies an improvement of another dimension of liquidity. In later periods, I have the opposite evolution: depth declines to its steady state, but also the spread reverts and becomes smaller. Also, I find evidence for asymmetries in the impact of shocks. Shocks on the ask side of the market have a larger impact than shocks on the bid side. This can be seen by comparing the responses of $\Delta \ln(A)$, $\ln(AD)$ and $\ln(\text{Dur})$ in Panel A with $\Delta \ln(B)$, $\ln(BD)$ and $\ln(\text{Dur})$ in Panel B. The median values in Panel A are always larger, in other words, a shock resulting from an aggressive buy order has a larger impact than a shock resulting from an aggressive sell order. The speed of recovery of the variables, or resiliency, is very similar, however. Escribano and Pascual (2006) also report asymmetric adjustments of ask and bid prices and asymmetric impacts of buyer- and seller-initiated trades. I show that this conclusion extends to other dimensions of liquidity such as depth and duration.

### 5.2.2 Spread and depth imbalances

An interesting transformation of my model allows for analyzing the behavior after a liquidity shock of the bid-ask spread, denoted Spread (in cents), and the log depth imbalance, $\ln(\text{BADR})$, defined as the log of the ratio of depth at the best bid and ask (in euro) $\ln(AD/BD)$. $\ln(\text{BADR}) = 0$ can then be interpreted as a balanced limit order book (i.e. depth at best bid and ask are equal), $\ln(\text{BADR}) > 0$ means that there is an imbalance at the bid side (i.e. larger depth at the bid side, compared with the ask side) and $\ln(\text{BADR}) < 0$ implies an imbalance at the ask side. I estimate a similar model as Equation (3), but redefine the vector of endogenous variables as

$$y_t = \{\text{Spread}_t, \ln(\text{BADR}_t), \ln(\text{Dur}_t)\}. \qquad (4)$$

The vector of exogenous variables $x_t$, number of lags and estimation procedure remain the same as before. Impulse responses after a liquidity shock are computed using the procedure outlined in the Appendix. Figure 2 draws these impulse response functions during a period of 15 orders ($x$-axis) after the shock. Liquidity shocks are again measured by an order of type MO_B1 in Panel A (shock on the ask side), and by an order of type MO_S1 in Panel B (shock on the bid side). The first graph in each panel draws the impact of such shock on the bid-ask spread Spread (in cents), the second graph the impact on $\ln(\text{BADR})$, the log of the ratio of depth at the best bid and ask (in euro) $\ln(AD/BD)$. The third graph shows the impact on log duration (in seconds) $\ln(\text{Dur})$. The simulation for the impulse responses is done for each stock separately, full lines in the graphs represent the median value of the responses across stocks, the upper (lower) dashed lines are the 95% (5%) percentile across stocks. The dotted straight lines are the steady-state values, measured as the average value of the variable over the sample period.

I find that the spread increases directly after the shock, to 11 cents (or ticks, since tick size in 1 cent for all stocks), which is almost double the value of the steady-state spread. This shows again that my measure for a liquidity shock indeed models indeed a significant event. Also, the order book becomes imbalanced: after a shock on the ask (bid) side, $\ln(\text{BADR})$ becomes negative

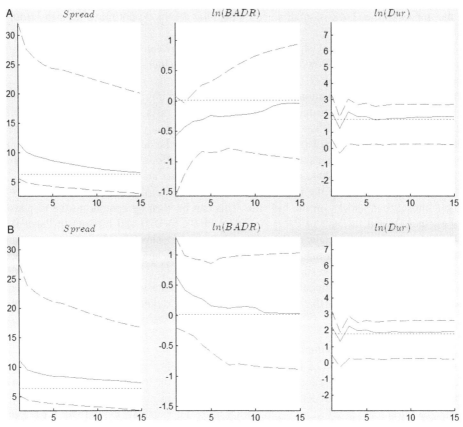

Figure 2. Spread model: impulse responses after a liquidity shock. (Panel A) Responses to liquidity shock on the ask side MO_B1. (Panel B) Responses to liquidity shock on the bid side MO_S1.

Note: This figure presents the impulse responses of a number of variables after a liquidity shock, during a period of 15 orders (x-axis) after the shock. This shock is defined as an order of type MO_B1 in Panel A (measuring a shock on the ask side), and as an order of type MO_S1 in Panel B (measuring a shock on the bid side). The definition of the order types can be found in Table 1. The first graph in each panel draws the impact of such shock on the bid-ask spread (in cents), the second graph the impact on ln(BADR), the log of the ratio of depth at the best bid and ask (in euro) ln(AD/BD). The third graph shows the impact on log of duration (in seconds) ln(Dur). The simulation for the impulse responses is done for each stock separately, full lines in the graphs represent the median value of the responses across stocks, the upper (lower) dashed lines are the 95% (5%) percentile across stocks. The dotted straight lines are the steady-state values, measured as the average value of the variable over the sample period. The computational details for the impulse responses can be found in the Appendix.

(positive), implying an larger depth at the ask (bid) side. The market is resilient, however. Both spread and depth imbalance revert to their steady-state values within around 15 orders after the liquidity shock. For log duration, the results are in line with the main model above.

### 5.2.3 Mid-price returns and average depth

In a next subsection, I implement another transformation of my model. More specifically, denote the return (in %) on the mid-price $M$ (the average of ask and bid) as $\Delta \ln(M_t)$, and let $\ln(\text{BAD\_Avg}_t)$ be the log of the average depth at the best ask and bid price. I then redefine the vector of endogenous variables as follows:

$$y_t = \{\Delta \ln(M_t), \ln(\text{BAD\_Avg}_t), \ln \text{Dur}_t)\} \tag{5}$$

The vector of exogenous variables $x_t$, number of lags, estimation procedure and computation of impulse responses remains the same as before. Figure 3 presents the impulse response functions, the interpretation of this figure is identical to the one in the previous subsection.

From Figure 3, it can be seen that a liquidity shock has a log-run impact on mid-prices. After a liquidity shock on the ask, the mid-price increases. In subsequent periods, returns are slightly negative meaning a small reversal of mid-prices. After a shock in the bid side, a symmetric result is found, which is slightly smaller in magnitude. Further, a liquidity shock induces an increase in the log average depth $\ln(\text{BAD\_Avg})$. It returns relatively quickly (within 15 orders) to its steady state after a shock at the bid side, but it takes longer after a shock on the ask side. This confirms earlier findings on asymmetries, i.e. that shocks on the ask side have a stronger impact.

### 5.2.4 *Trading frequency and relative tick size*

While the percentiles in the figures above already provided an idea of the differences in impact of liquidity shocks across stocks, I discuss this issue more in detail in this subsection. More in particular, I first divide the 35 stocks in my sample first on basis of their trading activity, i.e. the average daily number of trades (see Table 2). The most frequently traded sub-sample Most_Freq contains the 10 stocks that are most frequently traded, the least frequently traded sub-sample Least_Freq then comprises the 10 stocks who are least frequently traded (the 15 middle stocks are not considered). The distinction between frequently and less frequently traded stocks is motivated by the model of Foucault, Kadan and Kandel (2005), who show that resiliency is decreasing in the order arrival rate. The reasoning is that, when the order arrival rate increases, limit order traders become less aggressive in their price improvements. As a consequence, more orders are needed to bring down the spread to its competitive level, implying resiliency declines. I use trading frequency, i.e. the average number of daily trades, as a proxy for the arrival rate. Spierdijk (2004) shows that considerable differences exist between the price impact of trades for frequently and infrequently traded stocks. For both sub-samples, I repeat the same estimation and simulation as above. Important to stress is that the steady-state level is computed separately for the two sub-samples. The reason is that I am interested in reversion of liquidity dimensions to their normal level (steady state) and this level can be different across sub-samples. To save space, I do not report the estimation results or plots of the impulse responses, but just discuss the main findings. The results are available upon request. The key result of this analysis confirms the result in the model of Foucault, Kadan and Kandel (2005): I find a negative relation between resiliency and trading frequency. Although almost all liquidity dimensions[7] (i.e. spread, depth,[8] depth imbalance, average depth) do revert to their steady state within at maximum 30 periods, I find that reversion to the steady state occurs much faster, i.e. it takes less orders after the shock, for less frequently traded stocks. Given my and Foucault et al.'s definition of resiliency, this implies that resiliency is thus higher for less frequently traded stocks. Only for duration, I find little difference. Secondly, I find some differences in magnitude. The impact of a shock on returns is larger for stocks in the Least_Freq group, but still realized quickly. The impact on depth however is smaller for these stocks, compared with frequently traded stocks. The explanation for these findings is as follows. For frequently traded stocks, the second best price in the book and prices beyond are closer to the best one, while for the Least_Freq stocks, the difference between the subsequent prices in the book is larger. Furthermore, depth is more evenly distributed in the book

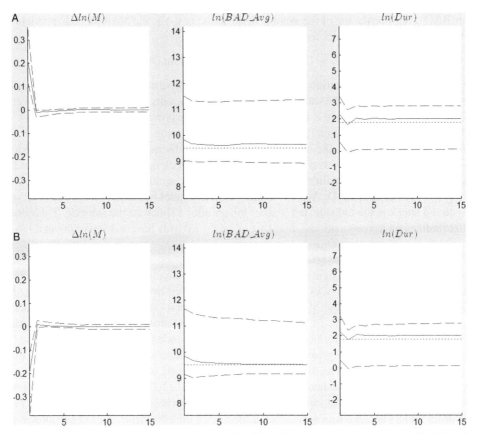

Figure 3. Mid-price model: impulse responses after a liquidity shock. (Panel A) Responses to liquidity shock on the ask side MO_B1. (Panel B) Responses to liquidity shock on the bid side MO_S1.

Note: This figure presents the impulse responses of a number of variables after a liquidity shock, during a period of 15 orders (x-axis) after the shock. This shock is defined as an order of type MO_B1 in Panel A (measuring a shock on the ask side), and as an order of type MO_S1 in Panel B (measuring a shock on the bid side). The definition of the order types can be found in Table 1. The first graph in each panel draws the impact of such shock on the return (in %) on the mid-price $\Delta \ln(M)$, with $M$ defined as the average of the best ask and bid. The second graph plots the impact on the log of the average of depth at the best bid and ask (in euro) ln(BAD_Avg). The third graph shows the impact on log of duration (in seconds) ln(Dur). The simulation for the impulse responses is done for each stock separately, full lines in the graphs represent the median value of the responses across stocks, the upper (lower) dashed lines are the 95% (5%) percentile across stocks. The dotted straight lines are the steady-state values, measured as the average value of the variable over the sample period. The computational details for the impulse responses can be found in the Appendix.

for Least_Freq stocks than for Most_Freq stocks for which depth beyond the best prices is larger. For duration, the impact of a shock is larger for Least_Freq stocks. Important to note is that while the recovery of variables, is expressed in number of orders for the two sub-samples, this takes much more time expressed in seconds for Least_Freq stocks than in the case of Most_Freq stocks, since the time between orders is larger for the latter. In other words, the period of 15 orders is much longer (in seconds) for these Least_Freq stocks, since the duration between orders is larger.

Next, I create two sub-samples based on relative tick size. The relative tick size Rel_tick for each stock is defined as the ratio of the tick size (in cent) to the average price mid-price (in euro):

$$Rel\_ts = \frac{\text{tick size}}{\text{average mid-price}} \tag{6}$$

Creating separate groups based on the minimum price variation is in line with the model of Foucault, Kadan and Kandel (2005). They show that there exists a link between the resiliency of an order-driven market and tick size. More specifically, a smaller tick size reduces resiliency.[9] The reasoning is that when the tick size is larger, traders need to improve prices by more than they would with a smaller tick size in order to obtain price priority. This spread improvement effect causes the bid-ask spread to narrow faster between transactions, making the market more resilient. The sub-sample Small_Tick contains the 10 stocks with the smallest relative tick size, the sub-sample Large_Tick the 10 stocks with the largest relative tick size (the 15 middle stocks are again not considered). Again, I compute the steady-state level separately for the two sub-samples. To save space, I do not report the estimation results or plots of the impulse responses, but discuss the main findings. I find that – as predicted theoretically by Foucault et al. – that resiliency is higher for stocks with a larger relative tick size. For the Large_Tick subsample, all liquidity dimensions (i.e. spread, depth, depth imbalance and average depth) return faster to their respective steady-state levels, compared with the Small_Tick subsample. Secondly, I also find some differences in magnitude. The results show that the impact of an aggressive order on returns is much larger for large tick stocks. Thirdly, the impact of aggressive orders on depth is also larger for large tick stocks. This is the case both at the side of the market at which the aggressive order was submitted as on the other side. This comparison between both groups for returns and depth suggests that the larger relative tick size is a binding constraint for this group of stocks. These results are in line with the literature that investigates tick size. When faced with a smaller tick size, traders use more intermediate prices, but the depth at these prices is lower. Finally, the impact of a shock on duration is comparable for stocks with large and small tick size.

## 6. Conclusion

In this article, I analyze resiliency in an order-driven market. I develop a VAR model that captures different dimensions of liquidity, being prices, depths and duration. My econometric model allows for taking into account relations between bid and ask sides of the market, as well as between liquidity dimensions. I use the estimated VAR to simulate liquidity shocks, measured by very aggressive buy and sell orders that at least consume all depth at the first three ask or bid prices in the book. A liquidity shock is found to have a permanent effect on prices at the side of the market at which the shock occurred, but the impact is realized almost instantaneously. However, in line with Rosu (2009), I also document an effect – though smaller in magnitude – on the best price at the other side of the market, which partly offsets the effect of the own side. Depth at the best prices increases after a liquidity shock, but mainly at the side of the market of the shock. Duration declines just after a negative shock, but increases quickly again to converges within a few orders to its average value.

My results clearly demonstrate the importance of incorporating different dimensions of liquidity in the analysis. After a liquidity shock, I find a permanent effect on prices, with returns (in absolute value) of initially around 0.4% (realized on an order-by-order basis) and a widening of the spread (almost doubling compared with its steady-state value). On the other hand, depth at the best prices increases, initially with up to 20%. This implies, on the one hand, a deterioration of liquidity since the spread widens, but at the same time, another dimension of liquidity improves since depth at the best prices increases. In subsequent periods, I observe the opposite evolution: the spread reverts (declines) back to the steady-state level but also depth declines. These results demonstrate the need to account for interaction and complementarity between different dimensions of liquidity. The Spanish market is found to be resilient, since all dimensions of liquidity revert to their steady-state level within around 15 orders after the shock. Furthermore, an analysis of liquidity should also allow for asymmetries in dynamics at bid and ask side of the market, since I find that shocks at the ask side have a larger impact compared with stocks on the bid side. These findings thus comprise relevant recommendations for theoretical modeling and empirical research.

In addition, some differences between groups of stocks are found. The effect of shocks on both returns and depth is larger for stocks with a larger relative tick size. This may indicate that the tick size is a binding constraint for these stocks. The impact of a shock on returns is also larger for less frequently traded stocks, but still realized relatively quickly. The impact on depth, however, is smaller for these stocks.

Concluding, the analysis in this article indicates that despite the absence of market makers with an obligation to maintain an orderly market and provide liquidity, pure order-driven markets seem able to cope with large liquidity shocks. They recover quickly from the impacts of such shocks. In other words, the limit order book is able to provide sufficient liquidity to the market. As a qualification, it needs to be remarked, however, that although the stocks in my sample account for both a large part of trading and market capitalization at the Spanish Stock Exchange, I did not consider very infrequently traded stocks.

## Acknowledgements

I would like to thank the editor Ingmar Nolte and the anonymous referee for their very helpful and interesting comments and suggestions to improve this article. I also thank Hans Degryse and Frank de Jong for detailed comments on an earlier draft, as well as Hans Dewachter, Dirk Heremans, Patrick Van Cayseele, Marno Verbeek and participants to the EFMA 2007 conference for their very valuable comments. I gratefully acknowledge financial assistance from FWO-Flanders under the contract G.0567.10.

## Notes

1. They measure a liquidity shock as a shock to market depth, defined as total depth six ticks away from the quote mid-price.
2. This is the so-called diagonal effect, see Biais, Hillion and Spatt (1995) and Degryse et al. (2005). An order of a given type is more likely to be followed by an order of the same type, relative to the unconditional probability of the order type.
3. Trades themselves then reveal information about the direction of the information event.
4. This effect might, for example, be due to the U-shaped pattern of trading activity during the day (see Biais, Hillion and Spatt 1995 for an illustration of this phenomenon on the Paris Bourse).
5. Recall though that these papers use a slightly less detailed classification scheme, see Section 3.1.
6. A *negative* return on the ask means an improvement of the best ask. On the other hand, a *positive* return on the bid points to an improvement of the best bid. Both imply a narrower spread.
7. Recall that we do not investigate reversal for prices, as they are non-stationary.
8. The only exception to this result is $\ln(BD)$.
9. To be precise, they prove that a market having a minimum price variation is more resilient than a market without.
10. The values for $x_0$ are those of the initial shock and are determined in step 1.
11. As a robustness check, we also take the unconditional mean over the sample period. The interpretation of this alternative is that, in this way, the system starts from a 'stationary' or 'steady-state' situation, after which an unexpected shock arrives. The results are unchanged and are available upon request.

## References

Beltran, H., A. Durré, and P. Giot. 2009. How does liquidity react to stress periods in a limit order market. *Global Finance Journal* 20, no. 1: 80–97.

Biais, B., P. Hillion, and C. Spatt. 1995. An empirical analysis of the limit order book and the order flow in the Paris Bourse. *Journal of Finance* 50, no. 1: 1655–89.

Bien, K., I. Nolte, and W. Pohlmeier. 2011. An inflated multivariate integer count hurdle model: An application to bid and ask quote dynamics. *Journal of Applied Econometrics* 26, no. 4: 669–707.

Coppejans, M., I. Domowitz, and A. Madhavan. 2006. Electronic limit order books and resiliency: Theory, evidence, and practice. In *Advances in quantitative analysis of finance and accounting – Vol. 3: Essays in microstructure in honor of David K. Whitcomb*, ed. I. Brick, T. Ronen, and C. Lee, 19–38. Singapore: World Scientific Publishing Co. Pte. Ltd.

Degryse, H., F. de Jong, M. van Ravenswaaij, and G. Wuyts. 2005. Aggressive orders and the resiliency of a limit order market. *Review of Finance* 2, no. 2: 201–42.

Dufour, A., and R. Engle. 2000. Time and the price impact of a trade. *Journal of Finance* 55, no. 6: 2467–98.

Easley, D., and M. O'Hara. 1987. Price, trade size, and information in securities markets. *Journal of Financial Economics* 19, no. 1: 69–90.

Easley, D., and M. O'Hara. 1992. Time and the process of security price adjustment. *Journal of Finance* 47, no. 2: 577–605.

Engle, R., and A. Patton. 2004. Impact of trades in an error-correction model of quote prices. *Journal of Financial Markets* 7, no. 1: 1–25.

Escribano, A., and R. Pascual. 2006. Asymmetries in bid and ask responses to innovations in the trading process. *Empirical Economics* 30, no. 4: 913–46.

Foucault, T., O. Kadan, and E. Kandel. 2005. Limit order book as a market for liquidity. *Review of Financial Studies* 18, no. 4: 1171–217.

Griffiths, M., B. Smith, D. Turnbull, and R. White. 2000. The costs and determinants of order aggressiveness. *Journal of Financial Economics* 56, no. 1: 65–88.

Harris, L. 1990. Liquidity, trading rules, and electronic trading systems. New York University Salomon Center Monograph Series in Finance, Monograph # 1990-4.

Hasbrouck, J. 1991. Measuring the information content of stock trades. *Journal of Finance* 46, no. 1: 179–207.

Jang, H., and P. Venkatesh. 1991. Consistency between predicted and actual bid–ask quote revisions. *Journal of Finance* 4, no. 1: 433–46.

Large, J. 2007. Measuring the resiliency of an electronic limit order book. *Journal of Financial Markets* 10, no. 1: 1–25.

Nolte, I. 2008. Modeling a multivariate transaction process. *Journal of Financial Econometrics* 6, no. 1: 143–70.

Pardo, A., and R. Pascual. 2007. On the hidden side of liquidity. Unpublished working paper.

Parlour, C. 1998. Price dynamics in limit order markets. *Review of Financial Studies* 11, no. 4: 789–816.

Ranaldo, A. 2004. Order aggressiveness in limit order book markets. *Journal of Financial Markets* 7, no. 1: 53–74.

Rosu, I. 2009. A dynamic model of the limit order book. *Review of Financial Studies* 22, no. 11: 4601–41.

Spierdijk, L. 2004. An empirical analysis of the role of the trading intensity in information dissemination on the NYSE. *Journal of Empirical Finance* 11, no. 2: 163–84.

## Appendix. Simulation methodology: computation of the impulse response functions

Using the VAR model in Equation (3), the resiliency of the market can be investigated by simulating a liquidity shock on basis of this model. More specifically, I start from an order of type $i$, $i \in \{MO\_B1, MO\_S1\}$, and compute the evolution of returns, depths and duration during a period of $h = 1.15$ orders after the submission of the initial order. In the simulation procedure, which is inspired by Escribano and Pascual (2000), it is assumed that an aggressive order of type $i$ is submitted in interval nine (this is between 12h45 and 13h15). After having estimated the VAR model in (3), the simulation procedure proceeds through the following steps:

(1) As stated, a liquidity shock will be measured by an order of type $i$ in interval nine of the day. This is simulated by setting the relevant order type and time of day dummies equal to one. So, $T09_t = 1$, and either $MO\_B1$ or $MO\_S1 = 1$, depending on the value of $i$. The corresponding order size is set equal to the average order size of type $i$.

(2) In a second step, I need to compute the initial values for the lags of the endogenous variables ($y_{t-l}, l = 1 \ldots L$), as well as the lags of the exogenous variables ($x_{t-m}, m = 1 \ldots M$).[10] They are equated to their mean, conditional upon the submission of an order of type $i$ in period $t$. In this way, I consider in my simulation the average market conditions around a liquidity shock.[11]

(3) For each of the *exogenous* variables, a predicted value needs to be computed for $h = 1 \ldots 15$ periods after the shock (recall that one period refers to a trade). For predicting the *order type* and *order size* variables, I calculate the average

value of each of these variables in period $t+h$, $h=1\ldots15$, conditional upon the submission of a type $i$ order in interval 9, which is indexed by $t$. Finally, I need predicted values for the last group of exogenous variables, being the *time of day* dummies. For them, I assume that the 15 orders following an aggressive order, fall entirely in the ninth interval of the day (i.e. between the hours of 12.45 and 13.15), such that $T09_{t+h}=1, h=1\ldots15$. The summary statistics on duration indicate that this is a plausible assumption. Moreover, it is not a restrictive assumption since, as will turn out later, the coefficients of the time of day dummies often are not significant, neither econometrically, nor from an economic point of view.

(4) On the basis of the VAR in Equation (3) and the necessary data computed in the previous three steps, I am able to compute the impulse response functions for bid and ask returns, depth at best bid and ask and duration for each period $h=1,\ldots,15$ after the liquidity shock, i.e. the submission of the order of type $i$. Note that for each period $h$, the value of Spread is updated in the following way: $\text{Spread}_{t+h} = \text{Spread}_{t+h-1} + \Delta \ln A_{t+h} - \Delta \ln B_{t+h}$.

# Index

Note: Page numbers in **bold** type refer to **figures**
Page numbers in *italic* type refer to *tables*
Page numbers followed by 'n' refer to notes

For Product Safety Concerns and Information please contact our
EU representative GPSR@taylorandfrancis.com Taylor & Francis
Verlag GmbH, Kaufingerstraße 24, 80331 München, Germany